JOHN AND PHILOSOPHY

JOHN AND PHILOSOPHY

A New Reading of the Fourth Gospel

Troels Engberg-Pedersen

OXFORD
UNIVERSITY PRESS

OXFORD
UNIVERSITY PRESS

Great Clarendon Street, Oxford, OX2 6DP,
United Kingdom

Oxford University Press is a department of the University of Oxford.
It furthers the University's objective of excellence in research, scholarship,
and education by publishing worldwide. Oxford is a registered trade mark of
Oxford University Press in the UK and in certain other countries

Published in the United States of America by Oxford University Press
198 Madison Avenue, New York, NY 10016, United States of America

British Library Cataloguing in Publication Data
Data available

Library of Congress Cataloging in Publication Data
Data available

ISBN 978-0-19-879250-5 (Hbk.)
ISBN 978-0-19-880925-8 (Pbk.)

For Jonna

PREFACE

This book is an act of retrieval. I aim to retrieve the text itself: *from* the many attempts to separate layers in it and the even more speculative attempts to situate such layers at various stages of the historical development of the so-called 'Johannine community'; and *to* a process of rereading that focuses on the development of ideas within the text itself. Such a process must evidently rely on the broadest possible knowledge of the text's many contexts, but the aim must always be to draw on these contexts for heuristic purposes only in order to let them illuminate what the text itself aims to say.

Any worthwhile book on such a hugely studied work as the Fourth Gospel must spring from some form of dissatisfaction with previous readings, or at least from a sense of remaining problems in the text that have not yet been tackled well enough in previous scholarship. Here I identify two such problems. I believe they reflect a general bafflement that remains just below the surface of much scholarly analysis of this strange text and is probably supposed to be removed by the approaches hinted at above. First, there is a sense of its repetitive character: that it almost obsessively repeats the same ideas, metaphors, and locutions without making it entirely clear to the reader what is added from one moment to the next. Secondly, there is a sense of its 'riddling' quality: that it gestures towards enigmas (the 'mystery' of this text) which it ultimately leaves in the dark.

For a long time I have myself shared these feelings. However, on the basis of an intensive study shaped by my knowledge of ancient philosophy, I have become convinced that the supposed repetitiveness always has a distinct point and that its aim is not to gesture towards any enigmas, but quite the contrary, to generate an absolute clarity in the reader. John aims for clarity (in the reader, that is)—at the same time as the *lack* of clarity, indeed, the pervasive lack of understanding in all those with whom Jesus engages throughout the Gospel is a crucial theme of the text as a whole.

This book has had a long gestation. I have taught John for decades. In the middle of the 2000s while I was finishing a book on Paul entitled *Cosmology and Self in the Apostle Paul. The Material Spirit* (2010) I also began working on John. During that period, as I was working on Paul and the *pneuma* ('spirit') I also supervised a PhD thesis by Gitte

Buch-Hansen on John, which focused on the concept of *pneuma* in John. Dr Buch-Hansen's book was published in 2010 entitled *»It is the Spirit that Gives Life«. A Stoic Understanding of Pneuma in John's Gospel*. I fully acknowledge here the mutual give-and-take that went into that scholarly process. I also explicitly refer to this book which, in the footsteps of Adele Reinhartz's concept of a 'cosmological tale' in the Fourth Gospel (Reinhartz 1992), successfully develops the idea of a 'meta-story of pneumatic trans-formations' in the Gospel that runs from the baptism scene in John 1 to the resurrection scenes in John 20. The present book adopts a different strategy, however. I stay closer to the ground and attempt to cover the whole of the Gospel by applying a so-called 'narrative philosophical' approach that aims to show how John's narrative argument proceeds step by step.

I was able to work seriously on this book from 2008 onwards when I was fortunate to direct (together with Professor Niels Henrik Gregersen, for the period 2008–13) a Centre of Excellence entitled 'Naturalism and Christian Semantics', generously funded by the Rector of the University of Copen-hagen, Ralf Hemmingsen. I am grateful to the Rector for funding the centre, which gave me a wonderful chance to work on the relationship between Stoicism and Platonism in the New Testament period (see Engberg-Pedersen (ed.), *From Stoicism to Platonism. The Development of Philosophy 100 BCE–100 CE*, Cambridge University Press, 2017) and also on the present book. I am also grateful to the Dean of the Faculty of Theology, Kirsten Busch Nielsen, who gave me a whole year's research leave in 2015 before my retirement on 1 February 2016. The book was actually written between 1 January 2015 and 1 June 2016. Thanks are also due to the Danish Royal Library for its professionalism in securing access to scholarship on John that in many cases had to be procured from abroad, as well as to the various publishers of Engberg-Pedersen 2012, 2013a, 2013b, 2015, 2016, and 2017 for allowing me to reuse (in greatly changed form) material from those articles. Finally, I wish to thank the Museo Civico di Sansepolcro, Tuscany, Italy, for allowing me to reproduce on the cover of the book a part of their magnificent Madonna della Misericordia by Piero della Fran-cesca. I saw the painting in 2014 in Sansepolcro itself—Piero's birthplace—and immediately decided that its representation of John the Evangelist would be highly suitable for the planned book. The Museo has generously helped to put this idea into practice.

Once I began to study John seriously, I acquainted myself with (sizeable parts of) the huge scholarship on John from the 1900s onwards (in particu-lar 1907, see Chapter I). I was happy to discover that Johannine scholarship is generally in excellent shape, not least as a result of the developments 'post-Bultmann' from the 1980s onwards. Where one may feel in other parts of New Testament scholarship that the constant production of new commentaries leads to surfeit, in John's case new distinguished commentaries are constantly being published that offer genuine help to the avid reader. Here I wish to mention the masterful work on John done by three Germans, Jörg Frey, Udo Schnelle, and Michael Theobald. Their command of the scholarly literature is magisterial—and exceedingly helpful to their co-workers. In Frey and Schnelle one also finds a concentrated attempt to get away from the speculative excesses of historical criticism (while both firmly remain historical critics themselves). Theobald has not relinquished operating with layers in the text, but his insight and 'ear' are admirable, even when the text goes against his own preferred reading.

My first scholarly monograph (on Aristotle's *Ethics*, Oxford University Press, 1983) was dedicated to my beloved wife, Jonna. In addition to so much else, she has been a constant support of my scholarly work over all those years, at the same time as she was herself engaged in equally taxing work, and we together brought up our three children, of whom we are so proud: Anna, Anders, and Astrid. Coming full circle, I dedicate this new book to her, in deep love and gratitude.

CONTENTS

I

A RETURN TO THE TEXT

THE ISSUES SINCE 1907

The Fourth Gospel continues to baffle its interpreters and for good reason. Had we only had the Synoptic Gospels and were then asked to imagine another gospel that would either continue their line or present an alternative, would we ever have come up with something like John? And so the theme of 'John and the Synoptic Gospels' has been on the scholarship agenda for ages. Indeed, what one of the Gospel's most acute readers, Rudolf Bultmann, wrote even more broadly in 1925 still holds true: 'The position of the Gospel of John within the history of early Christianity is in fact a riddle (or puzzle, *Rätsel*) that has not to my mind been solved to this day' (Bultmann 1925, 100/1967, 55).[1]

Then there are the internal difficulties. Is the text at all coherent? Does it not offer another range of 'puzzles' (*aporiai*) of narrative and thought that has generated an incredible ingenuity among scholars to 'solve' them since they were first pointed out in the first decade of the twentieth century by Julius Wellhausen (1907) and Eduard Schwartz (1907–8)?

Moreover, even if the text is taken to be coherent, how should one understand and explain the presence of so much repetition within the Gospel? John certainly has a style of his own. But why does he repeat himself so that another of his most acute readers, William Wrede, might react like this: 'Speeches of extraordinary length . . . turn in the manner of variations around certain main themes and leave behind not so much an impression of power and wealth as of diffuseness and monotony' (Wrede 1907, 181)? Much more recently, the experience of repetition in John has become the theme of a scholarly volume of its own (Van Belle, Labahn, and Maritz 2009).

Finally, when we move from style to content, what Bultmann termed 'the second big riddle' of the Fourth Gospel appears to be just as unsolved as

---

[1] Where nothing else is indicated, all translations—whether from the Bible or the secondary literature—are my own.

ever: 'What is its central viewpoint (*zentrale Anschauung*), its basic conception (*Grundkonzeption*)?' (Bultmann 1925, 102/1967, 57). Bultmann himself
took the key concept to be that of 'revelation' (*Offenbarung*) and then
famously stated as the big riddle that 'Jesus does not reveal any secrets of
an anthropological and cosmological or theological kind, but only this
single one: that he is (himself) the revealer' (1925, 102/1967, 57). Incidentally, back in 1907 Wrede had made exactly this point (Wrede 1907, 199, his
emphasis):

If one asks what especially Christ announces concerning the Father, the hidden
God, one will be surprised to see that there is no real answer to be found—other
than the answer that this God has precisely sent his *Son* for the salvation of human
beings. That means: Christ is in fact not only the one who brings the message, but
also its very content. What matters is this: *that* he has come from the Father, *that* he
is God's Son, *that* he deserves the same honour as the Father.[2]

Many more puzzles might be mentioned that have engaged readers of
John for more than a century. The aim of the present book is certainly not
to attempt to solve them all. But the book does spring from some degree of
dissatisfaction with the talk of 'puzzles', 'riddles', and 'mystery' in John.
One can well understand why scholars have been baffled, yet one may
also feel that the idea of mystery has itself been repeated so many times
that it has acquired a life of its own. Do we know that John was not, in
fact, aiming at clarity and transparency? May it be that some of the
'mystery' of this text may be dissolved if we try to address it once more,
based on all the insight that has been accumulated since the beginning of
scientific analysis, but also governed by a sense that some, at least, of the
puzzles raised in scholarship might be due to the scientific enterprise itself
rather than its object? To sketch this possibility, we need to have a firm
grasp of the development of scholarship on John since the first decade
of the twentieth century, beginning with Wrede, Wellhausen, and
Schwartz, all of whom published groundbreaking works on John more
or less in the same year. I will try to show that this development has had
a distinct internal logic to it. By looking at it from the perspective of
overall method, rather than the individual positions of substance, we will
be able to articulate a methodological position that both draws extensively on previous scholarship and also adds up to a new position with a
name of its own: a return to the text. The aim of this chapter is to perform
that exercise. I will quote quite liberally from the best scholars at either
end of the story I am going to tell. Only in this way will readers be able
to see exactly how we arrived at the various main positions that have

---

[2] John Ashton, too, begins his big book on John from the same two Bultmannian riddles
(Ashton 2007/1991, 2–11 *etc.*). It is worth noticing, however, that Wrede had already been there.

characterized Johannine research during the twentieth century and how we—almost—got out of them again.

CURRENT OVERVIEWS OF SCHOLARSHIP

Here we should acknowledge the help to be gained from the work over the last two decades of two German specialists on John: Jörg Frey and Udo Schnelle.[3] In his magisterial treatment (Frey 1997, 1998, 2000a) of the vexed question of the 'eschatology' of John, which had formed one kernel of the most important work on John during the mid-twentieth century by C. H. Dodd and Rudolf Bultmann, Frey thoroughly situated the whole issue in previous scholarship and in that connection covered almost all the scholarly handling during the twentieth century of the puzzles outlined earlier. Frey has continued this work in a series of substantial essays that address individually all the major issues: *Kreuzestheologie* ('theology of the Cross', 2002), John and the Synoptics (2003), John's context (2004) from the perspective of *Religionsgeschichte* (history of religion) and *Traditions-geschichte* (history of tradition), John and Qumran (2004), 'dualism' in John (2006), and more, all culminating in a substantial summary of the 'Paths and Perspectives of the Interpretation of the Gospel of John' in the form of Frey's 'Reflections on the Path towards a Commentary' (2013c) that he is currently writing. The latter essay introduces a volume (2013a) in which all the other essays are reprinted. This is a veritable treasury, a mine of information on previous scholarship presented with the utmost care and clarity and leading forward to Frey's own thoroughly argued positions on all the relevant issues.[4]

In Udo Schnelle's substantial scholarship on John, two extensive discussions of the current tendencies in Johannine scholarship are particularly worth mentioning here: first (Schnelle 2010) on the research tendencies in commentaries published between 1994 and 2010; and next (Schnelle 2013) on similar tendencies in monographs from the same period on Johannine eschatology and the so-called 'Farewell Speeches' (*Abschiedsreden*). These, too, are magisterial treatments, steeped in knowledge of the whole German tradition since the beginning of the scientific study of the New Testament.

---

[3] Other excellent overviews of current scholarship include Scholtissek 1999a–2004 and Moloney 2012a–b.

[4] Compare George Parsenios at the end of his brief review: 'This volume is essential reading for anyone who wishes to be attuned to the latest and most important scholarship of the Fourth Gospel' (Parsenios 2015, 27). And Klaus Scholtissek at the end of his more detailed review: 'Mit seinen Studien, die exegetisches Arbeiten heute selbstkritisch schulen, leistet er der gesamten wissenschaftlichen Exegese insgesamt einen kaum zu überschätzen-den Dienst' (Scholtissek 2014, 579).

But they are especially interesting in the present context since they to a large degree are in agreement with the picture given by Frey of where Johannine scholarship is at present. Both bodies of work constitute an excellent stepping stone for further reflection on how to proceed from where we are.

In this connection it is worth noting that both Frey and Schnelle are just as well informed on French, British, and American scholarship as they are on the German tradition. To mention a few names, central Johannine scholars such as Jean Zumstein (recently) for the French tradition, C. H. Dodd and C. K. Barrett (and many others) for the British tradition, and Raymond Brown, Wayne Meeks, J. Louis Martyn, R. Alan Culpepper, Harold Attridge (and many others) for the American tradition have all been incorporated into these overviews of scholarship. There is one striking omission, however. This concerns the turn to be noted in American scholarship from the 1990s onwards, as heralded, for instance, by the second of two volumes (Segovia 1998a) that reflected a series of meetings between 1991 and 1996 within the Johannine Literature Section of the American Society of Biblical Literature. In this volume there is a distinct move from the text—as analysed from so many perspectives—to its readers, to be understood here as its *real* readers, and moreover not just in their usual guise as White Academic Men (and Women), but as situated globally and reflecting the widest possible range of cultural and personal interests. This turn is not really incorporated into the overviews of Frey and Schnelle, nor will this perspective be in focus in this book. But it needs to be acknowledged as one highly significant trend in Johannine scholarship and constitutes a challenge to earlier forms of scholarship that need to be factored in one way or the other.[5]

A HIGH POINT IN HISTORICAL CRITICISM: WREDE, WELLHAUSEN, AND SCHWARTZ

More than fifty years have passed since Thomas Kuhn published *The Structure of Scientific Revolutions* (1962), in which he introduced the notion of a 'paradigm shift' in order to describe in more detail so-called revolutions in science.[6] Kuhn's book focused on natural science and one example is the

---

[5] See later in this chapter on the challenge. Here, too, we should mention the substantial amount of scholarship that has recently been addressed to gender in the Fourth Gospel (e.g. Conway 1999; Attridge 2003; Levine (ed.) 2003; Seim 2005 and 2010). Important as this theme is, it plays no role in this book, which is concerned to follow the text rather more from the inside. It is interesting to speculate, though, how the two approaches might be combined.

[6] For one recent discussion see Bird 2013.

huge change in the history of astronomy from a Ptolemaic world view to that of Copernicus, as described by Kuhn in his earlier book on *The Copernican Revolution* (1957). In spite of the fact that Kuhn's theory has been enormously influential across all the sciences, great care is needed if one attempts to see shifts in a humanistic discipline such as Johannine scholarship in terms of Kuhn's theory. In fact, there is only one change in this field that might qualify as a genuine Kuhnian paradigm shift of the magnitude of the Copernican revolution, and that is the rise of historical criticism itself in the eighteenth century. Within that framework, however, it will be helpful to use some of Kuhn's concepts to describe the history of scientific change in the exploration of the Fourth Gospel since the first decade of the twentieth century. To begin with, I speak here only of 'paradigm shifts' in scare quotes since the positions to be mentioned all remained within historical criticism. Only later do we come across two changes that may qualify as genuine paradigm shifts in a Kuhnian sense, though not quite of the magnitude of historical criticism: narrative criticism and the kind of radical reader response referred to earlier. Even so, I believe that the Kuhnian theory will be helpful for understanding the character of the changes themselves and their relation to what came before.

One central Kuhnian idea is the rejection of the idea that scientific progress is linear and uniform as it moves cumulatively towards ever greater knowledge. In a way Kuhn did retain such a picture, but only within what he called 'normal science', which was defined as proceeding according to a certain basic paradigm, which it takes for granted and does not query as it proceeds. A paradigm consists of a certain set of concepts or basic assumptions about the shape of the scientific field to be investigated, often found to be exemplified in certain classical works. Such works, Kuhn claimed, have two essential characteristics (Kuhn 1962, 10):

Their achievement was sufficiently unprecedented to attract an enduring group of adherents away from competing modes of scientific activity. Simultaneously, it was sufficiently open-ended to leave all sorts of problems for the redefined group of practitioners to solve.

Thus understood, a paradigm both guides and constrains research. It guides research by setting up the parameters within which scientific progress may unfold, and constrains it by not allowing the scientist to move completely outside those parameters.

In Johannine scholarship, historical criticism as articulated in the eighteenth-century Enlightenment constitutes such a paradigm. A single, splendid quotation from Johann Gottfried Herder will show its shape. Speaking of the relationship between the four Gospels, Herder said in 1797: 'What cannot be combined, must stand alone, each evangelist with his own credit.... Four evangelists there are, let each one have his own purpose, his own facial colour, his own time and place'.[7]

One hundred years later, the rigorous focus of historical criticism on understanding any given New Testament in its historical context and the constant aim of criticizing the dogmatic use of the texts by systematic theologians are features that were massively present in the so-called *religionsgeschichtliche Schule*, of which William Wrede may be taken as a stellar exponent.[8]

In Wrede's reading of John, the text was drastically removed from having any historical reference back to Jesus. Instead, it was taken to reflect the historical circumstances of its own writing, chief among which was a conflict with Judaism. Only here may one really reach what Wrede, 207) called 'an historical understanding'. But then one also gets it: '... an historical understanding is only reached when one sees the gospel as *a text that has been born out of a struggle and written for a struggle*' (Wrede 1907, 208, his emphasis). This, for Wrede, constitutes the key to the whole 'character and tendency' of the Fourth Gospel, a text that he also does his best to remove from having any immediate meaning of the kind cherished by systematic theologians. Here Wrede certainly did not introduce a wholly new paradigm (of historical criticism): he only took it to its radical extreme, in a manner that would have huge consequences for the rest of the twentieth century.

Exactly the same may be said of the other breakthrough in Johannine scholarship presented in the same decade by Julius Wellhausen and Eduard Schwartz. Coming from two neighbouring disciplines—of Old Testament scholarship and Classics, respectively—Wellhausen and Schwartz put their historical perspective to use by destroying the unity of the transmitted text of John. As Wellhausen (1907) showed in a booklet of thirty-eight pithy pages, the transmitted text of John was full of *Erweiterungen* (additions) and *Änderungen* (changes). Moreover, these were of such a kind that Wellhausen was able to detect behind them the single hand of a *Redaktor* (editor), who had transposed the text to such an extent that 'it is no longer transmitted to us in its original edition, but only in a second, extended and improved one' (Wellhausen 1907, 38).

Wellhausen's booklet was followed by the publication of a series of lectures by one of its dedicatees, Eduard Schwartz, who in his much more extended account identified the *aporiai* of narrative and thought that have

---

[7] 'Was sich nicht vereinigen lässt, stehe einzeln da, jeder Evangelist mit seinem Verdienst.... Vier Evangelisten sind, und jedem bleibe sein Zweck, seine Gesichtsfarbe, seine Zeit, sein Ort.' (I am quoting from Frey 2003, 68/2013b, 247.)

[8] On Wrede—one of my scholarly heroes—there is an interesting account in Strecker 1960.

set the scene for one powerful research trend ever since: that of Johannine *Literarkritik* (source criticism or 'literary criticism' in this old, German sense of the term). As with Wrede, neither Wellhausen nor Schwartz created a wholly new paradigm, but they took historical criticism to a logical extreme, again with huge consequences for scholarship for the rest of the twentieth century. From then on, it became 'natural' within Johannine scholarship to look for literary strata within the text and try to combine these with specific stages in what one took to be the development of the so-called Johannine community. In this sense the change brought about by Wellhausen and Schwartz came to have the unquestioned status of a genuine paradigm—as it were a 'paradigm' within the overarching paradigm of historical criticism.

RELIGIONSGESCHICHTE, LITERARKRITIK, AND EXISTENZTHEOLOGIE: BULTMANN

Exactly the same status should be assigned to the change brought about by Rudolf Bultmann from the 1920s onwards. It became a 'paradigm' that was unquestioned in principle, at least within German scholarship on John, until well into the second half of the twentieth century, and its shadow has loomed large ever since.

What Bultmann did, basically, was to bring together two scholarly disciplines that were, and have continued to be, central in the exploration of John, and then to add a third one that was wholly his own. The two basic ones were: *Religionsgeschichte* (the older of the two) and *Literarkritik* (the more recent one, as applied to John). Within the former, Bultmann explicitly rejected the tradition (which had been the leading one around 1900) of finding the most appropriate context for John in Hellenized Judaism, to some extent influenced by Greek philosophy in the shape of Platonism and with Philo of Alexandria as its star specimen.[9] Instead, he focused on a range of 'Mandaean' and 'Manichaean' sources that had newly been published (compare Bultmann 1925). New evidence, then, would give rise to a new 'paradigm' (within the paradigm of historical criticism).

On the basis of these sources Bultmann constructed a (supposedly) Gnostic *Erlösungsmythos* (redeemer myth) that he also found behind the Gospel of John.[10] Bultmann's myth itself is more complex than is normally

---

[9] In this rejection, too, Bultmann was preceded by Wrede: 'Nicht selten hat man dem Verfasser eine philosophische Lehre zugeschrieben. Schon die Andeutungen, die ich gegeben habe, dürften ausreichen, um das Grundlose einer derartigen Ansicht zu erkennen' (Wrede 1907, 201).

[10] Compare again Wrede: 'Ich bin geneigt zu glauben, dass dem Evangelium gnostisch geartete Anschauungen zu grunde liegen' (Wrede 1907, 201).

understood. For our purposes, it is sufficient to indicate one of its basic features, which concerns the role of the messenger from heaven (Bultmann 1925, 104/1967, 59):

> To the soul that is imprisoned on earth the messenger who comes from heaven brings revelatory news (*Offenbarung*) about its origin, its home and its return there. The messenger appears in earthly human dress, but he ascends in glory.

Armed with this conceptual figure, Bultmann went on to analyse the Gospel text into sources and layers which he ascribed to the Evangelist himself and a later Church-oriented 'redactor'. And in finding the criteria for this operation, Bultmann introduced a perspective derived from the third discipline referred to above: a wholly modern, existentialist approach ultimately derived from Martin Heidegger.

What matters here is not so much the substantial content of Bultmann's overall picture, which, as comprehensively articulated in his great 1941 commentary, was at the same time exceedingly complex in its details and strikingly powerful in its basic message. More important is the methodological shape of this reading. What Bultmann did was to combine an intensive study of the text itself with perspectives on it that were derived from outside the text: from the *religionsgeschichtlich* positioning of the text within one specific context and from a modern, *existenztheologisch* framing of the question of the text's overall message. The result was his extremely complicated *literarkritisch* dismembering of the transmitted text—which was then also taken in a hermeneutic circle to corroborate the approach itself. There was nothing wilful in this procedure. Bultmann did read the text itself most carefully and saw that it fitted his own framing perspectives. It remains the case, however, that it was those framing perspectives that gave his reading of the text itself its power. As soon as they had lost their persuasiveness, the reading itself could not be maintained. It is also this tight combination of a range of central scholarly perspectives on John that turns Bultmann's reconstruction into a genuine 'paradigm' (within the fundamental paradigm of historical criticism). Here was a combined set of basic assumptions within which scholars might continue to work by querying details, suggesting minor amendments, and the like without directly addressing the basic props on which the whole theory was based.

AVOIDING EXCESSES: DODD AND BARRETT

Side by side with Bultmann and his followers, Britain produced leading explorations of the Fourth Gospel in the period just after the Second World War. Two deserve to be mentioned here, not just because of their influence, but also because of their respective profiles with respect to *Religionsgeschichte* and *Literarkritik*. In neither respect is it appropriate to speak of a paradigm shift. Rather, what we see are moves within the basic paradigm of historical criticism that in their slightly different ways point forward to where we are at present by curtailing some of the excesses of which Bultmann was a prime example.

The two figures I have in mind are C. H. Dodd and C. K. Barrett: Dodd in his two monographs on John, *The Interpretation of the Fourth Gospel* (1953) and *Historical Tradition in the Fourth Gospel* (1963); and Barrett in his magisterial commentary (1978/1955). Both were well aware of Bultmann's reading, with which they engaged whenever appropriate. But both also basically rejected the basic props of that reading. This is most strikingly the case with regard to Bultmann's *literarkritisch* dismembering of the transmitted text. Neither Dodd nor Barrett would have any of it. On the contrary, in Part III of his great book of 1953, Dodd gave a reading of the Fourth Gospel viewed as a single, coherent text that pointed forward, well before its day, to the narrative critical reading that was only introduced into Johannine studies by R. Alan Culpepper in 1983.[11]

With regard to Bultmann's Gnostic reading of John, Barrett was basically not persuaded. He felt that to the extent that a tradition historical positioning of the Fourth Gospel was required, one would have to draw quite broadly on the Old Testament, Hellenistic Judaism, early Christian traditions, and even, to some extent, on Greek traditions that would include philosophical ones (1978, 3–41). Dodd (1953) made much more in Parts I and II of his book of placing John within a *religionsgeschichtlich* context. He rejected a specifically Gnostic and Mandaean reading of John and instead elaborated the Hellenistic Jewish philosophical traditions with input from Plato, as seen primarily in Philo. In doing so, Dodd, like Barrett, opened up a broad view of the context of John which cut across the traditional divide between Jewish and Hellenistic traditions.

Why did both Dodd and Barrett reject Bultmann's positions with regard to *Religionsgeschichte* and *Literarkritik*? On the first point, Dodd did take up the challenge and he responded with what proved to be the fatal objection to Bultmann's Gnostic and Mandaean anchoring of the Fourth Gospel: that it is anachronistic (Dodd 1953a, 98, 130). The sources for anything like Bultmann's Gnostic redeemer myth are much later than John. With regard to *Literarkritik*, Jörg Frey has suggested that the 'independent profile' of British scholarship on John, which 'came from a profound tradition of conservative-theological and philological-historical interpretation', 'only slowly and guardedly let itself be influenced by German criticism' (Frey 1997, 246). He sees the work of E. C. Hoskyns,

---

[11] Compare Culpepper's own recent account of Dodd in Culpepper 2013.

Dodd, R. H. Lightfoot, W. F. Howard, and Barrett as being very close to one another 'in their *literarkritisch* abstinence (*Abstinenz*)'. Whether or not this abstinence (always a good thing!) is due to a conservative theological outlook, it seems fair to see it also as reflecting a kind of scepticism vis-à-vis more fanciful proposals that is emblematic of British scientific solidity. What we find here is a rejection of a supposedly new 'paradigm' (within the shared paradigm of historical criticism) that points forward, not only de facto to narrative criticism, but also to the more cautious historical-critical position which, as we will see, Frey has himself commendably ended up articulating.

THE JOHANNINE COMMUNITY: MARTYN AND BROWN

A much more daring approach, one that also took up impulses from German scholarship directly, was adopted by a group of American scholars who from around 1960 onwards moved on to centre stage in Johannine scholarship. The primary focus here was to reconstruct a picture of the so-called Johannine community that was taken to lie behind, issue in, and perhaps also help in revising the Gospel of John, thereby being ultimately responsible for the Gospel as we have it. Two central figures in this were J. Louis Martyn and Raymond E. Brown.

In his very influential book, *History and Theology in the Fourth Gospel*, which was first published in 1968, but reissued as late as 2003 in an expanded version, Martyn made two claims that may well be seen ultimately to derive from Wrede. First, in introducing his famous two-level reading of the Fourth Gospel, Martyn, as Wrede had done before him, argued that John's account of the stories in which Jesus was involved reflected John's own time much more than they did that of Jesus himself. Martyn even contended, for instance in his analysis of the healing of the man born blind (John 9), that when the Johannine text tells a story of an event in Jesus' time it also refers to a similar specific event in the writer's own time. These are the two levels at which the text is taken to be operating. The underlying 'redaction critical' point had been clearly articulated already by Wrede in 1907, even though 'redaction criticism' only became a recognized scholarly tool around fifty years later.

Secondly, like Wrede, Martyn saw the conflict with Judaism as the central theme of John's reconfiguration of the Jesus story. But Martyn went one step further by claiming that it was possible from the Gospel text itself to detect a number of stages in the community's development in its relations to the Jews: an early, middle, and late period, ending with the complete separation of the Johannine Christ believers from the synagogue. In this last endeavour Martyn was clearly influenced by German *Literarkritik*, but his focus was not so much on the text itself as on getting behind the text to a picture of the community that was supposedly reflected in it.

The same interest in getting behind the text is to be found in Raymond Brown's *The Community of the Beloved Disciple* (1979). However, since Brown had already published his great commentary on John in the years 1966–70, he remained more focused than Martyn on the text itself. In the commentary Brown distinguished between five stages in the composition of the Gospel, two of which lay before the written Gospel. Where stage three consisted of 'the first edition of the Fourth Gospel as a distinct work' (Brown 1966, xxxv), stage four was seen to contain a '[s]econdary edition by the evangelist' (xxxvi) and stage five was a 'final editing or redaction by someone other than the evangelist' whom Brown called 'the redactor' (xxxvi) Brown further claimed that 'while preserving the substantial unity of the Gospel, this theory explains the various factors that militate against unity of authorship' (xxxix), a list of which he had initially produced (xxivxxv). But careful as he always was, Brown also noted that '[t]here remain many inadequacies and uncertainties in such a theory' (xxxix), which is why he decided to 'comment on the Gospel in its present order without imposing rearrangements' (xxxiv). Still, the uncertainties did not prevent him from going behind the text and combining his understanding of the genesis of the text with a four-stage picture of the growth of the Johannine community.[12]

What we see in both Martyn and Brown, then, is an acceptance of German *Literarkritik*, though one may also notice that neither practised it in the extreme form done by Bultmann. In spite of this commendable caution, however, the idea itself that the transmitted text of the Fourth Gospel had layers in it that were more or less identifiable allowed both Martyn and Brown to propose historical reconstructions of the development of Johannine community that was supposed to lie behind the text itself. Moreover, these reconstructions, which might at least be said to have had a kind of conceptual predecessor in Wrede, went much further than Wrede in speaking of several stages of development, specific historical situations (such as expulsion from the synagogue), and the like.

Understood in this way, the scholarly trend inaugurated by Martyn and Brown of focusing on the Johannine community in no way constituted a genuinely new Kuhnian paradigm within Johannine studies. But it did set the scene for a period of scholarship after Martyn and Brown that was

---

[12] Brown retained his overall picture of text and community in his later thorough revision of his introduction to the commentary (Brown 2003), even though—under the influence of literary criticism—he distinctly played down its importance for the study of 'the Gospel as it now stands' (Brown 2003, 86, compare 6). As he himself added: 'that is the only form that we are certain has ever existed' (6).

concerned with the same issues.[13] More importantly, it may well be said to have taken to an extreme Wrede's line in earlier scholarship of looking towards the historical situation behind the text. In this respect, the Martyn–Brown approach is comparable to Bultmann's approach, where the same line in earlier scholarship (*Literarkritik*) was also taken to an extreme, though in a quite different direction.

A GENUINE PARADIGM SHIFT: CULPEPPER

We have not yet come across any real paradigm shift in Johannine scholarship from Wrede to Brown. Rather, what we have seen is that historical–critical approaches that had been introduced more or less explicitly in the first decade of the twentieth century had been taken to extremes in ways that differed widely, but agreed in one crucial respect: they were not focused rigorously on elucidating the transmitted text in the form in which we have it. Instead, what they were after was either (in Bultmann's case) the theological shape of one *part* of the text (that of the 'evangelist') or else (in the case of Martyn and Brown) historical phenomena that were supposed to lie *behind* the text and were then taken to be reflected in it and give it part of its meaning. Towards the end of the twentieth century, however, we do come across a genuine paradigm shift, which aimed to focus sharply on the transmitted text as it now stands.

I am referring here to the literary critical reading of John that was inaugurated by R. Alan Culpepper (1983). Curiously, this type of 'literary criticism' is as far removed as one can imagine from *Literarkritik* of the original German type. In Culpepper's version, which reflects a much broader understanding within the modern study of literature, literary criticism is directly opposed to *Literarkritik* (Culpepper 1983, 5):

According to this model [Culpepper's own], dissection and stratification have no place in the study of the gospel and may distort and confuse one's view of the text. Every element of the gospel contributes to the production of its meaning, and the experience of reading the text is more important than understanding the process of its composition.

Against this methodological background, Culpepper then proceeds to discuss the whole range of topics that form the core of what may be called 'narrative criticism': narrator and point of view, narrative time, plot,

---

[13] It thus took the considerable intellectual powers of Adele Reinhartz to start querying, in particular, Martyn's theory of the supposed expulsion of the Johannine Christians from the synagogue (see Reinhartz 1998). On the historical issues surrounding the *Birkat Ha-Minim*, the supposed 'Synod of Jamnia', and the like, see Frey 2013b, 362–5.

characters, implicit commentary (including misunderstanding, irony, and symbolism)—all to be understood as phenomena that take place between the so-called implied author of the text (as opposed to its real author) and the implied reader (as different from any real readers). In an elegant diagram (Culpepper 1983, 6), adapted from Seymour Chatman's *Story and Discourse* (1978), Culpepper was able to show the connections between these various topics *within* the world of the text itself.

With literary criticism understood in this way we have a genuine paradigm shift, even with Culpepper's book as its founding text. It fundamentally rejected the basic assumptions that went into and served to define its predecessor, historical criticism. And it installed a new set of assumptions within which scholars might then go on—as they did—to extend, qualify, and supplement the overall picture presented by Culpepper without querying the fundamental shape of the new approach.[14] It is also noteworthy that Culpepper's model fits Kuhn's notion of a genuine paradigm shift in that it is possible to see it as a reaction to an impasse in previous scholarship, precisely the turn away from the text itself that we noted in Martyn's and Brown's version of historical criticism. For readers of John who took up the text to get to understand *that* text better, speculative reconstructions of the world outside the text in the form of the Johannine community were just not enough.

If literary criticism constituted a genuine paradigm shift, which must by Kuhnian definition be 'incommensurable' with its predecessor, it is all the more striking that Culpepper did not actually reject historical criticism altogether. Instead, he posited the new approach as an alternative (Culpepper 1983, 5, his italics):

While the approach of literary criticism is clearly distinct from that of historical–critical scholarship, there needs to be dialogue between the two so that each may be informed by the other. This book ... is intended not as a challenge to historical criticism or the results of previous research but as an alternative by means of which new data may be collected and readers may be helped to read the gospel more perceptively by *looking at* certain features of the gospel. This process is to be distinguished from reading the gospel *looking for* particular kinds of historical evidence.

This statement raises two serious questions. Was Culpepper right not to challenge historical criticism? *Why* should it not be challenged? And exactly how may the two approaches 'inform one another'? We will come back to these questions later.

---

[14] See, e.g., Duke 1985; Stibbe 1992 and 1993; Frey, van der Watt, and Zimmermann (eds) 2006; Thatcher and Moore (eds) 2008; Bennema 2009; Frey and Poplutz (eds) 2012a; Skinner 2013; Hunt, Tolmie, and Zimmermann (eds) 2013.

ONE MORE GENUINE PARADIGM SHIFT: SEGOVIA

Towards the end of the twentieth century things began to move very
rapidly in New Testament scholarship as a whole and in Johannine scholarship as well. Thus, in the last decade of the century another change was
articulated which once again had the form of a genuine paradigm shift:
'intercultural criticism' as presented by Fernando F. Segovia in two volumes already mentioned, '*What is John?*' I–II (1996 and 1998a).

In the present context, intercultural criticism derives its basic shape from
the discipline of cultural studies in the humanities. Here is how Segovia
identifies the central idea (Segovia 1998b, 187):

[*i*] To begin with, cultural studies questions the construct, howsoever formulated,
of the informed and neutral reader, universal and disinterested, and posits instead
the very different construct of the real or flesh-and-blood reader, always positioned
and interested. . . . [*ii*] Consequently, cultural studies sees real readers as lying
behind all reading and interpretation—all interpretive models and reading strategies as well as all retrievals of meaning from texts and reconstructions of history—
so that all such models and strategies, retrievals and reconstructions, are regarded
as constructs on the part of such readers . . . [*iii*] Cultural studies calls, therefore, for
joint analysis of the texts (the remains of the ancient world) as well as the readers
and their readings of such texts (the representations of the ancient world) . . .

Since the beginning of historical criticism, all new approaches within
New Testament scholarship have reflected not only developments within
the discipline itself, but also (and quite often with a marked time lag)
developments within neighbouring disciplines in the humanities and the
social sciences. In addition, there is a match with the general cultural
situation or *Zeitgeist*, which again reflects a whole number of social, political, and economic features in the societies in which these disciplines are to
be found. This is certainly true of literary criticism in New Testament
studies, which had a long pedigree in the modern study of literature before
being applied to the New Testament. It is also true of intercultural criticism
in New Testament studies, for which the ground was laid far away from
Biblical studies in cultural studies, postcolonialism—and in the kind of
globalization and democratization that the world has seen during the last
few decades. There is absolutely nothing wrong in this influence from
factors outside the individual disciplines. In the present context, however,
it is of greater interest to consider the relationship within New Testament
(and Johannine) studies between the three paradigms we have identified:
historical criticism, literary criticism, and intercultural criticism.

Very basically one may say that historical criticism was specifically
concerned with the past, aiming to go behind the text back to whatever
historical features might help to explain its meaning. In comparison,

literary criticism was specifically focused on the text itself in the present as captured within Alan Culpepper's diagram that leaves out both the real author behind the text and any real readers in front of it. Intercultural criticism, then, is specifically focused on the future in the sense of what lies in front of the text, and here primarily on its real readers. Thus understood, intercultural criticism is a development of so-called reader-response criticism, which in one of its forms, at least, was itself a form of *literary* criticism. The point here is that in addition to all the influences from beyond the various scholarly disciplines themselves, there is an internal logic to be found in the development of the three paradigms we have articulated—just as there is an internal logic in the development from Wrede, Wellhausen, and Schwartz to the radicalized historical–critical positions of Bultmann, Martyn, and Brown.

This raises the same question with regard to intercultural criticism as articulated by Segovia as we noted in connection with literary criticism as articulated by Culpepper: exactly how are they related to historical criticism? Culpepper did not reject historical criticism. Similarly, when Segovia speaks of a joint analysis of 'the texts themselves', understood as 'the remains of the ancient world', and then also of the readers and their readings of those texts, how are we to understand the proposed analysis of 'the texts themselves'? Is it to be understood as being historically informed? And if so, does such an idea invoke the notion of a (real) reader who is not *just* situated or 'positioned and interested', but perhaps performing *like* an 'informed and neutral reader, universal and disinterested'?

We will leave these questions hanging and take a look at the development of the historical–critical approach to John *after* Bultmann, Martyn, and Brown. For this we turn once more to German scholarship.

A SANITIZED HISTORICAL CRITICISM: FREY AND SCHNELLE

Jörg Frey and Udo Schnelle are both expert Johannine scholars who have reached their views independently of one another. It is all the more striking, then, that in their recent assessments of the current state of Johannine scholarship they reach closely similar conclusions about what are, by now, valid approaches and what are not. This pertains to all the subdisciplines we have mentioned: *Literarkritik*, *Religionsgeschichte*, *Traditionsgeschichte*, the Johannine community, and literary or narrative criticism. We should first take note of this basic agreement. Since it is so well argued, we may also see it as expressing where Johannine studies are at the present junction, as a carefully weighed result of the various developments over the last one hundred years. Based on this agreement, I go on to consider how an apparent, shared tension in the positions of Frey and Schnelle between

their positive attitudes towards literary criticism of John and their expressed
desire to stay historical–critical may be solved in such a manner that the
two paradigms may, in fact, be put to use together, as Culpepper had called
for (though in fact not by 'informing one another'). In the same connection
I also suggest a way in which Segovia's emphasis on the situated and
localized, non-universal real reader may be combined with the universal
perspective of historical criticism. In this way I articulate the methodological perspective that underlies the present book in its call for a return to the
text.

We may begin with Schnelle's position on *Literarkritik* (Schnelle 2010,
288):

It is doubtful to me whether the understanding of the current text (*der Jetzttext*) is
helped in this way [that is, by taking *Literarkritik* as one's methodological starting
point]. . . . The source critical arguments have remained the same for one hundred
years; they are most often repeated with small variations and often with the claim
that one confronts the problems instead of evading them.

Again (Schnelle 2010, 269):

It is not a possible pre- or post-history that determines the meaning of Johannine
texts; instead, the key to the understanding of the individual texts always lies in the
intra-textual world of the whole Fourth Gospel.

Correspondingly, Schnelle is very positive towards literary criticism of the
modern kind (Schnelle 2010, 287):

Within Johannine studies one may note a clear tendency during the last two
decades towards a basically synchronic analysis. . . . As a text, the Gospel of John
is a coherent, intrinsically unified literary form.

Even more (Schnelle 2010, 280, repeated 287):

Whereas (previously) abrupt transitions, unprepared time indications or sudden changes of perspective were taken as indications of a break in the meaning
and therefore as the basis for *literarkritisch* considerations, they are now seen
from a reception aesthetic perspective as elements that activate the process of
reading.

Against this general background, it comes as a great surprise when
Schnelle also makes the following statement: 'Precisely in John it becomes
clear that the current text [again *der Jetzttext*] cannot be appropriately
interpreted without bringing in its prehistory' (288). What we see here,
I believe, is a superficial inconsistency that is due to the fact that the
relationship between a literary–critical and an historical–critical approach
has not been precisely determined. We must attempt to sort this out.

Schnelle's position on how to contextualize John in terms of *Religionsgeschichte* is just as clear as his (basic) rejection of *Literarkritik*. He is against

any form of 'monocausality' (read Bultmann). Indeed, '[i]t is possible to show that the Johannine texts can be sufficiently explained within a framework of the traditions of the Old Testament, ancient Judaism, and pagan Hellenism' (Schnelle 2010, 296). This is quite broad, of course, and that is precisely the point. Schnelle is also keen on emphasizing the role of 'pagan Hellenism' here: ' . . . in any case it is obvious to me that John cannot in any way be understood within bringing in Greco-Roman culture' (299). As he says (quite rightly): 'The phrase πνεῦμα ὁ θεός [God is spirit] is an equally crucial idea in Hellenistic history of religion and in Johannine theology' (299). And he adds this wonderful sentence (299):

In terms of method, the distinction between on the one side 'Jewish' or 'Christian' and on the other side 'pagan' should be abolished just as the division between philosophy and religion inasmuch as ancient philosophy as a concrete form of life and religion and ethics were constantly intersecting with one another and were understood—differently from today—as a unity.

This is sweet music in the ears of one who once edited a volume on Paul entitled *Paul Beyond the Judaism/Hellenism Divide* (2001).

How far away this takes us from historical criticism at its various peaks in the twentieth century. It constitutes a sanitized form of historical criticism, one that has learned from its excesses. We also note, however, that the precise relationship between this sanitized historical criticism and literary criticism was not determined sufficiently clearly.

A SANITIZED HISTORICAL CRITICISM: FREY ALONE

Jörg Frey has gone over all these issues even more extensively than Schnelle. Here I employ his overall statement of the current state of the art in Johannine scholarship in Frey 2013c as a wholly convincing positioning of valid and invalid approaches to John resulting from the hundred years of scholarship that we have surveyed earlier. At the same time I identify two remaining problems in Frey's account that call for further clarification.

On the Fourth Gospel in relation to *Religionsgeschichte*, Frey makes two basic points. First, he argues against any kind of biased decision to begin with (*Vorentscheidung*, 2013c, 35). This is closely similar to Schnelle's warning against 'monocausality', and it is directed against Bultmann's Gnostic reconstruction and against Klaus Wengst's decision to draw almost exclusively on rabbinic material (Frey 2013c, 36):[15]

---

[15] For the latter see, in particular, Wengst 1981.

Such a restriction of the comparative material—to Gnosticism, philosophy, rabbinics, or 'merely' to Old Testament writings—constitutes a problematic narrowing of the interpretative enterprise that should be avoided.

This is exactly right. Secondly, Frey raises a crucial question concerning the whole point of the *religionsgeschichtlich* comparison (35):

The huge number of parallels that are noted, but quite often not put to any real use, in any case raises the question of what is actually learned (Frey: *erklärt*) from the 'parallels'. Ultimately, it should be less a matter of genealogical derivations than of a contextualization that shows the profile of the text to be interpreted within the group (*Gefüge*) of other comparable texts of its time and world.

Here, then, is the same kind of broadening of the comparative horizon as in Schnelle, and Frey adds the vital question of the whole point of engaging in comparison. We will return to this issue later on.

On *Literarkritik* Frey has even more to say. His basic position comes out as follows (18):

The lack of any objective criteria for distinguishing sources and layers, a process that cannot at least be verified in terms of language and style, suggests a certain scepticism towards *literarkritisch* approaches.

And again (34):

So detailed a reconstruction is certainly not able to generate a consensus (*konsensfähig*); an author here moves around in a circle created by himself, in which many things may well fit, but which does not add to the historical probability (*Wahrscheinlichkeit*) of the reconstructions. The degree of the hypothetical is enhanced at every step, the validity . . . can no longer be controlled. The unified overall picture turns into a fiction, a lovely 'glass bead game' (*Glasperlenspiel*).

It would be difficult to state this point in a better way. What it shows is that as a consequence of the way *Literarkritik* has been performed throughout the twentieth century, a mature scientific self-consciousness now tells us that this whole approach went too far. To achieve any solidity, Johannine scholarship will have to retrace its steps in this specific regard.

Frey also makes this point with regard to the attempt to draw conclusions from the stratified text back to the Johannine community that is supposed to lie behind it. Here his target is an attempt in that direction made at the time of Martyn and Brown by a group of German scholars (Georg Richter, the early Hartwig Thyen, and Jürgen Becker).[16] Frey comments (19):

---

[16] See Richter 1977; Thyen 1971; and Becker 1969/70, 1970, 1974, and 2006.

The assignments [of textual bits to extra-textual phenomena] and the stratifica-
tions of the texts often appeared wilful (*willkürlich*) and came out differently in
accordance with the criteria that had been chosen in each particular case.

He does not deny that the text may well reflect historical developments in
'Johannine community circles', but concludes (Frey 2013c, 19, my
emphasis):

The critical question remains whether any of these [positions and discussions in the
Johannine community circles] *can any longer* be identified, isolated, and assigned [to
any particular group] and whether this history *can any longer* be recovered through
the 'window' of the Gospel and the letters.

Immediately Frey goes on to pose this critical question to 'what is perhaps
the most influential community historical model, viz. the reconstruction by
Raymond E. Brown' (19). Earlier he has also called into question whether
the two horizons in Louis Martyn's two-level drama can be kept separate in
the way claimed by Martyn. He does not deny that (15–16):

in the Johannine text the story of the events that belong to the horizon of the
earthly Jesus in terms of place, time, and content is combined with problems,
theological insights, and forms of language that belong to the horizon of the
Johannine author and his addressees.

Indeed, he claims, quite rightly, that (17):

a large number of elements of the Johannine story—not only its picture of the Jews,
but also of the disciples, the style of Jesus' speeches, and the specific Christology and
soteriology—reflect features and insights that fit the time of writing and the first
readers much better than the time of Jesus.

But he also insists that 'both horizons are fused together in complex ways
that can no longer be clearly dissolved' (16, my emphasis).[17]
 All in all, then, Frey speaks distinctly for a certain 'sobriety' (*Ernüchte-
rung*) vis-à-vis Johannine *Literarkritik* (19). As regards the unity of the
transmitted text, he does acknowledge (20) that the Fourth Gospel:

can hardly count as a text that was 'cast in one piece', as a completely homogenous
literary unity. . . . At least with regard to chapter 21 one may think of a secondary
addition or even edition of an existing text.

But then again 'the question what in such a case might possibly have been
added may only be approached with cautious considerations (*vorsichtige
Erwägungen*)' (20). The same scepticism holds for the question of sources
and traditions behind the text: 'It seems clear that the evangelist drew on

---

[17] Here I am interested in Frey's observation of a complexity that cannot be dissolved, not
in his notion of a 'fusion of horizons'. I will return to that in Chapter XII of this book.

sources and traditions', but 'if one presupposes some knowledge of the Synoptic traditions [a view for which Frey argued convincingly in Frey 2003]', then the various substantial sources that have been reconstructed 'can hardly any longer be reconstructed'. And so Frey concludes that 'the key to the interpretation of the Fourth Gospel can hardly be expected to come from *Literarkritik*' (21).

Particularly interesting for our purposes is Frey's attitude to the in principle ahistorical approach of literary criticism. Here he is divided. On the one hand, he is very positive—and I quote again because Frey expresses so well an understanding of John that is surely correct (37, Frey's italics):

> In fact, an awareness of the *literary*, narrative, and dramatic elements of the Johannine text, of the progressive development of motifs and themes, of the subtle pattern of implicit comments to the reader and aids to the understanding, indeed of the whole, didactic dynamics of the text belongs to the most important results of recent Johannine scholarship. The Gospel is precisely not a secretive work that closes in on itself,[18] but one that aims to communicate its own understanding of the story of Jesus by a variety of means. But these means can only be grasped when one looks at the text in its totality (*Gesamtheit*), as a 'functioning' whole.

And he continues (37):

> The synchronic–narrative approaches tie the interpretation back to the literary form (the *sprachliche Gestalt*) of the transmitted text, to what is actually there (*was faktisch vorliegt*), and they give rise to a cautious scepticism (*vorsichtige Skepsis*) towards all hypotheses concerning sources and redaction processes, which are often launched with a much too high degree of self-confidence.

This is extremely well said. But Frey then also adds, on the other hand, a crucial qualification (38, Frey's own italics):

> Nevertheless, we cannot avoid the *historical* questions and *aporiai*, not even when we are operating within the horizon of synchronic approaches.

Even more explicitly (38):

> Although I therefore consider the synchronic, text-oriented approach to be the one that promises most for interpretation and is methodologically most appropriate, yet I can neither abandon the historical question of the possible author and the first...readers nor the question of the appropriate historical and tradition– or religion–historical contexts...even when precisely these questions can only be answered tentatively (*in Ansätzen*), very hypothetically, or perhaps even not at all (*oder vielleicht auch gar nicht mehr*).

---

[18] In Frey's wonderful German: '*ein verrätseltes, sich abschliessendes Werk*'.

Since this is such an important point, I give a last long quotation that shows how Frey wishes to address the questions even when they probably cannot be answered (25):

> The complex questions regarding the unity (of the text), the author, the situation of writing, and the historical context, and also the literary relationship between the Gospel and the letters do not allow themselves to be pushed completely back. The claim that an historical explanation (*die historische Erklärung*) is superfluous for a reading of the text and an understanding of its textual world is unsatisfactory as long as our involvement with Biblical texts is undertaken within the framework of an historical paradigm, and this remains determinative at least in a European context. Whether the questions that are posed may (then or in fact) be answered with a sufficient degree of plausibility (*Plausibilität*) is a moot point (*sei dahinge-stellt*)—and scepticism towards all reconstructions of sources and strata is fully justified (*sehr berechtigt*)—but in a big scientific commentary one cannot to my mind abandon the attempt to illuminate the genesis of at least individual bits of the text, no matter that the possibility of answering these questions is strongly reduced (*sehr eingeschränkt*).

The caution and forthrightness of all this are equally impressive. But has the problem of relating literary criticism to historical criticism been solved? And has the insistence been justified on continuing to raise those historical questions that probably cannot be answered?

A RETURN TO THE TEXT—WITH REGARD TO *RELIGIONSGESCHICHTE*

Schnelle and Frey have identified with exceptional clarity the state of the art of Johannine scholarship at present. Our task now is to determine where this leaves us as we engage in an overall study of the Fourth Gospel. What methodological position should direct our reading of this extraordinary text?

There are three main issues to be addressed. One concerns the relationship between the historical–critical paradigm and the two later paradigms of literary criticism and intercultural criticism. We will attempt to resolve that issue towards the end of this chapter. Meanwhile, if we also wish to operate within the historical–critical paradigm, there are two further issues to be considered: how to handle the discipline of *Literarkritik* (and the types of tradition history that are often combined with it); and how to handle the discipline of *Religionsgeschichte*. It will be easiest to discuss these two issues in reverse order.

With regard to John and *Religionsgeschichte*, Schnelle and Frey have made one important point that must surely be allowed to stand. The *religionsgeschichtlich* context of the Fourth Gospel must be understood very broadly. Themes and motifs in the Old Testament that are relevant for a better understanding of that Gospel are certainly to be included. And the same goes for Hellenistic Judaism in its broadest sense (e.g. as including both Qumran and Philo). But the same also goes—'beyond the Judaism/ Hellenism divide'—for any kind of material from the Greco–Roman world, which includes not only history of religion and philosophy, but also a range of topics on the literary side, such as genres, imagery, and more.

There remains a genuine problem, however, which Frey raised head on: what is the point and purpose of bringing in all this material for comparison? This question has long been on the agenda in New Testament scholarship— one thinks of Samuel Sandmel's classic article on 'Parallelomania' (1962) or Jonathan Z. Smith's incisive chapter 'On Comparison' (1990)—and I propose an answer which, while remaining within the historical–critical paradigm, pushes the focus distinctly in one direction, that of the text itself.[19]

It seems that scholars may have two interests in trying to contextualize a text such as the Fourth Gospel. One is to situate this particular text, in Frey's words, within 'the group (*Gefüge*) of other comparable texts of its time and world' as a question of its religion– and tradition–historical '*Einordnung*' (Frey 2004a in 2013a), which means something like 'classifi- cation' or even 'pigeonholing'. The idea behind this is a genuinely historical one: here is one text in its historical situation; can we find other texts (in their respective historical situations) that are similar? If we can, then we have 'situated' this particular text. We have, as it were, put it in its place as part of a wider group of texts.

But then there is also another interest, to which Frey's question itself rightly points. Here one is not interested primarily in 'situating' the text. Instead, one wishes to understand the text itself better *through* all the contextual material that scholarship puts at one's disposal. This exercise is certainly also an historical one. It presupposes the belief that the text belongs somewhere or other in the *Gefüge* of other similar texts. It has not dropped down from heaven, but belongs either here or there. But that is not the present concern. Rather, without feeling certain about where exactly the text belongs, this approach is focused on the text itself and proposes to employ *whatever* contextual material may be seen to *work* in order to elucidate its meaning.

Such an approach draws on contextual material for a purpose that we may understand as being exclusively *heuristic*. It aims to find as much coherent sense as possible in the text that is studied. When one speaks

---

[19] For a treatment of the issue, see Seelig 2001. Seelig discusses Jonathan Smith's position (296–300), but ends up rejecting 'the retreat from drawing historical conclusions that Smith in fact calls for' (299). He would probably not be happy with the proposal I am about to make either.

here of looking for what 'works', one is making the point that the criterion of verification for the use of any kind of contextual material lies in the text itself and the act of reading it. To the extent that the text comes out as being coherent and making some striking point, one may say that the text has been illuminated through the reading that draws on the given contextual material and that the reading itself and its use of that material have been verified in the same process. Then this particular use of contextual material has also been shown to 'work'.

I have already said that this heuristic approach remains historical. It acknowledges that the text itself does belong in some specific time, place, and context. And it also draws on a large range of contextual material that is itself historical. (This does not exclude, of course, that one may *also* bring in much more modern, theoretical perspectives that may *also* illuminate the text and, if so, also 'work'.) Still, the focus here is not on the historical *Einordnung*, but on the text itself, on understanding *that* specific text better. But then again, if one does adopt this text-focused approach, there is nothing to prevent one from *moving on* from there to some kind of *Einordnung*. If any given application of the heuristic approach has been seen to work, then one may well move on to do some historical situating of the text. Only, it should be quite clear that this exercise is a different one from the heuristic, text-oriented one on which it was based.

In this book I put into practice this heuristic approach. Out of the wide range of historical contextual material that is, in principle, *all* relevant to the Fourth Gospel, I propose to draw on one particular field: that of Greco-Roman philosophy, and even more narrowly, that of Stoicism. This might seem the kind of narrow approach to which Frey and Schnelle have objected in connection with Bultmann. But it is not. I am not excluding anything whatever in the wide range of potential contextual input into the reading of John. On the contrary, I am attempting to keep the horizon as open as possible. When I bring in motifs and ideas from Stoicism, the only criterion for determining whether this is justified or not is whether it works. If anybody can come up with alternative contextual motifs and ideas that will work equally well (or even better), I will greet this with enthusiasm. The whole point of the exercise is to better understand the text itself, to bring as many of its widely different themes and motifs together into a coherent, powerful, single reading.

Methodologically, then, with regard to contextualizing the Fourth Gospel in terms of *Religionsgeschichte*, I adopt the heuristic approach. Contextual *Einordnung* must come, if at all, at a later stage as a result of intensive work on the text itself.[20]

[20] I will make an attempt at such an *Einordnung* (in relation to Mark and Paul) in Chapter XI.

A RETURN TO THE TEXT—WITH REGARD TO
LITERARKRITIK AND LITERARY CRITICISM

Here, too, Schnelle and Frey have drawn the proper conclusions from the development of Johannine scholarship in the twentieth century. They are right in claiming that the *literarkritisch* approach has directly *shown* itself to be illegitimate in the way it has been performed. They are also right in claiming that literary criticism as introduced in the 1980s has proved to be an immensely valuable tool that actually 'works': it throws a flood of light on what is actually going on in the text and between the text and its reader.

There is one point, however, where we need to go one step beyond Schnelle and Frey methodologically. When addressing the rewards of the narrative approach, they both insist that this approach must not exclude the historical questions, but Frey at one point also states that 'synchronic and diachronic methods continue to be insufficiently combined in New Testament exegesis' (Frey 2013c, 36)—which I take to mean that it remains unclear exactly how they may and should be combined. Here I propose a two-pronged position. First, it is correct to insist that the whole range of historical questions are, in principle, available as questions to be asked. *However*, the development of scholarship has shown that by far most of these questions are, *in fact*, no longer available for such questioning. Or more explicitly: we should give up asking those questions—though definitely not forget that they *have* been asked. Instead, we should look at the transmitted text as a whole. That is where our focus should be. It is important to see—once again—that this position does not leave historical criticism behind. On the contrary, it is an historical–critical position. There *are* historical questions to be asked (in principle); *only*, since they are (as we have now learned) impossible to answer with any degree of certainty so as to generate the required consensus, they should no longer be asked. In relation to such questions, we should take up the position of Greek sceptical *epochê* (suspension of judgement) or, in another ancient language, of a *non liquet* ('it is not clear').[21] Here, then, I wish to go distinctly further than Frey, though within the same historical–critical paradigm and based on the same perception of the development of that paradigm. In any case, there remains a wealth of contextual, *historical* material that may be brought in for heuristic purposes to elucidate the text.

The other prong concerns the relationship of narrative criticism to the historical–critical enterprise. Alan Culpepper expressed his wish that they might 'inform one another', but it was unclear exactly how that might be

---

[21] Here, too, belongs the vexed question of the relationship between the Johannine Gospel and Epistles. In this book I will stay rigorously focused on the Gospel itself.

since theoretically narrative criticism did constitute a genuinely different paradigm from historical criticism. Here the best solution seems to be as follows. Let us go back to the model of past, present, and future: of (i) reading the text 'backwards' (that is, going beyond the text itself back to the various conditions in the past that may lie behind it); (ii) reading the text 'itself'; and (iii) reading it 'forwards' (that is, by considering its later reception among real readers in what is the future vis-à-vis the text itself). In relation to that model we may well say that the narrative approach is of immense value in connection with stage ii, only while it does illuminate the text very importantly by using its various tools that are not necessarily 'historically specific' (on the contrary: they are fundamentally modern, though with ancient ancestors), there are also other literary tools that may be applied in addition, precisely such historical and contextual ones as considerations of ancient literary genres and the like. Understood in this way the in-principle ahistorical discipline of narrative criticism may be seen as *one tool among others* which does not in itself, and should not, exclude that other literary (and broader) considerations that *are* historically based may *also* be brought in. The narrative perspective alone is not all, but may be employed—extremely usefully—as part of a more comprehensive approach in which the reader operates with a *range* of perspectives. While narrative criticism and historical criticism are indeed in principle 'incommensurable' taken as wholes, there is no incommensurability in the actual *use* by the *reader* of a narrative and an historical perspective since they are both applied to the only thing that matters: understanding the text itself.

The case is similar here to the use of another type of modern conceptuality which has also been brought to bear on the Fourth Gospel: one informed by modern social theories about sects, their use of language, and the like. I have in mind illuminating works by Wayne Meeks (1972) and Norman Petersen (1993). The issue here is not whether such approaches have been successful or not, only that it is, in principle, fully possible to bring to bear a modern conceptuality on ancient texts and then to weigh its usefulness in relation to whatever historical information one *also* possesses. In the same way, in studying the text itself within a narrative perspective, one may certainly draw on the modern insights of narrative criticism and *also* relate the results to more historically informed literary perspectives.

We should conclude that even though historical criticism and narrative criticism constitute different, and in principle, 'incommensurable' paradigms in a Kuhnian sense, both may be *employed* by the same scholar who—in an interpretative enterprise that may also be open to reading in all three directions we have noted—wishes to focus on the text itself. In so doing, the scholar may let the results from using either paradigm fertilize one another in his or her own mind.

In this book I do precisely this. While being open to reading in all three directions, my focus is on the text itself, and here the reading is informed both by modern narrative criticism and also by historical, literary and other considerations. The justification for this approach must be found in whether it works. The proof is in the pudding.

It follows from these considerations that since *Literarkritik* must now be put aside (in fact, though not in principle) even by a scholar who is (also) working within the historical-critical paradigm, the text analysed in this book is the whole of the Fourth Gospel as we have it. But precisely because this scholarly decision is not based on the narrative paradigm alone, I also claim that the text in focus is the whole transmitted text minus 7:53–8:11 (on the woman caught in adultery), which is excluded in some manuscripts, and minus chapter 21, which has all appearances, as Frey rightly stated, of being a *Nachtrag*. All the rest is *the* object of study here.

A RETURN TO THE TEXT—WITH REGARD TO INTERCULTURAL CRITICISM

The methodological paradigm articulated by Fernando Segovia constitutes a direct challenge to historical criticism in a number of respects, one of which is the rejection of the idea of a single interpretation as being *the* best one, inasmuch as it is claimed to be the one that best holds together all the historical information available to the interpreter. Here is Segovia's way of drawing the contrast (Segovia 1998c, 322):

With the emergence of diversity in method and theory (in reader constructs and strategy) as well as in readers and interpreters (in real readers), the traditional quest for the one original and definitive meaning of the Gospel has yielded to an ever-increasing production of readings and interpretations on the part of increasingly self-conscious readers and interpreters.

Is intercultural criticism, as explained by Segovia, incompatible or incommensurable with historical criticism, as it should be if it constitutes a genuinely new Kuhnian paradigm? And where does the present book place itself in relation to intercultural criticism?

Let me state from the outset that the present reading of John in no way purports to give us 'the one original and definitive meaning of the Gospel'. This would be wholly presumptuous precisely in view of the many different readings that have been offered even within the historical–critical paradigm. Here, too, one must insist that the history of scholarship has taught us something important, namely, that a scholarly claim to be in possession of the one original and definitive meaning of the Gospel is wholly vacuous. One must always keep one's mind open to better readings.[22]

It does not follow, however, that *aiming* at the best historically informed reading of the text is wrong. The idea itself—and this is one central claim of historical criticism—that there is *a* (more or less clearly circumscribed) accessible meaning of an ancient text and that it must be accessed through the best knowledge of all relevant historical factors, this idea is not made questionable by the fact that nobody can justifiably claim to have reached that meaning and articulated it to the full. Rather, it lies as a kind of regulative idea behind any such endeavour.

But may Segovia not argue—with a basis in much postmodernist reflection—first, that the idea of a text's *own* meaning is vacuous, and secondly, that the situatedness of *any* reader should force us to admit the 'local' as opposed to 'universal' character of any reading whatsoever? Obviously, these are fundamental issues that call for far more extensive treatment than they can be given here. However, let me make just a few points.

On the issue of the text's own meaning it seems an incontrovertible fact that any text provides some degree of resistance to interpretation. Not all interpretations will work, just because they run up against features of the text itself (as understood by anyone who reads it) that will not allow them. This fact is certainly not sufficient to point in the direction of a single best reading of the text—the one that runs against no features at all of the text. But it shows that reading a text cannot *merely* be a matter of articulating 'where the reader comes from'.

Conversely, one may well ask what the point should be of reading, for instance, an ancient text if one puts all the weight on the side of the local reader. Do we not read in order to learn something *different* from what we knew beforehand? If so, even an intercultural critic must allow that the aim of reading that underlies historical criticism has a legitimate role to play within any kind of reading, no matter the extent of its local situatedness. Indeed, aiming at *that* kind of understanding must be a central element in any kind of reading that also aims in reading to understand better the world as a whole.[23]

---

[22] Compare Udo Schnelle's pithy formulation of this point: 'Die Ergriffenheit von der eigenen Erkenntnisfähigkeit und Logik sollte nicht dazu führen, andere Sichtweisen zu vernachlässigen' (Schnelle 2010, 274). Let me add another quotation: 'Natürlich habe ich nicht vor, sämtliche Probleme des Evangeliums zu erörtern oder gar zu lösen. Die von mir gestellte Frage muss das Ganze im Auge behalten, braucht aber nicht alles Einzelne zu behandeln' (Käsemann 1966, 5–6).

[23] Acknowledgement of the *difference* of ancient texts seems implied when Segovia operates with the notion of a 'resistant' reader (see Segovia 1998c). For a splendid example of how to read John from a number of 'local' perspectives ('compliant', 'resistant', 'sympathetic', and

It remains the case that the intercultural approach puts its finger on another incontrovertible fact: that all readers do read, not from nowhere, but from somewhere. Intracultural criticism is quite right to remind us of this and insist that we do not forget it in our practices. In that way one may indeed hope that we as readers and interpreters become 'increasingly self-conscious'.

With these remarks it should be clear that in presenting the reading of John that is developed in this book I am not forgetting where I am coming from as an author. At the same time, I am attempting to live up to the regulative idea that underlies historical criticism of getting as close as possible to the historical meaning of the text, or—in the language of literary criticism—of articulating the message that the implied author has sent to the implied reader. And that task requires a thorough historical awareness, since the text is itself an historical one.

THE METHOD TO BE ADOPTED: A NARRATIVE PHILOSOPHICAL READING

In light of all these considerations, we may call the type of reading to be presented in this book a 'narrative philosophical' one. It is a narrative reading since it builds on the demise of *Literarkritik* and the arrival of literary criticism. This means that throughout we are concerned to see how the text may make sufficient literary sense—across all apparent *aporiai*—not only as a whole, but also in individual sections. I presuppose here all the usual modern literary critical tools as explained by Culpepper and others.[24] These include (from Culpepper): narrator and point of view, narrative time, plot, characters, implicit commentary (misunderstanding, irony, symbolism), and the implied reader. Resseguie 2005 basically agrees: rhetoric (repetition, which includes *motifs* and *themes*, framing narratives, rhetorical figures, figures of thought), setting, character, point of view, and plot.[25] I do not, however, plan to provide a narrative analysis that constantly appeals to the various technical terms within narrative criticism. They are all presupposed, but will be used (more implicitly) to bring out the basic issues with which the text seems to be struggling.[26]

'engaged'), see Reinhartz 2001a. Here, too, the idea of the (historical) meaning of the text itself seems implicitly acknowledged.

[24] In addition to Culpepper 1983 and Resseguie 2005, special mention may be made of O'Day 1986b and Stibbe 1992.

[25] For motifs and themes, which are important in this book, see, e.g., Resseguie 2005, 45–8.

[26] Recall how narrative criticism developed out of so-called New Criticism with its overall double emphasis on seeing the text as an organic whole and doing close reading of it; see Resseguie 2005, 21–30.

Any *literarkritisch* concern with strata and the like are kept rigorously at bay. Building on that platform, I will be concerned to give the text one more chance by trying to show that it hangs intimately together in larger sections (often two whole chapters). Of these, some have already been recognized as being coherent in literary terms, others have not.

Once that has been established, I turn to the philosophical, heuristically contextualizing side of the reading and try to show that the sections that have been identified as units on purely literary grounds also constitute individual units of content. This unitary character comes out when one sees that relatively early in each section a question of a philosophical character is raised in the narration, to which an answer is then also given—and again in the narration—towards the very end of the given section. An example of such a question might be: why is it that some people respond positively to Jesus' teaching so as to 'obtain faith in' him (Greek: *pisteuein*), while others do not?[27] This question is a properly philosophical one. It belongs within the philosophical discipline of epistemology. It calls for reflection on a number of concepts and ideas that may all be seen to be addressed in the Johannine text: what it is that people believe about Jesus when they have faith in him; how they may be brought to have such a belief; who or what brings it about, and more. Such questions have also been asked in traditional readings of the Fourth Gospel when they addressed what is most often called the theology of the text. That is a fact to be greeted with enthusiasm. When I speak of philosophy here, I do not consider it in any way to be opposed to, or different from, theology. I prefer the broader term since it covers everything that needs to be addressed—not just theology in the narrow sense of thoughts about God (or Christ)—but also precisely epistemology, cosmology, and ethics. (In John's case this is all *within* a setting of thinking about God and hence theology.) Similarly, when I address issues that theologians have traditionally articulated under such terms as 'Christology', 'eschatology', 'soteriology', 'ecclesiology', *Kreuzes-theologie* versus *Gesandten-* or *Herrlichkeitstheologie* ('messenger theology' or *theologia gloriae*), and the like, I do so in terms that are immediately *philosophically* intelligible. The aim is to spell out the meaning of these technical theological terms, instead of merely taking them over. In doing this, I translate them back to the level at which John himself speaks. The result is a new account of 'the whole of John' which, hopefully, gets to the heart of what this great text was meant to say. In the final two chapters, I will relate the resulting picture to a number of issues that have been discussed

---

[27] Judith Lieu once reminded me that while John speaks a great deal about 'believing' or 'having faith' (*pisteuein*), he never speaks of 'belief' or 'faith' (*pistis*), which is so common in Paul. The point is important to remember, but cumbersome to follow when one is paraphrasing Johannine statements.

intensely in scholarship: John's relationship with the Synoptics (not least Mark), with Paul, and with the Jews (Chapter XI), and John's use of imagery and his special—or rather, not so special—eschatology (Chapter XII).

THE RESULTING PICTURE IN OUTLINE

To help the reader grasp where the argument is going, I provide a brief outline of the most salient features of the reading I am proposing.

(1) Jesus—so the text aims to show—had a double identity during his earthly life. On the one hand, he was fully a human being, Jesus of Nazareth, who went around acting and preaching in Galilee, Samaria, and Judaea, who engaged directly with other people in bodily and emotional ways, who was killed by crucifixion, and was then resurrected into heaven. The last event is certainly not a 'merely human' one, even though it should be understood wholly literally within a concrete cosmology. It reflects the fact that, on the other side, Jesus was also identified as 'the Son of God' by John the Baptist when he, Jesus, received the spirit (or *pneuma*) from God. From then on, as Jesus *Christ*, Jesus was also the (bearer of the) *logos* (God's plan for the world) which had been with God from the beginning but which was fixed on Jesus precisely when he received the *pneuma*. In everything Jesus did after that moment (his wondrous acts and divine speech), Jesus acted precisely as Jesus (the human being) *Christ*, the (unique) Son of God. His resurrection, which was engineered by the *pneuma*, was the final confirmation of this divine side of Jesus' double identity.

In this picture, both the facts of Jesus' crucifixion and of his resurrection are given equal weight. The fact of Jesus' crucifixion is meaningless (in John's conception) without that of his resurrection. Conversely, the fact of his resurrection is meaningless without that of his crucifixion. It is the crucified Jesus Christ—who by his death has 'taken away the sin of the world' (1:29)—who has also 'conquered the world' (16:33) through resurrection. Jesus Christ *must* die to be resurrected.

(2) However, that is not the end. Jesus will return to the disciples immediately after his death and resurrection, namely, as *pneuma* (the 'Paraclete'). And Jesus will also return at a later date, which lies in the future, beyond the time of both his immediate disciples and John and his readers. At that time he will call all the living and the dead to either eternal life in heaven or eternal death, thereby confirming a destiny that has already been settled in people's reactions to Jesus in his earthly life (or at least in the reactions of people living later to the message about Jesus).

This whole set of events—as described in points 1 and 2—was part of the *logos* that was with God before the creation of the world. It is this set of events and Jesus' own role in bringing it about that constitutes the content of the message (the *Offenbarung*, 'revelation') that Jesus is constantly trying to communicate in speech to his listeners in his earthly life and aiming to make them see through his wondrous works. Jesus' message is therefore far from vacuous, but full of content.

(3) On the side of the recipients of the message, there are clear demarcation lines. Some people (the most intransigent among 'the Jews')[28] do not receive the message at all, and John is careful to explain why that is so. Others receive parts of it, in that they come to 'have faith' in Jesus. Such faith may take different forms, and here the various descriptions people give of Jesus (his 'titles') play an important role in differentiating between types or degrees of faith. The first disciples (John 1) see him in a number of ways, none of which is *the* proper one. Other people (such as the Samaritan woman and her male compatriots in John 4 and Martha in John 11) also see him in different ways, but again insufficiently.[29] And the same holds even for Peter (John 6). In fact, as John 13–17 brings out, before Jesus' death *and* resurrection *nobody* had the proper faith in Jesus since nobody understood fully who and what he is—in spite of the fact that he had constantly told them all about it. It is only in John 20 that Thomas finally gets it. In itself this lack of understanding is not surprising. What people did not understand is specifically the fact that Jesus was resurrected and went back to the Father, that is, his *return*, as opposed to his having *come* (in some sense) from the Father, a point that many understand. It is the fact of his return that shows *fully* who and what Jesus is. But who could have understood *that* before it had actually happened?

(4) Again, that is not all. The reader of the Gospel is made to believe that *after* Jesus' death and resurrection, the disciples (and their successors, the readers of the Gospel) will finally come to see fully and know who and what Jesus is. In this they are crucially helped by receiving the *pneuma* in the shape of the 'Paraclete'. For them, then, the Gospel has been written in order that they may *fully* 'believe that Jesus is the Christ, the Son of God', and moreover, in order that 'having that (*full*) belief' they may also have (eternal) *life* in his name (20:31). Here, then, there is a clear distinction between levels of belief about Jesus; and it is only full belief that will give

---

[28] All through this book I adopt the scholarly convention of speaking of 'the Jews' in quotation marks, not in order to rescue John prematurely from the charge of 'anti-Judaism', but merely to indicate that there is a difficult issue here that should always be kept in mind—and will, in fact, be discussed later (see Chapter XI).

[29] The Samaritans actually appear to get it right ('the Saviour of the world', 4:42). See more on this in Chapter IV.

believers what was part of God's plan for human beings right from the start—that they obtain (eternal) *life*. They do this quite literally when they, too, are resurrected (by means of the *pneuma*, one must suppose) into eternal life in heaven together with Christ and God, who is himself, of course, also *pneuma* (4:24).

In this picture there is no room for the notion of 'realized eschatology' that C. H. Dodd placed firmly on the map of Johannine scholarship in the mid-twentieth century, suggesting that John had the idea of understanding eternal life as the already realized 'life by which men live now and always' (Dodd 1953a, 365). Nor will there be room for the comparable Bultmannian idea that those who come to believe in the earthly Jesus already have eternal life, without having to wait for the *pneuma* and the final consummation on the final day to come—in other words, that sheer faith (unspecified) in Jesus is 'eschatological' and *is* eternal life. On the contrary, John is throughout much closer to traditional Christian 'apocalyptic eschatology' as found, for instance, in Paul and Mark.

This overview will hardly surprise specialists on John, even though it contains a few points that may raise an eyebrow. In a way, however, that is only the surface story. For underneath there is a substructure that *explains* the surface story or spells it out in a vocabulary that is philosophical in the sense given earlier and thus speaks directly of cosmology, epistemology, and ethics.

(5) At this deeper level we will find that there is a whole Johannine theory centred on the meaning of the *logos* throughout the Gospel that is introduced in the Prologue—and, not least, on the intimate relationship between the *logos* and the *pneuma*, which Jesus received at his (divine) baptism and which stayed with him all through and guided him in everything he did and said. In bringing this out, I rely on the intimate relationship between *logos* and *pneuma* in the type of Greco-Roman philosophy that had played a leading role within philosophy in the four centuries up until the time of John: Stoicism. The claim here is certainly not that John had 'studied' Stoicism. Instead, I adopt the heuristic approach developed earlier, seeing whether reading John through a Stoic lens *works* (better than any other lens).

(6) As already noted, this approach in no way denies the relevance of the Old Testament and Hellenistic Jewish texts for elucidating John. On the contrary, it is obvious that, for instance, the Prologue to the Gospel draws heavily on Genesis 1 and on various texts inside and outside the Old Testament in the Jewish wisdom tradition. However, it is also clear that John's account in the Prologue belongs at a higher level of abstraction—in fact, a philosophical one—than the Genesis account of creation. This is precisely due to the fact that he also draws on the Jewish wisdom literature, which, for instance in the Wisdom of Solomon, had directly incorporated a

certain amount of Greek philosophy, including Stoicism (but also Platonism). This is one main reason why John's *logos* should not be translated in the traditional way as 'Word'. John is *interpreting* the Genesis talk of God's word *philosophically*, showing what that talk *means* in philosophical terms, just as Philo had done in his *De opificio mundi*. John's *logos* is God's 'rational plan' for the world.

(7) If John belongs at this level of abstraction one might be tempted, as many scholars have been, to see some form of Platonism, e.g. as represented by Philo the Jew, as the type of philosophy most likely to illuminate John. Is this not the philosophy that will help us best to understand the kind of dualism that seems to pervade the Fourth Gospel?[30] No, that is what I deny. Moreover, we will see that it matters greatly whether one reads John through a Platonic lens or a Stoic one.

Platonism, certainly as developed by Philo, is a form of ontological dualism that distinguishes sharply between the world of the senses and the world of ideas. By contrast, Stoicism is basically a form of ontological monism. This does not exclude the Stoics from thinking 'dualistically' about the one world they were describing. This happens in ethics, in the radical distinction between the extremely rare 'wise man' or 'sage' and all the rest of us 'fools'. But it also happens in cosmology in the distinction between the world 'below' (basically made up of earth and water) and the world 'above' (from air upwards into fire in heaven). And it even happens in Stoic theology in the distinction between God and matter, the two primary principles of the world. Still, in Stoicism *all* this remains part of God's good world, which is good because it includes and is directly structured and governed by God himself.

(8) With two such different conceptions it will be clear immediately that the consequences of reading John through one or the other lens are momentous. For instance, the disagreement in German scholarship about how to combine the human and the divine aspects of Jesus Christ that is expressed in the battle over *Kreuzestheologie* versus *Gesandten-* or *Herrlichkeitstheologie* may well be due to the fact that scholars have been reading John through a Platonic lens.[31] In Platonism, the relationship between the world of the senses and the world of ideas is one that can only be expressed in terms of an 'image' (*eikôn*) vis-à-vis its 'model' or 'paradigm'. There is no physical connection between the immaterial (*a-sômatos*) world of ideas and the material world of the senses. If, then, Christ is divine *logos* in that sense, how can he also be a human being of flesh and blood? Thus, underlying the

---

[30] For illuminating discussions of the Johannine 'dualism', see Frey 2004 and 2006.
[31] An excellent introduction to this battle is Frey 2002. See also Schnelle 2008.

famous description of the protagonist of the Fourth Gospel as an *'über die Erde schreitender Gott'* ('a God who strides across the earth', Käsemann 1966, 22) there may well be a solid portion of Platonism, which we have all inherited from the Platonizing Church Fathers of the second century CE onwards.[32]

By contrast, I show that if we employ monistic Stoicism as our reading lens, then not only will the problem of Jesus' two natures disappear, but we will also be able to understand better a wide range of other themes that are due to the dynamic manner in which the Stoic-like, material *pneuma* is thought to operate in a monistically conceived world: it comes down on Jesus, thereby making him *literally* one with God (who is himself *pneuma*); it comes to direct expression in what Jesus is able to *do* (e.g. in resurrecting Lazarus from death)—and in his *speaking*, thereby *explaining* the power of his words on those who come to believe in him; it resurrects Jesus into heaven and makes him reappear on earth more or less immediately afterwards *as pneuma* in the form of the 'Paraclete'; it *makes* the disciples on their side (once they have received the *pneuma*–'Paraclete') finally understand in the full sense who and what Jesus is and so *also* makes them one with Christ and *therefore* also one with one another; and finally (and in the future), it will *literally* resurrect them all into eternal life in their heavenly abode.

All these events together constitute a kind of *Grundgerüst* (scaffolding) of the Johannine Jesus story that shows its basic progress and purpose. It all hangs together in terms of the activity of the (*logos-*) *pneuma* when this is understood cosmologically as a (cognitive and) material entity along Stoic lines that literally and concretely acts on all involved: on Jesus and on those who follow him. Only a reading of the *logos–pneuma* along such lines will do justice to all the references to *logos* and *pneuma*, respectively, throughout the Fourth Gospel. And only such a reading will bring out the sheer power of God's plan and action in Jesus Christ (the *logos* itself and its execution), as this is expressed *in nuce* in the Prologue and followed up in the rest of the Gospel.

Where, then, did the 'mystery' go that readers of John have from very early on connected with seeing John as the 'spiritual gospel'?[33] God's love, as expressed in 3:16 in his aim of generating eternal life for human beings, remains a mystery, but the way in which he meant to achieve this aim does

---

[32] Käsemann refers to F. Chr. Baur, G. P. Wetter, and E. Hirsch for this idea. But see also Wrede, who in 1907 spoke of Jesus' 'more than human majesty (*übermenschliche Hoheit*)' and continued: 'It is a wandering God (*ein wandelnder Gott*) who is being depicted' (Wrede 1907, 206).

[33] It is a curious fact that on the reading of John through a Stoic lens presented in this book, this Gospel is indeed a preeminently 'spiritual gospel'—though in a quite different sense from the one intended by the late second century Platonizing Christians who coined the phrase.

not. It is spelled out clearly by John in the hope that those who read his account may finally come to understand it fully and so gain eternal life.

Here, too, belongs the 'riddling' quality of John's writing, which scholars have been fond of emphasizing, not least in more recent scholarship.[34] Why does Jesus so often speak in ways that initially, at least, sound rather baffling to anybody who hears him, e.g. when he claims that he is 'the bread of life'? And why does John again and again describe a whole sequence of dialogue in which Jesus speaks in ways that continue to be misunderstood by his immediate interlocutors, e.g. when he speaks of being born 'again/from above'? My answer is: for the sake of clarity. This is a tool that John uses almost to excess with a view to his readers, in order that *they* may grasp the full meaning of what Jesus is saying. When Jesus speaks in baffling ways, the readers *should* initially be tantalized—and so tuned into trying to understand *fully* Jesus' meaning, which he almost always goes on to spell out clearly enough. And when readers see how Jesus' immediate interlocutors do *not* understand, they are themselves spurred on to celebrate and cherish the understanding that they themselves do have. In both cases the ultimate aim is clarity and full understanding. The text is working on its reader in order to make the reader work. Quite often, moreover, the reader's work has not been correctly done until he or she has grasped the direct reference of much of the superficially riddling talk: that it refers to the one thing that ultimately matters to all concerned, the *pneuma*.

---

[34] See in particular Leroy 1968 and Thatcher 2000. Attridge 2002a is also relevant. Brown in his review of Leroy is refreshingly outspoken: 'I do not find the Johannine usage so obscure or so clever in what English-speaking readers would normally call riddles. While in the Gospel narrative Jesus' audience fails to understand what he is talking about, the reader of the Gospel, even in his initial effort, can easily comprehend the "special meaning". Thus, the exclusive and recondite qualities of the Johannine understanding of revelation are rather superficial' (Brown 1970, 154). Specifically on John's use of imagery, see Chapter XII.

II

THE UNITY OF *LOGOS* AND *PNEUMA* IN JOHN 1

READING THE PROLOGUE

In this and the next chapter we consider the relationship in John between *logos* and *pneuma*, first in John 1:1–34 and then in the rest of the Gospel. John 1:1–34 contains the famous Prologue (1:1–18), which is probably the single text in the New Testament that has most often been analysed. Innumerable readings have been proposed and this constitutes a scientific problem in itself. Are they all in some way right? How, if at all, may they be combined? Who can take them all in? And how may any given reading be rejected? These are questions that are genuinely pressing if one cares about New Testament scholarship as a science. In this chapter I do two things. First, I aim to set aside a number of questions and answers that cannot achieve a sufficient amount of scientific solidity. The questions themselves are often sensible enough, but the many answers suggest that there is no way of answering them that commands a sufficient degree of scholarly consensus. Secondly, I argue for a single new proposal on an issue of considerable importance, namely, how the *logos* 'became flesh' in Jesus (1:14). This is the philosophical question that guides the investigation. In addressing it I am very much concerned to integrate the proposal with what other scholars have said. Only in that way will it be possible to make a contribution to scholarship that has some chance of generating a consensus.

In the first part of the chapter we consider the Prologue and only gradually turn to its connection with the text that immediately follows it: 1:19–34 on John the Baptist's witness. We therefore need some methodological rules to help us see what can and what cannot be done in reading the Prologue—and what should be done.[1]

---

[1] A very helpful analysis of main issues in the scholarly discussion of the Prologue in the period 1987–2010 is Theobald 2010b.

(1) On reading the Prologue as a hymn. The approach of trying to find a so-called hymn behind 1:1–18 that was then edited to serve as the Prologue to the Gospel gathered momentum in twentieth-century scholarship up until and including, for instance, John Ashton (1998a, 6). In light of our methodological considerations in the previous chapter we must conclude that this *literarkritisch* approach can no longer be adopted. Recently, Martinus de Boer (2015, 456) has reminded us of the pervasiveness of this approach in the second half of the 20th century: 'Well-known and highly respected Johannine scholars are associated with this hypothesis of an edited hymn (e.g. J. H. Bernard, Rudolf Bultmann, Ernst Käsemann, Ernst Haenchen, Rudolf Schnackenburg, Raymond E. Brown)'. De Boer also notes that already in 1985 Gérard Rochais had reviewed thirty-seven proposals before articulating his own. Add to this the fact that it is notoriously wholly unclear what is required to make a piece of written text an ancient 'hymn' and the conclusion should be obvious: this approach has no future. Here the sanity of C. H. Barrett's comment is striking. Having divided the Prologue into four sections (1:1–5, 6–8, 9–13, 14–18), he comments (1978, 150, my emphasis):

These divisions are of roughly equal length, but it does not seem possible to split them up further into poetic structure, either in Greek or in a conjectured original Aramaic. . . . The Prologue is better described as rhythmical prose. If this is true, it is impossible to strike out certain passages as prose insertions into an original 'logosode'. This is confirmed by the fact that the whole passage shows, on careful exegesis, a marked internal unity, and also a distinct unity of theme and subject-matter with the remainder of the gospel; *and by the variety of attempts which have been made to restore the original form of the Prologue.*

In the italicized words Barrett articulated the scientific rule I proposed in Chapter I: the many individual proposals have reduced themselves *ad absurdum*.

(2) On finding a highly specific structure in the Prologue in its present form. A number of scholars have attempted to find a carefully wrought structure in the Prologue as a whole, precisely without attempting to break it up into historical layers. In itself the attempt is laudable, but here, too, the fact of radical disagreement and a lack of any likelihood that a consensus may ever be reached suggest that scholarship must retrace its steps. For instance, one of the most insightful of Johannine scholars, Ignace de la Potterie (1984), divided the proposals that had been made regarding the Prologue's structure into 'deux types fondamentaux de structure': (i) the concentric structure, which sees the whole of the Prologue as being 'embraced' (sandwich-like) between 1:1 and 1:18, and (ii) the parallel structure, which sees the Prologue as moving forwards in a 'spiral' (Potterie 1984, 355) through a 'repetition of the same themes in a number of series that are

symmetrically parallel (*a, b, c / a´, b´, c´*)' (357).[2] An immediate reaction
would be: why cannot we have both at the same time? But more important is
the fact that Potterie's own proposal (which is of the second type) as
summarized graphically on p. 358 of his article is so fine-tuned that it is
certain from the very beginning that it will never be able to generate a
consensus. How much more satisfying it is to stay with the structure just
quoted from Barrett: John 1:1–5, 6–8, 9–13, 14–18, which is also the one given
in the Nestle Aland twenty-sixth and twenty-seventh editions and, in fact,
that of a German Johannine *savant* such as Michael Theobald (2009), in spite
of the fact that he also operates with a hymnic *Vorlage*.[3] Andrew Lincoln
(2005, 94) is pithy and convincing:

In its present form the prologue falls into four parts: (1) vv. 1–5—the Word in
relation to God and creation; (2) vv. 6–8—the witness of John the Baptist to the
Word as light; (3) vv. 9–13—the Word in the world and the two types of response;
(4) vv. 14–18—the community's confession about the Word.

(3) On contextualizing the *logos*. Here again the proposals are many. The
traditional translation of the *logos* as 'Word', 'Wort', 'Verbe', or 'Parole'
takes up directly the Hebrew *dabar* in Genesis 1:3. Many scholars similarly
find the basic context for John's *logos* here. Others agree, but also bring in
the wisdom tradition in or after the Hebrew Bible (Proverbs, Ben Sira, the
Wisdom of Solomon),[4] which itself speaks of God's *logos* in a manner that
takes us back to Genesis, but also develops this *logos* into the figure of
'wisdom' (*sophia* in the Septuagint), which is a much more independent
figure than God's 'creative word' in Genesis. Then there is Daniel Boyarin
(2001), who (preceded by Peder Borgen 1970 and 1972) saw the Johannine
logos as a parallel to the *Memra* of the Aramic Targums to Genesis 1: the
'Word' based on Genesis 1, but now to be understood in a midrash-like form
as also drawing on the wisdom tradition (specifically, Proverbs 8:22–31) in a
tradition which Boyarin called Jewish 'Logos theology' that was also to be
found in Philo of Alexandria. Finally, there is the position of C. H. Dodd,
who—although presented back in 1953—actually attempted to hold all the
proposals together (though without Boyarin's special *Memra* twist): the
Genesis *dabar* supplemented by the wisdom tradition and by Philo in his full

[2] Among proponents of a concentric structure Potterie mentions M-E. Boismard (1953),
Peder Borgen (1970), and Alan Culpepper (1981). Proponents of the parallel structure include
H. Ridderbos (1966).
[3] 'In fact': Theobald operates with only three 'circles' divided into 'sequences': 1:1–5
(namely, 1:1–2 + 1:3–5), 1:6–13 (namely, 1:6–8 + 1:9–13), and 1:14–18 (Theobald 2009, 104).
But the effect is much the same as in Barrett and Nestle Aland (and a host of others).
[4] The date of Wisdom is uncertain: sometime during the first centuries BCE and CE.
I personally prefer the date proposed by Hans Hübner (1999, 15–19) of around 30 BCE.

Platonic shape, which Boyarin played down quite radically.[5] We come back to Dodd's account later in this chapter. In addition, there is the whole Greek tradition, on whose relevance Udo Schnelle, for instance, has insisted. How, in light of these many proposals, should one address the question of the context for John's *logos* as employed in the Prologue?

Here we should make use of another methodological rule presented in the previous chapter. It all depends on the *heuristic benefit* to be derived from bringing in any form of contextual material, where 'heuristic benefit' is determined by the degree to which the material proves genuinely illuminating in helping to *solve distinct and urgent issues of understanding* in the text itself. In this present chapter I argue that we may keep in the picture the whole Jewish tradition from the Genesis concept onwards, but also need to include (with Dodd) the full *philosophical*—and hence 'Hellenistic', that is, Greek—development of this concept that one finds, for instance, in Philo.[6] Only, one should not have recourse to this philosophical development in the ontologically dualistic Platonic form it has in Philo, but in the monistic form it has in the philosophical movement of Stoicism that came after Plato and Aristotle. Only that type of context gives full meaning to the *logos* as described in John 1:1–5—and also solves the distinct and urgent issue in our philosophical question of explaining precisely how 'the *logos* became* flesh'.

READING WHAT?

The Prologue of John is no easy text. For one thing, in two places it is unclear how the text should be construed syntactically. The two places are 1:3–4 and 1:9. At 1:3–4 the New Revised Standard Version (NRSV) of the Bible translates as follows: '³All things came into being through him [that is, the *logos*], and without him not one thing came into being. What has come into being ⁴in him was life . . .'. But they also add another possible

---

[5] This, to my mind, is one of the least convincing sides of Boyarin's stimulating article. He goes so far as to say that it 'becomes . . . less and less plausible to speak of Philo as having been influenced by Middle Platonism. Instead, insofar as the Logos theology, the necessity for a mediator, is intrinsic to Middle Platonism, that form of "Hellenistic" philosophy may simply be the Judaism of Philo and his fellows' (Boyarin 2001, 251). Boyarin has never been afraid of tearing down scholarly constructs. Here, in spite of his caveats, he has definitely gone too far. For much more properly Platonic readings of Philo in relation to the Prologue, see Tobin 1990 and Leonhardt-Balzer 2004. On Philo and Middle Platonism in general, see Dillon 1996, Runia 1993, Sterling 1993, and Dillon 2008.

[6] Of the two articles mentioned in the previous note, Tobin (1990) is fully alert to the distinctly philosophical character of Philo's *logos*. To my mind, Leonhardt-Balzer (2004) still finds too much of the pre-philosophical Genesis 'Wort' in Philo. As Tobin shows, Philo's account of the *logos* is a philosophical *interpretation* of the Genesis 'Word'.

translation in a footnote: '³All things came into being through him [that is, the *logos*]. And without him not one thing came into being that has come into being. ⁴In him was life . . .'. At 1:9 NRSV translates as follows: '⁹The true light, which enlightens everyone, was coming into the world.' But they also add the following translation in a footnote: '⁹He was the true light that enlightens everyone coming into the world'. I adopt here NRSV's secondary translation in the first case and their primary one in the second case. Of these issues the former does not matter so much for understanding the overall line of thought in the Prologue.⁷ The latter does.⁸

Another issue of translation concerns the rendering in 1:5 of the final verb in the Greek (*katélaben*). Is the meaning this: '⁵The light shines in the darkness, and the darkness did not *overcome* it' (NRSV)? Or this: '⁵The light shines in the darkness, and the darkness did not *understand* it'? I take it that the intended meaning is 'overcome',⁹ but Barrett may be right that 'John is . . . playing on the two meanings' (1978, 158).

A further thing that makes the Prologue less than easy is the fact that it is pregnant with ideas which—as befits this 'overture' to the whole Gospel—are not fully spelled out in the text itself. Nevertheless, the primary task is to consider all the important connections between concepts and ideas intrinsically within the Prologue itself—at the same time as we must allow ourselves to draw heuristically on the rest of the Gospel and contextual material where this pays off.

However, there is one important point about what constitutes the text that has been made in recent scholarship, which tends to loosen the sense of 1:1–18 as a wholly independent 'Prologue' to what comes after. Michael Theobald has insisted that the *corpus* of the Gospel only begins with 2:1 and not 1:19. Chapter 1 is then taken up by the Prologue (1:1–18) and 'the story of John the Baptist and his disciples who go over to Jesus (1:19–51)' (Theobald 2009, 100).¹⁰ However, Theobald also very suggestively sees an inner connection between 1:1–18 and 1:19–34 in terms of a negative and a

⁷ Classic defenders of NRSV's primary translation are Potterie 1955 and Aland 1968, to whom may be added Thyen 2007b. De Boer 2015, 450–1, too, defends this translation. Counterarguments: (i) the perfect in γέγονεν fits better when taken with οὐδὲ ἕν than with ἦν in 1:4; (ii) starting 1:4 with 'in him' gives the desired weight to this that continues 'by him' and '(not) without him' in 1:3. The best counterargument is perhaps that (iii) the various suggested ways of rendering the text preferred by the scholars mentioned are 'almost impossibly clumsy' (Barrett 1978, 157).

⁸ For good arguments see Barrett 1978, 160–1, Brown 1966, 9–10, Lincoln 2005, 101, Theobald 2009, 122, and Painter 2014, 53. (Schnackenburg 1965–84, vol. 1 [4th ed. 1979], 230–1, is very complicated and unpersuasive.) The best argument is this (in Brown's formulation, 10): 'It seems, finally, that the contrast of vs. 9 with vs. 8 also demands this interpretation: John the Baptist was not the light; the real light was coming into the world'.

⁹ See, e.g., Brown 1966, 8, and Theobald 2009, 115–16, both with good arguments, including the reference to John 12:35.

¹⁰ Theobald first made these points in Theobald 1988.

positive witness to Jesus Christ in the following way (2009, 101). In the first half of the Prologue (1:1–13), the Baptist is described as being '*not* the light', whereas in the second half (1:14–18), he is quoted as pointing positively towards Jesus as the one who is. Similarly, in the 'first scene of John the Baptist' (1:19–28), the Baptist is quoted as saying that he is '*not* the Messiah, *not* Elijah, *not* the prophet', whereas in the 'second scene of John the Baptist' (1:29–34) he is again quoted as pointing positively towards Jesus (1:30). Theobald's point is extremely well taken. It shows that even if one sees the whole of John 1 as the beginning of the book, there is an especially close relationship between 1:1–18 and 1:19–34.

A complementary point has been made even more recently. Peter J. Williams (2011) showed that in the ancient manuscripts, lectionaries, early versions, and exegetes there is no indication that John 1:1–18 should be separated from the rest as constituting a 'Prologue' to the rest (2011, 376–80). Indeed, that notion is perhaps a nineteenth-century invention (381–2). By contrast, were one to base oneself on the appearance in the manuscripts, one would rather have to see 1:1–5 as the 'Prologue'. Martinus de Boer (2015) took up that idea and argued that it is, in fact, 1:1–5 that constitutes 'the *original* Prologue to the Gospel and, as a corollary, that this passage can still be regarded as the Prologue to the Gospel' (2015, 452, his emphasis).

What we have here are two perspectives on 1:1–5 and 1:19–34 respectively that together tend to make the granite character of 1:1–18 as *the* Prologue to John a little more porous. At the same time, they need not be taken to suggest (against de Boer) that we may no longer see and speak of 1:1–18 as 'the Prologue' to John. For 1:1–18 certainly has a *ductus* of its own that makes it utterly appropriate as a summarizing entry into what follows.[11] However, it *also* makes excellent sense to see 1:1–5 as having a special role within 1:1–18 and to see 1:19–51 (especially 1:19–34) as being extremely closely connected with the Prologue in a manner we will consider. I thus propose to read 1:1–18 as a textual unit as it stands, but also with 1:1–5 possibly having a special role within it and with 1:19–34 having especially close ties to 1:1–18 itself. We may also bring in whatever contextual material proves genuinely illuminating, but only once we have identified a serious issue of understanding that appears to call for outside help. Until that happens we will be satisfied to state the overall meaning of the text as this is likely to command *general* agreement among most scholars. All readings that display an advanced degree of ingenuity on the part of the reader will be put aside—and I am intensely concerned not to add any of my own! And the point of the whole exercise? First, to

---

[11] John Painter (2008, 38–9) well brings out the *inclusio* that is created by 1:18 in relation to 1:1–2.

answer our philosophical question by making a single new point that will deepen our understanding of 1:1–34 as a whole. And secondly, to lay the ground for the analysis of the rest of the Gospel.

The line in what follows may appear a little surprising. Having identified the overall message of the Prologue, I first follow this up by considering how the end of the Prologue, 1:14–18, both summarizes and specifies what comes before and also leads into the rest of the Gospel. Then I go back to 1:9–13 to consider certain issues that show the full depth of our philosophical question. Only then, in discussing 1:1–5, 1:14 and 1:19–34, will I address the philosophical question head on. The new point to be made is the topic of these last sections. But we must set aside certain issues in 1:14–18 and 1:9–13 before we can address that topic.

THE DUAL MESSAGE OF THE PROLOGUE

The overall message of the Prologue is not in doubt. It is a double one, with its first half focusing on the identity of Jesus: that Jesus of Nazareth (the human being), who is only identified towards the very end (1:17) and here as 'Jesus Christ', *is* the *logos* that *was* with God even before creation (1:1–2); that was *active in* the creation (1:3); that 'came into the world' (1:9) and 'became flesh' (1:14); and is now (once again) back and present as 'God the only Son' in the bosom of the Father (1:18). The story that is articulated in this way is one that is absolutely crucial for the rest of the Gospel, and Bultmann was right to focus on it as the central one: Jesus *came* from God and has *returned* to God. Later we shall see that while many characters in the Gospel came to understand the first half of this (on Jesus' origin) in a general way, none—not even the disciples apart, at the very end, from Thomas (20:28)—managed to grasp the second half (on Jesus' final destination). But the writer of the Prologue knew it.

To this theme about Jesus we must add, however, as an equally important part of the Prologue's message, that Jesus Christ came into the world (1:9–11, 14) for the specific purpose of giving those 'who received him' and 'who believed (*pisteuein*) in his name' 'power to become children of God' (1:12), those who were '(re-)born or -begotten of God' (1:13). The point here is that Christ's coming and departing had a specific purpose which rests in his intended reception among human beings. He came as a 'light' in order to give human beings a chance—if they *saw* the light—of achieving 'life'. In the Prologue itself this second theme is played out in its first half (1:1–13), which combines the motif of Christ's coming from God with that of his reception by human beings. The eventual purpose of this reception, namely, 'life' for human beings, is implied in 1:4, where 'life' is actually mentioned, though not in the form in which it occurs in the rest of the Gospel, as 'life eternal'.

With this dual message in place we will look at the second half of the Prologue (1:14–18) before returning to its former half.

JOHN 1:14–17 AS A SPECIFIC APPLICATION OF 1:1–13 THAT LEADS INTO THE REST OF THE GOSPEL

In 1:14–17 the happy reception of Christ by some as already indicated in 1:12–13 is further described in some detail that both turns the description of Jesus Christ into a celebration of him and also makes it function as a summary of the rest of the Gospel before this is actually narrated. In both respects, 1:14–17 serves to give specificity to the general account of the *logos* and its arrival on earth given in 1:1–13. Let us take note of some of the motifs that have this focusing function.

It is noteworthy that the text is now talking of 'us': the *logos* 'took up its abode in us, and we saw his glory' (1:14); and 'from his fullness we have all received' (1:16). These statements, which move from the third-person plural in 1:12–13 to the first-person plural, evidently serve to focus quite drastically the general account of the *logos* given in 1:1–13. There now is a 'we' who, as it were, vouch for the story of 'his glory' that the 'we' have actually *seen*, a story that is now about to be told.

Another feature that gives specificity is the obvious one that the *logos* that 'became flesh' is now finally identified as Jesus Christ (1:17). This feature hangs closely together with the first part of the Prologue. It marks the end point of a movement in 1:1–13 that we will consider later, from the role of the *logos* in creation via the mention of its announcement by John the Baptist, to its arrival on earth in an unnamed individual (1:11–13) who is then given his specific name in 1:14–17. The same movement towards specificity is found in the dual mention of John the Baptist's witness. In 1:6–8 it is described in general terms. In 1:15 it is specifically directed towards Jesus, beginning with a strongly marked *houtos*: 'This is the one of whom I spoke . . .'.[12]

A third feature, which again points forward to the rest of the Gospel, is found in the claim that 'we saw his glory, the glory as of a father's only son, full of grace and truth' (1:14). Three themes in this—Jesus' glory (*doxa*), his status as the Father's only son, and the idea of truth—are repeatedly taken

---

[12] I translate 1:15 as follows: 'John testified to him and cried out. "This was he of whom I spoke (or whom I mentioned). He who comes after me ranks ahead of me because he was before me"'. For this translation of εἶπον in 1:15, see 8:27. (For the traditional understanding, compare NRSV: 'This was he of whom I said, "He who comes etc."'.)

up in the Gospel as a whole. By mentioning them here in connection with what 'we' saw in Jesus, the text not only makes the general story of the *logos* more specific, but also provides a set of basic categories under which the following account of Jesus' life and death is intended to be seen.

A fourth feature has the same function, though in a somewhat more intriguing manner. In 1:14 Jesus is identified as being 'full (*plērēs*) of grace (*charis*) and truth' and in 1:16 it is said that 'we' all received 'from his fullness (*plērōma*)', to which the text adds: 'and grace upon grace' (NRSV).[13] This is intriguing since the notion of 'grace' (*charis*) does not reappear in the rest of the Gospel. It is likely, however, that the reference to grace here is meant to be cleared up by 1:17, which introduces a theme that is quite central in the rest of the Gospel: 'For the law was given through Moses; grace and truth came (into being?) through Jesus Christ'. The question of the relationship between Moses (or 'the Jews') and Jesus Christ permeates the whole of the Gospel. Apparently, the text wishes the issue to be seen under the category of 'grace' (*charis*) even though the concept itself is not taken up again later.

We may conclude that 1:14–17 of the Prologue gives a high degree of specificity to the general account of the *logos* given in 1:1–13 in a manner that both makes this section the focal end point of that account by tying the *logos* specifically to Jesus Christ and also opens up for the rest of the Gospel: 'we saw his glory etc.'—the one that is now about to be narrated.

THE ROLE OF 1:18

The concluding verse of the Prologue also has a double role. On the one hand, it directly continues the line of 1:14–17 of pointing forward to the account given in the rest of the Gospel of Jesus' life and death. This happens when the verse claims that Jesus, the 'God, the only Son (*monogenēs theos*)', who now is 'in the bosom of the Father', has *expounded* (*exēgēsato*) God. One asks: where and how? And the answer must surely be: in his earthly life and death *as these are going to be recounted*.[14] Both the description of Jesus as

---

[13] This expression is notoriously difficult and potentially highly explosive regarding 'John and Judaism'. Is John referring to a continually renewed grace among Christ believers alone (thus Barrett 1978, 168; Theobald 2009, 133)? Or is he referring to the grace of the Christ event in place of the *grace* of the Mosaic law, as 1:17 might indicate (thus Brown 1966, 16; Lincoln 2005, 107)? In agreement with Thyen 2015, 101–2 ('*Gnade anstelle von Gnade*'), who builds on Edwards 1988, I opt for the latter, which appears to yield a tighter connection of the two verses.

[14] Exegetes—and I with them—are happy to find the term for their own activity (*exēgeisthai*, 'to expound' a text) in what Jesus is said to have done here. Potterie (1988) has argued that as used here in an absolute sense the term means 'has opened the way'. His main argument is that the term *is* used absolutely here. But it is difficult not to hear 'God' as the implicit object of the verb. However, *if* Potterie is right, that also makes excellent sense: Jesus has 'opened the way' to heaven (a crucial point in John).

monogenês theos (see the 'father's only son' in 1:14) and also as an 'exposition' of God in his life and death directly continue the line of 1:14–17,
thereby pointing forward. But 1:18 also takes up and brings to its conclusion the general story line of 1:1–13. The *logos was* with God to begin with,
then *came* to earth—and is now again to be found in the bosom of God.
With this striking formulation, the text is ready to recount how *during* his
life on earth Jesus 'expounded' God.

However, we have only scratched the surface of how the Prologue aims
to present Jesus. We must now go back to the general account of the *logos*
given in 1:1–13 and consider in more detail how the text aims to fit Jesus of
Nazareth into that account. Our ultimate aim remains that of answering
our philosophical question relating to 1:14. But we must start from considering a problem that has bothered scholars for ages: where in 1:1–13 does
the text begin to speak of Jesus?

A CONUNDRUM: WHERE DOES JOHN 1:1–13 SPEAK OF JESUS?

John 1:1–13 introduces and connects four entities: the *logos*, life, light—and
then probably an individual person (in 1:11–12), who, as we have seen, is
only towards the very end explicitly identified as Jesus (1:17), and indeed as
Jesus Christ.[15] The four entities are more or less said to be identical, but it is
our task to clarify their relationship.

Here we come across an issue that divides scholars into two radically
opposed camps. One group takes it that 1:1–5 is a kind of paraphrase over
Gen. 1:1–5, which therefore speaks cosmologically of the original creation
of the whole world in which the *logos* apparently had some important role
to play. Then came an individual, John the Baptist, who bore witness to the
light (1:6–8) that was about to come into the world (1:9), then the light (or
the *logos*) (finally) came to its own (1:11) in an individual person, Jesus, and
all this is then summarized in the statement in 1:14 that the *logos* became
flesh (in Jesus). On this view, the text moves from an original universal
cosmogony to speaking of Jesus at a much later stage in the world's
unfolding. But the two themes are closely connected via the notions of
life and light. The purpose of the *logos* that was the agent of the original

---

[15] I say 'probably' concerning the individual person in 1:11–12 since there are scholars
(e.g. Dodd and Boyarin) who think that 1:9–13 is *only* a description of the arrival on earth of
the figure of wisdom *before* Jesus and John the Baptist. It is difficult to see, though, how that
fits with the mention of the Baptist in 1:6–8 and the transition from 1:8 into 1:9ff. I return to
Dodd later on, but leave this reading out of consideration for the moment in order to present
the two other readings that do see Jesus as being involved already before 1:14—though in
two quite different ways.

creation was to generate life (1:4), and life was 'the light of human beings' (1:4), that is, meant to be understood by human beings as the aim of creation. It was this light to which John the Baptist then bore witness (1:6–8) when it eventually was coming into the world (1:9). It is only in 1:11, then, that the light (which in 1:10 is probably also equated with the original *logos*)[16] must at long last be taken to refer to Jesus, who 'came to his own' and so forth. With such a general understanding, translating 1:2 (with NRSV) as '*He* was in the beginning with God' completely misses the point. What was present with God in the beginning was the *logos*, which is only very gradually identified with Jesus. Here one insists on reading 'forwards'. As we open the book, we are only very gradually told that the *logos* of the original creation also came to be present in an individual human being, Jesus.

The other group of scholars, which is equally numerous, reads the text 'backwards'. Here one knows beforehand that Jesus was the original *logos* and if one then asks the forwards-reading scholar where exactly in the text the *logos* is identified as Jesus, the backwards-reading scholar is likely to react by saying 'Ah, if that is where it happens (e.g. in 1:11: "He came to what was his own"), then why not a bit earlier?'. And here one might well point to the connection between 1:9 and 10:

[9]The true light, which enlightens everyone, was *coming* into the world. [10]It/He *was* in the world, and the world came into being through it/him; yet the world did not know it/him.

Is this text not saying that the one who was *coming* into the world after John the Baptist *was already* in the world from the very beginning, precisely as 1:10 describes 'him' in drawing on 1:1 and 1:3? In this picture it makes excellent sense to translate 1:2 as speaking of *him*. Jesus was 'pre-existent'. He was with God to begin with, even before creation in which he was himself directly involved. Then he also came *into* the world as a human being—when the *logos* became flesh.[17]

Scholars have argued back and forth on this, and the theological charge of the issue is huge. A particularly interesting reading was given by Dodd (1953a, 263–85) in twenty-three extremely insightful pages on *logos*. Drawing on the whole Jewish tradition, which brings him from God's 'Word' in Genesis via the later Jewish wisdom literature to Philo, Dodd in a first round

---

[16] This is due to a fascinating—and probably intended—technicality in this verse: that linguistically the entity that 'the world did not know' cannot be the 'light' (which is neuter), but must be—*either* the *logos* (which is masculine) *or* the individual person (that is, Jesus), or indeed both.

[17] I confess that I find a difficulty in this reading that is rarely addressed: was the pre-existent Jesus *already* a human being? If not, what *was* '*Jesus*' as pre-existent? If the answer is: '*logos*', then we are back to zero.

(263–83) argued that 1:1–13 (before the *logos* became flesh in 1:14) was all concerned with the role of the *logos* in the world *before* the arrival of Jesus Christ. 1:1–13 speaks of wisdom, who was with God to begin with, then sought a place in the world, but did not find it—apart from in a very few. Only then came Jesus Christ (by 1:14), who took up that same role. In a second round (283–5), however, Dodd argued that there is a further level of meaning in the text, 'which comes to light only when the passage is re-read in view of the gospel as a whole' (283). Then it speaks not only of the history of the *logos* and wisdom, but also of the life of Jesus with the consequence that 'not only verses 11–13, but the whole passage from verse 4, is *at once* an account of the relations of the Logos with the world, *and* an account of the ministry of Jesus' (284, Dodd's emphasis). In finding a 'double significance' (284) in the text, Dodd is, in fact, drawing on the kind of Platonizing distinction between the 'eternal' and the concretely historical which permeates his whole understanding of John—and which is wrong. Still, Dodd's suggestion of a double significance points to a solution to the quandary (though a quite different one from Dodd's own) which will show that both parties in the battle are right in a way once the required distinctions have been made.

THE SOLUTION TO BE ARGUED FOR: THE *LOGOS*— JESUS—JESUS CHRIST

In a nutshell (to be cracked open in the rest of this chapter), what came into being was 'Jesus Christ' when Jesus—a human being who was born after John the Baptist—*became* Christ. What was from the beginning was the *logos* (and light) that would eventually *make* Jesus 'Jesus Christ'. Thus the forwards-reading group of scholars is right to see Jesus—even as Jesus Christ—as referred to only very gradually in 1:1–13. Neither Jesus (who came after the Baptist) nor Jesus Christ (who did the same) was present before the creation of the world. But the backwards-reading group is also right to see '*Christ*' as being present with God before creation since that is true of the *logos* which eventually became flesh in Jesus, thereby turning him *into* Jesus Christ. What the Prologue is saying is that Jesus Christ came into being after the Baptist when the *logos*-Christ became flesh in Jesus, the human individual, by turning him into Jesus Christ. But since the *logos*-Christ was already present before creation, it is also correct to say that from the moment when Jesus had *become* Jesus Christ, 'he'—that is, Jesus, the human individual, but now (also) *as* Christ—also *was* before creation. That is why Jesus may later in the Gospel (8:58) say of himself that 'Before Abraham was born, I am'.

At this point I have presented the solution to be argued for later in order to help the reader see where we are going. We must now go back to consider a number of features of the Prologue that will eventually bring us to the solution just given in a more concrete and developed form.

A CLUE TO THE SOLUTION

Let us first note that a somewhat paradoxical clue to the proposed understanding may be found in 1:15 taken together with 1:9–10. In 1:15 John the Baptist specifically identifies Jesus ('*This* one...') in two ways: he is one who 'comes after me', that is, was born after John himself, *and* he 'has come into existence before me', that is, existed before John himself and hence (this must be the intended meaning) was present with God from the very beginning. It is important to realize the paradoxical character of this statement: how can one and the same person both have come into existence after the Baptist and have existed a long time before him? Exactly the same paradox is expressed in 1:9–10. By 1:9, the light was 'coming into the world' (note again 'coming', *erchomenon*, as in 1:15, *erchomenos*). By 1:10, however, the light *was* already in the world, and the world 'came into being' (that is, *had* come into being) *through* it, but the world did not know it (here probably the *logos*). Here again there is a paradox, which appears to be intended by the sharp contrast between 'was *coming* into the world' at the end of 1:9 and 'was in the world' at the beginning of 1:10. How, then, is the paradox to be solved?

It seems clear that the paradox is intended to bring out two radically different points about Jesus, what I call the duality in Jesus. On the one hand, Jesus was an individual human being who was born after John the Baptist. On the other hand, this same individual also in some sense *was* the *logos* (with its life and light) that had been there from the very beginning. These two points together create the paradox that we need to resolve.

THE DUALITY IN JESUS AS DESCRIBED IN 1:9–13

First let us note how the duality in Jesus is brought out in 1:9–13. The following observations basically support the picture given by scholars who read the text forwards, by finding a clear progression in time from primordial cosmogony to the post-Baptist Jesus and seeing an only gradual introduction of Jesus in the text. But we noted that the final reading will also acknowledge the insight about Jesus in relation to the primordial *logos* on the part of scholars who read backwards. The Jesus Christ who came into being also *was* present (as Christ) from the very beginning. We may put it in a form that sounds paradoxical, but precisely is not: Jesus *came* to be *primordially* present—when he became Jesus Christ. Consider then the duality in Jesus in 1:9–13.

The fact that 1:15, which explicitly mentions the duality in Jesus, may be seen to spell out something that was already said in 1:9–10 strongly suggests that 1:9–13 is not meant (as Dodd took it in the first round of his reading) to speak *only* of the myth of wisdom seeking an abode on earth. It is highly likely that that myth is indeed also recalled, as 1:10 in particular suggests (the world did not know the *logos*). But in spite of the fact that 1:9–13 does not *mention* Jesus, it seems certain that this part of the text, which to begin with, at least, speaks of the light and the *logos*, is also already *referring* to Jesus, the human individual. So, the duality in Jesus is present already in 1:9–13.

In addition there is the fact already noted, which can hardly be denied, that 1:9 (on the preferred reading of this verse) directly takes up and continues 1:6–8, which has spoken of the Baptist's witness to Jesus. '[8]*He was not the light, but <he came> to bear witness to the light. [9]The true light . . . was coming into the world.*' Once the Baptist had appeared (or indeed, been created, *egeneto*, 1:6) and *came* (*êlthen*, 1:7) to bear witness to the light, the human individual Jesus is already in the picture, at least from 1:9 onwards, where the light is said to be *coming into* the world. But since he is spoken of as the light, the other side of the duality is present too.

A third argument for finding Jesus as the (unnamed) referent already in 1:9–13 may be found in the content of 1:11–13. While 1:11 (if we translate it as 'It came to what was its own, and its own people did not accept it') might still be understood to refer to the Jewish myth of wisdom's arrival on earth, it seems impossible not to see what is described in 1:12–13 as the result of *Jesus*' arrival. After all, in light of what is said later in the Gospel (3:8), the chance of 'becoming children of God' (1:12), which belongs to those who have been 'born or begotten of or from God' (1:13), is one that is given only to those who are followers of Jesus, and not of wisdom.

We should conclude that the whole of 1:9–13 is *referring* to Jesus throughout without actually mentioning him. But we should also conclude that the text is obviously keen on drawing *into* the *description* of Jesus in 1:9–13 (as the figure *referred* to) as much as it can from the description of the *logos*, life, and light given in 1:1–5 and the underlying myth of wisdom's coming to the earth. This is just another way of saying that in bringing out the duality in Jesus the text aims to insist on the apparent paradox that Jesus both *came into* the world at a specific point in time—and that he also, in some sense, *was* in the world from the very beginning. Apparently, the *gradual* movement from speaking of the *logos* and the light to speaking of, that is, referring to, Jesus is *part of the point*, which is then brought to the level of explicit consciousness in the paradoxical statement (of 1:15 and

1:9–10) that he both *came into* the world and also *was* there right from the beginning. Are we then ready to resolve this paradox?

TIGHTENING THE PARADOX

For the benefit of the reader I have already stated my solution, which first distinguishes between Jesus (the individual human) and Christ and then brings the two together. However, it is important to note that *apart from the clue given in the two statements in 1:15 and 1:9–10* the text does not itself explicitly move in the direction of that solution. Instead, it operates at a wholly realistic and dynamic level of *things happening* or, indeed, being *created* when it speaks of the *logos* (and light) as '*coming into* the world' and as '*becoming*' flesh. I allow myself the heavy use of italics here since the point is so important. It shows that the text's own answer to the paradox is the one given in 1:14: that the *logos became* flesh—that what *was* there from the beginning (the *logos*, life, and light) in some way came to *be* an individual human being, Jesus. Initially, however, this answer is just as baffling as the paradox itself. And so the text's own attempt at a solution to the paradox raises more questions than it answers. In particular, what *is* the *logos*? And once we know that, how might that kind of thing '*become*' flesh? In short (our philosophical question): *how* did the *logos* become flesh?

We may first note that on the reading of 1:9–13 (or even 1:6–13) just given, the famous statement at the beginning of 1:14 comes as a concluding and summarizing statement that brings out explicitly what had already been implicitly stated in 1:9–13. From then on it is clear *who* we are talking about: Jesus (even though he is not explicitly mentioned until 1:17). What is not yet clear is how one should understand Jesus as one in whom the *logos* has become flesh.

We may also note that this lack of clarity extends to the description given of Jesus in 1:14–18. How is Jesus meant to be *understood* when he is said in 1:14 to be *monogenês* ('a father's only son')? The only help we get from the Prologue itself lies in the fact that those who receive him according to 1:12–13, have just been said—at the very end of 1:13—to have been 'begotten from God' (*ek theou egennêthêsan*). Here the repeated use of the same verbal root (*gennan* for begetting) points in the direction of some similar idea, but which one? Similarly, at the end of the Prologue (1:18), Jesus is once more described as *monogenês* and now even as *monogenês theos* ('God the only Son', NRSV). But in what sense? The issue remains, therefore, of exactly how to understand the statement that the *logos* became flesh. As long as we do not understand that, we cannot either resolve the paradox on which the text itself insists, that Jesus both came into the world and was also present right from the start. Nor can we explain in what precise sense Jesus was *monogenês*.[18]

In order to answer our philosophical question, we need to retrace our steps even further and address 1:1–13 from the beginning, focusing on how to understand the *logos* with which the text begins. Let us first consider what the text of 1:1–5 is actually saying. Here we will leave the term *logos* untranslated. Next we will bring in the various proposals that have been made in scholarship as to how the *logos* should be understood and translated.

THE NORMATIVE COSMOLOGY OF 1:1–5

In 1:1–5, John wishes to say two apparently opposed things about the *logos* that reflect its mediating role between God and the world. One concerns its relationship 'upwards' with God: 'the *logos* was with God, and the *logos* was God (or divine)' (1:1). Here John clearly wishes to connect the *logos* as closely as possible with God—but also to maintain a distinction. The *logos* is not just identical with God. Still, it is as closely connected with God as is possible when the two entities are *not* identical.

It is important to note that this particular feature of the *logos* in the Prologue fits exactly the picture given in the rest of the Gospel of Jesus', the Son's, relationship with the Father. For instance, 'the Jews' repeatedly attack Jesus for '*making himself equal to* God' (5:18, NRSV) or for '*making yourself* God' (10:33, NRSV). And Jesus himself agrees: 'The Father and I *are one*' (10:30, NRSV). Still, throughout the Gospel, Jesus also insists that he is only the Son, not the Father himself (see e.g. 8:42, 49–50). Thus the double aspect of the *logos* in its relation to God as given in the Prologue is maintained in Jesus' self-descriptions throughout the Gospel.

From this description of the relationship of the *logos* with God, the Prologue next describes the downward relationship of the *logos* with the

[18] Mention should be made here—if somewhat proleptically—of a splendid article by Adele Reinhartz (1999c), in which she argues that the Aristotelian theory of *epigenesis* in his embryology as spelled out in the *De Generatione animalium* lies behind John's talk both of the 'begetting' of the 'children of God' (1:12–13) and of Jesus as '*monogenês* from the Father' (1:14). ('*Epigenesis*' is a later term of art to be contrasted with '*pangenesis*' in the Hippocratic tradition.) I wholly applaud this approach, including Reinhartz's claim (1999c, 98) that 'the power of this language lies not only in its metaphorical aspects but also in its literal meaning'. In proposing here a broader Stoic meaning, I also attempt to take into account the overall cosmological framework in John, which Reinhartz does not consider here (but had seen, if perhaps not in a wholly literal sense, in Reinhartz 1992)—while also remembering that Stoic cosmology has been plausibly understood (by Hahm 1977) as a development of Aristotelian biology. Gitte Buch-Hansen (2010) took the same step from Aristotle, who was Reinhartz's topic, to Stoicism and partly for the same reason (Buch-Hansen 2010, 21–3).

world (1:3–5) in a description of creation in which the active role of the *logos*—in what an Aristotelian would call an 'efficient cause'—is particularly emphasized. The *logos* is involved in every form of creation (1:3b), everything being in fact created *through* (*dia*) the *logos* (1:3a). Some scholars (e.g. Ashton 1998b, 19–21) argue that the text is not so much about creation as about God's continued and providential maintenance of the world (through the *logos*) once it has been created. That is implausible, however. The relationship between 1:1–2 and 1:3 clearly suggests that the *logos was* (Greek: *ên*) with God *before* things began to happen (*egeneto*). Those things, therefore, are most naturally taken to be the things that did happen at the beginning of the world. Also, the use of the verbal root *gignesthai* three times in 1:3 (and again in 1:10 and 1:15) strongly suggests that the theme is precisely 'coming into being', that is, creation. Finally, almost all scholars agree that John 1:1–5 is a kind of paraphrase on the account of creation in Genesis 1:1–5. And 'genesis' is, of course, derived from the same Greek root as we find in 1:3. All this shows that in using the term *gignesthai* the text is distinctly speaking of creation, not of a sustaining function once the world has been created.

This is quite important. It suggests that when John employs the same verb in 1:6 (*Egeneto anthrôpos*: 'A man came into being'), he is suggesting that the Baptist's appearance was part of the same type of creation. Similarly, and extremely importantly, our guiding statement that the *logos* '*became*' (*egeneto*) flesh makes use of the very same term. Thus the appearance of the *logos* in Jesus is another example of the creation brought about *by* the *logos*.

In 1:3–5, however, this text again aims to say two apparently opposed things, and here about the role of the *logos* in creation. First, *all* things (Greek: *panta*) were created by the *logos* (1:3). By the division introduced in 1:5 this must include both light and darkness. Secondly, however, out of all those things the *logos* was particularly concerned with life and light (1:4). Thus, while the *logos* was responsible for everything in creation, it was apparently particularly concerned with those two things on the good side that one might well say constitute the whole point of creation. This connection between life and creation is made at the beginning of 1:4. After we have heard about the role of *logos* in creation (1:3), we are told that there was life *in* that *logos* (1:4 init.), presumably in the sense that the *creative* activity of the *logos* was intended to bring about *life*. The dual role of the *logos* as responsible for both light and darkness, but *particularly* concerned with life (and light) is obviously of crucial importance. It comes close to saying that although creation also contains things that are bad, creation itself is basically good. *In* the *logos* that was instrumental in creating the world, there was both life and light.

This brief account of the creation of the whole world should clearly be understood as a genuine cosmogony. It is about the way the whole world (*panta*) was brought into being. At the same time it is crucial for understanding the Prologue as a whole that the account is not just a cosmological one. It is also normative, distinguishing as it does between light (which is good) and darkness (which is bad). Furthermore, when it states that the life that was to be found in the *logos* was 'the light of human beings', it also moves from mere (normative) cosmology to epistemology, to the way the world is and appears (or *should* appear) *to human beings*. Saying that the life contained in the *logos* is also 'the light of human beings' is saying that human beings should *see* what the created world is all about normatively: life. This is where many scholars begin to speak of 'soteriology', and in a way rightly. But there is no contrast between cosmology (or even cosmogony) and soteriology here.[19] On the contrary, their inner connection is precisely the point. The world that has been created by the *logos* is a normative one and this immediately raises the ('soteriological') issue of how human beings should respond to it in order to obtain what the world was made for: life.

What we have, then, in 1:1–5 is a normative cosmogony that ties the purpose of creation—understood as life and light—directly back to God through a mediator—the *logos*—that was as close to God as possible without being identical with him. In order to understand how *this* kind of *logos* might be said to become flesh in Jesus Christ, we need to consider the various types of contextual material that scholars have brought in to elucidate the *logos*.

THE *LOGOS* IN SCHOLARSHIP—AND DODD

Any commentary on John will have its section on how to understand the *logos* in the Prologue. And any commentary will line up all the possible candidates. For our purposes in getting an answer to our philosophical question, the best strategy is to take as a basic text C. H. Dodd's (1953a) account, to which I have already referred (263–85). It covers all the most important candidates that have been brought in (with the *Memra* addition made by Boyarin) and it most importantly explains why one must, as it were, go from one to the other while also keeping them all in place. In addition, it shows why one has to go to an understanding of the *logos* that is properly philosophical (namely, as found in Philo of Alexandria). Finally, it

---

[19] Such a contrast is important to de Boer (2015, 464–7). But why?

will allow us to see why Dodd was wrong in the end to rely so much on Philo, the Platonist. Instead, he should have given pride of place to an understanding of the *logos* that he does mention, one that is found in Stoicism, where the *logos* stands for 'the rational principle in the universe, its meaning, plan or purpose' (280). We already know what that meaning, plan, and purpose was, according to John. It was life. Let us consider the steps in Dodd's argument. He begins from his 'main question':

is the term λόγος to be translated 'word', and is the whole Logos-doctrine to be understood from the Hebraic conception of the דבר יהוה ['word of Jahve'], or has λόγος a sense approximating rather to the Stoic 'rational principle', on the analogy of its predominant use in Philo? (Dodd 1953a, 268–9).

This very much speaks for the former solution, not least if one is prepared to see the דבר יהוה as being 'largely interchangeable' with תורה (the Torah, 269). Various sources influenced directly by Genesis 1:3 show that there was a widespread idea within Judaism that 'by His utterance [in Genesis 1:3] God brought into being a word which existed substantively, and mediated creative power' (269). It also existed 'before the world was' and even 'as a hypostasis distinguishable from God' (269). In addition, there are 'rabbinic sayings which (interpreting the Scriptures) declare the Torah (which is the word of God) to be life and light to men' (269). So, is John's *logos* not this original creative 'word' of God, so substantial that it deserves to be written with a capital W as Word—or, as argued by Boyarin, the *Memra* of God?

No, says Dodd, not quite. For there are two propositions in 1:1–14 'which present great difficulty, if λόγος be taken as precisely equivalent to "word", or "Torah"' (273) and these two are the claim in 1:1 that 'the *logos* was God'—and then our primary quarry in 1:14 that the *logos* became flesh. Of the latter Dodd even notes that it is 'difficult on any construction of the term λόγος' (273)—which is, of course, why we took it as our philosophical question. For this reason, and particularly in order to find a precedent for the 'personification' and 'hypostatizing' of the *logos*, Dodd turns to Jewish wisdom literature. Here 'the concept of חכמה, σοφία ["wisdom"], . . . represents the hypostatized *thought* of God, immanent in the world' and as such '*replaces* the Word of the Lord as medium of creation and revelation' (274, my emphasis). Dodd then refers to the classic account by J. Rendel Harris (1916) and lists the 'obvious and striking similarities between certain of the propositions of the Prologue and passages in the Wisdom literature' (274). This is all persuasive and it has been generally accepted by scholars. John's *logos* is not *just* the 'word' ('Word'!) of Genesis, but *also* that 'word' as elaborated in the wisdom account of *sophia*. In particular, it is noteworthy that while a late piece of wisdom literature such as the Wisdom of Solomon develops its understanding of *sophia* in a direction that is clearly philosophical and draws directly on both Stoic and Platonic ideas (see later), it may also continue to speak of the *logos* as something God *said*.[20]

So is this the contextual material from which we may draw our solution for a better understanding of the two intriguing propositions? No, says Dodd again. With regard to our special quarry, he does find it 'somewhat less difficult to find an approach to the enigmatic statement' that the *logos* became flesh within a setting of wisdom literature, where 'the idea of the immanence of Wisdom in men, making them friends of God, provides a kind of matrix in which the idea of incarnation might be shaped'. But he also adds that 'it would be idle to look for any real anticipation of the Johannine doctrine of incarnation' (275).[21] For the other proposition, that the *logos* was God (or divine), he can find no help in wisdom literature. Instead, he turns to Philo for this. Why? Because here one finds a notion of *logos* 'not simply' as 'the uttered word or command of God', but as (277, with my emphasis):

the meaning, plan or purpose of the universe, *conceived as transcendent* as well as immanent, as the thought of God, *formed within the eternal Mind* and projected into objectivity. From the human point of view it is a rational content of thought, expressed in the order of the universe, but it is this *not, as with the Stoics . . . but* in the sense that its order and meaning express *the mind of a transcendent creator*.

Since this is such an important point, it is worth quoting a bit more from Dodd. On Stoicism and Platonism (that is, 'Philonism') in John he says:

It is perhaps worth observing [indeed, it is crucial to observe!] that the propositions ἐν ἀρχῇ ἦν ὁ λόγος—θεὸς ἦν ὁ λόγος—πάντα δι᾽ αὐτοῦ ἐγένετο ['in the beginning was the *logos*—God was the *logos*—all things came into being through it'], are *such as would have been directly intelligible and acceptable to any Stoic*. They would have seemed to him a paraphrase of his own doctrine: . . . (Dodd 1953a, 280).

Here Dodd quotes from Diogenes Laertius 7.134 on Stoic doctrine:

The passive principle, then, is a substance without quality, that is, matter, whereas the active principle is the *logos* that is in it (the matter), that is, God. For being everlasting he creates (*dēmiourgein*) each and every thing.

Dodd continues:

It is surely not to be supposed that the coincidence is accidental. Where the Stoic could not have followed John is in the proposition ὁ λόγος ἦν πρὸς τὸν θεόν ['the *logos* was with God']. The assumption of a God *beyond* the world would have seemed to him uncalled for. But it is just here, of course, that Philo, under the influence of Platonism as well as of the Old Testament, differs from the Stoics with whom he has so much in common (Dodd 1953a, 280, my emphasis).

---

[20] See Wis. 16:12 and 26, which first speaks of God's *logos* and then of his *rhēma* ('spoken word').

[21] This off-hand remark reveals what one is up against in trying to *understand* John's claim in 1:14: the whole 'mystery' of Christianity.

Dodd concludes about the opening sentences of the Prologue as follows:

They are clearly intelligible only when we admit [!] that λόγος, though it carries with it the associations of the Old Testament Word of the Lord, has also a meaning similar to that which it bears in Stoicism as modified by Philo, and parallel to the idea of Wisdom in other Jewish writers (280).

From God's 'word' to 'wisdom' to Philo—but then also, in effect, to 'Stoicism as modified by Philo': Dodd's reasoning is cogent and it leads us to the only type of contextual material that will help us genuinely to understand the crucial claim that the *logos* became flesh in Jesus.

PHILONIC PLATONISM OR STOICISM IN JOHN 1:1–3?

At this point we need to become a bit more technical. Which type of contextual material—Philonic Platonism or Stoicism—will help us better understand two claims about the *logos* made at the beginning of the Prologue: (i) that the *logos* was 'with' God (1:1) and (ii) that everything came into being 'through' (*dia*) the *logos* (1:3)?

As to question (i), Dodd might immediately seem right in preferring Philonic Platonism, not because we need the notion that God is '*beyond*' the world in Dodd's distinctly 'transcendental' sense (after all, whether that is John's picture is precisely the point at issue), but because in Stoicism the relationship between the *logos* and God is even closer than as indicated by *pros* (being 'with' God), namely, one of identity.[22] In Stoicism, God *is* the *logos* that is operative in the world. In Philonic Platonism, by contrast, for example, as Philo develops the relationship between God and the *logos* in his own rewriting of the Genesis story in the *De Opificio Mundi* (in particular *Op.* 13–36), the *logos* is an immaterial entity consisting of the intelligible world of ideas that serves as a blueprint for everything to be created in the present, sensible world (see 20 and 24). In that guise, the *logos* might well be said to be 'with' God, who is himself above or 'beyond' even the intelligible world of ideas which constitutes his thoughts.

Here, then, we have a picture that might account for John's talk of the *logos* as being 'with' God. But we get it at a huge price, which has to be paid in two directions. In relation to God, although the Philonic *logos* may be said to be 'with' God in the sense explained, Philo also distinguishes God's 'firstborn, divine *logos*' (*De Somniis* 1.215) quite sharply in good Platonic manner from 'the God (himself) who was *before* (*pro*) the *logos*' (*Somn.* 1.65).

---

[22] There is an interesting topic within Stoicism regarding the relationship between God and *logos*. After all, Cleanthes' famous hymn was not a hymn to 'the *logos*', but to Zeus. For a good discussion of Stoic theology, see Algra 2003.

This means that God himself must remain inaccessible to human beings even when they have become able to grasp the *logos*. In John, by contrast, the *logos* is very closely connected with God himself, and when human beings 'see' the *logos* in Jesus (see 1:14), they also *see God*—albeit indirectly—since Jesus has 'expounded' God to human beings in his life and death (1:18). Thus the connection between the *logos* and God is much closer in John than in Philo. Conversely, and in relation to the world, when Philo connects the *logos* with the transcendental and wholly immaterial God and gives it the role in the creation of the world of articulating the *intelligible* world that functions as God's blueprint for the sensible world, he inserts a whole layer *between* God and the sensible world. How the *logos* may then also be *directly* involved in creating the present, sensible world (as it appears to be in John 1:3) becomes something of a mystery.

What Philo does, then, is to construct a layer between a remote God and the sensible world. In other words, he separates God and the sensible world from one another. John, by contrast, apparently aims to connect them. The conclusion to be drawn is that the price to be paid for bringing in Philo to elucidate the claim in John that the *logos* was 'with' God is simply too high. And so it seems much better to understand John's locution here as a *direct* appropriation of the idea in Jewish wisdom literature that wisdom, *sophia*, was seated next to God's throne—better, that is, than bringing in the whole Platonist *development* of that idea to be found in Philo. In trying to understand John, who appears to be much more direct, we should avoid being saddled with all the Philonic, Platonist paraphernalia.

The same issue—Philo or wisdom?—comes into focus in connection with question (ii). In what way did everything come into being 'through' (*dia*) the *logos*? Thomas Tobin (1990, 257–60) has helpfully collected some of the most important material in Philo that might illuminate John's use of *dia* in 1:3. There are two main points. First, Tobin rightly draws attention to Philo's fondness for the expression *di' hou* ('through which') to indicate the role of the *logos* in the creation of the world. Together with this goes his use of the term *organon* ('instrument'). The *logos*, in Philo's picture, was the actual 'instrument through which' God created the world. A good example of this idea is to be found in *On the Cherubim* 125–7, which Tobin quotes. Here is the beginning (Loeb translation with their emphasis):

God is the cause [*aition*] not the instrument [*organon*], and that which comes into being is brought into being *through* an instrument [*di' organou men*], but *by* a cause [*hypo de aitiou*].[23]

---

[23] Strangely, Tobin translates (1990, 257, my emphasis): '. . . is brought into being *not* through an instrument . . .' The 'not' is not in the text. Other passages that speak of the *logos* as an instrument in world creation include *Allegorical Interpretation (L.A.)* 3.96 and *On the*

Tobin also connects this way of speaking with a 'metaphysics of prepositions' that was 'part of the emerging Middle Platonism of the late first
century B.C.E. and the first century C.E.' (259) and he sees Philo's use of
this way of thinking as 'Platonic rather than Stoic' (259).

The second point is that the use of the expression *di' hou* in John 1:3 'is
not simply an alternate formulation for an instrumental dative' (which one
finds in the Jewish wisdom tradition, Tobin 258). Instead, as found elsewhere in the New Testament (1 Cor. 8:6 and Heb. 1:2) it is used to highlight
'the creation of the world through an intermediate figure' (259).

These two observations raise some questions. The second point is not so
easy to understand. Tobin is right to refer to the use of an instrumental
dative in the Jewish wisdom tradition. But in that tradition, *sophia* is
precisely an 'intermediate figure' that was involved in the creation of the
world. It is not clear, therefore, that the expression *di' hou* in Philo is
intended to distinguish Philo's picture from the one he had inherited from
the wisdom tradition. On the contrary, it is likely that when Philo spoke of
the *logos* as an 'instrument through which' God created the world, he
precisely intended to draw on the well-known picture of the role of wisdom
in that connection.

There may even be a good reason for this. In the wisdom tradition, the
figure of wisdom is *directly* involved in the creation of the present world,
the 'sensible' world if one speaks in Platonic terms. Not so in Philo. If one
tries to figure out exactly how *this* world was created 'through' the *logos*
in Philo's picture, one comes up with a number of ideas that articulate
Philo's basically Platonic conception, but do not explain how that conception may then be directly operative in creating the present world. As a
good Platonist, Philo saw the sensible world as an 'image' (*eikōn*) and
'imitation' (*mimēma*) of the ideal world (see *Op.* 16–19, 25). He also speaks
of it as being 'moulded' (*typōthēnai*) by the 'seal' (*sphragis*) that is the *logos*
(see *Op.* 25). In fact, in his account of the creation of the world 'through'
the *logos*, his whole interest lies in the 'ideas, measure, types, and seals
which, being themselves *im*material [NB], serve for the creation of something else: bodies' (*Op.* 34).[24] I suggest, therefore, that Philo's fondness for
the expressions 'through which' and 'instrument' is an attempt to draw
on the idea of wisdom's direct involvement in the creation of the present
world in order to create something that is *not* to be found in Philo's own
picture when he develops it Platonically: a genuine explanation of exactly
how the present, so-called 'sensible' world was, in fact, literally created

---

Migration of Abraham (*Migr.*) 6. The expression *di' hou* is used in the same context in *On the
Sacrifices of Abel and Cain* (*Sacr.*) 8 and *On the Special Laws* (*Spec.*) 1.81.

[24] I am attempting here to bring out the meaning of ἄλλων in Philo's sentence '(they are)
πάντα ἰδέαι καὶ μέτρα καὶ τύποι καὶ σφραγίδες, εἰς γένεσιν ἄλλων ἀσώματα σωμάτων'.

'through' the *logos* as God's 'instrument'. As a good Platonist, Philo *could* not give such an explanation. His use of the terms 'through' and 'instrument' is an attempt to conjure up something that is not actually there.

It is interesting to note that Philo is well aware that somebody might feel a gap between the Genesis account of the creation of the world, which appears to be quite direct (God spoke, and the world—meaning *this* 'sensible' world—was immediately created), and Philo's own account, which precisely removes God from the world by inserting the intelligible world as a layer between the two and focusing on that instead. At *Op.* 129–30 he first quotes directly from Gen 2:4–5 ('This is the book of the genesis of heaven and earth etc.') and then comments:

Is he [Moses] not manifestly (*emphanôs*) describing the incorporeal and intelligible ideas (*asômatoi kai noêtai ideai*), which functioned as seals for the sensible objects that resulted from the process (*ta aisthêta apotelesmata*)?

Well, not quite 'manifestly'.

One more point: for the metaphysics of prepositions Tobin refers (259) to Seneca's account in Letter (*Ep.*) 65.7–10 of Plato's causal scheme. Note, however, that Seneca's scheme, which builds on a mixture of Aristotle and Plato, only mentions a single 'active cause', exemplified by the 'craftsman' (*artifex*, 65.7) in earthly matters (where he is called *id a quo*, 'that by which', 65.8) and by God (65.9) in heavenly matters (where he is called *faciens*, 'the agent'). When Philo distinguishes, in the quotation from *Cher.* 125 given earlier, between God as the 'cause by which' (*aition* and *to hyph' hou*) and the 'instrument through which', he is precisely *changing* or *adding to* the Aristotelian–Platonic scheme. Indeed, it is even here that one must locate the *formal* and *ideational* causes (from Aristotle and Plato, respectively) that go into Seneca's scheme in two separate versions, but are not at all present in Philo's scheme in that passage.[25] The reason, I suggest, is that he wanted to find room for the *logos* (but in his own 'ideational' conception of that) *by* drawing on the idea in the wisdom literature of 'an intermediate figure' who was directly active in the creation of the world.[26] This difference between Seneca and Philo brings out very clearly what Philo was up to: *making* the *logos* conceived as an immaterial entity the *direct* cause of the present world. But it cannot be done! In developing the creative *logos away*

---

[25] Seneca (65.8) speaks of *id ex quo* (the material cause), *id a quo* (the agent or active cause), *id in quo* (the Aristotelian formal cause), *id ad quod* (the Platonic model or ideational cause), and *id propter quod* (the end in view or final cause).

[26] For wisdom as the one who is directly active, see Wis. 12:1 in relation to 11:24. First on God (11:24, NRSV): 'For you love all things that exist, and detest none of the things *that you have made*, for you would not *have made* anything if you had hated it'. Then on wisdom (12:1, NRSV): '*For* your immortal spirit [*pneuma*] is in all things'. That the *pneuma* equals wisdom is made clear from the very beginning (1:4–7). But note: this is *Stoic pneuma*.

from the world to be created, Philo created a gap between the ideal and the sensible worlds that can only be bridged by various types of speech that are fundamentally metaphorical.

Where does that leave us with respect to understanding John 1:3, in particular *John's* use of the preposition *dia*? What we need is a picture according to which it makes sense to say that 'everything' (*panta*) in *this* world was directly brought into being *by* the *logos*. Since, as we have just seen, that picture cannot be Philo's Platonist one, we must conclude that spelling out John's use of *dia* by reference to Philo's highly contrived use of *dia* and 'instrument' is a cul-de-sac. It leads to more problems than it solves. Instead, an adequate picture may be found in Stoicism. Here the whole world (and there is only this one) is created out of the big, ultimate flash of light that is also God. As Dodd said, it is wholly Stoic to say that everything in the world came into being directly *through* (*dia*) the activity of the *logos*. It is true that the Stoics did not often use the term *dia* with the genitive in the sense of 'through'. Seneca shows why. In Stoicism there is only a single cause: the maker (*id, quod facit*, 65.4).[27] Seneca therefore objects to the 'throng of causes' posited by Aristotle and Plato (65.11). Instead, he is looking for 'the primary and general cause' (*prima et generalis causa*, 65.12). And that is 'creative reason' (*ratio faciens*), 'that is, God' (*id est deus*, 65.12). This cause, then, is a wholly adequate candidate for the idea expressed in John 1:3 that everything in the world was created 'through' the *logos*. And if it be asked why John employs the preposition *dia* with the genitive in the sense of 'through' to express this idea, the most obvious answer appears to be that *like Philo*, John, too, is drawing on the picture of wisdom in the wisdom literature as seated at the throne of God, but also the direct agent through which the (present) world was created. *Only*, we are not now required to go via the route adopted by the Platonist Philo, which raised more problems than it solved. In John 1:1–3, the *logos* is one that 'wisdom-like' is present 'with' God from the very beginning, but 'Stoic-like' is also directly active in creating the present world. That is what John expresses by his use of *dia*—and that is what Philo, too, *attempted* to suggest (but inadequately due to his Platonism) by his own use of *dia* and 'instrument'.

PHILONIC PLATONISM OR STOICISM IN 1:14?

We are now at long last ready to address our philosophical question directly on how to understand the claim in 1:14 that the logos 'became flesh'. Dodd in effect gave up finding material that might give direct and precise

---

[27] Compare also the fragments collected by von Arnim in *SVF* 2.336–56 (*De causis*).

meaning to this claim. (He even made a virtue of necessity.) The best he could do was to refer to the myth of wisdom coming to be present on earth. He could not find any idea in Philo's conception of the *logos* that might be of help. We know why: as Philo develops his notion of *logos* in *De Opificio Mundi* and elsewhere, it is utterly incomprehensible how that type of distinctly immaterial *logos* could become flesh. Here Dodd's move to Philo loses its power. Philo is of no help whatsoever for understanding Dodd's 'enigmatic statement' in John 1:14.

Thomas Tobin (1990) acknowledged this: 'Philo and Hellenistic Jewish exegetes of like mind would certainly have found such an identification ["of the *logos* with a particular human being, Jesus of Nazareth"] impossible' (267) and the idea 'that the *logos* had become incarnate in Jesus of Nazareth ... would have been unimaginable for someone like Philo' (268). Yet he also attempted to employ Philo's notion of 'the heavenly man' as an intermediary between the *logos* and Jesus of Nazareth: 'The identification of the *logos* with the heavenly man of Gen 1:27 [in Philo's interpretation of this text] provides the middle term, if you will, between the *logos* and Jesus of Nazareth: *logos*—heavenly man—particular man (Jesus of Nazareth)' (267). 'If you will': I certainly will not! For as Tobin both knows and shows, Philo's heavenly man is just as incorporeal as his *logos*. In what precise way may he then serve as a 'middle term' between the *logos* and Jesus?

This, however, is where monistic Stoicism comes off much better. Here there is no unbridgeable gap between the *logos* understood as God's active power in creating the world and the idea that this *logos* came to be present in all its fullness in a single individual. (a) The Stoic *logos* is present as the world's active power in everything that is, operating as it does in the whole world as an energy that guides and maintains it. (b) It is also present, at the level of consciousness, in human beings as a power ('reason' or *nous*) that makes them capable of understanding the world's order, for which the *logos* was responsible in the first place. (c) That power, however, is insufficient in ordinary human beings. And so the Stoic *logos* is finally present in the world in its most powerful form in one being who may be as rare as the phoenix: the Stoic sage or 'wise man'.[28]

In this picture it is essential to remember that when the Stoic *logos* is present in the world in these three forms, it is present *not* as an immaterial entity that relates—one does not know how—with matter, including the human body. Instead, it is a material power *within* matter (an especially

---

[28] The Stoic *logos* is also present in consciousness and in its full form in the Stoic God. But it is not clear that there is, in the end, any distinction between the Stoic *ideal* 'sage' and God. Systematic theologians will raise an outcry here. But what we are trying to understand is how the *logos* might become *Jesus Christ*.

vibrant 'tension' in matter), and here we speak of both the matter of the whole world and that of the human soul (and body). In both cases, the Stoic *logos* is a material power that 'energizes' the matter and enables it to relate to the rest of the (material) world.[29] If, then, this *logos* has come to be present in its total fullness in an individual human body (as in the case of the imagined sage), then the universal *logos* has 'become flesh' in him—as it did, according to John, in Jesus. Then this individual, who remains an individual bodily human being, has also literally become the bearer of the full divine *logos*. The individual's body will be literally informed by the divine *logos*. This whole conception, then, is much more helpful than a Platonist one in bringing us to see exactly how John's *logos* might become flesh. It apparently happened literally in Jesus just as it might conceivably happen in the ideal Stoic sage.[30]

Here, then, I propose, is a piece of contextual material that genuinely illuminates John's claim that in Jesus the *logos* became flesh. The idea is certainly not that 'John is a Stoic', only that the picture one finds in Stoicism helps to give precise meaning to John's claim. We also saw that there is at least one other claim in the Prologue that does *not* immediately fit with Stoicism, namely, the claim that the logos was 'with' God. Here we preferred to see John to be drawing on the idea in Jewish wisdom literature of wisdom being 'with' God. So, John is John and not a Stoic—and definitely not a Philonic Platonist either. With regard to the latter, Philo comes out as being much too sophisticated for John, who is much more direct, simple, and Stoic-like. Where Philo separates, John connects.

Scholars will probably continue to be sceptical about this reading for a host of reasons, some of which are due to the fact that from the second century onwards we have been accustomed to understanding Christianity in general and John in particular within a Platonist framework. This unquestioned truth is the one I am querying for (parts of) earliest Christianity. In such a situation it is particularly helpful that one of the writings that scholars traditionally draw on to elucidate John's *logos* in the Prologue, the Wisdom of Solomon, contains a number of texts that connect the *logos* of Genesis (and here to be understood as the 'Word') with a way of speaking

---

[29] I am getting a little ahead of myself here. According to Origen (see *SVF* 2.1051), the Stoics claimed that 'the *logos* of God, which descends (*katabainein*) as far as human beings, even the lowest ones, is nothing other than material spirit (*pneuma sōmatikon*)'. It is in connection with this 'spirit' (*pneuma*) that the Stoics spoke of 'tension' (*tonos*), see e.g. *SVF* 2.447 (for the world as a whole) and 3.112 (in an epistemological context).

[30] Let me just add that the basic idea behind this interpretation of John 1:14 is one I have advanced elsewhere (2010, ch. 1) for an adequate understanding of Paul's talk in 1 Corinthians 15 of a future *sōma pneumatikon* ('spiritual body', 15:44) of Christ believers alongside their present *sōma psychikon* ('psychic body'). The *logos* became flesh in Jesus, according to John, in the way the fleshly bodies of believers will eventually, according to Paul, become *pneumatika*.

in connection with wisdom (*sophia*) herself that is generally recognized as being not just philosophical, but also distinctly Stoic. This happens when Wisdom speaks of *sophia* in terms of *pneuma* (spirit). In looking at these texts, we are leaving behind our basically heuristic approach, which remains sharply focused on the text to be understood, and instead claiming that within a broader contextual perspective there is evidence that Stoic ideas were historically available in milieus that are recognized as being quite close to John. This should diminish the gap that scholars often feel between Stoicism and Jewish–Christian texts such as Wisdom and John.

STOIC *LOGOS* AND *PNEUMA*—AND THE WISDOM OF SOLOMON

Before turning to Wisdom, we should note that in Stoicism there are two ways of describing the entity we have hitherto spoken of as the *logos*: as *logos* and as *pneuma*. The point apparently was to identify two different aspects of the single entity that they had in mind: the fact that it was supposed to be both cognitive (for the *logos*) and so a matter of information, as in the sage—and physical (or material, for the *pneuma*) and so a matter of some form of extension, which was what made it a *sôma* (a body).[31] It is helpful to introduce the Stoic notion of *pneuma* here because it shows clearly that the *logos* we have employed to elucidate John is, in fact, a material entity, and hence entirely able to 'become flesh'. Stoic *logos* and Stoic *pneuma* are two sides of the same coin, seen in one respect as a cognitive entity and in another as a bodily one. The point, therefore, of speaking of it as *logos* is to emphasize that it has rational content, is part of a plan, and indeed is such that it may be understood by human beings, who may come to grasp the content and see the plan. The point of speaking of it as *pneuma* is to emphasize that it is a material power that is active in things in many different ways, including that of *enabling* human beings to grasp the rational content and see the plan.

It is in this context that the universally recognized talk of specifically Stoic *pneuma* in the Wisdom of Solomon becomes noteworthy. Let us consider a few passages in Wisdom.

Wis. 9:1–9 directly recalls Genesis 1 and also plays on the idea of *sophia* as being 'with' God (NRSV):

[31] That the Stoic *pneuma* is a material entity is wholly clear from the fragments collected by von Arnim in *SVF* 2.439–62. For the connection between *pneuma* and *logos*, see the quotation from Origen given earlier (*SVF* 2.1051). That *logos* itself is (also) cognitive is clear, for instance, from Chrysippus' definition of it as 'a collection of certain notions (*ennoiai*) and preconceptions (*prolêpseis*)' (see *SVF* 2.841, from Galen). There is a fine account of the Stoic notion of *pneuma* in Tieleman 2014.

[1]O God of my ancestors and Lord of mercy [says Solomon], who have made [*poiein*] all things [*ta panta*] by your word [*en logôi sou*], [2]and by your wisdom [instrumental dative] have formed ['created', *kataskeuazein*] humankind to have dominion over the creatures you have made [*ta hypo sou genomena ktismata*]...[4]give me the wisdom that sits by your throne...[9]With [*meta*] you is wisdom, she who knows your works [*erga*] and was present when you made [*poiein*] the world [*kosmos*].

Wis. 7:21–4 describes how Solomon has learned from *sophia*, who turns out to be *directly* the creator or 'fashioner' of all things and who is still operating in the world. Here the description of the *pneuma* that she contains is in part unmistakably Stoic (NRSV, Stoic terms emphasized):

[21]I learned both what is secret and what is manifest, [22]for wisdom, the *fashioner* [*technitis*] of all things [*panta*], taught me. [23]There is in her a *spirit* [*pneuma*] that is *intelligent*, holy, unique [*monogenes*], manifold, *subtle*, *mobile*, clear, unpolluted, distinct, invulnerable, loving the good, keen, *irrestistible*, beneficent, humane, steadfast, sure, *free from anxiety*, all-powerful [*pantodynamon*], overseeing all, and *penetrating* through all spirits that are intelligent, pure, and *altogether subtle*. [24]For wisdom is *more mobile than any motion*; because of her pureness *she pervades and penetrates all things*.

Elsewhere, Solomon describes God's aim in creation as being life and here again recalls Genesis 1 directly, only to go on to spell this out in terms of the *pneuma* that is present in *sophia*. See Wis. 1:12–15 (NRSV), where Solomon addresses the kings of the earth (compare 1:1) (NRSV):

[12]Do not invite death by the error of your life, or bring destruction by the works of your hands; [13]because God did not make death, and he does not delight in the death of the living. [14]For he created all things so that they might exist [*einai*]; the generative forces [*geneseis*] of the world are wholesome, and there is no destructive poison in them, and the dominion of Hades is not on earth. [15]For righteousness is immortal.

And 11:24–12:1 (NRSV, already partly quoted earlier):

[24]For you love all things that exist [*ta onta panta*], and detest none of the things that you have made, for you would not have made anything if you had hated it. [25]How would anything have endured if you had not willed it? Or how would anything not called forth [NB, the 'word'] by you have been preserved? [26]You spare all things, for they are yours, O Lord, you who love the living. [1]*For your immortal spirit* [*pneuma*] is in all things.

These passages give us a picture of God and *sophia* that is very close to the picture of God and the *logos* in John 1:1–4. Furthermore, the precise manner in which *sophia* is operating in the world through the *pneuma* is one that is universally agreed to be conceived in a distinctly Stoic terminology. This suggests that the Stoic-like reading I have offered of John's claim about Jesus in 1:14 is not only heuristically helpful but may also be said in a general historical way to lie within the conceptual horizon of the Prologue itself.

Is this enough to make such an historical claim plausible? Indeed, how may one go from what Wisdom says of *sophia* and the *pneuma* to what John says about the *logos?* Such an objection might be made if one insists that John had in mind *only* the old Jewish idea of God's 'word' and then sets aside the fact that Wisdom, too, speaks of God's 'word', and then goes on to *spell this out* in terms of *sophia* and *pneuma*, as we just saw. For it might be objected that Wisdom's *sophia* and *pneuma* are simply different from John's *logos.* Here, however, we are helped by John's own text since *he too* goes on to speak of *pneuma* (in 1:32–3). This is the ultimate point in the line of argument I have presented. We were able to give heuristic meaning to John's statement in 1:14 by bringing in contextual material from Stoicism that spoke about the *logos.* We saw that Wisdom is at least operating in the same field using clearly Stoic terms, which we took to point to a general historical horizon that it shares with John. To the objection that Wisdom speaks of *pneuma* where John speaks of *logos* we may now reply by connecting the 1:14 statement in John's own text *directly* with the other side of the Stoic concept of *logos:* the *pneuma.* For John himself spells out the meaning of 1:14 in terms that explicitly bring in the other term. To see this, we must focus on the narrative role played by John the Baptist in the whole text of 1:1–34.

THE MOVE TO GREATER SPECIFICITY IN JOHN THE BAPTIST'S WITNESS IN 1:1–34

The normative and epistemological dimension we have noted of the account of creation given in 1:1–5 is taken up directly in 1:6 when the Prologue brings in an individual person, John the Baptist, whose role it is to bear witness to Jesus. Of the three concepts of *logos*, life, and light we have noted in the cosmological account itself, it is the idea of the light, and hence of how human beings should *respond* to the *logos* (and eventually Jesus), that is now in focus (1:6–8): John came into being[32] in order to 'bear witness to the light' (1:7 and 8). Clearly, then, the Baptist is important as a witness. Equally clearly, however, he is wholly unimportant in comparison with Jesus himself. His *only* role was to bear witness to him. For our purposes, however, the heavy emphasis on the Baptist's role as a witness is of the highest importance for seeing how the Prologue is tied together with what immediately follows in 1:19–34.

---

[32] Note the forceful way in which the Baptist is introduced: *Egeneto anthrôpos* ('A man came into being'). And compare the introduction of the Baptist in Mark 1:4: *egeneto Iôannês* ('John came into being'). Is John here drawing directly on Mark? Indeed, when one notes that Mark's *egeneto Iôannês* articulates the content of the *archê* ('beginning') with which he begins his Gospel (Mark 1:1), might one also see John's own beginning (*en archêi*, 'in the beginning') as a reflex of the Markan text?

There are two points. The first concerns 1:19 in relation to 1:6–8:

[19]*This, then, is the witness of John when* the Jews from Jerusalem had sent priests and Levites to ask him, 'Who are you?'.[33]

What the Evangelist does here is to *spell out* the precise content of John the Baptist's witness as already introduced in general terms in 1:6–8. Thus the section beginning at 1:19 *directly* continues the movement towards greater specificity that we already noted in connection with 1:14–17, but now focusing on the Baptist.

The second point concerns the repetition of what the Baptist actually says about Jesus. In 1:15 of the Prologue itself, once (the unnamed) Jesus *has* appeared on the stage (in 1:11–14), the Evangelist brings in John the Baptist once more. We already noted that this constitutes one step in the direction of greater specificity as seen in relation to 1:6–8. We also noted that the Baptist's statement is highly paradoxical: how may one and the same person be both before and after the Baptist? We will see, however, that the paradox is actually resolved in 1:30 when it is repeated in a context that goes directly on to add even more specificity by explaining, in 1:31–4, the precise manner in which Jesus was singled out to the Baptist himself by God.

In these two ways the Prologue is tied exceedingly closely together with what immediately follows through its emphasis on the witness of John the Baptist given in 1:19–34. The literary movement towards ever greater specificity that we found within the Prologue itself extends beyond the Prologue into the rest of John 1 (up until 1:34). In the Prologue there is a clear progression of specificity from 1:6–8 to 1:15. But this movement is repeated in 1:19–34 by 1:19 itself, which takes up 1:6–8 and then moves much further in spelling out the content of the Baptist's witness—and then by 1:30, which both actually quotes 1:15 and also moves much further in explaining (1:31–4) the precise manner in which Jesus was singled out to the Baptist himself by God. We have a parallelism here between two sets: (a) 1:6–8 (A^1) and 1:15 (B^1) and (b) 1:19 (A^2) and 1:30 (B^2). What the parallelism suggests is that the event described in 1:14, which the Baptist immediately greets in B^1, *happened in the specific manner* that his repetition of the greeting in B^2 goes on to describe in 1:31–4: when God sent his *pneuma* to rest upon Jesus.

JOHN THE BAPTIST'S WITNESS IN 1:19–34

To see this development in the text itself, we must look at the way John the Baptist's witness is described from 1:19 onwards before and into the

---

[33] I understand καὶ (and) at the beginning of 1:19 as being 'resumptive' ('So')—just as in 1:14.

'baptismal' scene (1:19–34). This part of John 1 may be read as consisting of two main sections (1:19–28 and 1:29–34), each divided into two subsections (X^1: 1:19–23; Y^1: 1:24–8; X^2: 1:29–31; Y^2: 1:32–4) that correspond to one another across the main sections: X^1–X^2 and Y^1–Y^2.

In the first main section, the theme all through X^1 and Y^1 is a dialogue between various groups of 'Jews' and John the Baptist that begins with discussing who he is himself and ends up making him point away from himself towards Jesus. In this way 1:19–28 can be seen as a greatly expanded version of 1:6–8. In text X^1 (1:19–23) the Baptist is asked by some priests and Levites sent by 'the Jews from Jerusalem' whether he is 'the Christ' (1:20), Elijah (1:21), or 'the prophet' (1:20), all of which he denies. In spite of the Baptist's denial, the reader is made to understand that there is an issue here. People are looking for 'the Christ', 'Elijah' (presumably *redivivus*), or 'the prophet'. It is this theme that ties the X^1– text together with text X^2, where John does say who *Jesus* is. However, it is striking to note that in X^2 the Baptist does *not* say that Jesus is any one of the three figures mentioned. Instead, Jesus is something *more*.

The interrogation of John is continued in text Y^1 (1:24–8). Why, people ask, does John baptize if he is neither the Christ, nor Elijah, nor the prophet (1:25)? John answers (1:26–7, NRSV):

[26] ... 'I baptize with water. Among you stands one whom you do not know, [27]the one who is coming after me; I am not worthy to untie the thong of his sandal.'

How does this statement answer the question? Partly if we understand it in terms of 1:23 as saying that John only baptizes in *preparation* for 'the one who is coming (*erchomenos*) after me', and partly in terms of text Y^2, where the Baptist himself quotes God as saying of Jesus that *he* is 'the one who baptizes *with holy pneuma*' (1:32) as opposed to his own baptism that is with water. In fact, it is the motif of baptism that connects texts Y^1 and Y^2 with one another.

The next main section (1:29–34) can then be seen as another greatly expanded version of something said in the Prologue (here 1:15), which is now focused, not on who the Baptist is (or is not), but on Jesus.[34] Text X^2 (1:29–31) takes up again the question of 'titles' (like in text X^1) when John sees Jesus 'coming' (*erchomenon*, see 1:9, 15, 27) towards him and says: 'Look, here is the Lamb of God who takes away the sin of the world' (1:29). The 'title' given to Jesus in this verse is hugely important for the rest of the Gospel. As will become gradually clearer later, Jesus is actually the 'lamb of

---

[34] Let me emphasize this: 1:19–28 is an expanded version of 1:6–8, and 1:29–34 is an expanded version of 1:15. Noteworthy here is the change from οὗτος ἦν in 1:15 to οὗτός ἐστιν in 1:30. The former refers back to 1:6–8, spanning the bridge between prediction and fulfilment; the latter rather actualizes in the narrative present.

God' who by his own death 'lifts up and takes away' (the meaning of the Greek *airein* in 1:29) the sin of the world, thereby enabling the world to attain eternal life.[35] What matters at present, however, is the fact that John the Baptist identifies Jesus positively here in three different ways. There is first (1:29) the prospective identification of Jesus that reaches to the heart of who and what Jesus is. Next (1:30) there is the retrospective identification of Jesus as the *logos* described in the Prologue, a claim that ties the present passage very closely to the Prologue since the Baptist is actually quoting himself from 1:15. Finally (1:31) there is a present point about Jesus which spells out the answer given by John in text Y[1] to the question of why he baptized. He did this (and again: 'with water') in order that the one he has just identified in 1:29–30 might be *revealed* to Israel. This point takes up the idea in the Prologue that Jesus has come to 'shine upon' every human being (1:9), not least 'his own' (1:11). But what does the Baptist mean by saying that he himself 'came baptizing with water' *in order that* Jesus Christ—the one he has just described in 1:29–30—might be revealed to Israel? The answer is given in the second half of the Baptist's witness, text Y[2] (1:32–4), which brings in an altogether different kind of baptism:

[32]And John bore witness saying, 'I have seen the *pneuma* descending from heaven like a dove, and it remained on him. [33]I myself did not know him, but the one who sent me to baptize with water, *he* said to me, "The one on whom you see the *pneuma* descend and remain, *he* is the one who baptizes with holy *pneuma*." [34]And I myself have seen (it) and have borne witness that this one is the Son of God.'

This is the crucial text. John the Baptist does not baptize Jesus. But he came—as sent from (1:6) and by (1:33) God—baptizing with water in order to become able to bear witness to an entirely different kind of baptism: that of Jesus, who was baptized, not by the Baptist, but by God himself and with *pneuma* that literally descended from above and was seen by the Baptist (as God had himself foretold) to remain on Jesus.[36] Furthermore, the *pneuma* that Jesus received in this way is also something with which he himself baptizes (as God had further told the Baptist). Finally, the ultimate claim to which the Baptist bears witness is that Jesus is, not just 'a' son of God, but *the* Son of God—presumably in the sense of the Prologue: the 'only Son of the Father' (see 1:14), which is also the sense given in the rest of the Gospel

---

[35] It seems highly likely that John's use of the verb *airein* here plays on the salvific role of Jesus' crucifixion, in which he was notoriously 'lifted up' (*hypsôthênai*), both on the cross and into heaven. Compare 19:15, where the 'Jews' cry out (NRSV): 'Away with him (*aron*)! Away with him (*aron*)! Crucify him!' 1:29 is a central verse for those who believe (as I do) that the idea of Jesus' death on the cross is very much alive in the Fourth Gospel.

[36] Scholars often deny that 1:32–4 is a 'baptism scene' because Jesus is not described as actually being baptized by the Baptist. But Jesus is baptized by *God* (as the Baptist testifies). Is that not enough of a 'baptism scene'?

whenever Jesus speaks of himself as 'the Son', namely, of 'the Father'. In the rest of the Gospel nobody apart from Thomas at the very end understood fully who Jesus was. Right at the beginning, however, John the Baptist did. He bore witness to it and the reason he was able to do so was that God had himself told him so when he, God, who had sent the Baptist to baptize with water (1:33), told him about (1:33) and then executed (1:32 and 34) an entirely different baptism of Jesus: the one with *pneuma*.

In this way, what 1:19–34 does—in addition to repeating (1:19–28) the point from 1:6–8 that the Baptist was not the light but had come to bear witness to it—is to *make the Baptist provide the full identification* (1:29–34, as anticipated by 1:15) *of who and what Jesus is*: not just the Christ, or Elijah, or the prophet, but the lamb of God who is also God's one and only Son and who *became* this when he was baptized by God himself with *pneuma* that stayed upon him and with which he will then himself baptize. What Jesus became in the Prologue has now been *spelled out* in the Baptist's witness (1:29–34)—in great detail, in a different terminology, and in a text that is now wholly narrative in form, thereby leading directly into the Gospel's narration of Jesus' life and death. But it is one and the same event that is described in 1:14 and 1:32–4.

What John does in 1:29–34, then, is to spell out in terms of the *pneuma* precisely what happened when the *logos* became flesh.[37] God's own *logos*, which was with him before the creation of the world, came down upon Jesus in the form it presumably also had all along: as *pneuma*. If we recall that in the Genesis account of creation there was also a *pneuma* (Gen. 1:2: and the *pneuma* of God 'swept over the face of the waters', NRSV) when God spoke his creative 'word', then we may conclude that the (Stoic-like) combination of *logos* and *pneuma* that we have found in John's own text is itself *a highly developed, philosophical uptake* on that basic text, Genesis 1:1–5.

We will not consider the rest of John 1 here, only note that it moves very smoothly from John the Baptist to two of his disciples, who go over to Jesus (1:35–7); that it then recounts how more disciples are made to follow Jesus; and most importantly, that it is structured around a number of descriptions (or 'titles') given to Jesus by these disciples, all of which are in a way true

---

[37] This interpretation is (fortunately) not quite new, see Theobald 1990 (in Theobald 2010a, 16), who refers to Reinhold Seeberg (1915b) and Jürgen Becker for the same idea, which was also independently suggested by Francis Watson (1987). Theobald's own rejection is based on two points: that the Baptist's function is only to *reveal* Jesus and that no actual baptism is being told. But surely, there is a specific content to the Baptist's 'revelation', namely *that* the *pneuma* did come down upon Jesus; and that event must suffice as a (divine) 'baptism'. Watson argues that John's conception is an 'adoptionist' one. I prefer to steer clear of this heavily loaded concept and consider only what is actually being said. None of my three predecessors, however, has employed Stoicism as part of their arguments.

enough, but none of which is wholly adequate. For as Jesus concludes by telling Nathanael (1:50–1):

50 . . . '. . . You will see *greater* things than these.' 51And he said to him, 'Very truly, I tell you (all), you will see heaven opened and the angels of God ascending and descending upon the Son of Man.'

The interpretation of John 1:51 is one of the most 'open' in the whole Gospel, where commentators go in very different directions.[38] Methodologically, we should focus, first, on the additions made by John to the quotation from Gen. 28:12 on Jacob's dream: 'opened' and 'the Son of Man', and secondly, on the ideas of 'seeing' and 'ascending and descending', which are taken up later in John 3:13 ('Nobody has ascended to heaven other than the one who has descended from heaven, the Son of Man') and 6:62 ('What, then, if you see the Son of Man ascending to where he was before?'). Thirdly, we should consider whether there is anything to be gleaned from the full story of Jacob's dream in Gen. 28:10–22.

In light of this, I hesitantly propose that we read the verse as talking about the *ascension* of the Son of Man (Jesus himself). This is the one fact about him that the disciples do *not* understand throughout the Gospel. But this is also precisely what they will eventually come to see ('you will see', see 6:62). They will see heaven being 'opened' to receive the Son of Man. And they will see the angels 'ascending and descending', presumably in a situation of ascent and descent (like on the ladder in Jacob's dream), just as the Son of Man has both descended from heaven and will ascend into it (3:13). Moreover, they will see the angels 'descending *down upon*' (*epi* with the accusative) the Son of Man, presumably to help *him ascend* together with them. All this fits the description given in the story of Jacob's dream of the place where he had his dream. On waking up, Jacob said: 'How awesome is this place! This is none other than the house of God, and *this is the gate of heaven*' (Gen. 28:17, NRSV), that is, the place from which one may get *into* heaven.

If we understand 1:51 in this way, what 1:19–51 does is to spell out once more in a narrative key the fundamental point made in more abstract terms in the Prologue of Jesus as having *come from* God and *returning to*

---

[38] Brown 1966 rightly notes that 1:51 is 'a verse that has caused as much trouble for commentators as any other single verse in the Fourth Gospel' (88), adding (90): 'When scholars try to be more precise, their different answers are ingenious'. Compare, e.g., Barrett 1978, 186–7; Lincoln 2005, 122–3; Theobald 2009, 195–7. Reynolds (2013, 71–2) acknowledges the possibility that 1:51 refers to 'Jesus' glory' in the sense of 'Jesus' future glorification' (Reynolds 2013, 72), but ends up agreeing with Ashton (2007, 249–51) that it is Jesus as the Son of Man 'who establishes communication between earth and a heaven which is now (permanently) open' (Ashton, 250). This seems much too general. Léon-Dufour (1988, 197–202) also gives the verse a present sense: 'c'est *ici bas* que le Fils de l'homme relie terre et ciel' (201–2, his emphasis). He does not, however, comment on the future in 'You will see'.

God. He came from God (the *logos* became flesh) *when* he was baptized by
God with God's own *pneuma* (1:32–4) and he will return to God in the
manner described in 1:51—to be in the bosom of the Father (1:18).[39]

SUMMARY ON 1:1–34: THE *LOGOS* AND THE *PNEUMA* ARE ONE AND THE SAME THING

Having set aside a number of traditional issues surrounding the Prologue,
we have been reading a text while keeping an open mind to what follows in
the rest of the Gospel and to whatever input from the text's many contexts
might appear fruitful for elucidating the text itself.

Among these contexts we have been drawing on three very different
ones: Genesis 1; the wisdom tradition as articulated in the Wisdom of
Solomon and by the most philosophical among Hellenistic Jewish wisdom
writers, Philo; and finally, Stoic philosophy. We have been concerned never
to give exclusive preference to any single one of these contexts. It seems
highly likely that all three are lurking historically somewhere in the
background of our text: Genesis 1 definitely so, the Jewish Hellenistic
wisdom traditions (as in the Wisdom of Solomon and Philo, where 'wisdom'
turns overwhelmingly into philosophy) with very high probability,[40] and
Stoicism (at least as received within those wisdom traditions) with a certain
degree of probability. However, this has not been the point. Instead, we
have attempted to employ heuristically whatever contextual material
appeared fruitful for elucidating the text.

Methodologically, what we did was to identify a philosophical question
derived from John's statement about the *logos* in 1:14, then to search for an
answer based on a reading of the text itself and on whatever contextual
material might help us to provide such an answer. We may also note that
the philosophical question raised (in our minds as readers) by 1:14 was

---

[39] This reading is not so very far from that of Burkett (1991, 112–19) who saw the vision as
being about 'the union of heaven and earth', which is 'prefigured by the lifting up of the Son
of the Man on the cross' (118) where his 'head ... reaches symbolically to heaven, while his
feet reach downward to earth, where the cross is planted' (119). Only, I take John to be
referring to a literal event: Jesus' resurrection and ascension that together create that union.
Compare for this the incomparable Nils Dahl (1962, 159): '... the main point of the Johannine
text seems to be clear. Nathanael is to see "greater things"; in analogy with 5:20 and 14:12
this promise will refer to the ascension of Jesus.... The main meaning of the promise given to
Nathanael and his fellows is that they shall see the glory of the Son of Man; they shall see the
Son of Man glorified'.

[40] I am not suggesting, though, that John had read Philo. The differences between John
and Philo that have come out in this chapter suggest that even if he had, he would not have
been impressed. Understanding Jesus in a Philonic manner would have gone against John's
basic claim that *in* seeing Jesus Christ, human beings may actually see God (1:18).

answered by the text itself towards the end of the whole text of 1:1–34, in 1:32–4. Only, it was not answered until we had been alerted, through the use of the relevant contextual material, to the possibility that an answer to our philosophical question might in fact be discovered there.

The answer that we found posits an intimate relationship between *logos* and *pneuma* in the Johannine text. This point is so important that it bears repeating, which will also help to clarify two central notions in the traditional thinking about John: of Jesus' 'pre-existence' and his 'incarnation'. As they appear in the text we have been discussing, the two notions of *logos* and *pneuma* constitute the two sides of the same coin, where the *logos* stands for the cognitive side and the *pneuma* for the purely material one. Both were present at creation, moreover, both were operative in it. Both also came to be present—in a uniquely forceful manner—in the individual human being of Jesus of Nazareth when he received the *pneuma*. As a result, *he* became the bearer of the whole point of creation, which is life and light. He *became* 'the light of the world' (8:12) so that 'whoever follows me will never walk in darkness but will obtain the light of life' (8:12).

But who is this 'he'? He is Jesus the *logos*, or Jesus the *pneuma*, or Jesus the only Son (1:14 and 34), or Jesus Christ (1:17), but he is definitely not just Jesus of Nazareth, the son of Mary (2:3). Of that exalted 'he' it is entirely true to say (and let himself say, 8:58): 'Before Abraham was born, I am'. Jesus *Christ* was 'pre-existent', that is, 'He' was with God before creation. By contrast, Jesus of Nazareth, the son of Mary, was not. He came into existence when he was born by Mary after John the Baptist had come into being (1:6). And he *became* Jesus *Christ*, and wholly literally Jesus the only Son, *begotten* by God (*monogenês*, 1:14, 18) *through* the *pneuma*, when at a quite specific point in time the *logos* descended upon him in the form of *pneuma* from above and remained on him. That was the moment when 'the *logos* became flesh'. *Jesus* was not 'incarnated'. Jesus *Christ* was—when the *logos* was literally 'incarnated' in him in the way just described.

In this way we have also been able to solve the paradox that was highlighted by John the Baptist in 1:15 and 30 and also stated by the Evangelist in 1:9–10. The one who came after the Baptist was Jesus, as an individual, and also Jesus *Christ* as a result of the descent of the *pneuma* on Jesus. The one who was *before* the Baptist was the *logos*–Christ who Jesus of Nazareth then also *became* when the Christ–*pneuma* descended upon him and turned him into Jesus Christ.

Everything in this summary has been about how to read a text—and then about how to understand what this text says about God's handling of creation, both originally and then again in the 'sending' (through the *pneuma*) of Jesus Christ, that is, when Jesus of Nazareth became Jesus Christ. It is all about God, creation, the *logos*, the *pneuma*—and Jesus Christ.

It is all about God's creative intervention with and in the world through the *logos–pneuma*. But there is also another, equally important side to the story, which we highlighted to begin with as being connected with the normative and epistemological side of the cosmological events. It has to do, both with the normative side of creation itself—that its point lies in life and light—and also with an epistemological dimension of the same side: that the normative point of creation was meant to be *understood* by human beings, that the light that shone in the created world (1:5) and fell upon human beings so as to 'enlighten' them (1:9) was meant to be seen *by* them. Only then would they become able to gain the life that was the whole point of creation.

The epistemological side of the account of creation is already strongly present in the Prologue with its focus on the cognitive *logos*, and for good reason. After all, the main theme of the rest of the Gospel is precisely whether Jesus (Christ) is actually *seen by people as being* what the Prologue has described him to be. And here, too, the underlying thought is that only when people see Jesus as what he fully is will they become able to gain the kind of life that is in play: eternal life. But the same epistemological side of the account of creation is also strongly present towards the end of our text when John the Baptist explains that he came to baptize (with water) 'in order that he (Jesus, the Son of God, 1:34) might be *revealed* to Israel' (1:31). In this way, once again, the Prologue and John the Baptist's witness hang exceedingly closely together. What the Prologue describes in abstract terms is spelled out in narrative terms in the Baptist's witness. The *logos* of the Prologue and the *pneuma* of the Baptist's witness are two sides of one and the same thing.

III

LOGOS AND *PNEUMA* IN THE BODY OF THE GOSPEL

THE ISSUES

If the *logos* and the *pneuma* of John 1 are the same thing, how does the Evangelist treat the two concepts in the rest of the Gospel? It is often said that the *logos* of the Prologue disappears in the rest, but can that really be? And while it is fully acknowledged that the *pneuma* does turn up again in crucial places, do its appearances result in a coherent picture that might even be related to what is said of the *logos*? In the first part of this chapter we focus on the *logos* side and only bring in the *pneuma* side when necessary. In the latter half we will focus specifically on the *pneuma* side.

We may articulate the issue by looking first at what is said about *logos* and *pneuma* in the rest of the Gospel by two scholars who have addressed the question in sufficient depth, C. H. Dodd (1953a) and Felix Porsch (1974). Next we set out in some detail the Stoic theory of the relationship between *logos* and *pneuma* as centred on a distinction that has already made its way into New Testament scholarship: between 'spoken *logos*' (*logos prophorikos*) and 'interior *logos*' (*logos endiathetos*). Then we are ready to address *logos* and *pneuma* in the rest of the Gospel in the manner indicated above. The ultimate aim is to articulate what I will rather grandiosely end up calling John's theory of *logos* and *pneuma*.

DODD ON *LOGOS* AND *PNEUMA*

In his 1953a book, Dodd discusses *logos* and *pneuma* separately (263–85 and 213–27). Towards the very end of his discussion of *pneuma*, however, he does bring in the *logos* from the Prologue and connects it with the *pneuma*:

The only way for man to rise from the lower life to the higher[1] is by being born ἐκ πνεύματος [from *pneuma*], which is also to be born ἐκ τοῦ θεοῦ [from God]. This

---

[1] Remember here that Dodd was a Christian Platonist.

rebirth is made possible through the descent of the 'Son of Man' from τὰ ἄνω [above] to τὰ κάτω [below]. This descent is *otherwise expressed* in the terms ὁ λόγος σὰρξ ἐγένετο [the *logos* became flesh]. The Logos, being θεός [God], *has the nature of* πνεῦμα [spirit] ... *Being* πνεῦμα [spirit] ... He became σάρξ [flesh] ... (Dodd 1953a, 226, my emphasis).

This is quite striking since Dodd implicitly recognizes here the virtual identity of *logos* and *pneuma* that we discovered in the previous chapter. But he does not in the least allow this to influence the rest of his account. In what he says of the *logos* in the rest of the Gospel (265–8) there is no whisper of the *pneuma*, nor, conversely, does the *logos* play any role in his account of the *pneuma* in the Gospel as a whole (222–6) up until that last passage. In spite of this, what Dodd does say about the *logos* in the rest of the Gospel is worth our notice.

He distinguishes between four usages (265): '(i) The term λόγοι [words] in the plural is used in the plain and simple sense of "words" spoken by Jesus or by others. It is interchangeable with ῥήματα [spoken words]'. Dodd is right here, as shown by 7:40, 10:19, 19:13. '(ii) The singular λόγος [*logos*] is used for a "saying", "statement", or "discourse"'. Here again Dodd is right and he gives some examples to which we will return. Then (iii), there is '*logos*' 'used collectively for the whole of what Jesus said to His disciples and to the world, His "message" ...' (265), 'the sum total of His spoken words ..., regarded as *containing His thought or meaning*', 'His total message to the world' (266, my emphasis). Finally (iv), *logos* 'is used of the "Word of God"' (266), 'the content of Christ's teaching', which 'is *a rational content of thought* corresponding to the ultimate reality of the universe' (267, my emphasis). But Dodd is keen on emphasizing that this 'rational content of thought ... is always in some sense uttered, and because it is uttered becomes a life-giving power for men' (267).

What Dodd says under (iii) and (iv) is, in a way, correct enough. When he speaks of Jesus' 'spoken words' as 'containing his thought or meaning', he even implicitly draws on the distinction between *logos prophorikos* (the spoken words) and *logos endiathetos* (the thought or meaning) that we mentioned earlier—and from which Dodd actually begins (263). In his very brief attempt to connect the use of *logos* outside and within the Prologue (267–8), he focuses only on the idea in the Prologue that Christ *is* the divine *logos*. What is missing is any attempt to connect the later usages of the term with what constitutes the two central elements in the *logos* of the Prologue: its actual content—that creation was meant for life (see 1:3–4); and its communicative role—that the life it contained was also a light that was meant to be understood by human beings (see 1:4–5). It is only by attending to these two features that Dodd might have been able to find the deeper meaning of the idea that the 'rational content of thought'—namely, what?—must be *uttered* and '*because* it is uttered becomes a life-giving power for men'—namely, how? Differently put, it is only if Dodd had fully realized the connection between *logos* and *pneuma* that we have found in 1:1–34 as a whole and which Dodd himself does recognize at the end of his discussion of *pneuma*, that he would have been able to see the full role played by Jesus' *logos* in the rest of the Gospel.

That role is as follows: Jesus' full *logos* (which is also God's *logos*, as the Prologue explains) is his understanding (brought to him by God's *pneuma*) of the whole point of creation, which is life for human beings, and of his own role in bringing that point to fruition so that human beings might *obtain* that life—in short Jesus' understanding (as an *endiathetos logos*) of God's rational plan (the *logos* itself) as described in the Prologue. For purposes of clarification we may distinguish between the following three versions of the *logos*: (i) the original *logos*, which is God's thought in and plan with creation including its final realization in Jesus Christ; (ii) the Prologue's *account* of the original *logos* and its final stage; (iii) and finally Jesus' own (*endiathetos*) *logos*, which *refers back* to the whole content of (ii) the Prologue's account of (i) the original *logos*. To this we must add— for the communicative role of Jesus' *logos* viewed as (iv) a *prophorikos logos* and now with a view to his listeners—that when Jesus articulates his message of (ii) and (i) in what he literally says, he is transmitting the message to his listeners in streams of language that flow out of his mouth borne by the *pneuma* that carries his (*prophorikos*) *logos* and aiming to hit the ears of potential listeners who are able to 'hear' it.[2]

PORSCH ON *LOGOS* AND *PNEUMA*

Felix Porsch managed to reach a much better understanding of the connectedness of *logos* and *pneuma* in spite of the curious fact that his account is permeated with Protestant, Dialectic Theological, and indeed Bultmannian formulations (Porsch being a Roman Catholic). Here is a quotation from his summary:

Again and again our exegesis led to a point where the activity (*Wirksamkeit*) of the Word and the Pneuma appeared to overlap with one another (*ineinander überzugehen*). 'Word event' (*Wortgeschehen*) showed itself to be a pneumatic event and vice versa.[3] The attempt to give a more precise account of this relationship led to the conclusion that the Pneuma must be understood as the genuine 'power' (*Kraft*) that gives God's Word its active force (*Wirksamkeit*) and renders the Words of revelation (*Offenbarungsworte*) 'Words of eternal life' (Porsch 1974, 406).

---

[2] The preceding paragraph summarizes the role of the *logos* in the case of Jesus (as different from the 'believers'). Compare footnote 5 below.
[3] Bultmann could not have said it better.

This conclusion is reached on the basis of a careful exegetical analysis of a number of passages which we will consider in the present chapter: John 1:32–3 (which we already know), John 3:3–8, 3:34, 4:23–4, 6:63, and 7:37–9, and then the various references to the *pneuma* in the Farewell Discourse and John 19–20. In this Porsch managed to spell out the basis for the verdict of Hans Leisegang (1922, 13) on the role of the *pneuma* in the Fourth Gospel, which Porsch quotes to begin with (1974, 2): John is, in comparison with the Synoptics,—

the only evangelist who has connected the concept of *pneuma* so intimately with his whole gospel that one can never detach it from the individual ideas without at the same time destroying it all.

In spite of his clear grasp of the interconnectedness of *logos* and *pneuma* and the active role of the latter, Porsch's reading fails in two respects. The first is his view that Jesus *gives* the *pneuma* to those among his listeners who respond by 'hearing' what he says. This cannot be right since, as Porsch himself at least half admits in his exegesis of 7:37–9 (53–81), *nobody* other than Jesus himself came into possession of the *pneuma* during Jesus' lifetime.[4] Instead, we may guess, what happened when (some) people 'heard' Jesus was that they *reacted* positively *to* the *pneuma* that was streaming out of his mouth. They did not actually receive it.

That Porsch did not distinguish between these two aspects of the matter is clear in his summary of his exegesis of 3:34:

In this way the central relationship between Word and Pneuma has been established which must be considered characteristic of the Fourth Gospel. In his Word, which is (also) God's Word (3:34; compare 7:16, 8:26, 28, 40, 14:24), Jesus *gives* the Pneuma, or in other words in Jesus' Word the Pneuma communicates itself to believers (Porsch 1974, 211, my emphasis).

The second half of this is entirely correct, but the former half is false: Jesus does not *give* believers the *pneuma* since nobody in Jesus' entourage actually came to possess it.

The other—connected—point where Porsch goes wrong is one he shares with an overwhelming majority of commentators:

This Pneuma [of 6:63b] is in the former half of the verse (v. 63a) explicitly said to be 'life-creating'. It is clear from the context that this '$\zeta\omega o\pi o\iota\epsilon\hat{\iota}\nu$' (*sic*) ['life-creation'] *consists in* this: to awaken faith in Jesus, the messenger and revealer of God ... This faith is—*in its full form* (*Vollgestalt*)—also true cognition (*Erkenntnis*) of Jesus, his

---

[4] Leisegang (1922, 13), by contrast, got this exactly right: 'Solange er [Jesus] der Träger des Geistes ist, kann er [der Geist] in seiner ganzen Fülle nicht auf andere übergehen. Erst muss Jesus sterben, auferstehen, wieder zum Vater zurückkehren; dann nimmt der Vater in seinem Namen das $\pi\nu\epsilon\hat{\upsilon}\mu\alpha$ und sendet es als Paraklet von neuem in die Welt.'

person and his works (cf. 17:3, 8). The awakening of faith (and cognition) is the real aim of the working of the Pneuma, according to 6:63 (Porsch 1974, 211, my emphasis).

Note here how Porsch implicitly distinguishes between two forms of 'faith' in Jesus, one as the messenger of God and one in its 'full form', which is also true cognition—German *Erkenntnis*—of Jesus' person and work. Where Porsch ends up bringing the two together, they must, in fact, be sharply distinguished, even though both forms may fall under a single term: *pisteuein* ('believe'). 'Believing in' Jesus at an initial stage as this or the other type of figure is what might come about by *reacting to* the *pneuma* transmitted by Jesus without actually coming to possess it. By contrast, 'believing in' Jesus in its *full form* was only possible once people had themselves come to *possess* the *pneuma*. That only happened after Jesus' death. Then they would see him not just as one who had 'gone out from God', as the disciples in the end managed to do (16:30), but also as one who had *returned* to God (through his resurrection and ascension). That *full* story is the one Jesus has just articulated in that passage (16:28). It is also central in the Prologue's account of the *logos* (see 1:18). And so, when human beings would receive the *pneuma*, they would also be in possession of God's divine *logos* in and behind creation as this was comprehensively stated in the Prologue. *Then*—and only then—they would have 'faith' in Jesus in its full form of *Erkenntnis*.[5]

PROPHORIKOS AND *ENDIATHETOS LOGOS*: THE STOICS ON LANGUAGE AND KNOWLEDGE

I have already hinted at the help we may get from the Stoic theory of *prophorikos* and *endiathetos logos* in explicating John's handling of the whole complex of *logos, pneuma, lalia* (speech), and *rhêmata* (spoken words). But we need to have the full theory in front of us.

The Stoic theory belongs within several philosophical disciplines. It is part of their philosophy of language (including semantics and the physiology of human speech) and also immediately opens up to their theory of knowledge (epistemology). But since in Stoicism *logos* as found in human beings is also directly related to the *logos* (and *pneuma*) that permeates the universe as a whole, the theory is also directly related to Stoic ontology. Here we may begin from its role within its primary discipline: the philosophy of language.

---

[5] The preceding paragraph summarizes the role of the *logos* and *pneuma* in the case of 'believers' (as different from Jesus). Compare my earlier footnote 2.

Sextus Empiricus writes as follows (*Against the professors* 8.275–6 = *SVF* 2.223, part = Long and Sedley 53T, their translation, my additions of central Greek terms in round parentheses):

They [the doctrinaire philosophers] say that [(1)] it is not uttered speech (*prophorikos logos*) but internal speech (*endiathetos*, sc. *logos*) by which man differs from non-rational animals (*ta aloga zôia*); for crows and parrots and jays utter articulate sounds (*enarthroi...phônai*). (2) Nor is it by the merely simple impression (*haplê...phantasia*) that he differs (for they too receive impressions), but by impressions produced by inference and combination (*hê metabatikê kai synthetikê*, sc. *phantasia*). (3) This amounts to his possessing the conception of 'following' (*akolouthias ennoia*) and directly grasping, on account of 'following', the idea of sign (*sêmeiou noêsis*). For sign is itself of the kind 'If this, then that.' (4) Therefore the existence of signs follows from man's nature and constitution.

We will return to points (3) and (4) much later (Chapter VII) in connection with the Johannine notion of a 'sign' (*sêmeion*). Here we focus on the basic difference between human beings and non-rational animals as developed in points (1) and (2). Parrots may produce sounds that are 'articulate' in the sense that they *might* have a meaning (to human beings), but in fact—so the Stoics postulated—do not when uttered by the parrots. Similarly, non-rational animals may well have 'simple' impressions of external things, but they cannot combine them and draw inferences from them—literally 'go from one impression to the other' (*metabainein*). And so one does not find in them what Chrysippus is elsewhere quoted as having described as 'a *collection* (*athroisma*) of certain notions and preconceptions'.[6] The consequence is that non-rational animals cannot be said to have *endiathetos logos* and so their 'articulate sounds' (in crows, parrots, and jays) do not amount to a full *prophorikos logos*, they do not have a meaning that reflects an *endiathetos logos*.

The physiology of language is explained as follows by Diogenes of Babylon (second century BCE) in the translation of LS 53U (once again with my own additions in parentheses):[7]

(1) The source of articulate utterance (*hê enarthros*, sc. *phônê*, 'voice') is the same as the source of utterance (*phônê*), and therefore meaningful articulate utterance (*hê sêmainousa enarthros phônê*) has that source too. (2) But this is language (*logos*). (3) Therefore language (*logos*) and utterance (*phônê*) have the same source. (4) But the source of utterance is not the region of the head, but evidently somewhere lower down; for it is obvious that utterance passes through the windpipe. (5) Therefore language too does not have its source in the head, but lower down. (6) But that too is certainly true, viz. that language (*logos*) has its source in

---

[6] Galen, *On Hippocrates' and Plato's doctrines* 5.3.1 (*SVF* 2.841, also in LS 53V).
[7] Galen, *On Hippocrates' and Plato's doctrines* 2.5.9–12 (*SVF* 3 Diogenes 29, part).

thought (*dianoia*); for some actually define language as meaningful utterance sent out from thought (*phônê sêmainousa apo dianoias ekpempomenê*). (7) It is also credible that language is sent out imprinted (*eksesêmasménos*), and stamped (*ektetypôménos*) as it were, by the conceptions (*ennoiai*, 'notions') present in thought, and that it is temporally coextensive with both the act of thinking (*to dianoeisthai*) and the activity of speaking (*hê kata to legein energeia*). (8) Therefore thought too is not in the head but in the lower regions, principally no doubt around the heart.

The Stoics had a special term for this area 'around the heart'. It was called the *hêgemonikon*, the 'commanding faculty', which was the seat of 'seven parts of the soul which grow out and stretch out into the body like the tentacles of an octopus' (LS 53H, from Aetius). It works like this (LS 53G, from Calcidius, with my additions in parentheses, apart from the sharp one):

> The soul's parts flow from their seat in the heart, as if from the source of a spring, and spread through the whole body. They continually fill all the limbs with vital breath (*vitalis spiritus*), and rule (*regere*) and control (*moderari*) them with countless different powers—nutrition, growth, locomotion, sensation, impulse to action.... The soul as a whole despatches the senses (which are its proper functions) like branches from the trunk-like commanding-faculty to be reporters of what they sense, while itself like a monarch (*ut rex*) passes judgement on their reports.... It is the function of internal reflection (*intima deliberatio*) and reasoning (*consideratio*) to understand (*intelligere*) each sense's affection, and to infer from their reports what it [i.e. the object] is, and to accept it when present, remember it when absent, and foresee it when future.

In addition to the five senses, of the two remaining 'parts of soul'

> one is called seed (*sperma*), and this is breath (*pneuma*) extending from the commanding-faculty to the genitals. The other, ... which they also call utterance (*phônê*), is breath (*pneuma*) extending from the commanding-faculty to the pharynx, tongue and appropriate organs.[8]

I have quoted extensively here in order to provide a flavour of the Stoic form of theorizing—so different from anything in John—and also to bring out how Stoic theory aimed to hold tightly together what we might wish to separate as the cognitive aspect of thought and language and its physiological 'realization'. In Stoicism these two things are one—even though they are certainly *conceptually* distinct—and they are concretely located in the same place (the heart) from where they literally extend to whatever organs are involved, e.g. the pharynx, tongue, etc. in the case of speech. This extending function is performed by the material *pneuma*, but once again, this *pneuma* evidently 'carries' the cognitive content that turns an

---

[8] LS 53H, from Aetius, *SVF* 2.836.

utterance into a 'meaningful articulate utterance', in fact into a *prophorikos logos* that reflects and expresses the *endiathetos logos* that is uniquely found in human beings.

To this picture of language—*from* the 'commanding faculty' into actual speech—we should add that in Stoicism the 'thought' (*dianoia*) that is another term for the *endiathetos logos* is connected 'outwardly' with the world as a whole. As present in the commanding faculty it is itself 'carried' by *pneuma* and this *pneuma* is operative in the world at large, the one that is identical with the kind of *universal logos* that is also identical with God. That is why the Stoics spoke of *logos* in human beings as an *apospasma* from the universal *logos*, a 'portion' of God.[9] We already noted this side of the Stoic theory in Chapter II of this book, when we referred to the role of *logos* and *pneuma* in the world at large, in human beings in general, and specifically in the one human being who is precisely one with the universal *logos* (and God): the human sage.

What we have in Stoicism, then, is a theory of *logos* and *pneuma* with three components that will prove helpful in articulating what we also find in the Fourth Gospel. (x) There is the universal *logos* and *pneuma* that is active in God's continuous creation of the world. (y) There is the *endiathetos logos* to be found in any human being, a *logos* that reflects—if things go well, in the human sage—God's universal *logos* and *pneuma*. (z) And there is the *prophorikos logos* through which human beings articulate in speech—with cognitive content literally borne to the speech organs by *pneuma*—whatever part of the universal *logos* they have managed to grasp. And here again it is only the words of the ideal human sage that will express the full truth and nothing but the truth which is to be found in his *endiathetos logos*, the one that constitutes (y) a *grasp* at the level of consciousness of (x) the *facts* about the world in the sense of the actual behaviour in the world as a whole of God's universal *logos* and *pneuma*.

All three components are obviously important. With a view to the Fourth Gospel, however, special emphasis must be placed on the *endiathetos logos* (y). In John, this is the key that holds together Jesus' grasp—in one direction—of the divine, universal *logos* (x) that has been described in the Prologue and—in the other direction—his actual words (z, his *prophorikos logos*) that are given in the rest of the Gospel. In what follows, I am asking the reader to consider what comes out of reading the Johannine text through this Stoic lens. In particular, we should pay attention to the fact that on such a reading, Jesus' words are to be understood as being both cognitive and at the same time also material and directly acting on the ears and bodies of his listeners. The ultimate goal here is to understand exactly how Jesus' words may—in the end—generate eternal life in the listeners.

---

[9] For *apospasma*, see, e.g., Marcus Aurelius 5.27 and *SVF* 2.633 (from Diogenes Laertius).

BACK TO THE FOURTH GOSPEL: FROM A BLAND USE
OF *LOGOS* TO A MORE POTENT ONE IN JOHN 4

Let us consider the use of the term *logos* in the rest of the Gospel. We will see that while the term may be used in an entirely neutral sense, signifying (as Dodd noted) nothing more than a 'statement', in a number of passages it has a much richer meaning in which it refers to the full content of what Jesus claims about his own relationship with God: his having been sent by God and his eventual return to God. Here 'Jesus' *logos*' signifies, or at least rehearses important elements in, the full content of the story about Jesus that has already been recounted in the Prologue. Thus understood, Jesus' *logos* is obviously much more than just a 'statement' of his. In fact, John operates with a clear distinction between Jesus' *logos* (in this full sense) and his *lalia* (speech) and *rhêmata* (words, sayings as they actually come out of his mouth). A corresponding distinction may be found in the term 'hearing' (*akouein*). It is one thing to literally hear the sounds that stream from Jesus' mouth and a different thing to hear them and 'take them in' and 'believe' their meaningful content. In Chapter VI of this book we will return to the question of what explains, on the side of the recipients, that some people may in fact 'hear' what Jesus says in the full sense while others do not. In the present chapter we stay focused on Jesus' side: on the apparent power of his words to 'move'—through the *pneuma*, as I suggested—some (at least) to hear (parts of) the full *logos* in what he says and hence to come to believe in him.

Before we begin, I should warn the reader that the following remarks on some crucial passages in the Gospel are not intended as 'full exegesis' of those passages. Instead, I am trying to gauge what is implied when John speaks of the *logos* (and later the *pneuma*) in those passages and how this may give meaning to what else he is saying. I will readily admit that there is an element of circularity in this. From repeated study of the text I have become convinced that there is a coherent, philosophical theory of the meaning and behaviour of *logos* and *pneuma* that underlies the actual references in the text to the two phenomena. In what follows I attempt to show this by 'teasing out' such implications from the text itself. The truth value of my claims will depend on whether they will be felt to add substantial meaning to the text.

We may first note two examples of the use of *logos* in the bare sense of a statement. This is uninteresting in itself, but provides the background against which to see the richer uses. In 2:19, Jesus makes a striking statement to the effect that if 'the Jews' will destroy the temple, he will raise it up again 'in three days'. John comments (2:22, NRSV with my own parenthesis):

²²After he was raised from the dead, his disciples remembered that *he had said this*; and they believed the scripture *and the word* (*logos*) *that Jesus had spoken*.

It is unclear why the NRSV translates the *logos* here as 'the word'. More idiomatic would have been 'the statement that Jesus had made' or just 'what Jesus had said', not least because it directly takes up that 'he had said this'. Here it seems pretty obvious that the *logos*—even as important as the one Jesus makes here—means nothing other than 'statement'.

Similarly, towards the end of the Gospel 'the Jews' tell the Roman governor, Pilate, that according to their own law Jesus must die 'because he has made himself the Son of God' (19:7). John continues (19:8): '⁸Now when Pilate heard this *logos*, he was more afraid than ever'. No matter how important the accusation of 'the Jews' was, the term *logos* clearly carries no special weight here. Indeed, the NRSV just translates the verse as follows: 'Now when Pilate heard *this*, he was...'.

However, there are other examples of the use of *logos* in the Gospel which are far more potent. Let us consider one example from John 4. In this chapter, once the Samaritan woman has had a long conversation with Jesus, she returns to her city and tells the inhabitants this (4:29): '²⁹Come and see a man who told me everything I have ever done. Might he perhaps be the Messiah?'[10] The result is given in 4:39–42:

³⁹Many Samaritans from that city came to believe in him because of what the woman said (her *logos*) when she witnessed that 'He told me everything I have ever done'. ⁴⁰So when the Samaritans came to him, they asked him to stay with them; and he stayed there for two days. ⁴¹And many more came to believe (in him) because of his *logos*. ⁴²To the woman they said, 'It is no longer because of your speech (*lalia*) that we believe, for we have heard (*akêkoamen*) for ourselves (*autoi*), and we (now) know (*oidamen*) that this man is truly the Saviour of the world'.

It is clear that this text aims to distinguish between hearing at second hand and 'hearing for oneself' so that one gets to know. In 4:39 the woman's *logos* is therefore close to being just a 'statement'. It is also characterized by her (male) compatriots as mere *lalia* (4:42), mere (babbling) speech, as one might expect from a woman. By contrast, once the men had spent a couple of days with Jesus, they came to believe in him 'because of his *logos*'. That this is a fuller form of believing in him is made clear in two ways: they claim to have 'heard' 'for themselves' (*autoi*) and

---

[10] NRSV translates the last half of this as follows: 'He cannot be the Messiah, can he?' Lincoln (2005, 179) makes her just as cautious: 'This is not the Christ, is it?'. But the Greek locution seems more positive here. By contrast, Theobald (2009, 301) is probably too positive: 'Sollte dieser nicht der Christus sein?'. The point is important for gauging the level of the woman's grasp. Danker (2000, 649) places the verse—I think rightly—under 'questions in which the questioner is in doubt concerning the answer, *perhaps*', as different from the use, e.g., in Mark 4:21.

got to 'know' the truth about Jesus; and they acknowledge Jesus as 'truly the Saviour of the world'. This, by John's lights, is what Jesus most truly was. So these Samaritans apparently got it exactly right—whereas the woman did not quite do so (compare 4:29).[11]

Why then the difference—apart from the fact that the Samaritans were men! There are two answers. First, there must be something about *Jesus' logos* (as opposed to the woman's mere *lalia*) that generated full insight in the Samaritans. Secondly, the happy result must be due to the fact that the Samaritans had listened to Jesus in person. Both conditions are fulfilled if we take it that Jesus' *logos* is not just some individual statement, but the full story about himself, and also that this story worked its magic on the Samaritans because they were able to react to something that was only present in the direct, face-to-face encounter with Jesus. And what might that be? Is it too fanciful to suggest that it is the *pneuma* that uniquely streamed out of his mouth when he made the full *logos* known to them? True enough. There is no explicit reference in 4:39–42 to any particular element in the bit of theory I am invoking here to explain the text: that Jesus' *logos* is his full *endiathetos logos*; and that the Samaritan men were hit by the *pneuma* that carried this *logos* out of Jesus' mouth. But it is at least worth entertaining the possibility that that is what explains why Jesus was more successful here than in the case of the woman.

Why then did Jesus' *logos* not work its magic on the woman—and again apart from the fact that she *was* a woman? The answer probably lies in what appears to be the point of the whole story. The conversation with the woman seems to be aimed at showing the reader once more—like in the conversation with Nicodemus in John 3—the discrepancy between what Jesus says and implies and what is actually understood. But there is also the difference from the Nicodemus story that the Samaritan woman is described as gradually moving towards *some* kind of understanding of Jesus, as Nicodemus was precisely not. Both themes—the discrepancy and a gradual move towards overcoming it—are central in the Gospel as a whole. In addition, there is also a 'Samaritan' theme in the conversation with the woman: the suggestion in 4:21–4 that what Jesus has to offer reaches beyond both Judaism and Samaritan religion to all people who worship God 'in *pneuma* and truth' (4:23–4). That theme appears to reach its conclusion in what is said about the Samaritan men. By seeing Jesus as the 'Saviour of the world' these Samaritans, who were not well recognized

---

[11] I thus read the relationship between the 'transformation' of the Samaritan woman and that of the Samaritan men somewhat differently from the way it is taken by Attridge (2013b on the woman) and Peter Phillips (2013 on the men). Phillips (2013, 298): 'As the woman encounters Jesus and, arguably, is transformed by the encounter [so also Attridge], so the Samaritan chorus affirms her response by being transformed themselves.' But more is going on in 4:39–42.

by 'the Jews' (compare 4:9), instantiate the movement even beyond traditional Samaritan religion. There are good reasons, therefore, why John
describes Jesus as succeeding somewhat differently with his two conversation partners. It remains the case, that one needs some kind of explanation for
the difference, apart from the difference of gender. The simplest solution—
which may in the end be insufficient—might be that while the woman
only had a fairly brief conversation with Jesus, he stayed for two whole days
with the men. In any case, 4:39–42 appears to aim at bringing out some
feature of *Jesus' logos* that explains why it might have such a striking effect.

THE MEANING OF JESUS' *LOGOS* IN 5:19–38

Another set of relevant passages follows in John 5:19–38. Our discussion of
this passage will stay focused on how to understand the *logos* that Jesus is
talking about. In this connection we are also forced to bring in the *pneuma*
and some of the themes we consider will be taken up more thoroughly later
on. All of this makes for a somewhat convoluted discussion. But it also
shows how much richer John's (and Jesus') use of the term *logos* is than just
as a 'statement'.

Early in the speech (5:19–46) that Jesus gives in response to the accusations of 'the Jews' (5:16–18), he makes this famous statement (5:24):

[24] Truly, truly I tell you, anyone who hears my *logos* and believes in him who sent
me (already) *has* eternal life and will not come under judgement, but has (already)
passed from death to life.

What *logos* is Jesus talking about here? Clearly not just any particular
'word' (NRSV) of his. On the contrary, it is likely that it is closely connected
with what may be its effect, namely, that the person who 'hears' it will
thereby also 'believe him who has *sent me*'. This already indicates that the
logos is a much more comprehensive thing than a simple statement and is
meant to encapsulate everything Jesus has been saying in the immediately
preceding text, 5:19–23. This text more or less contains the whole message
of John's Gospel *in nuce* (NRSV, my square brackets—and the italics to
indicate the progression of thought):

[19] ... Very truly, I tell you, the Son can *do* nothing [like healing the man on the
Sabbath] on his own, but only what he sees the Father doing; for whatever the
Father does, the Son does likewise. [20]The Father loves the Son and shows him all
that he himself is doing; and he will show him *greater works* than these, so that you
will be astonished. [21]Indeed, just as the Father raises the dead and gives them life,
so also the Son *gives life* to whomsoever he wishes. [22]The Father judges no one but
has given all *judgement* to the Son, [23]*so that* all may honour the Son just as they

honour the Father. Anyone who does not honour the Son does not honour the Father who sent him.

Here we get a whole range of the essential claims that were already made in the Prologue (though in slightly different terms): the sending of the Son, the unique status of the Son vis-à-vis the Father, the ultimate aim of it all, which is raising human beings from death to life, but also its opposite outcome, which is judgement, and finally, the idea of honouring the Father *through* the Son. If people 'hear' *this logos*, then they will also 'believe him who has sent me'—and then they will also, as Jesus goes on to promise in 5:24, already have eternal life, and so forth.

Scholars have quite rightly struggled to understand the time frame in all this.[12] Does Jesus mean to speak of the future or the present or both, and if so how? Where 5:20–1 suggests that making alive belongs to the future, 5:24 speaks distinctly of the present. The same lack of clarity is found in the passage that immediately follows and that precisely addresses again the question of (eternal) life (5:25–9):

[25]Truly, truly, I tell you, the hour is coming, *and is now here*, when the dead shall hear the voice of the Son of God, and those who (will) have heard shall live. [26]For just as the Father has life in himself, so he has given to the Son also to have life in himself; [27]and he has given him authority to execute judgement, because he is the Son of Man. [28]Do not be astonished at this: for the hour is coming when all who are in their graves shall hear his voice [29]and shall come out—those who have done good, to the resurrection of life, and those who have done evil, to the resurrection of condemnation.[13]

This text spells out much more clearly the point about life already adumbrated in 5:20–1. And as we recall from the Prologue, life is the ultimate purpose of creation. But what is the point of basically speaking of things that will happen in the future (5:20–1, 25, and 28–9), but also from time to time speaking as if these things had already happened (in 5:24)? Indeed, what is the point of placing the two ways of speaking directly against one another, as in 5:25, which has even led some manuscripts—probably falsely—to delete the reference to the present in order to avoid the clash?[14]

---

[12] The fundamental scholarly work that both summarizes previous research and argues the case anew is Frey 1997–2000. An excellent later collected volume of essays that still struggles to give meaning to John's talk of the 'eschaton' as both present and future is Koester and Bieringer 2008. See, e.g., the essays by Attridge, Painter, Koester, Zimmermann, Zumstein, Schnelle, and Culpepper. I return to the issue more substantially in Chapter XII. Meanwhile, I will try to give meaning to what John says as we go along the text.

[13] I have translated quite stiltedly here in order to bring out that in verses 25, 28, and 29 the Greek text employs a genuine future tense.

[14] We know, of course, that the scholarly tradition of the whole twentieth century has been keen on finding different chronological layers in this text. However, that is not an option for us (and should no longer be so for anybody).

Before attempting an answer, we should note that all through the text of
5:19–29 there is also talk of Jesus' role as a condemning judge (5:21–2, 24,
26–7, 29), which means that the text is basically speaking of the *future*
'hour' of resurrection to either life or condemnation (*krisis*).[15] Indeed, the
text is clearly speaking—in a wholly traditional Jewish and early Christian
apocalyptic manner—of the future events on the last day. But then Jesus
also refers to the present in 5:24 and 25. Why?

Here we need to observe that although the *pneuma* is not explicitly
mentioned in our passage, it is implied in it. How has the Father '*given*'
the Son to '*have* life in himself' (5:26)?[16] And how has he '*given*' him
'authority (*exousia*) to execute judgement' (5:27, compare 22)? The most
straightforward answer seems to be that God gave these two powers to Jesus
when he sent his *pneuma* down upon him. The *pneuma* gives life (see 6:63) of
the ultimate kind that matters: eternal, physical life.[17] Similarly, when God
gave Jesus the authority to 'execute judgement' (5:27), he also gave him the
power—can it be anything other than a pneumatic power?—of generating
a universal resurrection (*anastasis*) on the day of judgement (5:28–9). In both
cases the *pneuma* is a power for life. The implication appears to be that the
future resurrection into life is generated by the *pneuma*.

There is another pointer to the *pneuma* in 5:25–9. Twice (5:25 and 28) the
text speaks very precisely about Jesus' *voice* (*phônê*) and its effect on the
dead people who hear it. Apparently, it is some characteristic of Jesus'
voice—his *prophorikos logos*—that explains why it may have its tremendous effect on the dead: that hearing it they will come out of their graves for
resurrection into life (hopefully, 5:28–9) or alternatively (5:25) just for life.
What could explain this feature of Jesus' voice? Again the most straightforward answer appears to be that he has in him divine *pneuma* (as the
other side of his full *logos*) which works for life as it streams out of his

---

[15] Culpepper (2008, 254–5) brings out well that the four times in the Gospel (5:28–9 and
11:24–5) where John employs the term *anastasis* (resurrection), they all refer to resurrection
in the eschatological future.

[16] Compare the careful discussion in Theobald 2009, 397–8 (also referred to by Zumstein
2016, 227). Having listed five different proposals that he rejects, he ends up suggesting,
somewhat disappointingly, that 'der Evangelist über die Art und Weise des »Gebens« nicht
reflektiert' (398). But he might presuppose it. From my perspective, it is noteworthy that the
first three proposals (Wengst: at the resurrection, Becker: at the baptism, Theobald himself: at
the sending) all refer to the same agent: the *pneuma*. Of these, the latter two in effect come to
the same thing.

[17] In all this I am taking John to be speaking straightforwardly of physical life, and here
eternal physical life. Compare this with Thyen 2015, 311–13, who argues well against the
'gänzlich unbiblische [!] Unterscheidung zwischen "*geistig*" und "*physisch Toten*"' that goes
with the 'questionable' 'Schlagwort der ,präsentischen Eschatologie' (312). Whether 'biblical'
or not, it is definitely not Johannine (but rather a reminiscence from a Platonizing reading
of John).

mouth. This is one very specific place where the Stoic lens appears particularly illuminating.

If the *pneuma* has this life-generating role in the future eschatological events, how should we understand the passages in 5:24–5 that speak about the present? I believe that there are two fairly simple answers to this question that can be seen once we realize that the focus in the two verses is primarily on Jesus himself and the *logos* that he speaks and only secondarily on the recipients of Jesus' *logos*. First on 5:24: if we recall that the content of 'my *logos*' in that verse is the one indicated by the preceding five verses (5:19–23) and also that those verses were referring to the *pneuma* that Jesus has received from God, then it will also follow directly that the person who genuinely hears *this* kind of *logos* will *ipso facto* have eternal life and have gone over from death to life. All that is required for that is *already* present in that *logos* of Jesus. In 5:24 Jesus is not saying that there *are* people who have heard his *logos* properly and hence have already gone over from death to life. Instead, he is saying that *if* people respond to the full *logos* of 5:19–23, *then* they will have eternal life. We know that as Jesus is speaking *nobody* will genuinely hear his full *logos*. To do so they would need to be themselves in possession of the *pneuma* (to match the *pneuma* that carries Jesus' *logos*), and this they have not yet. But that is not the main point either. Instead, Jesus is primarily speaking of himself and his *logos*—and for very good reason contextually since he is replying to an accusation of 'the Jews' that precisely concerns himself.

Then on 5:25: here it may be possible to give a similarly simple interpretation of the superficially paradoxical statement that 'the hour is coming, and is now here' if we relate the verse to 5:28–9, which again speaks of hearing Jesus' voice. Indeed, if 5:25 (speaking only of 'the dead') prefigures particularly the raising of Lazarus, whereas 5:28–9 (speaking about '*all—pantes*—those in the graves') is about the *general* resurrection and so remains distinctly future, 'the hour is coming, and is now here' in 5:25 may refer *both* to the future general resurrection after Jesus' death ('is coming') *and* to the raising of Lazarus during Jesus' own lifetime ('is now here'). In this way what continues to be something that will happen in the future has also already happened (partly, at least) during Jesus' lifetime in the raising of Lazarus. What this verse then does is once again to insist and emphasize that everything that is needed for human beings to come to life (and this includes the *pneuma*, which *they* do not have *then*) is *already* present in *Jesus*.

Summarizing on 5:24–5, we may say that in his use of the present tense in the two verses Jesus is drawing something that fundamentally belongs to the future *into* the present, and for good reason: it is all there *in Jesus' own presence* since *he* has the full *logos* of the Prologue together with the *pneuma* he received in his baptism. In 5:24 Jesus is drawing something that will only happen once believers have themselves received the *pneuma into* the present since on his own side everything is *already* there (in the *pneuma* and *logos* that he has). Similarly, if we take 5:25 to be also referring to the raising of Lazarus, in that verse, too, Jesus will be speaking of an event in his own presence that precisely prefigures the later, general resurrection. It remains the case that what he is talking about will fundamentally only happen in the future, as 5:28–9 shows.

We will return to the problem concerning the relationship between present and future in John. On the suggested interpretation there is *precisely* no so-called 'realized eschatology' in John (at least not in 5:24–5), meaning an eschatological event that is already present *without* calling for any future follow-up. If we think of believers during Jesus' time on earth, no eschatology is realized in their case since they do not yet possess the *pneuma* that is a necessary condition for that. If we think of believers after Jesus' death, we may well speak of an eschatology that is (partly) 'realized' (they do have the *pneuma*), but only in the sense that it will not be fully realized until the day of judgement. There is no 'realized eschatology' in John in Dodd's sense, in which 'realized' means 'present *and not* future'.[18] John's full eschatology is future, but Jesus' presence on earth was such that the basic *condition* for the eschatology to be realized was present already in him.[19]

However, what matters in the context of the present chapter is something else: first, that the *logos* of which Jesus speaks here as 'my *logos*' (5:24) is the full *logos* (like a Stoic *endiathetos logos*) with the specific content that we know from the Prologue to the effect that creation was made to bring eternal life to human beings; secondly, that in order to make sense of what the text says of how 'eternal life' may be generated, one has to bring in the other side of Jesus' *logos*, which is the *pneuma* that he also has. I said that 5:19–29 contains the basic message of the whole Gospel *in nuce*. That is wholly appropriate contextually since the text comes at the first climax of Jesus' confrontation with 'the Jews'. But what this text then also shows is what was already stated in the Prologue: that the basic message of the Gospel as a whole is Jesus' role in bringing eternal life to human beings.

---

[18] Dodd did not remove such clearly future eschatological references as 5:28–9 from the Evangelist's text, but claimed that they were 'reinterpreted' by the rest. Compare the helpful analysis and comparison with Bultmann's reading in Frey 1997, 247–51. I will return to this issue in Chapter XII.

[19] This interpretation of 5:19–29 should be compared with Jörg Frey's extensive discussion of the same text in Frey 2000a, 322–402. Frey sees no intrinsic contrast between 'present eschatological' and 'future eschatological' statements in the text, but places the main emphasis contextually on the present. I have suggested, however, that 5:24 is not really about any 'present eschatological' state of believers, but primarily about Jesus.

He came with it all (both the *logos* and the *pneuma*). He had it all. The only
thing that was lacking was that human beings might *fully* grasp it.

From 5:31 onwards Jesus' speech turns to another theme that we know
from the Prologue: that of the witnesses to Jesus. The Baptist is mentioned
(5:33–5), but Jesus continues as follows:

> [36]I, however, have a witness of my own (that is) greater than John's. The works
> (*erga*) that the Father has given me to complete, the very works that I am doing
> bear witness on my behalf that the Father has sent me.

When and how did God 'give' (Greek: *edōken*) Jesus that task?[20] Once again,
when he gave him the *pneuma*. Through the agency of the *pneuma*, which
has come *directly* from God, God *himself* bears witness to Jesus *in* those
works he has given Jesus to perform.

Then follows another passage that brings out one more time the comprehensive meaning of the text's use of *logos* (5:37b–38):

> [37] ... You have never heard his [God's] voice nor seen his form, [38]and you do not
> have his [God's] *logos* abiding in you, because the one whom *he* [God] has sent, *him*
> [that is, Jesus] you do not believe.

This text speaks not just of Jesus' *logos*, but of God's, too. The point that 'the
Jews' have never heard (*akouein*) God's voice (*phōnē*) nor seen (*horan*) his
form (*eidos*) refers directly back to the Prologue (1:18) and so God's *logos* will
stand for the whole story told in the Prologue. The reason why Jesus can
say that they do not have this whole *logos* abiding in them is that they do
not 'believe him whom God has sent' (Jesus himself). For the *logos* of the
Prologue is *about* him.

However, the text also appears to be saying something more, which is
suggested both by the reference back to 1:18 and also by the fact that it
speaks of 'having God's *logos* abiding in you'. If *they* have neither heard nor
seen God nor have his *logos* abiding in them, then it is quite clear to the
reader that somebody else has: Jesus himself. And how did that happen?
Once again, when he received the *pneuma*. Moreover, and extremely
importantly, it seems to be precisely this event that is being specifically
referred to when the text speaks of having the *logos* 'abide (*menein*) in you'.
What came to 'abide' (*menein*)—admittedly, not *in* Jesus, but *upon* him
(1:32–3: *menein ep' auton*)—was the *pneuma*. And so it seems that 5:37b–38
almost explicitly connects God's *logos*, which will abide as an *endiathetos
logos* in those who really 'believe in the one God has sent', with the *pneuma*.
But something else seems implied, too. Not only has *Jesus* heard and seen

---

[20] It is perhaps worth noting that Theobald (2009, 411–13) does not address this question
at all. The same goes for Brown, Schnackenburg, Zumstein, and Thyen. Barrett (1978, 266)
only refers back to 5:20.

God and has his *logos* abiding in him from when he received the *pneuma*: this is also something that human beings other than 'the Jews' addressed by Jesus can do—if and when *they* will receive the *pneuma*. 'The Jews', by contrast, so Jesus continues, search the Scriptures in the vain belief that they 'will have eternal life *in them*; and yet (*kai*) it is they [the Scriptures] that bear witness on my behalf' (5:39). It seems, then, that in his criticism of 'the Jews', Jesus is also implicitly contrasting them with others who will believe in 'the one whom God has sent' by having God's *logos* abide in them through the *pneuma*—and who will therefore in this way obtain through *him* what 'the Jews' were vainly seeking to find in the Scriptures: eternal life.

I think we are forced to conclude that the texts we have considered in John 5 contain a large number of elements from the comprehensive theory of *logos* and *pneuma* that I am ascribing to John. Even more, these elements together serve to bring out what is the basic point of the whole Gospel: to show that—and not least how—human beings may gain eternal life through Jesus. Basically, I have argued that these texts do not merely speak of the *logos*: in what they say about the *logos* and its various functions, they are also constantly referring to and recalling—without explicitly mentioning it—the power through which the *logos* is working: the *pneuma*.[21]

THE MEANING OF JESUS' *LOGOS* IN 8:33–44

There are many more passages throughout the Gospel that speak revealingly of Jesus' *logos*, for instance 12:48.[22] We will consider them in their respective contexts. Here we may conclude these remarks on the meaning of *logos* throughout the Gospel by moving forward to the climax of Jesus' confrontation with 'the Jews' towards the end of John 8.

In this passage Jesus is again on the warpath. When 'the Jews' declare that they are descendants of Abraham (8:33), Jesus famously claims that on

---

[21] The distinction I invoke here between an implicit *reference* to and an explicit *mentioning* of the *pneuma* will turn up a number of times. Here we may note that it is the same distinction we found in 1:9–13 of the Prologue with its various references to Jesus that did not actually mention him. The distinction has wide implications. It concerns the fundamental claim I am making that there is a well-developed concrete cosmology 'underlying' John's superficially more 'metaphorical' ways of speaking.

[22] NRSV (with corrections): 'The one who rejects me and does not receive my word [or better words, *rhêmata*!] has a judge; on the last day the word [*logos*!] that I have spoken will serve as judge . . .'. This is one clear example of how lack of attendance to the difference in this area between, for instance, *rhêma* and *logos*, covers up a whole lot.

the contrary their father is the devil (8:44). On his way to this accusation Jesus states the following (8:37–8):

[37]I know that you are descendants of Abraham; yet you seek to kill me, because my *logos* has no room (*chôrei*) in you. [38]What I say (*lalein*) is what I have seen at my Father's. Similarly you too do what you have heard from your father.[23]

Here again we find two elements in the underlying theory. One is that there is a difference between *logos* and *lalein* ('speak'). The *logos* clearly is something more comprehensive, which may or may not 'have room' in one— literally so, just as one might say of the *endiathetos logos* in Stoicism. By contrast, what Jesus says specifically (*lalein*) in his *prophorikos logos* will most often only be parts of that comprehensive *logos*. The other element is that Jesus has *seen* what he says when he was with God (compare again 1:18). We may ask: when and how? And answer: when God made himself known to Jesus by sending him his *pneuma*.[24] It is curious to observe that this self-description is then applied directly (though with negative connotations) to Jesus' opponents. What they do on their side is something they have 'heard' from their own father, the devil, who according to 8:44 'speaks (*lalein*) falsehood'. With regard to Jesus himself, 8:37–8 implies that what he speaks is something he has seen with God *in the sense that* it is a verbal expression of the interior *logos*—or *knowledge* of *God's logos*—which he received from God by means of the *pneuma*.

Immediately after, Jesus also brings in the notion of 'truth' (8:40):

[40]As things are, you seek to kill me, a man who has spoken (*lalein*) the truth (*alêtheia*) that I have heard from God. This is not what Abraham did.

What Jesus 'speaks' (*lalein*) are of course sheer words. Their content, however, is something much more comprehensive. It is the truth, says Jesus, which he has himself heard from God. We know what the content of Jesus' words is: the original *logos* or comprehensive plan that was with God to begin with and was then made to abide in Jesus when he received the *pneuma* so as to acquire knowledge of it. In this way God's *logos* became

---

[23] I read 38b as indicative (as against the imperative in, for instance, NRSV: 'as for you, you should do what you have heard from the Father'). Brown agrees with the NRSV (1966, 356). And Lincoln (2005, 262) and Zumstein (2016, 341) adopt the imperative without discussion. Barrett (1978, 347) disagrees, pointing to the 'true parallel' in 8:41, where the verb is an indicative. Theobald too adopts the indicative (2009, 599), as does Thyen (2015, 437) without discussion and if I understand him correctly. To Theobald's argument that 8:38 constitutes the 'title' (*Leitsatz*) of the whole following discussion, one may add that the reference to what 'the Jews' have 'heard' from their father is taken up again in 8:44, which speaks precisely of what the devil 'says' (*lalein*).

[24] Highly relevant here is also 3:32 on 'the one who comes from above' and 'from heaven' (3:31): 'what he bears witness to is what he has seen and heard', namely, in heaven. See Chapter IV on this.

Jesus' *logos*. When Jesus then articulates this knowledge in his own speech, his *prophorikos logos*, of what is this *logos* the truth? Only one answer seems possible. The truth about creation: *that* it was engineered by God's original thought in the way described in the Prologue; *that* it was directed towards life and light; *that* John the Baptist was sent out by God to bear witness to the light, etc., including, not least, that in one final creative act the plan in creation had issued in the figure of Jesus Christ himself who came to turn human beings into children of God. The truth thus articulated by Jesus is the truth about the form and content of God's creation of the world.[25]

Finally, just before Jesus accuses 'the Jews' of having the devil as their father (8:44), he says the following (8:43):

[43]Why do you not understand my speech (or with NRSV: 'what I say', namely, my *lalia*)? It is because you cannot hear my *logos*.

Here the translation in NRSV becomes strangely tautologous: 'Why do you not understand what I say? It is because you cannot accept my word'. This will only make sense once one adds some much fuller interpretation of the 'word'. By contrast, we know the meaning: 'the Jews' are unable to understand Jesus' actual words (his 'speech', the *lalia*) *because* they are unable from the very beginning to 'hear' and accept the much more comprehensive *logos* that Jesus is drawing on in articulating it in his individual words. And the reason for *that* is that they have an utterly different 'father' from God (8:44): '*You* are from your father, the devil etc.' The lies of the devil—when he 'speaks what is false (*to pseudos*)'[26]—are so widely removed from the truth about creation, which is contained in Jesus' *logos*, that 'the Jews' are entirely unable to connect in any way with the latter—and so do not understand anything of what Jesus literally says.

THE MEANING OF JESUS' *RHÊMATA*

We have already seen the difference between Jesus' *logos* and his 'speech' (*lalia*, *lalein*). Let us now spend a moment on John's repeated use of another term, briefly referred to above, within the same semantic field: *rhêmata*. The lexicon (e.g. Danker 2000, 905) gives the meaning as follows: 'that which is said, *word, saying, expression, or statement of any kind . . . the words* (opp. *ta erga*)'. That is entirely right: *rhêma* in Greek means '*that which is said* or

---

[25] I will not discuss elsewhere the meaning of John's repeated and important references to 'truth' and the like. As I see it, the notion has the very precise epistemological meaning just given (and none other).

[26] Note again the distinctly epistemological term employed here: 'the false' or 'falsehood' as the direct opposite of 'the truth' (*alêtheia*). The NRSV translation ('When he lies . . .') does not capture this.

spoken, word, saying', as Liddell/Scott/Jones has it (under the term). It is somewhat problematic, therefore, that when it comes to the Johannine cases, Danker elevates this meaning markedly: 'Of pronouncements of (Christian) teaching or of divine understanding'. Why not keep the ordinary Greek meaning?

Here is the NRSV translation of 5:47 (my parentheses):

[47]But if you do not believe what he [Moses] wrote (*grammata*), how will you believe what I say (*rhêmata*)?

Here Moses' *grammata*—his writings or what he wrote—are straightforwardly contrasted with Jesus' *rhêmata*: what he said.

Or take another text, 14:10, in the NRSV translation (my parentheses):

[10]Do you not believe that I am in the Father and the Father is in me? The words (*rhêmata*) that I say (*legein*) to you I do not speak (*lalein*) on my own; but the Father who dwells in me does his works (*erga*).

Here we have two things that should not be confused: first, that the text is just talking about what Jesus *says*; and secondly, that it also has Jesus claim that what he himself says is directly derived from God, it is *God's* 'work'. There is absolutely no reason to elevate these *rhêmata* into some special *type* of 'pronouncement' (other than remembering that they come from God). They are just 'sayings' that stream out of Jesus' mouth—though we know, of course, that these sayings are also borne by the *pneuma* of God. Incidentally, that must also be what Jesus is directly referring to here when he speaks of God as 'dwelling in me'. God (who is himself *pneuma*) is present *in* Jesus *as pneuma*, which then also streams out of Jesus' mouth in his sayings.

This combination of Jesus' sayings (*rhêmata*)—to be understood simply as his 'speech' (*lalia*)—with the *pneuma* is made as explicit as one could wish in 3:34, which NRSV translates as follows (my parentheses):

[34]He whom God has sent speaks the words (*rhêmata*) of God, for he [God] gives [him] the Spirit (*pneuma*) without measure.[27]

It is hard to find any better support for a crucial part of the theory of speech we have suggested underlies John's account of Jesus' speech. Jesus has

---

[27] Commentators are divided on whether the giver is Jesus (thus, e.g., Brown 1966, 158; Porsch 1974, 103–5; and Frey 2000a, 302 n. 296) or God (thus, e.g., Barrett 1978, 226; Lincoln 2005, 162; and Theobald 2009, 292–3, with a good discussion). The basic argument must be that taking God as the giver accounts both for the logical connection of 34b back to 34a ('for', *gar*) and for the point of 3:35 ('the Father loves the Son and has given everything in his hand'). If one thinks that Jesus 'gives the *pneuma* without measure', one must explain how he does this only after his death. Zumstein (2016, 160) agrees and wonderfully adds: 'Im Übrigen weiss der Leser dank des eröffnenden Taüferzeugnisses bereits (vgl. 1,33), dass es Jesus ist, der die Gabe des Geistes . . . empfangen hat.'

received the *pneuma* from God. Whatever Jesus says are therefore literally 'the words (*rhêmata*) of God'. They are the individual expressions of the comprehensive *logos* that Jesus got to know when he received the *pneuma* and God came to dwell in him. It is a very small step from this to 8:47 (NRSV with my parenthesis):

[47]Whoever is from God hears the words (*rhêmata*) of God. The reason you do not hear them is that you are not from God.

Here Jesus is talking of those who hear *himself* speak 'the words of God'. The reason why some of those will actually 'hear' what he says is that they are themselves (already) 'from God' (more on this in Chapter VI). Others, by contrast, do not 'hear' properly since they are not 'from God'. What matters in the present context, however, is that the one who *speaks* 'the *rhêmata* of God' is Jesus himself. He does this since in receiving the *pneuma*, which God gave him without measure, he also came to know the full *logos* that is articulated in those words.

We should conclude that even when Jesus says (6:63, NRSV, my parentheses) that 'The words (*rhêmata*) I have spoken (*lalein*) to you are spirit (*pneuma*) and life' or when Peter confirms (6:68) that 'You have words (*rhêmata*) of [that is, leading to] eternal life', what they are referring to is just what Jesus says, his spoken words and not some special 'pronouncements'. That these words have such a huge power is due to the fact that they are the individual expressions of the much more comprehensive *endiathetos logos* that is Jesus' and (as described in the Prologue) God's. And their power is literally to be explained by the fact that Jesus' *prophorikos logos* is borne by the *pneuma* he received when he was baptized from above. What 'moves' in Jesus' words (*rhêmata*) and speech (*lalia*) is the cognitive content of the underlying *logos*, but it is that content as borne by the *pneuma*. It is the *pneuma* present in Jesus' words and speech that hits.

THE USE OF *PNEUMA* IN THE REST OF THE GOSPEL

We have hitherto focused primarily on the *logos*, Jesus' *lalia*, and his *rhêmata* and not squarely on the *pneuma*. Even so, we have repeatedly seen that the texts make a much more striking point when we bring in the whole (Stoic) theory of *logos* and *pneuma* as a reading lens. It is now time to catch up with what is said about the *pneuma* in the rest of the Gospel, after its momentous introduction in 1:29–34. Since, as has been rightly claimed by Udo Schnelle (1998), the fourth evangelist was through and through a *Geisttheologe* (theologian of the spirit), this theme plays an extremely important role throughout the Gospel, much larger than is normally recognized.[28] However, we will not consider all the relevant material here. Some of it, for example, the account in the Farewell Discourse of the 'Paraclete', who is explicitly said to be the 'spirit of truth' (*to pneuma tês alêtheias*, 14:17), will only be discussed when we take up that text. Also, when we discuss passages on the *pneuma* in texts that will be more fully discussed later, we will try to focus exclusively on what they say about the *pneuma* and nothing else. What matters at present is the overall shape and role of the *pneuma* in the story about Jesus as a whole.

THE *PNEUMA* AS A NECESSARY CONDITION FOR RESURRECTION (JOHN 3)

The first text after John 1 in which the *pneuma* makes an appearance is John 3. Here the *pneuma* is explicitly mentioned twice. To begin with, possession of the *pneuma* by human beings is a necessary condition for them to come to 'see the kingdom of God' (3:3) and 'enter' it (3:5). The latter claim is then explained: 'What is born of the flesh is flesh, and what is born of the Spirit is spirit' (3:6, NRSV). As shown by 3:3 and 5 the text identifies this (re-)birth 'from the *pneuma*' as a matter of being 'born from above (*anôthen*)', where the play in 3:3–8 on the meaning of *anôthen* ('again' or 'from above'?) makes it certain that Jesus' intended sense is the latter: from above. But what does that mean? Commentators regularly read this in a metaphorical manner, which they also apply to the talk in 3:3 of 'seeing' the kingdom of God and indeed also to the notion of the 'kingdom of God' itself to be taken not at all in a spatial, locative sense. What it all comes down to is 'the believing realization . . . that *in* and *with him* [Jesus] God's own reality takes place'.[29] This is not wholly persuasive as a reading of John. First, it seems clear that the term *anôthen* is taken up directly a little later in the text (3:11–13) when Jesus introduces the contrasting pair of 'earthly' versus 'heavenly' matters and even begins to speak of 'descending from heaven'. That fact in itself suggests that 'from above' should be understood wholly concretely and cosmologically: from heaven. Secondly, it seems clear that the initially

---

[28] Let me give one quotation from Schnelle (1998, 23): 'Weil der Geist bleibend auf Jesus ruht und zu einem Attribut seiner Person wird, kann das gesamte Auftreten Jesu, seine Taten und Reden, als ein Geschehen in der Kraft des Geistes verstanden werden. . . . Die Pneumatologie erweist sich bereits zu Beginn des Evangeliums als Tiefenschicht der johanneischen Theologie'. Another small article that brings this out beautifully is Bieringer 2007. My own attempt, of course, is to spell out these insights in as much coherent and precise detail as possible.

[29] Theobald (2009, 248, his emphasis): 'das gläubige Wahrnehmen . . . dessen, dass *in* und *mit ihm* Gottes Wirklichkeit selbst Raum greift'. It is this (beautiful) kind of metaphorical understanding that I am querying in this book.

somewhat vague talk in 3:3 of 'being born from above' in order to 'see' the kingdom of God is meant to be made more precise in 3:5, where it is said to consist in 'being born from water and *pneuma*' (evidently playing on baptism) and '*entering*' the kingdom of God, which has far more specifically local connotations. Thirdly, in light of the two previous points it is surely relevant that when Jesus himself was baptized (by God), what happened was that the *pneuma* came down explicitly 'from heaven' (1:32).[30] All of this strongly suggests that the idea of 'seeing' and 'entering' the kingdom of God should also be taken wholly literally. If so, possession of the *pneuma* is a necessary condition on the part of human beings *for resurrection into heaven*.

This point may be strengthened by considering what Jesus says in 3:13, and here evidently of himself: 'nobody has *ascended into heaven* except the one who has descended from heaven, the Son of Man'. Here the '*has ascended*' is clearly proleptic relative to the narrative present. The 'has descended', however, has already happened: when Jesus received the *pneuma* from heaven. Though the *pneuma* is not literally mentioned in what this text says about Jesus, the context makes it overwhelmingly likely that it is implicitly referred to here as the agent underlying both Jesus' having descended and his prospective ascension. In that case this text is directly relevant to the claim made in 3:3–8. No human being will be able to enter the kingdom of God *by ascending into heaven* unless the person has before that 'descended *from* heaven' in the sense of having been baptized by water *and pneuma that has descended from heaven*. Jesus is the forerunner. Believers are meant to follow in his footsteps. Thus, (re-)birth by the *pneuma* in a wholly literal sense is a necessary condition both in Jesus and also in human beings generally for resurrection into the kingdom of God.

Later in the chapter, the Evangelist connects the *pneuma* explicitly with Jesus, and here in particular with his spoken words, as we already know:

[31]The one who comes from above is above all; the one who is from the earth is from the earth and speaks from the earth. [32]He bears witness to what he has seen and heard [namely, in heaven], and nobody accepts his witness... [34]He whom God has sent speaks the words of God, for he [God] gives the Spirit without measure. [35]The Father loves the Son and has placed all things in his hand. [36]The one who believes in the Son has eternal life; but the one who disobeys the Son shall not see life, but God's wrath remains upon him.

Jesus (Christ) has come from heaven; he bears witness to what he has seen and heard (in heaven); God has sent him (to earth), where he speaks the

---

[30] The claim I am arguing for here—that John in general thinks in wholly concrete, cosmological terms of heaven and earth and the like—is so important that I allow myself the following question: does anyone doubt that in 1:32 the *pneuma* is meant to have come down *literally* from heaven (in John's view, of course)?

words of God; and God has given everything in his power ('hand'): it seems highly probable that the explicit reference to the *pneuma* in connection with what Jesus *says* (3:34) is meant to cover all the rest, too. It might be objected that where the *pneuma* is actually mentioned in this text, it is only specifically tied to Jesus' *words*. However, that can be explained by the fact that the text is focused on how people will *respond* to Jesus (in 3:36), coming as he does from heaven in the way explained. And what they will 'respond' to are his words. Also, the other point of the passage is obviously to explain the pneumatic power of Jesus' words *by* all the other features told of him. That purpose is achieved much more easily if the *pneuma* is also taken to lie directly behind those other features. He came from heaven, has seen and heard things in heaven, was sent to earth by God, speaks the words of God there, and has everything on the earth in his hand—this *all* happened through the *pneuma* when he received that from God.

We may conclude that just as it is explicitly stated that the *pneuma* is involved in connection with Jesus' words, so it is highly likely that it is also meant to be involved in the rest of the story about Jesus. And just as it is explicitly stated that the *pneuma* is involved in connection with the prospective resurrection to heaven of human beings, so it is highly likely that it is also involved in Jesus' own resurrection. In fact, it is only on condition that having 'descended from heaven' in Jesus' case *means* having 'received the *pneuma*' that the parallel between the eventual fate of human beings and of Jesus will be complete. And in that case, having received the *pneuma* is a necessary condition for resurrection in Jesus' case, too.

The overall point is that the *pneuma* is here considered *the* agent in a wholly literal sense of everything that has happened to Jesus, happens to his addressees, and will happen to both parties. John was truly a *Geisttheologe*.

THE *PNEUMA* AS GOD'S ADDITIONAL GIFT WITH A VIEW TO SALVATION AND ETERNAL LIFE (JOHN 4)

The story given in John 4 of Jesus' meeting with the Samaritan woman contains two important references to the *pneuma*, one implicit and one explicit. The implicit, but still certain one is contained in Jesus' talk of 'living water' in 4:10–15. (i) Jesus defines the 'living' quality of the water he offers as follows:

[14]The one who drinks of the water that I will give him will never, ever, be thirsty; instead, the water that I will give him will become for him a spring of water gushing up to eternal life.

As is well known, the motif of living water that will quench a person's thirst is taken up again in 7:37–9, to which we will return. There the living water is explicitly identified as *pneuma*. That also fits here. The living water is (implicitly) said to be 'the gift of God' (4:10), which fits the description in 3:2–8 of the *pneuma* as the agent of a veritable rebirth in the baptism of Christ believers. (ii) Furthermore, just as Jesus is implied to be 'greater than our ancestor, Jacob' (4:12), so the water he provides is much better than the water to be found in Jacob's well. Here the contrast is taken up from 1:17 between a major representative of traditional Judaism (there Moses, here Jacob) and Jesus and what he brings. This theme is again addressed in the second passage of John 4 that we will consider (4:21–6), and there the contrast is explicitly drawn in terms of the *pneuma*. (iii) Finally, when in 4:14 Jesus' living water is said to 'gush up to eternal life', the reference to the *pneuma* is unmistakable. As we saw in connection with John 3, the *pneuma* appears to be the agent both when Jesus will ascend to heaven and when believers will enter the kingdom of God. We may conclude that according to this passage the living water that Jesus brings and offers is the *pneuma*, which will help human beings obtain eternal life.

The second passage (4:21–6) spells out the relationship between what Jesus brings and the kind of 'salvation' (*sôtêria*) that may be obtained by the Samaritans, who worship God on Mount Gerizim, and the Jews, who worship God in Jerusalem. Actually, it is only in the latter case that one may speak of salvation: 'for salvation is from the Jews' (4:22, NRSV). However (4:23–4, *allá*):

²³the hour is coming, and is now here, when the true worshippers will worship the Father ['*neither* on Mount Gerizim *nor* in Jerusalem', 4:21, *but*] in spirit and truth, for the Father seeks such as these to worship him. ²⁴God is spirit, and those who worship him must worship in spirit and truth.

This text very emphatically connects the *pneuma* with what Jesus *adds* to the worship performed by both Samaritans and Jews in their temples. Since God himself is *pneuma*, he must be worshipped by people who on their side possess *pneuma*. We will see in greater detail that these are not just people who 'believe in' Jesus Christ; it is possible to 'believe in' Jesus at an initial stage without having the *pneuma*. What, then, is it that possession of *pneuma* adds so as to make believers worship God in the proper manner? Here we may note that Jesus is speaking in the passage of 'salvation' and later in the chapter is acknowledged by the Samaritan men as 'the Saviour of the world' (4:42). If we connect this with what was clearly (but implicitly) said of the *pneuma* at the beginning of Jesus' conversation with the Samaritan woman (4:7–14)—the 'water' he will give is 'a spring of water gushing up to eternal life' (4:14)—the following conclusion suggests itself: the kind of pneumatic worship of God that Jesus adds to those undertaken by Samaritans and Jews is required (and enabled) by the fact that *through possession of the pneuma* human beings have now at long last obtained access to *salvation* in the form of (resurrection to) *eternal life*. On this reading, the text does not just make two distinct points about the role of the *pneuma*. It connects them into a coherent story. Exactly how, then, does one worship God appropriately through possession of the *pneuma*? Here the answer blows a little in the wind. Only, the answer must square with the suggestions given much later in the Gospel of the lives of people who will receive the 'Paraclete' after Jesus' death. They will also worship God in the required manner.[31]

Back in John 4, what time frame does Jesus have in mind when he stipulates the character of the right kind of worship of God? Here again we meet the paradoxical phrase 'the hour is coming and is now here' (4:23), which takes up and sharpens an exclusively future tense in 4:21 ('the hour is coming . . . when you will . . . '). Here it is indeed tempting to introduce the reading preferred by many commentators: that the present refers to the 'author's present'. The time is *now* here, says the author to his readers, when God is worshipped in *pneuma* and truth. However, I prefer our earlier solution, which does not make Jesus break out so rudely of the horizon of the story itself. And the main reason is that it makes a sharp point. The hour is 'coming'—after Jesus' death and resurrection—when the true worshippers will worship God in *pneuma* and truth. That claim does refer to the 'author's present' by referring *forward* to it. But the hour is also 'now here'—in Jesus' present—when true worshippers *would* worship God in *pneuma* and truth if only they knew and understood what was *present* in Jesus. Only, we know that on the human side what is necessary—the *pneuma*—is not yet present. What we see here is again that John lets Jesus draw something that belongs to the future *into* his own present— and for 'Christological' reasons: because it is all already present in Jesus as he now is. The point about the present in this drawing-the-future-into-the-present is made wholly explicit in 4:25–6 immediately after, when the woman says (4:25, NRSV): '"I know that Messiah is *coming*" (who is called Christ). "*When* he comes, he *will* proclaim all things to us." '—and Jesus then answers (4:26, NRSV): '"I am he, the one who is speaking to you"'. Thus when John lets Jesus make his 'realized' statements, he is giving expression to his distinctive Christology: it was all there already in Jesus (Christ) during his life on earth.

We may conclude that John 4 refers to the *pneuma* in two closely connected ways. The *pneuma* that people may drink as 'living' or life-*generating*

---

[31] A very important theme opens up here on the relationship between Jesus (indeed, Jesus' body, see John 2:18–22) and the temple. For our purposes, however, we need not address this theme in detail. (On temple 'symbolism' in John, which probably is not just a matter of 'symbolism', see, e.g., Coloe 2001. Also, recall Paul in 1 Cor. 6:13 and 19: 'The body is meant . . . for the Lord, and the Lord for the body. . . . Or do you not know that your body is a temple of the Holy Spirit within you, which you have from God . . . ?' NRSV.)

water is the means to eternal life. When one is in possession of *that* means to salvation, one will worship God in the proper manner since God is himself *pneuma*. We have already seen that the story ends (in 4:41–2) in such a way that one might expect the Samaritan men to have already received the *pneuma*. That is probably not intended, but it remains the case that the story of the Samaritan woman and even more the Samaritan men points forward to a future when 'the true worshippers will worship the Father in *pneuma* and truth' (4:23).

As a footnote to this reading we may ask what is meant in another text of the chapter (4:32–4) when Jesus declares to his disciples that 'I have food (*brôsis*) to eat that you do not know about' (4:32) and then explains what that food is: 'My food is to do the will of him who has sent me and to complete his work' (4:34). Strange food, indeed. But *if* there is anything at all for Jesus to have consumed, it could hardly be anything other than the *pneuma* which he received from God.[32] For that is precisely what lays upon him the task of doing God's will and completing his work—and what also *enables* him to do just that. Once again—and not at all surprisingly in light of the Gospel's later talk of 'food' (in John 6) and the talk of drink earlier in this very chapter—there seems to be here a direct *reference* to the *pneuma* even though it is not explicitly mentioned.

THE *PNEUMA* AS THE 'BREAD OF LIFE' (JOHN 6)

This leads directly into John 6, where the *pneuma* is explicitly mentioned towards the end (6:63) in a way that shows it has played a central role all through the chapter. The 'bread of life' (6:35, 48) or 'living bread' (6:51), which is also 'God's bread that descends from heaven and gives life to the world' (6:33, see 41, 50) and is Jesus himself ('*I am* . . .', 6:35, 41, 48, 51), indeed, is his very 'flesh' (*sarx*, 6:51–8) that is consumed in the Eucharist, all of this turns out to be—the *pneuma*. Here the *pneuma* comes in at the end to mark once again its crucial role for generating life (6:63, NRSV with my parenthesis):

[63]It is the spirit that gives life; the flesh is useless. The words (*rhêmata*) that I have spoken to you are spirit and life.

Or as Peter has it a few verses later (6:68):

You have words of eternal life (*rhêmata zôês aiôniou*).

Since we will look closely at John 6 as a whole later, we need only take note here of this exceedingly strong articulation of two elements in John's theory

---

[32] Paul shows in 1 Cor. 12:13 that early Christians might at least speak of 'drinking' the *pneuma*: 'we were all made to drink of one Spirit' (NRSV, compare John 6:35).

of *logos* and *pneuma*: the *pneuma* 'gives life' in the sense of producing life (it is *to zôiopoioun*); and it (and life) is somehow present in Jesus' actual words, thereby (if things go well) leading to eternal life for those whom he addresses. These are highly suggestive sayings. What the underlying theory of *logos* and *pneuma* does is to spell out exactly how the *pneuma* may generate life in those who hear Jesus' words.

THE *PNEUMA* IN THE DISCIPLES ONLY AFTER JESUS' DEATH (JOHN 7)

In 7:25–7 some people in Jerusalem speculate whether Jesus might after all be the Christ, but immediately correct themselves (7:27, NRSV):

[27]Yet we know where this man is from; but when the Messiah comes, no one will know where he is from.

This is a wonderful cue for Jesus (7:28–9):

[28] . . . You both know me and also know where I am from. *Yet* (Greek *kai*) I have not come from myself, but the one who has sent me, he is truthful, and him you do not know. [29]I know him, because I have come (and am) from him, and he has sent me.

Jesus' claim, which we should see as referring to his reception of the *pneuma* without actually mentioning it, has a very mixed reception (7:30–2), which only goads him on (7:33–4, NRSV):

[33]Jesus then said, 'I will be with you a little while longer, and then I am going to him who sent me. [34]You will search for me, but you will not find me; and where I am, you cannot come.'

So, in 7:28–34 Jesus has told the two crucial things about himself: that he has both been sent *from* God and is about to return *to* God. Against this background he immediately proceeds (though on a slightly later occasion) to make an emphatic statement about his followers (7:37–9):

[37]On the last day of the festival, the great day, Jesus took a stand and cried out, 'Let anyone who is thirsty come to me, and let the one drink [38]who believes in me.[33] As the scripture has said, "Rivers of living water shall flow out of his belly." '[39] This he

---

[33] I strongly prefer taking 'who believes in me' together with the end of v. 37 so that the belly from which the living water will flow is Jesus', not any given believer's. The issue is a famous *crux interpretum*. Barrett prefers the alternative reading (1978, 326–7) while also thinking that '[c]ertainty is not attainable'. Brown (1966, 320–1) argues well for the reading I have chosen, as do Lincoln (2005, 254–5) and Theobald (2009, 537–9), both with strong arguments. Zumstein (2016, 309) agrees without discussion. Thyen (2015, 398–401) too, agrees on the basis of a very complicated discussion. For further literature, see Theobald's references (2009, 537).

said about the spirit, which those who had come to believe in him were to receive; for as yet there was no spirit, because Jesus had not yet been glorified.

Taken in conjunction with Jesus' statement about his own going away this text says that when he has gone to the Father, that is, has died and been glorified in his resurrection, *then* the *pneuma* will come to be present on earth more widely, and then those who have *already* come to 'believe in' Jesus may *also* come to him and '*drink*' the *pneuma*.

There are two points in this that are of the greatest importance for understanding John's overall conception of the *pneuma*. First, before Jesus' death and resurrection the *pneuma* was only present on earth in a single person: Jesus himself. After his death and resurrection, however, it came to be present also among his believers. We know from later in the Gospel in what form this will happen: the *pneuma* will come as the 'Paraclete'.

Secondly and quite crucially, there are two stages in the reception of Jesus, which are very far from being kept sufficiently distinct in scholarship. One is that of 'believing in' him. This is the stage around which the whole Gospel is turning: do the people who come into contact with the earthly Jesus 'believe in' him, or do they not? We will return to this theme repeatedly and see that nobody (other than Thomas) captures the whole truth about Jesus: that as the one who has been sent by God *and will (and did) return to God*, Jesus is the figure who has been described in the Prologue in all its aspects. That truth may only be fully grasped once believers have also *themselves* received the *pneuma*.

In itself this is not at all strange. For receiving the *pneuma*—on the part of a believer—implies a full understanding of three things: that Jesus was himself resurrected from death by the *pneuma*; that he is now present with God as *pneuma* (God himself being *pneuma*); and that he (and God) would (and did) send the *pneuma* down on earth in the form of the 'Paraclete' upon Jesus' death and resurrection. These things had to happen *before* believers might themselves receive the *pneuma* (not least through baptism and the Eucharist) and in that way come to understand fully that Jesus, too, only came to be the *logos* and Christ of the Prologue when he on his side received the *pneuma* (according to 1:32–4).

Thus understood, 7:37–9 places a founding stone in the theory of *logos* and *pneuma* that the Evangelist is articulating and presupposing all through the Gospel. It both points backwards to the talk in John 4 of drinking living water and forwards to the talk in John 13–20 of the 'Paraclete' and Jesus' return after his death and resurrection. It ties in the idea of a full understanding of Jesus with three events: his resurrection, his being with God (see 1:18), and his (and God's) sending the 'Paraclete'. Only after these events had happened was it possible for human beings to receive the *pneuma*. And only then were they able fully to understand who Jesus was and is.

FURTHER TEXTS THAT BRING IN THE
PNEUMA (JOHN 9–17)

John 9–10 hangs together in a manner to which we will return. Though there are plenty of texts here which de facto reflect the presence of the *pneuma*, there is only one that, without actually mentioning the word, brings it in almost explicitly: 10:36.

The context is highly charged. 'The Jews' threaten to stone Jesus 'because you, though only a human being, are making yourself God' (10:33, NRSV). Jesus rebuts them with a quotation from Scripture about some people who are there called 'gods' and comments (10:35–6):

³⁵If those to whom the word (*logos*) of God came were called 'gods'..., ³⁶do you mean to say of the one whom the Father has sanctified (*hēgiasen*) and sent into the world that he is blaspheming because I said, 'I am God's Son'?

God has at some specific point in time *sanctified* Jesus and sent him into the world: it is difficult not to suppose that this happened when God gave him the *pneuma* and so 'sent' Jesus 'into the world' *by* 'sanctifying' him—Jesus of Nazareth—with *pneuma*.³⁴

John 11–12 also hangs together intimately in a manner that we will consider later. Here there is one explicit mention of *pneuma*, which we must take up in detail later: the statement in 11:33 that just before Jesus went out to raise Lazarus from the dead he 'was greatly disturbed in spirit and deeply moved' (NRSV). It is likely that Jesus is described here as 'collecting' the *pneuma* that is in him in order to be able to call out 'in a loud voice' the words that will make Lazarus come out of the tomb (11:44).

It is impossible to leave John 11–12 without taking note of one of the truly high points in the Gospel, even though the text does not explicitly mention the *pneuma* at all: 12:28. Here, on the verge of his death, Jesus prays to God not to be saved from his 'hour' (12:27), but on the contrary to go through it to his glorification (NRSV):

---

³⁴ This is one place where Theobald's perceptiveness comes into its own (2009, 701). He himself distinguishes between Jesus' pre-existence, his 'sanctification' (*Heiligung*), and his being sent (*Sendung*). In spite of this, he admits that 1:33, 3:34, and 6:27, 63, and 69 'lay an alternative reading near', namely, to see the idea of Jesus' sanctification as referring to 'seine Ausrüstung mit der Fülle...des Geistes *anlässlich seiner Taufe*' (Theobald's emphasis). His further reflections also seem to me to point strongly in the direction of tying the *Heiligung* and the *Sendung* very closely together (and of forgetting about Jesus' pre-existence). Contrast Zumstein (2016, 406 n. 46, my emphasis), whose comment well articulates the position against which I am arguing: 'Gelegentlich ist die "Heiligung" an die Gabe des Geistes bei der Taufe gebunden (1,33; 3,34; vgl. auch 6,27.69; 17,19). Dies ist hier *jedoch nicht* der Fall. [Denn:] Jesus ist als *präexistenter* Logos in die Welt gesandt'.

[28]'Father, glorify your name.' Then a voice came from heaven (*ek tou ouranou*), 'I have glorified it, and I will glorify it again.'

This is truly shattering. People in the crowd take the sound to be thunder, others to be an angel that has spoken to Jesus. Only Jesus (and the reader) understands the truth: that it is God himself who has spoken.[35] And said what? The promise that God will glorify Jesus makes immediate sense:[36] God will raise him to glory in his death and resurrection.[37] We already know from John 3 that the *pneuma* will be operative in that event. But when *did* God glorify Jesus if that is intended to refer to some special event, as the verbal form suggests? The most likely answer is: when he 'sanctified' him, that is, sent his own *pneuma* down upon him.[38] In this way, this verse, which in narrative terms is undoubtedly a high point in the Gospel as a whole (after all, God only very rarely intervenes wholly directly),[39] manages—more or less right in the middle of the text—to hold together the two glorifying events that frame the story of Jesus' life on earth. his baptism with *pneuma* at one end and his resurrection as also effected by the *pneuma* at the other.

John 13–17 of the Gospel constitutes a unified whole of great complexity and power. Here the *pneuma* plays a role of the greatest importance in the form of the 'Paraclete' alias 'the *pneuma* of truth' (14:17, 15:26, 16:13). For present purposes we may only notice that Jesus is wholly explicit in claiming that 'it is to your advantage that I go away; for if I do not go away, the "Paraclete" will not come to you; but if I go, I will send him to you' (16:7). In other words, the *pneuma* will only come to the disciples once

---

[35] To whom? Zumstein (2016, 458) says: 'nicht an Jesus (vgl. V. 29–30), sondern an das versammelte Volk'. Theobald (2009, 809) is better: 'der Vater antwortet seinem Sohn'. It seems to me of crucial importance that here God is meant to be directly interacting with *Jesus*—and *not* to be understood by all the others. For here God makes the whole content of his 'plan' (*logos*) explicit: 'I have glorified and will glorify'. *Nobody* but Jesus could understand that at the time.

[36] It is true that the object of the glorification done by God is specifically God's own name, but Léon-Dufour (1990, 472) is right to take this to imply also Jesus himself, *in* whom God glorifies his name.

[37] See Barrett 1978, 426: 'in the death and exaltation of Jesus'. Theobald concurs (2009, 810).

[38] For four other possible readings, see Theobald 2009, 809–10. What is the precise import of the verbal form used here (the aorist)? Even if it is understood as being 'complexive' (Brown 1966, 476), does this quite fit the idea for which both Bultmann (1941, 328) and Schnackenburg (1965–84, vol. 2 [3rd ed. 1980], 486) settle of taking it to refer to 'Jesus' activity as a whole' (Bultmann) or his 'whole earthly work . . . up until his "hour"' (Schnackenburg)? (For this reading see also Léon-Dufour 1990, 472, and Zumstein 2016, 459 n. 110.) Barrett and Lincoln think that the term refers to Jesus' signs. But the first sign (2:1–10) was one in which Jesus '*revealed*' his glory (2:11). So he had it before. When, then, did God *give* it to him?

[39] In fact, the only other place this happens—though only according to John the Baptist's witness—is in 1:32–3, where God first speaks to the Baptist (as reported by him, 1:33) and then sends the *pneuma* down upon Jesus (1:32). The fact that these are the only two cases of direct divine intervention is surely highly significant.

Jesus, in whom alone the *pneuma* was present during his life on earth, has left. Here the distinction between the *pneuma* in Jesus and in believers is spelled out explicitly.

Before leaving John 13–17, we may just note the implications of speaking of the 'Paraclete' as 'the *pneuma of truth*'. Truth about what? As we are interpreting the Fourth Gospel, the answer is quite unproblematic and straightforward. The person who possesses the *pneuma knows* the truth about God's creation, as this was set out in the Prologue: that it was meant for life and light and that it included in its final stage the sending of Jesus for the purpose of bringing human beings *to* life and light through his death and resurrection (and eventually through their own obtaining the *pneuma*). This is, of course, also the whole story that the Gospel is telling. That story is an *account* of creation that may be either true or false—and is, of course, overwhelmingly true. But in order to see that truth in its full form one needs a cognitive power to match it. And that power is the *logos*-carrying *pneuma* (of truth).

THE *PNEUMA* IN JESUS' DEATH AND RESURRECTION (JOHN 18–20)

The Johannine account of the passion (John 18–19) follows the Synoptic accounts relatively closely. Here, in the description of the events leading up to Jesus' death, there is little room or need for talk about the *pneuma*. Even a distinctly Johannine purple passage such as the report on Jesus' conversation with Pilate (18:28–19:16) does not mention the *pneuma*. That is not very surprising, however. After all, this conversation is with an outsider, whereas the *pneuma* distinctly belongs with insiders. However, in light of what we have seen so far there is one point in that text that comes very close to bringing in the *pneuma*. Once Jesus has said that '[m]y kingdom is not from this world' and 'my kingdom is not from here' (18:36, NRSV), Pilate perceptively asks: 'So you *are* a king?' (18:37, NRSV), to which Jesus answers:

[37]You say that I am a king. I, however, was born for this and have come into the world for this: to bear witness to the truth (*alêtheia*). Everyone who is from the truth hears my voice. [38]Pilate asked him, 'What is truth?'

Jesus was 'born' in a certain way like those in the Prologue and John 3 who have been 'born' from above through the *pneuma*. And he has 'come into' the world to bear witness, that is, to *say* something for which the *pneuma* was made responsible in 3:34. Furthermore, to 'hear' his voice, that is, the *pneuma* streaming out of his mouth, a person needs to be 'of or from the truth'. Most importantly, however, what Jesus bears witness to is 'the truth'. About what? We already know the answer: the truth about the ultimate purpose and meaning of the created world, which is life and light. That kind of witness is one that only Jesus can bear, because through possessing the *pneuma* he knows God's original *logos* in creation. No wonder, then, that Pilate, who is and remains a person of this world and not 'from the truth', is puzzled and asks, quite derisively, 'What, now, is *truth*?!'[40]

The only place in the Johannine passion story where the *pneuma* is explicitly mentioned is at 19:30 (NRSV): 'Then he bowed his head and gave up his spirit'. So, did the *pneuma* actually leave Jesus when he died? One might say that this is just a reflection of the Synoptic account to the effect that Jesus 'breathed his last (*exepneusen*)', as in Mark 15:37 and Luke 23:46, or 'let go or gave up his life-spirit (*aphêken to pneuma*)', as in Matthew 27:50. Perhaps the *full pneuma* in some way remained in him? However, since what Jesus did in John was to 'yield or hand over (*par-edōken*)'— namely, one must presume, to God ʹthe or his *pneuma (to pneuma)*', it is more likely that John intends to say that at his death, when Jesus 'breathed his last', he also literally gave the full *pneuma* he had received from God back to God.[41] That only makes what happened afterwards all the more striking: Jesus was resurrected and *again* came to possess the full *pneuma*.

That is the theme of John 20, where Peter and 'the other disciple' first enter the tomb and realize that Jesus has gone (but his wrappings remain, 20:1–10); where Mary Magdalene next meets Jesus in the garden (20:11–18); where Jesus then himself appears on the same day to the disciples in Jerusalem (20:19–23); and where he again appears a week later to them all, now also including Thomas (20:24–9). It is clear that as this story progresses, the Evangelist is intensely concerned with the question of the exact form of Jesus' appearance.[42] Peter and the other disciple just see the

---

[40] Lincoln thinks that Pilate's 'famous question ... is best taken neither as sneeringly sarcastic nor as profoundly philosophical but simply as an attempt to evade Jesus' witness and a sign of his failure to understand' (2005, 463). Brown agrees, but also toys with the idea of 'the politician's impatience with Jewish theological jargon' (1970, 869). That seems to fit better with Pilate's attitude in 18:35: 'Am I then a Jew?!'

[41] Brown (1970, 931) speculates that Jesus might hand over 'the (Holy) Spirit to those at the foot of the cross', a pious suggestion that Barrett well rebutted by pointing to 20:22 as 'the occasion on which Jesus imparted the Holy Spirit to the church' (1978, 554). Schnackenburg (1965–84, vol. 3 [3rd ed. 1979], 332–3) also denies that 'the *pneuma*' here may refer to 'the divine spirit' but he does recognize the special force of the verb used (*paradidonai*, 'hand over'). Danker (2000, 761) thinks the sense is that Jesus '*gave up his spirit* voluntarily'. However, if Jesus' reception of the *pneuma* in the first place is as important as I have argued, it seems probable that 'handing over the *pneuma*' in 19:30 is intended to cover both his human and his divine *pneuma*. What was left on the cross was just a dead body.

[42] See the analysis in Buch-Hansen 2010, 395–402. As Buch-Hansen rightly notes (395), '[t]he narrative of these successive encounters includes different stages in the process of ascent: from the "not-yet" in the encounter with Mary to the (nearly) fulfilled transformation in the scene with Thomas'. See also Frey (2002/2013a, 547), who well notes that '[d]ie Erzählung scheint besonderes Augenmerk auf die physische "Beschaffenheit" des

wrappings, whereas Jesus himself is nowhere to be seen. Mary goes a bit further in the intended direction since Jesus is now both present—though appearing to her as a gardener—and she is also able to recognize him, though not from sight, but only—and surely highly significantly—from his voice (20:16). This fits the role of Jesus' *phônê* earlier in the Gospel, which we saw carries his divine *pneuma*. Apparently, Jesus is once again in possession of the *pneuma*. Next, on the two occasions when Jesus appears to the disciples *en masse* and they are at long last able to see him, he is able to go through closed doors (20:19, 26). So he is definitely not just a human being, but in some way a pneumatic one. At the same time, he is also present to them in ordinary bodily form since he is able to show them his hands and his side as they were pierced at his crucifixion, a feat that then becomes the topic of the last scene with Thomas. How are we to understand all this?

Two texts help to provide an answer. At 20:17 Jesus famously forbids Mary to grasp or hold on to him, 'because I have not yet ascended to the Father' (NRSV).[43] And at 20:21–3 he says to the assembled disciples (NRSV):

[21]'Peace be with you. As the Father has sent me, so I send you.' [22]When he had said this, he breathed on them and said to them: 'Receive The Holy Spirit. [23]If you forgive the sins of any, they are forgiven them; if you retain the sins of any, they are retained.'

The latter text is clearly a mission statement. By having the *pneuma* literally blown into them (the Greek *emphysan* is both strong and wholly concrete),[44] the disciples are authorized and enabled to forgive sins—as it were as stand-ins for Jesus himself (and God behind him). Even more important for us is the fact that the risen Jesus sends the disciples into the world by blowing the *pneuma* into them *just as*—so he says—*he was himself sent into the world by God*. Here the text almost explicitly—and strikingly—acknowledges that Jesus was sent into the world when he himself received the *pneuma*, just as it now happens to the disciples.

Auferstandenen zu legen'. Frey also notes (547 n. 274) that the episode with Mary Magdalene is 'noch von einer eigentümlichen Vorläufigkeit geprägt'.

[43] The meaning of this is highly controversial. It seems certain, however, that the overall point is to focus the reader's mind on Jesus' bodily appearance as he is *about to* ascend to heaven. For a characteristically careful discussion see Bieringer 2008. He takes the perfect ἀναβέβηκα ('I have [not yet] ascended') 'as indicating an action that is still in progress', with reference to ἀναβαίνω ('I am ascending') later in the verse, but also claims that 'John 20:17 is a theological, not a chronological interpretation'. The former seems exactly right—and is not excluded by the latter.

[44] This is well brought out in Levison 2009, 370–2.

So, in the form in which Jesus appears to the disciples, he has the *pneuma*. That is why he can go through closed doors. And that must also be the reason why he forbids Mary to touch or hold on to him. In his present form, *before* he has (finally) ascended to heaven (compare 20:17), he both has his ordinary, fleshly body—and is also filled with *pneuma*. What kind of being is that? It is presumably exactly the kind of being that Jesus also was during his life on earth after he had been baptized with the *pneuma*—*only* he is now on his way to heaven. During his earthly life, when the *logos* had become *sarx*, Jesus was a full human being, whose fleshly body had also been infused with *pneuma*. The Gospel gives no hints at what kind of being *that* was. But one might find an at least intelligible idea in the Stoic doctrine of *krasis* or the complete interpenetration of two substances that may nevertheless be separated from one another at a later stage.[45] In that case, we might also—if we so wished—think of the rising Jesus of our chapter along similar lines.

How, then, should we conceive of him once he has finally 'ascended to the Father' (20:17)? Once again, there is no wholly clear answer to be found in the text. On the other hand, the point of emphasizing (in 20:17) Jesus' *intermediary* state when he meets Mary Magdalene will presumably be that at the end of the whole process, the fusion of *pneuma* and *sarx* in Jesus during the intermediary stage will have been resolved: when Jesus finally ascended to God, he was only *pneuma*. Two further bits of evidence support this picture. First, God himself is *pneuma*, as we know (4:24), and upon his return to God, Jesus will 'be in the Father's bosom' (1:18). Secondly, both God himself and Jesus will be able to become present again on earth in the form of the 'Paraclete', who is himself *nothing but pneuma*. (For this reading of 14:15–26, see Chapter IX.) All this is highly speculative, of course. What it shows is merely that by heuristically adopting a Stoic lens on John's handling of the *pneuma*, we may also throw *some* light, at least, into the murky area of the exact physical nature of Jesus in his relationship with God and the 'Paraclete' after his ascension.

We may conclude that in spite of the fact that the Fourth Gospel to a large extent follows the Synoptic Gospels in the story it gives of the passion, John also makes room for a highly profiled account of the resurrected Jesus that is distinctly focused on Jesus' appearance and explicitly makes the *pneuma* play a major role under this theme. This fact itself strongly supports

[45] In the words of A. A. Long, 'complete blending' refers to 'a form of compounding whereby "two or even more bodies are extended through one another as wholes through wholes, in such a way that each of them preserves its own substance and qualities in a mixture of this kind . . . For it is the special feature of things which are blended that they can be separated again from one another; and this can only take place if the things blended preserve their own natures in the mixture"' (Long 1982, 38–9, Long's translation of a text by Alexander of Aphrodisias, see *SVF* 2.473).

our claim about the central role played by the *pneuma* in this Gospel's account of Jesus' life on earth from his baptism with *pneuma* up until his death: *after* his death, the role played by the *pneuma* in Jesus' earthly life is brought completely into the open.

THE JOHANNINE THEORY OF *LOGOS* AND *PNEUMA*

In this chapter we set out to consider separately what John says about *logos* (with *lalia* and *rhêmata*) and *pneuma* in the Gospel after chapter 1. However, we ended up seeing that the two concepts could not be separated. In some places, both were invoked in the very same verse, e.g. 3:34, 6:63, and 6:68. This was only to be expected if John is drawing on something like the understanding of the relationship between *logos* and *pneuma* that one finds in the theory we employed as a heuristic lens: the Stoic theory of *endiathetos* and *prophorikos logos* with its distinct, ontological underpinning. In this theory *logos* and *pneuma* are two sides of the same coin: one cognitive and epistemological; the other ontological, physical, and directly active in bringing about things in the world. The main result of our analysis is that what John says of *logos* (with *lalia* and *rhêmata*) and *pneuma* must *always* be held together and seen to imply one another since it expresses the cognitive and the physical sides of the same coin.

Here, then, is a summary of the theory of *logos* and *pneuma* I am claiming underlies everything John says about Jesus' sayings and doings:

(1) Jesus received the *pneuma* directly from God at his baptism as witnessed by John the Baptist (John 1), thereby becoming the *logos* and Christ of the Prologue, God's messenger on earth whose task it was to execute God's original plan (*logos*) and bring to completion the whole point of creation, which is eternal life for human beings. He gave the *pneuma* back to God at his death (John 19), but received it again at his resurrection (John 20), which also enabled his final ascension to God (John 20). In this way, eternal life was realized in Jesus Christ as a forerunner for believers. In the middle of the Gospel (John 12) God himself bears witness to these events when he states that he *has* glorified Jesus and *will* glorify him. It is in this heavily loaded sense that Jesus has both 'come' from God—bringing the message of the *logos* that he, Jesus Christ, both knows and is—and will again 'return' to God.

(2) The latter part of this story (the 'return') is relatively carefully spelled out with regard to the question of Jesus' appearance during this stage of his life. At his resurrection he appears as an amalgam of *sarx* and *pneuma* (John 20). At his ascension, by contrast, he is probably to be understood as being wholly pneumatic. It was also in this form that he

might more or less immediately come to be present again on earth among those who believed in him: in the form of the 'Paraclete', who is nothing but *pneuma*.

(3) During Jesus' earthly life the divine *logos* and *pneuma* was present in him alone. The *pneuma* was the agent behind everything Jesus said and did at this stage, reflecting the fact that by bringing the divine *logos* of the Prologue to Jesus it also made him the carrier of that *logos*. In particular, the *pneuma* came to be articulated in Jesus' actual speech, his *logos* in the sense of his *lalia* and the *rhêmata* that streamed out of his mouth. This *prophorikos logos* should be understood as the literal articulation of Jesus' *endiathetos logos* that in itself reflects God's original *logos* in creation as described in the Prologue. In addition, it is highly probable that the *pneuma* in Jesus should also be understood as lying behind his *erga* ('works'), e.g. his raising of Lazarus, which pointed directly forward to his own resurrection and that of his followers.

(4) With regard to those followers, the *pneuma* was *not* present in any of them during Jesus' lifetime, which again had consequences for the level of cognition that they were able to achieve in 'believing in' Jesus. The *pneuma* only became available to them (in the form of the 'Paraclete' and through baptism and the Eucharist) after Jesus' death. Here it had two functions, which we must investigate further: one epistemological and one ontological. Epistemologically, it at long last enabled believers to grasp the *logos*, that is, to understand the full truth about Jesus as described in the Prologue, including the points that are only explicitly mentioned later in the Gospel of his resurrection and ascension to God and his (and God's) sending of the 'Paraclete'. Thus to believers, too (as to Jesus), the *pneuma* brought the *logos* and so full knowledge. Ontologically, when they had received it in baptism and the Eucharist, the *pneuma* also enabled them to obtain what Jesus had himself already obtained: eternal life through resurrection into heaven.

In developing this theory, we became able to see the inner connection between a number of themes that scholars have not connected so closely:

– Between (i) the *logos* of the Prologue and (ii) 'Jesus' and God's *logos*' as this is mentioned in the rest of the Gospel; the latter is the original *logos* of the Prologue (God's plan) *as* present in Jesus in the form of an *endiathetos logos*.
– Between (i) God's activity in creation through the original *logos* (and *pneuma*) and (ii) his sending of Jesus by the *pneuma* to bring about for human beings what had been the point of creation from the very beginning—and to achieve this through *Jesus'* handling of *logos* and *pneuma* during his life on earth; here the connection focuses on the communicative *pneuma* side of Jesus' articulation of his *endiathetos logos* in his *prophorikos logos*.

- Between (i) Jesus' possession of the *pneuma*, his *pneuma*-borne speech, and his eventual sending of the *pneuma* (the 'Paraclete')—and (ii) the final goal of it all: the future resurrection of Christ believers to eternal life, for which Christ's own resurrection acts as a forerunner; that future event would be generated by the *pneuma*, too, once it had become available to believers after Jesus' death and resurrection; in this process, the *pneuma* plays a central role that is both cognitive (as bringing full knowledge of the *logos* to believers) and also ontological in literally bringing them to eternal life.

What is striking about this picture is its stark and direct realism, so strongly removed from any form of Platonism as one can imagine.[46] God has been directly and creatively active from the beginning of the world through his *logos and pneuma*; and he continues to be so in sending, first John the Baptist and then Jesus Christ. In the latter case, God's creative, *pneuma*-driven action goes via what Jesus *says* on the basis of his own possession of the *pneuma*— and also via what he does (which has not been our theme so far). Let me put it all in a single sentence: it is Jesus' *pneuma*-driven *prophorikos logos*— reflecting (backwardly) his *pneuma*-shaped *endiathetos logos* that contains (even further back) the whole truth about God's plan for creation—and the extent to which it influences and is understood (forwardly) by human beings, thereby eventually generating a dynamic change in them, that together constitute the conceptual nucleus of the Fourth Gospel.

With this picture in mind, if we go back to the beginning of the previous chapter of this book and recall the tradition of understanding and translating the Johannine *logos* of the Prologue as God's creative 'Word' (as found in Genesis), we can now say that it is indeed that—*but* to be understood in the far more developed philosophical manner that we have unearthed. This conclusion is reassuring since it both maintains the contextual position and rootedness of the Fourth Gospel within Judaism and also allows for an extensive novelty of this text that matches contemporary ideas within Greco–Roman philosophy.

Now that we have before us John's combined theory of *logos* and *pneuma*—the cognitive meaning of God's creation and the physical agency of its actual operation—we are ready to address in more detail a range of narratively coherent passages of the Gospel and consider how they operate philosophically on a number of distinct themes that are all related in one way or another to the underlying theory of *logos* and *pneuma*.

---

[46] This is where I see an interesting connection between the present philosophical reading of the Fourth Gospel and the recent attempts to connect John with Jewish 'apocalypticism' (see, e.g., Williams and Rowland (eds) 2013). At least, the one type of reading should not be played out against the other.

IV

THE PHILOSOPHICAL SEARCH
IN JOHN 2–4

A PHILOSOPHICAL NARRATIVE

We begin our consecutive reading of major parts of the Gospel In this chapter by applying our preferred reading strategy, which comes from seeing the Fourth Gospel as a 'philosophical narrative'. This term is intended to refer to a text that is fundamentally narrative in form. It tells a story and so makes use of all the features that have been highlighted by students of narratology. In addition to the usual features of time (when), place (where), characters (who), and plot (what), in the Fourth Gospel these also include more refined features such as misunderstanding, irony, and symbolism, which Culpepper brought together under the rubric of 'implicit commentary' (1983, 149–202). By his heavy use of such features John has immediately elevated the crude telling of a story to a quite different level that already points in the direction of a narrative that is also philosophical.

In the present context the latter term may be defined by two connected marks. As a necessary condition, for a narrative to be philosophical it must give unmistakable hints at having a secondary meaning in addition to the meaning of the storyline itself. An example would be a text that tells a story which also has an allegorical meaning: for instance, if one took it that the stories in the Pentateuch had the allegorical meaning attributed to them by Philo of Alexandria. In that putative case, those texts would contain markers that invite the reader to speculate about the additional meaning of the text. And a full account of the text's meaning would mention both levels of meaning.

However, not all texts that have several meanings of this kind will necessarily be philosophical. The second mark of a philosophical narrative, which constitutes a sufficient condition, is that the additional meaning to which the text points has the character of what I call a 'theory', that is, a coherent account at the *conceptual* level of a sizeable part of the world.

As an example we may take the theory of the connection in John between *logos, lalia, rhêmata,* and *pneuma* that we unearthed in the previous two chapters. This theory is philosophical since it operates at the conceptual level, as we were able to see by bringing in Stoic philosophy to articulate it. When a narrative introduces the idea of an additional meaning that takes the form of a theory of this kind, it is a philosophical narrative.

Another, more practical way of thinking of a philosophical narrative is to note that a narrative such as the Fourth Gospel constantly makes its readers ask questions. In John the narrative often leads its reader quite early on to ask some basic question as a result of what has been told in the narrative. For instance, if John has noted at an early stage that some people came to believe in Jesus, while others did not, the question immediately arises of *how* that is: *why* the difference? Furthermore, many sequences of text in John not only raise such questions to begin with: they also deliver material for an answer towards the end of the sequence. We already saw in Chapter II how this functions. In the rest of the book we will constantly be on the lookout for one or more philosophical questions raised at an early stage in the text and answered towards the end.

It is important to see how this approach differs from more traditional ways of reading the Fourth Gospel. Quite often commentators on an individual text sequence will also gather up their step-by-step readings in a section that articulates what Raymond Brown in his commentary calls 'theological motifs'. Moreover, perceptive commentators will also connect the theological motifs to be found in one text sequence with their presence in other text sequences of the Gospel. In this way commentators are providing answers to the (unarticulated) philosophical questions that the texts raise (in the attentive mind). Thus there is a sizeable overlap between the activities (and indeed, the results) of good commentaries and those that will be presented here.

However, there also is a clear difference. The most important is that while the narrative philosophical approach does aim to lay bare an underlying, coherent philosophical theory, it also stays very close to the ground in attending to the specific ways the philosophical issues are addressed in the narrative from one moment to the other. This is where this approach is similar to the analysis that focuses on those features of the text that Alan Culpepper identified as 'implicit commentary'. The secret lies here: in both cases John's readers are requested—in some cases even forced—to *ask questions* as part of the reading process since they are constantly being presented with obstacles to understanding, bumps on the smooth road of reading. For this reason the analyses of this book will have to stay close to the ground and repeat some of what has already been well said about the text. It is features of the narrative itself that raise the philosophical issues we are trying to elucidate.

This approach has certain advantages. By presenting the kind of 'conceptual readings' or 'theories' at which the best commentators often arrive as answers to philosophical questions raised by the text itself, we may reach several goals. First, we may see how the text hangs together thematically over fairly extensive stretches by the fact that it raises such questions and also attempts to answer them. Secondly, by focusing on philosophical questions of this kind, we may become better able to see that John does have a theory: that underlying the Johannine narrative in all its meanderings there is a fairly substantial, coherent, but also conceptually fine-grained general idea about Jesus and God in relation to the world as a whole. Thirdly, to the extent that there is such a theory, we will, by focusing on such philosophical questions and their implied answers, at a single stroke place and read John where he belongs: as a thinker and writer who in giving his *narrative* account of Jesus is *also* operating at an intellectual level that is genuinely theological, cosmological, and anthropological (in the sense of ancient philosophical anthropology)—in fact, genuinely *philosophical*. By approaching John in this way, we are freeing ourselves to *think* with John, instead of merely *celebrating* something that either cannot be understood (John's 'mysteries') or else belongs to a quite separate sphere of human thought that is wholly its own ('Christian theology'). Neither approach is in itself very satisfactory. We should give John the benefit of the doubt before placing him there.

In the present chapter we try out this approach in relation to John 2–4. As has been well recognized in scholarship, these chapters have a somewhat introductory character. They are not, therefore, perhaps the most obvious texts to show the benefits of the proposed approach. But since we aim to follow as closely as possible the progression of thought in the Gospel, we need to begin here. Also, I believe we will see that the proposed approach pays off even here.

THE STRUCTURE OF JOHN 2–4

There is little disagreement that a new sequence of texts in the Gospel begins with John 5.[1] At the other end of the text, some scholars have seen

[1] Dodd (1953a, 297–317) discusses 2:1–4:42 under the title 'The New Beginning' and then sees 4:46–5:47 as a new episode entitled 'The Life-giving Word'. Brown acknowledges that 'the brilliance of his [Dodd's] analysis of many of these units should leave a permanent mark on Johannine studies' (1966, CXLII), but also criticizes Dodd on this particular question (rightly, to my mind), which leads him to the division favoured here: 2:1–4:54, 'From Cana to Cana' (Brown 1966, XI). Barrett concurs in principle: 'This miracle (4.46–54) like that of 2.1–11 takes place at Cana—a fact that helps to bind the material together' (1978, 13). So do Lincoln (2005, 4, 7–8) and Theobald (2009, 29, 199–200).

2:1–11 or 12 as the conclusion to the sequence 1:35–51, in which a number of disciples are called. Does 2:11, in particular, with its concluding comment that 'his disciples believed in him' (NRSV) not bring to an end the whole sequence of the call?[2] However, the very obvious *inclusio* of 2:1–12 and 4:43–54 that the Evangelist has produced by referring explicitly back to the former story in 4:46 and counting the healing reported in 4:46–53 as the 'second sign that Jesus did after coming from Judea to Galilee' (4:54)—the first being at the wedding in Cana in 2:1–10—strongly suggests that he himself saw 2:1–4:54 as a coherent unit. And it seems that the disciples' coming to believe in Jesus in 2:11 is specifically tied to the preceding miracle. They came to believe in Jesus with respect to the 'glory' that he had revealed to them in this, the first of his signs (2:11). Conversely, Jesus' prediction as stated in 1:51 of what the disciples will come to see has very little to do with the wedding in Cana. It rather points forward to the *final*, *crucial* event that the disciples will eventually experience: Jesus' resurrection and ascension into heaven. In spite of the excellent principle formulated by Raymond Brown to the effect that 'the same scene can serve as the conclusion of one part and the introduction to the next'[3], it is best to let a new section begin at 2:1. What we get, then, is a section 'From Cana to Cana': 2:1–4:54.

Within chapters 2–4 considerations of place suggest the following divisions:

2:1–12. Cana in Galilee to Kapernaum (2:12)
2:13–4:3. Jerusalem (2:12–3:21) and Judaea (3:22–4:3) and from there towards Galilee (4:3)
4:4–43. Samaria (4:4–42) on the way to Galilee (4:43)
4:44–54. Cana in Galilee (and healing at a distance in Kapernaum).

This all makes for great structural clarity based on the places where the events occur. We should generally beware, however, of putting too much emphasis on the category of place. A good example of this is to be found in our text at 3:22–4:3. Here John has been very careful to point out a change of place on Jesus' part. Jesus goes with his disciples 'into the Judean countryside', stays there for a while, and baptizes (3:22). Then John the

---

[2] Brown (1966, CXLII) was attracted to this, claiming that 'the theme of John the Baptist and his disciples who become Jesus' disciples holds together i 19–ii 11'. When he then calls this section 'our Part One', he is refuted by his own better sense and practice in the next sentence in seeing 2:1–4:54 as 'our Part Two'. Barrett, too (1978, 13), took 1:19–2:11 together in spite of his recognition of the unity of 2:1–4:54 (see the previous note). Lincoln, Theobald, and Zumstein are less deterred (rightly, to my mind) by the connections one might see between 1:35–51 and 2:1–12.
[3] Brown 1966, 198. This is also the way (on p. CXLIII) in which Brown attempts to solve his indecision regarding where 2:1–11 belongs.

Baptist is introduced also as baptizing in the neighbourhood (3:23–4), and after an important speech by the Baptist, which is triggered by his disciples complaining (3:26 NRSV) that Jesus 'is baptizing and all are going to him', we hear (4:1–3 NRSV) that:

[1]when Jesus learned that the Pharisees had heard, 'Jesus is making and baptizing more disciples than John' – [2]although it was not Jesus himself but his disciples who baptized – [3]he left Judea and started back to Galilee.

Jesus' reason for leaving Judea is somewhat unclear.[4] And the remark about Jesus' *not* baptizing is (initially, at least) altogether baffling.[5] But the Evangelist's care in spelling out the changes of place is obvious. *However*, we will see that the intervening text between 3:22–4 and 4:1–3 (3:25–36) connects exceedingly closely with what comes before it in 3:1–21 *across* the change of place in 3:22. The lesson is clear: narrative breaks such as a marked change in location (or time) do *not* necessarily lead to breaks in thought.

Let us go through the individual sections of the three chapters and consider in what ways they may constitute a philosophical narrative.

WHAT DO JESUS' SIGNS SIGNIFY (2:1–12)?

John 2:1–12 is a very short text. It is unlikely that we will find the full shape of a philosophical narrative in this text. In particular, while it does raise a philosophical question, it does not answer it. It fits the fact that this text very much has the form of an introduction to the Gospel story as a whole.

In discussing this passage—as all others—there are numerous aspects rightly taken up by commentators that we will not attend to. Here belongs a number of tradition historical issues, for instance, the possible overlap of the Cana wedding with a well-known motif about the Greco–Roman wine God, Dionysus,[6] and any speculation about the early Christian

---

[4] The best guess (see, e.g., Theobald 2009, 297) is that John is taking up the motif of Pharisaic opposition to Jesus adumbrated in 1:24 and brought to fruition later (e.g. in chapter 9: 9:13 and 40) via another trip to Galilee by Jesus to avoid the Jewish plans for his death (7:1).

[5] Is it a secondary gloss (Theobald 2009, 297)? Or perhaps a gloss by the narrator himself (Lincoln 2005, 171)? In either case, it seems singularly inept. Two other possibilities seem more worth entertaining: (i) Might it be a *marginal* gloss by a later scribe that has then crept into the text? (ii) Or might it—going in an entirely different direction—be a hint by the narrator himself that Jesus himself did not 'really' just baptize with water, but—as 3:25–36 appears to suggest—with (water and) *pneuma*? In that case, the narrator is not so much correcting *himself* (Lincoln) as correcting a false *interpretation* of Jesus by the Pharisees (4:1) and the Baptist's disciples (3:26). If so, we might render the particle that introduces 4:2 (καίτοιγε, NRSV's 'although') as follows: 'in fact, however, (Jesus himself did not baptize)'.

[6] See for this in particular Theobald's excursus on the theme (2009, 203–8).

traditions—including the Synoptic Gospels—that may lie behind the text in its present form.[7] That kind of broader historical contextualization is certainly valuable, but it must show its relevance in practice. And here our focus will be constantly on the present text within its direct literary context, both more narrowly and including the Fourth Gospel as a whole. That is what we have directly in front of us and what we can actually see by turning the pages back and forth. That constitutes our primary empirical evidence.

The structure of 2:1–12 is immediately clear. There is first (2:1–10) the story of what happened at the wedding in Cana, next (2:11) a comment by the writer on the character and consequences of that event, and finally (2:12) a notice that Jesus went down from Cana to Kapernaum. This last verse nicely concludes the whole section by mentioning his mother and his disciples, all of whom were mentioned to begin with (2:1–2). The text is tied to what precedes it by an indication of time ('On the third day', 2:1 NRSV).[8] The place has also been prepared for—but no more than that—by the notice given in 1:43 that 'The next day Jesus decided to go away (*exelthein*) to Galilee'. Now he has arrived and on the third day there was a wedding in Cana.

The structure of the story itself (2:1–10) is equally clear (compare, e.g. Theobald 2009, 202). There is a setting (2:1–2), which mentions Jesus, his mother, and his disciples. Of these only turn up again in the writer's comment of 2:11. The mother and Jesus, by contrast, are the protagonists of the next section (2:3–5), which relates the usual kind of hindrance to be overcome before the agent of a miracle will do what he is asked to do. Memorably, Jesus at first denies because 'My hour has not yet come' (2:4). Which hour? What does he mean? His mother, however, is undeterred and arranges for her son's intervention to take place. And so he does in the next section (2:6–8), where one notices that the six water jars in which water turns into wine were originally meant for 'the Jewish rites of purification' (2:6). On Jesus' recommendation, the newly generated wine is brought to the *architriklinos* (2:8), who may be either a 'head waiter' or a 'toastmaster' or 'president of the banquet' (compare Barrett 1978, 192). The last section of the story (2:9–10) is taken up by the reaction of the *architriklinos*, who tastes the wine and comments to the bridegroom on the oddity that 'you have kept the good wine until now' (2:10).

This text relates a story of something that supposedly happened at Cana in Galilee on some (very) specific day. Jesus turned some water into wine when the wine had given out at a wedding. A little strangely, he was

---

[7] It is difficult, though, not to be reminded of the Markan saying of new wine in new wineskins (Mark 2:22), see Brown 1966, 105; Barrett 1978, 189; Lincoln, 132.

[8] For the meaning of this, compare in particular Brown 1966, 97 and 105–6.

goaded on by his mother against his own inclinations and he did it in spite of the fact that he had just very roughly rejected having anything to do with her. Even more strangely, Jesus almost disappears at the other end of the story when the *architriklinos* reports to the bridegroom and comments to him on the quality of the wine. This is where the miracle is acknowledged to have taken place, but the *architriklinos* completely misunderstands the situation, believing that the bridegroom has just—unaccountably— kept the best wine for a later stage of the party. In short, it is a miracle story, but it is also very odd.

This is the point at which the reader should ask a philosophical question: what on earth does this story—as recounted in this text—*mean?* This question is philosophical in the minimal sense in that it implies that the text has a much wider meaning than what appears on the surface. The question implies that there are two distinct levels of meaning—the story meaning and an extended meaning—and that one cannot properly be said to have understood the text until one has also settled its extended meaning.

The sense that there are two distinct levels of meaning is strongly confirmed by the writer's comment in 2:11. Here the reader learns three things: that this was the 'first of his signs'; that in it Jesus 'revealed his glory'; and that his disciples came to 'believe in him'. So, Jesus has turned some water into wine: of what is that a '*sign*'? How did he 'reveal his glory' in that act? And what kind of 'belief in him' did the disciples obtain through this admittedly quite miraculous, but otherwise also somewhat humdrum act—not least when they were already described in 1:35–51 as having come to believe in him? What 2:11 brings out explicitly—but what was already implied in the account itself—is a genuine clash between the event and story as understood at its most literal level and the wider meaning it is now explicitly stated to have. This clash raises the philosophical question in a more focused manner: of *what* was the story a sign? *What* kind of glory did Jesus reveal in it? What *kind* of 'belief in him' did the disciples obtain?

It is important to see that the philosophical question raised by 2:1–10 and 2:11 has two sides to it. One concerns the step from the literal meaning to the wider meaning. In my paraphrase of the text I attempted to bring out the character of this step: from the sheer event and a story about it that *might* have been told in much more realistic ways, to the story as we have it with its many oddities which give rise to the philosophical question, 'What does it (actually) mean?'. The other side to the philosophical question is raised particularly clearly by 2:11, which in a way already provides the answer to the philosophical question, but only in a manner that raises further questions. Thus 2:11 points in the direction of some more *developed* answer to the philosophical question, an answer that will spell out exactly what is signified by Jesus' signs, what his glory consists in, and what types of belief in him we may find among his followers. Or to put it differently,

2:11 points in the direction of a '*theory*' about Jesus, which will (hopefully) be spelled out fully in the rest of the Gospel. We may term these two sides of the philosophical question 'from literal meaning to wider meaning' and 'from wider meaning to a theory', thereby showing that they are connected on a single line.

Does the basic philosophical question also receive an answer in our text? Only partially, but also yes. The question raised by the story does receive a kind of answer in 2:11, but the more comprehensive meaning of it all (the theory) is not given in this text. This is where the approach adopted here to reading a Johannine text is in line with the usual way of reading it. For the many 'theological motifs' that commentators find to be taken up and played upon both in 2:1–10 and 2:11 will all enter into the full answer to the philosophical question that this text does not yet give.

Many of the oddities we noted above belong among these 'theological motifs'. (i) The role of Jesus' mother (2:3–5) evidently chimes in with her role at the foot of the cross towards the very end of the story (19:23–5). This tells the reader something about Jesus' status during his life on earth. He was wholly his own, completely independent of any people as no mere human being could have been, for the reason that he has a Father entirely elsewhere: in heaven. (ii) By speaking of his 'hour' (2:4) the text also points forward to the later references to Jesus' 'hour'. And this 'hour' is not just the hour of his death, but also of his being 'elevated' (the Greek is *hypsôthênai*: 'being lifted up', see 3:14, 8:28, 12:32, 34)[9] on to the cross and further into heaven. Jesus' 'hour' is that of his 'glorification' (see 12:28 and 13:31–2) in his resurrection, which is prefigured in the water that is turned into wine. (iii) Similarly, the fact that the newly generated wine is to be found in water jars 'for the Jewish rites of purification' (2:6) clearly plays on the qualitative difference that the Gospel sees between traditional Jewish practices and what Jesus brings. Once again, this motif will be spelled out later in a number of different ways that serve to make it part of John's overall theory about Jesus. (iv) Finally, what is perhaps the greatest oddity in the story—concerning the reaction on the part of the *architriklinos* (2:9–10)—also points clearly forward. He totally misunderstands what has happened.

---

[9] Let it be stated here once and for all: John's use of this term is clearly a pun. It evidently refers to Jesus being lifted up on the cross (see 3:14 and 8:28, where the grammatical subject of the act is 'the Jews'). But it certainly also *implies* (and so implicitly refers to) Jesus' being lifted up to heaven (and of course by God) *after* his death on the cross. Brown puts it well (1966, 146, my emphasis): 'It [Jesus' "being lifted up"] is the upward swing of the great pendulum of the Incarnation corresponding to the descent of the Word which became flesh. The *first step* in the ascent is when Jesus is lifted up on the cross; the *second step* is when he is raised up from death; the *final step* is when he is lifted up to heaven.' Compare also Theobald (2009, 264) who well rejects the (specifically German?) idea that the elevation is *only* on to the cross. (See also Frey 2000a, 277–80.)

But he inadvertently also states that the water that has been turned into wine is 'the better wine', meaning presumably the wine that Jesus either brings or even is. Finally, he even hints that this better wine has been 'kept or preserved' (by God?) for what is probably a hint of the eschatological 'now'. Is it totally by accident that this mediator of the Jewish purificatory water that has now turned into wine is also repeatedly called the 'chief' waiter (*archi-triklinos*) just as the Jewish 'high priest' is really a 'chief' priest (*arch-iereus*)? These are all hints and no more than that. But they are all hints at a full theory of who and what Jesus is—and here in relation to the rest of Judaism.

What we see here—and what commentators have been good at articulating—is what one might call a 'symbolic layer' of the story as told. Talk of a symbolic layer in John immediately fits the distinction we drew between two distinct levels of meaning and I have no objection to speaking of 'symbols' in John. However, I prefer to understand any symbols as pointers to a level of understanding that may be spelled out in the kind of philosophical theory of which we have spoken. As a sort of reading principle, I take it that a Johannine symbol is not just meant to evoke a sense of the mystery of Jesus Christ, but rather to point in the direction of an intelligible set of ideas—to be spelled out in a Johannine theory.

In summary, John 2:1–12 both answers (in 2:11) an initial philosophical question raised by the narrative itself and also raises the further philosophical question of the deeper meaning of that answer concerning the actual meaning of Jesus' signs and his glory and of believers' coming to believe in him. That meaning will only become clear as the text proceeds. In this way, the story truly serves an introductory purpose.

THE NEW TEMPLE (2:13–25)

The structure of this text is pellucid (see again Theobald 2009, 224). There is first a note on time and place (2:13): Jesus goes up to Jerusalem for Passover. Next follows an action of Jesus' in the temple (2:14–17), which ends (2:17) with a remark about something Jesus' disciples 'remembered' (after his death?) from Scripture as explaining his action. Challenged by a question on the part of 'the Jews' (2:18) concerning what 'sign' (again) he is showing them in his temple action,[10] Jesus next explains the meaning of his sign (2:19–22): he will raise the temple again—meaning 'the temple of his body', as John explains (2:21)—in three days if 'the Jews' destroy it. This section also ends with a note about something Jesus' disciples 'remembered', and

---

[10] I return to this reading of 2:18 later.

here explicitly 'After he was raised from the dead' (2:22, NRSV). The whole text then ends with a remark (2:23–5) about 'many' in Jerusalem who 'came to believe in his name because they saw the signs (!) that he was doing' (2:23). But it is also made clear (2:24–5) that this belief on their part was not worth much, as Jesus knew. 2:23–5 functions in relation to 2:13–22 in the same way the remark in 2:11 about the disciples coming to believe in Jesus functions in relation to 2:1–10. There is good reason, therefore, for taking 2:23–5 to belong together with 2:13–22, even though it is also clear that 2:23–5 serves to introduce the question of the proper understanding of Jesus that is then taken up directly in John 3 in the dialogue with Nicodemus.[11]

Is a philosophical question raised by this whole text? In fact, there are two. One, which is not answered in the text, is raised by 2:23–5: Why is it not good enough to believe in 'Jesus' name' (and what *is* that 'name'?) when one sees the signs he does? This is an epistemological question about the kind of understanding one must have in order to 'believe in Jesus' in the proper way. It is raised by 2:23–5, but not answered in that passage. It will receive a much fuller answer in John 3. This, incidentally, is one fairly strong argument for taking 2:23–5 together with that chapter, against what I have just claimed. However, this is probably as good an example as any of the validity of 'Brown's principle' that certain scenes may 'have a double role of concluding one part and opening the next' (Brown 1966, CXLIII). 2:23–5 appears to play that role.

The other philosophical question raised by our text is actually raised by 'the Jews' themselves in 2:18—on the understanding of that verse that I am adopting.[12] It is this: what 'sign' is Jesus showing in his temple action? Here 'the Jews' within the text itself ask on the readers' behalf the philosophical question of the wider meaning of Jesus' temple action in 2:14–16. It is noteworthy that this question is then answered by Jesus himself, even in this very short text, when he begins to speak of his ability to raise the temple in three days (2:19), meaning 'the temple of his body', as John

---

[11] Many commentators take 2:23–5 as both a 'transition' between 2:22 and 3:1 and an 'introduction' to the Nicodemus scene (Brown 1966, 126; Lincoln 2005, 144; Thyen 2015, 178; Zumstein 2016, 131). Theobald (2009, 238) even turns the passage into a 'scenic exposition' which he parallels with 3:22–4 in relation to 3:25–36. There is probably not much reason for disagreement. I just cannot get away from the sense (i) that 2:23–5 parallels 2:11, and (ii) that the opening of 3:1 introduces something (relatively) new in narrative terms: 'Now there was a Pharisee named Nicodemus, a leader of the Jews' (3:1, NRSV).

[12] NRSV translates: 'What sign can you show us for doing this?'. Brown is even more explicit (1966, 114): 'What sign can you show us, authorizing you to do these things?'. I prefer this rendering: 'What sign are you showing since you do these things', that is, 'in' or 'by' doing them? That is, *of* what is the act you are performing a sign? Then Jesus' answer in 2:19 becomes wholly apposite: what he has done is a sign of the eventual destruction of the temple and Jesus' re-erecting it in three days (namely, in his own resurrection). (Most commentators support Brown, e.g. Zumstein 2016, 128.)

immediately explains (2:20). What we have here is a use of the term 'sign' which—in full conformity with the way the prophets in the Hebrew Bible are said to do signs—points towards a wider meaning of some act or saying than the immediately apparent one. And John duly complies with the request when he explains, as it were on Jesus' behalf, what Jesus meant: the transformation of God's temple into one that is tied to Jesus' own resurrected body.[13] This is a stark and shattering statement. *However*, this answer to the philosophical question raised by Jesus' temple action only raises further questions: how on earth may Jesus' own resurrected body constitute God's temple? And that question is not answered in the present text. The reader must wait until at least John 4 (in particular, 4:23–4 on worshipping God 'in *pneuma* and truth') before that part of the overall theory is spelled out fully.

We noted that each of the two main sections of 2:13–22 (25) ends with a remark about the disciples 'remembering' something. This fact may give rise to one more philosophical question: what is the meaning of *that*? Once again, the answer is not given immediately, but it constitutes one of the major building blocks of John's overall theory, not least when the text says (2:22) that after Jesus had risen and the disciples had remembered, they *came to believe* both in the Scripture and in the *logos* that Jesus had spoken. Apparently, *full* belief in Jesus could only come about after his resurrection. But then: why is *that*? John 3 will suggest, as we have already seen, the answer that full belief in Jesus requires *pneuma* in the believer. As *we* know, but the reader will only be told in John 7 (7:37–9) and 20 (20:22), that requirement will only be fulfilled after Jesus' death and resurrection. What 2:12 and 2:22 do, then, is only to *raise* a philosophical question that will then be fully answered at a later stage.

THE ROLE OF BAPTISM WITH WATER AND *PNEUMA* FOR FULL BELIEF AND ETERNAL LIFE (3:1–4:3)—I (3:1–22)

John 3 is a justly celebrated text where the pattern of beginning with some kind of action and then moving into speech is adopted for the first time. The chapter has also raised a number of questions of understanding, which have given rise to the usual speculations about transpositions, earlier versions, and the like. Exactly when does Jesus' dialogue with Nicodemus

---

[13] Note that the explanation in 2:21 is not given by Jesus himself, but by John, who is informing *the reader* of what Jesus had meant. At the narrative level, 'the Jews' are left behind without an answer to their question in 2:20. This is a very clear example of the way in which John's interest in the *extended* meaning of his stories even wins over his mastery as a storyteller.

turn into the kind of monologue that it appears to be at its end in 3:21? Also, why do we hear about John the Baptist again in 3:23–30? And who is speaking in 3:31–6, a text that appears to refer back to and draw on 3:1–21, in particular?[14] Here, however, we will insist that while it is certainly valuable to be reminded of potential difficulties in understanding the text, addressing it in the way we are adopting may turn out to solve the same difficulties in a manner that proves more satisfactory.

The structure of 3:1–22 is clear enough (see Theobald 2009, 243–65). The text is structured by three interventions on Nicodemus' part, the last two of which are direct questions, and by three answers by Jesus. An introductory description of Nicodemus (3:1) gives rise (i) to his addressing Jesus (3:2), which leads to a statement by Jesus (3:3). Nicodemus addresses Jesus as a 'teacher' who has 'come from God' and claims that nobody can do the 'signs' (once again) that Jesus has done 'unless God is with him'. Jesus responds—somewhat enigmatically—by stating that 'no one can see the kingdom of God without being born from above'. Next (ii), a question from Nicodemus shows his total misunderstanding (3:4) and leads to a more extended answer by Jesus (3:5–8) that spells out the meaning of his first answer. (iii) Nicodemus' third intervention ('How can these things come to be?', 3:9) is then answered even more extensively by Jesus (3:10–15) in a manner that gradually leads into Jesus' account of the character and purpose of his own coming (3:16–21). The section is concluded by the usual piece of information about Jesus' change of place and a reference to his baptizing (3:22).

With regard to what follows, the fact that in 4:1–3 there is both a reference to Jesus (and his disciples) baptizing and attracting a larger group of disciples than John the Baptist (4:1–2) and also one more statement concerning a change of place—'he left Judea and went back again towards Galilee' (4:3)—shows that as we have it, the text is keen on *connecting* the text about John the Baptist (3:23–30) with the rest. There is thus a strong initial presumption that all the material we find in the text of 3:1–4:3 is meant to hang together in some way. What, then, about 3:31–6? Very much depends here on whether this is understood as being part of John the Baptist's speech that begins at 3:27 or as an independent comment

---

[14] Such issues are always well treated by Theobald (2009, 243–5, 279–80, and 289–91) in a manner that sifts the main positions that have been adopted and refers to the various protagonists of those positions. This is in spite of the fact that Theobald has much stronger confidence in the possibility of diagnosing 'tradition historical' layers behind the present text than may be warranted. But the issues themselves become very clear throughout. The same goes for Frey (2000a, 242–5), who is also particularly good at weakening some of the traditional issues, e.g. the question of the 'transition' from dialogue to monologue: 'a precise transition . . . cannot be identified' (243), or indeed rejecting them altogether, e.g. when he speaks of the 'connectedness (*Zusammenhörigkeit*)' of the whole chapter (244).

added by the writer. In the former case, the coherence of 3:1–4:3 will come out as being very tight, in the latter less so.[15]

Do we find somewhere at the beginning of this whole text a philosophical question that might then be answered at a later stage, but still within it? Here we may be helped by the fact that whenever John describes some misunderstanding among Jesus' interlocutors, the likelihood is great that there is precisely some issue that may initially appear opaque (and may thus lead the reader to ask a philosophical question), but needs to be understood through having the philosophical question answered in some way. The obvious question here is this: what is meant by being 'born from above', even when this is also said to happen through baptism (3:5) and reception of the *pneuma* (3:6–8)? And complementary to that, what is meant by 'seeing' (3:3) and 'entering the kingdom of God' (3:5), for which being born from above is said to be a necessary condition? If these are the two connected philosophical questions raised by the text in 3:3–8, then the answer should somehow be contained in Jesus' reply to Nicodemus' last question of the three: 'How can these things come to be?' (3:9). But then a further philosophical question arises: how on earth does what Jesus says in 3:10–21 constitute an answer to those two earlier questions? The ultimate philosophical question raised by 3:1–21 as a whole is therefore this: how does what Jesus says in 3:10–15 about *himself* and in 3:16–21 about *God* and judgement (*krisis*) of human beings answer the question concerning the meaning of his claim in 3:3–8 about the necessity of being 'born from above'?

Let us consider 3:10–21 in slightly more detail. In 3:10–15 Jesus makes two points that are held together by 3:13. The first is that what Jesus says is not an 'earthly matter', but something that belongs in heaven (3:12). This is an epistemological point. Jesus has seen and knows what he says and bears witness to (3:11), namely, as one may suppose, in heaven. Actually, in 3:11 and 12 he does not speak only about himself, but of 'we', thereby including those of whom he has been speaking in 3:3–8, those who *have* been 'born from above'. So far, then, Jesus has not yet answered Nicodemus' question of 'How these things can come to be'. He just presupposes that they *have* come to be and then uses that supposed fact in support of the claim itself: Jesus and 'we' have *seen* the heavenly things that lie behind the claim about being born 'from above' and 'from *pneuma*'.

Then comes the crucial verse 3:13. 'No one has ascended into heaven except the one who descended from heaven, the Son of Man' (NRSV). This

---

[15] Frey (2000a, 244–5) is splendid both in recognizing 3:31–6 as a 'monologue that is formally identified as a speech by the Baptist' and also in connecting this text with the picture of the Baptist given in John 1. He does not, however, quite spell out the focus on baptism with *pneuma* that we will find in the text.

clearly speaks of Jesus *alone*. *He* has 'descended from heaven' (we know how: when he received the *pneuma* from God), and for that reason he may also ascend to heaven again—and in two ways. One is epistemological in the sense that *by* having descended from heaven, that is, by possessing the *pneuma*, Jesus is also able to 'ascend into heaven' so as to *see* the 'heavenly matters' of which he has spoken in 3:11–12. The other way is ontological. Since Jesus as Son of Man has descended from heaven, he will also become able to ascend into heaven not only in thought (helped by the *pneuma* that he possesses) but also in body. And how will that be possible? Again, as we may postulate, he will be helped by the *pneuma*. However, the fact that Jesus as Son of Man undertakes these 'travels' goes nowhere towards explaining that the 'we', too, of 3:11–12 has or have the same access to heaven. For apart from the sheer assertion made by Jesus in 3:3–8 that this is necessary to both 'see' and 'enter' the kingdom of heaven, we have been told nothing to show that this being born from above has already occurred.

This is where the *ontological* side of 3:13 (as applied to Jesus himself) comes in. For as he now goes on to explain in 3:14–15, the Son of Man (Jesus himself) must be resurrected in order that *in him* believers may have eternal life. What this means—as the reader cannot yet fully understand—is neither more nor less than that Jesus' death and resurrection are the necessary condition for *the release to human beings of the pneuma*. When that has happened, then—and only then—will believers too be able to see (epistemologically) the heavenly matters (3:11–12), and *then they too* will become able (ontologically) to have eternal life just as Jesus will by then have it, namely, as resurrected into heaven.

On this reading of the intensely concentrated verses of 3:11–15, what Jesus does is to introduce the *pneuma*—as an entity that is active in himself both epistemologically and ontologically *and in believers (after his death)*—as what *explains* how *anybody* (apart from himself) may be 'born from above'. In this way Jesus does give an answer to Nicodemus' question of 'How these things can come about?'. The answer is: the Son of Man must die and be resurrected so that the *pneuma* may be released for the benefit of human beings, too.

However, one question remains: *how* may human beings come to obtain the *pneuma* that apparently is so important for the intended outcome of the whole story, namely, that they, too, will receive eternal life? This question is left open here, at 3:15 and also at 3:21, which ends Jesus' conversation with Nicodemus. But that is just the reason why John the Baptist is brought in again, from 3:23 onwards. For the answer to the 'how' is this: through *Christian* baptism (as hinted already in 3:5), that is, through the '*Jesus* baptism' whose superiority to the Baptist's own baptism John the Baptist himself points out in 3:27–36 as a whole.

In this wider context, what is the point of 3:16–21, with which Jesus' conversation with Nicodemus ends? The answer is pretty clear. Jesus spells out here—triggered by the idea that every believer will obtain eternal life in (the risen) Christ (3:15)—the *overall* character of God's intervention with Jesus Christ for the purpose of bringing eternal life (3:16) and 'salvation' (3:17) to 'the world' (3:17). As the text further explains (3:18–21), the outcome of this intervention is determined by human beings, namely, how they respond to God's 'only Son' (3:16): whether with belief in him (3:18) or with disbelief 'in the name of the only Son of God' (3:18, NRSV). Or again, since 'the light has come into the world' (3:19), what determines the fate of human beings is their actions. If they do evil they will not 'come to the light' in order to avoid being exposed by it (3:20). By contrast, if they do 'the truth', which presumably means what the world was *created* to make people see, then they will happily 'come to the light' to show that their actions have been 'done in God' (3:21).

Here the perceptive reader may well ask how all this is related to the point about the necessity of being born from above, through the *pneuma*. Is possession of the *pneuma* as spelled out in 3:3–8 a necessary condition for a believer to 'do the truth'? In that case, Jesus will be speaking of those who *after* his death and resurrection will 'believe in him' in the full sense of 'believing in the name of the only Son of God'. Since they already 'do the truth', that is, act in accordance with the truth about the world which they know by having the *pneuma*, they will 'come to' Jesus and let it be shown (on the day of judgement) that their acts have been done 'in God'. And so they will not be judged, but instead be saved. Or is the text speaking of good moral behaviour to *begin* with as a necessary condition for 'coming to the light' in the first place, and *then* possibly *receiving* the *pneuma*, and only *then* obtaining eternal life?

Two considerations speak for the former alternative. First, the more complicated second alternative makes it almost impossible to find a single thread in chapter 3 as a whole. What, on that supposition, is the point of introducing into the present context supposedly good moral behaviour as a condition for 'coming to' Jesus *at all*? Indeed, if 3:16–21 is meant to follow directly upon 3:15, we are *already* at a stage where the *pneuma has* been brought in. Secondly, when the text speaks of believing in God's 'only Son' (3:16) and (by implication) 'the name of the only Son of God' (3:18), it draws on a type of belief in Jesus that is distinctly above the kind of belief in Jesus that we met in 2:23–5 and that Nicodemus himself might be taken to exemplify. This elevated belief is precisely the kind that allows one both to 'see' the kingdom of God (3:3) and also to 'enter' it (3:5). It is the full, ultimate kind of belief in Jesus. It presupposes that a believer is in possession of the *pneuma*. *Then* this believer will also do 'the truth', 'come to the light', *and* receive eternal life.[16]

We may conclude from this discussion of 3:1–21 that a philosophical question was in fact raised by Nicodemus himself in 3:9 and that the question was answered by Jesus in 3:10–15 by explaining the conditions for human beings to receive the *pneuma*. What was not explained, however, is how that possibility might become actual so that human beings might in fact receive the *pneuma*. It is this further question that is answered in 3:22–36.

THE ROLE OF BAPTISM WITH WATER AND *PNEUMA* FOR FULL BELIEF AND ETERNAL LIFE (3:1–4:3)—II (3:22–36)

The basic consideration here is that this new piece of text speaks explicitly about baptism.[17] Jesus began to baptize in the Judean countryside (3:22). John the Baptist was baptizing nearby (3:23). The Baptist's disciples engage in a discussion about purification with a *Jew* (3:25).[18] They also come to the Baptist, remind him of his witness to Jesus, and complain that Jesus, too, baptizes—'and all are going to him' (3:26). Finally, the baptism motif is taken up again in 4:1–2. Why all this talk about baptism here? An answer suggests itself in light of the reference to Jesus' *pneumatic* baptism in 3:5: because baptism with 'water *and pneuma*', that is, *Jesus'* baptism as against that of John the Baptist, is the means by which believers in Jesus will, in

---

[16] In this connection it is worth asking about the meaning of the reference in 3:18 to '*the name*' of the only Son of God. Danker (2000, 713) seems right in explicating the sense in the present verse of 'believing in the name of someone' as having 'confidence that the person's name (rather in the sense of a title, see Phil. 2:9) is rightfully borne and encodes what the person really is'. In our context, the crucial idea is that of believing in Jesus *as* 'the only Son of God'. That kind of full belief in—and identification of—Jesus presupposes the presence of *pneuma* in the believer.

[17] Commentators have generally recognized that the theme of baptism is present throughout the chapter. See, e.g., the careful discussion in Brown (1966, 141–4) of 'the baptismal interpretation' of 3:5. Brown later (148) concludes (to my mind, rightly) that 'a baptismal motif permeates ch. iii of John'. Note also Barrett's comment on 3:5 (1978, 209): 'John in speaking of water had in mind not only John's baptism but also Christian baptism... It was the addition of "Spirit" which transformed John's into Christian baptism...'.

[18] This statement has always caused trouble and has even led to emendations (accepted by Theobald 2009, 285, but to my mind rightly rejected by Barrett 1978, 221). The fact that the dispute was 'about purification' suggests another solution. In 2:6 we heard about the Jewish water jars that were meant for purification, too, but that Jesus filled with wine. In 3:25 the dispute must be about the virtues of either Jewish purification in general or the one practised in his baptism by John the Baptist. Could it not be that this latter issue is introduced in connection with the Baptist's *disciples* in order to allow the Baptist *himself* in what follows to contrast even his own baptism with the much more important 'baptism' performed by Jesus, which is baptism with (water and) *pneuma* (corresponding to the wine in 2:1–10)?

fact, obtain the *pneuma*—as they need to in order both to 'see' and 'enter' the kingdom of God. Moreover, this is something that John the Baptist is himself made to say. Thus, the Baptist here spells out in his own words and as his own conviction what he has already in 1:33 reported God to be saying: that Jesus is 'the one who baptizes with holy *pneuma*'.

If in this way we understand the whole of 3:27–36 as being spoken by the Baptist, we can see a very clear line of thought.[19] To the implicit accusation of Jesus by John's own disciples, John replies about *Jesus* that: 'No one can take anything whatever unless it is given him from heaven' (3:27), that is, what Jesus has 'taken', namely, the ability to baptize, is something that has been given him from heaven. John next adds some remarks about himself by way of contrast, ending with the explicit claim that 'He must increase, but I must decrease' (3:30). Then, having as it were brushed himself aside, he *returns* to the one of whom he spoke in 3:27 (= Jesus), saying that 'The one who comes from above is above all' (3:31). And here he, to a large extent, repeats the content of what Jesus has himself said earlier in the chapter (3:11–21) both of himself and of believers, thereby making what Jesus has said his own. The message is that the baptism with which Jesus baptizes is of an altogether different kind from the Baptist's own baptism. Jesus baptizes with water *and pneuma*. This is because Jesus has himself directly *come* from above, sent by God (3:34) in a manner that is wholly different from the way in which the Baptist was sent (3:28): namely, when Jesus received the *pneuma*. And *this* then also means that the one who believes, not just in 'Jesus' in some noncommittal way, but in 'the Son' (3:36), whom God loves and in whose hand he has given everything (3:35), *that is*, 'the Son' who has *himself also* received the *pneuma* (namely, when Jesus himself was baptized with *pneuma*), *this* person '*has* eternal life' (3:36). For this person, too, has received the *pneuma* (in baptism).

Read in this way, 3:23–36 is not just the Baptist's 'second' witness, but his ultimate witness, in which he spells out the role that Jesus' being baptized by God with the *pneuma* (from his first witness) has *for believers*, the role in which Jesus as 'the one who baptizes with holy *pneuma*' (1:33) gives *believers* a *pneumatic* (water) baptism ('Christian' baptism) that will allow *them* both to 'see' and 'enter' the kingdom of God. Here what matters is the parallelism between what happens to Jesus and will happen to believers. Just as God

---

[19] Commentators regularly discuss who is speaking in 3:31–6 (e.g. Brown 1966, 159–60). Most, e.g. Brown himself, Lincoln (2005, 158–9), and Theobald (2009, 289–91), end up ascribing it to the Baptist, though often on the basis of complicated textual manipulations (Brown and Theobald). (Lincoln is better: 'whatever their origin or place in some earlier stage of composition', 2005, 159.) Léon-Dufour was more forthright: these verses 'peuvent *et même doivent* être laissés sur les lèvres de Jean, conformément au texte actuel' (1988, 326, my emphasis). Most recently, Rese (2014), Thyen (2015, 229–30), and Zumstein (2016, 158) concur.

gave Jesus the *pneuma*, which means that he will eventually be resurrected, so Jesus gives believers the *pneuma* (in 'Christian' baptism), which will have the same effect.

I have not seen this exact interpretation of the function of 3:22–36 in its context anywhere else. It follows, I think, once one recognizes the connection of what the Baptist says in 3:31–6 with what Jesus has himself said earlier in chapter, and then combines this recognition with the fact that baptism is a central issue both in 3:22–4:3 and *also* in 3:5–8. What the text as a whole brings out is the need for receiving the *pneuma*, which happens in 'Christian' baptism. Dodd's reading is pretty close to this (though his arguments differ). In light of 3:34, he says (1953a, 311, my emphasis),

we are led to the thought of Christ both as possessing the Spirit and as baptizing in Spirit, and in consequence *mediating eternal life to the believer* (iii. 36). We therefore conclude that the evangelist's intention is to link the ideas of ὕδωρ [water] and πνεῦμα [spirit] through the idea of baptism, and in particular baptism by Jesus (the Church's baptism), in contrast to John's baptism.

Jesus' ('the Church's') baptism gives the *pneuma*, and that makes a believer *have* eternal life (= certainty of seeing and entering the kingdom of God at some point in the future).

In sum, 3:1–4:3 can be seen to raise one philosophical question (Nicodemus' question in 3:9 as to how believers may come to receive the *pneuma*) and to answer that question by explaining its epistemological and ontological presupposition in the fate of Jesus himself (3:10–15). Next (in 3:23–36) the passage answers the remaining, almost practical question of precisely how that transfer from Jesus to the believers may concretely come about by having John the Baptist point to the kind of baptism ('*Christian*' baptism 'from water and *pneuma*'), which is the baptism *Jesus* gives, since *he* has come from above in a manner to which the Baptist cannot himself lay any claim.

Read in this way we may conclude that 3:1–4:3 constitutes a single, coherent literary unit in which a philosophical question is raised at the beginning and answered at the end. In addition, we may note that the section constitutes a literary unit *across* a change of place and time for Jesus and even a change of the main protagonist from Jesus to John the Baptist.[20] We will find such a practice later on in the Gospel, too. This is a sign that for John 'literary unity' is a matter not only of narrative features such as place, time, and agent, but just as much of themes or coherence of thought. In this fact we see particularly clearly that John's narrative is a philosophical one.

---

[20] I am happy to note that Frey, too, believes that with regard to 3:22 'die semantischen Beziehungen <scheinen> über den Szenenwechsel hinauszureichen' (2000, 244).

Before moving on, we should note one consequence of finding a basic contrast in this text between the Baptist's baptism and that of Jesus. This reading may suddenly give additional meaning to the various references to 'Judaism' in the chapter, going back to the fact that although a new section of the text begins at 3:1, the first half of the chapter still takes place literally in Jerusalem in direct continuation from John 2. What we have, then, are these references to 'Judaism': the location; the characterization of Nicodemus (3:1) as a Pharisee and, not least, 'a leader among the Jews'; Jesus' rebuff in 3:10: 'Are you a teacher of Israel, and yet you do not understand these things?' (NRSV); and finally, the dispute of the Baptist's disciples on purification with 'a Jew' (3:25).

It therefore seems that the text as a whole aims to bring out what is ultimately and crucially new in Jesus vis-à-vis both John the Baptist and (even further back) ordinary Jewish practices of purification: from the latter to the Baptist's baptism—and from there to Jesus'. Thus understood, the account of 'Christian' baptism in John 3 falls wholly into line with John having placed the temple event (2:13–25) at a very early stage of his account. There, too, the aim clearly was to contrast a central Jewish institution with what Jesus brings: resurrection (to eternal life).[21]

JESUS AND THE FULFILMENT OF GOD'S WORK (4:4–42)—THE PHILOSOPHICAL QUESTION

John has put a great deal of effort into making 4:4–42 a literary unit at the narrative level. (i) On his way through Samaria (4:4), which is well explained by his travel route given in 4:3, he comes to the Samaritan city of Sychar (4:5), outside of which is 'Jacob's well' (4:6). The action of 4:6–38 takes place here, only to be interrupted at 4:28–30 when the Samaritan woman leaves that place and goes into the city. As a result the inhabitants of the city set out to meet Jesus at the well (4:30 and 4:39–40), after which, on their invitation, he enters their city (4:40–2).

(ii) The narrative also accounts very carefully for the disciples. At 4:8 they had gone into the city 'to buy food' while Jesus remained at the well. At 4:27 they return and urge him to eat something (4:31) and when Jesus declares that he has 'food to eat that you do not know about' (4:32, NRSV), they misunderstand and ask themselves whether somebody else has brought him something to eat (4:33). In this way 4:31–8, which initially might seem out of place, is closely tied in with the rest.

---

[21] On John and Judaism see more in Chapter XI.

(iii) Also noteworthy is the way the gender of the Samaritan woman is handled throughout the text. At 4:9 she mentions the oddity that Jesus, a Jew, asks for something to drink from a Samaritan and (even) a woman. Upon their return, the disciples wonder 'that he was speaking with a woman' (4:27). Finally, the Samaritan men end up telling the woman of their belief in Jesus, which to begin with was triggered by her witness (4:39), but now is 'no longer because of what you have said' (4:42). We already saw that what is brought out in this way, which draws on the ancient, stereotypical understanding of women, is a distinction between her understanding of Jesus and that of the Samaritan men. Where she does acquire *some* understanding of who Jesus is, she does not reach the full understanding that is theirs.[22]

Does this whole text raise a question in the reader's mind that might be called philosophical? The most pressing question is quite simple: what is the connection between the various parts of this highly complicated text? In narrative terms, as we saw, it is carefully and coherently composed, but in thought it is far from straightforward. How, then, does it all hang together? Although this question asks about the coherence of thought, it is not yet a distinctly philosophical one. But once we consider the individual parts of the story in more detail, we will find that there is a more distinct question underlying that of coherence.

John 4:10–15 is a small section in which Jesus introduces the notion of 'living water' (4:10, 11), also identified as a 'spring of water' 'gushing up to eternal life' (4:14, NRSV). We already know from our discussion in Chapter III that this 'living water' is the *pneuma*, but that is not actually stated in the text. Characteristically, the woman completely misunderstands its character (4:15), a fact that in itself suggests there is some important point to be noted here. That is the first case for wonder. After another small section (4:16–19) that persuades the woman that Jesus is 'a prophet' (4:19), we get a second, contextually quite baffling statement by Jesus to the effect that even though 'salvation is from the Jews' (4:22), God must henceforth be worshipped neither on the Samaritan Mount Gerizim nor in the Jewish temple on Jerusalem, but, as we know, 'in *pneuma* and truth' (4:23 and 24). This has some effect on the woman, but not enough. She is led to speak, not now merely of Jesus as a 'prophet': instead, she brings in the 'Messiah', 'the one who is called Christ', who when he comes 'will proclaim all things to us' (4:25). However, even though Jesus explicitly tells her that 'I am he, the one who is speaking to you' (4:26, NRSV), she cannot, as we know, bring herself any further than to ask: '*Might* he

---

[22] It goes without saying that John 4 is *gefundenes Fressen* for any kind of gender-oriented analysis.

perhaps be the Christ?' (4:29). Thus Jesus' claim about the proper worship of God remains a second case for wonder. Finally, in 4:31–8 we get a third, very opaque statement by Jesus to the disciples, which is about sowing the seed and then particularly about reaping the fruit. This is truly a third case for wonder: what on earth is meant? At the end of the story, however, the Samaritan men declare—and now wholly to the point—that Jesus is 'truly the saviour of the world' (4:42).

As this brief summary shows, the reader is presented with three rather opaque statements by Jesus—on 'living water', on worshipping God 'in truth and *pneuma*', and on sowing and reaping—together with a clear development in the appreciation among those who are in contact with him of what and who Jesus is: from a 'prophet' to *possibly* the Messiah to *truly* the saviour of the world. This should give rise in the attentive reader to a philosophical question: what is it that these two things—what Jesus opaquely *says* and how he is *understood*—point towards? What is the ultimate *point* that the writer aims to bring across by describing, in a way that mixes the two things, Jesus' veiled statements and the way he is understood?

JESUS AS THE SAVIOUR OF THE WORLD (4:4–42)—THE ANSWER

If this is the question, is there also an indication of the answer? As we know, Jesus' first two statements on 'living water' as a 'spring of water' 'gushing up to eternal life' and the appropriate manner of worship both refer to the *pneuma*. If we read (as we did in the preceding chapter) the first statement (4:10–11 and 14) in light of 6:35, of 6:63, and of 7:37 (within 7:37–9) on drinking from the streams of living water (explicitly identified as *pneuma*) that flow from Jesus, then we can see that this is all about possession of *pneuma* as the thing that brings eternal life.

Similarly, when the second statement claims that people will worship God 'in *pneuma* and truth' (4:23–4) since God is *pneuma* (4:24), the meaning of the phrase 'in *pneuma* and truth' must be that they are themselves in possession of *pneuma*. Brown (1966, 180), who declines to see here a contrast between 'external' and 'internal worship', nevertheless rightly says this: 'God can be worshiped as Father only by those who possess the Spirit that makes them God's children . . . , the Spirit by which God begets them from above (John iii 5)'. Thus the claim that they must worship God 'in *pneuma* and truth' does imply that they are themselves in possession of the *pneuma*, 'internally' if one likes.

The third statement, however, is much more complicated. Here Jesus speaks of his own very exclusive form of food, which is 'to do the will of him who sent me and complete his work' (4:34, NRSV). We have already speculated that if one wants Jesus' food to be something that he may literally have consumed, then the *pneuma* he received from God at his baptism is the only likely candidate. But what is God's 'will' and what is God's 'work' that Jesus was sent to complete? This is where the second half of this passage (4:35–8) becomes relevant.[23] It says that in the case Jesus is talking about, the time period between sowing and reaping has been curtailed. The time is therefore ripe *now* for reaping so as to receive a recompense (*misthos*, 4:36) for one's labour (*kopos*, see 4:38) and to gather 'fruit for eternal life' (4:36). It seems likely that Jesus means to tell his disciples that *they* should now reap the fruit that he has himself just been sowing—sowing in the Samaritan woman and to be reaped in the Samaritan men who are now on their way to meet Jesus (4:30, 39–40). If that is what is meant, it seems clear that this text is pointing distinctly forward to a period of time that lies beyond Jesus' own lifetime. When Jesus says that 'I have sent you to reap that for which you did not labour' (4:34, NRSV), we must qualify this by noting that according to 20:22–3 the disciples were not sent out until after Jesus' death and resurrection when he blew the *pneuma* into them. In this connection it is important to see that the reader is also explicitly told in the passage what God's 'will' and 'work' are and how Jesus 'fulfils' them: by gathering people for eternal life (4:36).[24] That, too, seems to point distinctly into the future.

Our philosophical question concerns what the inner connection is between what Jesus opaquely says in the three statements we have considered and how he is understood by those who are in contact with him. We can now see the inner connection of the three statements. Jesus is talking all through of what he himself brings: the *pneuma* that gushes up 'to eternal life'; the *pneuma* that people must have to worship God 'in *pneuma* and truth'; and the *pneuma* that will bring Jesus' followers to harvest the recompense for their labour, a fruit that will result in eternal life. The *pneuma* is literally Jesus' food that will make him do the will of the one who has sent him (God)—*through* the *pneuma*, as we know—and so make him fulfil his (God's) work (4:34) of bringing human beings to eternal life (again through the *pneuma*). But what about the link to the other half of the question concerning the way Jesus is understood?

---

[23] For a good discussion of the issues, see Zumstein 2016, 189–92. I confess that I find 4:37 altogether baffling: 'For here the saying holds true, "One sows and another reaps"' (NRSV). Is *Jesus* here supporting something he has just said by referring to the truth of a well-known proverb? And what is the proverb intended to support? Could it not be that we have here a genuine scribal gloss that has crept into the text itself from the margin? The scribe *commented* on what Jesus has just said at the end of 4:36 and intended to say this: 'In this [namely, Jesus' statement] the (well-known) proverb comes out to be true that "One sows and another reaps"'.

[24] On this reading, God's 'will' is his original plan, *logos*, in creation. His 'work' is what he has done in Jesus to bring that will into operation.

Here the answer is finally given in the last few words of the whole passage, the confession of the Samaritan men that 'this one is truly the saviour of the world' (4:42). In John, salvation consists in obtaining eternal life. And we saw that Jesus' three statements showed that eternal life (for human beings) was precisely the point of God's 'will' and 'work' brought to them by the *pneuma*. In this way the two last sections of the whole passage (4:31–8 and 4:39–42) *together* give the answer to the philosophical question. Jesus' veiled statements and the way he is gradually understood by his hearers together make the point that he is the saviour of the world in the sense that he puts into practice God's 'will' and fulfils God's 'work' by making human beings obtain eternal life—and that the *means* by which he achieves this is the *pneuma*, which God gave him for the very same purpose, and which he himself transmits to his followers.

This reading presupposes that when the Samaritan men arrive at their final identification of Jesus, they are themselves to be understood as having come into possession of the *pneuma*. We saw in the previous chapter that they arrived at this identification 'because of his (Jesus') *logos*' (4:41) when he was with them, that is, by experiencing Jesus' full *logos* as distinct from merely hearing the *logos* of the Samaritan woman (4:39). This point hints that they have obtained the *pneuma* since elsewhere the full *logos* and the *pneuma* go so intimately together. Moreover, postulating that the Samaritan men are in possession of the *pneuma* is the only way to *connect* Jesus' veiled statements throughout the chapter (which are all about possession of the *pneuma*, as we saw), with the idea of a development in his listeners that ends with the full confession of the Samaritan men. This is not a very strong argument, of course, since there might not *be* any connection. But we are trying to find as much inner coherence as possible in the passage as a whole.

Here, however, we are distinctly helped by the fact that the various claims made in Jesus' veiled statements all point beyond Jesus' own lifetime: there *was* no *pneuma* on earth apart from in Jesus (for 4:10–15); people were *not* (yet) worshipping God in *pneuma* and truth (for 4:20–4); and the disciples had *not* (yet) been sent out to reap the fruit of Jesus' sowing (for 4:34–8). Similarly, it makes excellent sense to see the entirely appropriate reception of Jesus on the part of the Samaritan men as being in fact 'proleptic': it reflects a post-resurrection perspective when (*ex hypothesi*) some Samaritans did come to see Jesus as 'the saviour of the world'. Apparently, the whole Samaritan theme of John 4 belongs at a post-resurrection stage of the whole story. Why, then, might that be? What point might John be wishing to make by letting Jesus speak very prematurely about the future role of the *pneuma* in relation to the Samaritans, too? We will return to this question once we have considered the story that concludes John 4.

BELIEF IN JESUS BASED ON MORE THAN 'SIGNS AND WONDERS' (4:43–54)

This story, which in a neat *inclusio* brings us back to Cana, also strikes one as containing a number of oddities. (i) Jesus left Samaria and went on his way towards Galilee (4:43). But he *explains* this travel in the next verse (4:44) by proclaiming that a prophet has no honour in his country (*patris*). If Galilee *is* Jesus' *patris*, as I take it, then that reason is distinctly odd.[25] As it happens, the Galileans even 'welcomed him, since they had seen all that he had done in Jerusalem at the festival; for they too had gone to the festival' (4:45, NRSV). So there was *no* reason, after all, to fear dishonour from the Galileans?[26] (ii) Then we hear of a 'royal official' (*basilikos*), whose son was ill in Kapernaum, asking Jesus to come down to Kapernaum to heal him. But Jesus brusquely addresses him with an accusation that is (also) directed at them all: 'Unless you people see signs and wonders, you will never, ever believe' (4:48). What is the point of that rebuff, not least when the royal official was not at all asking for a 'sign'? (iii) Nevertheless, the royal official is completely undeterred and just pursues his own course: 'Sir, come down (to Kapernaum) before my little son dies' (4:49).[27] (iv) Surprisingly, then, and without further ado, Jesus obeys and heals the child, even at a distance.[28] (v) The royal official, on his side, immediately believes (*episteusen*) 'the *logos* that Jesus had said to him' (4:50), namely, presumably what Jesus has just literally said: 'Go, your son lives (or is alive)'. And when he later ascertains that the boy had been healed at exactly the moment when Jesus had said that his son was

---

[25] Commentators regularly discuss the issue of Jesus' *patris* in connection with this verse, e.g. Brown 1966, 187; Lincoln 2005, 184; Theobald 2009, 346. Meeks's alternative understanding remains worth considering (1967, 40): 'Jesus' πατρίς, his ἴδια [see 1:11], is Judaea. Jerusalem in John is the center of "the world," the place of decision. But the πατρίς is not Jesus' *native* land, but his *own* land. In his πατρίς he is not received, but when he goes to Galilee (his native land), there he is received (4.45).' However, I take it here that the *patris* is Galilee.

[26] 'These three verses constitute a notorious crux in the Fourth Gospel', says Brown (1966, 186), who goes on to analyse the difficulties (186–8). Lincoln 2005, 184–5, is also good on the issues as is Theobald 2009, 344–7, with good references to the secondary literature. The suggestion by some (including G. Van Belle 1998, J. Becker 1991, and J. Blank 1977, see Theobald 2009, 346–7) that the introductory *gar* ('for') in 4:44 has a 'continuing' sense, is attractive to my Greek ear: 'Of course (*gar*), Jesus himself had testified that a prophet has no honour in his own country'.

[27] Well expressed by Thatcher (2014, 138): 'John's βασιλικός shows none of the self-debasing humility of his synoptic counterparts.... [He] ignores Jesus' overt criticism of his faith and repeats his demand in even stronger terms'.

[28] Lincoln 2005, 183, well compares my oddities (iii) and (iv) in the present story with Jesus' rebuff to his mother in 2:4 and his subsequent unexplained compliance. Nevertheless, one needs to recognize the oddities as just that.

alive, he himself (and his whole house) *again* 'believed' (*episteusen*). A strange story, indeed.[29]

The first question that the attentive reader will ask is this: what is the point of the oddities? What on earth is this story *about*? As we know, this question is not yet a genuinely philosophical one. But once again by looking a bit more closely, the reader may well feel called to ask whether there is not a genuine philosophical question lurking within the story. In fact it seems as if the passage as a whole is focused on bringing out two different types of reaction to Jesus' 'signs', two types of believing. In that case, a genuine philosophical question arises: how do they differ? There is one type of believing that is directly tied to 'signs and wonders' (4:48). From the way Jesus addresses 'them', and not just the royal official, in making this point, one may guess that Jesus is targeting all the Galileans who 'welcomed' him since they had seen what he had done in Jerusalem (4:45).[30] As we know, the type of belief to be found among the people in Jerusalem was deficient too (2:23–5). In that case, Jesus' premonition concerning his likely reception in his *patris* (Galilee) was actually to the point.

But then there is also another type of belief as exemplified by the royal official. The fact that he asks Jesus to come and heal his son hardly makes it anything special. It is different with three other features of the story. First, he does not in the least let Jesus' rebuff deter him from his course (4:49). He also immediately believes the *logos* Jesus had spoken to him to the effect that his son lives (4:50). And here we should note that the son's 'illness' or 'weakness' (4:46) is twice described as one that is so severe that it risks leading to his death (4:47, 49), to which corresponds the fact that Jesus' cure is twice (4:50, 53) described as one of making him live.[31] Finally, and by far most importantly, once he has realized that his son had been cured at exactly the moment when Jesus had spoken his *logos*, he and his whole house 'believed'—but in what? Surely not just in the fact that the son had been healed, or healed by Jesus. Those were by now facts and both were the object of the royal official's 'believing' already in 4:50, where he believed in the 'word' or 'statement' that Jesus had just spoken to him. No, the kind of belief involved here must be something broader, namely, a belief *in Jesus*. In fact, when the royal official *and his house* 'believed', they became *followers* or

---

[29] Compare in general the analysis in Van Belle 1998, as also recaptured in Thatcher 2014, 120–40.

[30] Theobald argues well for seeing this connection (2009, 357–8).

[31] Theobald is right (2009, 358, my emphasis): 'Im Unterschied zu den Synoptikern [in the comparable healing stories] . . . geht es dem Vierten Evangelisten viel radikaler um die Opposition Tod und Leben, *auf die zuletzt alles hinausläuft*.' (Oddly, this feature is not at all dwelled upon in Thatcher 2014.)

disciples of Jesus, probably not so literally as to walk around with him, but so as from then on to belong to his group as residents in Kapernaum.

If this is what the story aims to convey, then the fact that the father of the story is a *basilikos* may suddenly become quite relevant. Commentators discuss what kind of royal position he may have had (e.g. Barrett 1978, 247). The only thing we know is that he was in some way attached to the court of 'King' Herod Antipas of Galilee. But is that not precisely what we need? In that case, the story is definitely not about a Gentile like the centurion in Matt. 8:5–13 and Luke 7:1–10.[32] Instead, it is about a *Galilean* who, *differently* from those Galileans who are referred to and mentioned in 4:44–5 and then directly addressed in 4:48, did obtain a more developed type of belief in Jesus. Of this type of belief we may say that even if it did not go the whole way towards full belief in Jesus, it nevertheless went much further than merely being a belief in Jesus' *miracles* (or in Jesus as a mere miracle-monger). Instead, it was a belief in *him* and in his capacity to make a person who is on the verge of dying come alive.

Perhaps we may go one step further and see a genuine point in the double description of the royal official's 'coming to believe' at 4:50 and 4:53. In the first case what he came to believe in was Jesus' '*logos* that he had spoken to him', that is, his 'word' or 'statement'. *However,* in light of the much wider and more semantically loaded meaning of the term *logos* elsewhere in the Gospel *and* the fact that Jesus' particular 'statement' here is that the royal official's son is (now) *alive*, it is difficult not to hear a little more in the use of the term here. This might be captured, perhaps, if we translated it here as Jesus' 'powerful word or statement'.[33] In short, it seems that there is *some* basis in the first instance of the royal official's belief that points in the direction (but no more) of the fuller belief in Jesus himself that he obtained when he heard about the manner of his son's recovery.

So, is there a genuine philosophical question and an answer in this text? On the proposed reading there is: one that concerns different types of belief, of which one is strongly deficient whereas the other goes a long way in the proper direction. And the difference lies in the extent to which the belief that is generated by Jesus' 'signs' is a belief in Jesus himself (though not explicitly *as* this or that) and not just a belief in 'signs and wonders' (*sēmeia kai terata*), as Jesus himself describes them somewhat derogatorily (4:48). Such 'signs' are not fully understood as the kind of 'sign' that Jesus is doing,

---

[32] This is spelled out well in Van Belle 1998.

[33] What Jesus literally says does sound quite powerful (in the circumstances): 'Go, your son lives', compare the famous 'stand up, take your mat and go to your home' in Mark 2:11. Strangely, the NRSV weakens the Johannine saying considerably by translating it 'Go: your son *will* live' (my emphasis). May we also find a hint in the royal official's 'coming to believe' in 4:50 that he responded to the presence of *pneuma* in Jesus' speech? Perhaps.

which is a sign about himself and his unique capacity to make somebody who is on the verge of dying come alive again.

We should conclude that the narrative oddities in this story serve to distinguish between two types of belief and in particular make the point that the proper reaction to Jesus' signs is believing in *him*, or understanding the sign event to show something about who and what Jesus is. Even if the royal official did not go the whole way, he prefigures others (such as the healed man born blind of John 9) who go a long way in the right direction.[34] At the same time, this story has made the reader aware of the issue of different types of belief in relation to Jesus that will be played out in the rest of the Gospel.

THE INNER COHERENCE OF THE FIVE STORIES OF JOHN 2–4

Can we see a pattern in the five stories that make up John 2–4: Cana, the temple, Nicodemus, Samaria, and the royal official?

It seems that there are several different themes here (the relation to ordinary Judaism, different reactions to Jesus, and more), which are all, however, connected by putting up front *what is uniquely special about Jesus*. There is wine instead of ordinary Jewish cleansing with water; there is the resurrection of Jesus' own body instead of the Jerusalem temple; there is the idea of a pneumatic rebirth that goes completely over the head of the Jewish leader, Nicodemus; there is a saviour of the whole world who will also integrate some Samaritans in something that goes beyond both ordinary Judaism and Samaritanism; and there are healing powers that verge on bringing life from death and thereby create a new form of follower of Jesus as against that of ordinary Galileans. In all this John appears to be keen on bringing out what is the ultimate truth about Jesus: that *he* brings (eternal) *life* to human beings and that he does it through the *pneuma*; *that*, then, is what human beings must understand, and that is also what some of them do understand, though only to varying degrees and in contrast to those who do not understand it at all (such as Nicodemus).[35] In this highly varied manner, John 2–4 constitutes a powerfully suggestive *introduction* to the account of Jesus' activities on earth that points far beyond his life and death towards two things: (i) an alternative community that is prefigured by the royal official's 'house', by the Samaritan men, who themselves prefigure a

---

[34] Following Van Belle 1998, Thatcher (2014, 140) well articulates this point: 'John's royal official is paradigmatic of those who move from an inadequate belief based on signs to a higher faith that trusts Jesus' powerful word. Here as elsewhere in John, Christ never changes, but people's beliefs about him sometimes do'.

[35] However, Nicodemus turns up later in the Gospel (7:50–2 and 19:39–42) as one who may have understood *something*.

worship of God that goes beyond Judaism and Samaritanism, and by those who are reborn by water and *pneuma* once Jesus has himself exchanged the temple in Jerusalem for his own resurrected body; and beyond that community towards (ii) the idea of eternal life for all (believers) in the form of a future human resurrection into heaven.

A NARRATIVE PHILOSOPHICAL SEARCH

We have now considered the individual texts in John 2–4 and their coherence in an attempt to see whether addressing these texts in terms of a philosophical question to be answered within the text itself constitutes a useful manner of approaching them. Readers will make up their own minds on this. I would emphasize two points that speak in its favour. The first is that as I have put the approach into practice, it will be immediately clear to Johannine experts that it to a considerable extent covers the same ground as is covered in more traditional approaches to the text, particularly when commentators address what they call 'theological motifs' in the text. That I consider a point in its favour. It would be very disquieting if the proposed way of reading this whole text were to differ radically from anything else that had been said about it over the last two millennia. The second point is that the present approach nevertheless differs by adopting a more rigorous way of asking questions about the text. It does this by focusing on coherence of thought at a level that may reasonably qualify as being philosophical and also by finding such coherence through attending closely to the level of the narrative itself and the many bumps it presents to the smooth understanding of the reader. These two sides of the search for coherence support one another. But it is the rigorous pursuit of coherence of thought in a close reading of the narrative that gives the approach adopted here its special profile.

THE SON EQUALS THE FATHER AND HIS PNEUMATIC BODY GIVES LIFE (JOHN 5–6)

THE SEQUENCE OF JOHN 5–6

Scholarship has traditionally queried the sequence of John 5 and 6. (i) At the end of John 4 (4:46–54) Jesus was in Galilee, in Cana but healing at a distance a boy who was in Kapernaum on the shore of the Sea of Galilee. John 6:1 runs: 'After this Jesus went to the other side of the Sea of Galilee...' (NRSV). Does that not fit exceedingly well together? From Cana to Kapernaum to the other side of the sea: why should we have a story that takes place in *Jerusalem* in the intervening chapter 5? (ii) Conversely, if we read the story in the transmitted sequence, how should we imagine that Jesus concludes a speech in Jerusalem at the very end of John 5 (5:47) and then moves with lightning speed to the *other* side of the Sea of Galilee in 6:1? (iii) And there is also the fact that John 5 in Jerusalem brings the confrontation with 'the Jews' to a first climax explaining why they 'started persecuting Jesus' (5:16, NRSV) and were now 'seeking all the more to kill him' (5:18, NRSV). Does that not fit exceedingly well as the first item in a sequence of chapters that continues directly into John 7 (in fact, John 7–12) in which there is an ever-mounting confrontation with 'the Jews', and precisely (for John 7–10, at least) in Jerusalem?[1]

However, there are several arguments on the other side against changing the order of John 5 and 6.[2] One is that there is no indication at all in

---

[1] Theobald (2009, 362–4) provides a good overview of the traditional arguments for switching around the sequence of John 5 and 6. He particularly focuses on the three 'seams' at 4:54–5:1, 5:47–6:1, and 6:71–7:1 and suggests (as a new argument why John 5 and 6 have been switched around) that John 5 later received a 'baptismal' interpretation that made it appropriate to place it before the Eucharistic chapter 6.

[2] At the end of his discussion (1966, 235–6), Brown convincingly states: 'The projected rearrangement is attractive in some ways but not compelling....No rearrangement can solve all geographical and chronological problems in John, and to rearrange on the basis of

the manuscripts of a different order from the present one. So, a supposed change must have been relatively early. A stronger argument is that the case for transposition may well be, as claimed by Lincoln, 'over-concerned with geographical issues at the expense of thematic links' (2005, 210). And in any case, 'the narrator has already prepared readers for swift moves between Jerusalem and Galilee in 2.12–13 and 4.54' (210). Indeed, as one might add, the geographical sequence of 2:1–11 (Cana), 2:12 (Kapernaum), and 2:13 (a festival of the Jews and Jesus in Jerusalem) is closely matched by that of 4:46–54 (Cana—but also the boy in Kapernaum) and 5:1 (a festival of the Jews and Jesus in Jerusalem).

There is also the following consideration. If John 5 is read together with John 7–10 (and 11–12) as being focused on confrontation with 'the Jews' in Jerusalem, then how should we evaluate 7:1, which runs as follows: 'After this Jesus went about in Galilee. He did not wish to go about in Judea because the Jews were looking for an opportunity to kill him' (NRSV)? This verse is followed by a complicated text (7:2–10) in which Jesus' brothers invite him to come with them to Jerusalem, but he at first declines and stays in Galilee (7:9) only to follow them clandestinely once they have left (7:10). In other words, within the supposed 'Jerusalem sequence' of John 5 + 7–10, we have a single verse (7:1, even extending up to 7:10) in which Jesus is *not* in Jerusalem, but in Galilee. We may conclude that in spite of the fact that the reference in 7:1 to the murderous intent of 'the Jews' directly recalls 5:18, the sequence of John 5 + 7–10 is not itself free of having Jesus move with lightning speed between the two geographical poles of Jerusalem and Galilee. Indeed, were one to ask where it is likely in narrative terms that Jesus had been staying just *before* 7:1 ('After this Jesus *went about* [*periepatei*] in Galilee'), the straightforward answer would be: somewhere *in* Galilee— where he was at the end of John 6 (Kapernaum, 6:59).[3]

There is another consideration suggesting that John 5 and 6 may well be read sequentially in the transmitted order once we place more emphasis on themes than on Jesus' supposedly real travels between the two geographical poles. This is not in the least to suggest that geography is unimportant in John. On the contrary, the fact that the first real confrontation with 'the Jews' takes place in Jerusalem (John 5) and that the feeding of the 5,000

---

geography and chronology is to give undue emphasis to *something that does not seem to have been of major importance to the evangelist*' (236, my emphasis). We will see in this chapter that geography does matter to John, but in a somewhat more 'symbolic' sense than envisaged by scholars who rearrange. For arguments against a mechanical 'change of pages', see, e.g., Kümmel 1980, 171, who is in general very good on the failure of all the suggested transpositions, additions etc.

[3] I have not seen this consideration elsewhere. It is not, of course, proof of anything. But it does seem noteworthy that 7:1 does *not* say—as does 6:1—'After this Jesus *went away* (*apēlthen*) to Galilee', but that he 'walked around *in* Galilee'.

takes place across the Sea of Galilee (John 6) may well be of the greatest importance precisely in connection with the two themes that are being treated. But it is geography of a different kind from the one that is concerned—quasi-historically—with Jesus' actual travels. The consideration is this: if John 5 concerns the crucial controversy with 'the Jews' about Jesus' status in relation to God, and if John 6 concerns, as we will see, the consumption of Jesus' pneumatic body in the Eucharist, then the reader is presented with exactly the same move here—*from* one thing *to* the other—as one may find between John 3 (Nicodemus in Jerusalem is incapable of understanding Jesus' *special* divine status in relation to Judaism) and John 4 (the Samaritan woman and her compatriots are geographically away from Jerusalem but gradually do become able to understand Jesus' special divine status). This consideration may be supported by another one about John 6 that follows from noticing that once Jesus has at long last spelled out the Eucharistic meaning of his claim to be 'the bread of life', the reaction (6:60–71) is a devastating loss of followers on Jesus' part. It is so great that at the end *only* the twelve original disciples are prepared to follow him (6:67–71). And the point? Out of this exceedingly small group—from which even Judas will defect (6:70–1)—will *develop* the later, much larger following that is centred on eating Jesus' pneumatic body in the Eucharist and not at all on Jerusalem and its temple. With that change, the movement away from 'the Jews' and Jerusalem will be complete.

The conclusion must be that there is very good reason to read John 5 and 6 in their transmitted order and indeed to see them as complementing one another in the way suggested.[4] They do not constitute a single unit of the type of John 7–8, 9–10, 11–12, and indeed 13–17. But it is likely that they were intended to be read sequentially in the transmitted order in the way we should also read John 3 and 4. In both sequences there is a move away from Jerusalem (John 3 and 5) to some other place (Samaria in John 4 and across the Sea of Galilee in John 6) and this move has a *thematic* point: from failure to understand Jesus in Jerusalem (John 3) to growing understanding in Samaria (John 4), and from open confrontation with 'the Jews' (John 5) to a loss of followers that leaves only the nucleus out of which grew an altogether *different* understanding of where salvation is to be found (John 6).[5] Let us now consider John 5 and 6 in more detail.

---

[4] Other scholars have seen a thematic connection between John 5 and 6, e.g. Borgen (1997, 111–13), who takes 5:31–47 as 'the thematic background of ch. 6' (111), and O'Day (1997, 156–7), who from a similar perspective focuses also on 5:19–30.

[5] This goes against even the supreme literary critic, Alan Culpepper, who at the time he edited a fine volume of essays on John 6 thought it likely that 'John 6 was added at a secondary stage to an early edition of the Gospel in which John 7 followed immediately after John 5' (Culpepper 1997b, 249). The year later, by contrast, he noted that the present order of the two chapters (though still generated at a later stage?) 'allows chapter 6 to develop

IS JESUS EQUAL TO GOD (JOHN 5:19–30)?

There is no serious disagreement about the structure of John 5. A story of a healing at a specific location in Jerusalem (5:2–9a) is followed by some action by 'the Jews', Jesus, and the healed man regarding the fact that it took place on a Sabbath (5:9b–16). The issue is raised to its highest possible level by Jesus (5:17) and in reaction to that by 'the Jews' (5:18), who now engage on the strategy that will lead to Jesus' death:

> [18]For this reason the Jews were seeking all the more to kill him, because he was not only breaking [better: abolishing][6] the sabbath, but was also calling God his own Father, thereby making himself equal to God (NRSV).

In response to this accusation Jesus launches a speech that has two parts. In 5:19–30 he makes a claim on his own behalf that would indeed confirm the suspicion on the part of 'the Jews' that he did make himself equal to God. In 5:31–47 he supports this claim by arguing that God himself bears witness to it.

The story of the healing itself has some interesting features that we should not pass over. One is that it is Jesus who takes the initiative to heal the man who has been unable for thirty eight years to get first into the healing pool. Another is that Jesus' healing order, 'Stand up, take your mat and walk', which is suspiciously similar to the one in Mark (2:11) in another healing story (2:1–12), circumvents completely the whole issue of the pool. It is as if John wishes his Jesus to behave in a manner that altogether bypasses any ordinary healer's practice. 'Do you want to be made well?' (5:6), then 'Stand up, take your mat and walk' (5:8). This healer is clearly more than just that.

Once the healing has been completed, the story becomes even more complicated, not just by the fact that it took place on a Sabbath, but also because it initially (5:10–13) concerns only the healed man and 'the Jews', who object to his carrying around his mat. Later, Jesus finds the man in the temple and tells him to sin no more (5:14), whereupon the healed man reports to 'the Jews' that it was Jesus who had healed him (5:15). 'Therefore the Jews started persecuting Jesus, because he was doing such things on the Sabbath' (5:16, NRSV). Why the complicated picture of who is addressing whom in this part of the story? The healed man himself is hardly in

the theme of the witnesses to Jesus introduced in the discourse in chapter 5 (God, Scripture, Jesus' works, and Moses)' (Culpepper 1998, 154).

[6] Theobald (2009, 381) is right: 'On the basis of a single breaking of the Sabbath there is a conclusion to the fundamental fact that Jesus "abolished" the Sabbath'. Danker (2000, 607) agrees: '*abolish the Sabbath* J 5:18 (in John, Jesus is accused not of breaking the Sabbath, but of doing away w. it as an ordinance)'. See also Liddell/Scott/Jones under the term.

focus. Instead, he has a narrative function of mediating between 'the Jews', who are concerned about the Sabbath, but have not yet found the proper person to whom they may address that concern, and Jesus. In narrative terms, this aftermath to the healing story itself describes in an exceedingly concentrated manner how the concern of 'the Jews' begins from being vague—relatively to its final goal: Jesus' death—and then eventually reaches its target, Jesus (5:16), only to be drastically sharpened in the statement that they were now 'seeking all the more to kill him' (5:18). But note that they are goaded into this by Jesus himself (5:17), who says this: 'My Father is still working, and I also am working' (NRSV). Once again we see that it is Jesus who is the sovereign agent behind it all. He *creates* the confrontation.

The attitude underlying Jesus' challenge to 'the Jews' comes to full expression again in the speech that follows. This is one reason why it is not wholly adequate to see the speech as an *apologia*, not even in its second half.[7] Basically, what Jesus does is first to *make* the claim that 'the Jews' take to mean that 'he makes himself equal to God' and then to *support* this claim by stating that God himself is a witness to it. This constitutes the highest challenge to 'the Jews' on Jesus' part and does not in the least reflect any 'defensive' mood.

The first half of the speech is very clearly structured in terms of Jesus' 'Truly, truly' sayings in 5:19, 5:24, and 5:25. We already spent some time on 5:19–29 in Chapter III. In the present context our focus will be on articulating exactly what Jesus is saying in this section regarding his relationship with God. As part of this we will be on the lookout for any difficulty of understanding that may raise a genuine philosophical question. The overall aim is to show that there is a very high degree of coherence of thought in the speech as a whole.

John 5:19–23 begins by arguing that whatever the 'Son' does is something he has learned from the 'Father'. This includes everything the Son does (5:20a) and in particular certain 'works (*erga*)' in the future that are going to be even greater than those they have already seen (5:20b). Here Jesus is referring to two future tasks: making people come alive (*zōipoiein*, 5:21b), which here must mean resurrecting them since it is paralleled with God's 'raising the dead' (5:21a), and judging them (5:22). These two tasks

---

[7] The term *apologia* is Dodd's (1953a, 320). Since Dodd the approach of seeing the Fourth Gospel as a whole through the lens of a lawsuit in a court of justice has gathered strong momentum, culminating in Lincoln's *Truth on Trial* (2000) and now Bekken (2015). (As noted in Chapter I, Wrede was already there.) However, we should beware not to let this slightly mechanical perspective (which may not be altogether wrong) prevent us from actually reading each particular text that might initially be categorized as being either for the prosecution or for the defence. Many other things than that may well be going on in these texts.

are then taken up in the second 'Truly, truly' saying of 5:24, which speaks both of obtaining eternal life and not coming under judgement.

We saw in Chapter III what this verse is likely to mean. Hearing Jesus' *logos* and believing in God who has *sent him* will amount to grasping the whole *logos* that has been described in the Prologue. That cannot, however, be fully done unless one is oneself in possession of the *pneuma*, and the *pneuma* will only be given to believers after Jesus' death and resurrection. Nevertheless, Jesus may well speak proleptically of such full believers even during his own lifetime since there is no more in terms of *content* to that future situation than what is *already* present in Jesus himself. Or more directly: in Jesus as he is *now* one may also find *God's* full capacity for raising the dead, giving them life, and saving them from judgement. This, then, is the actual *content* of Jesus' 'making himself equal to God'.

The third and last 'Truly, truly' saying (5:25–9) continues the strategy introduced with 5:21 and 22 of speaking first (5:25–6) of life and next (5:27–9) of judgement. But now the focus also becomes more explicitly on believers, in addition to Jesus himself. Where 5:24 brought 5:21–2 forward to its point within the context of Jesus' speech—namely, that *Jesus* has everything that is required for eternal life and escape from judgement— 5:25–9 now spells out that the whole thing is in the end about future resurrection to (eternal) life *for human beings*. Still, the point about *Jesus'* role in that scenario is also continued from 5:24 into 5:25–9: hearing '*my*' *logos*, the one who has sent '*me*', hearing the voice of '*the Son of God*', '*the Son's*' having life '*in himself*', his being '*Son of Man*', and finally hearing *his* voice, that is, the voice of 'the Son of Man'. In all this one may note a clear progression from 'I'/'me' via 'the Son (of God)' to 'the Son of Man'. What 5:24–9 does, then, is to focus very sharply on the role of Jesus—but in an eschatological scenario that concerns human beings. The role that Jesus claims to have, a role that does make him 'equal to God', *is all through directed at the eschatological fate of human beings*.

Once Jesus has spelled out his own role in the eschatological scenario, he is able in 5:30 to go back to his first claim (5:19) that he does nothing on his own. And so, since he only does what comes directly from God, the Son is— in a way—equal to the Father.

A PHILOSOPHICAL QUESTION IN 5:19–30

So far we have only followed the train of thought in the first half of Jesus' speech. Does the text also mean to say something at a deeper level on the issue that has triggered it, which here is the question of Jesus' relationship with God (compare 5:18)? In other words, does 5:19–30 give rise to a philosophical question, a query of some kind that will make the text 'work' in the reader's mind? There is one verse, 5:23, which I have hitherto neglected and which does seem to raise a further question. Moreover, we will see that the theme raised here is also given a hearing in the second half of 5:30 and again in 5:39–47. So perhaps we find here another example of a question being raised to begin with, which is then answered towards the end.

What 5:23 says is that God has given Jesus eschatological power—to make those come alive whom he wishes (5:21) and to judge (5:22)—*for a specific purpose* (*hina*, 5:23), namely, 'so that all may honour the Son just as they honour the Father' (NRSV). Superficially, of course, that makes good sense. If Jesus is, in effect, arguing that he is indeed 'equal to God', then it makes excellent sense to say that God has given him certain divine powers in order to make Jesus (the Son) honoured as God is himself honoured. But this is only a very superficial sense. It sounds as if it is primarily concerned with Jesus: God has acted in order to make *Jesus honoured*. Can that really be what is meant? After all, it chimes in somewhat badly—if at all—with what is said just before and after. For here it seems that those who are ultimately in view are human beings, not Jesus, those whom God had in mind *in giving* Jesus the eschatological powers. Is 5:23 then saying that No, the purpose with which God has put Jesus in charge of the fates of human beings is that he, *Jesus*, be honoured as God is himself honoured? If that does sound somewhat strange, then our philosophical question will be this: what is the point of bringing in the motif of Jesus' honour in 5:23?

It is noteworthy that the wonder lying behind this question is not alleviated by the second half of 5:23, where Jesus declares that '[a]nyone who does not honour the Son does not honour the Father who sent him' (NRSV). In other words, honour to God presupposes honour to Jesus. Again it is clear that taken by itself this claim supports the implicit claim that Jesus is in some way 'equal to God'. But again the observation is also somewhat baffling. Why should we hear here of honouring at all, whether the object be Jesus or God?

This question becomes even more acute when we come to the second half of 5:30. 'I can do nothing on my own', says Jesus (5:30a), referring back to 5:19. And '[a]s I hear, I judge' (5:30b, both NRSV), which continues directly the talk in 5:27–9 of Jesus' role in judging. But then the verse continues: 'and my judgement is just, because I do not seek my own will but the will of him who sent me' (5:30c, NRSV). How should we combine this claim to complete self-effacement on the part of Jesus vis-à-vis God with the self-*asserting* claim in 5:23 that God has given Jesus the power over human life and death *in order that Jesus be honoured*? Apparently, so it sounds, Jesus was meant to be honoured just as much as God (by 5:23), which would certainly give *him* the highest conceivable status. But then he also goes on to declare that he is entirely unconcerned about seeking his own 'will' (= what *he* wills) since he is always and only seeking the will of

the one who has sent him. If the latter is true, then what is the point of
bringing in the motif of Jesus' honour in 5:23? We will find an answer when
we consider what follows in the text after 5:30.

GOD'S WITNESS TO JESUS AND ITS PURPOSE (5:31–47)

The second half of Jesus' speech, 5:31–47, is often described by scholars (e.g.
Lincoln 2005, 205) as fitting particularly well with the idea of the whole
speech as a defence speech in a trial scene. Is not Jesus producing witnesses
here for his claim as stated in the first half of the speech? Moreover, do we
not see here that once he has produced the required number of witnesses
Jesus turns to attack his opponents towards the end of the speech?[8] It has
been well said that the connection of 5:31–47 with the first half of the
speech has the following form: 'Jesus has made remarkable claims [in
5:19–30]. Upon what evidence do they rest?' (Dodd 1953a, 328). But we
will see that the attempt to force 5:31–47 into a forensic straitjacket
threatens to misconstrue the progression of the line of thought.

We must first consider the structure of this section. Jesus begins by
stating that were he to bear witness to himself, his witness would not be
true (5:31). Instead, there is another one (*allos*) who bears witness on his
behalf (5:32). The question who this *allos* is is only answered in 5:37a:
'...the Father who has sent me, he (*ekeinos*) has borne witness on my
behalf'.[9] The text in between then concerns other possible witnesses. Here
it is important to note that the first witness listed, who is John the Baptist

---

[8] Lincoln speaks (2005, 208) of a turning of the tables: 'As the tables begin to be turned [in
5:41–4] and the defendant becomes the prosecutor,...'. Theobald (2009, 405) speaks of
5:31–47 as a whole as a 'Prozessrede Jesu: Zwischen Verteidigung und Anrede'. Apparently,
this perspective is now becoming a new truth in Johannine scholarship (see also Parsenios
2010). In fact, it is quite old. About fifty years ago Meeks (1967, 305) wrote the following: 'A
number of scholars in recent years have emphasized the significance of forensic terminology
in John. They have suggested that the action in the gospel adds up to a cosmic legal process,
in which witnesses produce their testimony, accusations and counter-accusations are
delivered, and judgment is rendered. The trial bears a highly ironic character, for the
principal witness, the "Son of Man," though he is "attested" by the Baptist, by his own
"works," by the Scripture of Moses, and by God himself, becomes the accused because "the
world" refuses to accept his "testimony" or his attestation. It is this very refusal, leading to
the condemnation and execution of the witness, which exposes "the world" as condemned in
the judgment of God. Thus the "trial" of Jesus becomes his enthronement as King and judge
and at the same time the "judgment of this world." There is no need to repeat in more detail
what has been said so frequently by others.'

[9] Neither the NRSV ('And the Father who sent me has himself testified on my behalf') nor
Lincoln (2005, 206: 'And this Father who sent me has borne witness about me') captures the
point of the *ekeinos*. Theobald is better, both in his translation (2009, 406) and his exegesis
(412). He also correctly concludes about the two witnesses—the 'works' and the 'Father'—:
'tatsächlich fallen...beide zusammen' (412).

(5:33–5), is rejected by Jesus as an appropriate witness even though he did witness to the truth (5:33). For John was only a human being and Jesus does not accept a merely human witness; he only referred to the fact that 'the Jews' had themselves sent messengers to John (5:33, compare 1:24–5) for the purpose of giving them one more chance of being saved (5:34): even the Baptist said it. But no, 'I (on my side, as opposed to you) have (as) my witness (one that is) greater than John's' (5:36a), namely what or whom? 'The works (*erga*) that the Father has given me to complete, the very works that I am doing, bear witness on my behalf that the Father has sent me' (5:36b). So are these the proper witnesses that Jesus may appeal to? In fact not. The *allos* of 5:32 is not just Jesus' 'works'; instead, 'the Father (himself) who has sent me' (5:37a) and who has *given* Jesus the power to do those works (5:36b)—as it were, the ultimate agent *behind* the 'works'—he (the *ekeinos*) is the one who has borne witness on Jesus' behalf (5:37a). Since this is the precise line of thought, it is not quite right to say that the passage consists in Jesus' producing several witnesses to defend his claim as if in a court of law. He only produces one. Also, it is noteworthy that the one witness he does produce (though admittedly as seen in his 'works') is not one who might very easily serve such a function in a defence speech. On the contrary, Jesus' reference to God as his one witness has much more of the character of a further claim. Jesus is challenging his opponents much more than defending himself.

Then follows 5:37b–38, which is best understood as an addition to 5:37a that brings out an implication of the statement in 5:37a that 'the Father… has sent me':[10]

37bYou have never heard his voice or seen his form, 38and you do not have his *logos* abiding in you, because you do not believe in him whom he has sent.

As we know from Chapter III, the implication is that the speaker, Jesus, *has* heard God's voice and even seen his form, and moreover, that *he* truly has God's *logos* abiding in him. This happened when he received the *pneuma*. By contrast, 'the Jews' have never experienced these things since they do not believe in 'him whom he has sent'. Here the point is again not just that they do not 'believe in Jesus' in some vaguer sense. What they do not believe is specifically that Jesus is one whom God has *sent*. We have already suggested that this means not just that Jesus has 'come from God' (e.g. in the way Nicodemus stated that Jesus had 'come from God', 3:2), but that he has been sent by God as a messenger who will also eventually *return* to God. We

[10] One may well say—with Bieringer (2014, 182)—that the *kai* at the beginning of 5:37 is epexegetical, thereby tying 5:37a closely together with 5:36. But there is no reason to separate 5:37b from 5:37a and thus to divide up the whole of 5:31–47 into the two sections suggested by Bieringer: 5:31–7a, 5:37b–47. (See later on this.)

also know that this is something human beings only *could* see and believe once it had actually happened, that is, after Jesus' resurrection. Then, when they have themselves received the *pneuma*, it might be true to say of them that they, too, have—in a sense and vicariously through Jesus—heard God's voice and seen his form and that they, too, have God's *logos* abiding in them. In the present passage, however, the point is that they are precisely *not* there and so cannot even understand the full import of Jesus' claim that '… the Father who has *sent* me, he has borne witness on my behalf' (5:37a).

With 5:39, as has been recognized,[11] an additional point is made. In two small sections (5:39–40 and 5:45–7) Jesus claims that the Jewish Scriptures, too (5:39)—later simply called 'Moses' (5:45) and 'his [= Moses'] writings' (5:47)—bear witness to him, but that his addressees do not understand that either. In between these two small sections comes another small section (5:41–4) in which the theme is suddenly again 'honour' (though the term differs: *doxa*, 'glory', instead of *timê*, 'honour', in 5:23). We must clearly consider the relationship between the three small sections in 5:39–47: 39–40, 41–4, 45–7.

It is important to get the sense of 5:39–40 right:

[39]You search the Scriptures because you think that in them you have eternal life. And yet (*kai*) they are the ones that bear witness to me. [40]And yet (*kai*, or Nevertheless), you are not willing to come to me to have life.

It is certainly true that these two verses continue the theme of witnessing from 5:31–7. The Scriptures bear witness to Jesus, too. It is also true that the two verses continue the theme of 5:37b–38 that Jesus' addressees fail in a number of respects because they do not believe in the one whom the Father has sent, that is, Jesus himself: *instead*, they search the Scriptures in the belief that they will have eternal life in *them* (*en autais*, emphatically positioned). However, the theme is no longer so much that of witnesses. Instead, it is one of a failure to understand on the part of 'the Jews' and—even more importantly—the *reason* for that failure.

That reason is given in the middle section, 5:41–4. Here Jesus first claims that he does not accept glory from any human being (5:41) and then that they on their side do not have the love of *God* in them (5:42). Why? Because they do not accept Jesus who has come in the name of his Father; instead, they are ready to accept anybody who comes in his own name (5:43). Indeed, they *cannot* believe in Jesus since they only receive glory from one

[11] For instance, by Theobald (2009, 408), who well contrasts the witnessing discussed in 5:33–8 with that of 5:39–47, which is focused on the Scriptures. The Nestle-Aland practice of beginning a new little paragraph at 5:41 would be all right if they had also done so at 5:39. Otherwise, it hinders a grasp of the line of thought.

another, that is, from human beings, but do not seek the glory that comes from the one and only God (5:44).

Here Jesus draws a contrast between seeking and accepting honour at the human level from other human beings, which prevents one from seeking it from God and is a sign that one does not love God—and then on the other hand receiving glory *only* from God. Basically, it is the contrast that we already know well from John 3 between being from the earth and being from heaven. But here it is applied to the specific topic of seeking honour either from below or from above. This raises a question: one can see why the distinction between *being* from below or above might be brought in to explain why 'the Jews' are unable to read their Scriptures in the proper way; but why does Jesus make that point in terms of where one seeks honour?

This is where the reader is *asked to think back* to what has been said earlier in the chapter about Jesus as the proper object of honour (5:23) and one who does not seek his own will (5:30). What the glory-seeking of 'the Jews' signifies is an attitude of horizontal, earthly inter-human glory-seeking that prevents them from the true, vertical glory-seeking from God. By contrast, Jesus, who precisely does *not* seek his own will, but only—exclusively vertically, as it were—the will of God . . . to him God has given the power to administer God's own major power over human life and death in order that *he* (Jesus) be honoured. Two things follow from this for the answer we should give to the philosophical question we raised in connection with 5:23. First, when God has acted in order that human beings may come to give honour to the Son, he does not do so because that is valuable for *Jesus*. For Jesus himself does not seek his own will, but only *God's* will. Jesus, then, will not *receive* honour from human beings (were he to be given it) for his own sake. And the intention behind his being honoured (by human beings) is that *God* should be honoured (by human beings) *through* Jesus. When God gave Jesus the power over human life and death, the aim was that *through* Jesus *God* should be genuinely honoured—as he was not by those who did not have 'the love of God' in them. Secondly, there is a further purpose, that comes out in the connection between what Jesus says in 5:39–40 of the failure on the part of 'the Jews' to read the Scriptures properly and what he says in 5:41–4 of their failure to seek glory from God. The point is that although 'the Jews' scrutinize the Scriptures in the hope of achieving eternal life (5:39), they do not reach that specific goal *since because* they seek glory only horizontally and not from God (5:41–4), and do not *therefore* 'come to' *Jesus* (5:40), who seeks it only vertically (5:41)—for that precise reason they do not *achieve* life (5:40), which only comes through Jesus from God. So the point about seeking honour in the wrong place has to do with what is the ultimate purpose of it all: how human beings may achieve eternal life.

This may sound quite complicated, but we may put the general idea like this. Jesus' coming on earth was staged by God in order to lead human beings to (eternal) life. In this process Jesus was only God's representative on earth and Jesus acted accordingly, never seeking to do his own will but only the will of God. Still, God intended *Jesus* to be honoured by human beings *as* the visible *stand-in for* God. If *that* were to happen, *then* the road would be open for human beings actually to obtain eternal life. For then human beings would obtain the proper relationship with *God through* Jesus. However, 'the Jews' were not prepared to recognize and honour Jesus, vertically as it were, as a stand-in for God. This reflects the fact that they did not in fact have the proper love for God but instead sought glory, *not* from God but from one another at the earthly level. For that reason, although they did seek eternal life in the Scriptures, they did not achieve it. They should have seen that the Scriptures bore witness to God's stand-in, *Jesus*.[12] But they were prevented from doing so by their own merely interhuman glory-seeking.[13]

In sum, the answer to the philosophical question that is raised throughout this text is that God intended his stand-in in the eschatological scenario, Jesus, to be honoured so that when that happened and God *himself* would be truly honoured *through* Jesus, *then* human beings might at long last be given eternal life. And if it is further asked how that might come about, the answer suggested by 5:24–9 is this: when they on their side would eventually receive the *pneuma*, just as Jesus, the mediator between God and human beings, had already received it.

CONCLUSION ON 5:19–47

Is Jesus equal to God according to the speech he himself gives in response to the accusation of 'the Jews' that he has made himself so? The answer is both yes and no. Yes, in the sense that the whole brunt of the speech is that God has in effect *made* Jesus equal to himself by giving him the power over human life and death and bearing witness to Jesus' status in giving him to do his 'works'. By having Jesus make this point in both the first and the second half of the speech, the Evangelist also makes Jesus continue his

---

[12] It is worth asking in what more specific way John may have thought that the Jewish Scriptures bore witness to Jesus. However, the question is immaterial for grasping the line of thought, where the point is just presupposed.

[13] Who are 'the Jews' in this text? This question is well addressed in Bieringer 2014. We should agree with his 'synchronic' reading: they are those Jewish contemporaries of Jesus (and of the Johannine community) who did not believe in Jesus (2014, 172). However, I read John's Jesus here as being much more accusatory of these Jews than Bieringer, who takes him to be issuing an 'invitation' (*Einladung*, 188) to them. On the general issue see Chapter XI.

challenge of 'the Jews' (as opposed to merely defending himself) in a manner that will goad them on in their strategy to have him killed. But also no, for in spite of the fact that God has acted in relation to Jesus for the purpose of making him honoured just as much as God is himself honoured, Jesus' speech also shows that he on his side is only doing the will of God (as opposed to his own will), and only receiving glory from God (as opposed to accepting it from human beings). He only acts as a mediator, in the shape of a visible *stand-in* for God, between God and human beings. The way this concretely came to be was when God gave his *pneuma* to Jesus—and to Jesus alone—in his earthly life. In doing so, God aimed to make himself (indirectly) visible on earth so that God's own aim for human beings, namely, eternal life, might at long last be realized when they reacted positively to Jesus and through him to God. Then they, too, might come to receive the *pneuma* and so eternal life. All through this, however, Jesus is only acting on God's behalf, as his messenger and stand-in: 'I have come in the name of my Father' (5:43).

What we see here is that this whole text makes a much wider and *much more precise* point (on glory-seeking, the relationship between Jesus and God, and the final purpose of it all)—in what one might call a 'conceptual story'—than merely giving a response by Jesus to an accusation of 'the Jews' or making him cite witnesses in his own defence. This wider point comes out once one tries to ask a philosophical question about an intriguing topic in the text that calls for an answer. Then one may begin to see how the whole text is exceedingly closely argued. Then, and only then, is one also invited to do the concentrated work that is required to see all the connections of thought that the text contains.

JESUS' PNEUMATIC BODY IS WHAT GIVES ETERNAL LIFE (6:1–71)

John 6 is one more example of John's pattern of beginning with a story about some spectacular doing of Jesus that is then followed by a speech.[14] In the present case the speech begins at 6:26 in response to a question asked by the crowd that has been following Jesus. In fact, Jesus' speech is more in the form of a continued dialogue, or better a set of relatively extended statements by Jesus interrupted by interventions by 'the Jews', and given in

---

[14] Here too, the unity of the text has been repeatedly questioned by scholars. The undauntedness of Léon-Dufour is refreshing, however: 'Certes ici aussi des sources ou des traditions diverses ont été utilisées par Jn, mais une lecture synchronique est possible, *nécessaire même*' (1990, 91, my emphasis). Léon-Dufour also refers (91 n. 2) to Borgen 1965, Dunn 1971, and Ruckstuhl 1987.

response to those interventions. This feature is in itself interesting. 'The Jews' are constantly asking questions, objecting because they do not understand, and the like. They thereby help to make explicit that there is some deeper meaning to what Jesus says that calls for elucidation. One might almost say that it is 'the Jews' who pose the philosophical questions raised by Jesus' statements. John is at work on behalf of his reader.

The beginning of the chapter (6:1–4) before the story proper gets started helps to introduce some of the themes that will be central in the chapter as a whole. (i) We are 'on the other side of the Sea of Galilee' (6:1). This area was basically non-Jewish, and it is likely that this forms an important part of the message: what happens in that area (the feeding of the 5,000, 6:5–13) and its meaning (6:26–71) are directly relevant to Gentiles, too. (ii) 'A large crowd was following him' (6:2). Later in the chapter (from 6:41 onwards) the crowd will gradually turn into 'the Jews'. In view of the fact that towards the end (6:60, 66) many (*polloi*) even among his disciples found what Jesus had said both 'tough' and unacceptable (6:60) and so defected from him (6:66), it is noteworthy that to begin with Jesus was followed by a 'large crowd'. Thus there is a quite drastic reduction in the number of Jesus' followers once he has articulated his central message. That must surely have a point. (iii) It is also explicitly stated that the eagerness of the crowd was due to the 'signs' they 'saw' him to be doing for the sick (6:2). We will see that the notion of 'seeing signs'—and seeing them properly—plays an important role at the beginning of Jesus' speech (6:26, compare 6:30). It introduces what Jesus then goes on to explain.

(iv) At the beginning Jesus 'went up the mountain and sat down there with his disciples' (6:3, NRSV). The mountain plays a narrative role in what follows. At 6:5 Jesus sees a 'large crowd coming towards him'. Once they have been fed, he 'withdrew again to the mountain by himself' (6:15), while his disciples 'went down to the lake' (6:16) and began to cross the lake to Capernaum (6:17). 'The next day the crowd that had been standing [all through the night?!] on the other [Eastern] side of the lake noticed...' something about the boats there (6:22). So, they too had 'come down' to the lake. Did the feeding then take place *on* the mountain? Yes, in the sense that it occurred somewhere 'up there'. But also no, in the sense that Jesus was able to withdraw even higher up in the mountain (by 6:15). The 'mountain' here functions as 'Jesus' place' (like Moses on Mount Sinai), to which the crowd did not have full access.

(v) The last bit of information given to the reader is that 'the Passover, the festival of the Jews, was near' (6:4). No explicit use is made of this in the chapter, but it must have some meaning. The best reading is the one that attempts to see what happened later at the final Passover as being connected with what John 6 as a whole is all about. That does make sense, as we will see.

The two stories of the feeding of the 5,000 (6:5–13) and Jesus' walking on the sea (6:16–21) follow the accounts given in Mark and Matthew quite closely.[15] One difference is that both Mark (6:41) and Matthew (14:19) employ the verb *eulogêsen* (NRSV: 'blessed') for Jesus' action just before he gives the multiplied bread to the disciples. John employs a different verb, *eucharistêsas* (6:11, NRSV: 'when he had given thanks'), which makes the 'Eucharistic overtones' of the feeding that are probably also *implied* in the Synoptics wholly explicit.[16] We will see that this has the greatest importance for understanding the whole of John 6.

Another difference is that the two stories of the feeding and the walking are separated in John by another revealing section (6:14–15):

[14]When the people saw the sign (*sêmeion*) that he had done, they said (to one another), 'This man is truly the prophet who is coming into the world'. [15]But Jesus, who knew that they were about to come and take him by force in order to make him king, withdrew again to the mountain by himself.

In view of the rest of the chapter, this indicates that the crowd's understanding of Jesus' 'sign' and Jesus himself is strongly deficient. Jesus is definitely *more* than 'the prophet who is to come into the world'. And he is not just a 'king', but if at all—as the reader will realize in his conversation with Pilate—a king of a quite different kind. To think the way the crowd does is to misread the sign.

The last thing to be noted is the entertaining account in 6:22–5 of the crowd's reflections on how Jesus had managed to leave the area on their side of the lake when he had not gone with his disciples in the only available boat (6:22) and was no longer to be found there either (6:24). (Fortunately, some other boats had arrived from Tiberias on which the crowd might then follow Jesus, 6:23 and 6:24b.)[17] We may note that John

[15] Commentators are strongly divided on the question of whether John knew those two accounts or not. Brown's discussion is particularly detailed (1966, 236–50). He claims that John was independent of Mark, as does Theobald (2009, 426–7). Barrett (1978, 271) finds 'many indications' to 'suggest that John knew and recalled the two miracle narratives of Mark 6.35–44; 8.1–9'. In 1997, Culpepper summarized the positions of the contributors to his volume on John 6 who discussed the issue by saying that apart from Schenke (see Schenke 1997, 218–19) they all felt that 'John 6 is informed by a synoptic-like tradition rather than by dependence on one or more of the synoptics' (Culpepper 1997b, 249). But what if John was an independently creative writer? Can we then distinguish between 'a synoptic-like tradition' and the Synoptics themselves? For more on John and the Synoptics, see Chapter XI.

[16] This issue is also controversial. Theobald (2009, 434–5) provides a good overview that supports finding the Eucharist to be prefigured here.

[17] Theobald (2009, 446) well rehearses the problems scholars have found in these verses, including Eduard Schwartz's judgement that they constitute 'ein wirres Conglomerat von sprachlichen und sachlichen Ungeheuerlichkeiten'. Theobald's own solution is redactional (446–8). Personally, I find the line of thought of the four verses pellucid once one reads them as characterizing the perplexity of the crowd vis-à-vis the miracle of Jesus' crossing the lake on foot.

once again (6:23) employs the *mot juste* for Jesus' act just before he gave them the multiplied bread to eat: 'after the Lord had given thanks (*euchar-istêsantos*)'.[18] We may also note that the concept that captures what the crowd's reflections on Jesus' whereabouts are intended to express is that of the crowd's 'seeking for' Jesus (*zêtountes* in 6:24). They are not just 'looking for' him (as NRSV has it), but much more strongly 'seeking for' him. What the rest of the chapter shows is what would go into the *proper* 'seeking for' Jesus, which requires quite a bit more than this crowd is able to deliver.

DIVIDING JESUS' SPEECH (6:26–58)

We noted that Jesus' speech[19] is interrupted by interventions from the crowd and 'the Jews'. This happens at 6:28, 6:30–1, 6:41–2, and 6:52. Instead of letting these interventions structure the speech, however, it is better to consider the themes treated by Jesus in his replies to the interventions. We will see that this leads to a division at 6:46, where 6:47 and 48 rather return to and take up from 6:33 and 35 the themes of having eternal life if one believes in Jesus, who is 'the bread of life'. With this return, the text is ready to move into a detailed discussion of the sense in which Jesus is the bread of life, thereby spelling out the meaning of 6:35 (and through that back to 6:27).

This division accords in a broad way with the view in much twentieth-century scholarship that what follows somewhere after 6:46 is a redactional addition to an earlier form of the speech.[20] Brown, in particular

---

[18] The quoted words are left out in a few manuscripts of less than the highest quality. One wonders why. According to the usual text critical criteria, they must be deemed genuine.

[19] For the structure of John 6 see, in particular, Beutler 1991. I am not persuaded by his wish to see Jesus' speech as beginning at 6:22, or his finding a concentric circle between the following sections: (A) 1–15, (B) 16–21, (C) 22–7, (D) 28–9, (E) 30–3, (E') 34–40, (D') 41–51, (C') 52–9, (B') 60–5, (A') 66–71. But he is right to place emphasis on vv. 27 and 35 as providing 'ein starkes Indiz für die innere Kohärenz der vorliegenden Lebensbrotrede einschliesslich ihres sog. "eucharistischen" Teiles' (102).

[20] For this whole approach, with which he agrees, see the fine summary of the argument in Theobald 2009, 454–5. He notes that 'massgebliche Forscher des 20. Jh.s' like Bultmann, Brown, Becker, and Dietzfelbinger all agree that 6:51–8 does not belong to the 'ursprüngliche[n] Brotrede des Evangelisten' (454), but also recognizes that this view remains controversial. However, already in 1997 Culpepper (1997b, 253) had concluded as follows: 'One of the chief contributions of this collection of essays, therefore, is to reverse the long-held view that John 6:51c–8 is a later redactional insertion that jarringly introduces a eucharistic interpretation of the bread of life theme. The continuities of theme and language are much stronger than was previously assumed, meaning that these verses should now be read as an integral part of the discourse'. Similarly, Frey (2000a), who provides good references on the controversy, himself agrees with Beutler 1991: 'Der eucharistische Abschnitt dürfte daher keinem anderen Autor als dem johanneischen Evangelisten zuzuschreiben sein' (393).

(1966, 284–94), makes a strong, post-Bultmannian case for this claim, which otherwise appears to have its root in Bultmann's famous theory of an 'Ecclesiastical Redactor' who in 6:51–8 aimed to correct the earlier speech in order to make room for the Church's practice of the Eucharist (see Bultmann 1941, 161–2, 174–7). Brown found that the 'first discourse', 6:35–50, has 'primarily, but not exclusively, a sapiential theme', whereas the 'second discourse', 6:51–8, has 'a much clearer eucharistic reference than the rest of the chapter' (1966, 290–1). He also admitted, however, that 6:51–8 has 'many features in common with the rest of ch. vi, and indeed extremely close parallels in structure to 35–50' (291). In fact, he insisted against Bultmann (and quite rightly, 286, my emphasis) that:

an insuperable objection to Bultmann's theory is the evidence of secondary [?!], eucharistic undertones in the multiplication, the transitional verses (22–24), the introduction to the discourse, and the body of the discourse (35–50). *This chapter would be eucharistic if 51–58 were not part of it*; and if 51–58 are a later addition, they were added not to introduce a eucharistic theme but to bring out more clearly the eucharistic elements that were already there.

Brown's solution lies in the observation that 'the juxtaposition of the sapiential and the sacramental themes is as old as Christianity itself' (290).

Against all this, my own line will be to show, not only that 6:47ff cannot in any way be dislodged from the speech as a whole, but also exactly why that is so. Indeed, the last part of the speech spells out and explains exactly what is meant by the two verses that come quite early in the whole speech, 6:27 and 6:35:

[27]Do not work at the food that perishes, but the food that endures for eternal life, which the Son of Man will give you. For it is on him that his Father has set his seal, God (himself).... [35]Jesus said to them, 'I am the bread of life. Whoever comes to me will never be hungry, and whoever believes in me will never be thirsty' (NRSV).

Without 6:47ff, I claim, the precise meaning of 6:27 would be wholly unintelligible.[21] Let us now consider the first half of the speech, 6:26–46.

---

[21] In making 6:27 the key of the whole speech, I am fortunately in accord with Lincoln (2005, 223–5). Lincoln also accepts Peder Borgen's well-known midrashic reading of the whole text (Borgen 1965), which sees the quotation from Scripture in 6:31 as the key verse that triggers the whole discourse. Theobald insists against this that 6:35 constitutes the 'core word' (»*Kernwort*«) of the whole dialogue (2009, 454). We will see, however, that 6:27 and 6:35 almost come to the same thing. Theobald's intuition that one should not let form (a midrashic homily) overrule content (the argument and the way it proceeds) seems to me exactly right.

TYING THE KNOT (6:26–35)

John 6:26–9. At 6:26 Jesus explicitly takes up two motifs from earlier in the chapter: (a) 'You seek me'; (b) but 'not because you saw (any) signs', but because they merely ate their fill of the loaves. Thus their search for Jesus both misunderstands who he is and does not see the proper meaning of what he does. Then, in the crucial verse 6:27, Jesus explicitly tells them what they should do instead: work at food that endures for eternal life. This is quite opaque as it stands. What does it mean to 'work at' some food? Does it mean 'work to obtain'? And what is meant by the food that 'endures for eternal life'? In what way will the Son of Man give this food to human beings, not least when this claim is justified by noting that God has set his 'seal' on him?[22] The last bit about the seal is perhaps not so difficult in itself. As commentators have seen, the seal here (*sphragis*) must refer to the *pneuma*. And we know, of course, exactly when God did 'put his seal' on Jesus: at his baptism.[23] But the rest of the verse calls for further explanation. Here, then, there is clearly a philosophical question: how may one 'work at' (*ergazesthai*) some kind of non-perishable food that endures for eternal life and which the Son of Man (on whom God has set his pneumatic seal) will give?

It is noteworthy that this question is also the one the crowd then asks of Jesus (6:28): 'What must we *do* (*poiein*) to work at (*ergazesthai*) God's works?'. The crowd has caught on to the term 'work at' in 6:27. And they correctly understand that it means both that they must themselves *do* something and also that what they are asked to do belongs among the 'works (*erga*) of God'. Their question then is *what* they must do under these rubrics. This comes very close to asking what the non-perishable food *is* of which Jesus has spoken and what one must do to 'work at' *that*. In effect, therefore, the crowd is itself asking what we have identified as the philosophical question of this text.[24]

---

[22] That the relative clause ('which the Son of Man will give you') refers to the 'food' and not to 'eternal life' is made explicit in Brown's and Theobald's translations (1966, 260; 2009, 451). Linguistically both are possible. But the two scholars seem right since it is the idea of the food to be worked at that is primarily in focus. In any case, the Son of Man will presumably give eternal life *through* that food.

[23] Theobald (2009, 456–7) is excellent on this. He even goes on (in a small section entitled 'The Holy Spirit as Food for Life') to connect this reading with 6:51–8, even though, as we know, he considers that section redactional. These are very good examples of Theobald's sensitivity to the deeper meaning of the text, even where it does not really fit his own overall reading.

[24] There may, however, also be an element of misunderstanding in the crowd's question. If the 'food' is the *pneuma*, as we will see (and as Theobald confidently took it), then it may be inappropriate to speak of 'working at' it. Correspondingly, as Jesus immediately goes on to say, the 'work of God' is that they '*believe in*' him whom God has sent. And this hardly requires much *work*. (What it does require is understanding—based, as we will see, on

Jesus' reply does provide an answer of some kind (6:29). There is apparently only one 'work of God': that they 'believe in (*pisteuein eis*) the one whom he (God) has sent'. Is this then the full answer to the philosophical question we have raised? Here we come across the well-known problem of how to understand 'believe in' Jesus. Must one 'believe in' Jesus *as* 'the one whom God has sent'? And if so, exactly what does that mean? Or is some vaguer content of belief sufficient? We know already from 6:14–15 that believing Jesus to be the prophet who is to come into the world is not good enough. We may also recall from John 3 that believing him to 'have come from God' in Nicodemus' sense (3:2) was not enough. By contrast, we know from 5:24 that there is a sense of 'believing in the one who has sent' Jesus that is precisely right. If 6:29 is meant to identify what was meant in 6:27, then believing in Jesus will have to include quite a lot, for instance, that he is the Son of Man, that God has put his seal upon him (perhaps even in the form of the *pneuma*), and the like. However, this is neither said nor directly implied in 6:29. Even if one takes it that people are required to believe in Jesus *as* one whom God has sent, it is not yet clear exactly how that may be identical with what they are required to do according to 6:27. Thus Jesus' claim in 6:29 precisely raises a *question* about the relationship between the two verses—because the requirement stated in 6:29 is underdeveloped when seen in relation to the much greater (but also superficially somewhat opaque) specificity of 6:27. We should conclude—and will see how this fits the rest of the chapter—that it is *unclear so far* how 'believing in him whom God has sent' (6:29) will actually fulfil the requirement stated in 6:27 of 'working at the food that the Son of Man will give'.[25]

John 6:30–5. At 6:30–1 the crowd again intervenes with a set of questions (6:30) and a challenge (6:31). Both show with exquisite irony that they have understood nothing. They first attempt to turn Jesus' talk of signs that they have seen but not understood (6:26) and his request that they should 'work at' something (6:27) against him: 'What sign will *you* then do in order that we may see it and believe you? What work will you do?' (6:30). This is in itself highly ironic since Jesus *has* just done a divine 'work' and *has* just made a sign, only they saw it without seeing it properly. To turn Jesus' request against himself, then, is doubly ironic. Next the crowd introduces a

---

reception of the *pneuma*.) So, the crowd may be misunderstanding Jesus' use of the term *ergazesthai* here.

[25] In a very personal reading of John 6 (Kysar 1997), Robert Kysar actually saw that the theme of 'believing in Jesus' is not just being taken for granted in the chapter, but precisely queried. Only, where Kysar saw the text to perform a 'demolition of any confidence in faith conceived as human decision' (179), which is a very post-ancient thought, I propose that the chapter aims to bring out as the proper reaction to Jesus a kind of 'believing in Jesus' that goes with possessing (or indeed, having been given and having literally ingested) the material *pneuma*, Christ himself.

reference to the eating of manna in the desert as an example of what they are asking Jesus to do now (6:31). But of course, that is also just what Jesus *has* been doing when he fed the 5,000. Thus the crowd's question and challenge only serve to underline their total lack of understanding.

However, they do more than that. For by quoting from Psalm 78 on the 'bread from heaven' that God gave them to eat, they also trigger Jesus' reply in 6:32–5, which moves the discourse forward in the direction of actually giving an answer to the philosophical question raised by 6:27.[26] Jesus first distinguishes between the manna given by Moses and the true 'bread from heaven' that his Father gives (6:32). This distinction is already similar to the distinction in 6:27 between food that is perishable and food that endures for eternal life. In both cases one may therefore ask, 'What, then, *is* that true bread from heaven?' This question is then answered in 6:33–5, though in a manner that does not yet make everything clear. Jesus first declares that 'the bread of God' is 'that which comes down from heaven and gives life to the world' (6:33). Here there is a double entendre in the 'that which'. As the crowd will hear Jesus, the 'that which' means 'the bread which' (in Greek: *ho artos ho katabainôn ktl.*). For the crowd immediately asks: 'Sir, give us this bread always' (6:34). A little later, however, when Jesus speaks of *himself* as having 'come down from heaven' (6:38, compare 6:41 and 42) it becomes clear that as intended by Jesus, the 'that which' in 6:33 meant 'the one who', that is, Jesus himself. This double meaning in 6:33 is then spelled out explicitly in 6:35 when Jesus declares that '*I* am the bread of life'. How does the crowd react to that? That comes out in their next intervention, 6:41–2, to which we will return: they do not understand a word!

Before we get there, however, we are given some further explanation by Jesus in 6:35 that should, in principle, begin to answer the philosophical question raised by 6:27. In fact, it only does so very gradually. And so, as I insist, while the latter half of 6:35 does point clearly forward to the later explication of the sense in which Jesus is 'the bread of life' (6:35a), and indeed, towards what the 'food' of 6:27 is, the full answer is not yet given. John 6:35b therefore primarily serves to raise further questions instead of providing the needed answer.[27] Once Jesus has declared that he himself is the bread of life, he adds: 'Whoever comes to me will never be hungry, and

---

[26] Note here how a formal analysis of the text in terms of a midrashic homily risks turning the reader's attention away from following the *argument* of the text.

[27] One scholar who has seen the progressive character of John's line of thought in the chapter is Francis Moloney (1997), who (drawing on Genette, Moloney 1997, 132) has introduced the notion of (a distinctly narrative) prolepsis into the analysis of the chapter. In particular, Moloney reads the reference to the remaining *klasmata* ('fragments') in 6:12–13 as pointing forward to 6:27, then to 6:32–3, then to 6:35, and finally to 6:51cff. He is quite right. Sadly, however, he does not take the full step intended by John of including also 6:62–3.

whoever believes in me will never be thirsty' (6:35b). This is striking in several ways. First, it speaks of 'coming to' Jesus and 'believing in' him as what appears to be synonyms. In fact, they are. Where 6:29 and 6:30 spoke of 'believing in', 6:36, 6:40, and 6:47 will do the same. But after 6:35 we also get 'coming to' in 6:37, 6:44, and 6:45. Clearly, when they are interwoven in this way, 6:35 does introduce the two expressions as synonyms. That only makes it all the more relevant to ask exactly what is meant by those two expressions. Secondly, the fact that Jesus now speaks (if only implicitly) not only of eating but also of drinking, certainly gives room for thought. When the crowd has just asked Jesus to *give* them (*dos hēmin*) 'that bread', namely, to eat, one cannot but be reminded of the similar request by the Samaritan woman (4:15) that Jesus may give her (*dos moi*) 'that water', namely, to drink. There we saw the 'living water' to be a pneumatic substance. In John 6, however, the reader has so far only been given fairly slight hints of what the bread (and the liquid, for 'drinking') might consist in, if indeed it consists in the *pneuma* that was hinted at already in 6:27.

Let us summarize briefly so far. We began with a question about the meaning of 6:27 on 'food for eternal life' etc. and the relationship between that verse and the request stated in 6:29 that the crowd must 'believe in the one whom God has sent'. We have now (6:32–5a) heard about Jesus himself as 'the bread of life' and been told that if one comes to and believes in him, one will never feel hungry or thirsty. What this section (6:32–5) does, then, is to repeat the two conceptual queries that were raised in 6:26–9. What should one do (*ergazesthai*) with the 'food' that leads to eternal life, according to 6:27? And what is the relationship between that 'doing' in 6:27, 'coming to' Jesus, and 'believing in' him in 6:35 (and 6:29)—and never being *hungry* or *thirsty*, according to 6:35? To put it another way, what 6:32–5 does in response to the misunderstanding displayed by the crowd's questions and challenge is to *begin* to give an answer to the two philosophical questions we articulated on the basis of 6:26–9, but an answer that also *develops* the conceptual *queries*. After all, what *does* it mean for somebody to say that he is 'the bread of life' and that whoever comes to and believes in him shall never be hungry or thirsty?

A FIRST ACCOUNT OF THE PROPER REACTION TO JESUS (6:36–46): BELIEVING IN JESUS

John 6:36–40. 6:36 begins with an *All* ('but', 'however') that is probably full of meaning. The line of thought appears to be this: '*However*, I already told you (presumably in 6:26) that you have both actually *seen* something (namely, the feeding sign) but nevertheless do *not believe* (in me); so, let me explain . . .' What he aims to explain in 6:37–40 is this: what they must do in order to obtain eternal life against the background of what God has done and does in order to bring them there.

This section, too, is extremely carefully constructed. (i) It speaks of human beings as 'coming to me' (6:37) and 'seeing' the 'Son', and 'believing in' him (6:40). These phrases, including the 'seeing', we should take as synonyms. They constitute what I will call Stage 2 in what comes out as being the 'will' (*thelêma*, see 6:38–9, 40) or plan of God for human salvation. (ii) But the section also focuses on how people may come to that second stage. Here the requirement is that God has 'given' the person to Jesus (6:37, 39)—call that Stage 1. The term 'stage' here is not meant in distinctly temporal terms, but rather logically. God gives (Stage 1) and *through* that gift the human being comes to and believes in Jesus (Stage 2). (iii) Then there is a third stage (Stage 3), which receives what are probably intended to be two connected descriptions. The first is that at this stage Jesus will not *reject, expel,* or *cast out* (*ekballein exô*, 6:37) the one who has come to him, nor will he *let him perish away from him* (*apolesai ex autou,* namely, from God, 6:39). Instead, and this is the second description, Jesus will raise him on the last day (6:39, 40). On this reading, what Jesus explains in 6:37–40 is that there is a line of three connected stages in God's plan for human salvation: (1) a person being given by God to Jesus, (2) the person coming to and believing in Jesus, (3) the person being raised by Jesus on the last day.

These three stages are already set out carefully in 6:37. In the rest of the section (6:38–40), Stage 3 is explicitly spelled out twice as being about resurrection on the last day. But this happens as part of an overall argument that provides an explanation (see *hoti,* 'because' at the beginning of 6:38) of what was stated in 6:37. The explanation runs like this. Jesus has descended from heaven not to do his own will, but the will of God, who has sent him (6:38). *And this is God's will . . .* , which is repeated at the beginning of both 6:39 and 6:40. Similarly, the content of God's will, namely (Stage 3), that Jesus will raise all that God has given him (6:39), or whoever sees the Son and believes in him (6:40), is expressed in almost identical terms at the end of both 6:39 and 6:40.

Thus 6:36–40 does two central things. It sketches three stages in the proper relationship with Jesus and explains that these stages are all an expression of God's will. Indeed, to bring them about was the whole point of God's sending of Jesus. *God* aimed to bring it about—by making human beings (Stage 1) 'come to', 'see', and 'believe in' Jesus (Stage 2)—that he, Jesus, might raise them on the last day instead of rejecting them and letting them perish away from God (Stage 3). And why did God do that? Because it was his will that they *should have* eternal life (6:40).

In this 'should have', is the 'have' (*hina . . . echêi,* 6:40b) to be understood as pertaining to the future or the present? Certainly *also* to the future since Jesus goes immediately (6:40c) on to say: 'and (= so that) I will [*anastêsô,* with a future tense] raise him up on the last day'. But does it also refer to the present? In answering this question now, we are getting a little ahead of ourselves since the text itself does not yet unequivocally suggest an answer. But the answer should be: Yes—and that is actually what the whole speech is all about. In other words, the sense that the text is attempting to bring out of (Stage 1) being given by God to Jesus (6:37 and 39) and (Stage 2) coming to Jesus (6:37), and seeing him and believing in him (6:40) is the one that *requires the presence of pneuma in the believer*. For it is only on that presupposition that it is possible to say that believers *already have* eternal life so that Jesus may without further ado raise them on the last day.

We are not yet quite there as the speech progresses, even though we can now see more clearly that both 6:27 and 6:35 appear to be about possessing the *pneuma*—which, as I am now suggesting, also underlies the whole of 6:36–40 with its talk of being given by God to Jesus and, not least, '*seeing*' Jesus in the *full* sense (compare and contrast 6:36 and 40), and believing in him, also in the full sense. *If* that is what is meant, then the sense in which God 'gives' a person to Jesus (Stage 1) will be a very simple and straight-forward one: God gives the person the *pneuma* (in baptism or the Eucharist). Similarly, since the *pneuma* gives access to full knowledge (in fact to God's and Jesus' *logos*), the sense in which a person *truly* 'sees' and 'believes in' Jesus will now be the one that contains a full understanding of who and what Jesus was and is. But as I said, this is getting ahead of ourselves.

If we go back to the stage to which the speech has itself progressed, it is at least clear that 6:36–40 must be understood as spelling out what was meant in 6:32–35 by the talk about Jesus as the bread of life that came down from heaven. Then it is particularly noteworthy that 6:36–40 speaks of all this in the language that is quite usual in the Fourth Gospel (for Stages 2 and 3), without ever bringing in the notions from 6:32–5 of 'bread', 'eating', 'drinking', and the like. Moreover, it generally (apart from the possible hint at the present tense in 6:40) speaks of a form of eternal life that lies distinctly in the future. It follows that while 6:37–40 does spell out the idea from 6:33 and 35 of Jesus' 'coming down from heaven', and also the idea from the same two verses that Jesus gives *life*, it does not really explain the talk in 6:32–35 of Jesus as *bread* nor the suggestion in 6:35b of eating and drinking. Clearly, there is a need for further explanation. The same is true, one might add, of the new idea that has been introduced in 6:37–40 concerning Stage 1: that God 'gives' a person to Jesus. How does he do that? And as we saw, the precise content of Stage 2—'coming to' Jesus and 'believing in' him—has not yet been fully explained.

John 6:41–6. This passage, which begins from having 'the Jews' (as they are now called) grumble about Jesus, is related to 6:32–5 and 6:37–40 in fascinatingly precise ways. 'The Jews' grumble about Jesus 'because he said, "I am the bread that came down from heaven"' (6:41, NRSV).

Actually, Jesus did not say this in so many words in 6:32–5, but it is a very precise combination of what he did say. Now 'the Jews' have apparently managed to understand the meaning of the double entendre in 6:33. In fact, however, they have understood nothing. For they go on to ask what he, the son of Joseph, means by saying that he has 'come down from heaven' (6:42)—and here with a reference back to 6:38, where Jesus did make that part of his claims in 6:33–5 wholly explicit. What 'the Jews' do is both to refer back to the *more* opaque section of 6:32–5 and also to the section 6:37–40 that has at least begun to spell out what might be meant in the earlier section. 'The Jews' understand neither claim.

Seen in this light, it is noteworthy that what Jesus goes on to do in 6:43–6 does *not* (yet) address and contribute to clarifying the more opaque section of the two (6:32–5). Instead, it repeats and expands on the message of 6:37–40. This is remarkable since it means that *by 6:46 the meaning of 6:35 (back to 6:27) that has hitherto not been made explicit* (but may well be presupposed in 6:36–40, and in 6:41–6, too) *has not yet been stated.* So, perhaps that will happen later in the text?

John 6:41–6 repeats 6:37–40 in a very precise manner. John 6:44 describes exactly the three stages we found in 6:37 and again in 6:38–40:

⁴⁴No one can come to me [Stage 2] unless drawn by the Father [Stage 1] who sent me; and I will raise that person up on the last day [Stage 3] (NRSV).

In 6:45–6, however, the text goes on to explain a bit more about Stage 1, the 'drawing'. As Jesus says, it is a matter of being 'taught by God', of having 'heard' and 'learned' from him (6:45). But how? *Not* from having *seen* God, for only 'the one who is from God' has seen him (6:46). This obviously refers to Jesus himself, who literally *is* from God. Instead, one must be *taught* by God, must *hear* and *learn* from him: how?

With this question, the reader may feel at her wit's end. Not only has a new question come up: it is also the case that by 6:46 the reader will *not* have become able to answer the philosophical questions we articulated with regard to 6:26–9 and 6:32–5. What is meant in 6:27 by 'working at the food that endures for eternal life' and exactly how does 'believing in' Jesus (6:29) relate to that earlier idea? Or again, if Jesus is 'the bread of life' in the sense of a person who has come down from heaven and gives life to the world (6:33, 35a), as this has been spelled out by Jesus in 6:37–40 in what one might well call 'sapiential' or cognitive terms, then how is that to be understood in relation to the claim of 6:35b that there is some actual eating involved in the matter (so as never to be hungry) and some actual drinking (so as never to be thirsty)? The point here is a threefold one. First, the passages that speak of 'food', 'bread', never being 'hungry', and never being 'thirsty' are those that relate directly to the miracle story from which the whole speech springs. Secondly, in 6:29 and 6:36–46 the text basically speaks in sapiential or cognitive terms about believing, but how is this vocabulary to be related to the passages that speak of eating? Thirdly, at the end of the part of the speech we have considered so far, the meaning of those references to eating and drinking has not been given in any precise way. So, what is the point of the whole text? It is about 'food', 'bread', never being 'hungry', and never being 'thirsty'. But what all this means has not been explained. But that explanation is precisely given in the rest of Jesus' speech (6:47–58).

THE SECOND STEP IN THE PROPER REACTION TO JESUS (6:47–58): EATING THE BREAD OF LIFE

John 6:47 begins with Jesus' emphatic statement: 'Truly, truly...'. It is likely, therefore, that this verse introduces the rest of the speech. What is particularly noteworthy, then, is that this verse no longer speaks of *obtaining* eternal life in the future by being resurrected on the last day, but of *having* it: 'Very truly, I tell you, whoever believes has eternal life' (NRSV). Here, then, the text explicitly adopts the understanding that we postulated for 'in order that he may have' (*hina... echêi*) in 6:40, too. Is the idea then that simply by believing (in Jesus, obviously, but understood in what way?) a person already has eternal life? That is the truly pious, but I believe hugely oversimplified understanding that has attracted so many readers that C. H. Dodd eventually baptized it 'realized eschatology'. We will see, however, that if there is any connection between 6:47 and what follows, the answer must be no. Something more is required, which will then fill in the content of 'believing' as employed here. The question raised by 6:47, then, is exactly the one we raised in our philosophical question concerning the relationship between 6:29 ('believing in the one whom God has sent') and 6:27 ('working at the bread that endures for eternal life').

With 6:48–9 Jesus explicitly takes up 6:31–5. 'I am the bread of life' (6:48) quotes 6:35, and the statement in 6:49 about 'Your ancestors' who ate the manna in the wilderness continues 6:31. In formal terms, this return to 6:31–5 suggests that the speaker now intends to say something *more* about those earlier passages. And this is confirmed by the specific point of 6:49: *in spite of* having eaten the manna, they *died*. By contrast, the bread that *Jesus* brings will *prevent* them from dying (6:50). In other words, 6:48–9 clearly suggests that the reader may now expect to learn more about the issues left hanging in 6:35.

John 6:50 is rarely understood entirely correctly. In the NRSV it runs as follows: 'This is the bread that comes down from heaven, so that one may eat of it and not die'. What does 'this' (the Greek *houtos*, which is very emphatic) refer to here? No answer seems possible if one reads the verse in the way NRSV does, entirely independently (grammatically, that is) from its surroundings. If, however, we place a colon at the end of the verse instead of the traditional full stop, the grammar becomes immediately clear. '*This* is the bread etc.: I am the living bread etc.' (6:50–1). Note also on this reading the nice correspondence between the two different forms of the same Greek verb in the two verses: 'This is the bread that *comes down* (*katabainôn*) from heaven etc.' (6:50); and then 'I am the living bread that *has come* (*katabas*) down from heaven etc.' (6:51). Where 6:50 gives a form of generalized talk of the bread of life, 6:51 refers specifically to Jesus: 'I' plus '*has* come'.

What happens, then, in the rest of 6:51 is that the idea from 6:50 of 'a' bread of life that is coming down from heaven so that people may *eat* (*phagein*) from it is spelled out in excruciating detail: 'Whoever eats (*phagein*) from this bread will live forever; and the bread that I will give is my flesh (given) for the life of the world'.[28] In short—this is the unavoidable conclusion—in order to have eternal life, one must *eat 'the bread of life'* = *Jesus* = *Jesus' flesh*. Note also that the verse refers back precisely to the two earlier passages in the speech that have not yet been elucidated. When Jesus says in 6:51 that he 'will give' the bread which is his flesh, he takes up his claim in 6:27 that the Son of Man 'will give' the 'food' that leads to eternal life. And when he says that he will give the bread which is his flesh 'for the life of the world', he is taking up his claim in 6:33 that God's bread is the one (namely, person) who comes down from heaven and 'gives life to the world'. By the end of 6:51, then, Jesus has managed to repeat the opaque idea introduced in 6:27 and kept alive in 6:32–5. But he has also given it a wholly concrete twist: it is a matter of eating his flesh. It is difficult to find stronger support for the conclusion we must draw: that 6:51 as a whole (that is, as including the claim that Jesus' bread is his flesh) is intended, not only to take up again ideas from 6:27–35, but also to *answer* what was left unclear there.

That answer, however, is developed through yet another confrontation with 'the Jews', who react with a heated dispute among themselves (6:52a). They ask a question (6:52b) which is wholly to the point—indeed, it is *the* philosophical question that underlies the whole of Jesus' speech: 'How can this man (again *houtos*!) give us his flesh to eat?' (6:52b). But in saying that this is the philosophical question, we should also add that as stated by 'the Jews' it expresses baffled misunderstanding, whereas to the reader of John's text it points to the deepest and truest understanding.

---

[28] Theobald (2009, 475) takes his 'Eucharistic insertion' to *begin* at 'and the bread etc.' in this verse. But that leaves the explicit mention of *eating* (*phagein*) the bread in the preceding sentence (and 6:50) wholly unexplained.

The question of 'the Jews' only gives Jesus a clue to persist even more emphatically (6:53–8, NRSV apart from 6:57–8):

[53]Very truly, I tell you, unless you eat the flesh of the Son of Man and drink his blood, you have no life in you. [54]Those who eat my flesh and drink my blood have eternal life, and I will raise them up on the last day; [55]for my flesh is true food and my blood is true drink.

[56]Those who eat my flesh and drink my blood abide in me, and I in them. [57]Just as the living Father has sent me, and I live because of the Father, so too whoever eats me, he too will live because of me. [58]This is the bread that has come down from heaven—not in the way your ancestors ate, but (nevertheless) died: the one who eats *this* bread will live forever.[29]

This is utterly magnificent. With extreme precision it identifies a number of crucial ideas. (i) The point is repeated from 6:27 that the whole thing is about eating the flesh of the Son of Man. That in itself points in the direction of understanding the 'flesh' as more than merely ordinary human flesh (see later on this). Still, it must (also) be and remain just that: human flesh. (ii) We now hear explicitly (6:53, 54, 56) that the whole thing is not just about eating but also about drinking. This takes up the talk in 6:35 of neither being hungry nor thirsty. (iii) We hear that it is a matter of having life 'in oneself' (6:53). Apparently, something ('the flesh and blood of the Son of Man') has to be consumed in such a manner that it will *enter the bodies* of those who eat and drink it. This idea is continued in 6:56, which very emphatically speaks of the result of the eating and drinking as being that eaters and drinkers remain 'in' Jesus and Jesus 'in' them. (iv) We hear that the result of the eating and drinking is a matter of '*having (echein)* life' in oneself (6:53). This fits 6:47, and the idea is clearly that by eating the flesh of the Son of Man and drinking his blood a person comes *already* to possess eternal life. Some readers will no doubt be reminded here of the modern idea of 'realized eschatology' that I am combatting. But 6:54 shows that that is precisely *not* the idea that is in play. For this verse speaks of both *having* eternal life and *also* being resurrected in the future on the last day as two things that are connected, but certainly not identical: one *leads to* the other. We may bring out this idea by speaking, not of 'realized eschatology', but of 'proleptic eschatology'. People who eat and drink in the required manner already *have* eternal life in the proleptic sense that they (already) *have* something in the present—that will then also lead to resurrection and eternal life in the future. (v) John 6:54 introduces a graphic synonym for 'eating' (*phagein*) when it speaks of 'munching' (*trôgein*) Jesus' flesh. This is

---

[29] I read 6:58 grammatically in the same way as 6:50–1. *houtos* ('This') is the grammatical subject, which is then pointing forward to and taken up by *touton* ('*this* bread') towards the end of the verse. The colon in Nestle-Aland after *apethanon* ('died') is just right.

continued in 6:56, 57, and 58, and the point is clearly to challenge 'the Jews' (and the reader) as much as possible: is the man talking about cannibalism? (vi) John 6:55 clearly takes up 6:27 when it begins to speak, not here of 'bread' but of 'food' (*brôsis*)—which is then explicitly supplemented by 'drink' (*posis*). The claim that 'my flesh is true food' thus makes the reader understand that when 6:27 spoke of 'working at the food that endures for eternal life', it was in fact speaking of munching the Son of Man's flesh. (vii) John 6:57 speaks of how the 'living' God has sent Jesus, who also 'lives because of' God. We already know that God sent Jesus when he gave him his *pneuma*. It now appears that Jesus is said to 'live' for the very same reason, that is, *because of* what God did then. This contains a hint that life of the kind Jesus is talking about is connected with possession of the *pneuma*. (viii) John 6:58 clearly takes up 6:50–1 even to the extent of adopting the same elegant way of letting the Greek *houtos* ('this') point forward to something later in the verse. What has been added, however, is the point about 'munching' this bread, a point that is intended to challenge 'the Jews' even more.

What we have at the end of the discourse, then, is 'the Jews' in heated dispute among themselves (6:52) about the meaning of Jesus' claim in 6:48–51 that he will give the world his flesh to eat—and then Jesus giving the screw another drastic turn in 6:53–8. 'The Jews' do not understand a single word of what Jesus has been saying and what he goes on to say even more challengingly. At the same time, and precisely as part of their lack of understanding, they ask the crucial philosophical question: How on earth is this man able to give us his flesh to eat?

The reader of the present book will know the answer. What the Son of Man is able to give is his flesh, which he will 'give' at his death on the cross 'for the life of the world' (6:51), but now *as transformed by the pneuma (of his own resurrection to eternal life) into a pneumatic substance that will similarly give those who consume it and take it into their own bodies access to resurrection and eternal life*. That *this* is the proper answer to our philosophical question is clear from a number of factors. First, this is already implied (but no more than that) in the statement of 6:27 that God has put his (pneumatic) seal on the Son of Man. Secondly, it is implied by the clearly Eucharistic connotations of the talk of 'eating and drinking' in 6:35, 53, 54, and 56. And here we may surely be allowed to bring in a direct reference to the same idea from outside the Gospel: at 1 Cor. 12:13, Paul claims that 'in (or through) the one *pneuma* we have all been baptized into one body ... and we have all been given to *drink one pneuma*'. Where the former alludes to baptism, the latter must allude to the Eucharist. So Paul, for one, thought that the Eucharist took the form of an ingestion of *pneuma* into the bodies of believers. Thirdly, if this is what is meant in John, too, then one can understand why Jesus goes to such extremes in the direction of suggesting that he is talking of cannibalism. Cannibalism is precisely *the wrong* understanding, the one 'the Jews' seem to adopt only to reject it immediately. I repeat: it is *precisely* the wrong interpretation. But then, what *is* the true interpretation? What *is* the 'true' food and drink that 6:55 is talking about if it is *not—against* what that verse explicitly says—Jesus' *flesh*? Answer: the other side of Jesus, his *pneuma*, or better: his flesh *as transformed* into *pneuma* at his resurrection into eternal life.

Is the reader not convinced? In that case it is good that Jesus himself makes the point explicit in what immediately follows:

61 ...Does this scandalize you? 62Then what if you were to see the Son of Man ascending to where he was before? 63It is the *pneuma* that generates life (is *to zôiopoiun*); the flesh is of no avail.

This text makes it utterly clear that what will give life to believers is the *pneuma*, which will be involved in their own resurrection just as it is in the resurrection and ascension of the Son of Man into heaven. Moreover, we already know that this *pneuma* only became available to human beings once Jesus had himself died, been resurrected, and ascended into heaven.

That this is the precise connection between 6:61–3 and 6:51–8 has fortunately been seen by at least one scholar, Ludger Schenke (1997), who described the Evangelist's view as follows (1997, 214, my emphasis):

the divine Logos had become "flesh," had become "human" (1:14) *and had ascended back to heaven "as a bodily human being," though not in an earthly bodily form, but in a form changed by the pneuma (compare 20:19–29).*

A page later he added a footnote, from which I quote (215 n. 21, my emphasis):

Just as Jesus was not only "merely human," but Logos and "flesh" at the same time, so too the Eucharistic gift is not mere "flesh and blood," but the "flesh and blood of the Son of Man," *of the pneumatic Jesus, that is.* In fact the Johannine Christians too do not eat and drink human flesh and blood during their Eucharistic rites (as in the misunderstanding of the Jews in 6:52), but "bread" and "wine" [to be understood as pneumatic stuff].

COROLLARIES FOR BEING 'DRAWN TO' AND 'BELIEVING IN' JESUS

Suppose, then, that what Jesus is in fact talking about in 6:27, 6:32–5, and 6:47–58 is consuming the *pneuma* in the Eucharist, an event that will evidently only take place after Jesus' death. This will make people 'have' eternal life in the readers' present in a sense that is itself proleptic: by being in possession of the *pneuma* already then, they may be certain that they will eventually be resurrected into eternal life—and presumably once again by the *pneuma*. However, we still have not answered the question of the relationship between that story and Jesus' talk in 6:36–46 (as prefigured by 6:29) of people as 'coming to' and 'believing in' him. Are 'coming to' and 'believing in' Jesus the same as receiving the *pneuma* in the Eucharist? Or do they differ?

We may answer this question by going back to the three stages in the relationship of human beings to God's plan for salvation that we found in 6:36–46 of the speech. In particular, we may note that the stage of being drawn by God towards Jesus (Stage 1) is in fact quite directly connected with what comes out of it at Stage 3. Thus in 6:37 we had it that 'everything that God gives me [Stage 1] will come to me [Stage 2] and I will not cast out [Stage 3] the one who comes to me'. It is likely, therefore, that 'coming to' and 'believing in' Jesus at Stage 2 have a much fuller sense than merely consisting in a vague 'belief in' Jesus. And so it may well presuppose the presence of the *pneuma* through baptism and the Eucharist in those believers of whom Jesus is speaking in John 6. In fact, if one asks exactly how God may 'give' people to Jesus (by 6:37) or 'draw' them towards him (by 6:44), the only really precise and sharp answer will be that this is something God does by giving the *pneuma* to *them* just as he has previously given it to Jesus. *Then* they will 'come to' Jesus and 'believe in' him not just as a 'prophet', the 'Messiah', or the like, *but* as God the Father's only Son, who has come down and been sent into the world (when he himself received the *pneuma*), and has then been resurrected (by the same *pneuma*), and ascended and returned to the Father, where he was before (compare 6:62). And *then* the road will also be open for them to their own resurrection and entry into eternal life.

The Fourth Gospel is very concerned all through about two themes: who Jesus is and how human beings may relate to him. The two themes are closely connected since 'relating to' Jesus is fundamentally a matter of understanding (or not understanding) who he actually is. This interconnectedness of the two themes is what accounts for the many different descriptions given of Jesus throughout the Gospel, many of which are true enough so far as they go but precisely also deficient in that they do not go far enough. It is also what accounts for the many different types of reactions to Jesus. In both cases there is a line: from wholly deficient descriptions of who Jesus is, to the completely correct one towards which everything in the Gospel is pointing—and again from wholly inadequate reactions to Jesus, to the completely adequate one that answers to who Jesus genuinely is. In John 6 we see the interconnectedness of these two themes, but here with special emphasis on the fully adequate reaction to Jesus.

The argument of the chapter is intended to show that since Jesus *is* the Son of Man who will ascend to heaven in pneumatic form, therefore, in order to *grasp* that fact, human beings must relate to Jesus not just in accordance with any of the many deficient descriptions of him; instead, *they must themselves come to possess the pneuma*, and this happens both in baptism as we know (John 3)—*and also in the Eucharist* (John 6). Then they will at long last understand fully who Jesus is, and then they will also themselves eventually reach the goal of the whole set of events that have been staged by God (see 6:36–46): their own resurrection on the last day. So, the food at which they must work, according to 6:27, to gain eternal life is this: the *pneuma* as consumed in the Eucharist. By ingesting that, they will never be hungry or thirsty, according to 6:35.[30] And so they will certainly (but only eventually) obtain eternal life.

THE DARING OF THE EVANGELIST

If we stand back for a moment and consider the whole of Jesus' discourse (6:26–58), we may be struck by three points. The first is how exceedingly carefully the line of thought proceeds through the whole of this text. John begins by laying out pointers in 6:27, 6:32–5, and 6:35, in particular, to the explicitly Eucharistic material that will only come in much later. He also lays out a pointer in 6:29 to the cognitive level (of believing in Jesus and the like) that will then be taken up in 6:36–46. In 6:47–8 he recapitulates material from 6:31–5 in order to spell out what has previously only been pointed towards.

The second thing to be noted is the Evangelist's daring, both in counting on his readers to be able to follow the train of thought along such lines and also in expecting them to be able to discover along the way the true meaning of Jesus' outrageous claims about munching his flesh—before he spells it out to the dumb in 6:62–3.

A third thing to be noted is that the approach of asking philosophical questions and seeking answers to them along the way has been—I would say amply—vindicated by a text like this one. Apparently, this approach reflects a feature of the text itself: that it is *meant* to proceed from opacity to illumination, thereby hopefully leading its readers to the only thing that really matters: full understanding.

Note also that underlying this whole reading is the philosophical point that we also find in Stoicism: that the *pneuma* is a material entity that also has a cognitive side to it. That is why it is needed for a full grasp of who Jesus is. Returning now to the story itself, we will see that the centrality of

---

[30] I do not in the least apologize for this 'Eucharistic' reading of the whole of John 6. I am trying to read a text. How we may react to what comes out of the reading (e.g. here: eating/drinking the material *pneuma*) is not my concern here.

the issue of understanding and the role of the *pneuma* in the same regard are shown quite dramatically in the rest of the story.

ONLY A SMALL REMNANT UNDERSTANDS THAT JESUS HAS WORDS OF ETERNAL LIFE (6:59–71)

The reaction to Jesus' strange claim about how human beings may obtain eternal life is radical. 'Many of his disciples' (6:60) react in exactly the same way as 'the Jews'. They declare Jesus' speech (*logos*) to be tough, ask (a bit like 'the Jews' in 6:52) whether anybody can accept it and end up 'grumbling' about it (6:61). This only leads Jesus to scandalize them even more by referring to his own future ascension into heaven (6:62–3a)—but in fact also, as we have just seen, to explain the meaning of what had scandalized them in the first place:

> ⁶²Then what if you were to see the Son of Man ascending to where he was before? ⁶³It is the *pneuma* that generates life (is *to zōiopoiun*); the flesh is of no avail.[31]

To this Jesus adds that the 'words' (*rhēmata*) he has spoken to them 'are *pneuma* and life' (6:63b), but also that he is well aware that there are those among them who do not 'believe' (6:64), including, as Jesus knew from the very beginning, 'the one that would betray him'. This is only confirmation of his earlier claim that 'no one can come to me unless it is granted by the Father' (6:65)—Stages 1 and 2 mentioned earlier. The consequence is immediate: 'Because of this many of his disciples turned back and no longer went about with him' (6:66, NRSV).

What this is all about becomes clear in the last few verses (6:67–71) when Jesus asks the remaining twelve disciples, that is, the nucleus of the movement, whether they, too, wish to defect. No, Peter declares on their behalf (6:68–9):

> ⁶⁸ '...You have words of eternal life, ⁶⁹and we have come to believe and to know that you are the Holy One of God'.

---

[31] Borgen (1997, 110 n. 44) found it 'difficult to define the exact meaning of John 6:62 because it has the protasis, but lacks the apodosis'. But Menken (1997, 202–3) got it exactly right: 'Jesus answers their offence with the anacoluthon: "Then what if you see the Son of Man ascend to where he was before?" ... Jesus' saying in v. 62 indicates the moment at which his preceding discourse will be verified, so that the suppressed words of the anacoluthon should be something like: "Will you then accept my words?"'. Moloney's honest perplexity about the content here (1997, 166–7, my emphasis) points forward precisely to the role of the material *pneuma* in the Eucharist: 'He [Jesus] claims that the "spirit gives life; the flesh is useless" and that his words are spirit (v. 63). *What can this mean in the light of what has just been said about the importance of eating his own flesh?* The shift to spirit suggests that the previous speech is not to be taken literally [No!]; but that leaves unresolved what sense it makes if one looks for the "spirit" in it.'

So, is the sense that at the end of a very long and taxing day, on which Jesus had been left by 'many of his disciples' (6:66), he at least had eleven followers (since Judas is explicitly excluded from the group in 6:64 and 70–1) who believed and knew completely who he was? That would be comforting to know. But if so, we also have a problem. For we have claimed that full knowledge of Jesus presupposes the presence of *pneuma* in the believer. And the *pneuma* only became available after Jesus' death.

However, what we have in Peter may be something else: the furthest one may go in one's relationship with Jesus *before* one has come into possession of the *pneuma* and has grasped what can only be grasped through its means. It is true that Peter declares that the disciples 'have come to' believe and 'have come to' know that Jesus is 'the Holy One of God'. Here the 'have come to' indicates that their belief and knowledge are settled: they firmly believe and know.[32] Furthermore, in view of the way John elsewhere speaks of 'holy' and its cognates,[33] the unusual title that Peter gives to Jesus is probably meant to suggest that Jesus possesses divine *pneuma*, which is, of course, one constitutive element in who Jesus *really* is. So, has Peter not got it right, even without himself being in possession of the *pneuma*?

But there are also considerations on the other side.

(i) Peter can, as it were, hear that Jesus' words are 'words of eternal life', thereby recalling what Jesus has himself just said in 6:63 but *precisely* without referring to the *pneuma*, which Jesus did mention. Is this not a way of marking almost explicitly that Peter has not grasped it all?

(ii) Correspondingly, there is no indication that Peter already understands what Jesus has explicitly told them in 6:62: that they will see the Son of Man ascending to the place where he was before. In fact, the Farewell Discourse precisely insists that this is the part of the whole story that the disciples were completely unable to grasp until it had actually happened.

(iii) Along the same line, Dodd (1953a, 392) refers to 16:30 as a brief confession by the disciples that 'may be regarded as a kind of doublet of Peter's confession' here at 6:68–9. But that reference actually casts grave doubts on 6:68–9, as we already know. At 16:29–30 the disciples happily exclaim: Now you speak plainly; now we know and believe 'that you have gone out from God' (16:30). But that is only the first half of what Jesus has just said himself in 16:28: 'I have gone out from my Father and have come into the world. *I again leave the world and go back to my Father*'. And in

---

[32] Compare the discussion (with references) in Frey 1998, 103–4. Frey rightly concludes that the perfect tense serves to express the '*Intensität* dieses Zustandes' (104, his emphasis).

[33] Compare 10:36: 'The one whom the Father has made holy (*hēgiasen*) and has sent into the world . . .', which we took in Chapter III to refer to Jesus' receiving the *pneuma*.

16:31–2 Jesus responds to the disciples' jubilation: [31]'...So, now you believe?! [32]See, the hour is coming, and indeed has come, when you will be scattered etc.' Clearly, whatever confessions the disciples may make should be taken with a considerable amount of salt.

(iv) This point seems strengthened by the fact that Jesus goes on to say in 6:70–1 that even though he has himself chosen the twelve, nevertheless (Greek *kai*) one of them (Judas) is a devil (who will betray him). This may not fall back only on Judas (or indeed on Jesus himself), but on all twelve disciples: no matter how much they agree with Peter's confession, they all still *risk* defecting (as Peter himself will famously do: 18:15–18 and 25–7), which means that their 'having come to believe and know' may still be somewhat defective.

(v) Then there is also this consideration. Peter's 'the Holy One of God' must clearly be related to the other titles for Jesus that are given throughout the Gospel. Then we can see that it is nearer the truth than, for instance, the titles given in John 1, but further from it than both the title given to Jesus by the Samaritan men in 4:42 and Thomas in 20:28. This difference can be easily explained. In John 20 the situation is after Jesus' death and resurrection when the *pneuma* has become generally available. In John 4 the description is given from a post-resurrection perspective. By contrast, in John 6, Peter's confession is so closely tied into the narrative of the feeding and its explanation by Jesus and the resulting defection among his followers in Kapernaum that it must be meant to be understood as a *direct part* of Jesus' Galilean sojourn: it is something that Peter might have said within the parameters of the story that happened *then*.

Seen in that light, it seems likely that the title given to Jesus by Peter should be understood along three lines: (a) It is one that is sufficiently high to explain why the twelve disciples continued to follow Jesus when everybody else had defected; (b) it is also one that has the *potential* to be filled with *true* knowledge of who Jesus was, once the group had been created (after Jesus' death and resurrection) for which the twelve disciples constituted the nucleus; (c) *but* it is also one that does *not yet* express the full truth about Jesus, which is why the risk of defection remained in place (as witnessed by Judas). 'The Holy One of God' seems to fulfil precisely these requirements, thereby fitting the narrative picture of Peter and the remaining disciples as the *remnant* when all others had defected—a remnant that then also pointed *forward* to the group of followers that would be created after Jesus' death and resurrection.

I conclude that we should understand Peter's identification of Jesus as 'the Holy One of God' as either going as far as one may go in the proper direction without actually hitting the mark—or else as hitting the mark, but without Peter's fully knowing it in the manner one may only know it after Jesus' death and resurrection.[34]

JOHN 5–6: THE SON EQUALS THE FATHER AND HIS PNEUMATIC BODY GIVES LIFE

John 5 and 6 complement one another in a number of ways. Here Jerusalem; there Gentile land. Here an almost ontological focus on Jesus alone—who he is and how he is related to God; there a much more epistemological focus on how human beings must relate to Jesus and how they may come to do so in the proper way. Here rejection by 'the Jews'; there rejection by the crowd, 'the Jews', even many of the disciples with only a small forward-looking group remaining that consists of the twelve original disciples. Taken together these different perspectives strongly suggest one thing: the idea of a movement *from* Jerusalem *to* the Gentiles. Jesus will be put to death among the Jews in Jerusalem, but he and Gentile believers will obtain eternal life through the *pneuma* that will only become generally available after Jesus' death. Where John 5 brings the confrontation with the Jews in Jerusalem to a first climax with their decision to have Jesus killed, John 6 points distinctly *beyond* Jesus' death to the new group that will emerge based on the original eleven remaining disciples. This group is constituted by reception of the *pneuma* in the Eucharist after Jesus' death, through which the purpose of the whole story of Jesus' coming and going will eventually be realized: eternal life for human beings. Thus we have Jesus' death in John 5 and his (6:62) and believers' resurrection to eternal life in John 6.

If the sequence of John 5–6 is understood in this way, it corresponds, as we already saw, to the sequence of John (2/)3–4, where John (2/)3 takes place in and near Jerusalem, but John 4 points distinctly beyond Jerusalem, into both Samaria and Galilee. In light of this correspondence and the fact that with the end of chapter 6 John also ends his whole account of Jesus' activities in Galilee, it is tempting to divide John 1–12, not as chapters 1, 2–4, and 5–12, but instead as chapters 1, 2–6, and 7–12. While John 2–4 constitute a single literary unit ('from Cana to Cana'), we may now supplement this section with John 5–6, which reiterate the pattern established in

---

[34] Contrast, for instance, Theobald's almost ecstatic celebration (2009, 495, his emphasis) of the 'erleuchteter Glaube, gesättigt durch Erfahrung, der sich in dem Bekenntnissatz ausspricht: »*Du bist der Heilige Gottes!*«'. Conversely, I am happy to note that Dietzfelbinger (2004, 186) finds the title 'the Holy One of God' 'etwas dürftig' and 'mager'. But his reasons are not so clear. Frey, who understands Peter's confession just as positively (see 2000, 373) as Martha's in 11:27 (see 2000, 412 and 436), does not relate it to Peter's defection in chapter 18, as predicted by Jesus himself (16:32).

chapters 2–3 and 4, but also add strongly to it. Jesus' relationship with Jerusalem is brought to a first climactic confrontation and his movement away from Jerusalem is extended even beyond Galilee.

Once the pattern established by John 2–3 and 4 has been developed in this manner, a new major section may then begin in 7:1 with an account of Jesus' stays in and around Jerusalem that will eventually lead to his passion. The focus on the passion is clearly introduced at the beginning of John 7, where we first hear that 'After this Jesus went about in Galilee. He did not wish to go about in Judea because the Jews were looking for an opportunity to kill him' (7:1, NRSV), and next (7:2–10) that he planned to stay away from Jerusalem during the festival of Tabernacles—but then ended up going after all, if only clandestinely to begin with. Whatever else this complicated first section of John 7 may mean, it certainly brings out that with Jesus going to Jerusalem *this* time, something new begins that will eventually lead to his death.

TWO TYPES OF BELIEF AND THE ROLE OF *PNEUMA* IN JOHN'S EPISTEMOLOGY OF FAITH (JOHN 7–8)

TWO SETS OF UNIFYING MOTIFS AND TWO THEMES IN JOHN 7–8

As we have understood the sequence of John (2)3–6, a new long section begins at 7:1, stretching up to the end of chapter 12. The overall theme is now the confrontation with 'the Jews' that leads directly into the passion story. A number of scholars have recognized that the first coherent unit in this long stretch is John 7–8, where Jesus brings the confrontation to a climax when he declares that 'the Jews' 'are from your father the devil' (8:44, NRSV).[1] But scholars also feel that the two chapters exhibit 'a collection of miscellaneous material', a series of confrontational dialogues that are 'often without clearly apparent connection' other than the confrontation itself (Dodd 1953a, 345).[2] If we wish to see the two chapters as a genuinely coherent unit we must therefore trace any connections between

---

[1] Dodd (1953a, 345–54), who had difficulty finding a single thread in the text, did connect the two chapters under the title 'Light and Life: Manifestation and Rejection'. Barrett (1978, 316) agreed that chapter 7 'must be read in close connection with chapter 8'. Brown (1966, xii, compare 202) collects an introduction and three 'scenes' (7:1–13; 14–36; 37–52; 8:12–59) under a single title: 'Jesus at Tabernacles'. Lincoln (2005, 241) agrees with this. In continental Europe the situation is different. Theobald (2009, 563) finds that the theme of Tabernacles is over in 7:52. He does recognize the close connection between chapter 8 and chapter 7 (2009, 562–3), but also argues (563) that a 'new sequence of scenes' begins at 8:12. Thyen (2015, 420) agrees but his structuring of 8:12–12:50 as a whole is very complicated (IX, 417–19)—and unconvincing to me. Zumstein (2016, 321) sees 'die thematischen und argumentativen Verbindungen zwischen Kapitel 8 und Kapitel 7' but also 'einige Unterschiede'.

[2] See also Lincoln (2005, 241): 'The sequence of argument in chapters 7 and 8 can appear rather disjointed. This may well be because the evangelist has brought together from his tradition smaller units relating various aspects of disputes with Jesus.' He does recognize, however, 'the sense of mounting conflict which they convey' (241).

their individual parts. My claim here will be that there is much more coherence at the thematic level than is usually acknowledged. If so, this will be one more example that theme trumps other relevant narrative categories such as time, place, and agency.

We may note two striking thematic 'motifs' that point towards two overarching themes.[3] The first motif is one of concealment and public appearance. At the beginning of John 7 there is an extended treatment of this motif. Jesus has decided to stay in Galilee 'because the Jews were looking for an opportunity to kill him' (7:1, NRSV). However, when the festival of Tabernacles was near, his brothers urged him to go up to Jerusalem to show his works to his disciples there (7:3); 'for no one who wants to be widely known (*en parrêsiai*) acts in secret (*en kryptôi*). If you do these things, show (*phanerôson*) yourself to the world' (7:4, NRSV). Jesus at first declines (7:6–9). But when his brothers had left, 'then he also went, not publicly (*phanerôs*) but as it were in secret (*en kryptôi*)' (7:10, NRSV). But of course Jesus cannot remain in secret: 'About the middle of the festival Jesus went up into the temple and began to teach' (7:14, NRSV), and here the people of Jerusalem recognize this: '"Is not this the man whom they are trying to kill? And here he is, speaking openly (*parrêsiai*)..."' (7:25–6, NRSV). Why all this play on secrecy and publicity? Jesus himself gives the answer: his time has not yet come (7:6–9). Why, then, did he go up to Jerusalem at all? Only one answer seems possible: in order to bring the confrontation with 'the Jews' to a climax in full publicity. Thus this narrative motif points in the direction of an overarching theme in the two chapters, which is that of Jesus' confrontation of 'the Jews' and their mounting opposition to him.[4]

Seen in that light, it is noteworthy that once this theme has been brought to a shattering climax at the end of John 8, Jesus again fades into secrecy: 'So they picked up stones to throw at him, but Jesus hid himself (*ekrybê*) and went out of the temple' (8:59, NRSV). From secrecy (*en kryptôi*) to full publicity (*en parrêsiai*) at the beginning of John 7 and back again into hiding (*ekrybê*) at the end of John 8: this kind of inclusion is a characteristically Johannine way of creating a thematic unit through the use of particular narrative motifs.[5] What it emphasizes is the overarching theme in the two chapters of confrontation with 'the Jews', a theme that is also marked at the beginning (7:1) by a reference to their decision to have Jesus

---

[3] On narrative 'motifs' and 'themes', see Resseguie 2005, 45–6 and 46–8, respectively.

[4] Note that it is repeatedly Jesus who challenges 'the Jews', e.g. in 7:19, 8:21, 24, and 32.

[5] Brown saw this (1966, 342): '...there is a certain unity between vii and viii...since vii begins with the theme of Jesus going up to the feast of Tabernacles in secret (*en kryptō*: vii 10) and viii ends with the theme of Jesus' hiding himself (*kryptein*).'

killed and at the end (8:59) when they try to stone him—but unsuccessfully since his time had not yet come.[6] That, then, is *theme one*.

The other thematic motif that creates unity at the narrative level is the repeated claim by Jesus' opponents that he 'has a demon'. At the beginning of his public appearance Jesus asks (7:19–20, NRSV):

[19]'Why are you looking for an opportunity to kill me?' [20]The crowd answered, 'You have a demon! Who is trying to kill you?'

This motif is taken up again at the very end (8:48–9 and 52):

[48]The Jews answered him, 'Are we not right in saying that you are a Samaritan and have a demon?' [49]Jesus answered, 'I do not have a demon; . . . [52]The Jews said to him, 'Now we know that you have a demon. . . . '

Scholars have seen the recurrence of this charge, but they have never asked what the overarching theme is that is marked by this use of the same motif and how it serves to keep the two chapters together as a single unit. We will see that the charge of being possessed by a demon—and correspondingly, of having the devil as one's father—forms part of the answer to a philosophical question that is raised by what is the second overarching theme of the two chapters. That theme—*theme two*—is that throughout the two chapters Jesus' claims are repeatedly met with a divided reaction. Some come to believe in him, others by contrast become more and more enraged. The first articulation of this theme is highly characteristic since it brings together many of its aspects (7:30–2, NRSV):

[30]Then they tried to arrest him, but no one laid hands on him, because his hour had not yet come. [31]Yet many in the crowd believed in him and were saying, 'When the Messiah comes, will he do more signs than this man has done?' [32]The Pharisees heard the crowd mutter such things about him, and the chief priests and Pharisees sent temple police to arrest him.

Here we first meet theme one: the gradually mounting confrontation that is not put into effect since Jesus' hour has not yet come. But we also hear of a divided reception of Jesus (theme two). In the present text, the 'chief priests' and the 'Pharisees' are on the side of the opposition and the crowd is more positive towards Jesus. However, there also is division within the crowd, as is shown by the relationship between verses 7:30 and 7:31. For the people described in 7:30 also belong to the crowd. Note also how the vacillation of the crowd is described in 7:25–9 that leads up to 7:30. At first they are positively struck by Jesus' daring in speaking out in public (7:25–6) and

---

[6] One might even ask whether this way of framing the whole sequence is not also a friendly sign to the reader that John is operating even more freely in this text than elsewhere (read: *inventing* it)?

continue: 'Can it be that the authorities really know that this is the Messiah?' (7:26, NRSV). But then they retrace their steps: 'Yet we know where this man is from; but when the Messiah comes, no one will know where he is from' (7:27, NRSV). So they end up being sceptical. And when Jesus then challenges them with the claim that they do not know where he is *really* from (7:28–9), they react as described in 7:30. *However, many of the crowd came to believe in him* (7:31).

The theme of the divided reception of Jesus comes up again in 7:40–4. Some people in the crowd reacted favourably: '"This is really the prophet"' (7:40). Others said: '"This is the Messiah"' (7:41). But yet others denied that the Messiah might come from Galilee (7:41–2). And then John has hit upon the term that best describes the situation: *schisma oun egeneto* ('So there was *a division* in the crowd because of him', 7:43, NRSV). And again the ritornelle, 'Some of them wanted to arrest him, but no one laid hands on him' (7:44, NRSV).

We may note that the motif of Jesus' escaping from the murderous designs of 'the Jews' is repeated in John 8, too, both at 8:20 and at the very end, in 8:59. Even more noteworthy is the inflection given in John 8 to the theme of the division among 'the Jews'. The theme comes up only once, at 8:30, and in a manner that has raised problems for scholars. Where, they ask, does the change occur that may account for the difference between 8:30 ('As he was saying these things, many came to believe in him') and 8:37 ('…you seek to kill me…')?[7] Let us consider what is said between 8:30 and 8:37.

Once Jesus has made one more of his major claims about himself in 8:21–9, the response is that 'many came to believe in him' (8:30). However, Jesus also immediately addresses 'the Jews who had come to believe in him' (8:31) in a manner that gradually alienates them completely. He first states that it is only if they 'remain in my *logos*' that they will be 'truly my disciples' (8:31). This is different from merely 'believing in him',[8] and Jesus' further claim that they need to be 'made free' (8:32) alienates them completely (8:33, NRSV):

[33] …'We are descendants of Abraham and have never been slaves to anyone. What do you mean by saying, "You will be made free"?'

---

[7] Compare Brown 1966, 354–5. Barrett (1978, 344) and Lincoln (2005, 269) half-see that John may be wishing to expose the 'grave deficiencies' (Lincoln) in the belief of the 'Jews' addressed by Jesus. Theobald (2009, 589) thinks that 'es bleibt das Problem, wie Menschen, die Jesus einmal geglaubt haben, dann aber von ihm abgefallen sind, ihm sogleich nach dem Leben trachten können'. But he has a fine sense that it is Jesus himself who in 8:37 ascribes to them the wish to kill him.

[8] Barrett (1978, 344) correctly senses this: 'Merely to place credence in Jesus' words is not enough; men must abide in his word'. But there is much more to it than that, as we will see (and partly already know).

Jesus' answer as given in 8:34–6 is full of central ideas. They *are* slaves, namely of sin (8:34). This will lead them into death (8:35). But 'the son/Son' may make them free (8:36), namely, of sin and death.[9] And so Jesus may conclude this first round by saying (8:37): 'I know that you are descendants of Abraham; yet you look for an opportunity to kill me, *because there is no place in you for my logos*' (NRSV, except for 'logos' instead of 'word'—and of course my emphasis). Here the italicized words refer directly back to Jesus' claim in 8:31 that they must 'remain in my *logos*'. This shows that there is no inconsistency or change at all between 8:30 and what follows. The 'many' in 8:30 did come to 'believe in him'; *only* that belief is in the end wholly insufficient: 'believing in Jesus' in the way of the many will not serve to keep them from trying to kill him. Why? That is what the text goes on to explain (more on this later).

We may conclude that John 7 and 8 are kept together by a number of connected motifs and themes. The first major theme of a mounting confrontation between Jesus and 'the Jews' is marked by the motif of Jesus' concealment and publicity at the beginning and end of the whole section and by the repeated ritornelle that 'the Jews' wanted to lay hold of Jesus, but were unable to do so. The second major theme of a divided response to Jesus is situated within the frame of a motif that is also rehearsed at the beginning and end of the whole section to the effect that Jesus 'has a demon'. While *all* 'the Jews'—whether the crowd or the Pharisees and the chief priests—are described as claiming that Jesus is 'demonized', there is nevertheless also a divided response, or *schism*, among them along the way: some do respond favourably to him, though in ways that are insufficient.

A PHILOSOPHICAL QUESTION: WHY A DIVIDED RESPONSE THAT NEVERTHELESS LEADS TO CONFRONTATION?

However, the attentive reader cannot stop here. How should one *explain* the fact that some of the Jews addressed by Jesus respond by coming to *pisteuein* in him—if only insufficiently—whereas others do not? It is not enough just to take the divisions that are mentioned as reported facts. John always has a further aim in describing the facts. Is he suggesting, then, that in spite of his rejection by the Jewish leaders, Jesus also had at least a potential following among ordinary Jews? But in that case, why does he let Jesus make his move in chapter 8 (from 8:30 onwards) of *challenging* precisely these potential followers into turning against him? Thus, the

[9] I write of 'the son/Son' here since 8:35 speaks of 'the son' in an ordinary household (*oikia*), whereas 8:36 transfers this to 'the Son' (Jesus himself).

repeated reference to a divided reception of Jesus makes little sense at the purely narrative level. Why, then, is it there?

This is where a philosophical reader may begin to ask questions. Could it be that John is less interested in the ostensive division among 'the Jews' than in understanding the *possibility* of such a division, not least the kind of 'believing in Jesus' that supposedly did occur among some Jews: *how* it came about in some and *why* it was *insufficient*, thereby risking to turn into the same type of rejection as found among the other Jews? Thus understood the repeated reference to divisions among 'the Jews' raises a question that is genuinely philosophical in character—in fact our philosophical question for these two chapters: how should one *explain* the fact that some of the Jews addressed by Jesus respond by coming to believe in him—if only insufficiently—whereas others do not? And *why* does that kind of believing remain insufficient?

We have already noted that the two major themes are interwoven with one another throughout the text. To see how the philosophical question is answered through the narration of the mounting confrontation which leads to the mutual charge of being 'demonized', we need to follow the text quite carefully by engaging in a slowly progressing, cumulative reading that the Fourth Gospel so often calls for.

THE INNER COHERENCE OF JOHN 7–8: THE FIRST WAVE (7:14–30)

In 7:14–30[10] 'the Jews' at first 'wonder' (*thaumazein*) at Jesus' teaching (7:15). Their reaction is neutral or just baffled and may go either in a negative or a positive direction. When Jesus then explains from where he has received his teaching (7:16–18) and challenges them with regard to their not doing the law of Moses (7:19), the crowd accuses him of being possessed by a 'demon or bad spirit' (*daimonion echeis*, 7:20).[11] Jesus

[10] Brown (1966, xii) sees 7:14–36 as 'Scene One' and 7:37–52 as 'Scene Two'. That might be defended by the fact that there is a change of time at 7:37. However, the fact that the Pharisees send out their servants in 7:32 and that these return in 7:45 seems to overrule the importance of the change of time. Thus 'Scene Two' may well begin at least with 7:32. Theobald (2009, 517–19) agrees with Brown, but finds a number of traditional problems in 7:14–36, which makes him (together with Bultmann, Schnackenburg, Becker, and Dietzfelbinger, see 517) produce a text that is quite different from the transmitted one. This is hard to follow. It destroys the *inclusio* of 7:20 and 8:48 and 52. Also, on a point of detail, note how 7:15–17 on the origin of Jesus' 'teaching' (*didachē*) directly continues 7:14: that Jesus went up to the temple *and taught* (*didaskein*).

[11] John 7:17–18 are very important in themselves as we will see later. John 7:19 on not doing the law is probably closely connected with the preceding two verses in the following way: 'the Jews' (says Jesus) do not do the law *since* they on their side (as opposed to Jesus himself) 'seek their own honour' instead of God's (7:18).

responds by explaining what is wrong in their understanding of the law as shown in their reaction to an earlier feat of his (the healing in John 5 of the man at the pool of Bethzatha; 7:21): if 'the Jews' allow 'a man' (*anthrôpos*) to be circumcised on the Sabbath (7:22–3) 'in order that the law of Moses may not be broken' (7:23, NRSV), then why are they angry with Jesus 'because I healed a man as a *whole* (*holos anthrôpos*) on a Sabbath' (7:23)? The result is now a reaction of initial wonder among 'some of the people of Jerusalem' (7:25), which, however, turns quite sceptical, as we saw (7:25–7). To this Jesus responds by making the first of his explicit claims in the two chapters that he has his origin in God, who has sent him (7:28–9). And then the reader for the first time gets the ritornelle that we noted: 'Then they tried to arrest him, but no one laid hands on him, because his hour had not yet come' (7:30, NRSV). We will see that this section contains *in nuce* much of what will be spelled out later in the two chapters. But the conflict between the two parties is only at its starting point:

– Jesus' interlocutors are a vague group of 'the Jews': 'the crowd' and 'some of the people of Jerusalem' who are distinctly said to be different from 'the authorities' (7:26).
– Their reaction is initially one of non-committal 'wonder' (7:15, again 7:21), which only gradually (7:25–7) develops into a rejection of Jesus (7:27) that only becomes quite firm right at the end (7:30).
– Conversely, while Jesus is reasonably clear in his claims about himself, it is only at the end (7:28–9) that he brings his divine origin entirely into the open.

THE INNER COHERENCE OF JOHN 7–8: THE SECOND WAVE (7:31–52)

John 7:31–52 begins by introducing for the first time the motif of a schism among the Jews. 'Many in the crowd believed in him' (7:31, NRSV), suggesting that he must be 'the Christ', but the Pharisees, who are now introduced for the first time, heard about this reaction in the crowd and together with the high priests sent their helpers to lay hold of Jesus (7:32). This both raises the stakes in Jesus' confrontation with 'the Jews' and sets the scene for the whole section, which ends with the helpers' return (7:45) and a discussion between the Pharisees and high priests and first the helpers themselves, then Nicodemus of how to understand Jesus (7:46–52). It is already clear that this constitutes an intensification of the initial mixed reaction described in 7:14–30:

– The opposing party is now explicitly divided into two, with 'many in the crowd' being on Jesus' side and the Pharisees and high priests opposing him.

– Moreover, even within the latter group, the helpers and Nicodemus turn out to be tentatively on Jesus' side; thus at the end of John 7 we have what I will call a triad: Jesus, his supporters among 'the Jews', and his enemies among them.

In the latter division we may note the helpers' claim that 'Never has a human being *spoken* like that' (7:46)—thus referring to Jesus' particularly impressive speech (*lalein*). And Nicodemus claims that before condemning Jesus on the basis of the law, one must 'first *hear* (*akouein*) from him and find out what he is up to' (7:51). Speaking and hearing: with respect to people's coming to believe in Jesus very much hangs on his speech and their hearing it.

In the midsection (7:33–44) we get three small passages (33–6, 37–9, 40–4) in which Jesus first tells of his upcoming departure to a place where 'the Jews' (7:35) cannot go (7:33–4), a claim that they completely misunderstand (7:35–6). Next he invites those who believe in him to come and drink from the *pneuma*, which those who 'had in fact come to believe in him' (*pisteusantes*) were only *about* to receive (*emellon lambanein*) 'since the *pneuma* was not yet present inasmuch as Jesus had not yet been glorified' (7:37–9).[12] Finally, we are told that some from the crowd 'who had heard those words' (of Jesus) took him to be a prophet (7:40), others to be the Christ (7:41), while yet others denied him to be the Christ (7:41–2). 'So there was a schism in the crowd because of him' (7:43, NRSV). And then the ritornelle: 'Some of them wanted to arrest him, but no one laid hands on him' (7:44, NRSV). Again we may note an intensification:

– Jesus now explicitly announces his departure (the readers know: to heaven), telling the baffled 'Jews' (unspecified) that they *cannot* go where he is going (7:34, also 36),
– Jesus also explicitly prophesies that those who have come to faith (note the aorist in the Greek) will *later* receive the *pneuma*; in light of 20:22, where the risen Jesus blows the *pneuma* into his disciples, this makes even clearer the overall direction of the story as leading towards Jesus' death and resurrection.
– Finally, the idea of a division among 'the Jews' that was implicit in the transition from the previous section into the present one (7:25–7, 30, 31) is spelled out explicitly (7:40–4) ending with the statement of a 'schism' in the crowd (7:43), which led *some* of them to try to kill him (7:44); this very

---

[12] Commentators rightly see a connection between the content of what Jesus says on this last day of the festival and the ritual events that took place on the same day (see, e.g. Theobald 2009, 536–7). Might *this* not be the explanation for the change of time at 7:36 which does *not* imply a change in the overall themes?

pointedly raises the question of why some reacted to Jesus in one way and others in another—our philosophical question.

We may conclude that the conflict between Jesus and 'the Jews' has now been greatly intensified. In particular, the theme of the division among 'the Jews' has been enhanced. 'Many in the crowd' were on Jesus' side (7:31), but the high priests and the Pharisees opposed him (7:32). In the crowd itself there is a division (7:40–4) as is the case among the high priests and the Pharisees (7:45–52). Conversely, the fact has been further emphasized that Jesus belongs in heaven, where he will eventually go, and that 'rivers of living water [= *pneuma*] will stream from his belly' (7:38), which believers will receive after his glorification (7:39). Clearly, the challenge that Jesus constitutes has been raised to a new level.[13]

THE INNER COHERENCE OF JOHN 7–8: THE THIRD WAVE (8:12–20)

John 8:12–20 should clearly follow directly upon 7:52.[14] After the interlude in 7:45–52 between the Pharisees, high priests, helpers, and Nicodemus, we are back with Jesus (8:12), who discusses directly with the Pharisees (8:12–19). Here we are presented with a number of claims on Jesus' part that clearly take up the presentation of the *logos* in the Prologue:[15] Jesus, so he claims, is 'the light of the *kosmos*' (8:12, compare 1:4–5, 9); the Pharisees impugn his 'witness' (8:13, compare 1:7–8); Jesus, however, insists upon it by bringing in the earlier motif of knowledge or the opposite of Jesus' origin and, not least, where he is going (8:14).

There is already some intensification here inasmuch as Jesus' implicit self-identification with the *logos* of the Prologue raises the stakes considerably. If Jesus is identical to the *logos* of the Prologue, then the question of how people will react to him must be a crucial one. Also, Jesus is now specifically addressing the Pharisees about both his origin and his goal. In

[13] It is interesting to note that the lack of understanding on the part of 'the Jews' about where Jesus is going is spelled out emphatically (7:36 in relation to 7:35) in exactly the same way as this happens in chapter 16 (16:16–19) in the case of his disciples. This fact—that Jesus is about to return to God—is what *nobody* understood during his lifetime.

[14] 'The *Pericope Adulterae*, vii. 53–viii. 11 in the Textus Receptus, is omitted as being no part of the original text of this Gospel' (Dodd 1953a, 346 n. I).

[15] This needs emphasis. For instance, for Jesus' claim (8:12) to be 'the light of the world', Barrett (1978, 335–7) has a long and illuminating discussion of the context for this idea in the Feast of Tabernacles, 'pagan religions', Judaism, and early Christianity. But the fact that Jesus is explicitly positioning himself (as he also does at the very end of the chapter: 8:58) within the cosmological framework presented in the Prologue scarcely receives mention. The same is true of Theobald's discussion of the verse (2009, 566–70), no matter how informative it is in other respects. Here Zumstein (2016, 324–6) is much better.

the conversation that follows (8:15–19), the contrast is again intensified by marking a radical distinction between the two interlocutors: when Jesus refers to the law of Moses as 'your law' (8:17) and then claims that his own witness is supported by God himself (8:18); and also when he speaks of God not only as 'the one who has sent me' but 'the one who has sent me, *the Father*' (8:16, 18). The use of the term 'father' is new here (in John 7–8) and it clearly adds to the sharp opposition between Jesus and his opponents. Here we may also note the first use of the phrase 'I am' or 'It is I' (*egô eimi*) in 8:18, which will become very important later in the chapter.[16] It is not yet used in the absolute form employed a few verses later (8:24). So here, too, we meet a gradual intensification. Still, the claim is strong enough:

[18]*I am* the one who bears witness for myself and (the one who) bears witness for me (is) the one who has sent me, the Father.

Note here how Jesus *almost* makes himself identical with the Father: the 'I am' at the beginning of the verse balances 'the Father' at the very end.

The reference to 'the Father' leads directly into the most direct confrontation we have had so far (8:19, NRSV):

[19]You know neither me nor my Father. If you knew me, you would know my Father also.

The Pharisees must have been affronted: do they not know God? However, we again get the ritornelle: 'but no one arrested him, because his hour had not yet come' (8:20, NRSV).

With this explicit confrontation with the Pharisees we are ready for the final confrontation, which follows in 8:21–59. The three sections of this passage are intimately connected. However, to see the cumulative force of the confrontation, we must consider them separately.

THE INNER COHERENCE OF JOHN 7–8: THE FOURTH WAVE (8:21–9)

The first section of 8:21–9 is introduced (8:21) as if Jesus was still in conversation with the Pharisees. However, it turns out that his interlocutors are now more generally 'the Jews' (8:22). There is an important point here since in the rest of John 8 the contrast from John 7 between the crowd and the Pharisees will disappear. Rather, Jesus is now said to be speaking to 'the Jews' quite generally (8:22, compare 31; 8:48, 52, 57). It is true that the

---

[16] Commentators often say (in an excursus) what needs to be said about John's use of this fascinating locution. See, e.g., Schnackenburg 1965–84, vol. 2 (3rd ed. 1980), 59–70 and Theobald 2009, 463–6. To these should be added Ball 1996.

old motif that 'many came to faith in him' is repeated once (8:30), but we saw that when Jesus goes on to speak to 'the Jews who had come to believe in him' (8:31), he quickly begins to treat them as if they belonged among the Jews who are hostile to him. The point should be clear. Whereas in John 7 we had a triad consisting of Jesus, Jews who had come to faith in him, and Jews who opposed him, in John 8 the triad has been reduced (but not quite, witness 8:30) to a dyad consisting only of Jesus and the opposing Jews. Thus we are now approaching the ultimate and final confrontation where there is only room for two opposing parties, Jesus and 'the Jews'. It remains the case, however, that the issue (our philosophical question) that has also been implicitly raised in John 7 when the text operated with two opposed groups of Jews—namely, why it is that some Jews come to believe in Jesus while others do not—this issue is *kept alive in John 8*. In fact, one may even say that 8:30 serves that very purpose.

Within 8:21–9 itself we note an intensification in the following respects:

- Jesus repeats the point about his going away to a place where the Jews cannot go, but he also very significantly adds that when that happens they on their side will 'die in your sin' (8:21), since they are 'from below' and 'from this *kosmos*' whereas he is 'from above' and 'not from this *kosmos*' (8:23); moreover, they 'will die in your sins' 'if you do not come to believe *that I am*' (8:24).[17]
- To their baffled question, 'Who, then, are you?' (8:25), Jesus answers: 'The one I have told you from the very beginning' (8:25), thereby presumably referring *explicitly* back (as against the more implicit backward reference in 8:12–20) to the beginning of the Gospel itself and its description of the 'light', the *logos*, and more.[18]
- Finally, Jesus intensifies his self-description in 8:28: 'when you have lifted up the Son of Man, *then* (*tote*) you will understand that "I am" and that I do nothing on my own (*ap' emautou*), but as the (or my) Father has taught me—those things I speak'; here the whole basic storyline of the Gospel (and God's plan for the salvation of human beings) is being referred to.

---

[17] It is worth speculating about the relationship between 'dying in your sin' (8:21) and 'dying in your sins' (8:24). The first probably refers to their not recognizing Jesus in the proper way. From this ultimate 'sin' then follow a host of more ordinary sins.

[18] The Greek of Jesus' answer here is a famous *crux interpretum*. Brown lets a thorough discussion (1966, 347–8) issue in the following translation: 'What I have been telling you from the beginning'. He thinks this is 'smoother than the Greek warrants' (347), but I believe he got it exactly right. The Greek τὴν ἀρχὴν probably means 'to begin with'. Is John not here having his Jesus refer directly back to John's own Prologue? Note also the Greek καὶ in the phrase: '(I am) from the very beginning what I have *in fact* been telling you'. Here 'from the very beginning' probably qualifies 'have been telling' (Greek λαλῶ). It is placed first to give it emphasis.

Jesus is the one who saves people from dying in their sins; he is from above and not from this *kosmos*; he is the one of whom he has told them from the very beginning; he is the Son of Man who is going to be both crucified and raised; and finally: I am. Can the stakes be made any higher than that? Not really. But they can be spelled out further so as to sharpen the confrontation with 'the Jews' even more. This happens in the last two waves.

THE INNER COHERENCE OF JOHN 7–8: THE FIFTH WAVE (8:30–47)

We know that 8:30–7 is framed around the movement from the initial statement that 'many came to believe in him' (8:30) to Jesus' claim that nevertheless 'you seek to kill me' (8:37). The reason why he can react to them in this way is that he has told them that '(only) if you remain in my *logos*, will you be truly my disciples' (8:31) and Jesus knows at the stage reached in 8:37 that 'my *logos* has no room in you'. We will return to the idea of having Jesus' *logos* in one (or conversely, of being in it).

In itself Jesus' claim that they seek to kill him is a challenge of 'the Jews'. The note of a challenge in 8:37 continues a series of challenges in 8:32–6. Only if they remain in Jesus' *logos* will they (in the future) 'learn the truth', which will then also 'free you' (8:32). So do they not already know the truth? And are they not already free? 'The Jews' choose to focus these objections on the figure of Abraham, who as the 'father of the Jews' will remain of central importance until the end of the chapter (8:33). But Jesus is undaunted: they *are* slaves, namely, to sin (8:34); but a slave has no permanent position in a household, only the (freeborn) son has this and cannot be dislodged from his position: it is always his (8:35); if, then, the *Son* will free 'the Jews' from their postulated slavery (to sin), *then* they will be (truly) free (8:36). The argument is somewhat contrived since it probably also plays on the freedom to live *forever* (*eis ton aiôna*, 8:35) that the Son will give to true believers, and this idea is not so easy to fit into the picture of the workings of a social household.[19] But Jesus' point is clear enough: the fact that 'the Jews' originate from Abraham does not prevent them from sinning and hence being in need of liberation from slavery to sin.

The talk of Abraham's seed and the Son leads to an extended discussion in 8:37–47 of who is the father of the two parties. The result famously is that while Jesus' father is God, the *father* of 'the Jews' is—the devil (8:44). By contrast, Abraham, whom 'the Jews' had introduced to give them unquestioned status (8:33), as Jesus recognized (8:37), does not help them. Though

---

[19] Is the idea that when (or if) they are liberated from sin, 'the Jews' will remain permanently in the position of 'sons' of the 'household' (of human salvation)?

they keep bringing him in (8:39, 52), he is superseded as the true ancestor by Jesus himself, who goes even further back than Abraham (8:56–8).

This, however, is to anticipate a bit. We should bring to attention a number of features in 8:37–47. First, there is again a clear intensification, not only in the explicit contrast of the two 'fathers', but also because Jesus' father is now explicitly identified as God (from 8:38 to 40, 41, 42). The contrast between the two 'fathers' is reached through an interchange on the relationship of 'the Jews' with Abraham. Jesus has said that he knows that 'the Jews' are Abraham's seed; *still* (Greek *alla*), they seek to kill him since Jesus' *logos* has no room in them (8:37). He then continues (8:38):

[38]What *I* speak is what I have seen in the Father's presence (or at my Father's: *para tôi patri*): what you too then (similarly) do is what you have heard from the father (or your father).[20]

With this (somewhat disputed) reading of the verse, Jesus is drawing up the ultimate contrast between himself and 'the Jews'. He speaks of what he has literally seen when he was with his own Father. Similarly, they do what they have (only) heard from *their* father (meaning, as will become clear, the devil). 'The Jews', however, misunderstand completely and stick to Abraham as their father (8:39). But Jesus insists that in that case they would not seek to kill him when he speaks the truth that he has heard from *God* (8:39–40); instead, 'you do the works of *your* father' (8:41a).[21] 'The Jews' are not dumb, however. They drop Abraham—or rather: keep him as their legitimate ancestor, whose pedigree goes even further back— and insist that they have a single father: God himself (8:41b). This, then, leads Jesus in 8:42–7 to a final, concentrated statement which focuses on the claim that since he himself comes from God (8:42), he speaks the truth (8:44–6) whereas his opponents' father, the devil, is the father of falsehood (8:44). Obviously, in this whole exchange the confrontation between Jesus and 'the Jews' is driven to a climax.

Secondly, 8:37–47 also shows an explicit interest in *explaining* just why the Jews are unable to understand what Jesus is saying:

---

[20] This translation reflects two decisions. First, it is often the case in John that the weight lies on the subordinate clause (here 'what I have seen' and 'what you have heard'). This should then be expressed in the translation. Secondly, I take the Greek *poieite* ('you do') as indicative and not imperative. Brown (1966, 356) in his discussion acknowledges that Bernard, Barrett, and Bultmann took it that way, but himself prefers the imperative since 'Jesus is still trying to convince his audience to obey the real Father, God'. No, he is challenging them. Lincoln (2005, 262) agrees with Brown but takes the father of 'the Jews' to be Abraham. Theobald (2009, 599: indicative and the devil) got it exactly right; Zumstein (2016, 333: imperative and Abraham) did not.

[21] Here there is no doubt about indicative and the devil.

- John 8:43: 'Why do you not understand what I say? It is because you cannot hear my *logos*.'
- John 8:47: 'Whoever is from God hears the words of God. The reason you do not hear them is that you are not from God.'

These verses clearly merit our close attention, for they explicitly maintain the reader's interest in the theme that had otherwise been in danger of disappearing in John 8 (apart from 8:30): how to *explain* that some Jews came to believe in Jesus, whereas others did not.

A third noticeable feature about 8:30–47 is that the themes of truth, falsehood, and sin continue to play a role here. God is responsible for truth (8:40, 45), whereas the devil is responsible for falsehood (8:44). And nobody may accuse Jesus, who speaks the truth (8:45 and 46b), of sin (8:46a). 'Then why do you not believe in me?' (8:46b). If truth (an epistemological notion) and freedom from sin go together in this way, there is all the more reason to try to explain—in what we may now call an epistemology of faith—*why* 'the Jews' are not able to hear what Jesus is saying (8:43 and 8:47).

THE INNER COHERENCE OF JOHN 7–8: THE SIXTH WAVE (8:48–59)

In the last wave, 'the Jews' finally come into the open: were we not right in saying that you are a Samaritan[22] and possessed by a 'demon' (8:48, referring back, as we know, to 7:20). Jesus explicitly denies this (*daimonion ouk echō*, 8:49): he honours his 'Father' (8:49) and does not seek his *own* glory (8:50). In other words, Jesus has *God* on his side. By implication, the *daimonion* belongs with *them* (as Jesus has just said in 8:44). To further tease 'the Jews' and bring out what this means with regard to his identity, Jesus then offers them the final bait: 'whoever will keep my *logos* will never in all eternity see death' (8:51). This is immensely important within the conceptuality of the Fourth Gospel. It speaks of eternal life, which is what the coming of the *logos* is all about. And it speaks of 'keeping' (*tērein*) Jesus' *logos*, which along with the notion of 'remaining in' it (8:31) goes well beyond

---

[22] There is every good reason to reflect on this mention of the Samaritans here in connection with John 4. However, I will not speculate on 'John and the Samaritans', only note the (probably deadly serious) humour with which John characterizes 'the Jews': where Jesus ('rightly') sees 'the Jews' as having the devil as their father, they themselves see him—in this climactic confrontation—as being . . . a Samaritan. Is this not a good example of John's manner of denigrating the super self-confident 'Jews'? (And it is also deeply ironical: Jesus *is* a 'Samaritan' who does have a 'demon' of an altogether different kind than they have in mind.)

merely 'believing in' him. 'The Jews', however, understand nothing, but are immediately duped: Abraham has died (8:52). So are *you above* 'our father, Abraham'? The reader knows that Jesus is in fact 'above Abraham'. And Jesus himself remains undaunted: yes (8:54–5),

> [54] ... it is my Father [here not just 'the Father'] who glorifies me, the one of whom you say 'He is our God'. [55]And yet (*kai*) you do not know him, but *I* (*egô*) know him. Were I even to say that I do not know him, I would become a liar [one who speaks falsehood, compare 8:44] like you are. No, I know him and keep his *logos*.

Nay, even more: 'Truly, I say to you: *before* Abraham was born, I am' (8:58). This is clearly another reference back to the picture of Jesus given in the Prologue, but it is also a shattering climax of the confrontation with 'the Jews' since Jesus is here explicitly laying claim to that picture, not just referring to it more or less vaguely. No wonder they once more attempt to stone him. 'But Jesus went into hiding and left the temple' (8:59).

Now the confrontation is complete: my Father is your God; I am. In this way the theme of a gradually intensified opposition between Jesus and 'the Jews' reaches its climax. Is the other theme of explaining why 'the Jews' do not get it also in play? Yes, implicitly when Jesus declares that 'I *know* him (*oida*) and keep his *logos*' (8:55, compare 8:51 and 52, where Jesus spoke of keeping his own *logos*, not God's). In light of Jesus' reference back to the Prologue both earlier in the chapter (8:25) and also a few verses later (8:58), it seems clear that the way Jesus 'knows' God is through having literally been together with him *at the beginning*. Jesus (Christ) *was* with God (as the *logos*) to begin with (compare 1:1). It follows that Jesus is *literally* 'from God' (*ek tou theou*, see 8:47), whereas the Jews are not (*ouk ... ek tou theou*, 8:47), but instead 'from your father, the devil' (*ek tou patros tou diabolou*, 8:44). Thus what we have is really an opposition between *God* (and Jesus Christ) and the *devil* (and 'the Jews'—and now with no ostensive divisions between them). We will see that it is this stark difference, which has now at long last been made wholly explicit, that in the end also *explains why* 'the Jews' do not get it even though some appeared to do so.

Let us go from this rather long-winded but necessary cumulative reading of the two chapters to a consideration of how they may be seen to answer the philosophical question that they raise.

THE PROPOSED ANSWER IN THE ABSTRACT

The proposed answer will focus on a motif in the two chapters that we noted in passing: whether people are able to 'hear' what Jesus is saying. This motif should be combined with the difference we noted between a triad of people in John 7 and a dyad in John 8. The group of people who are (almost) left out in John 8 (those who do come to believe in Jesus) are precisely those who are able to 'hear'. What, then, is the phenomenology of 'hearing'?

There are three features to be noted here. (i) One is that the eventual believers are characterized as being from the beginning 'willing to do the will of God' (see 7:17). Thus what we may call their default position is in a vague sense favourable towards listening to God (and hence also to his messenger, Jesus). (ii) A second feature is that the two other groups in the triad (Jesus and the non-believers) are both said—and this is one thing that only comes out *cumulatively* throughout John 8—to belong in a formally identical, but substantively directly opposed manner under two opposed powers: God and the devil. Whereas the non-believers accuse Jesus of being possessed by a 'demon', we know at the end of John 8 that while this accusation is precisely not true of Jesus, it is true—so Jesus says—of the non-believers themselves. They are possessed by a very 'bad spirit': the devil. (iii) The final feature to be noted is that in Jesus' case, his belonging with God takes a special form: Jesus *has* the spirit, he is 'possessed by' a spirit—namely, the *pneuma*.

The conclusion should be that those Jews who come to 'believe in' Jesus do so not because they already possess the *pneuma*, but because they are not already where the eventual non-believers are, namely, belonging under the devil; rather, they are—in principle—genuinely wanting to do the will of God. These two things make them able to *react* to the *pneuma* that is present in what Jesus is saying and to 'hear' it. The result is that they 'believe in' Jesus in some premature form—which *may* then *eventually* lead to their becoming themselves possessed by the *pneuma*. Then they will (or rather: might, if things did not go wrong) come to believe in him fully as who he is.

Of the three features that characterize the three different members of the triad, we need not spend much time on the second: that Jesus and the non-believers are directly opposed to one another as belonging under two opposed powers. We may just note that while the non-believers twice (7:20 and 8:48 and 52) state that Jesus is possessed by a demon, Jesus does not explicitly say the same of them. However, his statement that 'you are from your father, the devil' (8:44) does make that claim, though without using the exact term. Thus the opposition between Jesus and the non-believers is stark and direct and—most importantly for our purposes—it has the same formal character of people being 'from' this or the other 'father'.

The two other features need more careful consideration. We will begin by looking at the first feature (i): the default position of the eventual believers.

THE DEFAULT POSITION OF EVENTUAL BELIEVERS

The first statement on this matter is made in 7:17, where Jesus answers the question of 'the Jews' of how he has learned the law when he has not been taught it (7:15). His 'teaching', so he claims, is not 'my own', but that of the one who has sent him (7:16). And then (7:17):

> [17]If somebody wishes to do his (God's) will, he will come to know concerning my teaching whether it is from (*ek*) God or whether I speak on my own (or from myself: *ap' emautou*).

Here a presupposition is mentioned: that one wishes to do God's will. And a consequence is stated: then one will come to understand that Jesus' teaching 'is from God' and that he does not speak 'on his own'. Both claims point in the same direction: that the focus of attention on the part of both Jesus' ideal addressees and Jesus himself is God. The former wish to 'do God's will'. Then they will see that Jesus' teaching is 'from God' (and not from himself).

The idea of a contrast between focusing on God and seeking 'one's own' is further developed in 7:18 when Jesus states that the one who speaks 'on his own' (*aph' heautou*) seeks 'his own (*tēn idian*) glory', whereas the one (Jesus) who seeks the glory of the one who has sent him (God) is true and without injustice. This motif is also immediately spelled out in relation to the doing or not-doing of the law of Moses and to seeking to kill Jesus (7:19). Apparently, it is because 'the Jews' seek their own glory and do not (really) wish to do God's will that they do *not* themselves do the law *and* instead seek to kill Jesus for having violated that law (7:21–3). In so doing they 'judge superficially' instead of making a judgement that is truly just (7:24).

This is all very tightly connected. And the key is the initially stated idea of genuinely focusing on God through wishing to do his will.

The same idea comes out in 8:37–47, which is somewhat parallel to 7:19–24.[23] Only, where the earlier passage spoke of (the law of) Moses, the later one speaks of being Abraham's seed, with Jesus denying that his addressees are that. This is shown, he claims, by the fact that they seek to kill him (8:37 and 40, compare 7:19), even though he speaks the truth (8:40, compare 7:18). They, however, 'do not understand my speech (*lalia*)', because they 'cannot (*dynasthe*) hear (*akouein*) my *logos*' (8:43). And the reason for that is that 'being from your father, the devil', they 'wish (*thelein*, compare the opposite idea in 7:17) to do the desires (*epithymiai*, compare God's "will" in 7:17) of your father' *and* in him there is no truth since he is a liar and indeed

---

[23] Brown (1966, 356) at least notes the following on 8:37 ('a chance to kill me'): 'This theme last appeared in vii 19, 20, 25. Although these discourses at Tabernacles are loosely connected [!], some themes run throughout'. We have seen that the connections are much tighter than that.

the father of falsehood: one who speaks—precisely—'from *his own (ek + ta idia)*' (8:44).[24] If that is what the devil himself is, then it will also be true of those who are 'from' him. It is no wonder, then, that since Jesus on his side 'speaks the truth', they do not believe in him (8:45 and 46). *For* (8:47):

[47]The one who is from (*ek*) God hears (*akouein*) God's words (*rhêmata*). That is why you do not hear (*akouein*)—since you are not from (*ek*) God.

We may use what Jesus says here in John 8 of those who do *not* come to believe in him to bring out an understanding already stated in John 7 of those who do have a chance of doing so. The non-believers of John 8 do not 'hear' Jesus' *rhêmata* or his *logos* because they are not 'from God'. On the contrary, since they have the devil as their father, they belong wholly on the other side. We cannot conclude from this that the potential believers of chapter 7 are *directly* 'from God', only that they are *not* (yet) 'from the devil'. Instead, as Jesus says, they do *wish* to do God's will, but most likely in a vague and general way as opposed to the non-believers, who distinctly wish to do the devil's desires.

The general point is this: whereas the description of the non-believers given in 8:37–47 states quite clearly both that and why they come out on the wrong side, we should not understand the picture of those who do come to believe in Jesus as if they just and already belonged fully on the other side. Rather, while not yet being completely 'from God' (so far only one person is that in the literal sense it is meant: Jesus himself, who came to be so when he received the *pneuma*), they at least *wish* to do God's will. They are, we may say, in an intermediary state, which constitutes the (default) position that enables them to 'hear' what Jesus is saying.

We are attempting to explain the possibility of the division among 'the Jews' by focusing on what Jesus says of wanting (in a general way) to do the will of God as opposed to already belonging with the devil. However, there is one more presupposition of the theory we are developing. This has to do with what Jesus, on his side, is offering them—the third feature (iii) mentioned earlier.

WHAT JESUS HAS TO OFFER, I: THE *PNEUMA* SPEAKING TO POTENTIAL BELIEVERS

Throughout John 7 and 8, Jesus gradually discloses more and more about himself. In 7:16–17 he speaks of his 'teaching' (as opposed to himself) as coming from God and not from himself, though even here he speaks of God

---

[24] NRSV translates the last bit as 'according to his own nature'. They thereby miss completely the reference back to 7:18: 'the one who speaks on his own (*aph' heautou*) seeks his own (*tên idian*) glory'. Might one translate *ek tôn idiôn lalein* in 8:44 as 'speaking from his own interests'? The basic contrast appears to be between wishing to do the will of God and seeking one's own.

as 'the one who has sent me' (7:16). In 7:28–9, however, he comes more clearly into the open claiming that he has not 'come' 'from myself', but 'the one who has sent me, whom you do not know, is truthful' (7:28). And then quite clearly in 7:29: 'I (*egô*) know (*oida*) him since I am (*eimi*) from (*par'*) him and he has sent me'.

We already know that Jesus is 'from' God and was 'sent' by God when he received the *pneuma* from above. If so, his reply in 7:28–9 to the query of the people of Jerusalem *whether* he might be 'the Christ' (7:26) and what they themselves '*know*' about 'the Christ' (7:27) suggests an epistemological principle: he himself *knows* God (7:29) *since* he has received the *pneuma* from him. So, in whatever he says, Jesus is giving expression to the *pneuma*. We do not yet know that all of Jesus' talk about his origin and similar themes throughout John 7–8 should be taken to refer to his reception of the *pneuma*. But that is the possibility we should explore.[25]

A little later Jesus begins to speak about where he will soon be going (7:33–4), but this is misunderstood (7:35–6). Then comes the central statement (7:37–9) that those who have come to believe in him will at some later stage receive the *pneuma*. This coheres closely with the talk of going away: it is only when he has himself been 'glorified' that the *pneuma* will become available to believers (7:39). Conversely, it is also clearly presupposed that the *pneuma* is already present with Jesus himself while he is saying these things. After all, he speaks of 'rivers' *of pneuma* that will (eventually) 'flow from his *koilia* (belly or womb)' (7:38). And when did they *get* there? So, let us continue to look for further clues in the two chapters that the *pneuma* is actually in play in Jesus' speech.

Here we may note that immediately after 7:37–9 we get an indication of the effect of Jesus' words: people from the crowd—'having *heard* those *logoi*' (7:40)—become convinced that Jesus may truly be 'the prophet' or 'the Christ' (7:41). Not all are convinced, of course, and so we get a schism (7:43). But when the Pharisees' helpers return, they, too, say that 'Never has any human being *spoken* like that' (7:46). So, Jesus' words are repeatedly stated to be effective, presumably because he is in possession of the *pneuma*.

Next, in 8:12–19, Jesus advances his self-claim considerably by implicitly referring back to the picture given in the Prologue. Furthermore, where John 1 had a great deal to say about John the Baptist's witness to Jesus, in John 8 it is Jesus himself who claims to be a witness (namely, to his own identity), moreover, he even invokes God as the required second witness: 'it is the one who has sent me, *the Father*, who witnesses about me' (8:18). How? We already know the answer from 5:36–8: through 'the works that the Father has given me to complete' (5:36, NRSV). And how did God give

---

[25] Please note here—once more—the importance of the notion of 'reference': that the various locutions adopted by Jesus may be taken to '*refer*' to his reception of the *pneuma*.

Jesus that task? Answer: at Jesus' baptism, as we saw in Chapter V. Once again, the text of John 7–8 implies that Jesus' speech in these chapters reflects the fact that he is in possession of the *pneuma*.

Next, 8:21–9 both continues and sharpens Jesus' self-characterization. He tells 'the Jews' that he is on his way to a place where 'you cannot come (*elthein*)' (8:21). In light of 4:5, it seems obvious that 8:21, too, is playing on the *pneuma*: Jesus has the *pneuma* and so he can go there; 'the Jews' do not have it and so cannot go there. Similarly, when Jesus says that 'I am from above' (8:23), the meaning seems straightforward: through reception of the *pneuma*.

Jesus also tells them that 'unless you come to believe that I am, you will die in your sins' (8:24). What is the connection? Answer: if they do come to believe *that*, which is wholly different from the vaguer forms of 'believing in Jesus', then they will also have received the *pneuma*; and *then* they will not 'die in your sins', but instead have eternal life, *namely*, as engineered by the *pneuma*. When 'the Jews' then ask who Jesus is, he answers by referring them back to what he had said to them 'to begin with' (8:25) and tells them that 'when you have lifted up the Son of Man, then you will understand that I am' (8:28). How and why? Because then Jesus will blow the *pneuma* into them, as John says in the crucial verse, 20:22. Since possession of the *pneuma* is the ultimate condition for full knowledge, they will then at long last know about Jesus that 'I am'.

We should conclude that the reason why those who wish to do God's will may come to believe in Jesus at a certain level is that in all that he says he expresses the fact that he himself possesses God's *pneuma* and in that sense comes directly from God. Conversely, even though the eventual believers do not (yet) themselves have the *pneuma*, nevertheless, if they are, in principle, willing to do God's will, they will also be able to *react* to the *pneuma* that Jesus has. In that way they may come to believe in him, if only in the initial forms of such a belief. What Jesus offers, then, to human beings is the possibility of reacting to the *pneuma* that he himself possesses and that streams out of his mouth in his speech.[26]

WHAT JESUS HAS TO OFFER, II: THE PNEUMA WITHIN BELIEVERS

However, *from 8:31 onwards* Jesus begins to speak repeatedly of 'my *logos*'. How is talk of the *logos* related to the talk of 'believing in' Jesus of the type we have just considered? Here are the passages:

[26] Remember here the Stoic theory of *logos endiathetos* and *prophorikos* that we developed in Chapter III.

- John 8:31. 'If you remain (*menein*) in my *logos*, you are truly my disciples' (said to many people who *had* 'come to believe in him'—but then also immediately defected).
- John 8:37. 'You seek to kill me since my *logos* has no place (*chôrein*) in you.'[27]
- John 8:43. 'Why do you not understand what I am saying (my *lalia*)? It is because you cannot hear my *logos*.'
- John 8:51. 'If somebody keeps (*têrein*) my *logos*, he will never in eternity see death' (compare 8:52).
- John 8:55. 'I, by contrast, know him [God] and keep (*têrein*) his *logos*.'

There are two central issues here, the first of which is famous in Johannine studies: (i) What *is* Jesus' *logos*, which—by 8:55—is also God's, in terms of its content? (ii) And what is the relationship between coming to believe in Jesus and 'remaining' in Jesus' *logos*, 'giving it a place' in one, and 'keeping' it? Let us consider the second issue first.

John 8:31 suggests that coming to believe in Jesus is both a presupposition for, but also different from remaining in his *logos*. It is as if having come to believe in Jesus means having been initially struck by certain aspects of the understanding of Jesus that the Johannine Jesus is constantly articulating. By contrast, remaining in his *logos* refers to some form of being settled in the understanding of Jesus that constitutes or is part of having his *logos*. Then one is 'truly' Jesus' disciple (8:31) and then one will know 'the truth' (presumably about Jesus, 8:32). This does appear to be something more than just having come to believe in Jesus. The converse idea of the *logos* 'filling up' a person from the inside seems to be implied by 8:37, which speaks of Jesus' *logos* as 'having place or room in you'. But let us ask: is this 'remaining in' the *logos* and 'giving it a place within one' just a matter of cognition? At least, the expressions themselves suggest some kind of spatial metaphor that might give one pause. If one is sufficiently impressed by this, there is an obvious way of spelling it out. John, it seems, is once more relying on the idea that Jesus' (and God's) *logos* is literally borne by the *pneuma*, which is a physical phenomenon that may directly enter a person or, conversely, be something within which the person may be situated.

But will that do here? If Jesus' claim in 8:31 about those who have come to believe in him is taken to imply that when they 'remain in' his *logos*, then

---

[27] Both Liddell/Scott/Jones and Danker vacillate on the translation of *chôrein* here. Danker (2000, 1094) first translates: *my word makes no headway among you*, but then adds: 'Or perh. . . . *there is no place in you for my word* (NRSV . . .)'. Liddell/Scott/Jones similarly first translates *advance, succeed*, but then adds, as another possibility, *find room*. Theobald (2009, 599) rightly adopts the spatial interpretation, which he—equally rightly—relates to 8:31. We are clearly in the area of being and remaining 'in' Jesus (or the opposite) that will be fully articulated in John 15 (15:1–8).

they also have the *pneuma*, will this not go against the other claim that we should take as foundational in John: that during Jesus' lifetime the *pneuma* was present on earth only in him? Not necessarily. 'The Jews' who have come to believe in Jesus, according to 8:31, are precisely not *already* 'truly my disciples'. As 8:32 shows, their 'knowing the truth' and 'being freed' are matters that will only occur in the future—if all goes well (as it precisely did not in their case). The same will also hold of their being 'truly Jesus' disciples'.

John 8:37 allows for the same interpretation, which connects giving room within to Jesus' *logos* with oneself actually possessing the *pneuma*. For in this verse Jesus is precisely aiming to contrast those he is addressing, who are out to kill him, with himself. *They* are 'from your father, the devil' (8:44). *He* is from God, *his* Father (8:38 and 40). They do not therefore have what he has: the *pneuma*. On the contrary, as we saw, they have the direct opposite of that: the devil. *A fortiori*, neither does Jesus' *logos* have any place in them (8:37).

True enough, it may be said, but is there any explicit indication that the *pneuma* is invoked in all this? This is where 8:51 and 52 become relevant. These verses speak both of 'keeping' (*têrein*) 'my *logos*' and, as a direct result, of having eternal life instead of dying. How is the latter thing to be brought about? This is something we learn both from the description in John 20 of Jesus' own 'life after death' and also from John 6, as we have previously seen: eternal life is generated by the *pneuma*, which is 'what generates life' (6:63). In that case, 'keeping' Jesus' *logos* will also be a matter of having the *pneuma* in one and (presumably) letting it come to expression in what one says and does.

This understanding is strongly supported by 8:55, where Jesus says of himself that he himself 'keeps God's *logos*'. How? Answer: by having the *pneuma* in him that he received at his baptism and by letting it come to expression in everything he himself says and does.

It seems, then, that in everything Jesus is saying in 8:31, 37, 51–2, and 55 about various forms of relating to his (and God's) *logos*, he is *implicitly referring* to the possession of the *pneuma*, either among those who will truly become his disciples or by himself. That relationship with the *pneuma* is clearly different from the relationship we found in the initial believers, who were only able to *react* to the *pneuma* as present in Jesus but not in themselves.

There remains 8:43. Will that fit into this picture too? This verse is intriguing in two ways. First, it connects Jesus' *logos* with the idea of being able to 'hear' it. In itself this is not unusual (see 5:24), but it does strike a different note from speaking of 'remaining in' the *logos*, 'giving it room within oneself', or even 'keeping' it. Secondly, not being able to 'hear' Jesus' *logos* is apparently intended to *explain* why they do not (either)

'understand my speech (*lalia*)' (= what I am saying). How does the difference between *logos* and *lalia* fit into such a sequence, which superficially
appears to be the opposite of the most natural one (compare 8:31)?[28]

The best solution may be derived from looking at the immediate
context of the verse. It seems as if there is a progression here from (a)
not understanding my *lalia*, to (b) not being able to hear my *logos*, to (c)
being from the devil as one's father (8:44). In that case, what Jesus is
talking about in 8:43 is not a general epistemological principle to the effect
that one must (b) be able to hear the *logos* in order to (a) understand the
lalia. Rather, he is here speaking precisely of those who already (c) belong
with the devil. That fact necessarily means (b) that they are unable to
'hear Jesus' *logos*' in the sense that they are by definition completely
distanced from having any contact with the *pneuma* that carries Jesus'
logos. And in that case (a) neither will they actually understand anything
of what he concretely says.

It seems, then, that throughout these references to Jesus' *logos* towards
the end of chapter 8, John is not merely referring to Jesus' *speech*, his *lalia*.
Instead, Jesus' *logos* stands for the whole rationale of everything Jesus says
and does: what it all means—the full *logos* that we know from the Prologue.
That is all through *borne* by the *pneuma* that Jesus—and nobody else—has
already received. But here at the end of John 8, where he is partly speaking
of what the initial believers are still lacking and partly of what his direct
opponents are wholly lacking, Jesus introduces as something he eventually
offers not just the *pneuma* that is streaming out of his mouth, but also
the *pneuma within* believers. When (if) in the future the initial believers
will literally receive the *pneuma* in their interior, *then* they will also fully
understand the truth about Jesus, the full *logos*.

With this interpretation we have also answered the first question raised
above: what *is* Jesus' (and God's) *logos* in terms of its content? We know the
answer from our reading of the Prologue: it is the whole rationale or plan of
God's creation, the one that issues in God's sending of Jesus, in short, the
logos that was with God in the beginning; this *logos* lies behind everything
Jesus says and does, reflecting the fact that he received it when the *pneuma*
was sent by God to remain upon him. Jesus' and God's *logos* is the meaning
of the events that are described in the Gospel, a meaning that Jesus (Christ)
knows, understands, and in a way also *is because* he has the *pneuma* sent by
God remaining upon him. It is the plan for the salvation of human beings to
eternal life.

---

[28] Surely, the natural sequence would be that of being able to understand what Jesus is
literally saying and then to go on from there to being able to 'hear' his whole *logos* as implied
in what he has literally said.

WHAT JESUS OFFERS: THE *PNEUMA* IN TWO STAGES

Our question some way back was how to explain that those 'Jews' who were initially willing to do God's will might also be able to react to what Jesus says by coming to believe in him. The answer we can now give is this: even though they are not themselves in possession of the *pneuma* (that belongs to the future, if at all), they are able to respond to the *pneuma* as present in what Jesus says. He has the *pneuma*, and the *pneuma* is present in what he says (and does). They do not have it, but they are able to respond to its presence in Jesus, namely, to the way it streams out of his mouth.

We may also conclude that when Jesus urges those who have come to believe in him to 'remain in' his *logos* and 'make room for it within themselves', he is speaking *proleptically*, as we have previously understood this. What he says is something that may only happen after his own death when the *pneuma* will also be transmitted to his followers. Then they may truly 'remain in' his *logos* and 'make room for' it since then the phenomenon, which *carries* that *logos*, may actually be present in them: the *pneuma*. Understood in this way, Jesus may be said to offer the *pneuma* throughout the Gospel in two stages: in himself in the present (as something to which potential believers may react) and *eventually* in his followers (as something initial believers may then later come to possess in themselves).

It is the fact that the two stages at which Jesus offers the *pneuma* are separated in time that explains why those among 'the Jews' in John 7–8 who came to believe in Jesus by reacting to the presence of the *pneuma* in him, but without having it in themselves, might nevertheless also end up switching over and siding with the other 'Jews' who rejected Jesus out of hand because they had the devil as their father. We may say that the general desire to do God's will, which allowed them to come to believe in Jesus at some initial level, was not enough to ensure that they stuck to their belief. For that, they also needed the *pneuma*. As it was, however, since they neither belonged with the *pneuma* (only Jesus had it) nor with the devil (they were not completely unable to hear what Jesus was saying), they stood at a crossroads from which they might take one road down towards the devil, and another towards receiving the *pneuma* in themselves.

TWO TYPES OF BELIEF AND THE ROLE OF THE *PNEUMA*

The point of this whole analysis should be clear: John 7–8 are not only concerned to develop the first overarching theme of a confrontation between Jesus and 'the Jews'; they are also—and at the same time—

aiming to answer a question that is raised by the second overarching theme of a division *among* 'the Jews', a theme that forms part of the account of the increasing confrontation. That question—our philosophical question—was why is it that some Jews reacted favourably to Jesus' speech, whereas others did not. The suggested answer is twofold: those who reacted negatively to Jesus' speech did this—so John's Jesus claims—because they were themselves filled with the demonic power (the devil) that corresponded (at the opposite end of the spectrum) to the power that also filled Jesus himself (the *pneuma*). Those, by contrast, who reacted positively to Jesus' speech did so because *since* they were not (at least, not yet) filled with that demonic power, but instead in principle wished to do God's will, they were able to react to the *pneuma* that was present in Jesus' speech without themselves possessing that *pneuma*, thereby coming to believe in Jesus (though in a less than complete way). Only later they might also come to have the proper belief if they went on to receive the *pneuma*.

We may conclude that in chapters 7–8 John is developing and presenting a very careful, richly faceted *theory* of different reactions to Jesus, a theory that fully deserves to be seen as an epistemological one. John is doing philosophy here (in addition to all the rest) and relying for his epistemology on the idea of the two sides of the *logos–pneuma*: that this combined entity is both cognitive and material. At the same time, as we may add, he is tracing his epistemology back to a fundamental, ontological division in this world between God (and Jesus and the *logos–pneuma*) and the devil.[29]

Methodologically, we may conclude that the kind of cumulative reading of John that we have been engaged in is wholly necessary to get a proper grasp of what is going on in this text. Concretely: it is only once one sees how and why the triad of John 7 is narrowed down to a dyad in John 8 that one becomes able to answer the philosophical question that was itself raised to the attentive reader in John 7. In addition, it seems evident that precisely by writing in the way that the cumulative reading lays bare, John does far more than merely provide a narrative account of the sayings and doings of Jesus. He both draws on the comprehensive cosmological picture into which he has fitted Jesus Christ, the *logos*, and the *pneuma*, and he also suggests a precise answer through narrative means to a philosophical question that is raised by the narrative account itself but also belongs under philosophical epistemology: *why* it is that some people reacted to Jesus in one way and others in another and why the positive reaction might not be sufficient, after all. By giving such an answer, he also aims to tell his readers something of crucial importance to themselves that he will eventually identify as his whole aim in writing: exactly what kind of belief in

---

[29] By contrast, I do *not* believe that he also raises philosophical questions about 'determinism', 'freedom', 'responsibility', and the like.

Jesus is required for it to occur that '*through believing* you may have *life* in his name' (20:31, NRSV). The answer is: full belief.

Along the way we have also been able to explain a number of features of the two chapters that have hitherto escaped notice, for instance, what the precise role is of the motif of 'wishing to do God's will'; why we only hear once in John 8 of any 'Jews' coming to believe in Jesus; and why they immediately turn out, after all, not to do so in the proper way. Perhaps most important is the fact that we have found strong confirmation for the view that 'believing in Jesus' comes in basically two forms: first, reacting positively to Jesus in a number of ways that all fall short of being fully adequate since they do not contain a full grasp of Jesus' *logos*; and secondly, reacting to Jesus in the only manner that is fully adequate. We have come across this difference many times before, but may now speak of the two forms more formally as an 'initial belief' and a 'full belief'. The latter requires that one is oneself in possession of the *pneuma*, which is a stage that may only be reached after Jesus' death. It is present when the whole of Jesus' *logos* 'has room' in one (8:37), when one 'remains' in that *logos* (8:31), and when one 'keeps' it (8:51–2). Then—and only then—will it also be the case that one will 'never taste death' (8:52) but (already) has eternal life (though only to be fully obtained, of course, in the future).

VII

WHO CAN SEE WHAT JESUS' ACTS SIGNIFY (JOHN 9–10)?

THE SCHOLARLY SET-UP AND PRESENT QUERY

As John 9–10 has been read throughout most of the twentieth century, it presents one of the major obstacles to the kind of reading that is being pursued in this book.[1] According to many scholars, the two chapters must be divided into two or three distinct sections with divisions at 9:41 and 10:1 and at 10:21 and 22, each with their own separate histories. It is true that there is a recent tendency not to pay too much attention to this scholarly tradition. But the tradition is still very much around and it would be incorrect to say that it has been rejected conclusively.[2] In this chapter, I aim to present a number of arguments to suggest that the strategy of dividing up the text is not required by the text itself and so cannot call upon the kind of necessity often appealed to by dividers. If we are successful here, the road lies open for us to continue to look for philosophical questions in the text that are raised and answered through narrative means.

As always, the coherence we will find is primarily thematic. It centres on the ability to conclude from the acts of Jesus—not least the healing in John 9 of the man born blind—to his divine identity. At the beginning (9:16) *and* end (10:41) the text identifies this ability as that of being able to see Jesus' acts as 'signs' (*sēmeia*). In between, the text spells out the precise logical character of a 'sign'. We will see that the two chapters are held tightly together as a single unit by this all-pervasive theme. Nor is this fact in itself very surprising. It is no accident that scholars have called John 1–12 the 'Book of Signs'. In John 9–10, then—just before we hear of Jesus' last and greatest sign (the raising of Lazarus)—the Evangelist spells out the meaning of a 'sign' and of describing Jesus' various acts *as* signs.

---

[1] The substance of this chapter has been published before in a shorter version in a Festschrift and a longer one on the internet (2013a and 2013b, respectively). I have made a great number of changes and additions here.

[2] References concerning the claims made in this paragraph are given later in this chapter.

This identification of an overarching theme in John 9–10 should be compared with other attempts at finding a unitary theme. For instance, Raymond Brown (1966, 377) well brought out how John 9, in particular, makes much of the theme of light and darkness: 'The story starts in vs. 1 with a blind man who will gain his sight; it ends in vs. 41 with the Pharisees who have become spiritually blind'. Perceptive as this is, it only concerns John 9. Indeed, Brown later (1966, 388) toys with the idea of separating John 9 sharply from John 10 just because of the former chapter's emphasis on light and darkness. Fortunately, he ends up being more open to seeing literary connections between the two chapters. But there is no suggestion of a unifying theme across the chapter divide. In response to this, one should make two methodological points. The first is that if it is possible to identify a single theme for both chapters, then such a claim is logically stronger than any proposal that focuses on parts of the text only. The second is that identifying a single theme in no way excludes that we may also find subthemes in individual parts. What we are after is maximal coherence and this may be found in the combination of several different types of theme.

If we are right in identifying as an overarching theme of John 9–10 the issue of how to read Jesus' acts as signs, it follows that a reading of the text that is philosophically orientated need not look any further for a philosophical question to be raised by the text either explicitly or implicitly. For the theme is already a philosophical one: what *is* a sign, and just how are Jesus' acts to be read as signs? I will attempt to illuminate this theme by bringing in an explicitly philosophical analysis of 'signs' that is contemporary with the Fourth Gospel itself: the Stoic understanding of a 'sign' (again *sêmeion*) as reported by the second-century CE philosopher Sextus Empiricus. But we will also consider the exact ways in which John's concern with the theme of reading a 'sign' informs his overall narrative in the two chapters and gives meaning to everything in it. Here we address the broader contrast drawn in the text between the healed man who was born blind and 'the Jews'—together with the contrast between their understanding of Jesus and the claims made by Jesus himself about his own identity.[3] All of this, I claim, is informed by the theme of being able to read a 'sign'.

A final introductory remark relates John 9–10 to John 7–8. The contrastive connection is easy to find. If John 9–10 is about how to read Jesus' *acts*, then that theme immediately fits John 7–8, where the issue was that of

---

[3] In this chapter I continue my practice of speaking about 'the Jews' in inverted commas for reasons given earlier. The inverted commas around 'Christians' are inserted in order to leave open the question to what extent the Johannine group that is articulated in the Gospel should be understood as being separate from Judaism. The fact that I read the two chapters as being very much concerned about *separating* the two groups does not necessarily imply that they stand, respectively, for Christianity as a new religion and Judaism as the old one.

'hearing', that is, understanding, Jesus' *words*. In this way, John 7–10 together cover the whole issue of how to understand both what Jesus says and what he does.

ARGUMENTS FOR AND AGAINST UNITY

Traditionally, as we noted, scholars have felt the need to make a cut at two points in John 9–10: between 9:41 and 10:1; and between 10:21 and 10:22. Is Jesus not introducing a quite new topic at 10:1 in the parable of the good shepherd? And should we not acknowledge the change of place and time at 10:22, with a new festival as the occasion and a different location as well? As an example of this position one may mention C. H. Dodd who, while he did not allow himself to be seriously challenged by Rudolf Bultmann's extensive use of the cutter's knife, nevertheless felt that within John 9–10, which he did take as a coherent unit, something new began at both 10:1 and 10:22.[4]

More in line with Bultmann and the idea derived from Eduard Schwartz of a series of literary 'aporiai' in John, is John Ashton, who even in the slightly less adamantly literary critical second edition of *Understanding the Fourth Gospel* insists that the beginning of John 10 constitutes one of those insurmountable aporiai. On 10:1 Ashton comments (2007, 48, his emphasis): 'Between the end of chapter 9 and the beginning of chapter 10 *the situation has changed*'. I will suggest, however, that the supposed change in situation is engineered by the Johannine Jesus himself, as begun already at 9:39. And 9:39–41 clearly *also* belongs together with the preceding part of John 9.

More recent scholars have accepted that the arguments for introducing a cut at 10:1 are insufficiently strong. In fact, there seems to be a general pattern here. Whereas (for the German tradition) in 1971 Rudolf Schnackenburg divided completely between chapters 9 and 10, in 2000 Klaus Wengst (2000, 351) claimed that 'the later division of chapters suggests a new beginning with chapter 10 that is not there'. Similarly (for the American tradition), whereas in 1992 Charles Talbert took John 7–9 and 10–11 together (Talbert 1992, 143–78), in 2006 Gail O'Day and Susan E. Hylen claimed (O'Day and Hylen 2006, 97) that 'Chapter 9 should also be considered part of a larger unit that includes 10:1–21'. And correspondingly (for the French tradition), Xavier Léon-Dufour, S. J., wrote (1990, 327) that 'If one neglects the artificial chapter division, one sees that the discourse continues the controversy'.

---

[4] See the very nuanced discussion in Dodd 1953a, 354–62.

Most scholars, however, even among the most recent ones, feel that something new begins at 10:22. For instance, Wengst (2000, 351) finds that 'there is a clear division between 10:21 and 10:22' in terms of both time and place. This view is shared by most others, e.g. Theobald (2009, 624 and 687), who finds a connected unit in 9:1–10:21 and a different one in 10:22–39: 'At the Festival of the Dedication: The process against Jesus is in full swing!'. Lincoln (2005, 303) agrees that 10:22–39 'incorporates...the issues dealt with in the Synoptic tradition of Jesus' trial before the Sanhedrin', but also acknowledges that there is 'broad thematic continuity' with what precedes, not least because 'the sheep and shepherd imagery from 10.1–21 is taken up again in vv. 26–9 in a way that appears to presuppose the same audience'. He adds the following perceptive sentence: 'As always, the evangelist's eye is as much on his own audience as on what is appropriate for the audience of the narrative.' Only, take the full step and instead of 'his own audience' write 'reader'. John's eye is primarily on the thematic connections. Like in a musical 'theme with variations', he is playing a philosophical variation over the underlying melody of the narrative with the aim of instructing his readers.

In contrast to the current scholarly situation, it is noteworthy that a great Johannine reader such as Frédéric Godet from the pre-Schwartz and pre-Bultmann period was able to see the whole of John 9–10 as a single unit. Godet spoke (1903 [originally 1869], II. 354, my emphasis) of 10:22–42 as 'a second discourse that was admittedly given a little later and at a different visit to Jerusalem, but *in its contents is just a continuation of the preceding discourse*'. Even Godet, however, did not see the specific connection that I claim binds 10:22–42 tightly together with the rest of John 9–10.

A THEMATIC UNITY

As already noted, the decisive consideration lies in the way the two chapters develop the theme of concluding from Jesus' acts to his identity. (i) That theme is introduced already at 9:3–4 when Jesus claims that the man born blind has suffered from his illness 'in order that *God's works (erga)* may be *revealed* in him' (9:3) since Jesus 'must do the works of *the one who has sent me*' (9:4) as long as he is in the world (9:5). Here the theme is already aired of deducing something from Jesus' acts. (ii) After the man has been healed (9:6–12) and the Pharisees have begun to complain about Jesus' healing on a Sabbath (9:13–15), we get the by now well-known motif of a schism (*schisma*, 9:16). Some among the Pharisees declare that 'this man is not from God (*para tou theou*)' since he does not keep the Sabbath (9:16). But others say: 'How would a man who is a sinner be able to do such signs?' (9:16). The latter people, then, are able to conclude that

Jesus must be 'from God' and that his acts are precisely 'signs'. They see them in some way as 'God's works', as in 9:3.

However, 'the Jews' in general are not persuaded and address first the man's parents (9:18–23) and then the man himself (9:24–34) in what turns out to be a most striking conversation. To begin with the man declares that against what 'the Jews' have just declared about Jesus (9:24), he himself does not know whether Jesus is a sinner: what he does know is that Jesus has healed him (9:25). When 'the Jews' then declare that they do not know from where Jesus comes (9:29), the healed man states that that is just what is so 'illogical' (*thaumaston*) about the whole situation: *they* do not know from where Jesus comes—'*and yet* (Greek *kai*) he opened my eyes' (9:30). This leads to a very cogent piece of reasoning on the part of the healed man (9:31–3). (iii) He first establishes a premise that he takes to be shared by all ('we know ... ');

First premise (9:31). God does not listen to sinners; only if a man is pious (*theosebês*) and does God's will does God listen to him.

Next he recalls the enormity of what Jesus has done:

Second premise (9:32). It has never been heard since the beginning of time that somebody has opened the eyes of a man born blind.[5]

Then the conclusion follows:

Conclusion (9:33). *Had* he not come 'from God' (*para theou*—so that he is no sinner), he *would* not have been able to do anything (of that kind).

In other words, the fact that Jesus *has* performed such an unheard-of feat *proves* that he is no sinner, but instead comes from God. Once more—as in 9:16—the logic of a sign is explicated in counterfactual form: this man *would not have been* able to do anything *had he not been* 'from God'.

After a brief conversation between Jesus and the healed man, in which he confesses to the Son of Man (9:35–8), and another brief conversation between Jesus and the Pharisees, in which Jesus accuses them of spiritual blindness (9:39–41), we get the long speech about the good shepherd (10:1–18), which is followed by yet another schism (*schisma*, 10:19) among 'the Jews' (10:19–21). (iv) And here we get one more case of the theme of the sign when some of 'the Jews' declare against the others that Jesus'

---

[5] It has been suggested to me (by the late John Moles of Newcastle University) that the time reference in 9:32 ('Never since the world began has it been heard that ... ') may contain a hint back at 8:58 where Jesus has claimed that 'before Abraham was, I am'. Thus half-unwittingly, the healed man may be intimating already here what he is next led to believe in his conversation with Jesus in 9:35–8. The idea is suggestive and in reading the Fourth Gospel one must always keep one's ears open to such hints.

'words' (*rhêmata*, namely, the whole preceding speech) are not those of a man who is possessed by a demon (as the others have just claimed of Jesus): '*would a demon be able to open the eyes of the blind* [that is, to *heal* him]?' (10:21).

Then follows the new situation during the festival of the Dedication and an apparently new theme when 'the Jews' surround Jesus and ask him to declare himself openly: is he the Messiah (10:24)? Jesus' reply refers back both to John 9 (as did 10:21 about opening the eyes of the blind) and also to the shepherd speech at the beginning of John 10, thereby giving coherence to the text as a whole. He *has* told them, so he says—but they do not believe him (10:25a);[6] moreover, (v) 'the works (*erga*) that I do in my father's name, those bear witness about me' (10:25b; compare John 9)—*but* they do not believe him since they are 'not among my sheep' (10:26; compare 10:1–18).

What follows takes further the double theme of Jesus' flock and his relationship with God (10:27–30), which leads to one more abortive attempt by 'the Jews' to do violence to Jesus (10:31). Again, however, the theme of Jesus' works comes up (10:32): (vi) '[32]Many fine works (*erga*) have I shown you from the (or my) Father: which one of them is it that makes you (wish to) stone me?'.

'The Jews', however, are not interested in Jesus' works (10:33). Instead, we get a small conversation concerning the legitimacy of Jesus' claim to be 'Son of God' (10:34–6).

But the works come back once more (10:37–8):

(vii) [37]If I do not do my Father's works, do not believe in me. [38]But if I do them, even if you do not believe in myself, believe in the works *in order that you may realize and understand that* the Father is in me and I am in the Father.

Here, in spite of the conceit of distinguishing between Jesus 'himself' and the works, the latter retain their function as premises for a conclusion about Jesus.

Finally, after a change of place (not, now, of time) we get the last reference to what Jesus has done and this time by means of the technical term of a 'sign' (10:41):

(viii) [41]And many came to him and they said: 'John (the Baptist) did not do any sign (*sêmeion*), but everything that John said about this man was true'.

That is, Jesus *has* done 'signs'. 'And many came to believe in him there' (10:42).

Thus, eight times during the two chapters we get the theme of Jesus' works (*erga*) and what they should show. Twice—at the beginning (9:16) and

---

[6] When has Jesus told them this? Nowhere in so many words. But note 8:25. Here 'the Jews' ask Jesus who he is and he replies (on my preferred reading): 'The one I have told you from the very beginning'. There seems to be a pattern here: Jesus *claims* to have told them everything (even when he has not explicitly done so)—but they have not understood.

end (10:41)—the works are identified by the technical term as 'signs'. Twice, too—at the beginning (9:16) and end (9:30–3) of the story about the healed man—the logic of the sign is spelled out in counterfactual form. But the theme is also kept alive three times in John 10 (10:25, 32, 37–8) before being reintroduced as that of the 'sign' (10:41). Clearly, there *is* a unity of theme here focusing on the ability to read Jesus' works as signs of his relationship with God. But what exactly is the theme and how does it give meaning to everything else that is said in the two chapters? We will now address these two questions in turn.

WHAT IS A SIGN—THE STOICS?

Some of the first philosophers in the European tradition to reflect on the notion of a sign (*sêmeion*) were the ancient Stoics. Our best evidence comes from Sextus Empiricus (*Adv. Math.* 8.244–56, see *SVF* 2.221–3, pp. 72–4), but the theory itself no doubt goes back to Chrysippus. In his analysis, Sextus makes use of a number of examples. They all derive from medicine:

(1) 'If this woman has milk in her breasts, this woman has given birth'—namely, in the (recent) past.
(2) 'If this man has coughed up bronchial cartilage, this man has an ulcer in his lung'—namely, in the present.
(3) 'If this man has been wounded in the heart, this man will die'—namely, in the future.

A Stoic sign is defined in various ways. First, it is something 'intelligible' (*noêtón*). It is not a thing or event, for instance, the case of a particular woman who has milk in her breasts. Instead, it is a 'proposition' (a Stoic *axíôma*), namely, 'the fact that' (in Greek: the definite article *to* + the infinitive) this woman has milk in her breasts. This shows that in speaking of signs one is operating at the cognitive level of understanding the world and saying something about it.

Secondly, a sign is the antecedent in a logical implication, whose form is 'if this, then this'. Sextus therefore considers all forms of this implication that are logically valid depending on the truth value of its antecedent and its consequent. He decides that since a sign must be true and must also be 'representative of something true' (*alêthous parastatikon*), only the implication that has an antecedent that is true and a consequent that is also true qualifies for defining a sign.

Thirdly, Sextus also adds, however, that it is only one form of the 'if true, then true' implication that will serve to define a sign. In addition, it must contain a 'nature' that is 'revelatory of the consequent' (*ekkalyptikên echein physin tou lêgontos*). For instance, in example 1 'the former fact is revelatory (*ekkalyptikon*) of the latter. For by attending (*prosballontes*) to the former, we make a grasp (*katalêpsin . . . poioumetha*) of the latter'.

What is the 'nature' or 'character' that makes a sign 'revelatory' of the consequent? Sextus' examples suggest that it is the fact that the consequent either *causes* or *is caused by* the antecedent.[7] In example 1, the consequent (that this woman has recently given birth) *causes* the antecedent (that she has milk in her breasts). In example 3, the consequent (that this man will die) *is caused by* the antecedent (that he has been wounded in his heart). In either case, there will be a 'revelatory' process from the sign (*sêmeion*) to the 'signified' (called *sêmeiôtón* by Sextus).

A fourth and final feature of the Stoic theory is that sign and 'signified' are both present here and now. A sign is *parón paróntos*, a 'present' indicator of something 'present'. The reason is that both sign and 'signified' are 'propositions' and not actual things or events in the world. Thus, for instance, in example 1 the consequent is not 'this woman has given birth' (in the past, that is, as the event itself), but 'the (present) fact that this woman has (in the past) given birth'. Similarly, in example 3 the consequent is not 'this man will die' (in the future, and once again as the event itself), but 'the (present) fact that this man will die (in the future)'. The distinction may appear contrived (though in fact it is not), but it shows that in speaking of a sign of something, one is operating at the cognitive level, stating how the world should be *understood now*—as it were in *relation* to the way the world itself either *has* behaved, *is* behaving, or *will* behave.

WHAT IS A SIGN—JOHN 9–10?

In what follows, I will not be claiming that John explicitly presupposes the Stoic theory of signs. It is unlikely that John had read and directly applied the Stoic theory of signs to his own account.[8] Instead, the claim is that bringing in the Stoic theory throws additional—and quite striking—light on what is already there to be found in the Gospel itself. Thus we should apply the Stoic theory to John for 'heuristic' purposes: in order to find something in John that can then be seen actually to be there. The Stoic theory will help us to see more clearly two features of John 9–10 that have already been present—though only somewhat indistinctly—in the previous analysis of the text. One feature is fairly general, the other more specific. Let us begin with the latter.

---

[7] What follows slightly misrepresents the Stoic theory of causation. For the full version, see Long and Sedley (1987) vol. 1, 340.

[8] Why not? Because there is an insufficient amount of linguistic match in John with the technical vocabulary of Stoicism. Also, while I do argue that John is philosophical, it is obvious that his philosophizing is of a different kind from that of professional philosophers in the ancient world. In John, the philosophy is deeply integrated into narration.

John 9:30–3. Let us put this text under renewed scrutiny. 'You do not know from where he is, *yet* he opened my eyes!' (9:30). Here the healed man opposes a concrete fact to his opponents' bewildered, general speculations about Jesus. When he speaks of the situation as being 'illogical' (*thaumaston*), he also seems to be presupposing that they should have been able to do better, namely, to *deduce* an answer to their general speculations *from* the concrete fact. It is this deduction he goes on to present to them in 9:31–3. What is its exact logical form?

John 9:31. This verse states a general connection between an ability to do something and the moral character of the agent vis-à-vis God. Here the weight lies on the latter point: the agent must not be a 'sinner'; he must be *theosebês* ('God-fearing') and one who does God's will. Still, when it is said that God 'hears' him, it must be implied that we are talking about the agent's *doing* something that God *helps* him to do *since* he is not a sinner. We should understand this verse, then, as stipulating a general connection between acts and the *character of the agent* vis-à-vis *God*. This connection takes the form of a first, general premise:

(1)   God only helps people to act who are *theosebeis* and do God's will.

John 9:32. The text next describes the quite extraordinary character of what Jesus has already done, his particular feat that we already know (from 9:30) to be also a particular fact: 'he opened my eyes'. This description of Jesus' act takes the form of a second, particular premise:

(2)   Jesus' particular feat was quite extraordinary.

John 9:33. Then follows the conclusion, which is—informally put—that Jesus was only able to do (with God's help) his extraordinary act (compare premise 2) *because* he falls under the group of people who are *theosebeis* and do God's will (compare premise 1). Note, however, the exact logical form in which John puts this point. He *would not have been able* to do anything, *unless* he were 'from God'. This counterfactual may be directly converted into the following form: '*if* this, then this'—that is, *if* Jesus did do the extraordinary feat that was described in premise 2, *then* he has the *character* described in premise 1. *Quod erat demonstrandum.*

What we have in the whole argument of 9:31–3 are two things. One is a formulation in 9:33 in explicit, technical form of a 'sign' if one applies the Stoic theory of signs: if this, then this. As the Stoics said: by attending to the former (the healing: the sign), we make a 'grasp' of the latter (Jesus' identity: the signified). In accordance with the Stoic examples of a sign, we may articulate the 'Stoic' logic of Jesus' healing the man born blind:

(3)   If this man (Jesus) has healed a man born blind, then this man is from God.

The other thing we may derive from the healed man's argument is the point made in 9:31–2 about the inner connection between acts and the agent's character. What this point articulates is the feature of the Stoic sign that is spoken of as a 'nature' or 'character' in the antecedent that is 'revelatory of the consequent'. In other words, Jesus' acts as exemplified here by his healing of the man born blind (its extraordinary character which makes it the case that it can only be done by one who is *theosebês* and does God's will) are *intrinsically of such a kind that they reveal the consequent*: that Jesus himself, the agent of those acts, is from God. That is why some people draw the proper conclusion from Jesus' works (*erga*)— and others who do not *should* have done so.

We may note two other texts in John 9–10 that draw on the same logic of the sign. John 9:16 is an obvious example since here the Pharisees who respond positively to the healing do so by saying this: 'How *would* a man who was a sinner be able to (in Greek: *pôs dynatai*) do such signs?'[9] Since 'How would a man' of 9:16 equals 'Nobody would' of 9:33, the Pharisees are here making use of the very same logic as we found in 9:33. And the point is clear: if Jesus can do this, then *he must be 'from God'*. We have also already noted that the positive Pharisees even use the technical term of a 'sign' about Jesus' act: it is a *sêmeion*.[10]

The other relevant text is 10:37–8 (within the context of 10:31–9) right at the end of John 10. As we saw, Jesus here distinguishes explicitly between believing in 'me' and believing in 'my *erga*' and even states that 'the Jews' should do the latter *in order that* they may come to see something about Jesus himself (and hence come to believe in *him*). It is immediately obvious that this line of thought directly presupposes the understanding of Jesus' *erga* and their relation to his identity that has been spelled out in the two earlier texts in John 9. Indeed, one might even say that by spelling out in 10:37 that Jesus' *erga* are not just (as 9:3 had it) *erga tou theou* ('God's works') or (as 10:32 had it) *erga ... ek tou patros* ('works from the Father'), but even *erga tou patros mou* ('*my* Father's works'), Jesus points in advance (before the small argument of 10:38) to the conclusion to be drawn. Acts

---

[9] NRSV translate: 'How can a man who is a sinner perform such signs?', which is superficially quite all right. I sense, however, that in contexts like these, the Greek *dynasthai* ('to be able to do something') has a bit more of a modal meaning.

[10] Here one might feel that we are so close to the Stoic theory that one might be tempted to postulate a direct relationship. However, I will resist the temptation and stay with the 'heuristic' claim. The reader may dislike this kind of vacillation. But the claim for direct influence will always depend on the *extent* of overlap, either in thought or language. And there is no calculus that will determine when there is a *sufficient* overlap for it to be valid to claim direct influence. Also, the basic aim is to throw light on John's text. For that, any genealogical relationship is irrelevant.

like these are so intimately connected with God that their character falls immediately back upon Jesus. In that way they become '*my Father's* works'.

So much for the specific features of our two chapters that are—I would say—strikingly illuminated when one brings in the Stoic theory of signs as a heuristic tool. At a more general level the theory helps to emphasize another feature that is evidently there in the text, namely, its concern with understanding or knowledge. A few references will suffice. At 9:3 Jesus states that the man's blindness serves the purpose of making God's *erga* become *apparent* (*phanerôthênai*). So, people should *learn* from the healing. Then there is the fundamental idea that in making the blind man able to see Jesus is acting as the 'light of the world' (9:4–5). There is also the constant play on what people do or do not 'know' (*oida*; 9:12, 20, 21, 24, 25, 29, 30, 31). Finally, there is the emphasis in 10:14–15 on the mutual 'knowledge' (*ginôskein*) of Jesus' sheep and Jesus himself plus Jesus himself and God, an emphasis we may now supplement with Jesus' claim in 10:38 that 'the Jews' should believe in his acts in order that they may 'come to perceive (*gnôte*) and know (*ginôskete*)' the truth about himself. In fact, *everything* in these chapters (as elsewhere in this Gospel) is about knowledge. That immediately fits the Stoic theory of signs since it very distinctly places the sign at a cognitive level. Reading a Stoic sign is a matter of seeing conceptual connections *about* events that take place in the world itself. In the same way, all the dialogues and monologues that make up John 9–10 are about how to 'read' the facts about the world. The three specific texts we have noted that expressly address the issue of concluding something about the world from something else make this cognitive level transparent. But the whole text is operating at this level.

Let us now turn to our second overarching question. If John's handling of the notion of a sign in John 9–10 tallies with the way the notion is understood within Stoicism, then how does that handling give meaning to everything else that is said in the two chapters?

WHO CAN READ THE WORKS OF JESUS AS SIGNS?

Once one sees the pervasiveness in the text of the theme of being able to read Jesus' works as signs, one will also immediately see that the two chapters are structured around the idea of a contrast between some people who have or acquire that ability and others who do not. The stellar example of the former type is the man who was born blind. John 9 as a whole is clearly focused on showing a development that he undergoes from being a figure who is just around and is then healed by Jesus and repeatedly tells the story of that healing (9:1–17), to becoming a figure who gradually realizes for himself who Jesus actually is (9:24–38). Here the relationship between 9:17 and 9:38 is revealing. To begin with, when asked whom he takes Jesus to be, he replies with customary vagueness, 'a prophet'. At the end, however, he confesses to Jesus as 'the Son of Man'. There clearly is a development here.

Note then that the healed man does not by himself arrive at the conclusion that Jesus is 'the Son of Man'. He concluded on his own that Jesus was 'from God' (9:33), but is made to see by Jesus in *an additional exchange* (9:35–8) that Jesus is 'the Son of Man'.[11] Why does he need direct help from Jesus to take this step from 'from God' to 'the Son of Man'? We may find an answer by noting how he gets there. Jesus asks him whether he believes in the Son of Man (9:35). The man answers: 'Who then is he, Lord, so that I may believe in him?' (9:36). Jesus' reply ('You have both seen him and the one who is speaking with you is the one', 9:37) reminds one of his answer to the Samaritan woman in 4:26 ('I am the one, the one who is speaking with you'). But where the Samaritan woman only responds by musing about *whether* Jesus might be the Messiah (4:29), the healed man responds far more positively: '"Lord, I believe." And he (fell on his knees and) worshipped him' (9:38). However, does he know *what* 'the Son of Man' is? He definitely 'knows' *that* Jesus is that enigmatic figure. But to the extent that his baffled question in 9:36 not only concerns the reference of 'the Son of Man', but also the very sense of the term, he has been given nothing to build on. The conclusion must be that he is helped by Jesus to take a highly significant step from seeing that Jesus is 'from God' to confessing Jesus as 'the Son of Man'—whoever that figure really is—but only because Jesus has told him so. If this is right, one can also immediately understand why the text makes this complicated but also vitally important addition to the healed man's own deductions. For nobody *could* deduce, while Jesus was still on the earth, that he was 'the Son of Man' in the sense of a figure who would die, be raised, and sit in judgement on the final day.

It remains the case, however, that the healed man does undergo a development throughout the chapter. This development is in focus in his conversation in 9:24–34 with 'the Jews', which plays on what he 'knows'

---

[11] Barrett (1978) 364 comments on 'the otherwise surprising use of the title Son of Man' here by referring to 12:34 (itself referring back to 12:23) and suggesting that this title is specifically connected with the motif of Jesus appearing as judge: see 9:39. This is helpful since it connects directly the theme of judgement with that of seeing (the blind man healed) or not-seeing (the seeing Pharisees, who are actually 'blind'). Generally, the 'title' of Son of Man is connected with the motifs of Jesus' resurrection and return: compared already at 1:51, 3:13–21 etc. (See also Culpepper 2001, 70: 'the thirteen references to the Son of Man in John... consistently deal with his descent to earth and his ascent to heaven (3:13; 6:62), his exaltation (3:14; 8:28; 12:34), and his glorification (12:23; 13:31).') *That*, however, is something the healed man could not see by himself.

about Jesus (9:25 and 31–3) and what 'the Jews' 'know' about him (9:24, 29, 30). What 'the Jews' 'know' is either false (9:24) or a sign that they do *not* know the truth about Jesus (9:29). By contrast, what the man 'knows' is either a fact, namely, that he has been healed by Jesus (9:25, 30), or the truth about Jesus that *he* is precisely able to *deduce from* that fact (9:31–3). Thus the man becomes the stellar example of those who are able to read Jesus' works as signs when he *spells out* (in 9:31–3) the logic of the sign.

In spite of this, is the reader meant to understand the healed man as actually reaching, by 9:38, the full and final insight into Jesus' identity? Two points might suggest a positive answer: what he says *sounds* that way ('Lord'!); and his action (*proskynêsis*, 'prostration') suggests the same. However, we also know that one needs the *pneuma* to make a full confession, and there is no whisper of that here. Could it be, then, that the very fact that an additional exchange is needed is meant to suggest that the man only *half* gets what he confesses in 9:38 even when Jesus has explicitly told him? I think there are two answers to be given concerning the extent of the healed man's understanding. The first is that as he is described in 9:30–8 he does not himself reach the full and final insight in spite of his confession in 9:38. In this he may be compared with Peter in his confession at the end of John 6 (6:69). The healed man does two things. He draws his own conclusion that Jesus is 'from God' (9:33). And he confesses his belief that Jesus is 'the Son of Man' (9:35 and 38). But he does not *himself* conclude from the first thing to the second—which means that he does not understand his own conclusion in 9:33 in the way the *reader* knows it *should* be understood: that God helped Jesus *by giving him the pneuma*. Moreover, *that* is precisely implied—as the reader also knows—in Jesus' being 'the Son of Man' with all the tasks that go with that. Thus understood, the healed man does not *fully* know Jesus' identity. At the same time he is presented like that in 9:38. And the reason seems clear: he is to be understood as representing those among 'the Jews' who—in contrast to the healed man's diffident parents (9:22) and of course to his opponents, the Pharisees—came to constitute the new group of Jesus' followers. And these, as becomes clear in John 10, are to be understood as 'full believers'.

By contrast with the healed man, the Pharisees and 'the Jews' are precisely those who are unable to conclude to Jesus' identity from his acts. This is made abundantly clear in their conversations with the healed man both in 9:13–17 (especially 15–16) and in 9:24–34. And it is stated explicitly by Jesus himself in his reply in 10:25–6 to their question whether he is the Messiah (10:24): they are not able to believe him when he *says* that he is (10:25a), nor are they able to draw the appropriate conclusion from his 'works', that is, from what he *does* (10:25b–6).

In short, based on the idea of being able to conclude from Jesus' works to his identity, John 9–10 draws a picture of a contrast between some people who do have that ability and others who do not. Nobody, I should think, will disagree with this reading.

THE RESULTING CONTRAST: JOHN 9:34–10:21

Then comes a further point, which has not been generally seen. It is that the text connects the ability of the healed man with the inability of 'the Jews' in a manner that eventually results in a full and direct contrast between what the healed man has gradually come to represent, namely, the group of believers in Jesus (even as 'the Son of Man'), and 'the Jews' as representing a settled group of opponents of Jesus. This contrast is drawn in 9:34–41 but has wider implications for John 10, too.[12]

In 9:34 'the Jews' declare their superiority over the healed man. Reflecting the motif that was introduced at the beginning of the chapter (9:1–3), that there might be a connection between the man being born blind and some sin on the part of his parents (a suggestion Jesus rejects, 9:3), 'the Jews' now state that the healed man himself was born 'in sin', not just with respect to his eyes, but 'as a whole' (*hólos*): how then can he teach them anything? They therefore 'throw him out' (*ekballein*, 9:34). Here 'the Jews' insist on rejecting the conclusion that the healed man has gradually reached concerning Jesus' origins, and they cap their rejection by drawing a physical boundary between him and themselves.

When Jesus then hears that they 'had thrown out' the healed man (9:35, again *ekballein*), he himself seeks him out and engages him in the conversation about the Son of Man (9:34–8). But he also brings the contrast into the open between the healed man and the Pharisees (9:39–41). Where he was (literally) blind, but has now become seeing (both literally *and* 'spiritually'), the Pharisees, who are not literally blind and who claim to be ('spiritually') seeing, nevertheless remain in sin (9:41), obviously because they are '*spiritually*' blind. Thus when Jesus states that he has come into the cosmos to judge so that those who are not seeing may come to see and those who *are* seeing may become blind (9:39), he is directly contrasting the healed man with the Pharisees and 'the Jews' more generally. (In addition, it is wholly appropriate for Jesus to speak of his own task of 'judging' since

---

[12] For the chronological 'two-level drama', in which the blind man is not only someone healed by Jesus but also the representative of those Jewish Christians who have been expelled from the synagogue because of their confession of Jesus, see in general Martyn 2003. My own point rather concerns the way this theme is being *developed* in our text, and indeed from John 9 *into* John 10. Even if the healed man should probably not be understood to have reached the full insight, there can be no doubt that in the way he is contrasted with 'the Jews' he comes to represent the group of 'full believers' in Jesus.

this directly continues the previous conversation on his status as 'the Son of Man'.)

Now—and this is the structural point that has not been generally seen—the contrast between the healed man, who was 'thrown out' by 'the Jews', and the Pharisees and 'the Jews' themselves, as the contrast is spelled out in the final verses of John 9 (9:39–41), *leads directly into* John 10, where Jesus describes, in the form of a parable, the opposition between himself and his flock and his (and the flock's) enemies. Here the 'flock' clearly stands for those who have come to have faith in Jesus *on the model of the healed man.* By contrast, the shepherd's enemies are 'the Jews'.[13]

Then it is highly noteworthy—and additional proof of the textual connection across the chapter division at 10:1—that in the parable itself (10:1–5), Jesus employs exactly the term of 'throwing somebody out' (*ekballein*) that we found in 9:34 and 35. But here those who are 'thrown out', and indeed, by the shepherd himself (10:4), are *his own sheep*. Moreover, they are 'thrown out' from the original sheepfold, which in some way or other represents the boundaries of the Jewish people.[14] What we see here is that the text constructs a causal sequence: *because* 'the Jews' had in the first place thrown out the healed man, when he had drawn the correct conclusion about Jesus' origins from his acts, and when Jesus had then himself *reacted* to that violent act by helping the healed man to a final confession of Jesus as 'the Son of Man', *therefore* Jesus on his side is also forced to throw his own people *out of* the sheepfold and to walk away ahead of them (10:4). In relation to the imaginary centre of everybody's attention—the sheepfold—the acts of the two parties mirror one another exactly. Where 'the Jews' throw the healed man out in order to keep the valued object or 'field' for themselves, Jesus on his side throws his own people out of the valued object or 'field' and leads them away from it in order to keep *them* for himself.[15]

Read in this way, the theme in 10:1–18 is no longer how people may *come to* have faith in Jesus (as in the case of the healed man). Rather, Jesus' 'flock' is now already established (by 9:35–8 and 39–41 taken together) and may therefore be fully contrasted with 'the Jews'. Thus 10:1–18 should be understood as the *direct consequence* of the movement in John 9 that led to the drawing of a clear and explicit contrast between those who were able to

---

[13] This reading is also suggested by Léon-Dufour (1990).

[14] The precise interpretation of the various figures that turn up in the parable is highly contested. For the sheepfold, however, compare Barrett (1978, 369): 'This, then, is the fold of Judaism, which contained the first disciples and also the unbelieving Jews, of whom the former were to be joined by Gentile believers' (Barrett is here referring to 10:16).

[15] Lincoln (2005, 292) also notes the use of *ekballein* in both 9:34–5 and 10:4. When he states that the verb occurs with 'quite different connotations' in either place, he is in a sense right. In another sense he thereby misses the point I go on to articulate on the use of violence.

see and 'the Jews'. John 9 describes the development *towards* 'spiritual' sight, a development that then ends with an explicit contrast with those who have physical, but precisely not 'spiritual' sight. John 10:1–18 then rehearses the final character—and its contrast with 'the Jews'—of the new group that has been established as a result of the development described in John 9. However, in describing this change from 'becoming' to 'being' the text is also keenly interested in maintaining a distinct causal sequence. It was 'the Jews' who began using violence in order to keep the cherished value object for themselves. Then Jesus had to react, equally violently, by removing his own people from the cherished 'field'. Incidentally, this strategic claim about 'the Jews' is also very forcefully prepared for in 9:22–3, with the first of the three famous references to the practice of 'the Jews' of making anybody who confessed Jesus as the Messiah *aposynagôgós* ('thrown out of the syna-gogue'), which is almost identical in meaning with the use of *ekballein* in 9:34 and 35. In this way we can see how John's concern throughout the two chapters about how properly to read Jesus' acts as signs serves a further purpose of drawing a marked contrast between those who are able to do so and those who are not. The ability *or* inability to 'read' Jesus properly leads directly to a fundamental opposition, not just (as in John 5 and 7–8) between Jesus and 'the Jews', but now also between those Jews who, in spite of everything, did follow Jesus (= his 'sheep') and the other Jews.

It follows from this reading that the chapter division at 10:1 does violence (!) to the movement of the text. In fact, 9:39 (NRSV: 'Jesus said, "I came into this world for judgement so that those who do not see may see, and those who do see may become blind".') should be understood as a verse that both summarizes the development that has taken place in John 9 and also announces the contrast that Jesus draws in 10:1–18 between his own 'flock' and 'the Jews'. The Pharisees of 9:40–1 are 'spiritually' blind and remain in their sin. *In fact* ('Truly, truly I say to you ...', 10:1), they are like the thief and robber who enters the sheepfold illicitly (10:1). But the one who enters through the door is etc. (10:2).[16]

With this understanding of the relationship between John 9 and 10 we can see that John here repeats the pattern we also found in John 7–8 of speaking partly of 'initial belief' in Jesus and partly of 'full belief'. Thus in describing people's reactions both to Jesus' sayings (John 7–8) and his doings (John 9–10), John is concerned to keep in play the distinction between 'initial' and 'full belief'. And why? Because it encapsulates the one basic idea that holds the whole Gospel together: during Jesus' lifetime

---

[16] Léon-Dufour (1990, 327) is entirely right in his comment on the 'Truly, truly, I say to you': 'The double Amen of 10,1, with which the discourse begins, confirms the continuity of the text, for this formula normally introduces a more profound version of a preceding affirmation on the part of Jesus while the audience remains the same.'

nobody acquired full belief in Jesus or understood *fully* who Jesus was; and nobody *could* understand that since it presupposed knowledge of his resurrection and return to God which nobody could understand until it had happened and been made clear to (initial) believers when they would receive the *pneuma*.

We need not comment in detail on the parable of John 10 (10:1–5) and its exposition (10:7–18) by Jesus. Suffice it to say that it is full of themes that precisely reflect the self-understanding of the *fully* established 'Christian' group a long time after the events themselves, but once they had acquired full knowledge of Jesus: that the shepherd has come to give his sheep 'life' (10:10) so that they will be 'saved' (10:9); that he lays down his soul for them (10:11)—but also that he will recover it, as his Father has ordained (10:17–18); and that he has sheep from outside the sheepfold (of Judaism) who will join the other sheep so as to produce a single flock with a single shepherd (10:16).[17] Noteworthy, since it more or less accidentally keeps alive the probable connection between Jesus' possession of the *pneuma* and the effectiveness of his speaking, is the repeated emphasis on the shepherd's 'voice' (*phônê*) and the sheep's 'hearing' it (*akouein*). It is hammered out in the parable itself (10:3–5, NRSV):

[3]The gatekeeper opens the gate for him [the shepherd], and the sheep hear his voice. He calls (*phônei*) his own sheep by name and leads them out. [4]When he has brought out all his own, he goes ahead of them, and the sheep follow him because they know his voice.

[5]They will not follow a stranger, but they will run from him because they do not know the voice of strangers.

But the motif is also repeatedly taken up in Jesus' exposition of the parable, at 10:8, 16, and 27. All through, Jesus' sheep are those who are able to 'hear' his 'voice'.

Also noteworthy, and highly relevant to the talk of 'throwing out' the Jesus people, is the amount of violent language used by Jesus of the good shepherd's opponents. They attempt to force their way into the sheepfold (10:1). They only aim to steal and kill the sheep in order to offer them up for sacrifice (10:10). If they manage to take charge of the sheep, they will leave them in the lurch when they see a wolf approaching, 'and the wolf grabs (*harpazein*) and disperses them' (10:12). Here the term for 'grabbing' is taken up again at 10:28–9 when Jesus declares that he gives eternal life (!) to his

---

[17] Against Martyn (1996) and Ashton (2007, 113 n. 31), who take the 'other sheep' to be 'groups of "Jews" who professed faith in Jesus' (Ashton), I remain convinced by the traditional view among scholars that they stand for Gentiles. (See, e.g., Barrett 1978, 376.) Bultmann, of course, took 10:16 to be a later interpolation. But one needs to have Bultmann's confidence in one's own judgement vis-à-vis the transmitted text in order to be able to accept that.

own sheep (compare 10:26–7) so that they will never die (contrast this with 10:10) 'and nobody will (be able to) grab (*harpazein*) them from my hand' (10:28, 29). In all this, whereas the good shepherd is full of care for his sheep (10:11–18, 28–30), his opponents are full of violence. And the point? Once more that violence begins with 'the Jews'. When Jesus acts violently and 'throws out' his sheep from the sheepfold, he is only forced to do so by his opponents' behaviour and he acts in order to save the sheep.

We should conclude that 10:1–18 describes the fully 'Christian' group— probably the Johannine group itself—that has (*eventually*) been created when sufficient numbers of people had come to believe in Jesus on the model of the healed man of John 9. But the three verses that conclude this section of the text (10:19–21) also show that precisely this genesis of the group has not been forgotten. When 'the Jews' react to Jesus' words (note *logous* here, i.e. not his acts) in the usual way with a schism (10:19), many of them declare—in the manner we know from John 7–8—that he has a demon and should not be listened to (10:20, again Greek *akouein*), but others reply that those words (here *rhêmata*, that is, the actual sound-carried words that stream from Jesus' mouth) are not those of a man who is possessed by a demon. And then they refer, as we know, to Jesus' *acts*: 'would a demon have been able to open the eyes of blind people?' (10:21). Thus what is basically at stake in John 9–10 as a whole is the ability to read Jesus' *acts*, and to read them as the signs that they are. *Then* one will also be able to hear his words. In this way the end of 10:21 ties the whole of 10:1–21 tightly together with John 9. But we should also note that 10:19–21 in this manner ties the whole of 9:1–10:21 on how to read Jesus' doings together with the theme of John 7–8 on how to react to his sayings.

THE ULTIMATE ISSUE: JOHN 10:22–42

With 10:22 we get a change of scene, both in time and place. We already know the close thematic connections with both 10:1–21 and John 9. For the former note this: when 'the Jews' surround Jesus in Solomon's stoa and ask him to declare himself 'openly' (*parrêsiai*), *that is*, no longer in parables as in 10:1–18, whether he is the Messiah (10:24), Jesus' reply partly (10:26–7 + 28–9) refers back to the sheep of the parable. This gives two clear hints that 10:22–42 is meant to be read in direct continuation of 10:1–21. And for the latter: Jesus' reply also repeats the point from John 9 of the need to be able to read Jesus' works as witnessing about himself (10:25). As we also know, the same theme is taken up later in the new section (at 10:32–3 and 37–8) and in the concluding reference to the kind of *sêmeion* that Jesus' works constitute (10:41). In light of these connections across 10:22, what is the new point made in 10:22–42 as a whole?

The answer is not difficult to find since the new section is clearly focused on the question of 'the Jews' about Jesus' identity and their rejection of his answer—and conversely on the radical character of that answer. 'The Jews' ask whether Jesus is the Messiah (10:24) and Jesus replies in a way (10:25–9) that leads to the radical claim that 'I and the Father are one' (10:30), to which 'the Jews' react by trying to stone him (10:31). The reader will conclude that Jesus is the Messiah, but also much more than that. When Jesus then refers once more to his works, ironically asking 'the Jews' for which of those works they aim to stone him (10:32), they explicitly declare that they are unconcerned about any works: instead, they react to his blasphemy when he, a human being, makes himself (a) God (10:33). Here the text has 'the Jews' themselves *declare* what John 9 has already shown in practice: that they are entirely unconcerned with Jesus' acts; foolishly, they believe that Jesus' acts are one thing and his relationship with God another. However, in reply to the new charge on the part of 'the Jews' (10:33), Jesus engages in a teasing scriptural argument about who he is (10:34–6).[18] In all this, the central question remains that of his identity: is he the Messiah (10:24)? Are he and the Father one (10:30)? Is he (a) God (10:33)? And now: is he (the) Son of God (10:36)? Jesus' concluding claim again reverts to the question of his works (10:37–8). Again, however, 'the Jews' seek to catch him, but he left 'from their hand' (10:39)—just as they were unable to grab any of Jesus' sheep from his (10:28) and the Father's (10:29) hand. What 10:22–39 brings into the open as part of John 9–10 as a whole is clearly the *conclusion* that 'the Jews' *should* have been able to draw from Jesus' works: that he is the Messiah in the more developed sense that Jesus then spells out to them. One might say that this conclusion was already sufficiently clearly articulated in Jesus' conversation with the healed man concerning the Son of Man in 9:35–8. However, since John 10 (beginning at 9:39) has gone on to present the full contrast between the Jesus people and 'the Jews', it is wholly to the point that the conclusion to be drawn from Jesus' works should also be insisted upon vis-à-vis those who did *not* arrive at the proper conclusion. That is what happens in 10:22–39, which focuses on the conclusion itself while also keeping in the picture the theme of John 9 of how to arrive at that conclusion. Thus at the end of John 10 we have been given two parallel accounts of what people would conclude from Jesus' acts if they were able to see them as signs. The healed man came to see Jesus as being 'from God' and eventually as 'the Son of Man'. 'The Jews', by contrast, were unable to see him even as the Messiah. *A fortiori*, they were wholly unable to see him as what he

---

[18] Incidentally, note how Jesus here refers to 'your' law (10:34), thereby explicitly distinguishing between two wholly separate groups: 'the Jews' versus himself and his followers. (Much more on this in Chapter XI.)

really was: one with the Father, (a) God, (the) Son of God. They should have drawn this conclusion from his acts, but what the healed man had managed to do—at least to a large extent—they were unable to do.

If there is this parallel between what the healed man came to see—even if only three quarters of the way—and what 'the Jews' precisely did not come to see, then it is worth taking one more look at two of Jesus' self-identifications towards the very end of John 10. Just as the healed man needed some help to go from seeing Jesus as being 'from God' to believing in him as 'the Son of Man', so the two identifications at the end of John 10 add decisively to the notion of the 'Messiah' ('the Christ', 10:24) from which 'the Jews' began. The first is Jesus' claim to be *hyios tou theou* (10:36). This is backed by an argument that the Scriptures have already spoken of certain human beings as 'gods' (10:34–5); then why may the one whom God 'has sanctified' and 'sent into the world' not say '"I am *hyios tou theou*"' (10:36)? Two things are noteworthy here. First, it seems probable that the reference to God having 'sanctified' Jesus refers to a specific act that 'the Jews' might not really have heard about: Jesus' baptism from above when he received the *pneuma*. Secondly, the phrase *hyios tou theou* is ambiguous in an interesting manner. As part of the argument, it should mean 'a son of God'. However, in light of the (implicit) reference to Jesus' baptism from above and all that the *reader* knows about Jesus right from the beginning of the Gospel, it is also probable that the phrase is intended to mean 'the Son of God'. The latter reading is possible even without a definite article for 'son' (*hyios*). And it is the only reading that fits Jesus' earlier claim in the passage that 'I and the/my Father are one' (10:30).

The other self-identification made by Jesus is the one with which he ends: 'the/my Father is in me and I in the/my Father' (10:38). This is as close as anything to being the ultimate specification of the relationship between Jesus and God since it spells out the way in which 'I and the/my Father are one': Jesus and God are intimately connected—even in bodily form—by the fact that the *pneuma*, God's own *pneuma*, is present *within* Jesus—and vice versa.

With these two self-identifications, which clearly add tremendously to identifying Jesus as the 'Messiah', is Jesus then suggesting that 'the Jews' should have been able to deduce such an elevated status for Jesus from his *erga* ('works')? Both yes and no. Yes, in the sense that his *erga* are *erga theou* ('works of God', see 9:3) as performed by Jesus. So they do point to the identity that Jesus claims for himself. But probably also no. Here again—just as we saw in the case of the healed man—'the Jews' had no real chance of seeing this *full* identity of Jesus' since it involves a grasp of the presence of the *pneuma* in Jesus. That was something that nobody (apart from John the Baptist) was able to understand before Jesus' death and resurrection.

We on our side should conclude that 10:22–39, which scholars invariably separate from the rest, constitutes nothing less than the logical climax of the whole development that began in 9:1. Here the starkest formulations of Jesus' identity are given that 'the Jews' should in principle have been able to deduce from his acts. And here 'the Jews' are confronted most directly by Jesus himself with their inability to draw those conclusions from everything he has said and done. The confrontation is now total, also from the perspective of 'the Jews' since they now hear Jesus make claims about himself that they do not actually understand (as seen by Jesus himself and the Evangelist), but nevertheless understand well enough to find preposterous.

CONCLUSIONS ABOUT UNITY AND PHILOSOPHY

The reading we have given of the two chapters has, I believe, gone a long way to vindicate the claim that they constitute a tight literary unity. There is no textual necessity here that should force one to divide the text up at any of the places that have traditionally been proposed. On the contrary, seen from a narrative philosophical point of view such a procedure would do violence to the text in the strongest sense of this phrase: it would tear apart what belongs intimately together.

The claim has also been vindicated that there is a single theme that holds the two chapters firmly together: that of concluding from Jesus' works to his identity. Furthermore, we may confidently claim that John's manner of spelling out the theme of a 'sign' takes a form that it is fair to call philosophical, not least when it is also seen in light of the Stoic theory of the sign. Thus the two chapters are held together by the repeated use of a philosophical theme and the way this theme is intertwined with and gives meaning to the other themes that come up in the narrative: the conflict between the healed man and 'the Jews' (9:1–41); the contrast between a gradual movement of coming to believe in Jesus (9:1–41) and an account of the fully established group of Christ believers that results from such a process (10:1–21); the final clash between Jesus and 'the Jews' as a firmly established group of opponents with regard to the ultimate question of Jesus' identity (10:22–42).

We have not attempted to articulate the philosophical theme treated in the two chapters in the form of a philosophical question in our usual manner. It would be quite easy to do so, for instance in this form: what is it that is shown by seeing Jesus' 'works' (*erga*) as 'signs' (*sêmeia*)? But there is no need for this since the text itself already presupposes this question and then moves on to answer it, most clearly in the reasoning of the man born blind in 9:31–3. In this way the text is itself already one step ahead of the reader who is looking for philosophical questions to be answered during the reading. This text is already a philosophical one.

VIII

FROM BELIEVING IN JESUS
TO POSSESSING HIS *LOGOS*
(JOHN 11–12)

A THEMATIC UNITY

In this chapter I argue two points that have not been clearly seen by scholars.[1] The first is that John 11–12 constitutes a single, coherent narrative that is held together in strictly narrative terms by a number of internal references across the chapter divide. The second is that the two chapters also share a common overarching theme that has been more or less extensively touched on in earlier chapters (John 3, 5, and 8, in particular) but here is brought to its final conclusion in a manner that brings the reader directly back to the Prologue. This theme has a number of aspects that are all presented in the text, though under a huge caveat to be mentioned in a moment.

One such aspect is that the raising of Lazarus is a prefiguration both of the (death and) resurrection of Jesus and of Christ believers generally. Parts of this have been seen by scholars, but not in the strict form that ties the three cases of resurrection tightly together in a narrative logic: Lazarus' resurrection prefigures that of Jesus, which is the precondition for that of believers.[2]

Another aspect is that as a prefiguration of the resurrection of Jesus, the raising of Lazarus is meant to point explicitly towards the form of full belief in Jesus that goes distinctly beyond all forms of initial belief. Now the proper content of believing in Jesus is specifically that he will also *return to* God through his resurrection and that this has crucial

---

[1] A widely different version of this chapter with much less literary analysis of the text will be published on the internet in Engberg-Pedersen 2017.

[2] There is general agreement that John presents the raising of Lazarus as the direct cause of Jesus' death, but that is definitely not all.

consequences for human beings, who will also eventually be resurrected and obtain eternal life.[3]

Where these two points are basically matters of cognition, they are also inserted into a genuine epistemology when the two chapters address head-on the epistemological issue of exactly how human beings may arrive at obtaining the full cognitive insight. Here the two chapters at long last bring wholly into the open that in order to obtain full belief in Jesus, believers must themselves receive the *pneuma*—and *through that* access to the full *logos*. Moreover, it is also shown that reception of the *logos–pneuma* is what ensures in *ontological* terms that those human beings who have received it will themselves eventually be resurrected.

Thus it may be said that in spelling out the step from initial belief in Jesus to the full belief that he was resurrected and has returned to God and in suggesting that this step has crucial implications for human beings, John 11–12 takes a step from mere cognition via epistemology to full ontology, thereby showing how knowledge is connected with actual fact: in John's conception, epistemology and ontology are mutually intertwined.

But now for the huge caveat: at the narrative level where Jesus is still on earth and speaking in ways that have all these cognitive, epistemological, and even ontological implications, all the things that *should* have been understood were not yet fully understood. This crucial aspect of the overall theme is centrally marked in two places: in Jesus' conversation with Martha before the raising of Lazarus (11:21–7); and in the section that concludes John 12 (12:20–50). The lack of understanding shown here reflects the fact that at the time when Jesus was still on earth, nobody other than himself was in actual possession of the *pneuma*. But the *pneuma* must be present in a person both to generate a full understanding of the facts about Jesus and believers, as contained in God's and Jesus' *logos*, and also to enable the ontological realization of that understanding in the actual resurrection of believers. Lacking the *pneuma*, believers were unable to do more than react to the *pneuma* as contained in Jesus' *rhêmata*, thereby achieving only an initial understanding of Jesus' identity and only an initial belief.

Thus the thematic line runs like this: resurrection of Lazarus → resurrection to eternal life of Jesus → possession of the *pneuma*-carried *logos*, which is the full story of Jesus' descent and ascent → believing in Jesus' resurrection and return to God → resurrection to eternal life of believers.

---

[3] If one asks whether the full belief treated in John 11–12 differs from the one we have repeatedly been talking about, the answer is both that it does not fundamentally do so, but also that it is now very specifically focused on knowledge of Jesus' resurrection and what that implies for believers.

But it all stands under the huge caveat that during Jesus' lifetime these various connections were *not* understood. Somewhat ironically, one may say that John's story of the raising of Lazarus is itself intended to *show* that these things were *not* understood by the immediate agents.

In finding this comprehensive argument in John 11–12, we will rely on one presupposition that has been argued for in Chapter II of this book: that there is the tightest possible connection between *logos*, light, and *pneuma* (basically, they are the same thing as seen from different perspectives), and that as Jesus is described from John 1 onwards, he is to be understood as himself carrying, or being informed by, that trias. The task, then, for us as readers of John 11–12 is to note the places where this trias of concepts is invoked and activated.

We begin by considering the literary unity of the two chapters. Then we develop the single comprehensive theme of a fundamentally philosophical kind (cognition, epistemology, and ontology) that is articulated *through* that literary unity. We will do this by asking a philosophical question that is raised by the central conversation between Jesus and Martha in 11:21–7 and showing that this question is then answered by narrative means in the concluding section of John 12 (12:20–50).

ARGUMENTS FOR LITERARY UNITY: THE ROLES OF MARY, MARTHA, AND LAZARUS (11:1–12:19)

(i) Whereas Lazarus has a very passive role to play in the events described in John 11, Mary and Martha have more active roles, which are marked by the fact that at different points in the story they make an almost identical quasi-objection to Jesus (11:21 and 32). This active role is not forgotten in chapter 12 either, where Martha is said to 'serve' (12:2), while Mary famously anoints Jesus' feet and dries them with her hair (12:3–8). Lazarus is not forgotten either (12:1, 9–11, 17). In itself, this only shows that the story of John 12 has not forgotten that of John 11. But there is far more to these connections across the chapter divide.

(ii) In fact, when Mary is introduced at the beginning of John 11, she is presented as the better known of the two women (Martha is 'her sister', 11:1). Moreover, in a curious flash forward (11:2) she is said to be 'the Mary who' (had) anointed the Lord with unguent and (had) dried his feet with her hair. The reference is curious since it twice makes use of the Greek aorist verbal form that would immediately suggest that at the level of the storyline this was something that had already occurred. Perhaps, however, the two aorists rather suggest that the writer is momentarily looking at the story from the outside, or from his own time perspective: 'this Mary is the one, you know, who anointed the Lord' etc.[4] If so, his use of the aorist is an almost explicit way of tying the story of John 11 together with the one that will then be told in John 12.

(iii) It is well known that the story of Lazarus' resurrection directly triggers the decision of the high priests and Pharisees to kill Jesus (11:45–6 + 47–53, 57). In John 12, however, this is extended to include a decision to kill Lazarus himself (12:10–11) since many Jews went to see not only Jesus, but also the raised Lazarus and came to believe in Jesus because of him. Once again, this might be taken only to show that the story of John 12 has not forgotten that of John 11. However, it now begins to look as if John 12 has been deliberately constructed so as to follow on John 11. Apparently, John wished to emphasize even more than he had already done in John 11 the role of the story of the raising of Lazarus in the decision to have Jesus killed.

ARGUMENTS FOR LITERARY UNITY: THE ROLES OF THE CROWD AND THE AUTHORITIES (11:45–12:19)

(iv) The importance of the raising of Lazarus for the events described in John 12 is brought out especially clearly when one considers the role of the crowd, both 'the Jews' who were with Mary (11:31) or had gone up to her and seen what had happened to Lazarus (11:45; 12:17), and also 'the Jews' who had gone up to Jerusalem for the festival (11:55–6; 12:12) and then went out to meet Jesus (12:12–13) because they had heard about Lazarus (12:18).[5] For analytic purposes we may speak of the 'Lazarus crowd', the 'pilgrim crowd', and the 'Jerusalem crowd'. We will see that John is exceedingly careful across the chapter divide about both separating and eventually bringing together these three crowds. The apparent aim is to bring out the crucial role that the raising of Lazarus had for the story about Jesus himself. Also, it brings out very strongly the importance of 'the crowd' in the proceedings leading to Jesus' death. Let us consider the whole text of 11:45–12:19.

The positive reaction to the raising of Lazarus by the 'Lazarus crowd' in 11:45 is counterbalanced in 11:46 by some, who reported the events to the Pharisees. This leads to the decision in 11:47–53 of the high priests and the

---

[4] Thus also Theobald 2009, 725. There does not, however, seem to be any need to see the verse as a 'later gloss' (Theobald 2009, 726, referring to Bultmann, Brown, Schnackenburg, Becker, Dietzfelbinger, Lincoln). On the contrary, it may well be seen as yet another small feature that ties John 11 and 12 together.

[5] Barrett (1978, 417) rightly states on 12:13 that 'the crowd was in Jerusalem already and came out to meet Jesus' and adds that 12:17–18 'suggests two crowds, one accompanying Jesus, the other going out of the city to meet him'.

Pharisees to have Jesus killed. 'But Jesus (*Ho oun Iêsous*)...' (11:54) went into the countryside (*eis tên chôran*). Here we have a sequence: the 'Lazarus crowd', the authorities, Jesus. Then there is a change of time and place which scholars have found to be very important.[6] John himself probably considered the change of less importance. 'Now the Passover of the Jews was *near*' (11:55, NRSV)—so the time difference was not that marked. Similarly, John is keen to connect the verse that marks the change geographically with the immediately preceding verse about Jesus: 'and many went up *from the country* (*side, ek tês chôras*) to Jerusalem' (11:55, NRSV). These people are not the 'Lazarus crowd'. They are the 'pilgrim crowd' who end up being part of the 'Jerusalem crowd'. In Jerusalem, they seek for Jesus (11:56), not because of the events concerning Lazarus, but because the high priests and Pharisees had given orders to denounce Jesus' whereabouts so that they might arrest him (11:57). 'But Jesus (*Ho oun Iêsous*)...' (12:1) came to Bethany, where Lazarus and his sisters threw a party for him (12:2). Here again we have a sequence right across the chapter divide: the 'Jerusalem crowd', the authorities, Jesus.

After Mary's anointment of Jesus (12:3–8), the crowd and the authorities turn up again. The 'great crowd of the Jews' (12:9) must be the 'Jerusalem crowd'. They now realize that Jesus is in Bethany and go out there 'not only because of Jesus but also to see Lazarus, whom he had raised from the dead' (12:9, NRSV). How did they know about that? We must wait and see. But the mention of the crowd is immediately followed by two verses (12:10–11) on the authorities, who planned to put Lazarus to death as well (12:10) since it was because of him that many Jews came to believe in Jesus (12:11). Here Jesus himself is not immediately connected with the crowd and the authorities, but the nucleus of the sequence is intact: the crowd and the authorities. Moreover, the pattern that was begun in 11:45–53 (54) is now strengthened. There it was only the 'Lazarus crowd' leading the authorities to their decision to have only one person killed: Jesus. Here it is the much more important 'Jerusalem crowd', with the consequence that the authorities now decide to kill Lazarus *too*.

At 12:12–13 we again hear of 'the great crowd'. Now it is explicitly identified as the 'pilgrim crowd' that had come up for the festival (see 11:55) and then become part of the 'Jerusalem crowd'. When they hear that Jesus is on his way to Jerusalem, they 'went out to meet him' (12:13,

[6] Theobald, for one (2009, 761), lets a whole new section begin at 11:55 stretching up to 12:36 when Jesus' 'public ministry' is concluded. Barrett, too (1978, 408), lets a new section begin at 11:55. So does Lincoln (2005, 315–17), who while good on the question of how far the account of the raising of Lazarus extends, nevertheless concludes that '11.54–7 mark a definite break and point forward to the last Passover in Jesus' mission' (317). It is as if the fact that *we* know the importance of the Passion has prevented readers from following John's own line of thought.

NRSV). Whether this 'great crowd' is identical with the 'great crowd' that went out to Bethany the day before (12:9) is unclear. The point is that the 'Jerusalem crowd', which now includes the 'pilgrim crowd', *has now heard about the events concerning Lazarus*, which is why they both go out to Bethany and the next day go out to meet the approaching Jesus. How did they hear about that? Again we must wait and see. And then we get Jesus' entry into the city (12:12–16).

Next, in 12:17–19, the pattern of a sequence from the crowd to the authorities is repeated one last time and here in a very specific way that finally explains how the 'pilgrim crowd', who had eventually become part of the 'Jerusalem crowd', had got to know about the events concerning Lazarus: they had been *told by* the 'Lazarus crowd'. Here is the text (12:17–19, NRSV):

[17]So the crowd that had been with him when he called Lazarus out of the tomb and raised him from the dead continued to testify. [18]It was also because they heard that he had performed this sign that the crowd went to meet him. [19]The Pharisees then said to one another, 'You see, you can do nothing. Look, the world has gone after him!'

It is clear that John here aims to explain why the 'pilgrim and Jerusalem crowds' both went to Bethany and also—and not least—went out to meet Jesus on his approach to Jerusalem: they had been informed by the 'Lazarus crowd'. In this way John brings all three crowds together or even turns the 'pilgrim and Jerusalem crowds' *into* a 'Lazarus crowd'. The aim is clearly to explain the importance of the 'sign' connected with Lazarus (12:18) for the positive reception of Jesus by the 'pilgrim/Jerusalem/Lazarus crowd'. '*The*' crowd was very positive towards Jesus because it knew of his having raised Lazarus. That only makes the reaction—in our pattern—of the authorities even more apposite. They had made two decisions, one (in 11:47–53) to have Jesus killed and another (in 12:10–11) to have Lazarus killed *too*. And they now realize their failure: the whole world has gone after him (12:19).

In light of all this narrative care about the various crowds, it seems wholly impossible to break up the storyline at either 11:55, 12:1, 12:9, or 12:12. If one believes—and there is very good reason for that—that 11:45–54 belongs together with the story of the raising of Lazarus, then that story *and its aftermath* must go the whole way up to 12:19.[7]

We on our side should conclude that not only do Mary, Martha, and Lazarus play carefully defined roles across the chapter divide, but the importance of the raising of Lazarus, in particular, is equally carefully shown in the reactions of the various crowds to Jesus and the decisions of

---

[7] Lincoln (2005, 316) finds this solution 'enticing', but nevertheless decides to end the Lazarus story at 11:53.

the authorities in light of those reactions. In all this it is very difficult to see anything but a very tight narrative construction of a storyline from 11:45 up to 12:19—right across the chapter divide.

We may further note how extremely skilfully John has incorporated the two traditional stories he chose to recount here (Mary's anointment of Jesus, 12:3–8, and the entry into Jerusalem, 12:13–15) into the wider framework of 11:45–12:19. These two stories are not just given on their own as part of the tradition. Instead, they are subsumed under a single storyline that centres on the reactions of the crowds and the authorities. In John's account it is the development in the reactions of the crowds and the authorities that holds the text together.

ARGUMENTS FOR LITERARY UNITY: THE FRAMING OF THE STORY ABOUT LAZARUS' RESURRECTION (11:3–16)

(v) John is often very careful when he introduces his major stories. He seems particularly concerned to lay out some of the basic ideas that will make the deeper point of the story intelligible to the attentive reader. In John 11 this initial framing occurs in 11:3–16. What it pinpoints is partly the misunderstanding of his disciples, capped—hardly by accident—by a brief, completely mistaken statement by 'unbelieving Thomas' (11:16), and partly the character *and wider implications* of the upcoming story of Lazarus' resurrection. There is something here that should be understood, but in fact was not.

The first sign that something more is in play in the story is Jesus' reply to the message of the two sisters that his friend 'is weak' (or ill, 11:3): 'This weakness is not one that will lead to death; it is for the glory (*doxa*) of God, in order that the Son of God may be glorified through it' (11:4).[8] This is frightfully loaded with double meaning. First, Lazarus' 'weakness' was in fact one that did lead to death: he died. But then he was also resurrected, so his 'weakness' also led to life *beyond* death. Secondly, it has occurred 'for the glory of God', that is, to allow God's power over death to be revealed. And thirdly, it has occurred in order that the 'Son of God' may *himself* be 'glorified', that is, brought both to death and resurrection through the power of God. Just as Lazarus *will* die, but then also be raised, so the Son of God will die, but then also be resurrected and glorified through the power of God. Differently put, Lazarus' death allows Jesus to show what is about to

---

[8] The importance of this verse is noted by most commentators, e.g. Theobald 2009, 726, who rightly speaks of it as constituting 'the hermeneutic key to understanding the story of Lazarus'.

happen to himself. Lazarus, as it were, had to die—*in order to* be raised and made to live. *That* is what his interlocutors should but do not understand.

The next stage (11:6–10) consists of Jesus' waiting two days where he was—no doubt in order to make sure that Lazarus had died (see 11:14)—and then telling his disciples that he plans to return to Judea and why that is necessary. Apparently, his argument has nothing to do with Lazarus. It is about walking during the day, which has twelve hours (to work in?) when one can also see 'the light of this world'—as opposed to walking during the night (11:9–10). Is Jesus saying (as in 9:4): 'We must work while it is light'? Presumably yes. But there is also something here about not stumbling (*proskoptein*) while it is day, but precisely risking stumbling at night 'because the light is not *in one*' (11:10). What is meant? If we keep relying on 9:4, the idea will be that Jesus must work while it is still day and there is light to be seen in this world since when night has fallen, *that is*, when Jesus has himself gone, nobody will be able to work since they will no longer have the 'light of this world', that is, Jesus himself, within or among them.[9] If this is correct, then one is immediately reminded of the Prologue and its talk of the *logos*, which in the form of 'light' (1:2–5) was about to come into this world (1:9). This suggests at a very early stage that the story about the raising of Lazarus is not just a story about that singular event. It is also about Jesus, who is the ultimate light of this world, and it even contains a hint that it will soon enough be night, when this Jesus is no longer there.

The final stage (11:11–16) focuses even more specifically on the misunderstanding of the disciples. Jesus deliberately leads them astray. Lazarus has 'fallen asleep' and Jesus plans to 'wake him up from his sleep' (11:11). They quite reasonably misunderstand this: Ah, he is asleep; then he will be saved (11:12). Wild irony here: yes, he will indeed be 'saved'—from having been completely *dead*. Then Jesus speaks out: No, Lazarus is dead (11:14). And I am happy we were not there for your sake, *in order that you may come to believe* (11:15). Believe what? Believe—precisely—in the resurrection, and here we may confidently add (from 11:4): not just that of Lazarus, but also that of Jesus—and, as we will see a little later, *through* him that of all Christ believers. Are the disciples able to believe that? Not at all. The unbelieving Thomas makes that explicit: OK. Let us follow him—into *death* (11:16). If somebody should wish to celebrate John's use of irony, this would be one spectacular place to do it.

We may also note from a purely literary perspective that the (implicit) motif in 11:9–10 of Jesus being 'the light of this world' is taken up again twice towards the very end of what I am arguing is a single literary piece: at 12:35–6 (end of the speech that begins at 12:23) and again at 12:46 (in the

---

[9] I confess that this explication of the meaning of 11:10, in particular, is no more than a guess. The commentaries do not give much help here.

speech that concludes the whole of the Book of Signs). Just as Jesus' talk of his own *doxa* in 11:4 and 12:23–8 frames the rest, so does his talk at 11:10 and 12:35–6 and 46 of the 'light' that he himself is. This is one more example of a conceptual connection between beginning and end which, as we will see, is loaded with meaning.

ARGUMENTS FOR LITERARY UNITY: THE HOUR HAS COME; 'I HAVE GLORIFIED AND WILL GLORIFY' (12:20–50)

(vi) Once the story about Lazarus has been framed (11:3–16), once we have heard the story itself (11:17–44), and heard about its immediate consequences pointing towards Jesus' own death (11:45–12:19), there follows a final section of John 12 (12:20–50) which has the overall character of bringing the whole story line that began in John 1 to an end. After a highly peculiar introduction on Gentile interest in Jesus (12:20–2), we first get an extremely powerful statement by Jesus (12:23–33)—duly interrupted by a divine intervention from above (12:28)—to the effect that 'the hour has now finally come' (12:23). This is followed by a passage (12:34–43) on the perplexity (12:34) and unbelief (12:37–43) of the crowd and other Jewish figures, which is most cogently answered by Jesus (12:35–6). And finally, we get a concluding speech (12:44–50) by Jesus, once again of huge power, which appears to show what the 'hour' is all about. We will come back to some of the central ideas articulated in this whole section. Here what matters is seeing the literary connection of it all with what comes before.

The transition is made in 12:20–2. 'Some Greeks' among those who went up to Jerusalem for the festival wanted to 'see' Jesus (12:20–1). This connects directly back to the Pharisees' claim in the immediately preceding verse (12:19), which we saw to conclude the section that began at 11:45, to the effect that 'the whole world' (*ho kosmos*) is running after Jesus. Also, it takes up the motif from 12:12 and 11:55 of those who went up to Jerusalem because of the festival. The narrative connection, then, with what precedes is tight. Not so with what follows. Jesus 'answers them and says' (12:23)... what? 'The hour has come for the Son of man to be glorified'. Not much of an answer here, one should have thought. By contrast, it is difficult to find a stronger way of marking that now, finally, the moment to which everything else has been pointing is actually there. It is as if Jesus is saying: 'Enough! The hour has come etc.' If this is right, one may certainly go on to articulate the following connection: up until now everything has been focused on the attitude towards Jesus of various groups among 'the Jews'. Now, suddenly, 'some Greeks' are brought in. Could it not be because what is now coming directly into focus—Jesus' death and resurrection—is also *precisely* the one thing about him that immediately opens up what he stands for to Greeks, too?[10] Whether this suggestion is correct or not will to some extent depend on what the content is of Jesus' revelations in the three concluding sections of 12:23–50. That is not our concern right now. Here we may just suggest in more immediately literary terms that there may be a special fit between the fact that it is 'Greeks' who approach Jesus for the first time here and his claim that 'the hour has now (finally) come'. In strictly literary terms this suggestion also fits the fact that in the second of the three sections (12:34–43) John will go out of his way to explain why it is that 'they', i.e. presumably 'the Jews' in general, did not believe in him (12:37). This is a well-crafted summary of the whole picture of 'the Jews' given in the earlier part of the Gospel and it supplements the brief introduction of some 'Greeks' at 12:20–2. Thus at the precise point where it is claimed that the 'hour', which has been so well prepared for in John 11, has finally come, we both get a novel statement about 'some Greeks' and a concluding summary about 'the Jews'. In literary terms, this makes excellent sense and strongly supports the claim for unity right back to the beginning of chapter 11.

Here it is worth noting that the vital moment of 'the hour', which was implicitly referred to as early as 11:4, is not just marked by Jesus' actually speaking of 'the hour' (*hê hôra*) in 12:23. John does something more to mark it. He lets his Jesus invert the Gethsemane scene in Mark 14, by having him ask whether he should pray to God to 'save me from this hour (*tês hôras tautês*)' (12:27a). Of course not. For 'I have come to this hour (*tên hôran tautên*) for that very purpose' (12:27b). And so he even affirms this by praying directly to God that he, God, should 'glorify your name' (12:28a), which presumably means that God should set in motion the events that will eventually lead to Jesus' own glorification, that is, his *death*—and resurrection. The shocking result immediately follows: 'Then came a voice from heaven: "I have glorified (it or you) and I shall glorify (it or you) again."' (12:28b–c). We have already discussed the precise meaning of this. What matters here is only that the divine statement very clearly divides up Jesus' life into two consecutive parts: his life on earth (reflecting the fact that he 'has come' from heaven), in which God *has* shown his glory, and his death and resurrection (reflecting the fact that he will return to heaven), in which God *will* show his glory. If the divine voice carries this huge weight, then it is all the more noteworthy that John's initial framing of the story of Lazarus' resurrection began with Jesus claiming that it all happened 'for the glory of God, *in order that the Son of God should be glorified*' through Lazarus' illness (11:4). It is difficult to find a clearer sign of the overall unity

---

[10] See Barrett 1978, 420: 'They [the Gentiles] cannot see Jesus yet, but their presence is an indication that the hour of Jesus' death and glory is at hand, since it is only after the crucifixion that the Gospel compasses both Jew and Gentile.'

of John 11 and 12 as a whole than the one marked by the correspondence between 11:4 and 12:28.

THE UNITY OF THEME: MISSING THE POINT

Throughout the two chapters runs a single theme, which is that none of the people involved understands what the story of Lazarus' resurrection is ultimately about: Jesus' and their own resurrection.

(1) We saw that the first half of this topic is very clearly thematized in the initial framing of the Lazarus story (11:3–16), where Jesus goes out of his way to tell Mary and Martha (and the reader) that Lazarus' illness has come about 'in order that the Son of God should be glorified through it' (11:4). Similarly, the disciples very distinctly miss the point that the whole event is about life, not death, both of Lazarus and Jesus (11:11–16).

(2) The next person who misunderstands—and now all three parts of the topic, the resurrection of Lazarus, Jesus, and believers—is Martha (11:20–7).[11] First, and in a narratively ironic way, she complains to Jesus that 'if you had been here, my brother would not have died' (11:21). This is a complete misunderstanding since Jesus precisely stayed away in order that Lazarus might die—and so to show that he will not die *after all*, against what Martha takes him to have done. Martha continues by stating her confidence in Jesus (11:22). This is probably not to be understood as being directly related to any hope about Lazarus, but rather as stating a sort of general confidence in Jesus. For when Jesus declares that her brother will 'be resurrected' (11:23), meaning that he will be so in a moment, Martha takes him to be talking in the best Jewish manner of the general resurrection on the last day (11:24). In short, she again misunderstands. Then Jesus finally comes entirely into the open (11:25–6):

[25]I am the resurrection and the life. The one who believes in me shall live even though he may also die. [26]And anybody who lives [on the last day] and believes in me shall never die. Do you believe that?

---

[11] I am going somewhat against the current here (but see n. 15, this chapter). For instance, Theobald 2009, 733, says this: 'here there are no misunderstandings … step by step Jesus here leads Martha on her road towards understanding, and Martha allows herself to be led'. O'Day 2013 agrees (499) and carefully discusses the relationship with 11:39–40 (500–1). I am unconvinced, though, by her solution that 'Jesus' words to Martha [in 11:25–6] moved in a different direction than a particular miracle'. Ashton, in an incidental remark (2007, 370 with n. 5, my emphasis), shows greater perceptiveness: 'Even in the first part of the Gospel, in which the dominant note is one of Jesus' failure to win over his own people, there are frequent indications that he was nevertheless accorded a partial welcome [n. 5] *though it should be added that few, perhaps none, of those who acclaimed him fully appreciated who he really was*.' Would that Ashton had insisted on this insight and spelled out its full significance.

Here Jesus says two things. First, he speaks about himself, and the idea must be that in doing what he is about to do to Lazarus, Jesus will also be showing something about himself: that he, too, will be resurrected into life and that it is because he has this power in him that he is able to do the same to Lazarus.[12] Secondly, and most importantly, he now also speaks explicitly about those who believe in him: even if they *die* (physically, in this world), *they* shall also *live* (equally physically, but in heaven), and anybody among them who remains physically alive in this world (upon Jesus' return, one must suppose) shall never die in eternity, but will continue living (physically and in heaven).[13] In other words, believing in Jesus (repeated twice) secures eternal life, even beyond death.[14] Here we are presented with the full content of the belief in Jesus that is brought out by the Lazarus story: (x) Lazarus will be resurrected to life; (y) he will be resurrected by Jesus, who on his side stands for resurrection and life and will himself be resurrected into eternal life by the power with which he is also able to resurrect Lazarus; (z) finally, it is because of this side of Jesus that those who believe in him will similarly be resurrected into eternal life. So, Martha, do you believe this? Martha happily replies: 'Yes, my Lord' and solemnly states that she has 'come to believe' (*pepisteuka*)—that Jesus is 'the Messiah (or Christ)', 'the Son of God', 'the one who comes into the world' (11:27).

Let us take stock here. Does Martha finally understand? Or does she continue to misunderstand? We may focus this question on two questions of content (philosophical questions): if we have given correctly the full meaning—points x, y, and z—of what Jesus is saying in 11:25–6, *how* is it that he may actually be 'the resurrection and the life', and in particular how may he give life to the person who believes in him? Furthermore, is Jesus' 'being' as stated in 11:25–6 covered by the titles that Martha ascribes to him in 11:27?

---

[12] Argument: *can* Jesus say in the context of chapters 11–12 that he is 'the resurrection and the life' without this implying that he himself will (also) be resurrected to eternal life?

[13] Note the extremely careful pairing of 11:25b and 26a. If one *believes* and *dies*, one shall nevertheless come to *live*. If one *lives* and *believes*, one shall *never die*. For this pairing to work, 'living' and 'dying' must—respectively—refer to exactly the same kind of thing in either half-verse: physical life and physical death.

[14] As part of his extensive analysis of the Lazarus story (Frey 2000a, 403–62), Jörg Frey also discusses 11:25–6 (445–57), which he rightly considers a 'core logion' ('*Kernlogion*', 452) and characterizes as an 'interpretive saying' ('*Deutewort*') and 'an interpretive key to the whole Lazarus pericope' (453). Following his general approach, Frey also rightly takes 'he shall live' in 11:25 to have a future meaning (451) and 'even though he may also die' in the same verse to refer to physical death. I cannot agree, however, that 'shall never die' in 11:26 should be taken in 'a spiritual sense' (451), even though it is difficult to find somebody who does *not* agree with Frey. As I read the passage (and John in general), Jesus is all through speaking of 'physical life'—before and after (physical) death and so either on earth or in heaven. For comparison, see Paul in 1 Thess. 4:13–14 and 17 and 1 Cor. 15:51. This is one of many places in John where a simpler and more straightforward reading is preferable to a more complex one.

These are genuinely philosophical questions. The first asks for further elucidation of the ontology and cosmology that may give meaning to those claims. The second asks whether the traditional Jewish titles employed by Martha either already had or could be given or were intended by John to be given the precise meaning underlying Jesus' claims. Depending on how we answer the second question, we may say that Martha either finally understands or else continues to misunderstand. We will see that as the remaining text *answers* the two questions, the answer concerning Martha should be negative: Martha continues to misunderstand.[15]

In order to make the issue wholly clear, we jump a little ahead of ourselves. When scholars comment on Martha's ultimate confession in 11:27, they regularly—and quite rightly—refer to 20:31: 'These things have been written in order that you may (come to) believe *that Jesus is the Christ, the Son of God...*' This is all in close conformity with Martha's statement. However, that is not the whole of 20:31, as commentators tend to forget: '...and in order that *believing that (pisteuontes)* you may have *life* in or through his *name*'.[16] *That* is what Martha should have understood, but does not understand. In fact, she does not even understand that her dead brother, Lazarus, is about to obtain life again. And so Jesus later has to tell her when she warns him that Lazarus stinks (11:39): '*Did I not tell you that if you believe,* you shall see *the glory of God*' (11:40; that is, Lazarus being resurrected through God's power for life). This was what Jesus *meant* to tell her in 11:20–7 and which she did not understand. Moreover, this is what, from the beginning of the Lazarus story, 'believing in Jesus' now means: *full belief in the one who says that he is the resurrection and the life with all that this implies for the resurrection of Lazarus, of Jesus himself, *and* of those who follow him in having that belief. The importance of this can hardly be overstated since it pinpoints the theme that runs through the whole of John 11–12 of not understanding the *ultimate* thing about Jesus: that he is about to return to God through his death and resurrection (and that this has crucial implications for human beings). Seen in that light, it is not enough to believe in Jesus as 'the Christ', 'the Son of God', or 'the one who comes into the world'. In themselves, those titles describe Jesus quite

---

[15] I am happy to note that Ruben Zimmermann (2008a, 90–3) agrees on this. Drawing on Moloney 2003 he lists five problems (92) for seeing Martha as 'the great confessor of faith' (91). Of these the following three stand out: i) the incompatibility of Jesus' question and Martha's answer; ii) Martha's way of speaking of Jesus in the next verse (11:28) as a *didaskalos* (= Rabbi, 'teacher', compare 11:8); iii) her behaviour and Jesus' reply at the tomb (11:39–40). For the second point compare Barrett's surprise (1978, 397): 'The description is surprising after the exalted terms of Martha's confession of faith.'

[16] What is that name? Fortunately, passages such as 3:18, 3:16, and 1:14 make the answer clear: the name of the *only, unique* Son of God—with all that is implied by that (descent and ascent etc.).

well. But they precisely do not go far enough. They only express what we have earlier called initial belief. They say nothing about what really matters: that Jesus is 'the resurrection and the life' in the sense that he will himself undergo death and resurrection to eternal life and draw those who believe in *that* up to the same kind of life in the precise manner he has stated in 11:25–6.

(3) There is one more feature of the Lazarus story that speaks about understanding. At 11:41, just as the actual resurrection of Lazarus is about to begin, Jesus lifts up his eyes to heaven and thanks God that he has heard him. He immediately adds, though, that 'I myself knew that you always hear me, but I said it [presumably the prayer quoted in the previous verse] because of the crowd around me, *in order that they might believe that you have sent me*' (11:42). This is most peculiar. That Jesus has been sent by God is the content of the initial belief in Jesus as we know it further back in the Gospel. And it is precisely this content that must now be *added to*: Jesus is also the one who will return to God through his death and resurrection. So why does Jesus perform this little act of ostensive praying to God for that other purpose?

I suggest that this has to do with a feature of Jesus' resurrection of Lazarus that is precisely highlighted in this roundabout way. At 11:41 Jesus thanks God that 'you *have* heard me' (using the Greek aorist), which leads directly to his calling Lazarus out of the tomb in 11:43 (after the second-order explanation of his prayer in 11:42). So, where and how was Lazarus actually revivified?[17] This is where the storyline becomes relevant that begins a little further back with *Mary*'s complaint to Jesus that 'if you had been here, my brother would not have died' (11:32). Jesus' reaction is marked by an *oun* in the Greek (11:33): 'Now Jesus, on his side . . .'. This focuses the reader's attention on Jesus: there is something *he* now wishes to say or do. It is true that Jesus goes on to engage on the level of the bystanders and Mary. He sees them crying (11:33) and himself bursts into tears (11:35). But as the comment of the bystanders shows (11:36–7), that is not the level that really matters for a proper understanding of Jesus here. When they say: 'Would this man who has opened the eyes of the blind man not have been able to secure that this other man did

---

[17] Barrett (1978, 402) notes that '[n]o prayer of Jesus has been recorded earlier in the chapter; perhaps we should think that it was offered at the time of great emotional disturbance (vv. 33, 38). But much more probably . . . no specific moment of prayer is in mind; Jesus is in constant communion with his Father'. Theobald (2009, 742) agrees: 'Wir sollten nicht (wie manche Kommentatoren) fragen, wann Jesus nach der Vorstellung des Evangelisten sein Gebet an den Vater gerichtet hat (*Lagrange*, Joh 308, etwa denkt an den Moment der inneren Erregung Jesu V. 33). Denn »Jesus steht in ständiger Verbindung mit seinem Vater . . .« (*Barrett*, Joh 399)'.

not die?' (11:37), they precisely show—by the irony of their remark—that they do not understand either. For Jesus is precisely about to revivify Lazarus.

So where does he do it? There is a very good answer to this question. It happens twice: at 11:33 (after the first *oun*) when Jesus 'snorted in his *pneuma* and agitated himself' and again at 11:38 (after the second *oun*) when Jesus 'again snorted in himself'.[18] What this says is neither more nor less than that Jesus activated the *pneuma* that he was constantly carrying around after having received it in John 1. That explains why he already knew in 11:42 that God had heard him.

This reading presupposes two points. The first is that Jesus' 'snorting' in 11:33 and 38 is not in direct reaction either to his seeing people crying (11:33) or to the observation that he should have been able to prevent Lazarus from dying (11:37). These things happen at the human level and Jesus participates in them (at least when he bursts into tears, 11:35). His 'snorting', by contrast, is much more directly focused on his ultimate goal of making Lazarus come alive. This is suggested by the twice repeated use of *oun* in 11:33 and 38. The other point is that the inner *pneuma* through which Jesus 'snorts' is neither just a bland expression for 'himself' nor just for some *pneuma* (which one?) other than the 'Holy Spirit'.[19] On the contrary, it is precisely *the pneuma* that Jesus has been carrying around with him ever since his 'baptism' that he is now activating. It is difficult to provide any knock-down argument for this claim. It seems supported by its obviousness as soon as one allows it to be entertained. To put the point in its most provocative form: Jesus is here described as acting as a magician when he directly activates the Holy Spirit of God that he received at his baptism.

This is such an important point that it requires an extra word. When this text gets to the stage where it wishes to show that Jesus is 'the resurrection and the life' (11:25), thereby aiming to make people see 'the glory of God' (11:40), *it brings in directly the pneuma that Jesus is constantly carrying around*. Why? Because that *pneuma* is the power that explains all the other things that are told about him.

Seen in that light, what John says about Jesus' peculiar purpose in publicly praying to God (11:41–2) is meant to mark the *difference* between what people are actually able to understand about Jesus (namely, that he is sent from God) and the real facts: that he possesses God's *pneuma* and for that reason himself stands for resurrection and life. In a way, Jesus' prayer to God at 11:41 is only a sham and it is marked as such at 11:42 in order to

---

[18] I am happy to note that Theobald (2009, 738) at least considers this possibility 'worth mentioning': 'Erwähnenswert ist die These, dass *embrimasthai* ursprünglich ein thaumaturgischer Terminus ist, der die pneumatische Erregung des Wundertäters vor seiner Tat bezeichnet (»er schnaubte auf«, seine ganze göttliche Kraft zusammennehmend)...'

[19] Compare Barrett 1978, 398: '$\tau\hat{\omega}$ $\pi\nu\epsilon\acute{\upsilon}\mu\alpha\tau\iota$ has no reference to the Holy Spirit, but is synonymous with $\grave{\epsilon}\nu$ $\grave{\epsilon}\alpha\upsilon\tau\hat{\omega}$'.

make clear—and now we must say: *to the reader*—that there is much *more* to Jesus than people were able to understand. This something consists in the fact that Jesus has in himself the power of life over death in the form of the *pneuma*.

(4) In this long series of misunderstandings or only half-understandings, we next hear about the high priests and Pharisees (11:47–53), to whom Jesus' magnificent feat in Bethany has been reported (11:46). They do not understand either. On the contrary, they only think that 'this man does many signs' (11:47), a claim that is not false, but also very far from being the whole truth. They certainly do not understand that an even more important 'sign' is about to be realized once their plan to have Jesus killed has been put into action. Nor, as the text makes explicit (11:51–2), do they understand that by making Jesus die 'for the sake of the people' (11:50), they are making him die not only 'for the *ethnos* (= the *Jewish* people)' (11:51) in an altogether different sense from the one intended by Caiaphas, the high priest, but also in such a way that he might bring *all* 'God's children' 'together into one' group (11:52), no matter where on earth they are 'scattered' (which certainly means that they include Christ-believing Gentiles).[20] That is precisely the purpose of Jesus' dying *and* being resurrected, which is what the story of Lazarus is also about. In short, the high priests and Pharisees misunderstand wildly.

(5) There is one person, however, who does understand (though still somewhat implicitly): Mary. In 12:1–2 John takes care, as we have seen, to locate the foot-anointing scene very explicitly in Bethany in the house of Mary, Martha, and Lazarus. And here, while Lazarus (the male) participates in the meal they have produced for Jesus, and Martha (the female) helps out (*diakonein*) with the meal, Mary does something rather more unusual. She anoints Jesus in a manner that he, at least, interprets as an anointment for his burial (12:7). Thus, while the point is not at all made explicit, the manner in which John has integrated this story, which nowhere else is connected with Mary, the sister of Lazarus, into the storyline about Lazarus' resurrection, shows that the point of that story did get through, if only implicitly, to Mary. She half-grasped that the whole thing was (also) about Jesus.

(6) Another group of people who half-gets the point is the great 'pilgrim and Jerusalem crowd'. As we know, they had heard from the 'Lazarus crowd' about the 'sign' that Jesus had done in Bethany (12:17–18). And that

---

[20] John 11:52 is explosive in the context of John's relation to 'Jews and Christians'. I side here with Lincoln (2005, 330–1), who claims that 'the term for "nation", *ethnos*, is not spiritualized here or in its usage in 18.25. It is the Jewish nation that it is in view'. As for '[t]he notion of gathering the dispersed children of God', which is 'used in the prophets for the expectation of the end-time salvation of diaspora Jews', 'it now refers to those who believe in Jesus (see 1.12–13). Jesus' death, then, is here seen as on behalf not only of Israel but of all who believe, both Jews and Gentiles' (330). All of this seems just right.

was the reason why they went out to greet him as the 'king of Israel' (12:13) and of 'Sion' (12:15). They thus greet him as 'king of Israel' because they have heard about his raising of Lazarus. However, do they understand the special, highly paradoxical character of Jesus' kingliness, which John brings out—in accordance with the tradition—by having him enter the city riding on a donkey? Hardly, for John goes out of his way in 12:16 to state that the disciples did not understand the character of Jesus' entry into Jerusalem until 'Jesus had been glorified—then they remembered that those things were written about him and that they had done those things to him'.[21] And if the disciples did not understand it, then presumably the crowd did not either. They only half-grasped that the raising of Lazarus was in some way especially significant.

In this way John appears to have connected this second traditional story with what is his own overarching theme in John 11–12: Jesus' own death and resurrection as prefigured in that of Lazarus and with similar consequences for Christ believers. In both stories, the recognition (by Mary and the greeting crowd) of something unusual is only implicit. Though positive towards Jesus, neither Mary nor the crowd understands the full meaning of the raising of Lazarus. What the *text* shows its *readers*, by contrast, is that *they* must make the recognition completely explicit by grasping that believing in Jesus is not just believing in him as having come from God (or as a victorious king or the like) but also as having returned to him through death and resurrection for eternal life with all the consequences this has for believers themselves.

THE UNITY OF THEME IN 12:20–36: SPELLING OUT THE POINT (12:23–33), I

The long, concluding section of chapter 12 (12:23–50) then spells out what the story concerning Lazarus has actually been about: Jesus' own death and resurrection and its consequences for human believers. The hour has now come for the Son of Man to be glorified (12:23), which refers to his resurrection. But first he must die. And this holds for everybody. Only by dying may a person (Jesus obviously included) preserve his soul 'for eternal life' (12:25), as Jesus spells out in a marvellous combination of motifs from 1 Corinthians 15 and Mark 8.[22] Here, moreover, it is explicitly stated (John

---

[21] Barrett grasps this wonderfully (1978, 419, my emphasis): 'By emphasizing their failure *John probably intended to bring out the necessity of the glorification of Jesus (and by implication the gift of the Spirit) before* even his closest followers could understand him.'

[22] I am not necessarily saying that John drew directly on these other texts—though I believe he did.

12:26) that this is not just relevant to Jesus. Instead, by 'hating their own souls in this world' (12:25) Christ believers will follow in Jesus' footsteps and come to be where he, too, is, that is, in heaven: to them, too, God will give 'honour' (*timan*, 12:26), which is another way of saying that he will 'glorify' them.

If this is the overall plan, then it is also clear why Jesus should not wish to shy away from the 'hour' (12:27). On the contrary, it makes sense that he should even pray to God to put the plan of his death and resurrection into action (12:28). And God duly confirms this. Importantly, however, it is only Jesus who understands the voice from heaven (12:29), though he does not, in fact, need to hear it. Instead, the voice came 'for your sake' (12:30). Though not understood at the time, it explicitly states what now *should* be understood. This is then explained: *now* is the moment of ultimate judgement of this world, *now* its leader (Satan) will be thrown out; and when Jesus has been 'lifted up from the earth' (12:32; both on the cross, 12:33, and also in his resurrection), then he will *draw all to himself.*

So far we may say that the passage (12:23–33) is about this: what the content is of the present 'hour' and its significance for Jesus (namely, judgement, death, and resurrection, 12:31–2)—but also with some indications that this 'hour' is crucially relevant for believers. By hating their souls 'in the present world', they may keep them 'for eternal life', may follow in Jesus' footsteps to heaven, and be drawn there by himself. The question then is: how? How may Jesus 'draw' them? And how may they themselves go to heaven? How, that is, may we go from Lazarus' and Jesus' resurrection to the resurrection of believers? This is the question that is answered in the remaining text of John 12: 12:34–50. Here we should just note that this question is identical with our philosophical question concerning the meaning of the connection in 11:25–6 between Jesus' claim that he is the resurrection and the life and his claim that believers—whether dead or alive on Jesus' return—will come to live eternally. How, then, is this question answered in 12:34–50?

INTERLUDE: THE NARRATIVE LINE OF 12:34–50

Before looking at the way 12:34–50 answers our question, we should consider the narrative line of this last section of John 12. Scholars often let the storyline of John 12 end with 12:36, which itself ends as follows (NRSV): 'After Jesus had said this, he departed and hid (*ekrybē*) from them'. John 12:37–43 is a writer's comment on 'their' failure to believe in Jesus and since this refers to the 'many signs' (12:37) Jesus had performed in their presence, it seems natural to see this comment as rounding off the whole

Book of Signs. In 12:44–50 when Jesus suddenly appears again and makes a kind of concluding statement, the reader is told neither when nor where.[23]

This all makes sense to begin with. However, there are some indications that both 12:37–43 and 12:44–50 should be understood to conclude the much more specific narrative line that began in 11:45. First, at 12:34 John reintroduces the crowd, which had been left behind at Jesus' entry into Jerusalem. There they were positive, but had only half understood what the raising of Lazarus had shown about Jesus. Now, by contrast they are wholly negative. Jesus then gives them a kind of answer in 12:35–6, which is followed by the statement that he departed and hid from them. But in 12:37 John states (NRSV) that 'Although he had performed so many signs in *their* presence, *they* did not believe in him'. There is no indication of any change in who 'they' are. So they must still be the crowd—and still around.

Secondly, at 12:42 John takes up the other group of agents from 11:45 onwards: the high priests and the Pharisees. Now it is said that in spite of everything 'many, even among the authorities (*archontes*, presumably including the *archiereis*, "high priests")' did believe in him but did not confess it out of fear of the Pharisees. This suggests that it is the specific line from 11:45 onwards of the reactions of the 'high priests and the Pharisees' (11:47) that is now brought to a conclusion. *Even among the leaders* many did come to believe in him. Apparently, however, their belief was not wholly sufficient since they were afraid to confess it.

Thirdly, once we have heard about these failures of belief, John reintroduces Jesus with a contrasting *de* in the Greek and the use of a striking verb (*ekraxen*): Jesus, *however, cried aloud*: . . . What he begins to speak of is 'the one who believes in me'. In other words, *in direct contrast* to those who *failed* in their belief in Jesus, he himself now emphatically states what *proper* believing looks like. If one reads 12:44–50 in relation to 12:37–43 in this way, that is, thematically, the fact that there is no specific indication of any time and place for 12:44–50 becomes wholly irrelevant.

It looks, then, as if John is out, in the whole section of 12:34–50, to show two things: first, that in the end neither the crowd nor the authorities believed in Jesus in the proper way; and secondly, what that way was. Even though the crowd had been impressed by the raising of Lazarus, they did not in the end believe in Jesus in the full way that Jesus was actually spelling out to them in 12:34–6 (see more on this in a moment). Similarly, even though 'many', even among the authorities, did come to believe in him, their belief was insufficient since they were not prepared to confess it. Let us now consider what the content of full belief is as spelled out in the three sections.

---

[23] For this overall understanding of 12:37–50 see, e.g., Theobald (2009) 820–1.

THE UNITY OF THEME IN 12:20–36: SPELLING OUT THE POINT (12:34–6), II

In response to Jesus' statement in 12:23 that 'the hour has come for the Son of Man to be glorified' and his statement in 12:32 that he will soon be 'lifted up' from the earth, the crowd comes in again at 12:34, saying this:

> [34] ... We on our side have heard from the law that the Messiah [which they apparently still take Jesus to be] remains forever. How can you then say that the Son of Man must be lifted up? (In any case,) Who is this Son of Man?

It is extremely noteworthy that when the crowd is now described as being negative—actually, in a most elegant manner through the very form of what they say—they hit upon (out of everything Jesus has said in 12:23–32) precisely these two things that they do not understand: that the Son of Man must be 'lifted up' (implying that he will not remain forever) and who this Son of Man actually is. This is noteworthy since these are precisely the two things that people must understand in order to become full believers and so be drawn by Jesus into heaven where he himself is (see 12:32). Thus at the beginning of the text (12:34–50) that is meant to show how human beings may follow in Jesus' footsteps to obtain eternal life in heaven, it is explicitly stated what it is that they must believe: that as the Son of Man, Jesus has been resurrected from the cross. But if that is what people must believe—and that the crowd precisely does *not* understand—then how will they get to understand it, and how will their understanding it actually lead them into heaven?

It initially looks as if in his reply to the crowd Jesus does not answer their two questions at all. In fact, however, he does. What he says is this (12:35–6):

> [35] ... The light is among you only for a little longer. Walk as you have the light lest darkness should catch hold of you; and the person who walks in darkness does not know where to walk. [36]As you have the light, *believe in the light in order that you may become sons of the light* ...

Here Jesus is talking about the ultimate kind of belief that the two chapters are addressing by constantly bringing out that the various agents described precisely did not achieve *that*. This kind of belief is not just a matter of having read this or the other thing in the law, e.g. about 'the Messiah' (12:34)—or even of believing in 'the Son of God' or 'the one who is about to come' as understood by Martha in 11:27. It is about 'the Son of Man' and about his being 'lifted up' in the form in which his destiny was presented in the Prologue. For it is about Jesus as the *light* from the Prologue who *came into* the world (1:9) and is now about to leave the world *behind* in order to *return* to God (compare 1:18). And Jesus' exhortation in 12:36 is an exhortation to believe in *that light* since only if they do that, may they themselves *become* 'sons of the light'.

That there is an explicit reference back to the Prologue here is made clear in two ways. First, Jesus exhorts his addressees to walk 'as they have the light' in order that darkness may not 'overtake' or 'overcome' (*katalabein*) them. This is exactly the term that was also used in the Prologue with the same meaning and in the same context, only here in John 12 it is used about them, not about the light itself.[24] Secondly, Jesus also exhorts his addressees to believe in the light in order that they may 'become (*genésthai*) sons of the light'. Again, this is exactly the term that was also used in the Prologue with the same meaning and in the same context (1:12, NRSV): 'But to all who received him, who believed in his name, he gave the power to become (*genésthai*) children of God.'[25]

We must conclude that 12:35–6 brings the reader directly back to the general picture of Jesus and believers that was already given in the Prologue. There is one vital difference, though. Where the Prologue spoke in very general terms of the *logos* and the light as coming into the world to be found in Jesus Christ and then (implicitly) of their/his return to God, 12:35–6 must be understood to be speaking much more concretely. For the theme now is that the 'light' (of the Prologue)—*that is, Jesus himself* who is at this very moment speaking to them—is about to go away. Let us hold on to this difference between the Prologue and the present passage. Then we will be immediately reminded that the generality of the Prologue was *itself* made concrete a long time before John 12. This happened in two areas. With regard to the central notion of the Prologue, the *logos*, and its coming to be present in Jesus Christ, the mechanism was spelled out wholly concretely in the story of Jesus' reception of the *pneuma* later in John 1. With regard to believers' 'becoming children of God', the mechanism was similarly spelled out wholly concretely in John 3 when the reader was informed that this would happen when *believers* would receive the *pneuma*. Where the Prologue spoke of human beings 'becoming children of God' (1:12) through 'believing in his name' (1:12) *and* 'being born from God' (1:13), 'not through the will of flesh' (1:13), we were later told that the concrete meaning of this was that they should be born 'from above' (3:7), namely, 'by the *pneuma*' (3:8).

---

[24] Brown (1966, 479–80) makes nothing of the reference back to the Prologue. He does note (469) the use of the same term, but translates it differently ('darkness will come over you' as against 'overcome' in 1:5). Theobald does not even refer back to 1:5 in his note on 12:35 (2009, 817–18). Neither does Zumstein (2016, 463–4). Lincoln (2005, 353–4) sees the connection.

[25] No commentator I have consulted makes anything of this link. Lincoln, however (2005, 354), does note that 'this final encounter of Jesus' public ministry . . . sets it in cosmic perspective with the light symbolism (cf. 1.4–9 . . .)'.

Seen in that light, how are we meant to understand in concrete terms what is now *about* to happen to Jesus here in John 12, where this event is not just described in abstract terms as a 'return to the bosom of the Father' but quite concretely as a matter of being 'lifted up' on the cross and into heaven? Only one answer seems possible: just as Jesus' coming was spelled out in terms of his receiving the *pneuma* from above, so his returning to God must also be thought of as being brought about by the *pneuma*. Jesus will literally be 'lifted up' to God by the power of the *pneuma*. God's power of glory, that is, of resurrection, is the *pneuma*. Thus the very meaning of the claim that 'The light is among you only for a little longer' is that Jesus–the light, who also has the *pneuma* in him, will soon be transported to heaven by the same *pneuma*.

What, then, about the rest of 12:35–6, in particular the exhortation that as they have the light, they must believe in the light in order themselves to become sons of the light? If we work back from the end of this, we must take the phrase of becoming sons of the light to refer to their own resurrection, an event for which they themselves need to be in possession of the *pneuma*. That was the unmistakable message of Jesus' conversation with Nicodemus: in order to 'see' and 'enter' 'the kingdom of God', one must be in possession of the *pneuma*. What the present text says, however, is that they must 'believe in the light' '*in order to*' become 'sons of the light'. Once again we see that there are two types of belief in Jesus. The initial belief that we know well is also exemplified here in John 12 by the reaction of the crowd. Full belief, by contrast, is 'belief in the light' in the sense of everything Jesus has been telling about himself and believers in John 11–12, as exemplified by his statement in 11:25–6. To have *this* belief people must *themselves* be in possession the *pneuma*. Only then will the road be immediately open for them also to 'become sons of the light'.

That this is what is meant in the present text by 'believing' is suggested by the fact that Jesus precisely speaks of believing in *the light*, that is, the full figure that was described in the Prologue. Since that figure, namely, Jesus Christ as light and the *logos*, was generated and carried by the *pneuma*, it is wholly appropriate philosophically to say that people may only understand and believe in *that* figure on the supposition that they are also themselves in possession of the *pneuma*. This is where the step is taken from cognition (believing this or that about Jesus) to epistemology, that is, to accounting for the *conditions* for full knowledge of who Jesus is. Apparently, that step is needed for it to be possible to take the final step the whole way to ontology (in the claim about *becoming* 'sons of the light').

On this reading Jesus is not talking in 12:36 of some romantic form of 'believing in the light' while they have 'the light' among them and so becoming—even more romantically—'sons of the light'. He is speaking wholly concretely and cosmologically. While they have this pneumatic being ('the light') among them, they must acquire full, cognitive belief in that being (by themselves coming to possess the *pneuma*) in order for themselves to become in that way similar pneumatic beings. This is not just 'cognitive' or 'metaphorical' in a vaguely romantic way; it is wholly real.

There is one striking twist to this reading of 12:36. If, as I am claiming, the verse is meant to be talking of full belief, which presupposes possession of the *pneuma*, then how may Jesus exhort his addressees to have *that* kind of belief 'as you have the light', that is, while the light is still among them? For during that period the *pneuma* 'was not yet' (7:39) anywhere else than in Jesus himself. So, is Jesus exhorting his immediate addressees to have a belief in him that nobody *could* have at the time? Answer: precisely! That point is actually at the very heart of the overall theme of John 11–12. Jesus *is* 'the resurrection and the life' in all the various respects that are described in these chapters, and that, of course, is what should be understood about him (recall 11:26: 'Do you believe this?'); but it is precisely also what was *not* understood at the time by anybody and *could* not be understood—*because* the *pneuma* 'was not yet'. The solution to the apparent paradox is a double one (as we have repeatedly seen). John is writing for his readers: (a) *they* both will and can understand (b) what was in fact there to be understood all along.

If we read Jesus' statement and exhortation in 12:35–6 in this way, they do answer the crowd's perplexed questions. He, Jesus (as the 'Son of Man' who effects a *krisis*, judgement, of the world) *must* (see the Greek *dei* in 12:34) be resurrected by means of the *pneuma in order that* those who believe in him as *that* figure and with *that* destiny may themselves also come to experience the same destiny by means of the *pneuma*. What Jesus then does in 12:36 is to exhort his addressees, the perplexed crowd, to believe in just that. We will see in a moment that the concluding section, 12:44–50, refers even more explicitly back to the Prologue and brings us even closer to the combined picture of the light, the *logos*, and the *pneuma* that I am relying on here. But we must also note that the central point in 12:35–6 (and also in what follows) is precisely the notion of '*believing in* the light'. What this text is primarily about is *full* belief, which is belief in the full destiny of Jesus-the-*logos* that includes his death and resurrection (concretely, through the return of the *pneuma* to heaven). This is the belief that believers *should* have and that the text directly exhorts them to have, well knowing, as it goes on to explain in the very next section, that nobody among them did have it (to the full). If my readers find this construction too baffling (they *should* understand but *could* not), then they must be comforted by realizing that in all this John is writing for his own *readers*: *they* must *and will* understand what the characters in the story *could* not understand even though it was all there to *be* understood.

Before we look at the next two sections, I wish to repeat the argument I have constructed for bringing in directly the *pneuma* in 12:35–6 as what ultimately explains what is about to happen to Jesus and the implications it has for believers: (i) John 12:35–6 directly refers back to the Prologue; (ii) parts of the general or abstract picture given in the Prologue—the 'incarnation' of the *logos* and the idea of believers 'becoming children of God'—have already been spelled out concretely in John 1 and 3 in terms of the presence of the *pneuma*; (iii) the events referred to in 12:35–6—the light's going away and believers 'becoming sons of the light'—must in themselves be understood wholly concretely and not merely as given in the general or abstract picture of the Prologue; (iv) it follows that they, too, must be spelled out in the concrete terms that have already been introduced in John 3 *if* the idea of 'becoming sons of the light' in 12:36 is actually the same as that of 'becoming children of God' in 1:12. If all this is true, then it appears impossible to escape the conclusion (v) that Jesus' being lifted up to heaven is also meant to be understood as being directly operated by the *pneuma*; and furthermore (vi), that *all* of this can only be understood (in 'believing in the light') by people who are themselves in possession of the *pneuma*.

THE UNITY OF THEME IN 12:20–36: SPELLING OUT THE POINT (12:37–43), III

The failure to believe in Jesus in the only wholly adequate way is then spelled out and explained in 12:37–43. Scholars usually take John here to be merely recapitulating the theme that has been running through the whole of the Book of Signs: that 'they' ('the Jews') did not believe in Jesus in spite of all the 'signs' he had performed (12:37)—though many did believe in him, even among the leaders, without, however, daring to confess it for fear of the Pharisees . . . (12:42). But the meaning of the passage becomes much more pointed if we take it to continue directly the line about the crowd and the authorities that was begun in 11:45. Then it will not only be about 'believing' in Jesus, but about full belief.

This suggestion is independently supported by the fact that John brings in the notion of *doxa* ('glory') towards the end of the passage. Isaiah had spoken in the way quoted in 12:38–40 'because he saw his [Jesus'] *doxa*, and he spoke about him' (12:41). By contrast, those believers who did not dare to confess their belief in Jesus did so because 'they preferred the *doxa* of human beings *to the doxa of God*' (12:43). When John begins to speak of seeing Jesus' and God's *doxa*, he is no longer speaking of merely initial belief. Apparently, Isaiah had seen Jesus' *glory*. Scholars rightly discuss exactly what it is that Isaiah saw. But it will in any case include the status that Jesus had received from God at his baptism, which is also the status he is about to receive at his resurrection (compare 12:28: 'I have glorified and will again glorify'). Conversely, those who did 'believe in Jesus' (presumably at some lower level, e.g. that Jesus was 'from God'), but did not dare to confess it, did not see God's glory in him since they preferred the much lower 'glory' of human beings. *Had* they believed in Jesus in the only wholly proper way, namely, as the figure described in the Prologue who was meant to return to God in order to draw people there, they would presumably never have given in to that much lower 'glory'.

What we see here is that in 12:37–43 John is not, after all, just repeating the hackneyed motif from earlier in the Gospel that some came to believe in Jesus while others did not. Instead, he hints that *genuinely* believing in Jesus is much *more* than that: it is a matter of seeing Christ's full glory, which concerns both his having received the *pneuma* from God in the first place (and in that sharpened sense being one who has 'come from God'), and also, and even more importantly, his *returning* to God (in the blazing glory of the *pneuma*, one suspects). John 11–12 is intended to show that seeing *that* in its full power is what constitutes *full* belief in Jesus, and in 12:34–43, where John brings in the crowd again, he aims to show that *in the end* neither the crowd nor those among the authorities who did come to believe in him (12:42) obtained the only form of belief that is full belief, the one that Jesus had explicitly spelled out in his conversation with Martha (at 11:25–6). They did not understand Jesus' talk of 'lifting up the Son of Man' (12:34). They did not 'believe in him' in *that* sense in spite of the many 'signs' he had performed, including raising Lazarus (12:37). Thus they were unable to read the 'signs' correctly. Nor did they grasp the glory of Jesus, of which Isaiah had spoken (12:41). Or if they did believe in him, it was only in such a manner that they missed 'the glory of God' that was revealed in Jesus (12:43).

THE UNITY OF THEME IN 12:44–50: SPELLING OUT THE POINT (12:44–50), IV

Then comes the concluding passage, 12:44–50. Taken in one way, it directly spells out what the overall theme of John 11–12 has been. At the same time, since those two chapters also constitute the climax of all the earlier chapters, it also constitutes an apt conclusion to the whole of the Book of Signs. It is now shown what all those signs were ultimately about: not just showing that Jesus was *from* God, but also that he was meant to return *to* God in order to save mankind.

It is exceedingly important to note how carefully the argumentation progresses in 12:44–50.[26] One recurrent and gradually developing theme is that in, or better, behind, Jesus one should see God. (i) If one believes in Jesus, one believes in 'him who has sent me' (12:44). If one 'sees' Jesus, one 'sees' 'him who has sent me' (12:45). This already points back to the Prologue, where it was said that 'nobody has seen God', but Jesus Christ 'exegetes' him (1:18).[27] (ii) The theme is taken up again in 12:47 when Jesus claims that *he* does not judge anybody (for instance, if somebody 'hears' his words, *rhêmata*, but does not keep them). Instead, it is *'the' logos* which Jesus has spoken and that as it were stands behind him that judges him (12:48).[28] Once again the reader is clearly referred back to the Prologue, which was primarily about the *logos*. (iii) Jesus has not spoken anything 'from himself': it is God, who has sent him, and who has given him in command (*entolê*) what to say and speak (12:49). In short, *in* whatever Jesus has said, one should 'see' God and 'hear' the *logos*. (iv) Moreover, Jesus knows that this command of God's is (geared towards) 'eternal life'; and so, whatever Jesus says he speaks as God has told him to do (12:50).

This concatenation of the same theme in various guises is then interrupted in 12:46, where Jesus states (and now quite openly) that '*I have come as light* into the world in order that anyone who believes in me may not remain in darkness'. This verse is of the greatest importance since it wholly explicitly ties the whole passage back to the Prologue. In the rest of the passage, the overall theme is the relationship between Jesus' *rhêmata* (what he has literally said, the 'words' that have flown out through his mouth, compare the use of the term *lalein* in 12:48–50) and the underlying *logos* (12:48), which is soon identified with a command (*entolê*) that God has given to Jesus, a command that is for 'eternal life' (12:49–50).[29]

---

[26] Barrett rightly notes (1978, 433) that 'it is important to note the points that are selected and the way in which they are combined'. I am not convinced, however, that he himself quite succeeds in this. Ashton (2007, 518) rightly states that the passage 'is a carefully constructed piece, belonging . . . to the last stage of the composition of the Gospel'. His own suggested 'chiastic' analysis (2007, n. 42, 518–19) is neither very convincing nor very helpful. Theobald (2009, 837) ascribes the passage to a 'Redaktor' who intended 'ein kleines johanneisches Glaubenskompendium zu schaffen'. As we will see, both Ashton and Theobald miss one crucial point about the text, which is due to the fact that they do not read it closely as part of its immediate context.

[27] It hardly matters that the term for 'seeing' is *theôrein* in 12:45, but *horan* in 1:18.

[28] Compare for the move here Mark 3:28–30 (NRSV): [28]'"Truly I tell you, people will be forgiven for their sins and whatever blasphemies they utter; [29]but whoever blasphemes against the Holy Spirit can never have forgiveness, but is guilty of an eternal sin"—[30]for they had said, "He has an unclean spirit".' John 12:47–8 similarly distinguishes between Jesus (12:47) and the *logos* (12:48).

[29] Barrett (1978, 434, my emphasis) sees the importance of the relationship between the 'words' (*rhêmata*) and the *logos*: 'The *rhêmata* are the *logos*, which Jesus bears [good!], as it is split up into particular utterances; *logos* is *a kind of collective noun for the rhêmata*.' However, the *logos* is something more than just a 'collective noun' for the *rhêmata*. It rather refers to

With these two explicit references back to the Prologue (the light and the *logos*) we are entitled to read what is said here in 12:44–50 in the closest possible connection with the Prologue.

Then the overall meaning of these verses becomes clear. It is that Jesus is God's agent who mediates to human beings the whole plan that has been described in the Prologue. He is the 'light' that has 'come into the world' (12:46). What he says (his *rhêmata*) are articulations of the underlying *logos* (12:47–8) that he may even be said to have 'spoken' *in* those *rhêmata* (12:48). Again, what he says articulates what God has 'commanded' him to speak and say (12:49). And as God's mediating agent, Jesus 'knows' that God's command means 'eternal life' (12:50). Light, *logos*, and (eternal) life: these were also the main entities whose entry into the world was described in the Prologue. In the present passage Jesus claims that they are all contained in what he has said, precisely *as* God's agent vis-à-vis human beings.

That, then, is how human beings must understand Jesus in relation to God. And this constitutes one main theme of the passage. But of course they must also 'believe in' Jesus (12:44), 'see' him (12:45), 'hear' his *rhêmata* (see 12:47), and 'receive' them (see 12:48). That is, they must also *relate directly to* Jesus. And that is another pervasive theme in the passage. But—and this is the point that holds the two sides of the text together (speaking of Jesus' relationship to God and of how human beings must relate to Jesus himself)—in 'believing in Jesus', 'seeing' him, and the rest, they must believe in Jesus *as* that other figure who is directly mediating God to human beings. In other words, they must believe in him *as* the figure described in the Prologue. That, and only that, constitutes full belief.

How, then, may that level of understanding actually be reached? Here it is not enough to say—as we did earlier when we were only talking about initial belief—that people must react to the *pneuma* which, as a carrier of the *logos*, is literally streaming out of Jesus' mouth in his *rhêmata*. By now they must relate to (Jesus as) the whole *logos* itself that *underlies* those *rhêmata*, and this can only be done once they have themselves received the *pneuma* that carries that *logos*. Otherwise, the risk continues to be there that they may indeed 'hear' Jesus' *rhêmata* but not *keep* them (compare 12:47). Once again, for people to respond 'in kind' to what Jesus has now explicitly stated himself to be, namely, God's whole *logos* for judgement or salvation (again 12:47) in the form of eternal life (12:50), they must themselves be in

---

God's unified plan with Jesus, which is also expressed in his individual sayings. Ashton (2007, 517–21) makes little of the intricate relationship between the *rhêmata* and the *logos*. Similarly, Theobald (2009, 839–40) fails to grasp this relationship since he invariably translates the *logos* as 'the Word'.

possession of the *pneuma. Then* the whole aim of that plan will also be fulfilled: then they *will* have eternal life (but still only proleptically so).

Thus understood 12:44–50 constitutes an extremely powerful summary of everything Jesus has been aiming to show and say throughout the Book of Signs—but not least in John 11–12—about himself and the purpose for human beings of his 'coming into the world as light' (12:46). We know, of course, that nobody understood this to the extent that would constitute full belief in Jesus. But we also know that this is what everybody *should* have understood. When Jesus ends by saying that God has given him 'a commandment about what to say and what to speak' (12:49, NRSV) and that this commandment 'is (for) eternal life' (12:50), then the implication is that by God's command human beings *should* grasp the whole content of the *logos* as expressed in Jesus' individual *rhêmata* so that they might in that way obtain eternal life. Such an understanding would imply that believers would already themselves begin to be transformed into that kind of life since grasping the whole story presupposes that one has oneself received the *pneuma* that lies behind the 'words' of Jesus through which it is being told. In this way God *creates* (by means of his *pneuma*) that of which Jesus *speaks* (as an expression of the same *pneuma*): eternal life for human beings.

Objection: there is not a single whisper about the *pneuma* in either 12:35–6 or 12:41–3 or 12:44–50. Here are four replies. (i) We saw that the concrete content of what is about to happen to Jesus when he will be 'lifted up' invites us to recall the manner in which both Jesus' own destiny and the destiny of believers as initially described in the Prologue were later spelled out much more concretely and precisely in terms of operations of the *pneuma*. (ii) We have seen independently that John 11–12 constitutes a single literary unit; the question then is whether there is also a single theme that is being developed throughout this single unit; and we have seen that there is: 'believing in' Jesus is not just a matter of believing that he has 'come from God'; it also includes his return to God through death and resurrection and the whole point of that for believers in the form of eternal life in the hereafter. (iii) We saw that at a crucial point in the story of Lazarus' resurrection, namely, where the change from death to life actually took place in Lazarus' case, this text *explicitly* brings in—even twice—the *pneuma* as the tool with which this change was effected. (iv) Then there is also a final consideration: why, if that is what is actually meant, does Jesus not explicitly say in 12:34–50 that one needs to be in possession of the *pneuma* to understand the full content of the story of Jesus' life and death, and hence to have 'full belief' in him? There is a very good answer to this question. It is that in the whole of the Book of Signs, and not least in John 11–12, the basic concern is with the degree of understanding or misunderstanding on the part of '*the Jews*'—as represented in John 11–12 by the crowd, the high priests, and the Pharisees. And 'the Jews' constitute the group of people who did *not* end up believing fully in Jesus. Then there is not much point in saying that in order to obtain the kind of belief that they *should* have obtained, they only had to wait for the *pneuma*. For these people precisely did *not* wait. Instead, they ended up killing Jesus. If this consideration is apt, one might expect that when John addresses the question of full belief in relation to *the disciples*, who did end up obtaining precisely that belief, *then* he would bring in the *pneuma*. That, of course, is precisely what he does in the Farewell Discourse. Here, Jesus is also concerned with what the disciples understood at the time of speaking, but here, too, he brings in directly a reference to their future possession of the *pneuma* in the form of the 'Paraclete'. Once that had arrived *after* Jesus' death, *then* the *disciples* would fully understand.

THE ROLE OF THE *PNEUMA* IN JOHN 11–12

Summarizing, we may say that John 11–12 concludes the Book of Signs by describing the last and biggest sign. But the two chapters also point very strongly forward to the passion story in the rest of the Gospel. They bring out with tremendous force—and through John's usual means of emphasizing what people did *not* understand—that what is shown by all Jesus' 'words' (and his acts, that is, his 'signs') is that the way in which Jesus 'exegetes' God (1:18) is this: by himself undergoing death and then being resurrected through the *pneuma* with which he was initially endowed. Once believers understand *that*, they are saved—by themselves having obtained a share in the all-important *pneuma*, which will eventually resurrect them, too, to eternal life.

We are now able to answer the philosophical question we formulated in relation to 11:25–7. How is it that Jesus may actually *be* 'the resurrection and the life', and how may he give life to the person who believes in him? Answer: because Jesus has the *pneuma*. The *pneuma* is a power of life over death. Jesus has it, he lets it work on the dead Lazarus, and it is also the power that is at work in his own resurrection. Furthermore, Jesus may give life to people who believe in him, once again by making them partake of *pneuma*. Initially, they may come to believe in him in some lower form when they respond to the *pneuma* that streams out of his mouth in his *rhêmata*. Later, however, they may also themselves receive the *pneuma*. Then they will possess full belief in the form of access to Jesus' (and God's) full *logos*. And then they will also themselves be able to obtain eternal life. From then on, the *pneuma* will be directly operating in them to bring them there.

JOHN 11–12 IN RELATION TO JOHN 3, 5, AND 8

The overall theme of John 11–12 that we have now articulated has been prefigured in a number of ways earlier in the Book of Signs. C. H. Dodd (1953a, 380–1) pointed to John 3, 5, and 8, and that is obviously right. Let us recall, as an example, how a passage such as 3:13–21 (+ 3:31–6) in fact presents what we may call the 'salvation cluster' of concepts in an exceptionally concentrated form. The concepts are: the 'Son of Man', who has not only 'come down' from heaven, but will also 'go up' to heaven again, thereby giving 'eternal life' to those who 'believe in him'.[30] At present, however, we should rather take note of the difference between the three chapters (John 3, 5, and 8) and John 11–12, a difference that helps to pinpoint the specific purpose of the last two chapters.

Very briefly, what John 3 does is to let Jesus present the salvation cluster in a manner that is somewhat abstract or generalized. First, Jesus speaks of 'the Son of Man', 'God's only Son', and the like, but not *directly* of himself. Secondly, and probably connectedly, while Jesus speaks to Nicodemus, he is not directly addressing 'the Jews'. In 5:17–47, by contrast, Jesus both speaks distinctly of himself and also directly addresses 'the Jews'. Here Jesus brings out the salvation cluster not so much in order to convince anybody ('the Jews') or because the cluster itself is in focus, but rather—as part of his confrontation with 'the Jews'—in order to mark a clear and sharp contrast to the traditional, Jewish understanding of all these matters. Exactly the same is true of 8:12–29, where again one finds a high concentration of the salvation cluster, beginning with Jesus' direct claim that 'I am the light of the world' (8:12). In comparison with John 5, the only difference is that in John 8 the confrontation with 'the Jews' is even more direct and explicit. Up until and including John 8, then, we may say that Jesus' development of the salvation cluster is either preparatory (John 3) or forms part of an independent storyline, namely, of a gradual intensification in the confrontation between Jesus and 'the Jews' (John 5 and 8).

How different, then, with John 11–12. Here the salvation cluster is found scattered throughout the two chapters from beginning to end, coming almost explicitly to the fore towards the end of John 12. Thus it is directly in focus so as to constitute the overall *theme* of the two chapters. In addition, there are two points that have not hitherto played a similar role. One is that the moment has now finally arrived when all these things—meaning Jesus' death and resurrection—are actually about to happen. Previously, they have only been 'told about' (John 3) or 'foretold' (John 5 and 8). Now, however, in and through the resurrection of Lazarus

---

[30] And please note the central importance of the *pneuma* in this chapter (3:3 + 5–8 + 34).

they are directly about to occur. The second point is the one on which I have put much emphasis: in John 11–12 the salvation theme is constantly presented as one that Jesus' interlocutors do not understand, or at least only half understand, the point being that that is precisely what they—all of them, including such worthy believers as Martha and even Mary—*should* understand (or have understood). That is what makes this the unifying theme of the two chapters. Together, these two points give John 11–12 its special profile: it all happens *now*, and *that* is what 'you must all understand' (compare 12:36) in order to be *saved*. They must go from 'believing in' Jesus in a more or less bland, traditional sense to believing in him in the fullest sense that includes the fact of his resurrection. If they do that they will be in possession of God's full *logos*. And when they are in possession of that (including its carrier, the *pneuma*), then they both are and eventually will be saved.

Thus understood, John 11–12 takes several additional steps in comparison with what precedes. It spells out forcefully the full content of the belief one must have in believing in Jesus, a belief that is focused on resurrection and life. It hints that this full content is what brings Jesus into the reach even of Gentiles. And it in the end (12:44–50, as anticipated in 12:35–6) implicitly addresses this full content in almost hortatory form[31]—to whom? Answer: not just (but certainly also) to the immediate interlocutors at the level of the story, but also to the readers of the text itself, those who will be explicitly addressed at the very end of the Gospel, in 20:31.[32]

---

[31] On hortatory form: 12:36 is explicitly hortatory. Similarly, when Jesus says that 'I have come as light into the world *in order that* the one who believes in me may not remain in darkness' (12:46), it is difficult not to hear an implicit exhortation: 'Believe in me lest you remain in darkness!'

[32] There is a kernel of truth, therefore, in Theobald's view of 12:44–50 as a 'small Johannine *Glaubenskompendium*'. But the passage is also very clearly situated as a concluding climax to John 11–12.

IX

THE FAREWELL DISCOURSE AS PARAKLESIS (JOHN 13–17)

THE RUN-UP (13:1–30) TO THE FAREWELL DISCOURSE (13:31–17:26) AND THE ISSUE IN THE DISCOURSE

John 13 begins with a splendid sentence, whose literary quality has only rarely been grasped. Here is the rendering of 13:1–5 in NRSV:

[1]Now before the festival of the Passover, Jesus knew that his hour had come to depart from this world and go to the Father. Having loved his own who were in the world, he loved them to the end. [2]The devil had already put it into the heart of Judas son of Simon Iscariot to betray him. And during supper [3]Jesus, knowing that the Father had given all things into his hands, and that he had come from God and was going to God, [4]got up from the table, took off his outer robe, and tied a towel around himself. [5]Then he poured water into a basin and began to wash the disciples' feet...

Would anybody who reads this understand that in the Greek, 13:1–4 constitutes a single sentence?[1] Much hangs on the meaning of the last part of 13:1, which looks almost tautologous in the NRSV rendering. In the Greek, the two verbal forms of 'love' (*agapan*) signify an occurrence in the past, not a past state. 'Having loved his own' should therefore mean 'Having come to love his own'. What, then, is the point of 'he loved them to the end'? Here one must keep reading the Greek, where 13:2 begins with an 'and' (*kai*) that is immediately followed by 'during supper', which the NRSV has moved much further down. If one then also notices that 'Jesus knew' in 13:1 and 'knowing' in 13:3 translates the same verbal form in the Greek, which just means 'knowing' and is best translated as a *subordinate* clause, one may render the whole text as follows:

---

[1] By contrast, Léon-Dufour, who read the Greek, rightly speaks of 'une phrase majestueuse' (1993, 13 n. 1).

[1]Now before the festival of the Passover, since Jesus knew that his hour had come to depart from this world and go to the Father, (and) since he (also) had come to love his own who were in the world, he expressed this love for them (right) to the end [2]and during a meal—since the devil had already put it into his heart that Judas son of Simon Iscariot should betray him[2]—[3]since he knew that the Father had given all things into his hands, and that he had come from God and was going to God, [4]he gets up[3] from the table, takes off his outer robe, and ties a towel around himself. [5]Then he pours water into a basin and begins to wash the disciples' feet...

Nobody will say that this translation is elegant. But it brings out that with all the knowledge that Jesus had, he *expressed* his love for the disciples right to the end *by* getting up during a meal and washing their feet.[4] In that way this meal *became* the 'agapic' meal, the Eucharist, that it precisely is not overtly in the Fourth Gospel, but is in the Synoptic Gospels. This is an excellent example of how freely John operates with the tradition. What is achieved by connecting the last part of 13:1 (on 'loving') with what Jesus actually does during 'the meal' in 13:4–5 is that the foot-washing, which takes up the whole of 13:4–17, is explicitly described as an act of love. It is difficult to see how anybody could get that out of the NRSV rendering taken on its own. But the point is immensely important since the Farewell Discourse itself contains and develops Jesus' 'new command': 'that you love one another' (13:34). What this actually means has been shown by Jesus himself in the foot-washing scene.[5]

In that scene there are a couple of other points that are also important for what follows. One is that when a somewhat bewildered Peter has asked Jesus, 'Lord, are you going to wash my feet?' (13:6, NRSV), Jesus answers, 'You do not know (*eidenai*) now what I am doing, but later you will understand' (13:7, NRSV). This introduces a major theme in the Farewell Discourse: that the disciples do not (yet) understand. In fact, once Jesus has finished washing their feet, he asks them whether they 'realize' (*ginôskein*) what he has done to them (13:12) and then explains it carefully, concluding

---

[2] For this rendition of a highly controversial text (into his own mind or into that of Judas?), see, e.g., Barrett 1978, 439, and the arguments already given by Schwartz 1907, 343. (Compare also 13:27: 'After he [Judas] received the piece of bread, Satan entered into him', NRSV.) Witetschek 2012 adds further arguments, both text-critical and syntactical. He rightly concludes (273) that 13:2 is part of a 'prologue' to the whole passion story in which it becomes 'in eine grundsätzliche, kosmische Perspektive gestellt'.

[3] Note the exquisite use here of the 'historical present', which strongly focuses the action after the background account in the preceding verses.

[4] It is particularly sad, therefore, that Brown (1970, 548), who translates the end of 13:1 quite well ('he now showed his love for them to the very end'), ends up separating 13:2 from 13:1 by a whole empty line. Neither Brown nor Lincoln nor Nestle Aland[27/28] sees 13:1–4 as a single sentence.

[5] I am not at all claiming to be saying anything new here, only trying to bring out the connections even more strongly than it is usually done. In addition, I wish to celebrate John's writerly skills.

like this: 'If you know (*eidenai*) these things, you are blessed if you do them' (13:17). In this way the run-up scene to the Farewell Discourse clearly identifies the disciples' lack of understanding as a major theme. It also hints that 'knowing' or *fully* understanding will also lead to acting on that knowledge ('... if you *do* them'). That is an interesting philosophical idea.

Another noteworthy point in the foot-washing scene is again triggered by Peter. When he has forbidden Jesus ever to wash his feet (13:8) and Jesus has declared that in that case he has 'no share' with Jesus (13:9), Peter with characteristic impetuosity immediately goes to the other extreme and asks Jesus to wash him feet, hands, and head (13:9). But again no (13:10):

> [10] The one who has been bathed has no need to be washed, except for the feet, but is entirely clean (*katharos holos*). And you [plural] are clean (*katharoi*) ...

So, the disciples are already *katharoi holoi*, 'entirely clean'. That is good to know when one comes to the Farewell Discourse, where it is precisely an urgent question whether or not the disciples are fully where they should be in terms of knowledge and action.

There is one among them, however, who is singled out already in 13:10–11 as being not at all clean: Judas. The rest of the run-up (13:18–30) to the Farewell Discourse is taken up by Jesus' almost forcing Judas to undertake his treachery, compare 13:21 and 25–7. Clearly, the actual events are part of God's initial plan: Jesus himself brings them about. Finally, when Judas had left, ' ... Jesus said, "Now the Son of Man has been glorified, and God has been glorified in him"' (13:31, NRSV). That is, now Jesus will die and be resurrected. And so it is time to say farewell.

The Farewell Discourse itself will be the topic of the rest of this chapter.[6] The line will be thoroughly well known by now. We will see that against a scholarly perspective that has been reigning for more than a hundred years, there are very good reasons for taking the Farewell Discourse to constitute a single literary unit through all five chapters: a single speech or discourse, *the* Farewell Discourse.[7] And we will see that there is a closely

---

[6] Parts of the following text have been published previously in Engberg-Pedersen 2015 and 2016, from both of which I have taken over some pages verbatim. There are always differences, however. And the present chapter contains a large number of substantial additions.

[7] A recent treatment of John 13–17 as a whole by Stefan Burkhalter (2014) similarly argues for the unity of the text. His reasons as stated in his introduction (2014, 16–39) are much the same as my own: the 'crisis' of the traditional '*literarkritisch*' approach, the influence from modern literary and narrative analysis, and the like. Though he has qualms with applying the concept itself of a 'farewell discourse' to the text, he continues to speak of the text as the 'farewell discourses' (*Abschiedsreden*) in the plural (2014, 26). Also, as will become clear later, his 'chiastic' or 'concentric' reading of 13:1–17:26 as a whole (33–65) differs wholly from the one to be proposed here. An excellent earlier essay by Klaus Scholtissek (1999c) also speaks of 13:31–17:26 as the Johannine '*Abschiedsrede*' in the singular (namely, in the form in which it is part of the Gospel as a whole, 348–50), but nevertheless

knit set of themes that are being developed all through this text so as to yield a precise answer to a central philosophical question that has been raised at the start.

THREE PROBLEMS IN THE SCHOLARLY UNDERSTANDING OF JOHN 13:31–17:26

Critical scholarship has been wrestling with three connected problems in this text.[8] There is general agreement about its overall shape. John clearly embarks on the passion story at 13:1, and indeed with the splendid sentence we found in 13:1–4. However, that story proper does not begin until 18:1. In between, after the foot-washing scene and the commissioning of Judas, the rest of the text (13:31–17:26), so it is claimed, bristles with problems.

The most fundamental problem is that of unity.[9] Scholars have generally preferred to see 13:31–17:26 as a conglomerate of several Farewell Discourses. And indeed, one can understand why.[10] Consider John 14, which looks like a single speech of its own. Is it not held together by an *inclusio* between 14:1 and 14:27 (on the disciples' troubled hearts)?[11] Moreover, does the end (14:27–31) not look distinctly valedictory ('Peace I leave with you...')? In any case the chapter ends with a famous interpretative crux when Jesus says in 14:31 'Rise, let us be on our way from here'—and then continues speaking for three more chapters. So, is 14:1–31 not an originally independent farewell speech that has later been developed into the present wider framework?

Even within John 14 itself (beginning at 13:36) there are problems, it seems. John is primarily concerned to show three things. (a) The disciples do not understand Jesus' talk about his departure (13:36–8, 14:4–7, 8–11; 14:22). They constantly ask questions: Peter in 13:36, Thomas in 14:5, Philip in 14:8. (b) Jesus promises to ask the Father to give them a substitute for himself, which he calls 'another Paraclete' (14:16). It is meant to stay with them forever (14:16) as 'the *pneuma* of truth' which the disciples will 'know'

---

subscribes fully to the traditional view that the text is the result of a literary 'Wachstums-geschichte' in the form of a *relecture* or, as he prefers, *réécriture* (336–9).

[8] For a good discussion of scholarship on the compositional difficulties of the text, see Segovia (1991a) 20–47.

[9] Hoegen-Rohls 1996 (82–92) gives a good overview over the various divisions of the text in German scholarship of the later twentieth century. She herself ends up speaking of 13:31–16:33 as a comprehensive textual unit which she, too, however, terms '*Abschiedsreden*' (in the plural).

[10] For a judicious sifting of the traditional objections to finding an overall unity, see Frey 2000a, 110–13.

[11] See, e.g., Ashton (2007) 427.

'because he abides with you and will be in you' (14:17, NRSV). Later, the 'Paraclete' is described as the 'holy *pneuma*', 'which the Father will send in my name', and which 'will teach you everything, and remind you of all that I have said to you' (14:26). (c) Jesus also promises his *own* return either sooner or later. It may happen in what is probably the distant future (14:1–3) when it is connected with heaven. Or it may happen very soon, where it is rather connected with the earth (14:23).[12] Much of this appears coherent enough, but points b and c do raise a question of how to understand the precise relationship between the 'Paraclete' and Jesus and the precise relationship between Jesus' distant and more immediate return. Is the text coherent even within John 14?

The question of unity becomes even more acute in what follows. John 15 consists of (x) a parable of Jesus as a vine (15:1–8), (y) an elaboration of the love command that was very briefly introduced in 13:34–5 (15:9–17), and (z) a section on the world's hatred for Jesus and the disciples (15:18–25). (x) In the parable, Jesus is the vine, God the vine-grower (15:1) and the disciples are the branches (15:5) that must 'abide' (15:4, 5, 6, 7) in the Jesus-vine in order to 'bear fruit' (15:2, 4, 5). Indeed, 'In this has my Father been glorified, (in order) that you may bear much fruit and become my disciples' (15:8). (y) Jesus' command that they love one another is based in his love for them (15:12), which is shown when he lays down his life for them as his friends (15:13). And they are his friends, both if they do what he has commanded them (15:14), namely, to love one another (15:17), and also because 'I have made known to you everything that I have heard from my Father' (15:15, NRSV), which is the kind of thing one will only do to one's friends. (z) Finally, the world will hate and persecute the disciples just as it has done to Jesus (15:18–20), indeed, *because* of how it has behaved towards Jesus (15:21–5). These are all basically new topics. In particular, it is false to say that the theme of 'loving' has already been voiced in John 14. For 'vertical' love between believers and Jesus and God and vice versa (as in 14:15, 21, 23, and 24) is wholly different from 'horizontal' love for one another among believers (as in 15:12–13), even though the latter may well be based in the former (compare 15:9).

By contrast, John 16 appears to repeat the content of John 14. (a) Again, there is emphasis on the disciples' lack of understanding (16:16–33), for instance, at 16:17–18. This basically repeats the same theme from John 14,

---

[12] The summary of John 14 just given relies on a number of exegetical decisions on points that have been endlessly disputed among scholars. I do believe, though, that my summary has quite general support. For instance, for a traditional 'apocalyptic' understanding of 14:1–3, see the extensive, persuasive defence in Frey 1997–2000, e.g. 2000a, 119. Hoegen-Rohls too (1996, 145–6) recognizes the future temporal dimension of 14:1–3 'in spite of his [John's] heavy emphasis on the time after Easter as *Heilsgegenwart*' (*presence* of salvation). The latter point is doubtful to me.

though it also enlarges on it. Similarly, at the end of the chapter (16:25–33) the text also addresses the disciples' lack of understanding, but now with an additional focus on exactly what it is that the they do not understand. (b) Again, in an interesting passage (15:26–16:15) that may well constitute a kind of bridge between John 15 and the rest of John 16 (see later), Jesus speaks of the 'Paraclete' (15:26–7 and 16:7–15), which will now be sent by Jesus himself (not by God on Jesus' behalf, as in John 14). This includes a comprehensive overview of the 'Paraclete''s tasks (16:8–11) and a specification of its relationship to Jesus himself (16:12–15). While this basically repeats what was said on the 'Paraclete' in John 14, it also goes into much greater detail about the 'Paraclete''s functions. (c) Again, there is the question of understanding the meaning of Jesus' claim that he will himself return (16:16 and 22): when and in what form? And how is Jesus' return related to the coming of the 'Paraclete'?

In short, if John 15 brings in something new and John 16 basically repeats (but also expands on) John 14, how do the three chapters *together* constitute a unity? Could it be that John 16 (from 15:26 onwards) is the result of a *relecture* of John 14 that has later been stitched onto the text? But where does that leave John 15?[13]

It is easier with John 17, which consists of a prayer by Jesus to God on behalf of the disciples. This looks like a conclusion to the whole scene. But here, too, there are difficulties. For instance, Jesus now explicitly states that the disciples do understand a lot (17:6–8), as they precisely did not in John 14 and 16 (though, as we noted, in the latter chapter they did understand some things). This confidence about the disciples extends through the whole passage of 17:9–19, as we may see from some examples. 17:9–11 constitutes a single sentence whose structure is rarely understood. Basically, the idea is that 'I am *asking* on their behalf [17:9] . . . : Holy Father, *keep* them in your name etc.' [17:11].[14] All the rest is a parenthesis that partly specifies, partly justifies the prayer:

[9]I am asking on their behalf—I am not asking on behalf of the world, but on behalf of those whom you have given me, (and) *because* (i) they are yours, [10](ii) and all my things are yours, and your things are mine, (iii) and I have been glorified in (or

---

[13] Jean Zumstein's own use of the notion of a *relecture* with regard to these texts is different. He basically sees the whole of what he considers 'the second Farewell Discourse' = 15:1–16:33 as a *relecture* of the first one (13:31–14:31). See his pithy analysis in Zumstein 2007, 91–3, where he relates all 'three large parts' (92) of 15:1–16:33, namely, 15:1–17 (92), 15:18–16:4a, and 16:4b–33 (93) to 13:31–14:31. As will become clear later, I read these texts somewhat differently.

[14] The line, then, goes directly from ἐρωτῶ ('I am asking') to τήρησον ('keep'). I confine myself here to merely making this proposal. The issue pertains to our whole understanding of the level of John's language (compare on 13:1–4). Superficially, it is quite simple. But once one brings in the idea of argumentative logic, John's language becomes much more sophisticated.

among) them, [11](iv) and I am no longer in the world, but they are in the world, and I am coming to you—: Holy Father, keep them in your name etc.

For our purposes, the point is that Jesus asks God to *keep* them in his name. Indeed, when he was with them '*I* kept them in your name' (17:12)—but now he is going away etc. (17:13). And again (17:15–17):

[15]I am not asking you to take them out of the world, but to *keep* them from the evil one. [16]They are not from the world, just as I am not from the world: [17]*Make* them holy in truth; your *logos* is truth.

Even though Jesus here ends up asking God to *make* them holy, as if they were not yet so, the overall line is that he is asking God to *keep* them where they already are, namely, as not belonging to the world (17:16). The term *têrein* ('keep') is used three times (17:11, 12, 15) and twice (17:11, 15) of the central content of Jesus' prayer. Thus we should probably say that the disciples are already—to some degree, at least—'holy in truth', just as they were earlier said to be 'clean' (*katharoi*), both in the foot-washing scene (13:10) and also, significantly, in John 15 (15:3).

   Finally, at the end of the chapter Jesus declares that 'they have come to know (*egnôsan*) that you have sent me' (17:25) 'and I have made your name known (*egnôrisa*) to them and will [!, *gnôrisô*] make it known in order that the love with which you have loved me may be in them, and I in them' (17:26). So, even though there may still be room for some growth in knowledge, the disciples basically already are where they were intended to be. In this, John 17 completely parallels the picture given of them in John 15, where Jesus at one point says that 'I have made known (*egnôrisa*) to you everything that I have heard from my Father' (15:15). How, then, will that cohere with the constant emphasis in John 14 and 16 that the disciples do *not* yet understand (but again we saw that the claim is slightly more differentiated in John 16)?

   In sum, does John 14–17 constitute a unity across all these difficulties?

   The second and third problems to be noted focus on two of the issues that played a major role in creating the sense of disunity. The second problem: do the disciples actually understand or do they not? *If* the text is a unity, then why does it describe their understanding in the complicated manner we have just noted? Is it possible to make sense of these apparently contradictory statements? And the third problem: how should one understand the relationship between Jesus and the 'Paraclete' and the time frame for Jesus' return? And why are the two issues described in such a complex way? In John 14, Jesus first mentions the coming of the 'Paraclete' in 14:15–17 and again in 14:25–6. In between (14:18–24) he speaks of *his own* return to the disciples (14:23). In 15:26–16:11 he refers for the third and fourth time to the coming of the 'Paraclete' (15:26 and 16:7–8, 13), but in

16:12–15 he affirms that everything the 'Paraclete' will say is something that 'he will take from *me* and declare to you' (16:14). John 14 contains a reference to Jesus' return both in the more distant and in the immediate future, as we saw. Similarly, in John 16 (16:16–19) he tells the disciples that they will see him again 'in a little while', but 17:24 seems to rely on the more traditional idea of Jesus' return in the more distant future when he will bring the disciples to be with him where he is (in heaven). So, what is the relationship between Jesus and the 'Paraclete' and how does that relationship match with the time frame for Jesus' return?

UNITY: THE STRUCTURE OF 13:31–17:26 AS A PIECE OF PARAKLESIS IN THE PAULINE SENSE

Scholars rightly agree that the literary genre of our text is that of the 'farewell speech', of which there were many examples in antiquity.[15] The farewell speech is defined by a number of features that scholars have well distinguished. However, one such feature of our text—and still viewed as a farewell speech—has not been given the emphasis it deserves. At the very beginning (13:33–5), Jesus makes two announcements that may in a precise way be taken to structure the text as a whole.[16] Here is the crucial text (13:33–5, NRSV):

> [33][i] Little children, I am with you only a little longer. You will look for me; and as I said to the Jews so now I say to you, "Where I am going, you cannot come." [34][ii] I give you a new commandment, that you love one another. [35]By this everyone will know that you are my disciples, if you have love for one another.

Jesus first states that he is about to depart from his disciples. Next he gives them a 'new commandment'. Together, these two announcements may be seen as constituting a rhetorical *propositio* for the whole ensuing speech,

---

[15] The classic account of the genre is Munck 1950. Compare also Brown 1970, 597–601, Winter 1994 (with serious qualms about the genre), and more recently Dietzfelbinger 2004, 2:26–31. Segovia has a good discussion with the relevant *Forschungsgeschichte* up to then in 1991, 5–20.

[16] Brown (1970, 586), 'along with Dodd' takes 'xiii 31–38 as the introductory part of Division 1 [13:31–14:31] rather than as an introduction to the whole Discourse (xiv–xvii)'. Personally, I find it exceedingly difficult to imagine that a text that would have contained the love command as given in 13:34–5 might ever have been part of an 'overture' (Brown, 608) to John 14 *alone*. Normally, a major theme that is presented in an overture will be taken up later in the piece for which it is the overture. But there is no trace of the (horizontal) love command in John 14. If, then, 13:34–5 should be taken as pointing towards John 15, one may either say that John 15 was part of the writer's original design (as I am proposing) or else that a 'redactor' later 'inserted' both 13:34–5 and John 15 (and 16), a position that very many scholars adopt. In the latter case, is not the 'redactor' an even more consummate thinker than the original writer?!

stating its overall themes.[17] Jesus' departure is treated in John 14 and 16, the love command in John 15. John 17 has a special function, but we saw that it belongs with John 15 with regard to the disciples' understanding. Whereas in John 14 and 16 there is much emphasis on the disciples' lack of understanding, in John 15 *and* 17 they are explicitly taken by Jesus to understand. This suggests that the text as a whole has an ABA¹B¹ structure that matches the two themes announced in 13:33–5. This idea will be spelled out in what follows.[18] As it stands, however, the suggestion does not yet show that the whole Farewell Discourse constitutes a coherent unity. We must be particularly concerned to see whether the repetition of section A in its second occurrence (15:26–16:33) is repetition only or whether it adds something that might help to explain the repetition itself. By contrast, the repetition of section B in its second occurrence (John 17) poses less of a problem since the form of a prayer adopted here more or less immediately serves to explain the repetition. Jesus' prayer to his Father on behalf of the disciples now that 'the hour has come' (17:1) is an apt conclusion to the whole Farewell Discourse.[19]

If 13:33–5 constitutes a *propositio* for the rest of the speech, the question arises whether there is any special connection between the two parts of the *propositio*, Jesus' departure and the love command. At its deepest level that is a philosophical question. If the sequence of the two themes is not just accidental but intentional, is there anything *about* Jesus' departure (which the disciples do not yet fully understand, according to John 14 and 16) that

---

[17] Scholtissek (2000, 211) speaks of a 'prooemium'. Dettwiler (1995, 128) uses the term 'prologue'. I prefer the more rhetorically precise term *propositio*, which emphasizes that the Farewell Discourse is fundamentally a speech. As I see it, it is a distinct weakness of Burkhalter's recent treatment (2014) that he ends up seeing 13:31–5 as 'a preliminary, concluding, summary interpretation (*Gesamtdeutung*)' (2014, 117) of *13:1–30*. I believe this is due to his attempt to find a 'concentric' structure in 13:1–17:26 as a whole (in the wake of, among others, Mlakuzhyil 1987 and Zorrilla 1995, see Burkhalter 2014, 44–6). This is unconvincing to me.

[18] It is instructive to compare the proposed reading of 13:31–5 with Jean Zumstein's treatment (2007, 44–50). On the one hand, Zumstein claims (44, like Brown) that '[l]es v. 31–38 forment . . . une introduction qui esquisse de façon programmatique la thématique du premier discours d'adieu' (= 13:31–14:31). On the other hand, he also claims (48) that 13:31–8 'peut être considéré à la fois comme introduction du premier discours d'adieu et plus largement comme introduction aux chs. 14–17.' Similarly, he both finds (48 n. 9) the 'motif fondamental' of *agapan* in John 14 (14:15, 21, 23, 24, 28, and 31), 15 and 17—and also claims (49, rightly to my mind) that '[l]a thématique ecclésiologique du commandement d'amour [in 13:34–5] fait figure de bloc erratique; absente du chap. 14, elle ne sera reprise que dans le second discours d'adieu (Jn 15-16 . . .).' This position appears to me too complicated. It seems dictated by Zumstein's notion of *relecture*. (Incidentally, Zumstein notes [49 n. 16] that Frey, Schnelle, Barrett, Blank, Brown, and Wilckens take 13:34–5 to be in their proper, original place—'et sont donc de la plume de l'évangeliste'.) To my mind, Vargas 2014 suffers from the same lack of differentiation between 'vertical' love and 'horizontal' love between the disciples.

[19] For the exact delimitation of the A, B, A¹, and B¹ sections see later in this chapter, where I will call them sections i, ii, iii, and iv.

explains that they should love one another as Jesus' friends—and will in fact come to do so once they have obtained the required knowledge (as stated in John 15 and 17)? I insist on calling this a philosophical question since it turns on the issue of a deeper understanding. In the Farewell Discourse Jesus apparently aims to tell his disciples something that pertains to their understanding both of *what* is going to happen (his departure etc.) and also of what this *means* for them (the love command). Similarly, we may say that the text itself aims to make its *readers understand* that logical connection. So (philosophical question): what is the logical connection between the two themes announced in 13:33 and 34–5?

To further clarify this question, we may consider the use of the notion of *paráklêsis* by the Apostle Paul. As is well known, Paul uses the term and its verbal counterpart, *parakalein*, in two senses. In the more common sense, the two terms mean 'moral exhortation' and 'exhort', respectively. Here they refer to the Pauline practice of *'paraenesis'*.[20] In another use, *paráklêsis* means 'comfort'.[21] But the term remains the same. We may bring out this fact by translating *paráklêsis* and *parakalein* as 'encouragement' and 'encourage'.[22] In his 'exhortation encouragement' (*paraenesis*) Paul 'encourages' his addressees to do what they *already* know should be done. This last aspect will prove immensely important in John too. In his 'comfort encouragement' Paul rather 'comforts' them by appealing—once again—to what they already know has happened in the Christ event and then spelling out how that should make them 'rejoice' (Greek: *chairein* and *chará*) vis-à-vis the suffering and tribulation (*thlipsis*) that they encounter in their relations with the world.[23] In both cases they are being encouraged. But the focus differs. Paul's 'comfort' focuses, in the firm belief that this will relieve their suffering, on what his addressees know has happened in the Christ event. His 'exhortation' focuses on how they, as they also already know, should behave *in light of* the Christ event. But a tight logical connection is implied by Paul's use of the same term for both. We will gradually spell out the connection and show its importance for John.

---

[20] For one account of the relationship between *paráklêsis* and *paraenesis* in Paul, see my 2004.

[21] A striking example is 2 Corinthians 1 and 7 where Paul repeatedly contrasts his own and his addressees' 'suffering' (*thlipsis*) with the 'comfort' provided by God (2 Cor. 1:3–8 and 7:4–6).

[22] The point of this translation is that it may cover both senses of *paráklêsis* and *parakalein* under a single term. It thereby hints at an inner connection between the two senses which may make speaking of two different 'senses' obsolete. I am specifically wary about translating *paráklêsis* as 'consolation' in Paul since that translation removes the concept fairly drastically from that of 'exhortation'. And we do not know beforehand that Paul saw the two postulated 'senses' as different.

[23] For *chara* in Paul in connection with *thlipsis* and *paráklêsis*, see 2 Cor. 7:4 and 7:5–7.

In light of the Pauline distinction, we may understand Jesus' first announcement in John (13:33) as spelled out in John 14 and parts of John 16 (in particular 16:16–33) as 'comfort encouragement'. Here Jesus encourages his disciples against the background of his departure, not least by telling them of his return and the coming of the 'Paraclete'. 'Do not let your hearts be troubled' (14:1 and 14:27). '[P]ain (*lypê*) has filled your hearts' (16:6) and 'you have pain (*lypê*) now; *but* I will see you again, and your hearts will rejoice (*chairein*), and no one will take your joy (*chará*) from you' (16:22). This is closely similar to the 'comfort encouragement' that Paul gives to his addressees.

By contrast, Jesus' second announcement in the *propositio* (13:34–5) as spelled out in John 15 is clearly 'exhortation encouragement' (*paraenesis*). The parable of the vine (15:1–8) and the exhortation to love one another (15:9 17) are permeated with imperatives that have the same logical form as in Paul's *paraenesis*. They presuppose that the addressees already are where they are exhorted to be, and the imperatives are intended to make them stick to that. As Jesus says in John 15:4 and 15:9: 'Abide (*menein*, remain) in me', 'abide (*menein*, remain) in my love'. Similarly, as we saw, in John 17 we first hear that the disciples 'have kept (*têrein*) your *logos*' (17:6), after which Jesus goes on to ask (17:9, *erôtô*) the Father to '*keep* (*têrein*) them in your name' (17:11). Superficially, of course, this is not directed to the disciples, but to God. In an intriguing manner, however, it is definitely also paraenetically directed to the disciples, as is the whole of Jesus' prayer in John 17: *they* should abide (through God's help) in the *logos* they have already kept.

We may provisionally conclude that 13:33–5 constitutes a *propositio* for the whole text that leads directly into the basic philosophical question concerning the logical connection between Jesus' 'comfort encouragement' and his 'exhortation encouragement'. In this way 13:33–5 suggests that the text as a whole has a very high degree of unity, even though the purpose of the repetition of section A in 15:26–16:33 remains unexplained so far. We may also note, in connection with the question of genre, that on this reading the Johannine Farewell Discourse plays up the features of 'comfort' and 'moral exhortation' that form part of most farewell speeches by drawing on a central element from another genre that was also available to the earliest Christians: that of *paráklêsis* in the precise way this had (also) been developed by Paul.[24] What John has done is to tighten the various traditional elements in the genre of a farewell speech so as to make them all have a single focus: *paráklêsis* of the disciples, which they on their side

---

[24] It is immaterial here whether one takes John to have drawn directly on Paul or not. In accordance with more recent genre theory, I am only asking whether seeing the Johannine text in this light *works*.

(and the readers with them) will realize when they manage to see the inner connection in Jesus' death and resurrection between 'comfort' and 'exhortation'.

The suggestion here is that by subsuming everything in the Farewell Discourse under the two connected types of *paráklêsis*, John has turned the Farewell Discourse into one huge specimen of *paráklêsis* of the disciples. The underlying premise is that if they *understand* what Jesus is saying then they *will* be both 'comforted' and also made to do what Jesus has 'exhorted' them to do. However, since they do not quite reach that level of understanding in the narrative present (what we have called 'the fictional present'), the question becomes even more urgent as to how one should understand those sections of the whole text (basically, the B–sections: John 15 and 17) in which the disciples are described as having actually understood. This formulation of the question of the relationship of the A–sections and the B–sections already suggests a way in which that question may also be answered: in what Jesus is saying to and of the disciples in the B–sections, he is *also* speaking to and of Christ believers *after* his own death and resurrection.[25] That also includes the intended *readers* of the text. They should also understand. And if they do, then they will both be 'comforted' and actually do what Jesus has 'exhorted' them to do. Let us consider the time difference that appears to be involved in this picture.

THE DYNAMIC MOVEMENT IN TIME IN 13:36–17:26

Suppose that Jesus is engaged in 'comfort encouragement' in John 14 and 16, where it is also stated that the disciples do not *yet* understand, and in 'exhortation encouragement' in John 15 (and John 17), where they are explicitly stated to know. Then he will address the disciples in two distinct ways in the concrete narrative situation just before his death.[26] In John 14 and 16 he addresses them in the fictional present. They feel pain now (hearing of Jesus' imminent departure), but should also be comforted by the fact that certain good things will happen to them immediately upon

---

[25] This is the basic contention of Hoegen-Rohls 1996. She is quite right.

[26] The question about time to be addressed here has been extensively discussed, not only in German scholarship (see Frey 1997–2000, especially 1998, 208–83), but also in the American tradition that began with J. Louis Martyn's classic account (1968) of the 'two levels' that are present in the discourses of the Johannine Jesus. My own attempt remains strongly focused on the immediate narrative situation in which Jesus is speaking ('the fictional present') and aims to be as simple as possible. For this focus compare the excellent discussion in O'Day 1991, with which I share a great deal, not least its inspiration from Culpepper 1983 and Gérard Genette's concept of *prolepsis*.

Jesus' death. In John 15 and 17, by contrast, Jesus addresses the disciples, still in the fictional present, but now also somewhat *proleptically*, drawing on the way they are going to be once he *has* departed and once those good things have happened that will turn their present pain into joy. Then they will no longer need any comfort, but rather exhortation that they *remain* where they have by then come to be. We may express this proleptic perspective by speaking of 'the fictional future'.

This reading introduces an element of dynamic movement into the text. In John 14 Jesus gives comfort to his disciples in the fictional present in the way we have seen. By contrast, in John 15 (and *nota bene*: up until 16:15) he looks into the future and describes them as they will be once they have received the 'Paraclete'. This dynamic movement from (i) 13:36–14:31 (comfort in the fictional present) into (ii) 15:1–16:15 (exhortation in the fictional future) is reflected in a change in the way Jesus speaks of the world. In a moment we will consider two features of this change. The first serves to explain the step from section i *into* section ii, including the apparently insurmountable gap between 14:31 and 15:1. The second serves to explain the part (15:26–16:15) of section ii that leads from the primary part of that section (15:1–25) *into* what we will now call section iii: 16:16–33. For the sake of clarity, let us tabulate here the division of the Farewell Discourse that we will, from now on, adopt. It differs a bit from the transmitted chapter division.

John 13:31–5	Introduction (13:31–2) and *propositio* (13:33–5)
John 13:36–14:31	Section i (comfort in the fictional present)
John 15:1–16:15	Section ii (exhortation—plus comfort in 15:26–16:15—in the fictional future)
John 16:16–33	Section iii (comfort in the fictional present)
John 17:1–26	Section iv (prayer/'exhortation' in the fictional future).

THE ROLE OF THE WORLD IN THE MOVEMENT FROM SECTION I INTO SECTION II (ESPECIALLY 14:30–15:1)

Consider the role of Jesus' references to the world for the transition from section i into section ii. In section i, the world only makes a few brief appearances (14:17, 19, and 22). At the end of John 14, however, the world comes to play a much more important role when Jesus states that 'the ruler of this world is coming' (14:30). Jesus first reacts by saying that this 'ruler' (Satan, one suspects) 'has no hold on me' (14:30) and then utters the famous words: 'Rise, let us be on our way from here' (14:31). Whither?

Certainly not to *meet* Satan, as scholars have repeatedly suggested.[27] That might have been meant if John had just made Jesus say what he says in the Gospel of Mark: 'Get up, let us be going (*egeiresthe, agômen*). See, my betrayer is at hand' (Mark 14:42). However, John has no reference to the betrayer and instead adds a word that means '*from* here' (*enteuthen*): *egeiresthe, agômen enteuthen*. That fits. When Jesus goes immediately on to say that '*I* am (*Egô eimi*) the true vine' etc. (15:1) with much emphasis in the Greek on the '*I*', he is developing the image of the group of Jesus himself and his followers as one that has turned its *back* on the world and its ruler. This gives the following sense to the transition at 14:31/15:1. Where John 14 has gradually brought in the world until it ends up speaking of its ruler who is coming to bring Jesus to death, Jesus reacts by bringing in himself (contrastively matching the world's ruler) and the disciples as full members of the Jesus group (contrastively matching the world at large) which belongs *elsewhere*. In fact, as he says of them in John 17, 'They do not belong to the world, just as I do not belong to the world' (17:16). To *them*, that is, to the disciples who have now been *removed from the world* when Jesus tells them to rise and leave it behind, he may precisely say: '*Remain in* me or my love'. And *them* he may call his 'friends' because he has made everything known to them (15:15). By now, that is, *after* Jesus' departure, they constitute a group of their own that is directly attacked by the world, but has a high degree of inner cohesion, as explained by Jesus in 15:1–17.

It is worth spelling out this reading of the transition at 14:31/15:1 by looking at the text itself. Here are the three relevant verses:

[30]I will no longer speak much with you; for the ruler of this world is on his way, and he has no hold on me, [31]*but* (*all'*) in order that the world may know that I love the

---

[27] This is unfortunately the way it is almost invariably understood by commentators, who recall the somewhat similar expression in the Gospel of Mark (14:42). Against this, I am suggesting that Jesus is calling upon his disciples, as it were, to leave the world *behind*. Dodd's discussion (1953a, 406–9) is interesting. On the one hand, he connects John's ἐγείρεσθε, ἄγωμεν ἐντεῦθεν closely with Mark 14:42 and hence translates the phrase as a 'stirring battle-cry' (408, n. 1) meaning march 'to meet the approaching enemy' (406 n. 1) and 'let us go to meet the advancing enemy' (408). That must be wrong. First, we should at least attempt initially to make sense of John's sentence without thinking of Mark. Secondly, Dodd pays no attention whatever to ἐντεῦθεν (which is not in Mark). This suggests that John's Jesus is not inviting the disciples to go and *meet* Satan, but rather —since Satan is approaching and since he has no share in Jesus—to go *away* (with Jesus) *from* Satan's world. On the other hand, Dodd attempts a kind of 'spiritual' reading of the sentence (408–9), which Brown rejected as 'farfetched and unnecessary' (1970, 656–7). However, if we link the 'spiritual' reading directly with the Jesus-vine of 15:1–17, it makes a lot of sense: *that* is the goal towards which they should be going. (Incidentally, Dodd got the syntax of 14:31 exactly right [409], as Brown did not [651–2]—or for that matter Nestle Aland: a full stop before v. 31 and no full stop, but a comma after ποιῶ in v. 31.) For worthwhile objections to Dodd, H. Zimmermann, and Thyen, see Dettwiler 1995, 37–9. And for a completely different attempt at resolving the supposed 'aporia' of 14:31, see Parsenios 2005, 49–76.

Father, and that as the Father has commanded me, so I do ... : Rise, let us be on our way from here [that is, from the world]. ¹*I am the vine etc.*[28]

The world's ruler is on his way. He certainly has no hold on Jesus. *Nevertheless*, Jesus will do what God has commanded him to do, that is, go into his death. And in so doing he will—through his death and resurrection—also establish that '*other*-worldly' group that is described in the parable of the vine. In other words, 'Rise, let us be on our way *out of* this world' (namely, through Jesus' death and resurrection): *I am the vine*, etc.

On this reading, the transition at 14:31/15:1 is, if not smooth, at least highly suggestive. It also closely matches the transition we have discussed earlier in this book from John 9 into John 10. There, too, Jesus brought in at 10:1 a description of the Jesus group as fully constituted *after* his death and in the strongest contrast with the leaders of this world (there the Pharisees). And there, too, this was done by means of a parable. It is noteworthy that these are the two only extended parables in the Fourth Gospel. They appear to function in a closely similar way.

THE ROLE OF THE WORLD IN THE MOVEMENT FROM SECTION II INTO SECTION III (ESPECIALLY 15:26–16:15)

If we are right in seeing Jesus to be drawing the strongest possible contrast between the world and its ruler at the end of John 14 and his own 'rule' in the first half of John 15 (15:1–17), then it is noteworthy that this opposition is even further emphasized in the second half of the chapter (15:18–25) *and* in the part (15:26–16:15) of section ii that we may see as a bridge that leads into section iii. Here the disciples are first explicitly contrasted—as the group of Jesus' friends—with the world, which hates and will hate them just as it has hated Jesus (15:18–25). Next, the point is taken into John 16, focusing on the role the 'Paraclete' will play in their relations with the world (15:26–7 and 16:7–15). In this section, too, their future trouble with the world is described most explicitly and concretely (16:1–4) when Jesus says that '[t]hey will put you out of the synagogues'. Indeed, 'an hour is coming when those who kill you will think that by doing so they are offering worship to God' (16:2, NRSV).

---

[28] I thus agree with Dodd (1953a, 409) that the main clause after the subsidiary clause begun by 'in order that' comes with the two imperatives. The full stop after 'so I do' adopted by Nestle Aland 26–27 ed., and most commentators (e.g. Lincoln 2005, 383; Zumstein 2007, 84) is wrong. Léon-Dufour is an honourable exception (1993, 141): 'Bien plus! Pour que le monde reconnaisse que j'aime le Père en agissant comme le Père m'a commandé, levez-vous! Partons d'ici!'

In sum, the dynamic movement from section i into section ii turns on a change from the fictional present to the fictional future when the 'disciples' will have received the 'Paraclete' and then stand united as the group of Jesus' friends in direct confrontation with the world. In the second half (15:26–16:15) of section ii, this future confrontation is made wholly concrete (16:1–4), but the 'Paraclete' is introduced again (from section i) as a figure that will help the disciples in that future confrontation. It will do so by directly 'confronting' the world in the way described in 16:8–11.

This combination of the 'Paraclete' (from section i) with the theme of confrontation with the world that has been introduced earlier in section ii helps to explain why 15:26–16:15, where the 'Paraclete' is again in focus, is no mere repetition of section i. In John 16 it is combined with the theme of confrontation with the world. However, there are a few verses in the middle of 15:26–16:15 that might be taken to argue against this understanding: 16:4b–7. Do these verses not take up directly the line of section i, where Jesus speaks of his departure and comforts the disciples by pointing to the arrival of the 'Paraclete'? If so, should we not connect this part of the text with section iii (16:16–33), where Jesus again speaks of his departure (16:16–19) and the sorrow (*lypê*) this will cause them (16:20–2)?[29] In fact not. Since 16:4b–7 leads directly into the description in 16:8–11 of how the 'Paraclete' will help the disciples in confronting the world, it is better to see 16:4b–7 as providing the conceptual *background* to that claim—along these lines (I paraphrase): 'I did not tell you from the beginning when I was with you about all this future opposition from the world. Now, however, I am on my way to God—and you no longer even ask where I am going, but are only filled with pain. *However*, it is to your *advantage* that I shall go away and you will get the "Paraclete" instead. For *he* will *confront* the world, etc.' Thus understood, 16:4b–7 does not make an independent point where it stands, which would turn it into a repetition from section i. Rather, the text serves as a background to the claim that it is to the disciples' *advantage* that Jesus goes away, so that they may in *that* way obtain help in confronting the world.[30]

Why, then, does John's Jesus finally go back—in section iii: 16:16–33—to provide 'comfort encouragement' in the fictional present?[31] The reason

---

[29] Compare, e.g., Dettwiler 1995, 53–9, Zumstein 2007, 114, with references to Brown 1970, Beasley-Murray 1987, and O'Day 1995a. Frey 2000a, 111–12, is on the same line.

[30] Note what 16:5b–7 says of the disciples. Apparently, they *no longer* ask where Jesus is going (note καὶ in 5b: 'I go *and* none of you asks'; contrast this with the usual understanding, cf. NRSV: '...*yet* none of you asks...'). Instead (v. 6, *all*), they are (now) filled with pain. Yet (v. 7, *all*) it is all to their benefit since the 'Paraclete' will be coming. Thus, the focus remains on the 'Paraclete' and its importance in the future for the disciples now that Jesus is going away.

[31] It is worth noting that a nineteenth-century commentator on John, the excellent F. Godet (1869, 508–9), divided the text in the way I am also doing: (i) 13:31–14:31; (ii)

appears to be that he aims to focus on the precise content of the disciples' present lack of understanding. Here they are again explicitly described in the fictional present as lacking the understanding which we know they will eventually obtain. This is stated in 16:16–19, where the disciples are again musing among themselves. And it lies behind Jesus' claim that '[v]ery truly, I tell you, you will weep and mourn, but the world will rejoice ...' (16:20, NRSV). Then it is noteworthy that towards the end of the chapter Jesus begins to suggest that a time will come when the disciples will finally have achieved the required understanding. Is that time already there? Not quite (16:25–8): there is hope for the disciples; God loves them already now since they have felt love for Jesus and come to believe that he has come from God; but it is only on some day in the future that they may beg of God and he will give them; as yet, Jesus cannot even speak plainly about God. And why not? Since they will not understand. This latter claim is something the disciples do not understand either. They respond directly to 16:25–8 that 'Now we know ...' (16:29–30). But Jesus immediately rejects this (16:31–2): they will soon be scattered.

In light of this exchange one must conclude that just before the passion story is about to begin, John wanted to present the disciples as *not* fully understanding everything about Jesus. More precisely, while they did believe and understand that he had come from God (16:27 and 30), they did not understand the other half of 16:28: that he was now about to leave the world behind and return to God. What they could not understand is exactly the same as what we found to be unintelligible to everybody described in John 11–12: that Jesus' death was also his return to the Father and quite literally so, in his resurrection. Thus John is keen on emphasizing that the final point about Jesus, the climax of the story about him, could not be understood until it had actually happened. By contrast, in the earlier half of section ii (15:1–25) Jesus precisely presupposes that as the disciples are described *there*, namely, with a view to the fictional future, they do know everything about him, including the fact that he has returned to God in his death and resurrection.

Section iii ends in a striking manner. Once Jesus has declared that he will be left alone by the disciples, he concludes (16:33):

[33]'These things I have spoken to you in order that you may have peace in me. In the world you (will) have affliction. But take courage: I have conquered the world.

15:1–16:15; (iii) 16:16–33—and of course (iv) 17:1–26. Godet's title for 15:1–16:15 is particularly apt: 'The Position of the Disciples in the World after the Infusion of the Holy Spirit' (529). The equally admirable twentieth-century commentator, Dodd (1953a, 410–16), took the whole of chapters 15 and 16 together, but also in fact saw the special place of 16:16–33: 'With xvi. 16 we seem to be brought back to the theme of the dialogue in xiii. 31–xiv. 31' (415). Exactly—which is what raises the question I am addressing: why?

This verse very neatly summarizes both section i and section ii, the former when it speaks of peace (compare 14:27, end of section i) and the latter when it refers to the affliction that the disciples will suffer from the world (compare 15:18–16:11). That affliction is to be contrasted with the peace that they will have 'in Jesus', that is, in the group constituted by the Jesus-vine. Since this leads the reader back both to the conclusion of section i and to the beginning of section ii, it should come as no surprise that Jesus ends section iii with these unforgettable words: '*I have conquered the world*'. At 14:30 the ruler of the world was approaching. But the section on the Jesus-vine has shown that Jesus has *conquered* the world and its ruler.

In spite of the emphasis in section iii on the ultimate lack of understanding in the disciples, they are nevertheless addressed by Jesus in John 14–16 as being sufficiently close to the final stage of knowledge for it to be possible for him to go on in John 17 (section iv) to pray to God on their behalf, as if they already had a sufficient amount of knowledge. We saw in some detail earlier that the point of Jesus' prayer to God was to *keep* them where they had actually come to be. However, we should also note that when the disciples are praised in John 17 for having understood what should be understood, the content of the latter is actually *not* the one given in the *second* half of 16:28 (on Jesus' return to God), but only the one given in the first half (on his coming from God). Nowhere in John 17 are the disciples said to have understood that 'I am leaving the world and going to my Father'. What they have come to understand is only 'that all that you have given me is from you' (17:7), 'that I have come from you' and 'that you have sent me' (17:8) and again 'that you have sent me' (17:25). In this way the difference between what the disciples know in section iii and in section iv is not that big, after all. What the disciples need to understand, according to 16:28, is that Jesus not only came from God but also returned to God. What they need, according to 17:17–19, is to be 'made holy' ('sanctified'). Both needs will be fulfilled—when? Answer: when they will eventually receive the *pneuma*, the 'Paraclete'.

We may conclude that corresponding to the fact (on the proposed hypothesis) that Jesus is moving back and forth in the whole text between 'comfort encouragement' and 'exhortation encouragement', there is a dynamic movement from section i (13:36–14:31) into section ii (15:1–16:15) and again from section iii (16:16–33) into section iv (17:1–26). Here section ii is, in a way, the most important one since it describes both positively (with regard to the internal relations within the group) and negatively (externally with regard to the world) the state that the disciples will be in in the future *once* they have received the 'Paraclete'. We have seen that this reading also makes particularly good sense of the one rift in the text that has for more than a hundred years led scholars to question its unity: the transition from 14:31 into 15:1. This is another place—like 10:1—where the transmitted chapter division (and a too-bookish reference to Mark 14:42) seems to have led scholars astray.[32]

ANSWERING THE PHILOSOPHICAL QUESTION

We asked whether there is something in the motif of Jesus' departure (the first point in the *propositio*) that explains that the disciples should love one another as Jesus' friends (the second point in the *propositio*)—and indeed will come to do so once they have obtained the full knowledge of what goes into that departure. In other words, how should one understand the dynamic movement from section i into section ii and again from section iii into section iv? How will the disciples obtain full knowledge? What is its content? And how will it make them do what they should do as Jesus' friends, namely, act on the love command?

In a way we already know the answer: the disciples will receive the 'Paraclete', as Jesus *promises* in sections i and iii and the latter half of section ii. When that *has* happened (*after* Jesus' death), they will understand everything: that Jesus has died on their own behalf, as their friend (compare 15:13) and out of his love for them (compare 15:9); that he has been resurrected and gone to the Father; and that the appropriate response on their own part to Jesus' love for them is that they *similarly* love *one another* (15:12), whereby they will fully be Jesus' friends (15:14). All of this constitutes the actual content and meaning of the full Christ event, indeed its whole point (for life in the present): from God's love for Jesus to Jesus' love for human beings to mutual love among the latter (compare 15:9 and 12). This they will fully understand once they have received the 'Paraclete'. And so they will also apply it in practice.

And this they should. For it is only if they *keep* Jesus' commandments, that they will *remain* in his love for them (15:10), as expressed in his dying for them (15:13). The believers are Jesus' friends *if* they do what he commands them to do (15:13). And they *are* his friends because he has *made known* to them everything he has heard from his Father (compare 15:15). How, then, has he made that known to them? Not just by telling them when he was with them. For we know that the disciples remained ignorant to the very end of everything that had to do with Jesus' resurrection and

---

[32] It is interesting to note that Dodd (1953a, 411) does see the similarity between the transitions at 15:1 and 10:1: 'The closest parallel [to the transition from 14:31 to 15:1] is the transition from ix. 41 to x. 1.' Unfortunately, he does not make anything of this insight. But he should have done: the sudden shift to a parable that is about the fictional future ties these two transitions exceedingly closely together; thus, if John 9 and 10 are internally coherent, so are John 14 and 15.

what that meant. Instead, they came to understand it when they received the 'Paraclete'.

This is the answer that John himself gives. But this answer may be made much clearer if we remember that the 'Paraclete' is explicitly identified as *pneuma*—and then bring in once more for heuristic purposes the Stoic notion of *pneuma* in order to elucidate the logic of the 'Paraclete's identity and function. In Stoicism, the *pneuma* is both a material and a cognitive entity. It may be infused into human bodies and it may in this way generate knowledge in human beings. In John the same thing happened initially to Jesus himself in the baptism scene of John 1 when he became the bearer in his own body of the divine *pneuma*. This event also had a cognitive side to it. For the material *pneuma* is also the divine, cognitive *logos* from the Prologue. So, even Jesus came to know.

This is exactly what will also come to pass for the disciples when they receive the 'Paraclete', which is also called 'the *pneuma* of truth' (14:17; 15:26; 16:13). Then they will come to know the full truth that is 'Jesus' *logos*' (as opposed to merely believing in him in the many deficient ways we have constantly come across). They will know who he is, including that he *went back to* heaven, and what the purpose of that was. All of this they will at long last understand when they themselves come to possess the 'Paraclete'–*pneuma*. But in addition to this cognitive side of the disciples' experience, there is also a material one. The disciples will literally and substantively receive the *pneuma* within their bodies (thereby becoming able literally to remain *in* the 'Jesus–vine' just as he remains *in* them, 15:4), and this is what explains that they will henceforth 'bear much fruit' and act on the love command.[33] Not only will they now know: they will also act on their knowledge. When the *pneuma* has been infused into and taken over their bodies, they *cannot but* act on their knowledge.[34]

It is this precise idea of having the *pneuma* in one that fills in all the 'reciprocal statements of immanence' (*reziproke Immanenz-Aussagen*), of which there are so many in the Fourth Gospel and which go to the heart of what John aims to say.[35] Whenever John writes of God, Jesus, or believers as being 'in' one another, one should think: Ah, by means of the material *pneuma*! That is also what is meant in the concluding sentence of the whole Farewell Discourse (17:26, NRSV):

---

[33] We moderns may have problems about taking the 'in' relation so literally. It is a virtue of Stoicism—and one that helps strikingly to elucidate both Paul and John—to insist that it should be so taken.

[34] Why then *exhort* them? As in Paul, John's exhortation has the logical form of reminding the disciples of where they already are and asking them to put that into practice.

[35] For this, of course, compare Scholtissek 2000 (who does not, however, spell out the cosmology the way I do).

[26] ...so that the love with which you [addressing God] have loved me [as shown when God gave Jesus the *pneuma*] may be in them [by means of the same *pneuma*], *and I in them.*

Finally, it is the precise idea of having the *pneuma* in one that gives shape to what one may well call Johannine 'ethics' in the Gospel. Here, again, the crucial text is the first half of John 15 (15:1–17). Scholars have generally queried whether there was any genuine 'ethics' to be found in the Fourth Gospel, but it has also been recognized that this text in particular does address that issue.[36] Three features in it show this. There are first the many references to 'bearing fruit' (15:2, 3, 5, 8, 16), where the term for 'fruit' (Greek *karpos*) was almost a technical term in Early Christian texts precisely for ethical practice.[37] Secondly, there is the *topos* of friendship (15:13–15), which is a Greco–Roman concept that is exceedingly closely connected with ethical practice. It was central in Greco–Roman moral philosophy from Plato and Aristotle onwards. For its connection with ethics, in particular, we may quote this snippet from Diogenes Laertius on the Stoics (*SVF* III 631, DL 7.124):

They say that friendship is to be found only among the (morally) good because of their (mutual) likeness. They say that it is a certain partnership (*koinônia*) of all that has to do with life (*bios*) in which we treat our friends as (we would) ourselves. They claim that a friend is choiceworthy for his own sake and that having many friends is something (genuinely) good. Among bad men, however, there is no such thing as friendship and no bad man has a friend.

Thirdly, of course, 15:9–17 identifies the behaviour to which the disciples are being exhorted as that of mutual love (*agapê*, 15:12, 17, compare 13:34–5), and this constitutes *the* basic concept in other Early Christian reflection on the kind of 'ethics' which is the other side of the 'religious' relationship of human beings with Jesus and God.[38] Thus, for instance, Paul summarizes his *paraenesis* in both Galatians and Romans under that very term (Gal. 5:6, 13–14; Rom. 13:8–10). Indeed, *agapê* is the very first 'moral virtue' mentioned by Paul in Gal. 5:22 in a list of 'virtues' that spell out the content of the following thing: 'the *fruit* (*karpos*) of the *pneuma*'. This is almost identical with what one finds in John. And it has to do, precisely, with 'ethics'.

---

[36] For this whole issue see, in particular, van der Watt and Zimmermann 2012, which breaks new ground by extending the query beyond this central text.

[37] Danker (2000, 510) rightly understands *karpos* quite broadly in its use 'in the spiritual (opp. physical) realm' as '*result, outcome, product*'. But his references also show that the term is often used much more specifically for moral behaviour.

[38] As always, I place 'ethics' and 'religious' in scare quotes to indicate that the two concepts (at least, 'religious') are to a certain extent post-ancient and that the distinction between two fields of 'ethics' and 'religion' was actually not drawn in ancient thought, certainly not in the way it is in modern thought.

We should conclude that underlying the whole text of John 13:31–17:26 there is a philosophical question of what explains the logical connection between the two statements in Jesus' *propositio* for the whole speech concerning his departure and his love command. With the help of the Pauline distinction between two senses of *paráklēsis*, we reformulated that question as asking what explains the dynamic movement from the situation of the disciples in the fictional present (sections i and iii), when they receive 'comfort encouragement', to their situation in the fictional future (sections ii and iv), for which they receive 'exhortation encouragement'. We may now conclude that the text itself provides a simple and clear answer to that question. What accounts for the change is the fact that upon Jesus' departure the disciples will receive the 'Paraclete'—*and that the 'Paraclete' is pneuma with the features that we also know from Stoicism.*[39] When the disciples have received a 'Paraclete' of that kind, they will both fully know the complete Jesus story and also understand what it means for their own lives and how they should behave in that light. This includes the point that just as Jesus has died for them out of his love for them, so they must themselves love one another. Thus the disciples will fully understand everything that Jesus spells out to them in his exegesis in 15:9–17 of the parable of the vine (15:1–8). And they will also actually do it. In addition, we have seen that 15:1–17, in particular, brings out the precise effect of receiving the *pneuma* in terms both of the locution of being 'in' Jesus and God and also of a number of concepts that serve to identify this reception as constitutive of Johannine 'ethics'.

JESUS AND THE 'PARACLETE'; THE IMMEDIATE AND THE DISTANT FUTURE

Now we may also solve the second and third problems we identified to begin with, on the relationship between Jesus and the 'Paraclete' and between the immediate and the more distant future.

---

[39] It would be worth considering in more detail all the issues that surround the figure of the 'Paraclete' in John. That cannot be done, however. The classic, and still generally persuasive, discussion is Brown 1967. One basic conclusion, with which we should agree, is this: 'If there remains something unique in John's understanding of the Paraclete, so that the Christian concept goes beyond the mere sum of all the elements in the Jewish background, and no one translation of the Greek word can capture all its aspects, then the last approach to what is unique must be sought in John's own description of the Paraclete' (126). Here Brown in effect—and quite rightly—leaves the tradition historical analysis behind and focuses instead on what the text itself says about the *paraklētos*. For my own guess at the reason why John chose precisely this term for the 'holy *pneuma*', see later in this chapter.

Jesus and the 'Paraclete' are one and the same figure in a very precise way. The Jesus who is speaking and acting in John's Gospel is a (possibly Stoically conceived) 'amalgam' of two entities: Jesus of Nazareth and the *pneuma* he received in the baptism scene.[40] The Jesus who dies and is raised to heaven may or may not be the same composite figure. But that figure may come to be present on earth again, but now within the disciples and in 'disamalgamated' form, *as pneuma*. That *pneuma is* the 'Paraclete'. Though Jesus departs in one form, he also immediately returns in what is either the same or else a slightly different form, namely, as nothing but *pneuma*, which is nevertheless also the form that makes him be what he both was and is: Jesus *Christ*. There is absolutely no reason, therefore, to be surprised that Jesus speaks rather indiscriminately in John 14 of the coming of the 'Paraclete' and of his own (immediate) return: he is referring to the same event.

It is worth spelling this out by considering the whole text in John 14 (14:15–26) which contains the first and the second mention of the 'Paraclete'. The text begins by talking of the 'Paraclete' but also tying that figure closely to Jesus himself (14:15–17):

[15]If you love me, you will keep (*têrein*) my commandments.[16]And I will ask my Father, and he will give you another Paraclete, to be with you forever, [17]the *pneuma* of truth, which the world cannot receive, because it neither sees it nor knows (it). But you know it, because it remains with you and will be in you.

In this text, 14:15 is probably intended to bring out that loving Jesus himself *implies* a willingness also to keep his 'commandments', that is, to do whatever specific acts Jesus commands them to do. That, then, as 14:16 states ('And' = 'Then'), is also a *condition* for Jesus' asking the Father to give them the 'Paraclete'. That this is no stray thought is made clear by 14:21, 23, and 24, only here what will come about as a result is that God himself and Jesus ('*we*') 'will come' to believers. This in itself suggests that the 'Paraclete' is not different from Jesus himself (or indeed from God).

Here, however, we must also consider the matter a bit more carefully from the other side: that of believers. Note that what they will keep (*têrein*) is said in 14:15, 21, 23, and 24 to be either 'my commandments' (15, 21), or 'my *logos*' (23), or 'my *logous*' (24), that is, Jesus' 'words' (elsewhere called his *rhêmata*, see 14:10), which in 14:24 itself are implied to express the underlying *logos* which is both Jesus' and God's. There is a quite strong condition, therefore, on who will be able to receive the 'Paraclete', Jesus, and God. What is the point of this condition? And how far must believers

---

[40] The Stoic amalgam would be a case of proper, Stoic *krasis* (mixture), see *SVF* 2:463–81 (*De mixtione*) with the subtitle σῶμα διὰ σώματος χωρεῖ ('a body penetrates a body'). Here two types of matter are joined together while in principle remaining separable.

have gone in their relationship with Jesus in order to receive the 'Paraclete'? In particular, must they themselves already—strange as it may
sound—be in possession of the *pneuma?*

These questions are quite urgent in relation to the picture of two types of
belief in Jesus that we have been operating with in this book. Where initial
belief does not presuppose the existence of the *pneuma* in believers, full belief
does (so we said). Then where does 'loving Jesus' and 'keeping his commandments' (etc.) of 14:15–24 belong? It sounds as if that state presupposes
that one has full belief. But that cannot be if full belief only comes to apply
when a believer has received the *pneuma* as these people are only *about* to
do. So, is Jesus after all only talking of the relationship one has with him
when one has initial belief? That does not sound right either.

This whole issue is aggravated if we ask what Jesus' 'commandments'
actually consist in—and then bring in 15:9–12, where he again speaks of
'my commandments' (NRSV):

> [9]As the Father has loved me, so I have loved you; abide in my love. [10]If you keep my
> commandments you will abide in my love, just as I have kept my Father's com-
> mandments and abide in his love.... [12]This is my commandment, that you love
> one another as I have loved you...

This text comes immediately after the parable of the vine, where the idea of
the vine branches being 'in' the vine (15:4) distinctly appears to presuppose
that Jesus' addressees are (here) taken to be in possession of the *pneuma.* So,
is that idea also presupposed in 15:9–12? And if that text appears similar to
14:15–16, is John then saying that they will already be in possession of the
pneuma—when Jesus is also telling them that he *will* ask his Father to give it
to them?

The best answer to this genuine problem of interpretation may be derived
from noting an important difference between what Jesus says in 15:9–12
and 14:15–16 respectively, and relating that difference to the situation of the
disciples envisaged in 14:15–16. In 15:9–12 Jesus speaks of *abiding in* his love
(clearly reflecting 15:1–8); in 14:15–24 he just speaks of their loving him. If
we combine this with the situation of the disciples as envisaged in John 14,
where Jesus emphasizes that they do *not* (yet) understand well enough,
then it makes sense to see Jesus' injunctions in 14:15–24 as being directed
precisely to people who are not yet fully where they are headed. This is
borne out by the context. In 14:8–11 Jesus both criticizes Philip for his lack
of understanding (14:8–10) and also enjoins the disciples to believe in him in
a manner that amounts to full belief (14:10–11), which they are precisely
presupposed *not* to do. And in 14:12–14 he even spells out—but clearly
proleptically—what the situation of full belief among the disciples will be like
in *contrast* to where they are at present. Seen in that light, it makes
excellent sense that Jesus should go on to state a condition for their

receiving the *pneuma* that does not presuppose that they already have it but nevertheless moves distinctly in the proper direction. In that case the two texts will be playing on the difference between the disciples' loving Jesus and keeping his 'commandments' as an expression of their *less* than full belief—and their being fully 'in' Jesus and his love. In the former case they will then receive the 'Paraclete'–*pneuma*. In the latter case they already possess it.

On such a reading, what 14:15–24 is saying is that if the disciples will enter into the relationship with Jesus of loving him and keeping his commandments (and later his *logos* and *logous*) at an intermediary stage, that is, without *fully* understanding them and being *fully in* Jesus and his love, *then* they will also *eventually* receive the 'Paraclete'–*pneuma*, for which they have then qualified. And *then*—as we may fill out the thought—they will at long last also come to be fully 'in' Jesus and God—and they in them. If this is right, then it is another example of how extremely carefully John writes: 14:15–24 does *not* envisage the same situation of the disciples as 15:9–12 and this is brought out by the detailed phrasing—in particular, the talk of 'remaining in' Jesus and his love—even though the two passages might initially appear rather similar.

For our present question concerning the relationship between Jesus and the 'Paraclete', we may conclude that the very close but still insufficient relationship with Jesus that believers must have as a precondition for receiving the 'Paraclete' suggests that what their *eventual* reception of the 'Paraclete' will mean is this: the *fully* adequate relationship—with *Jesus*. And so, the two figures of (the risen and returning) Jesus and the 'Paraclete' are not in the end to be distinguished.

In the next small section (14:18–21), Jesus speaks of himself as one who will be 'coming' to them. He has just told the disciples that 'I am going to the Father' (14:12). But he now also tells them this (14:21):

> [21]The one who has my commandments and keeps them, he is the one who loves me; and the one who loves me will be loved by my Father, and I will love him and reveal myself to him.

Again we have the condition: the disciples must love Jesus and show this by having and keeping his commandments; *then* God and Jesus will love them in return and Jesus will reveal *himself* to them. Since when that happens the disciples will (finally) understand that 'I am in my Father and *you* are in me, and I in *you*' (14:20), it seems virtually impossible not to see Jesus here as talking of himself *as* the 'Paraclete'. The 'Paraclete' as *pneuma* is what is referred to by all this talk of being 'in'.

This is confirmed by the next small section (14:22–4), in which Jesus continues to speak of himself. One of the disciples asks why Jesus will reveal himself only to them and not to the world at large (14:22). He gets this answer (14:23):

²³If somebody loves me, he will keep my *logos*, and (*then*) my Father will love him and *we will come* to him and *(we will) make our home* with him.

How may both God and Jesus together come and make their 'home' or 'quarter' (*monê*) with a believer? Only one answer seems possible: as *pneuma*. It comes as no surprise, therefore, when Jesus goes directly on to the second mention of the 'Paraclete' (14:25–6):

²⁵These things I have spoken to you while I remain (*menein*) with you. ²⁶But the Paraclete, the holy *pneuma*, which (*ho*) the Father will send in my name, *he* (*ekeinos*) will teach you everything, and remind you of all that I have said to you.

Jesus 'remains' (*menein*) with the disciples in the present (14:25), but once he has gone to the Father, he and God will soon 'make their home' (*monê*) with them (14:23)—and the 'Paraclete', too, will soon 'remain (*menein*) with you and be in you' (14:17): again it seems impossible not to understand all this as saying that the 'Paraclete' *is* Jesus himself (and God), though certainly in a form that is sufficiently different for it to be possible for Jesus to refer to it as 'another Paraclete' (14:16). The best way to make sense of both the identity and the difference appears to be the one we suggested above when we distinguished between the 'amalgam' of *pneuma* and body of flesh and blood in the earthly Jesus—and the *pneuma* itself as both present *in* that 'amalgam' and also independently present in the form of the 'Paraclete'.

With this conclusion, it seems that we may also throw some quite striking light on the name itself of the 'Paraclete'. Scholars have rightly investigated this name and related it to the various functions that are ascribed to the 'Paraclete' in the text—such as 'teach(ing) you everything, and remind(ing) you of all that I have said to you' (14:26), 'witness(ing) about me' (15:26) and 'confront(ing) the world' in the ways described in 16:8–11.⁴¹ Here we may suggest an additional reading. First, when Jesus describes the 'Paraclete' as 'another Paraclete', he is evidently comparing it to himself in the role of a 'Paraclete' (as it were, the 'first Paraclete'). Now what does that mean? If we have been right in understanding the whole Farewell Discourse as a piece of (Pauline) *paráklêsis*, there is a striking answer to that question. Jesus is a 'Paraclete' (*paráklêtos*) *in what he says and does in the Farewell Discourse*. Secondly, how, then, will the *new* 'Paraclete' *be* a 'Paraclete'? Answer: by saying and doing exactly what Jesus has been saying and doing in the Farewell Discourse, that is, by reminding the disciples of that after Jesus' death. Is this not what Jesus

---

⁴¹ Compare Brown (1967, 114) on the functions of the Paraclete: '[T]he basic functions...are twofold: the Paraclete comes to the disciples and dwells within them, guiding and teaching them about Jesus; but the Paraclete is hostile to the world and puts the world on trial'.

himself says of it at 16:12–15? On this reading, then, the 'Paraclete' is called so because what he does is—*paráklêsis*.

In this connection we may also note the extreme care with which John describes the 'Paraclete' in both masculine and neuter forms (see, e.g., the quotation of 14:26 given above). The 'Paraclete' is a 'he', that is, a 'person', when described *as* a 'Paraclete', but an 'it' when described as *pneuma*. This is not at all surprising. The 'Paraclete' *is pneuma* and hence a (material and cognitive) power with the various functions we have identified, that is, a neuter being. But the 'Paraclete' is also Jesus (in that specific form, and hence as Jesus Christ) and so must be just as much a person as Jesus Christ is, that is, a male being. Incidentally, and probably not at all accidentally, we may recall that in the Prologue the *logos*, too, underwent a similar transformation, being first (e.g. in 1:2) described as a male being in accordance with its grammatical gender, then as a neuter being (namely, as *phôs*, 'light', see 1:9) and finally again as a male being (1:10)—when it was also meant to be understood as referring to Jesus. Such changes may appear strange to a modern sensibility. Apparently—and highly suggestively—they did not in antiquity.

If that is how we should understand the relationship between Jesus and the 'Paraclete', then we can also understand the relationship between the immediate and the more distant future in Jesus' statements about his own return. Jesus will return in the immediate future *as pneuma* (the 'Paraclete'). But Jesus will also return in the more distant future when human beings, too, will be resurrected according to the traditional picture. There is no need to choose here. Both events may well take place as two distinct events as soon as one sees how to differentiate between them.[42]

WHY DOES JESUS PRAY TO GOD ON BEHALF OF THE DISCIPLES IN JOHN 17?

The account we have given of the different levels of knowledge on the part of the disciples in sections i and ii and then again in sections iii and iv is, I believe, both clear and correct. We also noted, however, that John 17 appears to vacillate a bit between saying that the disciples have already come to know (compare 17:6–8) and praying to God that he may 'sanctify' them (17:17) even further. This suggests that we need to make an addition to our earlier picture of the ways people may relate to Jesus. Where we have previously distinguished between initial belief and full belief, it appears that in the case of the disciples as described in John 13–17, we must operate with

---

[42] This claim is in close agreement with the main result reached in Frey 2000a. The route and ontological underpinning differ widely, however.

a bit more than merely initial belief, while still insisting that none of them arrived at full belief, and indeed, that the aim of section iii is precisely to bring that out.

I am struck by the fact that when Jesus addresses the level of knowledge achieved by the disciples in John 17, what he says is that 'they have kept your *logos*' (17:6), which he then spells out in the next two verses (17:7–8) in terms precisely of the 'knowledge' they have acquired. But this idea of 'keeping the commandments and *logos*' was also the one we met repeatedly in our analysis of the section in John 14 (14:15–24) where Jesus spelled out the condition for—what? Answer: for his own '*asking*' (*erôtan*) God to give the disciples 'another Paraclete' (14:16). It seems, then, that what Jesus is saying in John 14 that they *should* do (keep his commandments etc.) in order to receive the 'Paraclete' from God is what he is saying in John 17 that they *have* done as a condition for his *now* 'asking' God (again *erôtan* several times: 17:9, 15, 20) *that* he should give them the 'Paraclete'. And as we saw, Jesus' prayer that God will 'sanctify' them (17:17) appears to have precisely that meaning: that they will receive the *pneuma*.

The proposal, then, is this: in John 17 Jesus is 'praying' ('asking') God to do to the disciples (upon his departure: 17:13) what he had himself told them in John 14 that he *would* ask God to do (14:16). The prayer of John 17 *is* the prayer announced by Jesus in John 14: the prayer that God may send the 'Paraclete' to the disciples, now that Jesus is himself going away. And the reason why he may ask for this is that in John 17 he is presenting the disciples as having fulfilled the condition for their reception of the 'Paraclete' that he had stated in John 14.[43]

With such a reading of Jesus' prayer in John 17, this chapter is tied very closely together with the preceding chapters of the Farewell Discourse in a manner I have not found articulated elsewhere. Jesus comforts the disciples in the fictional present (sections i and iii) and exhorts them (section ii) *as if* they were already in the fictional future. But he also prays (section iv) that God will act towards them in the way that will *bring them into* that fictional future (of section ii). The inner connections in all this are very tight, indeed. However, this is something one can only see by focusing sharply on the question of the levels of the disciples' understanding in relation to their receiving the *pneuma*.

If this whole reading is on target, we must conclude that precisely in the situation of the Farewell Discourse where Jesus is distinctly addressing 'his own', John adds to his previous notion of initial belief. As described in the

---

[43] This proposal concerning the precise reason why Jesus prays to God at this specific juncture is not intended to set aside the other thematic elements in the prayer, as well summarized, e.g., by Lincoln (2005, 432–4). It does add to them, including to the reflections in Attridge 2013a on the extent to which Jesus' prayer is a 'high priestly prayer'.

Farewell Discourse, the disciples do *not* (yet) have full belief (witness section iii). Still, they are closer to that than merely having initial belief. Their understanding of Jesus is in itself not necessarily more developed than in an initial belief. But they *have* 'kept your *logos*' (17:6) as one must in order to receive the 'Paraclete' (14:15–24). And this is due to the fact that they have also 'loved' Jesus (14:15, 21, 23). This picture of the disciples is not at all strange. For the Farewell Discourse as a whole is clearly—and wholly understandably in narrative terms—aiming to present the disciples *both* as being 'not yet there' and *also* as having nevertheless gone as far in the proper direction as one possibly can when one does *not* understand the ultimate thing about Jesus: that he will be resurrected and return to God.

SUMMARY OF 13:31–17:26: THE JOHANNINE VISION

Imagine a group of men (sorry about this!) standing in a circle in the middle of a stage holding one another's hands and turning their faces inward towards one another. The stage itself is dark, but right in the middle there is a pyramid of warm light of *pneuma* coming down from above that illuminates the men's faces while also contrasting that light with the darkness behind their backs. This is the group of men that John was trying to depict and also bring into existence by means of the Farewell Discourse he attributed to Jesus as he was leaving his disciples behind. The vision expresses the two main features of the whole speech, as these are articulated in its initial *propositio*: what will happen 'cosmologically' at Jesus' departure (the departure itself and the arrival of the 'Paraclete'); and what this will mean 'ethically' for the lives of the disciples. The vision pinpoints the connection between the two features, which is the arrival of the *pneuma* that turns the men into Jesus' friends and makes them love one another as Jesus has loved them. The aim of the text is, then, to make its readers grasp this vision by coming to see the connection between its two parts which is generated by the *pneuma*. By grasping that, they may also themselves come to realize the vision.

How, then, did John manage to present this vision to his readers? By working creatively with a large number of genre elements in these five chapters—a farewell speech that is held together by a regular rhetorical *propositio*, 'Pauline' *paráklēsis* of two kinds, a parable, a prayer, and more—but also with a set of philosophical strategies and motifs: asking for the logical connection between the two main themes announced in the *propositio*; drawing on the moral philosophical language of friendship in the way the text spells out in 15:13 the ethical implications of Jesus' dying for his 'friends'; drawing on a certain philosophical understanding of *pneuma* that gives immediate, bodily meaning to talk of being 'in' one another. There is not a single genre here or a single philosophical idea. But it is all kept together by the manner in which the text sets out from raising a philosophical question in the attentive reader and then continues through all its meanderings until it has provided a satisfactory answer to that question.

As regards these meanderings, I have argued that there is far more coherence to the whole of the Farewell Discourse than is generally accepted by scholars. In section i the text sets out the relationship between the promised 'Paraclete' and Jesus himself and the time frame of Jesus' returns on earth in a manner that is wholly coherent as soon as one understands that Jesus is talking all through of the presence of the *pneuma* among believers after his death (plus hinting at his own return in the more distant future). Similarly, in section ii John gives a picture of the fully established group of Christ believers after Jesus' death who have full knowledge of the meaning of the whole Christ event and its implications for their own lives, both internally and externally, a picture that makes excellent sense just because it presupposes that they will at that point have received the 'Paraclete'–*pneuma*. In section iii Jesus spells out the one key feature of the Christ event—of Jesus' return to the Father—that the disciples did *not* manage to understand during Jesus' lifetime but will precisely come to understand once they have received the 'Paraclete'–*pneuma*. Finally, in section iv Jesus prays to God that he may keep in them the level of knowledge that they have after all already achieved, namely, that Jesus has in an intensive sense 'come from God' (see 17:7–8). However, it also seems as if he is asking God to give them yet *more* knowledge so that they will eventually end up being truly 'sanctified' (17:17) and so that the love with which God loved Jesus—and indeed, Jesus himself—may also come to be fully present *in* them (17:26). I have suggested that Jesus' prayer in John 17 should be understood as *being* the prayer he has already announced in 14:16 that he will address to God: the prayer that God will give the 'other Paraclete', the *pneuma*, to the disciples. When *that* happens, they will *fully* know and be truly sanctified.

The whole of the Farewell Discourse, we should conclude, is held tightly together by the Johannine understanding of the *pneuma*, which provides the answer to the philosophical question we raised in relation to the *propositio* of the Farewell Discourse itself. Jesus will depart (13:33)—but that only makes possible the arrival of the *pneuma*; *then* they will also become able to live in accordance with Jesus' new love commandment (13:34–5). This inner connection constitutes the essence of the Johannine vision for the disciples (and his readers) as expressed in the whole of the Farewell Discourse.

X

THE EXECUTION OF THE PLAN
(JOHN 18–20)

THE SPECIFIC POINT OF JOHN'S ACCOUNT
OF JESUS' DEATH AND RESURRECTION

How, methodologically, should one read the passion narrative in the Fourth Gospel? Since this part of the Gospel—at least John 18–19—is the section that is most closely similar to the accounts given in the Synoptic Gospels, it might appear most straightforward to make a more or less detailed comparison with those accounts. What has John omitted, added, or transposed? What, in light of these operations, may one come to see as John's special profile in the passion narrative? Another approach might be to look for specific motifs that have come up earlier in the Gospel itself.[1]

It is not clear, however, that either approach would be sufficient. Rather, as we have been doing all through this book, we should ask about the *overall* point of this whole section, both the passion narrative itself (John 18–19) and the 'resurrection narrative' (John 20). What did he want to say as a whole about Jesus' death and resurrection? Is there a single theme that he wishes to articulate all through these three chapters? Such a theme may well be moderately complex, but for it to be a single one, whatever aspects it may contain must be held together by some single overarching idea. It goes without saying that there might not be such a theme. Instead, in this particular part of the story John might have felt 'constrained by the facts' (as recorded in the tradition) to such an extent that he would see his main task to be that of merely *stating* 'the facts', possibly by adding one or more of his own specific motifs here and there. On the other hand, we have realized again and again that this evangelist was constantly trying to articulate a

---

[1] Compare for this approach Dodd (1953a, 423): 'The question immediately before us is this: to what extent, and in what points, does the Passion-narrative in the Fourth Gospel appear to have been affected by motives (*sic*) arising out of the Johannine theology?'.

single theme for each individual episode over quite long stretches of text. Will he be doing the same in these concluding chapters?

In what follows we search for such a single theme, partly by drawing on a comparison of the Johannine account with those in the Synoptic Gospels, and partly—and rather more importantly—by drawing on the earlier chapters of the Fourth Gospel itself. The single theme we will discover is one that follows directly from John 11–12 and 13–17. We may articulate it as follows: *now* the plan is actually being executed that Jesus has been talking about (without being understood) all through the Gospel and not least from John 11 onwards. That is, first, Jesus, who is one with God and who is precisely not an earthly king, but one who has come from above and will return there, is now put to death and resurrected; and secondly, this is now finally understood by his closest followers.

It is reasonable to make explicit here that in this chapter we will not be following our previous practice of articulating a philosophical question to begin with and then considering how it is answered in the way the text proceeds. I have been unable to find such a question and it would be contrived to continue along that road. Still, the attempt to find a single overarching theme in the present text is closely related to the earlier search. Indeed, one may well say that the narrative philosophical approach of focusing on a philosophical question and its resolution precisely aims at discovering a single overarching theme in the text. Thus the difference from our previous approach is mainly rhetorical.

THE CENTRALITY OF THE PILATE SCENE
IN THE STRUCTURE OF THE THREE CHAPTERS

An attractive way of dividing John 18–19 has been suggested by Andrew Lincoln (2005, 441), who states that the two chapters consist of five distinct episodes: (i) Jesus' arrest (18:1–11); (ii) his interrogation by Annas (18:12–27); (iii) his trial before Pilate (18:28–19:16a); (iv) his crucifixion and death (19:16b–37); and (v) his burial (19:38–42).[2]

Of the Pilate episode Lincoln says (458):

Like the middle panel of a triptych, the Roman trial stands at the centre of the three equally long sections of the passion narrative, with Jesus' arrest and interrogation on one side (18.1–27) and his crucifixion and burial on the other (19.16b–42). It is another of the Gospel's episodes which has seven scenes and these follow the

---

[2] Zumstein (2007, 195–264) agrees completely. Brown 1970 (ix–x, 785–6) also basically concurs. In both, the trial before Pilate comes out as being central.

movement of Pilate back and forth between the praetorium and 'the Jews' (18.28–32; 18.33–8a; 18.38b–40; 19.1–3; 19.4–7; 19.8–11; 19.12–16a).

All of this appears exactly right. The only slight cause for hesitation is that with such an overall division of the two chapters, the section in John 19 (19:19–22) that concerns Pilate's inscription on the cross (19:19) and his discussion of the inscription with the leading Jews (19:21–2) is made to be part of Jesus' crucifixion, death, and burial and not of the Pilate episode itself. This is slightly unfortunate since this particular section does belong very closely with the Pilate episode. On the other hand, there is no doubt that the development that is indicated in 19:16 does mark a change (NRSV): 'Then he handed him over to them to be crucified. So they took Jesus . . .' and within two verses Jesus is crucified (19:18). The best way, therefore, to understand the progression of the text is to accept a major division at 19:16[3]—but then also to insist that 19.19–22, which in themselves fit in well where they stand, must also be understood as concluding the storyline of the battle between Pilate and the leading Jews that is played out in 18:28–19:16a.

With such a division, the reader first hears of Jesus' arrest in the garden (18:1–11), in which John has been very creatively at work. Then Jesus is brought to the high priest, Annas, who was the father-in-law of that year's high priest, Caiaphas (18:13). At Annas' residence two things happen. Peter denies Jesus for the first time (18:15–18) and Jesus is interrogated by Annas, again in a manner that has clear Johannine accents (18:19–23). After Peter's second and third denials (18:25–7), the Pilate episode begins with Jesus being brought from Caiaphas, to whom he had been sent in 18:24, to the Roman praetorium (18:28). Strangely, just as the interrogation at Annas' place was exceedingly bland (18:19), so nothing has happened at Caiaphas' residence, which is quite different from what one finds in the Synoptic Gospels. The best explanation is that John aimed to build everything the Jewish leaders had to say about Jesus and Jesus' own reactions to those accusations as closely as possible into the trial before Pilate. That,

[3] Thus also Bultmann 1941, Schnelle 1998, and many others. J. P. Heil (1995a, 78) also posits a division here, though a minor one since he places the major division between 'Jesus, the Jews, and Pilate (John 18:28–19:11)' and 'The Revelatory Death and Burial of Jesus (19:12–42)' (1995a, vi) already at 19:12. He does recognize, however, that 'as the final scene "outside" the praetorium', 19:12–16a 'climactically concludes the alternation of scenes "inside" and "outside" the praetorium (18:28–19:11)' (1995a, 78). Contrast Léon-Dufour, who moved in the opposite direction by taking 18:28–19:22 as a major unit. He accepts the seven scenes for the process before Pilate, but insists that 'la pointe de l'unité littéraire est la mise en croix avec le passage sur le *titulus* (19.17b–22)' (1996, 69). He certainly has a point, which was prefigured by Meeks (1967, 61): 'The movement of Pilate back and forth . . . serves to divide the second trial into successive scenes. Including the account of the crucifixion and the cross placard (19.17–22) the narrative has eight clearly marked stages'. In cases like this, no single reading is *the* correct one.

apparently, was meant to be the centre of the whole account. We will consider the Pilate episode in detail later.

After the Pilate episode, a new section (19:16b–42) describes Jesus' crucifixion, death, and burial and here there are some subsections that appear to place characteristically Johannine accents. The subsection on Pilate's inscription on the cross (19:19–22) is one of them. The subsection on how the soldiers divided Jesus' clothes (19:23–4) appears more traditional. By contrast, the subsections on Mary and the Beloved Disciple at the foot of the cross (19:25–7) and Jesus' actual death (19:28–30) both have a specifically Johannine profile. Since I am not addressing the role of the Beloved Disciple (or indeed, of Mary) in this book, we may leave aside the first of the two subsections. The account of Jesus' death, by contrast, is extremely important thematically and we will consider it more closely.

Finally, the aftermath (19:31–42) is taken up by two episodes: one (19:31–7) of breaking the bones (19:31–3 + 36) and piercing Jesus' side (19:34–5 + 37); and one (19:38–42) of having Jesus buried. In these subsections, too, there are characteristically Johannine accents. The account of the 'blood and water' that came out of Jesus' side (19:34) and the testimony to this given by an eyewitness (19:35) identify a very important motif to which we will come back. The remark about Joseph of Arimathea that he was 'a disciple of Jesus, though a secret one because of his fear of the Jews' (19:38) rings a characteristically Johannine bell and it is noteworthy that Nicodemus turns up again and is explicitly identified as the one 'who had first come to Jesus in the night' (compare 3:1). But these two remarks about Joseph and Nicodemus do not seem to have wide thematic implications. What they do, though, is to repeat the motif (e.g. from 9:22 and 12:42) that in spite of Jesus having been rejected by 'the Jews', some 'Jews' did believe in him—but were loath to make it public out of fear of 'the Jews'.

John 20 is best divided into two sections.[4] John 20:1–18 basically concerns the events that took place at the tomb, whereas 20:19–29 describes two appearances of Jesus (20:19–23 and 20:24–9) that took place among the disciples in Jerusalem, the first one in the evening of 'Easter Sunday' (20:19), the second a week later (20:26). These are all events that are almost completely specific to John. Correspondingly, they are full of Johannine meaning, as we will see.

In light of these various divisions of the text, we now proceed to identify its major themes. I believe we can see a single one that is generated by three

---

[4] Thus also, e.g., Brown (1970, x, 979, 1018) and Lincoln (2005, 487, 496). Schnelle (1998, ix) and Zumstein (2007, 270, 289) only find the four consecutive scenes that all agree on (20:1–10, 11–18, 19–23, 24–9). It does seem, however, that considerations of location and main protagonists suggest taking 20:1–10 together with 20:11–18 and 20:19–23 together with 20:24–9.

thematic threads in the overall tapestry that John has woven together to make clear his own understanding of these events to his reader.

THE OVERALL THEME I: JESUS HIMSELF MAKES IT HAPPEN THAT HE DIES AND IS RESURRECTED

In the chapters that lead up to the passion narrative, Jesus has again and again predicted what was going to happen: that he himself was about to die—and to be resurrected and hence to return to God by whom he had been sent into the world. That was the overall theme of John 11–12, where Jesus tried—vainly—to transmit this message to all the different types of Jews with whom he was in contact, and also of John 13–17, where Jesus tried to transmit the same message—but again in vain—to his disciples. Now it is actually happening, moreover, this whole set of events—the climax of Jesus' life on earth—is *made* to happen by Jesus himself.

That Jesus himself is directly active in bringing about his own death should come as no surprise.[5] That theme has been touched on several times in what comes before. For instance, we know from John 11 that when Lazarus had been reported to be ill, Jesus on purpose waited until he was dead—in order for it to become possible for him to raise Lazarus again with all the consequences that this would have, including his own death and resurrection. Similarly in John 12, Jesus explicitly rejected that he should pray to God to be spared his death. On the contrary, he prayed that God might glorify him, which means: lead him into his death and resurrection. Or recall John 13, in which Jesus almost commissioned Judas to betray him and asked him to do quickly what he was about to do (13:26–7). All through, Jesus is described as himself taking the initiative to bring about the death and resurrection that he has constantly been talking about.

The same is true in John 18–19. Consider the scene in the garden (18:1–11). Jesus is in the garden (18:1). Judas knows that he often came there (18:2). Judas comes to the garden with the full throng of soldiers (18:3). 'Then Jesus, knowing all that was to happen to him, *came forward and asked them*, "For whom are you looking?"' (18:4, NRSV). 'They answered, "Jesus of Nazareth." Jesus replied, "I am (he)" (*egô eimi*)' (18:5)—and then they stepped back and fell to the ground. Here we have two connected motifs: that Jesus takes the initiative, and that he describes himself in language that was normally reserved for God himself. Moreover, his

---

[5] Compare Frey (2002/2013c, 535–6), who well brings out Jesus' 'sovereignty vis-à-vis his fate'.

addressees recognize this by their action. Clearly, Jesus is here shown as one who makes what was to happen actually occur.[6] Next, this little scene is repeated (18:7) and Jesus tells them to let his followers go (18:8) and, by implication, be satisfied with arresting himself. Once again, Jesus is himself at work to make it all happen. Finally, when Peter thinks that they must defend themselves, Jesus orders him to put his sword back into its sheath: 'Am I not to drink the cup that the Father has given?' (18:11, NRSV). That is, these things are *intended* to happen. So, *let* them happen.

Next, consider the interrogation at Annas' place. The high priest asks exceedingly meekly 'about his disciples and about his teaching' (18:19, NRSV). But Jesus is on the attack. 'I have spoken openly to the world' . . . 'I have said nothing in secret' (18:20, NRSV). Then 'Why do you ask me?' And so forth (18:21, NRSV). This clearly constitutes a challenge. When one of the high priest's policemen then strikes Jesus because he has answered back to the high priest in this way (18:22), Jesus is not at all put off: 'If I have spoken wrongly, testify to the wrong. But if I have spoken rightly, why do you strike me?' (18:23, NRSV). Clearly, Jesus is here out to tease and challenge his opponents, not to placate them. He almost forces them to continue with their plan.

Finally, there is the account of Jesus' dying words on the cross: It is 'fulfilled' (*tetelestai*, 19:30 and 28). This draws strongly on earlier passages (e.g. 4:34 and 17:4) where Jesus states that it is his task to bring to completion (*teleioun*) God's 'work' (*ergon*). Now, as Jesus is about to die, the whole task that God had given him is about to be fulfilled. There is nothing more to be done. That was the end and purpose (in Greek, the *telos*) of it all. And that *telos* has now been reached.

In these three subsections of John 18–19, then, Jesus partly helps actively to bring about the final event, his death (and resurrection, we should add, see later). And once it is about to happen, he explicitly and self-consciously states that the *telos* has now been reached. Or as 17:4 had it, he has *himself* brought it to fulfilment.

We should conclude that in the way John has specifically told the story of the garden, of the interrogation among the Jews, and of Jesus' death, he has articulated an important aspect of the overarching theme: that Jesus himself precipitates his death (and resurrection), driving proceedings towards the moment when he may state that God's whole *ergon* ('work') has now been fulfilled.

---

[6] Zumstein (2007, 200, my emphasis) well notes that 'c'est Jésus lui-même qui sort . . . du jardin et qui va à la rencontre de la troupe. . . . C'est lui encore qui entame le processus d'identification en posant la question: « Qui cherchez-vous »?. Ainsi, que ce soit au niveau de l'agir ou du dire, *l'initiative lui appartient*'. Even more, Jesus *makes* the events happen.

THE OVERALL THEME II: NOT AN EARTHLY KING, BUT A HEAVENLY ONE; THE PILATE EPISODE (18:28–19:16A)

In his discussion of the Johannine passion narrative, C. H. Dodd rightly notes that John 'has laid much greater stress [than the Synoptic Gospels] upon the political charge brought against Jesus in the Roman court' (1953a, 426). But he also adds: 'This is not related to the distinctively Johannine theology, but seems to belong to a non-Synoptic version of the tradition'. This is most peculiar. We may recall the scene in John 6 when Jesus 'withdrew again to the mountain by himself' because he 'realized that they [the Jewish crowd] were about to come and take him by force to make him king' (6:15, NRSV). And we may recall that John 12 was concerned to show that the Jerusalem crowd who greeted Jesus at his entry into the city as 'the king of Israel' (12:13) and 'Sion' (12:15) precisely did *not* understand that the whole thing was not about the traditional 'Christ', but about the Son of Man who was about to be 'lifted up' on the cross (12:34). Seen in that light, the intense discussion of Jesus' supposed kingship in the Pilate episode clearly merits our close attention. What we find is that Jesus both is and is not a king. He definitely is not a king in the earthly sense with which the Jewish leaders and Pilate are operating. In another way, however, he certainly is, *but* that way is utterly paradoxical: Jesus is a king (a true king in his *heavenly* kingdom) *in* the miserable form in which he is presented by Pilate to the Jews, that is, as someone who is about to die. For Jesus, the heavenly king who has all God's power (*exousia*) at his disposal, *had* to die in order to go into his kingdom.[7] This theme, too, therefore belongs under the execution of the plan.

The Pilate episode is a fascinating piece of writing, utterly accomplished and suggestive. It has understandably evoked extensive scholarly treatment.[8] In relation to these readings my own interest lies not so much in Pilate as a character as in what the whole scene is intended to show about Jesus.[9]

---

[7] Josef Blank noted (1959, 61) that the Pilate episode contains a number of *Leitmotive* (fixed motifs) of which the one of 'glorification in lowliness' is the most 'general and well-known one'. However, he immediately adds 'the kingship motif', which he also brings out well (61–2). I suggest that a combination of the two motifs fits the Johannine irony best. (Compare also Frey 2002/2013c, 542–3.)

[8] Zumstein (2007, 216–17) has a helpful bibliography, to which may be added Bennema 2013 and Tolmie 2013. The latter is particularly helpful, first because it situates its own reading in relation to a number of readings from Culpepper 1983 to Bennema 2009, secondly in methodological terms through its use of the concept of 'a paradigm of traits' derived from Seymour Chatman, and thirdly by its emphasis on the many 'empty spaces' (Wolfgang Iser's *Lehrstellen*) in John's account that serve to explain the many different scholarly readings.

[9] See Tolmie 2013, 597: '... the large number of empty spaces can probably be ascribed to the fact that Pilate is not really the focal figure in these chapters. ... the focus falls primarily on Jesus ...'

Jean Zumstein (2007, 218) presents a refinement of the structure given above by Lincoln, by seeing 18:28 as an 'introduction', to which corresponds a 'conclusion' in 19:16a in which Jesus is delivered to his henchmen. In between, Zumstein finds an elegant structure which looks like this:

scene one = A (outside): 18:29–32;
  scene two = B (inside): 18:33–8a;
    scene three = C (outside): 18:38b–40;
      scene four = D (scourging of Jesus): 19:1–3;
    scene five = C' (outside): 19:4–7;
  scene six = B' (inside): 19:8–12;
scene seven = A' (outside): 19:13–15.[10]

What is striking here is the importance given to scene four (D), which is full of meaning.

In view of this structure we may say that there are two lines in it, with Pilate as the unifying figure—after all, he literally goes back and forth between 'the Jews', who are standing outside the praetorium, and Jesus, who is inside. The two lines consist of (a) Pilate and 'the Jews' (scenes A, C, C', and A'), and (b) Pilate and Jesus (scenes B and B'). Thematically, however, the two lines are closely connected. The first scene between Pilate and Jesus (B, 'scene two') explicitly discusses the theme of Jesus' kingship. The central 'scene four' (the scourging) and 'scene five', in which Jesus is brought out in front of the Jews—this scene, then, combines the two lines—mockingly dressed up as an inverted king, is also about Jesus' perverse form of kingship. 'Scene six' (B') relates to Jesus' kingship when Jesus claims against Pilate that he would have no 'power' (*exousia*) over Jesus, had it not been given to him from above, that is, from God. Finally, 'scene seven' is wholly about Jesus as a king, as is the 'appendix' to this whole episode in 19:19–22 on Pilate's inscription on the cross. And these two scenes belong to the line of Pilate and 'the Jews'.

Two lines, then, but also a single theme: that of Jesus' kingship. How does the episode progress from one scene to the other? And what does it aim to say about kingship in relation to Jesus?

At the uppermost level of the narrative, the episode clearly shows how the Jewish leaders succeed in having the Roman governor, Pilate, sentence Jesus to death by crucifixion. To begin with ('scene one') the odds are not so good. When Pilate asks them of what they accuse Jesus (19:29), they speak

[10] There is a small discrepancy vis-à-vis Brown's division (1970, 859), which takes scene six to cover only 19:9–11 and correspondingly enlarges scene seven by v. 12. Blank (1959, 61) took scene six to cover verses 19:8–12a and scene seven 19:12b–16. Sherri Brown (2015, 72) agrees with Zumstein on 18:28 and 19:16a, but otherwise divides chapter 19 as follows: 19:4–8, 19:9–11, and 19:12–15. (Thus also Tolmie 2013.) These slight differences probably do not matter.

lamely of Jesus as a 'wrongdoer' (19:30), which only makes Pilate suggest that they may take him and do with him what they want according to their own law (19:31). To this the Jews reply that 'We are not permitted to put anyone to death' (19:31). In historical fact, this does not seem quite accurate, but the next verse shows what is meant here. It was only the Romans who could sentence people to death by crucifixion and that is what 'the Jews' are after. Why? Answer: 'in order that Jesus' word (*logos*) might be fulfilled, the one he spoke by indicating with which death he was about to die' (18:32). This is an important verse. It probably refers back to 12:33, which contains a similar writer's comment on the action: 'He said this to indicate with which death he was about to die.' Also, it speaks of Jesus' *logos* as what was meant to be fulfilled. Here Jesus' *logos* hardly just means something Jesus had actually said (as in 12:33), but also the *whole logos* that is Jesus', that is, the whole plan that he is putting into action. In that case, what the present verse claims is that what 'the Jews' said—and so their whole attempt to have Jesus killed by the Romans—was dictated by the fact that *the plan was* that Jesus should die by crucifixion. This is one more example of John's basic idea that it all happened in that particular way because of the plan.

In 'scene two', Pilate then re-enters the praetorium and asks Jesus whether he is 'the king of the Jews' (18:33). We must take it that 'the Jews' have told him that Jesus had laid claim to being the Jewish king, as they directly say in 19:21. As shown in 'scene seven', this is the accusation on which the whole trial turns and which will in the end lead to Jesus' death by crucifixion. The handling of this accusation by (i) 'the Jews', (ii) Pilate, and (iii) Jesus is utterly sophisticated and full of meaning. Let us consider this in turn.

(i) The case of 'the Jews' is straightforward. They had long aimed to have Jesus killed, therefore they have now accused him before the Roman governor of having laid claim to being 'the king of the Jews', aiming in this way to have *him* kill Jesus as an insurrectionist against the Roman order. After a long struggle they manage to make him do that and so they reach their original aim.

(ii) The case of Pilate is much more complicated. Throughout the events he maintains a clear distance between himself and 'the Jews'. To begin with, he wishes to leave Jesus with 'the Jews'. When they have brought forward the political accusation of a claim to kingship, he interrogates Jesus concerning that claim—in 'scene two', to which we will come back.[11] The

---

[11] It remains a little strange that John has not found a way of explicitly making 'the Jews' state their political accusation if it is so important as it appears to be. Instead, John asks the reader to infer it from Pilate's conversation with Jesus on the matter (18:33–7). Perhaps, however, that is precisely the point: he wanted to reserve the issue of Jesus' kingship for that conversation—and for two reasons: first, to bring out the difference between Jesus' kingship

result, in 'scene three', is that he declares to 'the Jews' that he cannot find any case against Jesus (18:38b), but when he then asks them with a great deal of sarcastic irony whether they want him to release 'the king of the Jews' (18:39), they shout in reply that they want a bandit, Barabbas, instead (18:40). Obviously, Pilate does not in any way see Jesus as an insurrection-ist. In calling him 'the king of the Jews', he is teasing 'the Jews', thereby emphasizing his own superior position in relation to them.

In 'scene four', after 'the Jews' have prevented Pilate from releasing Jesus, he has him flogged and dressed by his soldiers in mock-kingly attire (9:2). The soldiers also mockingly address him with a 'Hail, King of the Jews!' and strike him (19:3). Scholars disagree on whether the scourging should be understood as punitive torture, aiming to inflict pain as punish-ment, or rather as judicial torture through which Pilate might extract a confession of some sort from Jesus.[12] One argument for the latter under-standing might be that John has moved the story of the scourging from its Synoptic place *after* Pilate has given Jesus over for crucifixion (Mark 15:15—and then the scourging in 15:16–20) to its present place in the middle of the proceedings. However, it is not clear that the issue (punitive or judicial?) is at all in focus in John's text. Instead, the main focus appears to be on the mocking homage paid by the soldiers in 19:2–3 to Jesus as king since this is immediately taken up by Pilate in the following scene (19:5). Moreover, if we ask why John has moved this scene forward, the best answer is that he needed to have Jesus clad in his mock-kingly attire for the *Ecce homo* scene that follows to have its tremendous effect.[13]

In that scene ('scene five') Pilate himself goes out to 'the Jews' telling them that he will lead Jesus out to them 'in order that you may understand that I find no case against him' (19:4). And when Jesus is then brought out in his perverse, 'kingly' outfit, which John spells out explicitly, Pilate says to the Jews: 'Look, here is the man!' (19:5). Here Pilate is clearly continuing his sarcastic talk of Jesus as 'the king of the Jews' from 18:33. He is saying to the Jews: 'Look at this guy (clad the way Jesus was)! Your *king*?! It's absurd. I can find no case against him.' What matters, however, are two things. First, that Pilate exhibits Jesus in a manner that *he* believes will show

and any earthly one, and secondly, to allow that difference to be spelled out in a genuine conversation between the protagonist in the whole episode (that is, Pilate) and Jesus.

[12] Compare Bennema 2013, 243, who follows Jennifer Glancy (2005) in adopting the latter understanding.

[13] Compare Meeks 1967, 69: 'In the Johannine version [of the scourging scene] Jesus, while still inside the Praetorium, is clad in the garb and crown of a king, which he wears throughout the rest of the proceedings as he is twice presented to the Jews with solemn proclamation (19.5, 13f.).'

anybody concerned that Jesus is definitely not a king. Secondly, that precisely in that guise Jesus *is* a 'king', namely, as it were, the ultimate king who is now about to die miserably, as he should (but then also to be resurrected). The end of Lincoln's comment on *idou ho anthrôpos* ('Look, here is the man') is so appropriate that it deserves to be fully quoted (2005, 466):

> By far the most plausible suggestion for a secondary and ironic connotation to the straightforward 'Here is the man [whom you have accused of claiming to be king]' is the one that points to 1 Sam. 9.17 LXX as the background. The correspondence in wording is precise. God is said to have told Samuel concerning Saul, 'Here is the man...He it is who shall rule over my people.' The irony is appropriate. John's formulation of Pilate's mockery of both Jesus and Jewish notions of kingship employs the words used of Israel's very first king and thereby reinforces Jesus' true identity as 'King of the Jews'. In this way 'Here is the man' anticipates Pilate's explicit 'Here is your king' in v. 14.

The only thing that needs to be added is that Jesus is that king precisely in his absurdly miserable attire: he had to go into his kingdom through death.[14] This is what makes 'scene four' and its immediate consequence in the *Ecce homo* scene absolutely central in the whole Pilate episode. Jesus *is* a king, indeed, a heavenly king alongside God himself, but he is this here on earth in the—by earthly standards—most miserable form imaginable. He will go into his kingdom through death. He will *die in order to* be with God, through resurrection. This is what makes 19:1–3 + 4–5 such a strong text. Through Pilate's statement 'Here is the man' it focuses the reader's attention on the very strong image of Jesus clad in his mock-kingly attire. And the point of that image is to bring out the unique identity of Jesus: a king who had to die—or conversely, a person who is about to die, but who *through* that dying will be shown in his resurrection to be the real king of the world.

In the rest of 'scene five' (19:6–7) there is no direct talk of Jesus' kingship, but it remains just below the surface. When 'the Jews' have seen Jesus in his strange attire, they make explicit their ultimate aim by repeatedly shouting 'Crucify him' (19:6). They do not give any grounds since there are no grounds other than the two we already know: that they had decided a long time ago to have Jesus killed, and that they attempt to reach that aim

---

[14] I miss an emphasis on this truly ironic character of Jesus' kingship in Meeks's otherwise splendid discussion of 18:28–19:22 (1967, 61–81), in which he among other things rightly emphasizes the political character of this text: 'Jesus' kingship is not "unworldly." Instead one of the characteristics of the Johannine treatment of the trial and the events that lead up to it is that the *political* implications are emphasized.... what the trial suggests is that the disciple will always have to decide *vis à vis* the Empire whether Jesus is the king or whether Caesar is' (1967, 64, Meeks's emphasis). (Meeks was always ahead of his times: see now Carter 2008.)

by having Jesus killed by the Romans since that was the only way in which he might be crucified, as Jesus had himself foretold should happen (see 18:32). But Pilate is not so easy to get on the hook. He answers, 'Take him yourselves and crucify him; I find no case against him' (19:6, NRSV)— which is again a case of bloody irony since the Jews precisely *could* not have him *crucified*. Is the point of Pilate's retort then (see Zumstein 2007, 232) that he wishes to *release* Jesus since everybody knew that the Jews could not have him crucified? Not necessarily. Rather, it seems that Pilate is merely saying this: '*You* can take him and crucify him!' (as they evidently could *not*): 'I don't find any case against him'.[15] In this way Pilate continues to taunt 'the Jews'.

In response to this impasse, 'the Jews' then answer by at long last bringing in what John considers their ultimate reason for wanting to get rid of Jesus: according to the Jewish law Jesus 'ought to die because he has made himself the Son of God' (19:7). If we recall the way Jesus was greeted by Nathanael in John 1 (1:49: 'Rabbi, you are the Son of God! You are the King of Israel!', NRSV) and note that in 19:12 'the Jews' will go on to accuse Jesus of 'making himself king', we should probably conclude that by accusing Jesus of making himself the Son of God, the Jews are in fact *not* changing the basis for their attack, *only* they are now appealing to the distinctly religious (as opposed to merely political) side of that accusation. Apparently, they hope that by mentioning what within their own system ('we have a law, etc.') is the ultimate reason for accusing Jesus, they will put enough pressure on Pilate to comply with their wish.

However, 'scene six', in which Pilate for the second time addresses Jesus directly inside the praetorium, shows that the Jews have misread Pilate. Instead of becoming convinced by their reference to the greatest crime within their own system, Pilate listens—and becomes 'exceedingly afraid' (19:8). 'The Son of God'? And he goes immediately in and asks Jesus, 'Where are you from?', meaning 'Are you by any chance from above?'. We will return to this scene and may just note that it ends with Pilate for the first time positively trying to find a way to release Jesus (19:12). Is the theme of kingship also involved in this scene? In fact, yes, though again only implicitly. This turns on Jesus' claim (see later)—against Pilate's claim to have 'authority/power (*exousia*)' (19:10) to either release Jesus or crucify him—that Pilate's *exousia* has been given him from above (19:11). The kind of *exousia* involved here is that of a king (or a Roman governor) in the earthly sphere—or of the ultimate king in the heavenly sphere, God.

Finally, in 'scene seven' the motif of kingship plays a major role. Against Pilate's wishes to have Jesus released, 'the Jews' now shout, 'If you release

[15] Compare the contrasting emphasis on 'you' (*hymeis*) and 'I' (*egô*) in the Greek.

this man, you are not the emperor's friend. Everyone who makes himself a king opposes the emperor' (19:12). Here 'the Jews' are attacking Pilate at his weakest point, where he would have believed himself to be invulnerable: his status as a 'friend' of the emperor, which was an almost official social and political position. Somebody who makes himself a king is an insurrectionist against the Roman order, and nobody who is a 'friend' of Caesar may release such a person.

Then comes a scene whose meaning is wildly contested by scholars. It all hangs on a grammatical feature which John has left unclear: is the sense of the Greek word *ekathisen* in 19:13 that Pilate, who had once again brought Jesus out from the praetorium, himself sat down on the judgement seat, ready to pronounce his verdict on Jesus? Or is the sense that he sat *Jesus* on the judgement seat? The former reading might be supported by the emphatic care with which John identifies both the place (19:13) and time (19:14): is this not the where and when of the ultimate verdict? Against this, and in support of the latter meaning, it must be noted that Pilate does not at all pronounce a verdict. Instead he states: 'Here is your king' (19:14) and when 'the Jews' then shout that Pilate should crucify Jesus, he asks a *question*: 'Do you want me to crucify your *king*?' (19:15). This consideration rather strongly supports the understanding that has Jesus sit on the judgement seat, and presumably still wearing his mock-kingly attire.[16]

On that reading we should understand 19:13–15 as Pilate's last attempt to avoid condemning Jesus to death after John has told us in 19:12 that he was keen on finding ways to release Jesus. Pilate in effect repeats the *Ecce homo* scene. He bombastically places Jesus—still clad in his perverse kingly attire—on the judgement seat. And then he declares to 'the Jews' (just as he had said his '*Ecce homo*'): 'Look, here is your king!' That is, 'Look at this guy. A *king*? It's absurd.' And now he has himself contributed even more to the absurdity by having placed Jesus on the judgement seat. Once again, however, we should also see all of this as being doubly ironic. What Pilate does is wildly ironic: nobody would consider such a person a king. But without in the least knowing what he is doing, Pilate also shows a

---

[16] We do not know for sure that Jesus was still wearing his 'kingly' attire, but have heard nothing to the contrary. On the issue of who is sitting on the judgement seat, Lincoln (2005, 469–70) ends with the understanding I have also adopted. Zumstein (2007, 235–6; 2016, 711) accepts it as a possibility. The fact that there are later witnesses (Justin, *Apol.* 1.35 and *Gos. Pet.* 5.7) that actually have a similar reading is, I think, strong support for its actual possibility. Basically, however, the decision is based on the meaning of that possibility, which I go on to develop. For an extensive treatment which favours the same reading see de la Potterie 1960, who according to Meeks (1967, 75), offered 'the final support' for it. On the whole, however, it is fair to mention that most scholars prefer the less spectacular reading. On its side see, for instance, the careful argumentation by Léon-Dufour (1996, 109–11).

Jesus who precisely in that attire and role *is* a king (and a judge), the ultimate one.

As in 19:6, however, 'the Jews' are not put off. They again shout, 'Take him away! Take him away! Crucify him!' (19:15). Actually, what they ask Pilate to do is to 'lift (up) and take away' Jesus, presumably from the judgement seat, and then to crucify him. The first verb here—*airein*—has been used in John 1 when John the Baptist sees Jesus coming towards him and says, 'Look, here is the lamb of God, the one who lifts and takes away (*airôn*) the sin of the world' (1:29). Now 'the Jews' ask Pilate to 'lift and take away' Jesus to be crucified. Is the correspondence intended? Who knows? But it is at least highly suggestive. Jesus will 'lift and take away the sin of the world' *by* being himself 'lifted and taken away' from the judgement seat and placed upon the cross.

Still, Pilate is not put off either. He answers, 'Do you want me to crucify your king?' (19:15). That is, he continues to tease 'the Jews' with sarcastic remarks in the hope that that will make them back off. But 'the Jews', who are now specifically identified as the high priests, respond with the terrible words: 'We have no king but the emperor' (19:16). These words constitute a violent denunciation of 'the Jews' by the Evangelist. 'The Jews' have, so he says, left behind the ultimate king who, according to John, is both Jesus and God, and turned instead to the Roman Caesar. But the words are also extremely cunning. By placing themselves so strongly on the side of the Roman emperor, the Jewish high priests practically force Pilate to act as they wish. Here they appear as more Roman than the Roman. And their success is immediate: 'Then he handed him over to them to be crucified' (19:16a, NRSV).

Summarizing on Pilate, we may say that John shows us a Roman governor who is highly conscious of his own superior political position, who considers Jesus innocent of the charge pressed by 'the Jews', who attempts by ironic statements (e.g. 18:39, 19:6, 19:15) and actions (19:1–5, 19:13–14) to get rid of having to sentence Jesus to death—but who is also forced to do so by 'the Jews' in a progressively more intense confrontation where the power of argument gradually tips over from Pilate to 'the Jews'.[17] And it all turns on the accusation of Jesus having claimed to be a king. As part of this development, Pilate twice shows Jesus to 'the Jews' in a kind of mockery of the attire and role of a king. Inadvertently, he thereby also shows in what way Jesus actually *is* a king, namely, as a person who while dying in miserable circumstances will next through his resurrection go into his heavenly kingdom.

[17] This summary is intended to be as 'minimalistic' as possible in the hope that it will generate a sufficient amount of consensus as far as it goes.

(iii) That Jesus *is* a king is brought out in 'scenes two and six', in which Pilate is talking to Jesus. In looking at these two scenes we consider the whole story from Jesus' perspective.

In 'scene two', Pilate has asked Jesus whether he is 'the king of the Jews' (18:33). Jesus replies by asking him whether he has put this question on his own or because others have spoken to him about Jesus (18:34), to which Pilate replies, in effect, that it is the Jewish people and the high priests who are responsible for the accusation (18:35). The purpose of this is clearly to mark Pilate's distance from 'the Jews' ('I am not a Jew, am I?', NRSV) and to make wholly explicit that the charge of 'making oneself a king' (see 19:12) comes from 'the Jews'. In response to Pilate's question Jesus then famously declares that 'My kingdom is not from this world (*ek tou kosmou toutou*)' or 'from here (*enteuthen*)' (18:36). So, Jesus *is* a king, though a heavenly one. Had his kingdom been from this world, his servants would have prevented him from being handed over to 'the Jews' (18:36).[18] Here Jesus evidently does lay claim to being a king, but of a different kind. His kingdom is a heavenly one, but no less strong for that. When Pilate hears this, he rightly concludes: 'So you are (in fact) a king?'. And what is the answer? When Jesus replies that 'You say that I am a king' and explains for what purpose 'I was born and for what purpose I came into the world', the reader is made to understand that although Jesus is a (heavenly) king with immense powers at his disposal, he is a king with a special task: 'in order that I may bear witness to the truth', with the consequence that only 'the one who is from the truth hears my voice' (18:37). To this the baffled Pilate famously and disparagingly comments: 'What (now) is *truth?*' (18:38a).[19]

Well, what is it? Evidently the truth that constitutes God's *logos* and plan: that Jesus was meant to come to earth, perform his signs, die on the cross, and be resurrected—all in order to give human beings a chance to be saved by believing in Jesus, receiving the *pneuma*, and eventually themselves being resurrected into heaven. So is Jesus a king? Yes, an immensely mighty one. But also with a task that in some of its details (especially his death) is most unkingly by normal, earthly standards. As we have already

---

[18] The animosity against 'the Jews' is violent when John's Jesus here speaks of his having been 'handed over to the Jews'. In John's perspective it is 'the Jews' who were responsible for having Jesus killed.

[19] Brown (1970, 869) well senses the meaning here: 'This question has been interpreted in many ways, for instance, as an expression of worldly skepticism or even as philosophical pondering. Even John is not likely to have painted a venal politician as a philosopher. On the level of the progression of the trial the evangelist may have meant the question to vocalize Pilate's failure to understand or perhaps the politician's impatience with Jewish theological jargon.' Methodologically, one must attempt (i) *not* to ascribe too deep a meaning to Pilate's question but instead (ii) to fit it into the overall depiction of Pilate's character as shown in his relationship with 'the Jews' and with Jesus.

seen, that picture of Jesus-the-king is then confirmed by Pilate himself—though wholly inadvertently—in the *Ecce homo* scene.

In the next conversation between Pilate and Jesus ('scene six'), the same double point is made: that Jesus is both a mightily powerful figure (more powerful than Pilate himself), but also one who is going to be crucified. When Pilate asks Jesus whether he does not understand that he, Pilate, has 'power (*exousia*) to release you, and power (*exousia*) to crucify you' (19:10), Jesus answers that Pilate does have this power—but only because it has been given him 'from above' (19:11), meaning from God, with whom Jesus himself belongs. *God* has this kingly power. Nevertheless, it is a power that has now been given to Pilate—and true enough: for both release and crucifixion, but as the reader knows, specifically for the latter. In other words, Pilate's kingly power is only delegated to him from above *in order that* what was planned might come to pass: that Jesus (the truly powerful king) is crucified. Once again, this picture of Jesus-the-king is then confirmed by Pilate himself—though wholly inadvertently—in what we may call the *Ecce rex* scene.

Summarizing on Jesus' perspective on the events, we may conclude that Jesus insists in his conversations with Pilate that he is himself a king though not just an earthly one: a heavenly king with a (real) power that by far exceeds the one to be found on earth (18:36). Also, the power that Pilate does have is one that has been directly given him from above (19:11). At the same time John's Jesus also goes out of his way to exonerate Pilate from being responsible for what is happening to Jesus, at the direct level of who is responsible for that. Twice he speaks of his own having been 'handed over'. In the first case (18:35) he has been handed over 'to the Jews'. In the second case (19:11) he has been handed over probably *by* 'the Jews' to Pilate (see 18:30).[20] So, from the perspective of John's Jesus it is 'the Jews' who are the real villains—as they *should* be (by John's lights) since they did not see that Jesus truly *was* the 'Son of God' (19:7) that they accused him of falsely claiming to be.

And then the appendix: 19:19–22. In the Pilate episode itself 'the Jews' end up outmanoeuvring Pilate. But he takes his sarcastic and mocking revenge when he places an inscription running 'Jesus of Nazareth, the King of the Jews' on the cross (19:19): Look, here he hangs, your king. When 'the Jews' object, Pilate closes the affair: 'What I have written I have written' (19:22), that is, Shut up, please, I can do what I want to do. This, then, is the third time—after the *Ecce homo* and the *Ecce rex* scenes—that Pilate inadvertently announces the truth: the person who is hanging on this cross *is* the king of the Jews. And why? Because the event of the cross

---

[20] The question who is hiding behind 'the one who has handed me over to you' in 19:11 is complicated. Lincoln (2005, 468) well reasons to the understanding I have also adopted.

was part of God's plan, the plan conceived by the almighty God, and set into motion with the mission of Jesus in order that the plan might reach its ultimate aim: that human beings would eventually obtain eternal life.

If we look back over the whole Pilate episode, we can see that it serves a single purpose: that of bringing out that the 'death of the king' was all planned and intended. Jesus himself twice (18:36 and 19:11) says that that is what was meant. The 'Jews'—for reasons wholly of their own—press the charge of 'making himself king' right to the end of having him crucified, thereby bringing about what was already *planned* to happen, a point that is made explicit in 18:32. And Pilate, on his side, as part of his vain attempt to *avoid* what was meant to happen from happening, three times in a highly theatrical manner—the *Ecce homo* scene, the *Ecce rex* scene, and the inscription on the cross for everybody to see (19:20)—*shows* what the whole thing is all about: the death of the true king.

And then the conclusion and overall point as part of the present inquiry: in the way John has staged the Pilate episode in all its fascinating details, he has been concerned to show that now—in these very events—what Jesus had foretold would happen not only happens but is *made* to happen by Jesus himself. 'The Jews' and Pilate on their side appear to be engaged in a fierce battle among themselves, the former wanting to make Pilate crucify Jesus and the latter wanting to avoid that outcome. In fact, however, both sides *together* bring about what was meant to happen. They behave almost like puppets on strings that are handled by Jesus and God. The plan is now being executed.

THE OVERALL THEME III: IN GIVING UP THE *PNEUMA*, JESUS PROVIDES THE *PNEUMA* OF LIFE

We have seen that Jesus' cry on the cross at the moment of dying celebrates that the ultimate goal (*telos*) of his mission has been reached. That *telos* consists in his death on the cross. However, let nobody think that the *telos* was *just* his death. In accordance with the motif we have just analysed of the death of the true king, and also with the whole of John 20 which is entirely focused on Jesus' resurrection, the *telos* that fulfils Jesus' mission is both his death *and* his resurrection: his *return to* God, from where he came, *through* his death.[21]

---

[21] Here as elsewhere I am opposing the idea of finding Jesus' 'salvific role' *only* in his death on the cross—in line with German *Kreuzestheologie*. I am firmly convinced that as in Paul, so in John there is no celebration of Jesus' death without it being implied that he was also resurrected. (Compare for Paul, 1 Cor. 11:26, which speaks of '*proclaiming* the Lord's *death— until he comes*'.) For the whole issue see the splendid discussion in Frey 2002.

That this is so is made wholly clear in John's account of Jesus at the very moment of his death: 'Then he bowed his head and rendered the *pneuma*' (19:30). He had received the *pneuma* at his baptism. Now he 'rendered' it. In using here the Greek verb *paredôke* (from *paradidonai*, 'hand over, give up') John differs from the Synoptic Gospels. Where Mark (15:37) has *exepneusen* (he 'breathed his last'), which was taken over by Luke (23:46), Matthew (27:50) has expanded on the notion of 'breath' that he found in *ex-e-pneu-s-en* and made the *pneuma* ('breath') the grammatical object of a new verb: *aphêken* ('gave up'), so that the result becomes that Jesus 'gave up his *pneuma* ("breath" or "spirit" in that ordinary sense)'. John is much more suggestive: Jesus 'rendered' or 'transmitted' the *pneuma*. Obviously, Jesus also died, that is, 'breathed his last'. But he apparently also did something else. To whom may he have rendered 'the' *pneuma*? Most likely (as we saw in Chapter III), to God. But in so doing he also made the *pneuma* available more generally—for instance, for infusion in his followers, as he goes on to do in 20:22: 'When he [the resurrected Jesus, who is apparently again in possession of *pneuma*] had said this, he breathed on them and said to them, "Receive holy *pneuma*".' Thus John's phrasing in 19:30 suggests that Jesus is engaged here in a veritable circle of 'giving the *pneuma*', where the participants in the circle are God, Jesus himself—and the apostles. The fact that Jesus is again able in 20:22 to participate in this circle strongly suggests that his 'giving up' the *pneuma* in 19:30 *implies* his (pneumatic) resurrection which will then allow him to act again as described in 20:22. He gives it up and receives it again so as to become able to transmit it to the apostles.

Another remark that points beyond Jesus' death to his resurrection and its consequences is the note that when Jesus' side had been pierced by the soldier's spear, 'at once blood and water came out' (19:34). This fact is vouchsafed by an eyewitness, who has borne witness to it (19:35).[22] So, it is obviously very important. Scholars have been quick to see why. Here is Lincoln (2005, 479):

Within the frame of reference of the Gospel itself the significance of blood and water is not hard to discover. The significance of the blood is set out in 6.52–9, where there are clear eucharistic overtones, but the basic level of reference is to the necessity of believing in the effectiveness of Jesus' death in order to have life—'unless you eat the flesh of the Son of Man and drink his blood, you have no life in you. Whoever eats my flesh and drinks my blood has eternal life' (6.53–4). In regard to the water, 7.38, with its talk of rivers of living water flowing from Christ's belly, provides the key. The water that comes from Jesus' side signifies the life of the Spirit that comes from Jesus' glorification.

---

[22] Since I basically leave out of consideration John 21, I will not go into the issue of the eyewitness.

The last point here is one that John himself makes wholly explicit in that passage (7:39):

Now he said this [about the rivers of flowing water] about the *pneuma*, which believers in him were to receive; for as yet there was no *pneuma* [on earth, outside in Jesus], because Jesus had not yet been glorified.

Thus, within a few verses of the account of Jesus' death, its significance for believers as transmitted through Jesus' blood (= the *pneuma*, as we have earlier read 6:53–4 in light of 6:63) and his (life-giving) 'water' (again = the *pneuma*, as read in light of 7:38–9) is shown with a concreteness that exactly matches the earlier talk of rivers of living water flowing from Christ's belly. Nobody should miss that point. It is the *pneuma* that was 'rendered' at Jesus' death that made available both resurrection and eternal life *for believers, too.*

SUMMARY ON JOHN 18–19

We have been looking for an overall theme in John's specific way of recounting the passion story which he had received from the tradition. We have found three threads that together constitute such a theme. The first is that of Jesus' active role in bringing to its final conclusion what had been planned to happen from the very beginning. The second is that of showing how all three agents in the Pilate episode work together (in the case of 'the Jews' and Pilate, wholly inadvertently) to bring about what was meant to happen: the death of the true king. And the third is that of reminding the reader of the wider purpose for believers of Jesus' death. As John has produced the tapestry of his account of Jesus' passion, all three threads are woven so carefully into it that they give it a single, powerful point: not only do the two chapters describe what happened as fulfilling what Jesus had foretold; they also describe it as having been *made* to happen by Jesus himself (and God behind him) in the way Jesus had foretold. Read in that way, the two chapters are held together by a single theme which is that of the execution of the divine plan.[23] The set of events told in them—the death of the true king that would generate life for himself and his followers through his own resurrection and his giving the *pneuma* to believers—was and is the true point of the whole story: what anybody should see, indeed, should *have* seen, but *could* not see until it had been made to happen.

[23] It has to be acknowledged, however, that the motif of the death of the true *king* (as part of the divine plan) constitutes something of an addition to the picture of Jesus given earlier in the Gospel, in spite of the fact that it has been well prepared in the ways we have seen.

THE OVERALL THEME IV: JESUS' RESURRECTION
APPEARANCES MADE HIS FOLLOWERS SEE AND BELIEVE

In Chapter III of this book, we noted one line of thought in John 20. We saw that this text is intensely concerned with describing the bodily form in which Jesus appeared to his immediate followers after his death. At first (20:1–10), he was merely absent; what was left of him was only his clothes, which lay scattered in different places inside the tomb (20:6–7). Next (20:11–18), Jesus was recognized by Mary Magdalene, but only gradually. At first when she saw him, she did not know it was Jesus (20:14). Instead, she took him to be the gardener. But then, highly significantly, she recognized his voice (20:16). Through this hearing, Mary also 'sees' Jesus, as she later tells the disciples (20:18). Indeed, she even clings to him so that he has to tell her, 'Do not hold on to me, because I have not yet ascended to the Father' (20:17, NRSV).

What is John telling his reader about Jesus' appearance in this scene in terms of hearing, seeing, and touching? Apparently, Jesus is (yet again) filled with *pneuma*, which is what Mary is responding to in hearing his voice just like people had done previously. But he is also sufficiently present in his customary bodily form for Mary to see him—and even cling to him—once she has recognized him through hearing his voice. In this dual form— 'sarkic' ('fleshly') *and* 'pneumatic' ('spiritual')—he is on his way to heaven. Thus the second scene at the tomb tells the reader much more about Jesus' physical appearance than the first one.

When does Jesus go up to the Father in heaven? It is truly hard to say. Andrew Lincoln (2005, 493) suggests the following solution:

> For the evangelist, Jesus' death, resurrection, ascent, and glorification can all be grasped as one event.... Jesus' brief appearance to Mary is a temporary stop in the one movement of ascent (cf. 3.13; 6.62). The later resurrection appearances to the disciples will, therefore, be appearances of the already ascended Jesus.

In Chapter III, we suggested another solution: that through the whole of John 20, Jesus' appearances in a 'sarkic' and 'pneumatic' form are all to be understood as appearances of Jesus at an intermediary stage before his final ascent. On Lincoln's picture, *if* the fully ascended Jesus, who is in the bosom of a Father who is himself *pneuma*, will also be just *pneuma*, his two (re-) appearances to the disciples in Jerusalem would require that he again also became 'sarkic'. That seems to require a quite baffling amount of bodily changes in Jesus over a very short time.

What clearly does matter throughout the text of John 20 is the progressive specification of Jesus' bodily form: from mere absence to a presence that is both 'pneumatic' and so 'sarkic' that Thomas is now invited to insert his hand into Jesus' side. That is one overarching theme of the chapter: to insist that Jesus was resurrected from the dead in such a form that he might be literally seen.

However, this theme also has another side to it, which concerns the disciples: that they—Jesus' immediate followers—did see him and hence came to believe in him *as* resurrected from death—and in the 'sarkic' and 'pneumatic' form that the chapter spells out, the one that precisely enabled the resurrected Jesus to be *seen*.

This topic is introduced at the end of the first subsection, when the Beloved Disciple went into the tomb, 'and he *saw* and *believed*' (20:8, NRSV). And the writer adds: 'for as yet they did not understand the scripture, that he must rise from the dead' (20:9, NRSV). The point of the explanation presumably is that the Beloved Disciple came to believe that Jesus had been resurrected simply by seeing the empty tomb, that is, without drawing on any insight into the scriptural truth that that was what would happen—and at this early stage also without seeing the resurrected Jesus in the form in which he might actually be seen.

The second subsection tells of how Mary Magdalene came to the same insight through an intermediary stage (of mistaking Jesus for a gardener and hearing his voice): she reported to the disciples that 'I have *seen* the Lord' (20:18). In the third subsection, the disciples similarly 'rejoiced... having *seen* the Lord' (20:20) once Jesus had appeared to them and shown them his hands and his side. Finally, Thomas famously reacts to Jesus' invitation to touch his wounds by confessing: 'My Lord and my God' (20:28), which leads Jesus to speak of him as 'having *seen* Jesus and come to believe' (20:29) in him in that way.

What all this shows is one thing: Jesus and behind him God (see 20:17) and two angels, whom Mary sees sitting in the tomb (20:11–13), are concerned to show *the fact* of Jesus' resurrection to the disciples by making the resurrected Jesus be *seen* in such a way that they would come to believe in his resurrection. Once again, just as John 18–19 did not just recount the unfolding of the events that had been foretold, but also showed how Jesus himself made them happen, so John 20 does not merely show that Jesus was resurrected, as he had himself repeatedly foretold. It shows in what physical form it occurred and also how Jesus made the disciples see and understand what he had previously foretold but what they had not understood at the time. In this way John 20 goes together intimately with John 18–19 in showing how Jesus was distinctly active in *making* the disciples understand the ultimate truth: that he was *meant* to die and be resurrected.

The importance of the motif of the disciples' belief is brought out very emphatically in the verse that concludes the scene with Thomas: 'Jesus said to him, "Have you believed because you have seen me? Blessed are those who have not seen and yet have come to believe"' (20:29, NRSV). The kind of belief of which Jesus is speaking here is evidently that of believing in

Jesus' resurrection. For that—meaning Jesus as resurrected—is what Thomas has seen. Blessed, therefore, are those later-living Christians who have come to believe in Jesus' resurrection *without* having seen him in resurrected form.

That this is the precise content of 'believing in Jesus' in this whole scene comes out very clearly in 20:25. When the other disciples declare 'We have seen the Lord', namely, as resurrected, Thomas answers that unless he 'sees' the mark of the nails in Jesus' hands, and puts his finger into the mark of the nails and his hand into his side—all of this is very emphatic—'I will never believe', namely, once more, that Jesus has been resurrected. So, 'believing in Jesus' means what we have called full belief. That is what is being negotiated in this text. And we have repeatedly seen the huge importance of the fact that *that* is what goes into 'full belief'.

This also explains that what Thomas does believe once he has been convinced by Jesus is that Jesus is both his 'Lord' and his 'God'. This is clearly the ultimate confession, in fact, the only genuinely true one. It corresponds (to their detriment) with two earlier, highly marked confessions, Nathanael's in 1:49 and Martha's in 11:27. When Nathanael said, 'Rabbi, you are the Son of God, you are the king of Israel', he was immediately corrected by Jesus, as we know, by a reference to what we took to be the resurrection of the Son of Man: 'Very truly, I tell you, you will see heaven opened and the angels of God ascending and descending upon the Son of Man' (1:51, NRSV). And when Martha said, 'Yes, Lord, I believe that you are the Messiah, the Son of God, the one coming into the world' (11:27, NRSV), the reader was later shown that that confession, too, was deficient, precisely because Martha did *not* include in it the whole dimension of resurrection that Jesus had just told her about. By contrast, Thomas' confession precisely consists in believing in Jesus ('my Lord and my God') *as* having been resurrected.

This leads directly into the last two verses of the chapter, with which the Gospel originally ended (20:30–1, NRSV):

[30]Now Jesus did many other signs in the presence of his disciples, which are not written in this book. [31]But these are written so that you may come to believe that Jesus is the Messiah, the Son of God, and that through believing you may have life in his name.

When NRSV translates 'so that you may come to believe', they also add in a footnote that 'Other ancient authorities read *may continue to believe*'. Everything hangs here on whether with NRSV one reads the so-called aorist of the Greek verb for 'believe' (*pisteuein*), as most ancient manuscripts do, or whether one reads the present of that verb, as the oldest and best (but fewer) manuscripts do. The issue is hotly debated in scholarship. In the present case, however, the choice should be an easy one.[24] First, and entirely without consideration of meaning, the relatively fewer manuscripts that read the present are also those generally considered the best (and oldest). Secondly, once one brings in the consideration of meaning, it seems much more obvious that the aorist should be a change from an earlier present introduced by scribes in order to turn 'may continue to believe' into an evangelistic 'may come to believe' that readers may generally have found preferable. That is, the present may be the so-called *lectio difficilior (potior)*: 'the more difficult reading' is 'the better one' since it is probably also the original one that has been changed to make the text run more attractively.

These two considerations from the art of textual criticism point quite strongly in the direction of adopting the present.[25] Will that then make any sense at all? Or is it after all too difficult? Here 'continue to believe' is perhaps not the best translation of the present. In light of the constant play on different forms of 'believing' that we have found to be articulated all through the Gospel, the sense may rather be this: 'in order that you may *genuinely* believe, etc.', as if the text is speaking of what modern philosophers call the 'intension' (as opposed to 'extension'; not 'intention') of the verb, precisely the 'full content' of believing in Jesus, which includes the fact of his resurrection. That this is what is meant is supported by what the verse specifies as the content of the belief: 'that Jesus is the Messiah, the Son of God'. For we know from comparison with Martha's confession in 11:27 that for these 'titles' to be adequate descriptions of Jesus, they are to be *understood* in a 'full' sense that includes a reference to Jesus' death and resurrection. That, after all, is the whole point of the account of Jesus that begins in John 11 and runs up to the present moment of the text. Moreover, that is also a necessary condition for the second clause in 20:31 to be true, the one that states the purpose for which all Jesus' signs have been written 'in this book': 'in order that *through believing* you may have *life* in his name'. In the Greek of this clause, 'believing' and 'life' stand next to one another, and that makes the whole point. The kind of belief that is involved here is the one that also generates (eternal) life. And we know what *that* type of

---

[24] I am happy to note that Zumstein (2016, 770) ends here too. However, he is much more cautious than I am (768) with regard to the text-critical arguments.

[25] May I be allowed to express my dissatisfaction with the practice in the Greek New Testament of Nestle Aland of putting letters or words on whose validity the editors could not agree within square brackets in the main text itself? As I see it, it is the editors' task to *decide*— in light of the available evidence—which text has the better claim to being the (more) original one and then to print the result of that decision in the main text itself. Any doubts and countervailing evidence may then be put into the textual apparatus. Moreover, in the present case the text critical situation distinctly speaks for only one reading as the more original one.

belief is like. It is our 'full' belief in Jesus as dead and resurrected (by the *pneuma*), which itself presupposes that believers themselves are in possession of the *pneuma* and may *thereby* themselves obtain eternal life just as Jesus has done. So, just as 'believing' at the end of the verse, where it is connected with 'life', is full belief, and just as the two titles given to Jesus in the middle of the verse must be understood in their 'full' sense—not just any old 'Messiah', but *the* Messiah and Son of God that Jesus has been shown to be—so 'believing' at the beginning of the verse is full belief: 'These (signs) have been written down in order that you may *genuinely* or *fully* believe that Jesus is etc.'.

JESUS' DEATH AND RESURRECTION AS EVENTS INTENDED TO GENERATE FULL BELIEF

In literary terms, 20:29–31 are three striking concluding verses. In 20:29, Jesus has been pointing into the future, speaking of those who in the future will not have seen the resurrected Jesus directly (as the disciples have just done), but will nevertheless (have) come to believe in him as being resurrected. In 20:30 the writer steps entirely outside the action by standing back from 'this book' and referring to other material that might have been, but was not, included in it. This step reveals the kind of second-order literary awareness that we have come to expect from John. Finally, in 20:31 he directly addresses in the second person plural those of whom Jesus had spoken in the third person plural in 20:29. *Having* come to believe in Jesus as the resurrected one (compare *pisteusantes* in 20:29), they are now described as the direct target of the book, those for whom it has been written with a specific selection of signs in order that they might come to *genuinely* believe that Jesus is the resurrected one and so have eternal life through that belief. From Jesus to the book to its intended recipients (including you, dear reader): here is a writer who knows exactly what he is doing.[26]

Even more, by concluding the whole book in this particular way, the Evangelist also shows that belief in Jesus as being both dead and resurrected has been the theme that explains all the specifically Johannine additions and changes in the passion narrative as a whole (John 18–20). What the

---

[26] I personally find that John is working at such a high literary level that it makes little sense to take him to have been writing *only* for some specific group of believers. Would anybody have sat down to produce such a sophisticated text that requires repeated rereadings for its full meaning to be grasped if he had only meant to address a specific group of believers, even including a 'study group' among them? Indeed, would anyone write this text—not only with its sophistication but also its extensive narration and its global perspective—for a 'study group'? This, however, is another hornet's nest of issues that cannot be adequately addressed here.

reader has been meant to understand is that Jesus, who was a kind of perverse, heavenly king who must die and be resurrected, was directly active both in bringing about his own death and also in showing his disciples that he had been resurrected from the dead. By coming to see this degree of direct activity on Jesus' part vis-à-vis his immediate disciples, later readers who had come to believe in Jesus as the resurrected one without actually having seen him (20:29) might be confirmed in that belief and thereby reach what had been the purpose of it all: eternal life. However, splendid as this conclusion is, it points to 'this book' as where it all happens. It is in the specific way the book has been written—about what *had* happened back then—that it will reach its aim. Thus the book literally ends up directing the reader's attention towards—the book itself.

XI

THE GOSPEL AS A WHOLE—MARK, PAUL, AND THE JEWS

SUMMARY AND FURTHER ISSUES

In the preceding ten chapters we have seen how the Fourth Gospel spells out in narrative terms a number of intrinsically connected themes. (1) There is the theme of Jesus' identity (who and what he is) and the way he himself proclaims it again and again to anybody who cares to listen. Correspondingly, there is the theme of a whole set of different receptions of this proclamation, from various kinds of initial belief among Jesus' inter-locutors (including many 'Jews') to an explicit, sharp conflict over Jesus' proclamation that generates disbelief in it among 'the Jews' in general and a more advanced belief among Jesus' disciples, which nevertheless remains less than fully adequate. (2) There is also the theme of the role of the *pneuma* in all of this. Its presence gives Jesus his special identity, its absence explains why even the few select disciples did *not* fully understand it during Jesus' lifetime; the *pneuma* further explains (as the 'Paraclete') why those living after Easter might obtain that full understanding—and finally how these people might then come to reach the aim of it all: to obtain eternal life (in heaven). (3) Finally, there is the theme of God's plan (his *logos*) behind it all: of sending Jesus Christ, his only Son, in order that through his life, death, and return to God he might bring salvation to humankind in the form of eternal life in heaven. All these themes are not just central to the Gospel, but also closely interconnected. Indeed, together they constitute a single conceptual tale.

In focusing on this set of themes, we have hitherto neglected completely a great number of other topics that have been intensely discussed during the last few decades of Johannine research. One of these we have already set apart in Chapter I: the attempt to correlate the text with this or the other historical 'situation' in 'the Johannine community'. But there remains a long list of other issues, of which the most important are the following:

– The text's relationship with Judaism, including the issue of how to translate the term οἱ Ἰουδαῖοι ('the Jews') and to whom it refers
– A gender-oriented perspective on the text that focuses both on its description of women and on its handling of the role of men
– The text's relationship with the Synoptic Gospels
– The text's relationship with Paul
– John and the historical Jesus
– A number of distinctly textual features: the use of various genre elements, images, symbols, irony, the style in a broader sense, including the use of repetitions, and finally, the overall 'riddling quality'
– The text's traditional historical position (including its role in the development of second-century Christianity) apart from its relationship with Stoicism and Platonism
– John and politics
– Finally (and most recently), John and ethics.

In addition, an issue that has already come up repeatedly in this book deserves further scrutiny: John and eschatology.

No single book can cover everything that can and should be said about this Gospel. In this and the next concluding chapters, I will not attempt to remedy the singlemindedness of my focus. Thus we will leave aside the following topics on the list: gender issues, the historical Jesus, further tradition history, and John and politics. Though they are in themselves distinctly well worth pursuing, none of these topics addresses directly the central *intentio operis* of the Fourth Gospel that I have been after.[1] Instead, I will address the remaining issues to see how they may cohere with and fit into the overall picture of the text's message that has been presented here. We may do this under three headings: (1) The secret of the Son of God, which discusses the relationship with the Synoptic Gospels, primarily Mark, and then goes back to Paul; (2) Salvation is from the Jews, which discusses the relationship with Judaism; and—for the next chapter—(3) Clarity for the reader, which focuses on some, at least, of the various textual features mentioned.[2]

Innumerable scholarly treatments have addressed all these topics. I have chosen a manner of discussing them that is far from conventional. I base my discussion of the first two main topics on a treatment that is more than

---

[1] This also holds, I believe, for John and politics, though this will evidently be denied by some scholars.
[2] The theme of John and ethics will come in under the third heading, as will that of John and eschatology.

a hundred years old—while also staying in touch with research of the last few decades. The treatment I have in mind is William Wrede's discussion of John in *Das Messiasgeheimnis in den Evangelien* (1901) and his general account of the 'Charakter und Tendenz des Johannesevangeliums' (1907). Wrede's discussion is generally of such a high quality that it deserves to be resuscitated from oblivion. We should not at all agree with everything in it, but its clarity, forcefulness, and general integrity is an absolute model of its kind. Furthermore, his (relatively) brief discussion in the two works is strongly directed towards what should be the ultimate aim for any work on this Gospel: an overall reading that attempts to hold all the major issues together in a coherent interpretation that is adequate to the text.

THE SECRET OF THE SON OF GOD: JOHN AND THE SYNOPTICS IN RECENT SCHOLARSHIP

As is well known, the treatment of the issue of 'John and the Synoptics' has taken a drastic turn over the last twenty-five years, not least due to work done in Belgian Leuven. Before the work of Frans Neirynck and his co-researchers, the general scholarly consensus—relying on a small book on this issue by John Gardner-Smith (1933)—was that John had been working independently of the Synoptic Gospels, based on other oral or written sources as the case might be. Not all scholars were convinced, e.g. C. K. Barrett (1978, 42–54) and W. G. Kümmel (1980, 165–83), but the topic appeared dead in scholarship until it was taken up again by Neyrinck. The result at the present time is not a general consensus on 'the Leuven hypothesis'. Indeed, the basic parameters behind the whole issue have recently been questioned. For instance, in a careful study of John 4:43–54 in relation to Mark 7:24–30, Matthew 8:5–13, Matthew 15:21–8, and Luke 7:1–10, Tom Thatcher (2014) has argued that the notion of 'dependence' (of John on the Synoptics) is invalid both historically and methodologically. Historically, it does not paint 'a credible portrait of early Christian media culture' (143) since it neglects its essentially oral character. Methodologically, it is 'less capable of explaining obvious differences between what appear to be parallel passages' (144), basically because Thatcher distances himself from notions such as 'John's fertile imagination' (144), 'the Fourth Evangelist's creative appropriation of the Synoptics' (144 n. 47), or 'free composition of original material' (144 n. 47). If Thatcher is right, the whole issue must be reconceived and no positive or negative answer may any longer be given to it as hitherto conceived.

I take it here, however, that Thatcher's objections are insufficiently strong. Were one to accept the historical point about 'early Christian media culture', one would also have to say two things that do not appear convincing. First, the relationship between Mark, Matthew, and Luke—indeed, the *dependence* of the two latter on the former—would also have to be accounted for in the same way. In view of the extremely close similarities between Matthew and Luke in relation to Mark, an understanding of *that* relationship along Thatcher's lines seems wholly unconvincing: both Matthew and Luke must have had direct access to a written Mark. Secondly, were one to accept Thatcher's picture for all four Gospels, one would also have to separate off completely these four written texts (as they are) from the whole literary practice and culture of contemporary Greco–Roman literature. This literary culture was certainly not oral in the way suggested by Thatcher for John when he at one point writes (of John): 'if he could in fact read' (143)! As I have analysed the Fourth Gospel in this book, its author could indeed read and he fully belonged to (Jewish–Hellenistic) Greco–Roman literary culture in the same way as, for instance, Philo of Alexandria.

On the methodological point, one must insist that finding John's supposed editorial creativity to be 'essentially synonymous with complete disregard for, or at least a profoundly corrective posture toward, the literary and thematic integrity of the source texts' (144) reflects a rather anachronistic understanding of an ancient writer's sense of obligation towards the 'integrity' of a source text. Instead, one might well take it as a wholly adequate description of John's actual literary practice.[3]

If we take it, then, that we may continue to speak of literary dependence in the sense that John may have had access to one or the other of the Synoptic Gospels as written texts, which he may have heard read aloud, have himself read, and have been able to consult as a written text, the most secure result of the Leuven hypothesis is that John has (in this sense) known the Gospel of Mark.

A good example of this position is Jörg Frey's convincing discussion of the issue from 2003. On the basis of a thorough account of the history of research, Frey makes two methodological claims. First, the reference to oral influence remains vague (necessarily so, one might add) and 'the assumption of interaction [with Synoptic material] at the stage of pre-Johannine tradition is hardly controllable' (258). Conversely, one would have to give up the hypothesis of Johannine independence 'if the dependence on a single redactional element in a single one of the Synoptic Gospels could be made sufficiently plausible in a single place [in John]' (258). In addition, Frey considers it likely that if the Johannine Evangelist was

---

[3] It is interesting to note that the idea of the oral transmission of stories about Jesus comes up particularly strongly among scholars who are interested in getting back as closely as possible to the 'historical Jesus'. Thatcher is one of them, just as the Swedish scholar Birger Gerhardsson (1926–2013) was in an earlier age, see his *Memory and Manuscript* (1961).

dependent on sources, he would not confine himself to the mere stitching together of pre-existing sources. On the contrary, 'he shows himself (explicitly in John 20:30–1) as an eclectic and independently creative writer—a point that does not exclude, but *includes* a reception of written sources' (259, Frey's emphasis).

Armed with this methodology, Frey focuses specifically on John's relationship with Mark, where there are both similarities of material (261–2) and compositional analogies (263). The latter suggest 'that the fourth evangelist knew at least the structure of the Gospel of Mark' (263). Frey adds that a consideration of the literary genre of the Fourth Gospel points strongly in the same direction (264):

> If John is to be included in the type of text that was created by Mark from the very beginning, it would be very improbable were one to posit one more analogous 'invention' of this genre parallel to Mark in a different 'trajectory of development'.... The 'composition' of a second narrative of the message of salvation in Jesus Christ that is no less impressively directed towards the Passion and Easter than in the work of Mark to my mind constitutes a very strong argument for the fourth evangelist's knowledge and (partial) reception of the Gospel of Mark.

All of this appears exactly right. And so does Frey's analysis of three paradigmatic texts in Mark and their reflections in John: Mark 14:32–42, Mark 1:4–11, and finally the Synoptic parallels to the talk of the 'kingdom of God' in John 3:3 and 3:5. Everywhere Frey is able to show 'how eclectically the fourth evangelist is at work with respect to the traditions and in how sovereign fashion with respect to his own formative intentions' (276). Even more, he speaks of a 'profound transformation' and claims that the Evangelist's approach was not just 'eclectic . . . and profoundly interpretative', but also in many places adopted a position of 'explicit disagreement' with the various elements of the tradition (281). What we find in John is 'a bold type of reinterpretation': 'Everything that is available is melted together linguistically and made to serve his own narrative interest' (287). Should we then say that John aimed to supplant or replace the Synoptic Gospels '(or at least Mark)' (291)? No. The reading of the Fourth Gospel 'implicitly plays on' the knowledge of the Synoptic material and thus presupposes it in its readers (291). Thus the literary working up of the older tradition about Jesus in the Fourth Gospel 'cannot really replace this tradition (and hardly simply aims to replace it): rather it presupposes it—in whichever form— and continues to do so' (291).

Basically, Frey's approach and his results are to be applauded, not least because they are—on the whole—'controllable'. In what follows, I aim to add to this by considering a single, central theme that is not addressed head-on by Frey (or anyone else I know of) but shows the same two points he has articulated: John's 'dependence' on Mark, in the sense given above, and his radical reinterpretation of Mark. That theme is the one Wrede put on the scholarly map: the 'Messianic secret'. I will attempt to show that John knew and adopted this motif, which is central in Mark, but turned it into something quite different: the 'secret of the Son of God'. What he did was to turn inside out the Markan motif (from secrecy to blatant proclamation) and to move it from being about the Messiah to concerning the Son of God.

THE SECRET OF THE SON OF GOD: JOHN AND THE SYNOPTICS IN WREDE

In Wrede's *Messiasgeheimnis* the main focus is on the Gospel of Mark and a key aim is to show that this Gospel is anything but an immediate rendering of the life of the historical Jesus. To bring that out, Wrede, among many other things, turns to a comparison of Mark with John:

The understanding of the writerly character of the Gospel of Mark that I have presented in certain respects in contrast to the normal critical treatment of that text corresponds to a certain extent with the understanding that critical scholarship— and here I mean the unprejudiced one—adopts in connection with another text: the Gospel of John. This needs to be emphasized . . . since one may learn from John about Mark (143).

Wrede does not deny that there are important differences between John and Mark, but concludes:

However—the fundamental similarity is nevertheless much greater than it is usually taken, just because Mark too is already very far removed from the real life of Jesus and is governed by dogmatic beliefs. *If one looks at Mark through a strong magnifying glass, one will get something like a type of writing shown by John* (145, my emphasis).[4]

Let us consider how Wrede brought that out.

Wrede found two distinct ideas in the motif of the 'Messianic secret' as he developed it for Mark. Here, again, is the point in Wrede's own, succinct rendering:

We find in Mark two ideas:
1) As long as he is on earth, Jesus keeps his messiahship a secret.
2) To the disciples he does admittedly reveal himself in contrast to the people, but to them too he remains incomprehensible in his revelations for the time being.

---

[4] The last sentence in this deserves to retain its German form: 'Man betrachte Markus durch ein starkes Vergrösserungsglas, und man hat etwa eine Schriftstellerei, wie sie Johannes zeigt.'

Behind both ideas, which to a large extent overlap, lies the same belief that real knowledge of what Jesus is only begins with his resurrection. This idea of the secret Messiahship extends significantly in Mark. It dominates many sayings of Jesus, numerous miracle stories, and the entire course of the narrative as a whole (114).[5]

We need not follow here Wrede's attempt to explain Mark's very peculiar idea historically. What matters is only that Wrede described the Markan idea as a 'transitional' one between an earlier conception, in which Jesus was not at all seen as the Messiah during his life on earth, but only became so at his resurrection—and a later one, in fact a bit like the Johannine one, in which he constantly reveals and proclaims his Messianic identity while still on earth.

When Wrede turns to the Fourth Gospel, he makes an important point:

The view of Jesus in the Gospel of John is not characterized by the concept of the Messiah..../ The only begotten Son of God, the *Logos*, the Light of the World, the Bread of Life, the bringer of Truth, these are predicates...(179–80).[6]

We know already that this distinction between 'Messiah' and 'Son of God' (etc.) is exactly right. To the extent that one may find a 'Messianic secret' in John, it will be a 'secret of the Son of God'. But do we find something like this?

Retaining his distinction between secrecy and misunderstanding, Wrede asks about the Fourth Gospel:

[i] Does Jesus keep his supramundane being and the divine truth concealed or [ii] do both of these in any case remain hidden in actual fact in his earthly life (180, my translation)?

To the first question Wrede answers—quite rightly—no.

What is the activity and the speech of the Johannine Christ if not a continuous revelation? Over all his speeches one might place as a motto the word he says to the high priest: 'I have spoken openly to the world...I have said nothing in secret (18_{20})' (180).

This is so obviously right that one often forgets to give the fact any further thought. What we see here is that John has taken the first half of the motif of the Messianic secret in Mark and—as I think we should see it—turned it inside out. Whereas in Mark Jesus is keen to keep as a secret (from 'the crowd') the identity that he is also there presupposed to have, in John he is overly keen to divulge it (to all). Since the motif of the Messianic secret is itself a very clearly redactional feature in Mark, the inverted relationship between John and Mark at this point strongly suggests that John knew

---

[5] My own translation with input from J. C. G. Greig (Wrede 1971).
[6] Translation Greig from Wrede 1971, 180.

Mark. John has taken up a motif in Mark and changed it drastically. Wrede himself did not quite see or say this. But the point is implied, I think, in the similarity between the two texts that we see him to be developing.

To the second question raised above by Wrede (Does Jesus remain hidden?) he—initially, at least—answers no, too:

> ...there is no lack of a true knowledge of his person. The Baptist does not stand alone in this; the disciples also very quickly know that they have found the Messiah. The Samaritan woman and her compatriots recognise him as the savior of the world (4_{42}) and Martha finds the same words for confessing him as does Peter (11_{27}, see 6_{69}) (181).[7]

This, as we know, is not quite right. While the Baptist does recognize Jesus' full identity, in the other cases there is more to be said. In fact, it is noteworthy that Wrede pays very little attention to the theme we have found to be central: that some Jews did come to 'believe in' Jesus, while others did not; and that the belief in those who did was never sufficient to count as full belief.

In spite of this deficiency, Wrede immediately goes on in a manner that shows that he has in fact grasped part of the point:

> Nevertheless the idea of the secret Christ—in the broadest sense—is not unknown to John (181).[8]

And then he goes on to show over several pages—and rightly—that *even in the case of the disciples* the full and final understanding of Jesus only came to be present after his death and resurrection. Here Wrede refers to John 2:22, 12:16, and 20:9 (183), all of which precisely focus on the resurrection and glorification. A page later he mentions 13:28 and concludes that 'such important hints and prophecies of Jesus...had to remain obscure to the disciples until the resurrection' (184, my translation). In short, Wrede fully sees the importance in John of the reference to Jesus' resurrection—and particularly to that very specific event—in connection with the second half of Messianic secret: the misunderstanding (or lack of understanding) of *all*, *including* the disciples, that will precisely only be lifted at Jesus' resurrection.

This second feature of John once again connects his text inseparably with that of Mark, where—as Wrede rightly insisted—the key text is Jesus' instruction to keep his identity a secret 'until the Son of Man has risen from the dead' (Mark 9:9). Wrede therefore concludes as follows:

> Thus we can already be in no doubt that with respect to the disciples' recognition of Jesus, John has a view that is very closely related to that of Mark. Here it is noteworthy that he explicitly singles out the resurrection as the decisive moment in time (185, my translation).

---

[7] Translation Greig (Wrede 1971, 182).   [8] Translation Greig (Wrede 1971, 182).

However, there is one point in Wrede's account of John where we must register a deficiency. Exactly what is it that John's Jesus constantly proclaims to anybody who cares to listen? Exactly what is it that no one among them finally understands? We have just seen that Wrede identifies the moment of final and complete understanding as that of Jesus' resurrection. But according to Wrede, the content itself of that understanding is not tied particularly to the resurrection. Instead, what people came to see is *everything* Jesus had been saying about his own identity: his being sent by God, his being one with God, etc. In this book we have reached a different answer. What people could not understand was this: that Jesus was the Son of God etc. *as shown by the fact that in his resurrection he returned to God.* That is the kernel of truth in Wrede's realization that the 'Messianic secret' in John is not really about the 'Messiah' but about the 'Son of God'. For Jesus is only the 'Son of God' (and 'the *Logos*, the Light of the World, the Bread of Life, the Bringer of Truth') *because* he was resurrected.

Since this is such an important point for the whole argument of this book, it is worth mentioning a few places where Wrede does see it, but only in order to immediately back down from it. At one point he admits that 'the weakness of the disciples' knowledge shows itself especially in the fact that the prophecy of dying and coming to life again or of going to the Father remains uncomprehended (14_5, 16_5 f., $_{16}$ff., $_{28(32)}$)' (192, my translation). However, that is only due to the 'situation' in which it is said. Or again:

> It is not possible to separate out any teachings which might be regarded as accessible once for all to the disciples or any that would be permanently barred to them. *One might, to be sure, make the second point with some justification in regard to the teachings about suffering and glorification.* But . . . (194, my emphasis, Greig's translation in Wrede 1971, 195).

Here Wrede is quite right about the second point, but wrong about the first one, as he half concedes. The overall point is this: only by understanding, grasping, and fully believing in the claim about Jesus' (suffering and) glorification will one be able to grasp and believe in the full content of all the remaining claims about him. It is his resurrection that shows that Jesus was (and is) the Son of God and that gives the ultimate and final content to that claim.

In spite of this difference, it remains the case that Wrede's whole discussion shows the direct influence of Mark on John on two specific points. First, John has turned the Markan point about the need to keep Jesus' identity hidden from the crowd completely inside out. In John he constantly proclaims it to anybody in his entourage. Secondly, John has taken up the motif of misunderstanding or lack of understanding of Jesus' true identity and extended it to cover not just those who do reach *some* understanding of Jesus, but also the disciples, who never reach the full understanding. Since the motif of the Messianic secret in Mark appears to be so very much a distinct, 'redactional' contribution of Mark himself, it seems impossible not to conclude that John knew Mark and that he transformed his Markan heritage in order to bring out as strongly as possible the full content of Jesus' identity: that he was not just the 'Messiah', but the 'Son of God' who had *come* from God in the sense already laid out to begin with (1:1–34) and had *returned* to God in his resurrection as confirmed by his resurrection appearances at the end (John 20).

Against this background, it must come as a huge surprise that Wrede concludes his discussion of John and Mark as follows:

> The Gospel of John reveals an understanding that is closely related to that of Mark, and accordingly also offers some confirmation of our interpretation of Mark. The importance of this understanding for the Gospel [of John] must admittedly not be overestimated, still it does have a substantial importance.... It seems... unthinkable that the mere influence of Mark or the other Synoptics should have produced it. For the mere similarity in general ideas (*allgemeine Gedanken*) does not in the least by itself make literary dependence likely. Instead, the *specific forms* (*die eigentümlichen Formen*) in which they appear in Mark or his successors had to be taken over. But that is not the case, or at least only in a wholly restricted sense (*in ganz eingeschränktem Sinne*, 203–4, my translation, Wrede's emphasis).

This paragraph is an excellent example of the care of Wrede's thought and writing. But for all that it does not convince. On the contrary, it seems that just the way John can be seen to have developed the two central—and in themselves highly specific—ideas in the Markan motif of the Messianic secret into something that served to bring out and indeed pinpoint his *own* understanding of Jesus is a strong indication that John did know Mark. How else would anybody come to focus one's whole narrative about Jesus on the two apparently contradictory—or at least, bafflingly opposed—points that Jesus loudly proclaimed his full identity to all and sundry from day one but nobody—not even his closest followers—understood it while he was with them? If one believes (as one should) that John must have taken over (and developed) from Mark the whole genre of the gospel narrative as this had been created by the latter, one must surely also agree that John has taken over and developed the much more specific theme of the Messianic secret that constitutes the 'inner form' in Mark of the genre of the gospel narrative, the theme that drives the story to its conclusion.

There is one more feature of Wrede's discussion of John in *Das Messiasgeheimnis* that we should at least mention here: in John, Jesus' speaking 'in parables' (which would explain why he was not understood) is transferred from being concerned with 'the crowd' (as in Mark 4) to pertaining to the disciples and *their* lack of understanding (see John 16:25–33). The point here is that the theme of Jesus' speaking somewhat 'obliquely' even to the disciples (as, e.g., in John 1:51) should probably not be explained in Wrede's manner by a reference back to the historical Jesus. Rather, in John the theme appears to be a literary device that brings a *third* 'actor' into this text, namely the reader. Where none of Jesus' hearers in the narrative fully grasps what Jesus is saying since it appears to require some code to be fully understood, the readers, who do possess that code, immediately understand everything, and are meant to do so. *They* have been given the necessary means for understanding—for instance, in John 1:1–34 up until the moment when the story actually begins. They therefore already know what the first disciples did not know until John 20. Let us call this theme the 'triangularity' of Jesus as narrated, his encoded hearers, and the reader, where the point is that the text establishes a collusion of understanding between the narrated Jesus and the reader across a lack of understanding in the hearers who are encoded in the narrative. If somebody would go on to claim that *this* feature of the Fourth Gospel is also derived from the Gospel of Mark, I should warmly agree. But enough is enough.

THE SECRET OF THE SON OF GOD LIFTED: JOHN AND PAUL

We now momentarily leave Wrede and turn to another issue that has come into focus again in recent scholarship: John's relationship with Paul. If we conclude that John did know and renegotiate the fundamental sketch of at least one of the Synoptic Gospels (Mark), should we also say that the same holds for his relationship with the figure who—at least in the New Testament—articulates *the* other basic, early Christian tradition about Jesus: Paul?

We may take as our starting point a helpful article by Christina Hoegen-Rohls (2004) in which she provides a sketch of the development of research on the issue and asks whether or not one should see Johannine theology 'in the context of Pauline thought'. What we find here is the usual picture of a development in three stages. Before the First World War, scholars regularly saw Paul as the 'yeast' that had a 'catalytic function' in relation to John's theology, in the words of Heinrich Julius Holtzmann.[9] Indeed, John 'stands on the shoulders of Paul' (*Johannes fusst auf Paulus*), according to Wellhausen, but also 'takes a major step beyond him'.[10] Adolf Jülicher spoke of an independent handling of Pauline theology in John: 'Half dependence . . . , half opposition' (Hoegen-Rohls 2004, 600). And Wilhelm Bousset concurred

---

[9] See the quotations from Holtzmann in Hoegen-Rohls (2004, 598–9).
[10] Again see Hoegen-Rohls (2004, 599).

about the Pauline shoulders (Hoegen-Rohls 2004, 601–3). Then came the reaction, as strongly articulated by Bultmann:

John does not belong to the school of Paul, nor is he influenced by Paul; rather, he is an original figure, who stands in a different atmosphere of theological thought.[11]

The third stage began in the 1980s with a list of articles by Schnackenburg, Zeller, Schnelle, Jürgen Becker, and others. What Hoegen-Rohls also brings out well is the fact that none of the pre-Bultmann scholars asked whether John knew and perhaps even used the Pauline letters '*literarisch*', as written texts. Instead, their primary interest (which went back to Baur) was focused on 'general conceptual features' of Johannine and Pauline theology, respectively (Hoegen-Rohls 2004, 603).

Hoegen-Rohls finds a corresponding distinction in more recent scholarship between a 'synchronically oriented model of a theological comparison that pays special attention to the similarities' (2004, 607) and a 'diachronically oriented model of tradition historical comparison that notes both similarities and differences' (607–8). She herself tentatively prefers the former approach. In the present context, however, what matters is, if not a 'tradition historical comparison', at least a comparison that aims to answer this question: did John know and even use the Pauline letters as written texts? However, we may also draw on the synchronic model by trying to answer the diachronic question not so much in terms of individual, highly specific terminology—such as the use of 'grace' (*charis*) in John 1:16 or 'justice' (*dikaiosynê*) in John 15:8 and 10, which in themselves sound strongly Pauline—as of overall conceptual themes. Only, and this is the challenge, such themes must remain sufficiently specific to Paul for their possible appearance in John to have any argumentative power with regard to the diachronic question. So, do we find in John any overall conceptual theme that is also to be found specifically in Paul?

What we are after will be rather like what we found in comparing John with Mark: a comprehensive theme that was specific to Mark—but was then also to be found (duly transformed) in John. Seen in that light there is one comprehensive theme in John which is not present in the other Gospels, but can precisely be seen as a development of a theme that is also fundamental and specific to Paul. What I have in mind is what the Fourth Gospel text says about the 'disciples', i.e. Christ believers, *after* Jesus' death and resurrection. In itself this theme is not quite new in John in comparison with the Synoptic Gospels. Two passages in Mark spring to mind, both with a clear connection to John.[12] (i) In Mark 8:34–8 Jesus stipulates as a condition for 'following him' that a person be willing to 'lose

---

[11] Quotation by Hoegen-Rohls (2004, 593) from Bultmann's *Theology of the New Testament*.
[12] I am not suggesting, though, that John took the two motifs from Mark.

his life (or soul) for my sake, and for the sake of the gospel' (35). This motif is taken up in John 12:25. In both texts, while the stipulation may certainly also be relevant while Jesus was alive, it points distinctly forward to the way Christ believers must live in the period after his death and before they will obtain eternal life. (ii) Even more strikingly, in Mark 10:41–5 Jesus explicitly tells the disciples how it 'is' (10:43)—and should be—among them:

[43] ...whoever wishes to become great among you must be your servant, [44]and whoever wishes to be first among you must be slave of all. [45]For the Son of Man has come not to be served but to serve, and to give his life (or soul) a ransom for many (NRSV, with two changes).

This motif is taken up in several places in John. The idea in the latter half of Mark 10:45 is reflected in John 10:15 and 15:13. And the idea in the former half of the same verse is spelled out in the foot-washing scene in John (13:1–17), culminating in Jesus' statement of its point in 13:13–15. In this way, two motifs in Mark that look distinctly forward to the period after Jesus' death are taken up in a number of places in John in which Jesus is speaking of the life of his disciples during that same period. It remains the case, however, that John has given added space within his own Gospel to this theme, and this is where Paul becomes directly relevant.

In thus moving back from Mark to Paul as models for John, we are extending our treatment of the Johannine reflection of the Markan theme of the Messianic secret. We saw that the latter theme has two parts in Mark and John, one concerned with who Jesus is and the other concerned with how he is understood. The latter focuses on Jesus' hearers, but precisely those hearers during Jesus' own lifetime. Moreover, the issue here is tied to the first half of the overall theme since it concerns their understanding of Jesus' identity itself. The new topic we are now addressing also concerns Jesus' 'hearers', but now explicitly after Jesus' death and not only as an issue of understanding Jesus' identity (since now they do understand that), but rather more broadly as the one of *how they should live* (in the period after Jesus' death) *in light of their new understanding*. This, I contend, is where John drew directly on Paul and for obvious reasons. For that is *the* theme of the Pauline letters.

We have just seen that *this* side of a focus on the hearers is also present in Mark and taken up again in the same way in John. We must now attempt to show that in addressing this issue, John does not just continue the Markan line but also develops it in a manner that must be derived specifically from Paul.

There are two themes in Paul that are particularly relevant. One is his special understanding of the character and role of baptism. The other is his understanding of the kind of life that follows from being baptized. In both cases, the central feature is the (reception and possession of) the *pneuma*. In what follows I am presupposing an interpretation of Paul that I have developed elsewhere.[13] That includes the view of a certain conceptual coherence in Paul's understanding throughout the seven genuine letters. Thus the fundamental role of baptism comes out in a number of places.[14] It is basically connected with reception of the *pneuma* since it is in baptism that believers will receive the *pneuma*. This is clear, for instance, from Galatians 3:14 taken together with Gal. 3:26–9 and Gal. 4:5–7. What Paul has in mind here is a clear and meaningful sequence: faith (in Jesus as Christ) leads to baptism; in baptism believers receive the *pneuma*; as a result they cry (when getting up from the bath?): 'Abba! Father!'. The same picture is articulated elsewhere. Romans 6, which explicitly spells out the content and consequence of baptism, does not mention the *pneuma*.[15] But after Paul's further exploration in Rom. 7:1–8:13 of the contrast (7:1–6) between living under the law of Moses (Rom. 7:7–25) and living in the *pneuma* (Rom. 8:1–13), the picture from Galatians is reintroduced (Rom. 8:14–15).

We may take it, therefore, that Paul's view of a Christ believer's full entry into the life of a Christian was the one given above: through reception of the *pneuma* in baptism. Moreover, the whole passage in Romans also shows the central role of the *pneuma* not only for the earthly life that would follow upon baptism, but also for what is eternal life through the resurrection. This comes out very clearly in the sequence from Rom. 8:9–10 into 8:11, where 8:9–10 speaks of the present and 8:11 of the future:

[9]You, however, are not in the flesh but in the *pneuma*, insofar as the *pneuma* of God dwells in you. Should somebody not have the *pneuma* of Christ, that person does not belong to him. [10]But if Christ is in you, while the body is dead because of sin, the *pneuma* is life because of righteousness. [11]If the *pneuma* of him who raised Jesus from the dead *dwells in* you, the one who raised Christ from the dead will also make your mortal bodies come alive *through* the *pneuma* that *dwells in* you.

What we have in Paul, then, is a view of the *pneuma*—which Paul identifies as both God's *pneuma*, Christ's *pneuma*, and indeed Christ himself—as having been received by Christ believers in baptism, as being operative in their lives after that, and finally as going to be operative also in their final resurrection into life (Rom. 8:6 and 11 in *zôio-poiein*), and indeed, into what Paul has himself earlier in Romans (2:7, 5:21, and 6:22–3) called 'eternal life' (*zôê aiônios*). This is all highly specific. It is a conceptual cluster that lies behind, and indeed spells out the precise shape of, the central Pauline idea of

---

[13] Most directly relevant is Engberg-Pedersen 2010.
[14] Though everything in Paul is controversial, the following remarks should not be contentious.
[15] The reason for this is presumably that Paul aims to spell out the *cognitive content* of baptism, for which a reference to the *pneuma* would not be enough.

being 'in' Christ, an idea that has given rise to talk about 'mysticism' in Paul, but should rather be understood in the down-to-earth manner of the operation of a heavenly, material *pneuma* on the bodies of Christ believers once it has been directly infused into them.[16]

Turn then to John. Here we find at an early stage the idea that those who received 'him', that is, Jesus Christ or the Jesus–*logos*, to those 'he' gave 'the power to become children of God' (1:12)—'those who had been begotten, not from blood, neither from the will of flesh, nor from the will of a man, but from God' (1:13). We already know from the way this is taken up in John 3 that the power behind this begetting is the *pneuma* as received in baptism (3:5–6). The language is to some extent different, but Paul, too, may speak of being 'begotten' in connection with the *pneuma* (Gal. 4:29) in opposition to the flesh (also Gal. 4:23). And he, too, may speak (compare 1 Cor. 6:9)— though just as rarely as John—of the 'kingdom of God' (as in John 3:3 and 5). What matters more—and this is where the synchronic approach to the issue becomes relevant—is the idea itself of reception of the *pneuma* in baptism—a *pneuma* which Paul identified with Christ (Rom. 8:10, compare 2 Cor. 3:17), and John even identifies with God (John 4:24)—and the central role played by that idea in the overall conception of the Gospel.

To see this we must move forward in the Gospel into John 13–17. We have already touched on the importance of the foot-washing scene for the theme of how the 'disciples' must live in the period after Jesus' death. Here we should note how the Farewell Discourse itself then spells out this theme in terms of two motifs that are intrinsically connected and show a very close connection with distinctly Pauline ideas. What I have in mind are, first, the idea of being 'in' Jesus (Christ), an idea that underlies one of the two main themes of the whole Farewell Discourse as announced in 13:33–5, namely, that of 'loving one another', and secondly, the idea of receiving the *pneuma* in the shape of the 'Paraclete' upon Jesus' death. The former idea is spelled out in 15:1–17, the latter in John 14 and 16. In Chapter IX of this book we saw how the two ideas are connected. Reception of the *pneuma* in the form of the 'Paraclete' is what enables the kind of life in the period after Jesus' death (and before the general resurrection) of mutual love that is the whole point of Jesus' coming (during that period). Believing in Jesus Christ, receiving the *pneuma* in baptism, being 'in' Christ, and living a life of mutual love (and then also being resurrected by the *pneuma* into eternal life together with Christ): that is the exceedingly tightly, intrinsically connected set of events that both John and Paul are primarily concerned to bring out.

---

[16] This is one central claim of Engberg-Pedersen 2010.

Please note here that in laying special emphasis on the Johannine Farewell Discourse for the comparison of John and Paul, I have made no use of the claim made in Chapter IX that the Farewell Discourse is structured around two senses of '*paraklêsis*' to be found in Paul. That claim had to stand or fall on its own, not as telling us anything about a relationship between John and Paul, but only as a heuristic device intended to make us grasp better the overall shape of the Farewell Discourse. Instead, what I have emphasized here is the role of the *pneuma* for the 'new commandment' of mutual love that John's Jesus introduces in 13:34–5 and spells out in 15:1–17. If *that* reading stands, then one may also employ the heuristic benefit from drawing on the two Pauline senses of '*paraklêsis*' in *further* support of the claim about a direct relationship between John and Paul. In the present context, however, the claim has been the different one of unpacking the conceptual grid underlying Jesus' new commandment, which I claim is also distinctly Pauline.

Is the tightly knit cluster of concepts that I have identified in both Paul and John sufficiently specific to Paul to allow us to conclude that John has taken it directly from him? Somebody might say: did not all early Christians think like that? Well, did they? Please, show us. If that cannot be done (as I do not think it can), then one might claim that surely—though unbeknownst to us—early Christians in general *must* have thought like that. But then Ockham's razor suggests that we should rather settle for the simpler and more straightforward alternative: John knew and understood Paul, and he employed a central Pauline idea in order to include in his Gospel, which was ostensibly only about the life and death of Jesus, the Son of God, a *fully developed* projection of the meaning of Jesus' death and resurrection for the earthly lives of his later 'disciples'. To bring that out he drew directly on Paul, who had been centrally preoccupied with the very same theme.

Do we need to make the implication clear? Perhaps yes: this, too, is where we find the 'ethics' (real and genuine ethics) of the Fourth Gospel—in addition to those many other places that are beginning to receive scholarly attention.

SALVATION IS FROM THE JEWS: JOHN AND THE JEWS IN WREDE

We now turn to an issue that has been a storm centre in scholarship for more than twenty-five years: John's relationship with Judaism. It is well known that the Fourth Gospel refers much more often than the Synoptic Gospels to Jesus' interlocutors and opponents simply as 'the Jews' (*hoi Ioudaioi*), instead of 'the Pharisees', 'the Sadducees' (never), 'the crowd', or the like. Who are 'the Jews'? To whom is this term meant to refer? Various possibilities have been canvassed, but if, as scholars have gradually come to realize, John's 'Jews' refers either straightforwardly to the Jews as an *ethnos* ('people') with defining characteristics of its own or at least to those Jews (as an *ethnos*) with whom Jesus was in contact, then one may ask whether John—and his Jesus—speaks of these Jews from the inside, as one of them, or from the outside, as an 'other' from whom he distinguishes himself. This question reflects the fact that the Gospel both speaks positively (or neutrally) about 'the Jews' and also decidedly negatively. After the Holocaust, the latter fact has—rightly—struck scholars, and the question has been raised forcefully whether the Fourth Gospel is 'anti-Jewish' and whether we should speak of 'anti-Judaism' in this text.[17] So, who are 'the Jews' in John? Why does he use this locution, in particular? Do we find 'anti-Judaism' in this text?

Before addressing these questions as they have been answered in recent scholarship, I propose to go back to William Wrede's account of John's relationship with Judaism (1907). In the present case the reason is not that we may derive valuable insights from Wrede that we may immediately take over. On the contrary, Wrede laid out a track on this issue that would be taken by scholars during the twentieth century until it was seen to reach an impasse. But he did it with a forcefulness that is all his own. Moreover, in developing his position he very emphatically articulated the methodological rule of historical criticism (in this case, as directed towards finding the extratextual historical situation that will illuminate the text). But this rule is put under pressure in relation to the present issue, not in principle, but in practice.

It should be emphasized that neither in my remarks on Wrede nor in those on much more recent scholarship do I aim to do justice to all sides of the impressive amount of scholarly thinking on this question. The aim here is to focus on the basic methodological issues underlying the ways scholars have answered the three questions listed above. In this manner I hope to clear the way for my own answers and thus to reach my ultimate aim of showing how the reading of John given in this book fits into an understanding of John's relationship with Judaism.

---

[17] One major contribution has been Bieringer et al. 2001a, who collect a number of important essays. In their introduction to the volume, Bieringer, Pollefeyt, and Vandecasteele-Vanneuville end up finding 'anti-Judaism' (Bieringer et al. 2001b, 32) and 'anti-Jewish elements' (33) in the Fourth Gospel. I query this conclusion while also insisting that the Gospel speaks in ways that fit hand-in-glove with anti-Judaism once the conditions for such a thing had become present. But I firmly believe that we must distinguish between the text itself and its *Wirkungsgeschichte*.

Wrede's 1907 account is divided into two halves corresponding to its title: first on the character, then on the 'tendency' (*Tendenz*). The move from one thing to the other shows Wrede's basic way of thinking:

An *historical understanding* is not reached by a mere description of the Gospel. How anybody got the thought to write such a text—that remains very unclear. We may understand that the writer wanted to enclose certain dogmatic ideas in his text, / but not at all thereby the real shape (*Gestalt*) of the Gospel, including not least why he wrote a Gospel at all (207–8, Wrede's emphasis).

Did he want to supplement the Synoptic narrative? No. Did he want to provide a dogmatic teaching (*eine Lehre*) about Christ? No. 'On the contrary, an historical understanding is only reached once we see the Gospel as *a text that was born from a fight and written for a fight*' (208, my emphasis). The Gospel is a piece of apologetics, which determines 'the character of it all': 'The Evangelist has to do with an opponent who determines everything he says' (208). This is clear, for instance, from the repeated use of the terminology of 'witnessing':

From time to time the form of this witnessing becomes almost pointedly juridical, as if it were a matter of conducting legal proceedings (209)....[18]

But who is the opponent? It is—primarily, at least—Judaism (*das Judentum*) or the Jewish school or church of the time during which our author is writing.

At this time Judaism had been shrugged off by Christianity a long time ago and already stood against it as a foreign religion....It is true that the Evangelist knows—how could he not?—that 'salvation is from the Jews'; but that is (only) a historical memory without any contemporary significance....In short, our Evangelist has his own share in the inheritance regarding its [Christianity's] relationship with Judaism that the whole of the post-apostolic church has Paul to thank for (209–10).

It goes without saying that the last part of this is wholly dated by now. The idea that Paul should have brought about an historical situation in which something called 'Christianity' had 'shrugged off' some other entity called 'Judaism' is a no-go in modern scholarship, which sees both Paul's own relationship with Judaism (to which we will return) and also the 'parting of the ways' between (what came to be) Christianity and Judaism in a much different light. But Wrede's exceedingly clear articulation of this position points distinctly forward to later developments in scholarship, as is clear from the immediately following section:

That it is Judaism that is the opponent with which he is engaged lies at hand from the fact that in the Gospel Jesus is contending precisely with 'the Jews' and that it is

---

[18] Here Wrede clearly prefigures the much later emphasis on the law-court character of much of the interaction between Jesus and 'the Jews'.

them to which his witness is addressed. These Jews are in a spiritual sense the Jews of the later period, against whose enmity the Christian congregation had to defend itself and which they had to face up to. In this way it also becomes somewhat more understandable to us why the Evangelist keeps talking in those general terms about 'the' Jews. That is a reflex of the situation in his own time. He and his people were in any case engaged with 'the' Jews; it was Judaism as such that stood against them (210).

This is almost prophetic if one thinks of the 'two-level' dramatic reading of the whole Gospel that was launched by J. L. Martyn in 1968. In this quotation from Wrede we find both the insistence on finding the background to 'the prominence [in John] of the Jews and their hostility to Jesus' in 'a genuine historical setting', and also the observation that 'the Jews in the Fourth Gospel reflected a Johannine conflict with contemporary Judaism'.[19]

Wrede goes on to rehearse a large number of topics of defence or attack (210–27) and concludes that:

...the apologetic aim does not just pertain to this or the other (individual topic), but determines the essence (*Wesen*) of this text. In its content the Johannine account is a direct predecessor to the anti-Jewish defence text (*Schutzschrift*) by Justin Martyr, the Dialogue with Trypho, the Jew (227).

Nevertheless, perspicacious (and honest) as he was, Wrede did admit as a 'limitation' (*Einschränkung*) of his reading that: 'In formal terms (*Formell*) the Gospel is not addressed to its opponents, nor to the general public, but to the Christian community' (227).

However, he concluded that: 'All in all (*In der Hauptsache*) the Gospel... remains an apology' (228).

Whether right or wrong, this is all magnificent. It articulates the insight that has been determinative for all later scholarship and remains so in spite of a number of later—in themselves both valid and important—'non-historical', additional perspectives: the insight that one central part of the meaning of an ancient text is to be found in its historical setting, in such a way that what the text itself actually says should be understood in intimate connection with the historical situation in which it was uttered. As we will see, it is the application of this fundamental principle (surely, correct in itself) that is at stake when we ask about John's relationship with Judaism.

[19] The two quotations are from D. Moody Smith's account of Martyn's position (Smith 2003, 6 and 7 n.14). In the latter text Smith did refer to Wrede, as Martyn himself had not done.

SALVATION IS FROM THE JEWS: JOHN
AND THE JEWS POST MARTYN

Who are 'the Jews' in John? In order to avoid the charge of 'anti-Judaism', various proposals were made after the Second World War. Perhaps '*hoi Ioudaioi*' was meant to refer not to the Jews as an *ethnos*, but merely to the people living in the landscape of Judea, and so an appropriate translation would be 'the Judeans' (Lowe 1976)? Or perhaps the reference of the term was not meant to cover *all* Jews, but only the leaders, those who were directly responsible for Jesus' death, so that one might 'translate' the term as 'the Jewish leaders' (von Wahlde 1981–2)? There is fairly general agreement in scholarship that these various suggestions do not succeed. For instance, it is extremely awkward to have Jesus address 'Judeans' in Galilee (6:41 and 6:52) and 'it remains very strange that the Galilean Jesus of Nazareth should be called a "Judean" and not a "Jew" by the Samaritan woman of John 4:9' (Frey 2013b, 345).[20] Similarly, the attempt to restrict 'the Jews' to being the religious authorities founders on the fact that when Jesus teaches in the temple (e.g. 7:14 and 8:20), his immediate hearers, many of whom even came to believe in him (8:30), are called 'Jews' (7:15 and 8:31). That fits 'the crowd' much better than 'the leaders'.[21]

The upshot of the discussion, as has been rightly insisted on by such Jewish scholars as Adele Reinhartz and Ruth Sheridan, is that John's 'Jews' refers to the Jews to be understood as members of 'a national, religious, cultural, and political group for whom the English word *Jew* is the best signifier' (Reinhartz 2001b, 221). We will see that this understanding fits well with the quite variegated use of the term in John. On two points, however, we must supplement this understanding. First, both Reinhartz and Sheridan from time to time suggest that John meant to refer to Jews in all times and places.[22] That seems unpersuasive. Surely, the Jews referred to in this text are those—within the narrative world of the text—with whom Jesus was engaged. It may well be that John also had in mind some other Jews in his own time and place, but to suggest that the text is meant to refer to Jews in *all* times and places seems too much. Secondly, both Reinhartz and Sheridan are averse to the practice of placing the Jews within scare quotes as 'the Jews'. For them, if the text speaks of the

---

[20] For the former point compare, e.g., Frey 2013b, 344–5, Reinhartz 2009, 383, and Sheridan 2013, 689.

[21] For other more restricted possibilities (e.g. specifically rigorously law-abiding Jews or Jewish Christians) see Frey 2013b, 343–4.

[22] See, e.g., Sheridan 2013, 691–2: 'I suggest that οἱ Ἰουδαῖοι has a broader referent point than a subset of Jews and that, as such, the text allows for an interpretation of οἱ Ἰουδαῖοι as the Jews of all times and places, then as now, in an ethnic, geographical, political and "religious"/sense'.

Jews as an *ethnos* and relates to them, then no palliative should be employed to soften the impact of what it does say.[23] Instead, one should acknowledge the force of the term and then go on to relate to it in accordance with the various types of reading that Reinhartz, in particular (2001a; 2009), has helpfully developed: from a 'compliant' reading via a 'sympathetic' and an 'engaged' one to a 'resistant' reading. The instinct behind the scepticism about the use of scare quotes is surely right. Nevertheless, while the scare quotes may well be understood in the falsely palliative way, they may also be understood as a neutral sign to the reader that there is an issue to be further considered about how this particular text employs this term—since it precisely does not just speak of Jews and Judaism in all times and places. It may well be that it will come out with a meaning that one should resist, but it may also come out in other ways. That remains to be seen. 'The Jews' in John's text are *John's* Jews—whoever they are. That is the way I have intended the scare quotes used throughout this book.

If we take it, then, that John's 'Jews' refers primarily to those Jews with whom Jesus was in contact within the narrative world of the Gospel, and secondarily—to the extent that this can at all be proved—to the Jews in John's own time and place, then a question arises on which we will from now on focus our discussion: does John speak from within Judaism or from the outside, as Wrede suggested by speaking of a *Kampfeslage* (229)? The question is 'whether and to what extent the coming into being of the work should be placed in an entirely Jewish context, that is, whether it is still a matter of an inner-Jewish controversy, or whether the polemics already come "from the outside"' (Frey 2013b, 346). Closely connected with this is the question why John decided to speak generically of 'the Jews' instead of specifying them into the various groups.

If we consider the development of scholarship from Wrede via Martyn to Reinhartz and Frey, we may note two things in relation to the question of the perspective from which John speaks. The first is that where Martyn went even further than Wrede in the direction of discovering a specific historical shape of a confrontation with contemporary Judaism behind the

---

[23] Reinhartz (2001b, 227) sees the attempts of New Testament scholars to 'limit the meaning of Ἰουδαῖος and to explain John's comments on Jews and Judaism as a response to Jewish exclusion' as a matter of 'dressing the Johannine Jews in quotation marks' and she fears that 'the effect of such interpretations...is to whitewash this text and absolve it of responsibility for the anti-Jewish emotions and attitude it conveys'. Sheridan (2013, 690, her emphasis) directly discusses the practice and finds that it contains 'an unstated commitment...to the notion that John's use of οἱ Ἰουδαῖοι never meant to incite incendiary attitudes and emotions against *real* Jews, thereby ignoring the *Wirkungsgeschichte* of the Gospel text, which reveals a targeted use of the text against actual Jews'. Once again, I believe one should distinguish rather more sharply between the textual meaning and its *Wirkungsgeschichte*.

text, the more recent development has not only queried Martyn's picture, but also the overall possibility of settling for one particular historical setting in preference to another.[24] Where Frey ends up suggesting that 'the battle with the synagogue and the exclusion of Jewish Christian members of the (Christian) congregation may well in fact go some time back' (2013b, 362), Reinhartz suggests *several possible* historical scenarios once she has disposed of Martyn's expulsion theory: 'the Fourth Gospel's negative comments about *hoi Ioudaioi* could be seen as part of the community's move towards self-definition, which would also entail differentiation from Jews who do not believe in Jesus'; or one might take it that 'the gospel intends the expulsion passages . . . as a warning to its earliest audiences not to return, or turn, to Judaism' (Reinhartz 2009, 391). In this way there is a distinct weakening in both Frey and Reinhartz of the attempt to find a single, specific historical setting behind the text.[25] This fits well with a fundamental caveat against this whole enterprise that Judith Lieu has well articulated:[26]

There is the necessary fragility of the circle that argues from the hostility within the text, to a social context that might generate such hostility, and so back to a solution to the textual hostility. The text we are seeking to explain—the Fourth Gospel—is the only certain evidence for the history of the community, which in turn is held to explain that text (2001, 108–9).[27]

The other thing to be noted is that in spite of this recent weakening of the direct historical impulse, which was so clear in both Wrede and Martyn, all four scholars from whom I have reported more or less explicitly take it that the answer to the question of John's perspective in relation to Judaism (from the inside or from the outside?) is: from the outside. This answer continues to be the preferred one even when scholars have (in practice) given up finding any specific historical sitting. But how do we know that?

In what follows, I present an argument to the effect that *for all we know* John *might* just as well be speaking from within Judaism. The point of this argument is not that that is what he does (we just do not know), only that if

---

[24] The arguments against Martyn's picture are well summarized (with the central bibliographical references) in Frey 2013b, 362–5. A fine statement of Reinhartz's objections, in particular, is Reinhartz 1998.

[25] Note how Frey (2013b, 373) introduces his final account of John's relationship with Judaism in this way: 'However, it would be a foreshortening of the perspective, were one to refer the anti-Jewish polemics of the Gospel of John [with which Frey continues to reckon] back only to its socio-political context'. This opens, rightly to my mind, for a more substance-oriented approach: 'What the battle is about is the high Christology of the Fourth Gospel' (374) etc.

[26] Frey, too, recognizes the methodological problems in this kind of 'mirror-reading' (2013b, 358–9) and quotes Thyen for speaking of a problematic 'Metabasis from the level of the text into history'.

[27] Lieu, to my mind rightly, repeats and develops this problem in Lieu 2008, 170–2.

the argument is valid, then we have *no way at all* to reconstruct a specific historical setting that has more claims than others to being the actual one. If that holds true, we should refrain altogether from positing one or the other specific setting, not because there is anything wrong with asking the question, but because we must recognize that with the evidence at our disposal we just cannot answer it. The circle to which Judith Lieu referred above will simply be too fragile. In that case, we should turn our attention exclusively to the text and try to make out what relationship with Judaism is implied there. In answer to *that* question, I will suggest that there is nothing that may reasonably qualify as 'anti-Judaism' in the text itself— but also that it certainly may have been *interpreted* in such a manner (in its *Wirkungsgeschichte*) once its readers found themselves in an historical situation with two distinct 'religions', Christianity and Judaism, and with one of them in political power.

For the sake of clarity, we should distinguish explicitly between 'John' in two forms. There is the actual writer of this text (no matter how we may further imagine him) and there is the 'author implied in the text'. I argue that just as we cannot make any inferences from the present text to an actual historical situation underlying it, so we cannot reach an answer to the question whether John, the actual writer, wrote from a perspective inside or outside Judaism. For all we know he may have done either. For the text itself does not point unambiguously in either direction. This leaves us with the other 'John', the one who is implied in the text itself. Here we see that *he* did speak from *within* Judaism, *as constructed and insisted upon by himself*—which is why in *that* sense we should not speak of anti-Judaism in the text.

'THE JEWS' IN JOHN: THE FACTS

Before considering the argument, we need to have before us the different ways in which John speaks of 'the Jews': both positively, neutrally, and highly negatively.

The most positive statement is without doubt the important one in 4:22 that 'salvation is from the Jews'. It is noteworthy here that salvation is said to be *from* 'the Jews', not just to be found *in* Judaism. The context clearly points away both from the Samaritan worship of God on Mount Gerizim and *also* from the Jewish one in Jerusalem (4:21) to the true worship of the Father 'in *pneuma* and truth' (4:23). Still, salvation *is* 'from the Jews' (4:22). And Jesus, who has earlier in the passage been identified by the Samaritan woman as a Jew (4:9), even states that 'we', which must here mean 'we Jews', 'worship what we *know since* salvation is from the Jews'. Attempts have been made to downgrade the importance of 4:22 (e.g. Bieringer et al.

2001b, 30–1). That is difficult to understand. The text clearly says two things: both that salvation, which is what Jesus has come to bring (see 4:42), has its *roots* in Judaism—and also that it takes a different form from what one finds in (traditional) Judaism. Thus understood, this text articulates what I call the double message of John's understanding of Jesus and Judaism: both yes (conformity with it) and no (difference from it).[28]

Then there is a large number of places that speak of the Jews in an entirely neutral manner. Here belong the many references to Jewish customs and rituals: 2:6 on 'the Jewish rites of purification'; 4:9 on Jewish practice with the Samaritans; 19:40 on Jewish burial customs and 19:42 on burial on the Jewish Day of Preparation; and a number of entirely neutral references to Jewish festivals (2:13, 5:1, 6:4, 7:2, 11:55).

More difficult are the references to Jesus' Jewish interlocutors. Some are positive. Nicodemus is first introduced as 'a Pharisee', but also 'a leader of the Jews' (3:1, compare 3:10). Though he understands very little in John 3, he turns up again later in the Gospel, where he appears much more positive towards Jesus (7:50, 19:39). He therefore comes to represent *those among 'the Jews'* who are positive towards Jesus. Of these there are many, e.g. in 7:40, 7:41, and 8:30–1. But we also saw that even 'the Jews who had come to believe in him' of 8:31 turned against him more or less immediately when they had been challenged by Jesus (8:31–2). Still, there are other 'Jews' who came to believe in him, e.g. in 10:21 or in 11:45. But then, there are also those 'Jews' whom Jesus challenges and ends up declaring to be children of the devil (8:44). Similarly, Jesus himself speaks of being 'handed over to the Jews' (18:36). As it happens, it is the chief priests Annas and Caiaphas (18:19–24) who deliver Jesus to Pilate (18:28), who then states that 'your own *ethnos* and the chief priests have handed you over to me' (18:35). In the further proceedings it is 'the Jews' (18:38) who 'shout' that they want Barabbas released (18:40). A moment later it is 'the chief priests and their helpers' who 'shout' 'Crucify him!' (19:6), then it is 'the Jews' who 'shout' that Pilate is no longer a friend of Caesar if he releases Jesus (19:12) and again 'shout' 'Crucify him!' (19:15), but the chief priests who declare that 'We have no king but the emperor' (19:15).

All this suggests two things, a fact and a question. First the fact: 'the Jews' are those Jews (understood as an *ethnos*, etc.) with whom Jesus was actually in contact. Some of them were positive towards him, others negative. All of them, however, were Jews. In fact, John has a very clear and pointed understanding of the Jews as an *ethnos*, exactly in the way this

---

[28] In speaking of such a double message, I am adopting the phrase from Turid Karlsen Seim's classic analysis of Luke on women (1994), which shows how Luke both makes extra room for women and also severely restricts their significance.

is also understood by modern scholars.[29] One might well say, therefore, that
John speaks of them as Jews—because they *were* Jews. Then the question,
however: if they were Jews, then why does John constantly speak of them *as*
Jews? Is there some specific perspective that explains why he speaks that
way? Has he some specific *aim* in doing so? This is the view of all four
scholars I drew on above. John, they would say, basically speaks of the
Jews from an outside position, as opponents of whatever sort. And this
reflects that the parting of the ways between something we may henceforth
call 'Judaism' and something we may henceforth call 'Christianity' has
already begun. However, we have seen that the line from the text to any
specific historical setting is extremely insecure. I am proposing, therefore
(and will give my reason in a moment), that we should give up trying to
secure that line and rather ask about the Johannine perspective from
within the text itself, without relying on any historical reconstruction
and without aiming to connect the text with any such reconstruction.[30]

First we need to conclude our rehearsal of the textual facts. In addition to
the positive usage of 'Jews' and the pervasive neutral one, we also found
some distinctly negative uses which raised the question of the point of the
generalized talk—already noted by Wrede—of 'the Jews'. We now need to
take note of some passages where Jesus speaks of things Jewish if not in a
necessarily negative way, then at least distinctly from a distance. For
instance, he at one point when he is actually quoting the Jewish law
against 'the Jews' (10:34–6, see 10:31 for 'the Jews'), famously asks them
whether 'it is not written in *your* law that "I said, you are gods"' (10:34).
Does this not mark a distance? Actually, it need not do so. Jesus might well
be asking pointedly whether the quoted statement is not written in 'your
own' law, in the sense of 'the law to which you are constantly appealing'.
For the sake of the argument, however, let us accept that there are places
where John distances Jesus from something as important to Judaism as the
law.[31] Does this then show us that John is speaking from outside Judaism?

---

[29] This is not always recognized, but see 11:48 where the high priests and the Pharisees
reflect as follows: 'If we let him go on like this, everyone will believe in him, and the Romans
will come and destroy both our (holy) place *and our ethnos*' (from NRSV). See also 11:50–2,
which clearly shows that the *'ethnos'* refers to the Jewish *ethnos* as a whole: [50]'... it is better
for you [says Caiaphas] to have one man die for the people [*laos*] than to have the whole
ethnos destroyed. [51] ... he prophesied that Jesus was about to die for the *ethnos*, [52]and not for
the *ethnos* only, but to gather into one the dispersed children of God' (from NRSV).
[30] Sheridan 2013, 676, takes a quite different route: 'The originating historical situation
behind the Gospel's composition plays a critical role here, as it determines what kind of
meaning we impute to the group referred to as οἱ Ἰουδαῖοι and, therefore, how we find an
equivalent term in English'. Methodologically, this appears to me to put the cart before the
horse.
[31] Frey 2013b, 358, lists the following references for this: 7:51, 8:17, 10:34, 12:34, 15:25,
18:31, 19:7. Of these, 7:51 (Nicodemus to the Pharisees: 'our law'), 12:34 (the crowd: 'we have
heard from the law'), 18:31 (Pilate to the high priest: 'in accordance with your law'), and 19:7

Here, too, we may take explicit note of the three famous passages that speak of people being 'put out of the synagogue' (*aposynagôgoi*, 9:22, 12:42, and 16:2) and of their 'fearing the Jews' (9:22, compare 7:13; 19:38, 20:19). We will return to the *aposynagôgoi* sayings. Here we should just note that in the last of the three sayings Jesus prophesies to the disciples in the Farewell Discourse that 'they will make you *aposynagôgoi*' (16:2). Does this not indicate that at the time of writing some Jewish Christians had in fact been made so? And if so, is Jesus not here made to speak at a considerable distance from Judaism?

From this brief overview we may conclude that while there are some passages speaking of 'the Jews' that appear quite positive towards Judaism and a large number of passages that speak entirely neutrally about them for the very good reason that Jesus' interlocutors were in fact Jews, the question of a certain distance from 'the Jews' is raised by the fact that John often *generalizes* negatively about them (not least in the passion story: *the Jews* were responsible for Jesus' death!)—and then also by the *aposynagôgoi* statements and the places where Jesus is made to speak of 'your law' and the like. In addition, some of the references to 'the Jews' are extremely hateful in tone, as, of course, in 8:44 where Jesus carefully argues that those 'Jews' that John has described a single page earlier as believing in Jesus (8:30) have the devil as their father.

These are the internal facts, to which more will be added when we broaden the perspective from merely looking at the use of the term *hoi Ioudaioi*. However, the strategy will be to stay all through within the perspective of the text itself and to ask whether it will be possible to identify in it a coherent position in relation to Judaism, one that also holds together the various uses of the term *hoi Ioudaioi* that we have just noted.

JOHN AND THE JEWS: THE ARGUMENT

I emphasize that what I am after is the possibility of identifying a coherent position in relation to Judaism within the text itself. Methodologically, we cannot begin from the outside, from some guess about the Evangelist's position on a trajectory that ends with a full 'parting of the ways'. For in order to support such a guess, we would always be thrown back on the text itself. We must begin, therefore (and end, as I will be arguing), with the text and with 'John' as the 'implied author' of that text. Our scholarly target is the understanding of Jesus' relationship with Judaism that the

(the Jews to Pilate: 'we have a law') do not seem distancing in the relevant sense. By contrast, 8:17 (Jesus to the Pharisees: 'it is written in your law') and 15:25 (Jesus to the disciples of what is written 'in their law') are.

implied author is aiming to transmit to the 'implied "model" readers' of the text itself.

I will now bring in for comparison a text from outside the Johannine corpus, about which we happily know more than about John. The aim is to show that this text, which denigrates 'the Jews' just as violently as John does, reflects a position on the part of the (actual) writer, which is not at all distanced from Judaism. On the contrary, it is written from within Judaism itself. I will also show what the rhetorical function is in that text of denigrating 'the Jews'. As already indicated, the argument to be constructed on this basis runs as follows. If I am right about the text to be quoted and what it tells us *as a possibility* about John, we must conclude, not that John, too, was writing from a perspective within Judaism, but instead that *we cannot settle whether or not* he was doing so. And then we are only left with one option: of trying to see whether we can make sense of John's handling of Judaism within the world of the text *completely on its own*. The move we are forced to make will be the one from John, the writer, to John, the implied author.

Here is the text I have announced: 1 Thessalonians 2:14–16. In 2:13, Paul has given thanks to God that his addressees, the Thessalonians, have received his own preaching 'not as a human word but as what it really is, God's word, which is also at work in you believers' (NRSV).[32] He continues:

[14]For you, brothers, became imitators of the congregations of God in Christ Jesus that are in Judea; for you, too, suffered the same things from your own compatriots as they did from the Jews, [15](those) who killed both the Lord Jesus and the prophets and drove us out (*ekdiôxantôn*) and who displease God and (are) opposed to all human beings [16]when they prevent us from speaking to the Gentiles in order that they may be saved. Thus they have constantly filled up the measure of their sins. But the wrath has overtaken them at last.

This passage belongs in the earliest written text in the New Testament.[33] It was directed to Christ believers who were not Jews, but it was dictated by a man, Paul, who was himself a Jew and who continued to the end of his life to understand the Christ faith that he preached to be a form of Judaism. This is clear from what is probably his last preserved letter, Romans, which

[32] Note here the almost Johannine thought—essential to Paul—of the 'word' (*logos*) being *active in* (*energeisthai en*) believers. How? Through the *pneuma* (even though Paul does not explicitly say so here).

[33] It should be explicitly noted that the passage has been frequently contested ('over the last two hundred years', says Malherbe 2000, 164) as an interpolation made by a later redactor. I take it, however (with Malherbe and many others, and crucially for my argument), that the text 'was written by Paul and that it belongs in the position in which the textual tradition has transmitted it' (Malherbe 2000, 165). For further discussion and references, see Malherbe's thorough analysis (2000, 164–79).

climaxes in Paul's claim (Rom. 11:13–36) that his immediate addressees, the non-Jewish Christ believers in Rome, are only wild branches that have been grafted into an olive tree whose rich root is solidly planted in Jewish soil, and then goes on to express the hope that eventually all Jews will turn to faith in Christ. But Paul's Jewish credentials are equally clear from 1 Thessalonians itself (e.g. 1:9–10). So, Paul, the Jew, who took the Christ faith to be a thoroughly Jewish form of 'religion', could describe those Jews who had not turned to God in order to be saved through Jesus in the extremely hateful ways just quoted, ways that are not a bit milder than John's in 8:44. That is the first point.

The second point is that the quoted passage is clearly part of Paul's paraenesis.[34] He is commending the Thessalonians for 'imitating' the Christ-believing congregations in Judea. This kind of 'imitation' is a thoroughly paraenetic tool. He is also comparing their present sufferings with those in Judea. That, too, is a paraenetic tool. Finally, he is implicitly comparing their sufferings with those of Jesus and the prophets and more directly with his own problems with the Jews who, as he claims, have tried to prevent him from preaching to the Gentiles, that is, themselves, so that they might be saved. All of this is thoroughly paraenetic.

The third point is that as part of his paraenesis, Paul clearly amplifies rhetorically whatever problems he may have had with the Jews (who *here* clearly stand for those Jews who did not turn to Jesus Christ). Not only have they 'prevented' him (though unsuccessfully, we must understand) from preaching to the Gentiles: they have also '*driven us out*' (*ek-diôkein*), which Paul places more or less on the same level as their having killed both Jesus and the prophets. Here one might well ask: have they both (tried to) *prevent* Paul from preaching to the Gentiles—and then also *driven him out* (presumably from Judaism), which would probably have *eased* his preaching strategy? But that question is precisely beside the point. Paul is out to construct as forceful a picture as possible of all the bad things the Jews have done to Jesus, the prophets—and himself.

Then the argument: if this is a correct reading of Paul, both in this specific passage and in general, then we must say that there is nothing in the Fourth Gospel that is, as it were, *more* 'distanced' from Judaism than this. And then we cannot conclude that John, as opposed to Paul, *must* have been distanced from Judaism. I am not suggesting here that John (the writer of this text) did have the kind of relationship with Judaism that Paul had and so that *he* positively did speak from *within* Judaism. I am only saying that he *might just as well* have done so. We cannot, therefore, on the

---

[34] It is impossible not to mention here the work of Abraham Malherbe on Pauline paraenesis and 1 Thessalonians, in particular, as a paraenetic letter. All the relevant articles (from 1970, 1983, 1990, and 1992) are reprinted in Malherbe 2014.

basis of John's text itself, say *anything* about any distancing or the opposite of John (the writer) from Judaism. For all we can know, he may have spoken from within Judaism—*or* from without it.

Once that question has been set aside (does the real author, John, speak from within or from without Judaism?), there remains the quite different task, for which we are much better equipped, of trying to make coherent sense of the position in relation to Judaism of the many things said about it in John's text itself. Can we succeed here?

JOHN AND THE JEWS: THE SOLUTION

I am insisting, then, on reading John's relationship with Judaism only from within the text as it is articulated in the text—what we might call *John's textual view* of Jesus in relationship to Judaism. Here I think we can find the double message I hinted at, one that is coherent enough in itself.

On the one hand, the Jews were responsible for the death of Jesus, and they were children of the devil. Here belongs anything that is said of any Jews in negative terms anywhere in the Fourth Gospel, for instance, when Jesus distances himself from 'your' law. In all this 'the Jews' continue to refer to real Jews, but here they refer to those (real) Jews who did not accept Jesus as the Son of God. Those are the main culprits—more so even than the rest of the non-believing world, which is also present in the Gospel's narrative world, but remains somewhat on the fringe. One can well understand this focus on those Jews: as John understood Jesus Christ, those Jews were, as it were, *closest* to having the proper understanding; *only* they did not have it *at all*.

On the other hand, many Jews did believe in Jesus, no matter how 'initial' their belief should be understood to be. There is therefore nothing wrong with Judaism *as such*. Quite to the contrary. What the Christ-believing Jews grasped was, for instance, that Jesus was 'the prophet' or 'the Christ'. On this side, then, belong all the claims in John that aim to situate Jesus Christ within Judaism as its 'fulfilment', e.g. 5:46 ('If you believed Moses, you would believe me, for he wrote about me', NRSV) or 10:35 ('If [the law] has called those "gods" to whom the *logos* of God has come—and *Scripture* [*hê graphê*] *cannot be annulled* [!]—etc.'). It is true that as seen from the perspective of traditional, 'normative' Judaism as represented by the Jews who did *not* accept Jesus as the Son of God (etc.), this supposed fulfilment is an odd one, indeed something of an affront. For instance, it resituates the temple completely (2:18–22). Nevertheless, it remains John's claim that Jesus constitutes the fulfilment of Judaism, the *true* Judaism that the non-believers just have not grasped.

The moment one begins to speak of 'fulfilment', the question immediately arises in the modern scholarly mind whether this is also a matter of 'replacement' or indeed (horror!) of 'supersessionism'. Here the answer must be that as long as we are trying to grasp the understanding of the implied author, we should answer no. In terms of what it was taken by him to be, the Christ Jesus fulfilment was neither a replacement nor a matter of supersessionism. What mattered was something else: that *all* Jews (and the rest of the world, in addition) should come to believe in this *fulfilment* of Judaism, that is, in Jesus as the Son of God.

I am fully aware that this understanding of John's double message on Judaism will seem unsatisfactory, certainly from a modern Jewish perspective (there is definitely no room for *us* in this), but also from an enlightened Christian or religious studies perspective, which will immediately ask this question: no matter what John himself *says*, how should we *actually* place him in relation to Judaism, not just from his own inside perspective, but from a coolly critical outside perspective (or even a Jewish one)? But that is where I am insisting that we do not know and cannot know the answer. For instance, did John, the writer, mean to 'abolish the temple' (for all or for Jews or ...)? We just cannot know. We do not have the required material for John—as we have it for Paul—that may help us answer such a question. (And in the case of Paul, too, it is frightfully contested.) What we *can* know and see in the text itself is that the implied author takes *everything* to be ultimately focused on Jesus as the Son of God. Grasping that—this is the text's ultimate message—is the *necessary and sufficient* condition for what the whole thing is all about: salvation for human beings (Jews and all others). John's double message regarding the Jews serves the point of inculcating precisely that more fundamental message.

This is where the present scholarly issue of the relationship of John to Judaism fits intimately into the argument of this book. What I have been concerned to show all through the book is the way in which John addresses in narrative terms a large number of philosophical issues that all point in the direction of showing who Jesus is and of bringing out (to the reader) the paramount importance of understanding just that. John's handling of 'the Jews', in *all* its facets, serves exactly that purpose, including, not least, his negative treatment of them. In one of her many helpful works on the matter, Adele Reinhartz wrote (2001, 225):

the Gospel's anti-Judaism is a by-product of the Evangelist's strong convictions regarding the identity and salvific role of Jesus.

We will come back to the idea of 'anti-Judaism' in a moment. Here I will just remark that John's handling of the Jews is not just a 'by-product' of those other convictions: it is there—and quite centrally—*in order to* bring *them* out. John does two things to bring his understanding of Jesus across.

The first and entirely positive one is to turn the inside out of Mark's 'Messianic secret' and make Jesus proclaim again and again who and what he is. The other, which moves from neutral to strongly negative, is to focus on the reactions of Jesus' addressees, and here to play up exceedingly strongly the opposition that Jesus' self-declarations met with. That happens when John describes the 'divisions' among the Jews and even more clearly when he recounts the verbal confrontations between Jesus and the distinctly non-believing Jews. All through, the aim is a single one: to bring out and insist as strongly as possible on Jesus' uniqueness as the Son of God vis-à-vis any other possible understanding of him.

Finally, to come back to Wrede, let us ask his question: for whom did John write in depicting the Jews in those many ways? As we noted, Wrede did see the correct answer, but he stepped back from giving it the significance it has in the text itself when John declares that he wrote for Christ believers 'so that *you* may (fully) believe that Jesus is the Messiah, the Son of God, and that through believing (in that way) *you* may have life in his name' (John 20:31). John's depiction of the Jews and their reactions to Jesus serves the aim of bringing out who Jesus was and is and of showing the already Christ-believing readers of the text ('you') that that is the only understanding that matters. In this way, John's approach is actually closely similar to what we found in Paul in 1 Thessalonians 2, where the denigration of the Jews also served a paraenetic aim.

If John is in this way strongly active in writing his whole account for a distinct purpose, which is now no longer that of confronting the (non-believing) Jews for its own sake, but the quite different one of *bringing across his own message to his Christ-believing addressees*, then it is worth spending a few words on his peculiar use of the term *aposynagôgos* in 9:22, 12:42, and 16:2, which is perhaps the feature of the text that points most strongly in the direction of a specific historical situation underlying the text—and certainly one that was understood in that way by Martyn. For comparison commentators regularly refer to Jesus' predictions of woe in Mark 13 and parallels (Matthew 10:17–18; Luke 21:12–13). Here is Mark 13:9:

[9]As for yourselves, beware; for they will hand you over to [Jewish] councils (*synedria*); and you will be beaten in synagogues; and you will stand before governors and kings because of me, as testimony to them (from NRSV).

This is somewhat vague and general in historical terms. Still, if one asks whether those addressed continue to be understood as members of the synagogue, the most plausible answer is yes. Being beaten in the synagogue certainly did not imply exclusion from it.[35]

---

[35] It is noteworthy that Matthew 10:17 appears to spell out the meaning of Mark's εἰς συναγωγὰς δαρήσεσθε in what is linguistically an even clearer form: 'they will flog you *in* their

Commentators also refer to Luke 6:22:

[22]Blessed are you when people (*hoi anthrôpoi*) hate you, and when they exclude (*aphorizein*) you, revile you, and defame you [literally 'cast out (*ekballein*) your name as evil'] because of the Son of Man (from NRSV).

This is also general in the sense that it speaks of all 'people' (as against the Jews), but at the same time quite specific when it speaks, not of being 'handed over' to certain institutions, as in Mark, but of what we may call 'social harassment' specifically focused on 'excluding' and 'casting out' the Christ believers.

In light of these texts, how should John's use of the term *aposynagôgos* be understood? Let us consider 9:22. Here the parents of the man born blind tell 'the Jews' (9:18), who are here identical with 'the Pharisees' (9:13), to go and ask their son himself about what they want to know. The reason is that 'they feared the Jews' (9:22). As we saw, 'fear of the Jews' comes up elsewhere in the Gospel (7:13; 19:38, 20:19). And this is now further explained in the rest of the verse:

[22.]...for the Jews had already (*êdê*) agreed that were somebody to confess him [Jesus] to be the Messiah, he should be put out of the synagogue [literally become *aposynagôgos*].

This is a very careful statement. Though the term 'agreed' (*syntithesthai*) may signify various levels of formality, the articulation of what had been 'agreed' upon sounds quite formal. And the whole thing becomes even more striking when one notes John's use of 'already'. He seems to be saying that the well-known (formal) decision to exclude explicit Christ believers from 'the synagogue', alias Judaism, that his readers know from their own time had *already*—*against* what they might otherwise have expected—been taken *then*. This may or may not stand in some tension with what Jesus says in the third *aposynagôgos* statement (16:2), where he *predicts* as something lying in the future that 'they' will 'put you out of the synagogue' (literally make you *aposynagôgoi*). In any case, it appears clear that in his statement in 9:22, John is presupposing some form of 'agreement' in his own time of excluding explicit Christ believers from Judaism. Or: that is how it has been almost universally taken by scholars.

However, in light of the comparable passages from Mark, Matthew, and Luke, *and* the care of John 9:22 itself, which includes both the invention of a new, highly suggestive, but also opaque term (*aposynagôgos*) and the almost perverse suggestion (by means of 'already', which cries out as a

---

synagogues (ἐν ταῖς συναγωγαῖς αὐτῶν)'. Luke 21:12 is more general: 'they will arrest you and persecute (διώκειν) you; they will hand you over to synagogues and prisons, and you will be brought before kings etc.'.

hoax) that there had been some form of formal 'agreement' against explicit Christ believers already in Jesus' own lifetime, it appears much more plausible that what we are witnessing here is in fact an invention by the Evangelist himself.[36] In order to bring out as sharply as possible what he was after (to show that Jesus was the Son of God), he *invented* an explicit, quasi-legal action (like a modern-day 'fatwa') by those on the other side of the divide and he did this as part of his comprehensive picture of an unbridgeable conflict between those Jews—here called '*the* Jews'—who did not believe in Jesus as the Messiah (and Son of God) and those who did.[37] In that way the absolute character of the turn to Jesus would become wholly clear. What John has done is to take the idea we found in Luke of 'social harassment' focused on exclusion and turn it into a much more formal practice of taking quasi-legal action. Where in Luke the idea pertained to 'all people', John has narrowed it down into being about the Jews. But he had a predecessor for this: Paul in 1 Thess. 2:14–16, who had spoken of the Jews who had killed Jesus and 'persecuted or driven us out' (*ek-diôkein*) and 'prevented (*kôlyein*) us'—in whatever way—from preaching the gospel. That it is this notion of 'exclusion'—fully present already in Paul—that John aims to employ for his own purposes becomes clear in chapter 9 itself when he notes that the Pharisaic Jews ended up 'throwing him [the man himself] out' (*ek-ballein exô*, 9:34, 35). In 9:22 John makes formal the Pauline and Lukan idea of social harassment focused on exclusion by turning it into a quasi-legal action. And he does this for a rhetorical purpose. He employs the resistance of 'the Jews' to make his own understanding of Jesus' uniqueness as clear as possible.

'ANTI-JUDAISM' IN JOHN?

So, is John 'anti-Jewish'? No. John did see Jesus as the fulfilment of Judaism, and his denigrating talk of 'the Jews'—always to be counterbalanced with his positive talk of those Jews who did come to believe in Jesus—is in no way worse than Paul's in 1 Thessalonians 2. We cannot therefore conclude that John (as the writer of this text) was any more 'distanced' from Judaism than Paul. (But we cannot either conclude that he was not.) What we can see is that in the text itself John elaborated with gusto a contrast with 'the

---

[36] While not going nearly so far as I do, Hartwig Thyen at least suggests (entirely rightly to my mind) that the term *aposynagôgos* is 'an ad hoc creation' by John himself (Thyen 2015, 465).

[37] Why was the supposed 'fatwa' directed against confessing Jesus as 'the Messiah' and not as the Son of God, which is John's own basic concern? Surely, because 'the Messiah' was the more traditionally Jewish title and so would be better suited for an invented quasi-legal 'agreement' among the Jews.

Jews'—to be understood here as those ('ethnic') Jews who did not believe in Jesus—in order to make his contrasting picture of Jesus as sharp as possible. This cannot be called 'anti-Judaism' as long as one stays with the view of the implied author in the text itself. In this sense there is not 'anti-Judaism' in the Fourth Gospel, nor is it 'anti-Jewish'.

But is John's 'high Christology' not in itself necessarily 'anti-Jewish', no matter what John himself may have thought? Do 'the Jews' not have a real point when they threaten to stone Jesus 'for blasphemy, because you, though only a human being, are making yourself God' (10:33, NRSV)? Here again we may deploy the argument I have constructed: Paul, too, describes Jesus in a closely similar way; but Paul himself did not consider this 'anti-Jewish'. The passage I have in mind is the famous Christ 'hymn' in Philippians 2:6–11, in which it is said that Christ 'though he was *in the form of God*, did not regard *equality with God* as something to be exploited' (6, NRSV) and so became human and died on a cross (7–8), with the consequence that 'God . . . highly exalted him and gave him the name that is above every name' (9, NRSV): . . . 'Jesus Christ is Lord' (11, NRSV). This text may be older than Paul himself (as many scholars believe). But Paul found it wholly adequate—and did not take it to be anti-Jewish. John may have thought the same.

It is entirely different when we consider later readings of these texts. Once 'Judaism' and 'Christianity' had come to be seen as two different religions, and once Christianity had come into power in the Roman Empire (and beyond), it became 'natural' for Christians to find those two religions in the text itself. Then John's 'Jews' would become the Jews as the Jewish *ethnos* who had *by definition* rejected Jesus—instead of merely standing for those *among* the Jews who had not come to believe in Jesus (as against those *other* Jews who had). And then the road was open to transfer all of John's (deplorable) hostility towards those (and primarily those *Jews*) who had not believed in Jesus onto 'the Jews'.[38] Then John (alias the Fourth Gospel) *became* anti-Jewish.[39]

---

[38] In calling John's hostility 'deplorable', I wish to indicate that I am personally against the whole literary strategy that I have attempted to lay bare and have ascribed to John of using a confrontation of opposed views to inculcate one's own view. As John himself clearly shows in the text, such a strategy both invites and condones the use of violence. My only aim here has been to show that the strategy is there in the text and that it has the functions I have stated. As we can then also see, it also has had ghastly *consequences* in its *Wirkungsgeschichte*.

[39] My conclusions on 'anti-Judaism' and John will appear unsatisfactory to those, like Adele Reinhartz and Judith Lieu (see also the latter's fine discussion in Lieu 2008), who have most strongly expressed their concern about the anti-Jewish dimensions of the Fourth Gospel. However, *if* one accepts the distinction I have relied on between John, the writer, and John, the implied author, and if one accepts that we cannot say anything about the former, then the basic issue is whether within the text itself John speaks from inside or

However, let me just repeat here the basic point that in these reflections on John and Judaism, I have been talking *only* of the relationship with Judaism (real Judaism, that is) *of the text itself.* What its real author 'meant' and where he and any 'Johannine community' belonged on the trajectory of the parting of the ways are wholly different issues on which we can say nothing at all no matter how much we might want to do so. I present this as a reasonably strong challenge to much scholarship on this issue.

outside Judaism. And here, although Lieu is right to claim that it would be a *non sequitur* to conclude from 'John's essential "Jewishness"' and his 'pervasive indebtedness to the Scriptures' that the Fourth Gospel 'cannot be anti-Jewish' (2008, 180–1), it seems clear that the Gospel *seriously claims* Jesus Christ to be the fulfilment of Judaism. If so, it cannot sensibly be termed 'anti-Jewish'. The Gospel precisely does have a double message about Judaism, which also includes a positive one.

XII

THE GOSPEL AS A
WHOLE—IMAGERY
AND ESCHATOLOGY

CLARITY IN THE READER: THE VARIOUS LITERARY TOOLS

One of the most stimulating, fruitful and, indeed, necessary developments in modern Johannine scholarship hs been the increasing attention given to a wide range of literary features of this text that cry out for further elucidation once scholars have recognized their existence. Here belongs, for instance, the attention given to questions of genre, including the recognition that many different ancient genres may be employed to illuminate this text. Another literary motif that has also received renewed attention is the lawsuit motif that may well be seen to underlie longer stretches of the text. While attention to such themes is often genuinely illuminating, it must always fulfil two requirements, first, that any outside material is put directly to use in throwing new light on the text itself, and secondly, that the resulting reading of the text is connected with other themes so that one may at least make a gesture towards an overall reading.

In the context of this book, the latter point is the more important one. Both approaches may be employed to that effect. For instance, a comparison with the concept of 'recognition' in drama may very easily be connected with the theme I have shown to be central of coming to understand who and what Jesus is.[1] Similarly, to the extent that the lawsuit motif can be shown genuinely to illuminate specific stretches of text, one can also almost immediately see its relevance to the theme of the confrontation with 'the Jews', whose purpose I have just explained.[2] The

---

[1] See, e.g., Bro Larsen 2008.
[2] For this theme, compare Lincoln 2000, Parsenios 2010, and Bekken 2015.

point here is the exceedingly banal one that any analysis of a given literary feature should never be left alone, but always connected with other aspects of the text.

Other literary features do not rely so directly on other texts but can be seen to be already present in the text itself the moment it is addressed from a general literary perspective. Here belongs the attention given to 'symbols' in the text in some early articles by John Painter (1979) and Xavier Léon-Dufour (1980–1) and then continued in Culpepper 1983 and Craig Koester (2003/1995). In fact, Dodd 1953a had already been there in ten pages (133–43) that attempt to cover both 'symbols', 'metaphors', and Johannine 'signs', and to connect them all with the (Middle) Platonic, 'allegorical' ways of thinking to be found in Philo of Alexandria. The result is emblematic of Dodd's form of Platonism (1953a, 140):

His φῶς ἀληθινόν ['true light', cf. John 1:9] is the archetypal light, αὐτὸ τὸ φῶς [never in John], of which every visible light in this world is a μίμημα ['copy', never in John] or symbol; his ἄρτος ἀληθινός ['true bread', cf. 6:32] is the reality which lies within and behind every visible and tangible loaf, in so far as it can properly be so called; and his ἄμπελος ἀληθινή ['true vine', cf. 15:1] is that which makes a vine a vine, at once its inner essence, and the transcendental real existence, which abides while all concrete vines grow and decay.

Beautiful, but is it John?

Another, later trend in scholarship has focused in particular on the careful analysis of 'images', including 'metaphors', and insisted—often recalling Paul Ricoeur's analysis of metaphors (1975, 1976)—on the genuinely metaphorical quality of this way of speaking, which means that it cannot be exchanged for some other form of speech that might spell out its meaning. Instead, the meaning is to be found both in the construction of the individual metaphor itself and in the network constituted by the varied use of any given metaphor throughout the whole text or even the overlapping networks of several distinct, but also intuitively connected networks of metaphors.[3]

Both types of focus—on 'symbolism' and 'imagery'—are valuable, even though there is also some lack of clarity when scholars speak of 'symbols' and when of 'metaphors' and exactly how these two are taken to differ. In the context of this book, I wish to pinpoint one feature that is shared by both forms of attention to the 'figurative' level of the Johannine text: that they ultimately aim to celebrate the supposed 'mystery' of the text and its message.

[3] An early, comprehensive example of this approach is van der Watt 2000.

CLARITY IN THE READER: CULPEPPER ON SYMBOLS

For a useful differentiation of 'metaphor' and 'symbol' we may draw on Culpepper's definitions in *Anatomy of the Fourth Gospel*. On 'metaphor' Culpepper (1983, 181) quotes the definition given by the literary critic Norman Friedman:

The basic definition of *metaphor* is that it is a device which speaks of one thing (tenor) in terms which are appropriate to another (vehicle), with the vehicle serving as the source of traits to be transferred to the tenor.

Culpepper continues:

When Jesus says, 'I am the bread of life' (6:35) in the context of a discourse on the true bread, the reader is given both the tenor ('I') and the vehicle ('the bread of life'). Our task is to infer the relationship between the tenor and the vehicle and in doing so to understand those features of the identity of Jesus which led the author to use the metaphor.

A symbol differs from a metaphor in that the symbol presents only the vehicle. Here the reader's task is both to discern the tenor and also (as in the metaphor) to construct the wider meaning of the symbol as referring to that tenor. Culpepper notes that 'a symbol is not arbitrary but bears some inherent analogical relationship to that which it symbolizes' (1983, 182). Nevertheless, 'the symbol means or expresses something more or something else than its plain or superficial meaning' (182). Culpepper therefore speaks of a 'surplus of meaning' or 'semantic energy' (182–3). Symbols 'call for explanation and simultaneously resist it' (183). And so one may speak of 'a residual mystery that escapes our intellects' (in a quotation from William York Tindall) and 'the mystery of a symbolic narrative' (183)—which is where I begin to have doubts.

Later Culpepper provides an excellent discussion of 'the three core symbols' in John, which are 'light, water, and bread' (189). He shows convincingly that they are 'expanding symbols' (189). For instance, by the latter half of the Gospel, the symbol of light has 'expanded to the point of explosion so that the mere suggestions of its presence [e.g. in 18:3, 18:18, 20:1, 21:4, and 21:9] evoke the heavy thematic and theological load it acquired in its earlier, more explicit development' (192). And the same holds for the two other symbols of water and bread (192–7).

This is all convincing, but a problem arises in Culpepper's conclusion to the chapter, in which he—in itself rightly—brings together what he has said about John's use of misunderstandings, ironies, and symbolism throughout the Gospel. The three themes 'are often interwoven' (199) in this way:

The metaphors and symbols are misunderstood by the dialogue partner, creating a setting for irony and underlining the importance of perceiving the symbolic meaning of Jesus, his words, and his works.

Again, however, there is a 'surplus of meaning' (199) and again Culpepper speaks repeatedly of 'the mystery made present in Jesus' that 'John points to' (200), ending as follows (201):

The world the reader knows points symbolically, at least when viewed from John's point of view, to the realm which neither author nor reader can fully comprehend. The symbols are in this regard bridges by which the reader may cross in some elusive sense into the reality and mystery, the life, which they represent. The symbols 'sing of the existence' of that which they symbolize, but more, they move us to sing their song as well. They give it immediacy, approachability, and even perceptibility, while never robbing it of mystery or relieving the judgment upon those who fail to understand it or its symbols.

Culpepper is certainly right to connect the three motifs of misunderstanding, irony, and symbolism. But the point of using these literary tools is in all three cases to generate clarity, not to point 'in some elusive sense' to any kind of residual 'mystery'. Recall the notion of 'triangularity' that I introduced to pinpoint the fact that this text operates with three agents: Jesus, his immediate hearers, and the reader. By showing how the immediate interlocutors misunderstand and how *they* do not grasp the tenor and wider meaning of the symbols that Jesus, on his side, relishes in dangling before their noses, the text implies that the real meaning of it all is quite clear—to Jesus and the reader. Jesus colludes with the reader above the heads of his immediate interlocutors in order to show *the reader* the full meaning in all its clarity.

There is a good reason why Culpepper does not see this. In his fine account of the symbol of water he says this of the 'living water' of 4:10: 'living water is a symbol for the new life *or the Spirit* of which Jesus is the giver and source' (194, my emphasis). Indeed, yes: Jesus' phrase 'living water' has all the richness of meaning as a vehicle for metaphorical speech that makes it a potent symbol. But it also has a distinct and direct *reference* (its tenor), which is not 'new life' in some 'spiritual' sense, but quite concretely 'the Spirit' in the form of the material *pneuma* that believers will receive. There is no residual mystery here. Instead, there is the clarity of a precise reference.

Culpepper half sees this—but then again does not. A little later he brings in 7:38:

The narrator provides a partial explanation which links the motif with the giving of the Spirit through Jesus' death (7:39). Living water therefore points to Jesus, the revelation, the new life, *and the means by which one enters it, the Spirit* (194, my emphasis).

No, the phrase 'rivers of living water' in 7:38 *refers* to one thing only: the *pneuma*, which believers will eventually receive upon Jesus' death. It does not just point (elusively) to 'Jesus, the revelation, the new life', and 'the Spirit'. *Rightly* understood, Culpepper is right: 'Jesus' does bring the *pneuma*; the 'revelation' is the *logos* (God's plan) that culminates in believers' receiving the *pneuma*; and the 'new life' is the resurrected life brought about by the *pneuma*. Only, the meaning of the symbol is much more direct than Culpepper suggests. And John counts on his reader to see it in all its clarity.[4]

Culpepper is not alone here. In his widely praised book on *Symbolism in the Fourth Gospel*, Craig Koester begins, as he should, by producing a definition of 'symbol'. He declares (2003, 3–4) that he will

draw questions and insights from various areas of research, while keeping our focus on the Fourth Gospel and trying to let our general observations about symbolism conform as much as possible to the distinctive contours of the text.

The result is this (4, my emphasis):

Here, however, we will focus the definition: A symbol is an image, an action, or a person that is *understood to have transcendent significance*. In Johannine terms, symbols span the chasm between what is 'from above' and what is 'from below' without collapsing the distinction.

Here the terribly question-begging notion of 'the transcendent' is built directly into the definition of the symbol. It should come as no surprise, therefore, that Koester may also say this (3, my emphasis):

The Gospel presents the paradox that the divine is made known through what is earthly and the universal is disclosed through what is particular. This gives Johannine symbolism a tensive, dialectical quality that *conveys transcendent reality without finally delimiting it*. The Gospel's testimony, given in symbolic language, is a vehicle for the Spirit's work; and it is through the Spirit that the testimony becomes effective, drawing readers to know the mystery that is God.

Here not only Johannine symbolism, but the 'Spirit' too is connected with 'transcendent reality'. This is something Koester apparently knows beforehand. From where? Surely, from a presupposed (but possibly unacknowledged) 'Platonic' understanding of the kind we noted above in Dodd.[5]

---

[4] One might well say that John has made John the Baptist literally *say* what he intends his reader to understand. When the Baptist states that he himself 'baptizes with water' (1:16, 33), while Jesus is one who 'baptizes with holy *pneuma*' (as God himself has told him, 1:33), then there is almost no step to an understanding of the 'living water' that Jesus gives, according to 4:10, *as* (holy) *pneuma*.

[5] See Koester's emphasis on what is available to the senses in his understanding of 'symbol' (2003, 5) '...we will include the images, the actions, and representative figures in our study of the Gospel's symbolism because they function similarly in the text. Each conveys something of transcendent significance through something accessible to the senses.'

CLARITY IN THE READER: ZIMMERMANN ON
IMAGERY (INCLUDING METAPHORS)

Ruben Zimmermann is the scholar who has done most to place Johannine imagery on the research map. Zimmermann 2006 is a superb overview (with a helpful *Forschungsgeschichte*, 2–9) that makes a large number of points that one can only applaud.

One such point is that against the background of a lack of relevant terminology in the Gospel itself,[6] Zimmermann elucidates the meaning of the single term that does belong here, that of *paroimia* (10:6, 16:25bis, and 16:29). In the ancient general understanding, the term may stand either for a 'proverb' or more broadly 'a manner of speech (*modus dicendi*) that—as shown in the parallels to metaphoric and allegorical speech—is characterized by its figurative quality and mystery' (12). Thus even such a translation as 'figurative speech' or 'riddle' might be appropriate. In John, however, as Zimmermann shows, the term is closely connected with the motif of the comprehension or otherwise on the part of the disciples. While it directly refers to Jesus' speech, it is used by John to focus on the enigmatic character of that speech to the disciples, and Zimmermann notes that this use is closely connected—not least in 16:25–9—with the Gospel's 'theological' time horizon, according to which the disciples only understood, and only *could* understand, after Jesus' death and resurrection (14). That is all fine. It is worth adding, however, that both in chapters 10 and 16 John's talk of *paroimia* is immediately preceded by two clear cases of 'figurative' speech by Jesus: the shepherd (10:1–5) and the woman giving birth (16:21). It is doubtful, therefore, that one may take the term to cover *everything* Jesus says and does in the Gospel as a whole. Once again, we should beware of finding 'mystery' where the text itself aims to be rather more precise.

Another helpful point is that Zimmermann provides a very broad definition of 'image' that allows it to cover 'metaphor', 'symbol', and 'narrative images' (15–16). He also attempts to 'describe text-immanent compositional techniques on a literary–synchronic level, which demonstrate how John formed and composed his images within the framework of his complete work' (30). Here he provides examples of 'clusters of images within a smaller passage of text', of variations in individual images across the whole Gospel, and of 'image networks within the entire Gospel' (30–6). All of this provides extremely helpful tools for analysing the

---

[6] See Zimmermann 2006, 15: 'John does not use any of the figurative terms such as *metaphora* (metaphor), *allēgoria* (allegory), *symbolon* (symbol), *mythos* (myth), *parabolē* (parable) or *ainigma/ainigmos* (riddle) that were already in use in ancient times and are seen particularly in the rhetorical tropes ("Tropenlehre")'.

pervasive figurative quality of this text. The overall picture is beautifully captured (33):

...the development of individual motifs in different forms can be seen as a recurring stylistic element of Johannine imagery. Instead of assuming that internal contradictions need to be smoothed out by means of literary–critical hypothesis or methodical synchronization, we must recognize that the formal diversity of the images is the author's conscious principle of presentation.

Finally, one should greet with enthusiasm what Zimmerman says of the 'pedagogical function' of the use of imagery in the Gospel (42, my emphasis):

The Johannine images work toward an inclusion of the recipient. The appeal to "see" Jesus and his splendour...can...be interpreted as a directive to the recipients of the Gospel. *The message of the Gospel reaches its true destination only with the reader* The Fourth Gospel contains Christology, theology, ethics, and ecclesiology not simply for their own sake, but always with a view that actual recipients should make them their own.

Earlier, Zimmermann has rightly said this of Jesus' speech (12 and 15):

Despite its figurative character, it does not intend to conceal but rather to draw the reader into a process of discovery.[7] ...In its vividness, Jesus' speech should not conceal but rather lead to a deeper understanding of his person.

In light of these statements, it seems fair to take Zimmermann to make a claim here that is close to my own 'triangularity' point: that the *readers* are meant to see *clearly* what the interlocutors in the story themselves are unable to see.

Once again, however, there are risks. For instance, Zimmermann at one point discusses so-called 'conceptual metaphor' in the terminology introduced by Lakoff and Johnson. As examples he gives the spatial metaphor of 'above–below' and adds the well-known Johannine phrase of the 'lifting up' of Jesus or the Son of Man, as in 3:14, 8:28, and 12:32, 34. But he never refers to a simple, straightforward cosmology on John's part. However, this is not an either–or. It is certainly true that the idea of things belonging 'above' and 'below' has a wide range of metaphorical associations tied to it. But it is *also* the case that 'above' *refers* directly to 'in heaven', just as 'below' refers directly to 'here on earth'. Similarly, the idea of Jesus' being 'lifted up' certainly refers to his being lifted up on the cross. But it equally certainly refers to his being 'lifted up' into *heaven*, namely, in his resurrection, and neither of these senses is merely metaphorical. They also have a direct, cosmological meaning.

---

[7] Actually, Zimmermann is talking here of speaking in *paroimiai* in the general ancient understanding. But he clearly intends this to cover Jesus' speech, too.

Another example of the risks may be found in Zimmermann's treatment of the category of 'symbolic narratives'. He refers to Dodd (1953a) on John 11, Birger Olsson (1974) on 2:1–11 and 4:1–42, Painter (1979) on John 6 and 9, Sandra Schneiders (1985) on John 13, and then Dorothy Lee (1994), who identified the following passages as 'symbolic narratives': John 3, 4:1–42, John 5, 6, and 9, and finally 11:1–12:11. This appears both right and wrong. It is certainly true that these texts—like almost all others in John—abound in misunderstandings, ironies, metaphors, symbols, and the like, all of which goes directly into creating the meaning that they have. But to see each whole narrative as 'symbolic' (of what?) is to bypass the specific themes of each of these texts that I have attempted to bring out in this book: what each text is specifically *about*. Thus, for instance, John 6 is not just 'symbolic' in a wider sense but very specifically *about* the sense in which Jesus (Christ) is 'the bread of life', namely, as bringer of the *pneuma*, which believers ingest in the Eucharist, whereby they will be resurrected into eternal life. Once again, focus on the 'figurative' level of the Gospel, which is certainly there, must not be pursued by neglecting its straightforwardly cosmological meaning. It is not an either–or.

Finally, when at the very end (42) Zimmermann considers the 'epistemological function' of John's use of imagery, we are suddenly back to Culpepper's talk of 'mystery':

> Images are the language of that which cannot be spoken. Images can put into words that which cannot be expressed in any other way...Images are concrete and vivid but they must not be identified with reality. They open up insights and thereby discovery, but also make clear that this discovery remains limited and in need of completion.

Is this a strictly literary observation? Or is it a theological one, reflecting a view that *God* can never be 'spoken' or 'expressed'? The Fourth Gospel famously states that 'No one has ever *seen* God' (1:18). But it immediately continues telling the reader that God could nevertheless be seen in the earthly life and heavenly fate of Jesus Christ. It is the concrete content of this claim (which was *shown* at the very end in his resurrection) to which all the Johannine imagery *refers*. At this epistemological level there is no opacity at all (as the *reader* will well see). It is all strikingly clear.

CLARITY IN THE READER (OR ITS OPPOSITE): ATTRIDGE AND HIRSCH-LUIPOLD ON JOHANNINE IMAGERY

In this connection, it is worth considering two recent attempts, by Harold Attridge and Rainer Hirsch-Luipold, to combine an analysis of the

Johannine imagery with a tentative location of the Gospel in the vicinity of Middle Platonic contemporary writings such as those of Philo of Alexandria and Plutarch. This goes to the heart of the critique I have presented in this book of a 'Platonizing' reading of the Fourth Gospel.

In a characteristically insightful and elegant essay, Harold Attridge has argued (2006, 47) that:

[t]he use of Johannine imagery reflects certain tendencies in the symbolic interpretation of sacred traditions that we find in the late Hellenistic and early imperial periods. These tendencies are (1) to overdetermine the significance of recognized images, in part by viewing them from different angles of vision, all of which seems to increase the complexity of the symbolic system, but (2) to focus thereby on the referents of the symbolic system, thereby striving to penetrate to the 'essence' of what is symbolized. I describe this tendency as 'cubist,' on a loose analogy with tendencies in early twentieth-century European art. Finally (3), the ultimate aim of such focusing is to provide an experience, mediated by images, of divine reality.

Applied to John, Attridge shows how a number of widely different images in John—the good shepherd, the 'Son of Man', the temple and its cultic cycle, together with the image of water—display what he calls 'the "cubist" principle of disorienting complexification deployed in the interest of ultimate focus' (51). There is both 'complexification' and also a single ultimate focus, which Attridge takes to be the cross (54):

The cross lurks in and around many, if not all, of the images in the gospel.... I would suggest that the gospel as a whole might be construed as one large cubist image, refracting the cross through other images, of light, water, shepherds, ladders, snakes.

Towards the end of the essay, Attridge then compares this with what one finds in Philo and Plutarch. And he concludes that a '(Middle) Platonic handling of religious imagery' as found in those two authors 'offers some interesting parallels to the Fourth Gospel' (60).

Two connected comments seem apposite. The first is that while Attridge is exactly right, as I have argued too, to find a single ultimate 'focus' of all the Johannine imagery, it does not appear to be 'the cross', at least in the shape of 'Jesus giving in word and deed the command to love' (60), as Attridge explicates it. Rather, it is the cross *and resurrection*, understood quite concretely as the two historical events—which are really just one— referred to and hinted at in John's talk of Jesus being 'lifted up'. We have seen throughout this book that that is the precise point that nobody saw during Jesus' life on earth, but everybody should have seen. It is the (pneumatic) event that people must understand in order to obtain the gift of eternal life for themselves.

The second comment is that when Attridge brings out what 'the focus or ultimate significance of religious imagery' is in Plutarch, he rightly claims it to be 'the Platonic structure of reality' (60) or perhaps rather, as Plutarch himself has it in *De Iside* 382D, the 'primary, simple, and immaterial principle' of the whole world, that is, the Platonic God.[8] But this identification is thoroughly indebted to Plutarch's Platonism. *And we do not yet know that John, too, was a Platonist.* In fact, if, as I have argued, the ultimate focus of the imagery in John is the cross and resurrection of the earthly Jesus who *became* Jesus Christ through receiving the material *pneuma*, then we are very far from a Platonic universe. For then God has been *directly active* in this earthly world, as no Platonic God could ever be. It is one thing, therefore, to say that John's handling of images has structural similarities of the kind identified by Attridge with what we find in Philo and Plutarch— and an entirely different thing to claim that John's ontology and cosmology are also the same as the Platonic ones to be found in the two Middle Platonist writers. There is no necessary step from the one to the other.

The Middle Platonic reading of imagery in John is taken one step further in a substantial essay by Rainer Hirsch-Luipold published in the same volume as Attridge's. Distancing himself from the attempts by Bultmann and Dodd to elucidate the Gospel on the basis of 'Platonist' ideas in the broadest sense (from Plato himself to 'Gnostic', Hermetic, and Mandaean writings), Hirsch-Luipold (2006) focuses particularly on Plutarch, on whose handling of imagery he is an expert (2002). The fundamental shape of his reading of John comes out in the following quotation (2006, 66, my translation):

That the divine *logos* enters into (the world of) becoming as a human being from its eternal being is an 'illogical' truth that runs against the nature of the divine *logos*. Under the conditions of the present world one can only approximate this nature, never grasp it completely. As a bridge to cross the dialectic between God and world one may employ the idea, already well known in Middle Platonism, that the divine *logos* is reflected in the present world and its history in the form of imagery (*bildhaft*) and that the traces of God may therefore be followed from (and out of) the world (*aus der Welt*) and back (to their origin).

For such a conception Hirsch-Luipold refers to Philo, *De opificio mundi*, and Plutarch, *De Iside* and *De genio Socratis*. In the same context he also refers to Clement of Alexandria and elsewhere (65 n. 16) to Origen. Thus the line is clear: this is indeed the 'Platonizing' understanding of John against which I have been arguing in this book. Hirsch-Luipold further articulates his thesis as follows (66):

---

[8] By contrast, when Attridge describes it as 'seeing the Divine present in and imaged by living elements of the physical world' (*De Iside* 382A–C), I believe he is misinterpreting the text.

If one may only speak in images (*bildhaft*) about God and never in discursive speech (*diskursiv*) because he is removed from being perceived in the categories of the (present) world, he has—according to the witness of the Fourth Gospel—become perceptible by analogy in Jesus Christ as his image (*Bild*), in his words and deeds, through the incarnation.

Hirsch-Luipold then attempts to show how this overall conception both works and is indeed both intended and 'signaled' in the text.[9] Here he addresses three Johannine conceptual complexes: the terminology of 'truth' and 'the true (light, bread, etc.)'; the concepts of *paroimia*, *parrhêsia* ('open speech') and acting and speaking *en kryptôi* ('in hiding'); and finally the notion of a 'sign'.

The essay is full of interesting ideas. For present purposes, however, the issue will be to consider what arguments Hirsch-Luipold is able to produce for his way of understanding John as depicting Jesus as an image (*Bild*) of God.[10] As far as I can see, the only real argument (beyond the overall approach of seeing John through a Middle Platonic lens) is to be found in Hirsch-Luipold's reflections on 'truth' and 'the true...'. In the important use of this concept in John, he finds an implication of two distinct (Platonic) 'levels of being' (*Seinsebene*), where truth itself stands for the divine level (or even God) and 'what is called "true" within the present world' is 'what has a part in the level of the divine truth and makes this visible (or perceptible: *sichtbar*) in the world' (69). As examples he mentions 'true light', 'true bread', 'true food', 'true vine'.

Let us consider, for instance, 'true food'. The idea itself has been introduced already in 4:32–4. John 6:27 then adds some clarification, which is further extended when Jesus speaks of himself as the 'true bread' (6:55) to be understood in the manner he then spells out in 6:58 and 6:60–3. Where in all this do we find something like the two Platonic 'levels of being'? What is meant here by 'true' is carefully explained: 'food' (and we know what that is: *pneuma*) that will lead to a kind of life that is 'true' *in the sense of* eternal: in connection with 'life', 'true' food is the one that leads to *eternal* life. We may then add something about how this eternal life is meant to be understood, by drawing, for instance, on 14:1–3. But the point for present purposes is that 'true' here has a straightforward meaning that is clearly explained. It does not in the least point to a level of being that cannot be discursively expressed, but must be hinted at through

---

[9] This is quite a stark claim: 'Eine solche Lektüre entspricht dem Johannesevangelium nicht nur, sie ist von ihm intendiert und wird durch eine Reihe von Textsignalen gefordert' (65).

[10] A few quotations: 'Die Zeichen...weisen *Jesus als Bild Gottes* aus und machen so mittelbar Gott selbst gegenwärtig' (96, my emphasis) and then: 'Die Zeichen zeigen...Gott selbst' (98), which leads Hirsch-Luipold to speak of 'eine bildhafte Präsenz Gottes' (96, 100).

the use of images. Thus what appears to be the strongest genuine argument for Hirsch-Luipold's reading does not deliver what he takes it to yield.

There are other features of Hirsch-Luipold's reading that one may find doubtful. It is not clear, though, whether they are to be understood as genuine arguments for the reading or rather as interpretive consequences *if* one has adopted a 'Middle Platonic' perspective. Here I will mention only one feature, which is Hirsch-Luipold's constant stress on God. For instance, in his (in themselves, very helpful) remarks on the notion of 'sign', he comments that 'there is a general consensus that the signs reveal Jesus' identity as Messiah and the Son of God' (97). But he immediately goes on to speak of the *theo*logical point of the signs: that they reveal God himself. This does not appear quite right. It is true that Hirsch-Luipold may refer to 1:18, which is extremely important. But the point of the signs is throughout focused on Jesus, aiming to show something about *him*, for instance, that *he* and God are 'one' (10:30). Of course, if that holds, then it also says something about God. What God is is shown in Jesus—what he says and does— *because Jesus* is 'one with' God. And it is the latter point that the Gospel is concerned throughout to make clear to all involved.

Why does Hirsch-Luipold insist on the other point? There are two connected reasons. One is that the issue of *how to know God* is precisely a central issue in Hirsch-Luipold's Middle Platonic writers. The other reason is that all through his analysis Hirsch-Luipold takes as his logical starting point a traditional understanding of the 'incarnation' (1:14) to the effect that the divine *logos* or even God himself literally (but in some mysterious and wholly unexplained way) 'became flesh' by 'entering the realm of becoming'.[11] (I repeat here that no '*Platonic*' *logos* or God could ever do this.) If that were the case, then one might well see the main focus to be on God. And then the road is open to speculate on God's 'presence' in the world, namely *als Bild*, that is, in his *image* (Jesus). However, we have found an altogether different picture. God stays in heaven. His *logos* becomes present in Jesus at the baptism as carried by the *pneuma*. And this means that *Jesus* becomes *divine*, not that God becomes human.

I conclude that what Hirsch-Luipold has very resourcefully done is to build on a traditional understanding of the incarnation, which is precisely (in a wholly unexplained manner) 'Platonic' (*from* the Church Fathers onwards)—and then to *find* in the near context of John (Plutarch) a set of (Middle) Platonic ideas that—wholly unsurprisingly—support such a reading. Hirsch-Luipold's sense that it fits John is due to the basically Platonist reading from which he begins. And that (I have argued) is not the best one available.

---

[11] For the divine *logos* see the quotation from Hirsch-Luipold given earlier (Hirsch-Luipold, p. 66, also p. 99). For 'God himself' see the claim on p. 82 that 'God became a human being'.

A final consideration on the whole issue of imagery in John is this. I have argued that one should not turn to 'Middle Platonism' to understand John's use of images.[12] How then should one explain his fondness for this kind of language? I believe there is a simple answer to this question, one that was already implied in Alan Culpepper's analysis when he described John's use of misunderstanding, irony, and symbolism *together* in a chapter entitled 'Implicit Commentary' (1983, 150–202). Here is a quotation from his conclusion (199, my emphasis):

> Our analysis of the misunderstandings, ironies, and symbolism of the Fourth Gospel highlights its 'deformation of language.'[13] Images, concepts, and symbols common in its milieu are de-familiarized, given new meaning, and used idiosyncratically. In succession various characters miss their meaning. The misunderstandings warn *the reader* not to mistake superficial for real meanings. By repeatedly exposing irony in the dialogue, the author calls *the reader* to share his elevated point of view on the story. Through the symbolism also the author tells *the reader* that things are more than they seem to be.

This seems exactly right. John's use of imagery functions in the same way as his use of irony and misunderstanding. It is a tool employed by John to create a direct relationship between Jesus *within* the narrative and the reader *of* the narrative, in the 'triangularity' of which I have spoken. Jesus knows and the readers know since John and his Jesus have constantly given them the necessary means for understanding. To them the whole imagery has the same degree of clarity (through its very precise reference, which John makes clear to them) as the misunderstandings and the ironies. Those to whom all three phenomena remain opaque are Jesus' immediate addressees within the narrative itself. *They* do not understand and only come to understand (if at all) after Jesus' resurrection. To the reader, by contrast, all that appeared opaque is bathed in the clear light of truth.

'REALIZED ESCHATOLOGY' IN JOHN?
THREE TEMPORAL STAGES

The precise character of John's eschatology continues to tease scholars. Throughout this book we have come across the issue repeatedly and

---

[12] It is noteworthy that Ruben Zimmermann explicitly sidesteps this issue: 'In this short approach to the compositional principles pf Johannine imagery I do not wish to go deeply into the religious-historical question as to the extent that the imagery in John can be incorporated into the horizon of contemporary writings, especially that of middle platonic philosophy' (Zimmermann 2006, 30).

[13] Culpepper here quotes from Beardslee 1970, 11.

provided the answers that seemed required in each case. However, in view of the significance of the topic for the thesis of this book, I will summarize here the overall conception of John's eschatology that we have hitherto articulated in piecemeal form.

The issues are clear enough. Do we not find in John what Dodd called a 'realized eschatology', meaning that although John may from time to time speak of eschatological events in the future, he also entertains the idea that *everything* is settled in the present, whether 'eternal life' for true believers or 'judgement' for non-believers?[14] Do we not find in John an 'eschatology', as developed by Rudolf Bultmann, that locates it squarely in the present (both then and now) in contrast with traditional Jewish, future-oriented 'apocalypticism'?[15] If so, should we not conclude that any future events are, in principle, irrelevant? Or if not, should we not at least agree with M. de Jonge (1992), who in an excellent, short article argued for both present and future aspects of eschatology in John, that '[n]obody will want to deny that the emphasis is on the present' (482)?[16] But in that case, how exactly may we connect those present and future aspects? Will we not have to admit that they stand in some 'tension' with one another, even if we are not prepared to relegate the various statements to different layers of the text?[17] There is a line here: from the wholesale denial of the relevance of the future (Dodd, Bultmann) via a recognition of both present and future aspects (de Jonge, Frey, and many others) to the continuing problem of precisely how to reconcile the two.

In this summarizing discussion, I attempt primarily to show the precise way in which the reading of the Gospel presented in this book may help to solve the problem. There are two basic questions: how may we read together statements in John about the present and about the future? And why is it that John has—apparently—put special emphasis on those

---

[14] As noted by von Wahlde (2013, 149), Dodd originally introduced the concept in order to account for Jesus himself, but he then attempted to show that the prime specimen of realized eschatology was to be found in the Gospel of John. Curiously, there is no explicit discussion of 'realized eschatology' in Dodd 1953a. But see his account of 'eternal life' (144–50), where his Platonic anchorage is made explicit: 'when the life of the Age to Come, with its specific quality, is transplanted into the field of present experience . . . , then the *chief* thing about it is its difference from merely physical life. Its everlastingness is a function of its divine quality. We may then recall that Plato . . .' (1953a, 149, Dodd's emphasis).

[15] For Bultmann's conception and importance here see Frey 1997, in particular 86–157. One of the glories of Frey 1997, 1998, and 2000a is that these three volumes once and for all showed that Bultmann's conception cannot be maintained.

[16] This statement is presumably meant to express what de Jonge in his title (but nowhere else) calls the 'radical' eschatology of John in comparison with the Synoptics. However, the whole burden of de Jonge's argument is that with respect to 'the expectation of a speedy completion [in the near future] of God's work on earth', 'Johannine believers are not different from their fellow-Christians', as reflected in the Synoptic Gospels (1992, 487).

[17] Attridge (2008), for one, insists on such 'tensions'.

statements about the present?[18] In answering these questions I follow the lead of Jörg Frey, who has strongly emphasized the role of time in this area, and then add one point that has come out in the present book concerning the role of the *pneuma*. I only bring in the relevant texts from John once the framework for a solution has been presented.

In accordance with our basic, narrative approach, we should keep sharply in focus what I will call 'Stage I' ('Jesus time'), that is, the 'fictional present' of the narrative itself in which Jesus acts and speaks as described in the Gospel. We know certain features that distinguish this stage: the *pneuma* is present in Jesus, but only in him; in particular, Jesus himself says that the *pneuma* *will* only become available to believers after his own death; also, at Stage I, no one (apart from John the Baptist in John 1, who was explicitly told by God himself) came to believe in Jesus in the proper way until after his death. These two features are closely connected. Reception of the *pneuma* is a necessary condition for acquiring the full faith in Jesus that sees him for what he was: the unique Son of God.

Within 'Jesus time' Jesus is made to speak in the 'fictional future' of a later stage (Stage II) that lies after his own death and resurrection. That stage is that of the disciples 'after Easter' and also the 'author's time'. At this stage ('believers' time') the disciples and other believers will have received the *pneuma* in the shape of the 'Paraclete'. Thus, they will have obtained full faith in Jesus as the unique Son of God, as opposed to the various types of 'initial belief' described in the Gospel itself.

However, various texts both in and before the Farewell Discourse also speak of a third stage (Stage III) which (though still foretold by Jesus in his own time) lies in the future vis-à-vis 'believers' time'.[19] These are the texts that speak of the traditional, future eschatological events connected with Jesus' second coming and the final judgement. This stage is often marked by the expression 'on the last day'. Since this time will apparently be connected with a general resurrection to either 'life' or 'judgement', we may call it 'resurrection time'.

There is nothing new in this separation of three stages, only it will prove helpful to keep them clearly distinct. Thus I am sceptical about speaking

---

[18] For the latter idea compare also Jörg Frey (2000a, 238): 'Der vom johanneischen Autor gesetzte Akzent liegt jedoch deutlich auf der *gegenwärtigen Gewissheit* des Heils' (his emphasis). This is also the idea that underlies Culpepper 2008, which begins: 'The understanding of resurrection and eternal life in the Gospel of John is distinctive, and often labeled "realized eschatology." Much that is anticipated, hoped for, and expected in the future in ancient Jewish writings and other books of the New Testament is understood to be *already present in a real sense* in the Gospel of John. There is still hope for the future realization of that which is not yet present, but *John is distinctive* in its proclamation that eternal life is *already a present reality* for those who believe in Jesus' (2008, 253, my emphasis).

[19] Here belong such texts as 5:27–9, 6:39, 40, 44, 51, 54, 11:25–6, 14:2–3, 17:24.

(with Frey 2000a, 234) of a 'temporal stereoscopy' in the Farewell Discourse, which practises a 'fusion (*Verschmelzung*) of the temporal and content-filled horizons of the time of Jesus and the time of the community'.[20] Frey has convincingly shown that John had a very clear sense of time differences.[21] I think we should stick to that sense.

ON HAVING ETERNAL LIFE IN THE PRESENT

Two issues should concern us now. First, we know that Jesus from time to time speaks (at Stage I) of phenomena that belong in the future, at Stage II. Why, then, does he also speak of such phenomena as belonging already at Stage I? A famous example is 4:23: 'the hour . . . when the true worshippers will worship the Father in spirit and truth' (NRSV) is 'coming' or 'about to come' (*erchetai*), but definitely not there yet. Then why does he also say that it 'is now here'?

Secondly, exactly how should we understand Jesus' repeated statements that the person who 'believes in' Jesus already *has* 'eternal life'? At what stage of the three should we place this person? And how does this person relate to what belongs to the two other stages? In particular, if, as seems likely, the person who is said to possess eternal life belongs at Stage II, exactly how is what holds of the person at that stage related to what will come about at Stage III?

We may begin from the second issue. John 6 contains a string of verses that distinguish between some 'present condition', including that of 'having eternal life', and its future result to the effect that 'I will raise him on the last day': 6:39, 40, 44, and 54. With this latter promise we are clearly at Stage III, but what about the 'present condition'? Is it meant to apply at Stages I or II? As we have interpreted John 6, the answer should be: at Stage II. Here belongs the one who '(already) has eternal life' either by 'seeing' the Son and (fully) believing in him (6:40), or else by munching his flesh and drinking his blood in the Eucharist (6:54), that is, by ingesting the *pneuma* (6:63). Such a person is certainly not 'resurrected' (yet). As Alan Culpepper rightly notes (2008, 255), 'John . . . maintains a distinction between [having] eternal life and resurrection [that is, being resurrected] that is most apparent in the separation of the present from the future in John 6:40 and 6:54', only we must understand 'the present' here to refer to Stage II and not

[20] Elsewhere (1998, 295) Frey speaks of a 'seeing together (*Zusammenschau*) of the time of Jesus and the time of the community'.
[21] Compare 1998, 294, where he speaks of the 'klare temporale Einordnungen und Differenzierungen' (of the various events), of the 'unauflösliche raum-zeitliche Konkretheit und historische[n] Einmaligkeit des erzählten Geschehens'.

Stage I. Jesus is himself speaking at Stage I, but both he and the reader know that it was true of no one at that stage that they actually 'saw the Son' and 'believed in him' so as already to possess eternal life. They *should* have done so, but no one did. For that, something more was required: that they themselves would receive the *pneuma*.

The same understanding lies behind another famous verse: 5:24. When Jesus says that 'the one who hears my *logos* and believes in the one who has sent me *has* (*echei*) eternal life and will not come to judgement, but has (already) gone over (*metabebêken*) from death to life', of what is he talking? We have already decided that this, too, belongs at Stage II. Only with the reception of the *pneuma* will human beings be able to 'hear my *logos* etc.' in the way that has this consequence.

We should take it, therefore, that what underlies any statement that a person 'has' eternal life is the fact that he has received the *pneuma* and hence belongs at Stage II. How then is that related to the resurrection, of which Jesus speaks so clearly in John 6 (39, 40, 44, 54) and indeed also in 5:27–9; in other words, how is it related to what will happen at Stage III?[22] The answer is made clear in another famous text: 11:25–6.

Jesus is 'the resurrection and the life', so he says at Stage I (11:25), that is, he will both himself be resurrected into eternal life and also give resurrection and life to believers (and, of course, to Lazarus). In the latter respect, 'the one who believes' in Jesus 'will live should (s)he even (beforehand) die (physically)'. Here the 'will live' (in the future, as opposed to '*has* life' in the earlier passages) clearly refers to Stage III. Thus the person who believes in Jesus will come to live (physically) through being resurrected into eternal life. This is closely parallel to the Pauline descriptions of those believers who may have died before the return of Jesus (see 1 Thess. 4:14 versus 4:17; 1 Cor. 15:51–2). Conversely, as the Johannine text continues, 'the one who lives', that is, remains alive (physically) at Jesus' return, *and* 'believes in' Jesus, 'will never die in all eternity': this person will live on (physically) in resurrected form in heaven (11:26). Who, then, is that person? Is it the one with the initial kind of 'believing in Jesus' that we hear about at Stage I (that is, in the Gospel itself)? Is that kind of 'believing in Jesus' sufficient? No, for Jesus immediately goes on to ask Martha whether she believes *this*, and while her answer (11:27) might in principle be sufficient (after all, she does mention the crucial title of 'the Son of God'), both the fact that she also speaks of Jesus in ways that are in themselves deficient (namely, as 'the Christ' and 'the one who is coming into the world'), and also that it is later

---

[22] If 5:24 is about Stage II and 5:27–9 is about Stage III, it is highly noteworthy that 5:25–6, which I have taken (together with 5:21) to refer to the resurrection of Lazarus, is about Stage I. This fact brings out the inner *connection* that we are after between the three stages, which nevertheless remain clearly distinct in temporal terms.

shown (11:39–40) that she precisely did *not* understand the crucial point about Jesus' being 'the resurrection and the life', must indicate that *her* kind of 'believing in Jesus' is *not* sufficient.[23] In other words, Jesus is once more speaking 'proleptically' at Stage I of believers at Stage II, those who will *by that time* have received the *pneuma* and will thereby have come to obtain the full faith in who Jesus was and is that was only fully revealed by his resurrection. If in that way the person described in 11:25–6 is a Stage II person who has received the *pneuma*, then one can immediately understand those two verses themselves and also the intended connection between Stages II and III. The person who has a *pneuma*-informed faith in Jesus will 'live eternally' already in the present by *eventually* (at Stage III) being resurrected into a heavenly life (either from death or while still alive) *through* the *pneuma* that he or she has *already* received (at Stage II). Of such a person it will also be true to say (with 5:24) that he or she '*has* (*echei*) eternal life [namely, already now] and will not come to judgement, but has (already) gone over (*metabebêken*) from death to life'. For (s)he has the thing that will eventually ensure a life that is truly eternal: the *pneuma*.

This is clearly not 'realized eschatology' in Dodd's original sense, meaning that any reference to future events is in principle irrelevant. On the contrary, a person will only 'have' eternal life at Stage II because (s)he at that stage already *has* the thing that will *eventually* secure a life that is genuinely eternal. That thing is the *pneuma*.[24] There is nothing in this that differs from what we find, for instance, in Paul, where believers also receive the *pneuma* in baptism 'as a first instalment' (2 Cor. 1:22 and 5:5, an *arrabôn*) or 'the first fruits' (Rom. 8:23, an *aparchê*), only to be put fully into operation at the general resurrection (1 Corinthians 15, compare Rom. 8:11). The only difference one might possibly find is that John is *perhaps* a little more prone

---

[23] I argued this point in Chapter VIII. I am delighted to see that Nils Dahl agrees on this vital point: 'The reader has to understand that her declaration, "I know that he will rise again in the resurrection on the last day" was both correct and inadequate, *as was her later confession that Jesus is the Christ, the Son of God* (11:21–7, *and see vv. 39–40*).' (1990, 329, my emphasis).

[24] For clarification, contrast this with Culpepper 2008, which is the most recent, substantial development of the idea of 'realized eschatology'. Here is one formulation: 'The Gospel of John reflects a realistic realized eschatology in that it recognizes the reality of physical death while maintaining that believers already participate in the eternal life *of the resurrection*' (263, my emphasis). And another: '…the distinctively Johannine [!] affirmation is that the judgement occurs in the present through one's belief or refusal to believe in Jesus, and that those who believe already have eternal life. That eternal life *continues after death through* the believer's future resurrection from the dead' (265, my emphasis). However, there is no eternal life '*of the resurrection*' at Stage II, only a real *possession* of the *pneuma* and thereby of a life that will *at Stage III* turn into and *become* a resurrected, properly eternal life. ('Eternal' means just that: that will continue forever and ever. It does not signify some timeless 'quality'.) There is no *fully* 'realized' eschatology at Stage II that may therefore merely 'continue after death' through the believer's future resurrection from the dead. Still, there *is* something that binds the two stages together: possession of the *pneuma*.

to emphasize the 'presence of salvation' (people *have* eternal life) in what is only the (Stage II) present *part* of a two-stage conception of salvation. *If* there is such an emphasis, we must try to account for it.

WHY AN EMPHASIS ON THE PRESENT (IN 'RETROJECTION')?

Back to the first issue: why then have scholars begun to speak of 'realized eschatology' in John? There are many reasons, of course. In Dodd's own case it was closely connected with his basically Platonic reading of John, which allowed him to 'find the eternal' in the 'world of becoming' exclusively through an act of faith. This was a kind of static and highly 'spiritualized' reading that does not do justice to John's very clear sense of the dynamic progression of time so clearly worked out by Frey, nor to the wholly concrete and indeed material character of the Johannine *pneuma*. In Bultmann's case this whole approach lies at the heart of his 'demythologizing' project and his 'existential' reading of the 'mythology'.

However, there are also texts in John himself which help to explain why scholars have gone down the cul-de-sac that Dodd's 'realized eschatology' or Bultmann's properly 'eschatological' reading have turned out to be. To see this we should consider those texts that appear to put special emphasis on the (Stage II) present part of the two-stage conception of salvation and also those texts that has Jesus speak of Stage II phenomena as already belonging at Stage I—the first issue above.[25] In both cases, we seem to be witnessing a strategy of 'retrojection' of ideas properly belonging at Stage III to Stage II and of ideas properly belonging at Stage II to Stage I.

Let us now consider the latter. Why does John make Jesus bring in his 'future-present formula' ('the hour is coming, *and is now here*') at 4:23? Here Jesus is clearly both speaking *from* and referring *to* ('now') his own time, 'Jesus time'. So, will people *now* (in 'Jesus time') worship God in *pneuma* and truth? Definitely not. For we know that at that time the *pneuma* was present to no one other than Jesus himself. Why, then, does Jesus *say* that 'people' will worship God in that manner *now*? Here we cannot answer that John has suddenly made his Jesus move from Stage I to Stage II. For the future tense in 'the hour is coming' will refer to Stage II. In that case it would be

---

[25] An example of the 'special emphasis' on what is present at Stage II is 17:3. God has given his Son eternal life so that he may pass it on to believers (17:2). And what is it? 'And this is eternal life, that they may *know you*, the only true God, and Jesus Christ whom you have sent' (17:3). Is that all? Indeed, yes. For this is something they will only know at Stage II and hence when they do have the *pneuma*. And then the road is also clear for a life that will eventually be a resurrected one and hence truly eternal. Thus 17:3 *sounds* as if it were only speaking of Stage II, but we know that that stage *implies* Stage III.

completely confusing were Jesus to say that, in spite of everything, that
time is already present. Instead, the point must be a different one, namely,
that *in and with* Jesus' presence on earth as bearer of the *pneuma*, the
conditions for worshipping God in *pneuma* and truth *were in fact fulfilled*
even though no one was able to live up to that situation. It was all already
there in Jesus himself. What John makes his Jesus do here is to draw
something that is actually future ('the hour will come') into the narrative
present *as part of his Christology*. In the quoted article, de Jonge makes the
same point (drawing on Josef Blank 1964) when he states that the
eschatological statements 'are preceded and followed by Christological
ones' (1992, 483). That is certainly true here. Indeed, we have already
noted the same move in 4:25–6 from future to present where Jesus is
speaking of himself: 'I am he, etc.'.

Then we can also understand John's special emphasis on 'present salvation' for believers at Stage II *if* it is there. We know that this should always
be understood as part of a two-stage conception of salvation (from Stages II
to III). Indeed, John maintains all through the sharp distinction from
chapter 6 between the present 'possession of' ('having') eternal life and
future '*resurrection*'. Nowhere does he either say or imply that (full) believers (at Stage II) are already *resurrected* now.[26] If he nevertheless puts
emphasis on 'present salvation', we should probably understand this in
light of our explanation of 4:23. If all was *already* present in Jesus (at Stage I)
then there is a temptation to say that once *believers, too,* have received the
pneuma (at Stage II), everything is also already present *to them*, including
the (clearly future) resurrection, for which the *pneuma* is responsible. This
temptation is even greater if one places strong emphasis on the 'Paraclete'
which believers will receive after Jesus' death and which is also—in a
clearly specified way—Jesus himself. If all was already present in Jesus
himself at Stage I, and if Jesus is fully present in believers (in the form of
the 'Paraclete') at Stage II, then one may well be tempted to say that
everything is also present in believers at that stage. *Only,* we know that
that is not so: in this interim period they 'only' have the 'Paraclete'
(corresponding to Paul's 'first instalment' of the *pneuma*) and even risk
dying (by 11:25). Thus, *if* there is a special emphasis in John on 'present
salvation' for believers (at Stage II), the most obvious explanation is—once
again—to be found in his high Christology, which makes him draw something that he himself *knows* belongs in the future into the present, either

---

[26] It is unfortunate that in the latter part of his excellent article, Alan Culpepper continues
to speak of living in 'the community of the resurrection' (2008, 269, 272, 273, 275). There is no
such thing in John. What there is is a community of full believers who 'have eternal life' in
the sense that they have already received the *pneuma* which will *eventually* secure truly
eternal life for them, through their resurrection. They (already) *have* eternal life by already
having the *pneuma*. But they are not yet resurrected.

Jesus' present at Stage I or the believers' present at Stage II. But both John and his readers know that this strategy only reflects his very high understanding of Jesus: with him (either before or after his death) everything was (in a way) already there.

I have spoken of the literary strategy and practice that we have just articulated as one of 'retrojection'. A feature of a later stage is 'retrojected' into an earlier stage. Earlier in this book I have spoken of 'proleptic eschatology'. The idea is the same. Whether you come to it from a later stage and find later material being 'retrojected' into an earlier stage or you come to it from an earlier stage and find later material being proleptically 'anticipated' at the earlier stage, the result is the same. What belongs at a later stage has been 'contracted' into an earlier one—and presumably in order to give that earlier stage maximum significance. It is all derived from John's extremely high view of Jesus and the power given to him when he received the *pneuma* from God. Here one should find the kernel of everything that would only come to pass much later: after Jesus' death (for believers, at Stage II) and in the eschatological future (for believers, at Stage III). It is the specific role of the *pneuma* to both bind together and separate the three stages. It is present in Jesus but nowhere else at Stage I, thereby making him speak and act as he does. It becomes present in believers at Stage II, thereby making them fully know Jesus and their own eventual salvation. (It also informs their communal life in that period before Jesus' second coming.) Finally, it is active at the second coming itself (Stage III) in bringing believers together with Jesus (and God) in heaven (14:3, 17:24).

I conclude that in spite of scholarly efforts to rescue the notion of 'realized eschatology' for a proper description of John, it should be jettisoned. It has too many overtones that are clearly false and to the extent that it might capture something that is actually there (as articulated by our notion of 'retrojection'), it should be understood in the way proposed here. John aims to bring out that with the reception of the *pneuma* (in Jesus at Stage I and in believers at Stage II), everything is in a way already there, including the *prospect* of resurrection into eternal life.

JOHN AND PHILOSOPHY

Philosophy stands for clarity. The reading of the Fourth Gospel that I have presented in this book has been aimed at bringing out the essential clarity of this text as opposed to celebrating the 'riddles', 'mystery', and 'spiritual' qualities that have traditionally been found in it. The way to expose this essential clarity has been to engage in a close reading that has focused on the text itself and kept its various contexts at a relative distance, not because they are intrinsically irrelevant (far from it), but because the gap between the text itself and the *range* of possible contextualizations is too big for it to be possible to rely on any of them. By returning to the text, the aim has been to discover a single comprehensive picture of Jesus and his interlocutors that might be seen to underlie what to begin with appears bewilderingly confusing and repetitive in the text—or even more explicitly: to display a striking simplicity underlying all the complexity (but then also to *explain* the complexity). In pursuing this line, I have been concerned to respond to the textual meaning at its own level, and indeed, to respond to what appears to be the work's own agenda: to bring out what John meant when he stated his aim to be that his readers might come to 'believe that Jesus is the Messiah, the Son of God', and 'through that believing' might 'have life in his name' (20:31).

The tool that I have put to use to achieve this aim has been the 'narrative philosophical' approach that has been developed for this purpose, reflecting the fact that we should understand the Fourth Gospel as a 'philosophical narrative'. No one will probably deny that it is a narrative. But we have seen that in two comprehensive respects this narrative is also a philosophical one. First, John has written the major sections (always covering several chapters, apart from John 1) in such a manner that certain questions of a philosophical type are raised to begin with by the narrative itself and then answered towards the end by narrative means. Secondly, we have seen that the clarity of the underlying, comprehensive conceptual story about Jesus and his believers comes out quite strikingly once one employs a specific type of philosophy, namely, contemporary Stoicism, as a heuristic reading lens. Here it is not just a matter of understanding specific textual issues such as the question of exactly how 'the *logos* became flesh', according to 1:14, or exactly how Jesus' announcement of his departure in 13:33 hangs together with his issuing a 'new command' of mutual love in 13:34–5. Rather, it is a matter of understanding how everything that is said of Jesus hangs together with everything that is said about the human beings with whom he is confronted: whether his direct opponents, who distinctly do *not* believe in him, or those with some 'initial' belief, or those (such as the disciples) with a somewhat fuller (though still insufficient) belief, or finally those who are described—proleptically—as having full faith. All these themes fall into place once they are understood in light of the role played by the *pneuma* when *this* is understood along the lines it had been developed philosophically within Stoicism.

If all this is accepted, then the reading we have been pursuing in this book opens up a number of ways of relating to this great text. There is the joy of delving into the text under these premises: of seeing where and how everything fits into the overall conceptual story. There is the complementary joy of being—as a reader—'in the know' in contrast with all those depicted in the text itself. There is the joy of admiration for the very high degree of reflectiveness in the text: that in reading one is in contact with a great mind. There is the joy of admiration for the starkness and clarity of the text's claims about Jesus. There is the joy of admiration for the daring of the text and the beauty of the simplicity of its focus—though certainly also combined with extreme worry about the *Wirkungsgeschichte* of those intrinsic virtues. Finally, there is a sense of the freshness of it all: how it constantly presents challenges to its readers and surprises them.

But all this can be seen and experienced in one way only: by reading the text, rereading it, and rereading it again. That is why the brilliantly red focus of Piero della Francesca's rendering of John on the cover of this book is: his book.

BIBLIOGRAPHY

The bibliography lists works that are quoted in the book. It also contains a number of unquoted works from which I have learned or against which I have tested my own view. The fact that a given work is not actually quoted does not imply any adverse opinion on its quality or importance.

ABBREVIATIONS

BETL	Bibliotheca Ephemeridum Theologicarum Lovaniensium
CBQ	*Catholic Biblical Quarterly*
FRLANT	Forschungen zur Religion und Literatur des Alten und Neuen Testaments
JBL	*Journal of Biblical Literature*
JSNT	*Journal for the Study of the New Testament*
NT	*Novum Testamentum*
NTS	*New Testament Studies*
SBLDS	Society of Biblical Literature Dissertation Series
SBLMS	Society of Biblical Literature Monograph Series
WUNT	Wissenschaftliche Untersuchungen zum Neuen Testament
ZNW	*Zeitschrift für die neutestamentliche Wissenschaft*
ZTK	*Zeitschrift für Theologie und Kirche*

BOOKS AND ARTICLES

ALAND, K. (1968) 'Eine Untersuchung zu Joh. 1.3–4: Über die Bedeutung eines Punktes', *ZNW* 59, 174–209.

ALGRA, K. (2003) 'Stoic Theology', in *The Cambridge Companion to the Stoics*, ed. B. Inwood. Cambridge: 153–78.

ARNIM, H. VON (1903–24) *Stoicorum Veterum Fragmenta*. 4 vols. Stuttgart.

ASHTON, J. (1986) 'The Transformation of Wisdom: A Study of the Prologue of John's Gospel', *NTS* 32, 161–86.

ASHTON, J. (ed.) (1986/97) *The Interpretation of John*. London/Edinburgh.

ASHTON, J. (1998a) *Studying John. Approaches to the Fourth Gospel*. Oxford.

ASHTON, J. (1998b) 'The Transformation of Wisdom', in Ashton (1998a), 5–35.

ASHTON, J. (2007/1991) *Understanding the Fourth Gospel*. Oxford.

ASHTON, J. (2014) *The Gospel of John and Christian Origins*. Minneapolis.

ATTRIDGE, H. W. (1980) 'Thematic Development and Source Elaboration in John 7:1–36', *CBQ* 42, 160–70.

ATTRIDGE, H. W. (2002a) 'Genre Bending in the Fourth Gospel', *JBL* 121/1, 3–21.

ATTRIDGE, H. W. (2002b) 'Argumentation in John 5', in *Rhetorical Argumentation in Biblical Texts*, eds A. Eriksson, T. H. Olbricht, and W. Übelacker. Emory Studies in Early Christianity 8. Harrisburg, PA: 188–99.

ATTRIDGE, H. W. (2003) ' "Don't Be Touching Me": Recent Feminist Scholarship on Mary Magdalene', in Levine (ed.) (2003): 2.140–66.

ATTRIDGE, H. W. (2005) 'Philo and John: Two Riffs on One Logos', *Studia Philonica Annual* 17, 103–17.

ATTRIDGE, H. W. (2006a) 'Johannine Christianity', in *The Cambridge History of Christianity*, vol. 1: *Origins to Constantine*, eds M. M. Mitchell and F. M. Young. Cambridge: 125–44.

ATTRIDGE, H. W. (2006b) 'The Cubist Principle in Johannine Imagery: John and the Reading of Images in Contemporary Platonism', in Frey, van der Watt, and Zimmermann (eds) (2006): 47–60.

ATTRIDGE, H. W. (2008) 'From Discord Rises Meaning: Resurrection Motifs in the Fourth Gospel', in Koester and Bieringer (eds) (2008): 1–19.

ATTRIDGE, H. W. (2010) *Essays on John and Hebrews*. Wissenschaftliche Untersuchungen zum Neuen Testament 264. Tübingen.

ATTRIDGE, H. W. (2013a) 'How Priestly Is the "High Priestly Prayer" of John 17?', *CBQ* 75/1, 1–14.

ATTRIDGE, H. W. (2013b) 'The Samaritan Woman: A Woman Transformed', in Hunt, Tolmie, and Zimmermann (eds) (2013): 268–81.

AUNE, D. E. (2003) 'Dualism and the Fourth Gospel and the Dead Sea Scrolls', in *Neotestamentica et Philonica*, FS P. Borgen, eds D. E. Aune et al. Supplements to Novum Testamentum 106. Leiden: 281–303.

BACK, F. (2013) 'Die rätselhaften "Antworten" Jesu: Zum Thema des Nikodemusgesprächs (Joh 3,1–21)', *Evangelische Theologie* 73/3, 178–89.

BALL, D. M. (1996) *'I Am' in John's Gospel. Literary Function, Background and Theological Implications*. Journal for the Study of the New Testament Supplement Series 124. Sheffield.

BARRETT, C. K. (1978/1955) *The Gospel According to St John*. London.

BARRETT, C. K. (1982) *Essays on John*. London.

BARRETT, C. K. (1992) 'The Place of John and the Synoptics within the Early History of Christian Thought', in Denaux (ed.) (1992): 63–79.

Bauckham, R. (ed.) (1998a) *The Gospels for All Christians. Rethinking the Gospel Audiences*. Edinburgh.

BAUCKHAM, R. (1998b) 'John for Readers of Mark', in Bauckham (ed.) (1998a): 147–72.

BAUCKHAM, R. (2006) 'Messianism According to the Gospel of John', in Lierman (ed.) (2006): 34–68.

BAUCKHAM, R. (2007a) *The Testimony of the Beloved Disciple*. Grand Rapids, MI.

BAUCKHAM, R. (2007b) 'Historiographical Characteristics of the Gospel of John', *NTS* 53, 17–36.

BAUCKHAM, R. and C. MOSSER (eds) (2008) *The Gospel of John and Christian Theology*. Grand Rapids, MI.

BAUER, W. (1933) *Das Johannesevangelium*. Handbuch zum Neuen Testament 6. Tübingen.

BAUM-BODENBENDER, R. (1984) *Hoheit in Niedrigkeit. Johanneische Christologie im Prozess Jesu vor Pilatus (Joh 18,28–19,16a)*. Forschung zur Bibel 49. Würzburg.

BEARDSLEE, W. A. (1970) *Literary Criticism of the New Testament*. Guides to Biblical Scholarship. Philadelphia, PA.

BEASLEY-MURRAY, G. R. (1987) *John*. Word Biblical Commentary 36. Waco, TX.

BECKER, J. (1969/70) 'Wunder und Christologie', *NTS* 16, 130–48.

BECKER, J. (1970) 'Die Abschiedsreden Jesu im Johannesevangelium', *ZNW* 61, 215–45.

BECKER, J. (1974) 'Beobachtungen zum Dualismus im Johannesevangelium', *ZNW* 65, 71–87.

BECKER, J. (1991) *Das Evangelium nach Johannes* I–II. Ökumenischer Taschenbuch-kommentar 4/1–2. Gütersloh.

BECKER, J. (1999), 'Geisterfahrung und Christologie: Ein Vergleich zwischen Paulus und Johannes', in *Antikes Judentum und Frühes Christentum.*, FS H. Stegemann, eds B. Kollmann et al. Beihefte zur Zeitschrift für die neutestamentliche Wissenschaft 97. Berlin: 428–42.

BECKER, J. (2006) 'Zu Hintergrund und Funktion des johanneischen Dualismus', in Sänger and Mell (eds) (2006): 3–73.

BECKER, M. (2014) 'Spirit in Relationship—Pneumatology in the Gospel of John', in Frey and Levison (eds) (2014): 331–41.

BEKKEN, P. J. (2015) *The Lawsuit Motif in John's Gospel from New Perspectives. Jesus Christ, Crucified Criminal and Emperor of the World*, Supplements to Novum Testamentum 158. Leiden.

BELLE, G. VAN (1994) *The Signs Source in the Fourth Gospel. Historical Survey and Critical Evaluation of the Semeia Hypothesis*. BETL 116. Leuven.

BELLE, G. VAN (1998) 'The Faith of the Galileans: The Parenthesis in Jn 4,44', *Ephemerides Theologicae Lovanienses* 74, 27–44.

BELLE, G. VAN (ed.) (2007) *The Death of Jesus in the Fourth Gospel*. BETL 200. Leuven.

BELLE, G. VAN (2009) 'L'unité littéraire et les deux finales du quatrième évangile', in *Studien zu Matthäus und Johannes/Études sur Matthieu et Jean*, FS J. Zumstein, eds A. Dettwiler and U. Poplutz. Abhandlungen zur Theologie des Alten und Neuen Testaments 97. Zürich: 297–315.

BELLE, G. VAN, M. LABAHN, and P. MARITZ (eds) (2009) *Repetitions and Variations in the Fourth Gospel*. BETL 223. Leuven.

BELLE, G. VAN, J. G. VAN DER WATT, and P. MARITZ (eds) (2005) *Theology and Christology in the Fourth Gospel*. BETL 184. Leuven.

BENNEMA, C. (2003) 'Spirit-Baptism in the Fourth Gospel: A Messianic Reading of John 1,33', *Biblica* 84, 35–60.

BENNEMA, C. (2007) 'Christ, the Spirit and the Knowledge of God: A Study in Johannine Epistemology', in *The Bible and Epistemology. Biblical Soundings on the Knowledge of God*, eds M. Healy and R. Parry. Milton Keynes: 107–33.

BENNEMA, C. (2009) *Encountering Jesus. Character Studies in the Gospel of John*. Louisville, KY.

BENNEMA, C. (2013) 'The Character of Pilate in the Gospel of John', in *Characters and Characterization in the Gospel of John*, ed. C. W. Skinner. London: 240–53.

BEUTLER, J. (1991) 'Zur Struktur von Johannes 6'. *Studien zum Neuen Testament und seiner Umwelt* 16, 89–104.

BEUTLER, J. (1998) *Studien zu den johanneischen Schriften*. Stuttgarter Biblische Aufsatzbände 25. Stuttgart.

BEUTLER, J. (2012) *Neue Studien zu den johanneischen Schriften. New Studies on the Johannine Writings*. Bonner Biblische Beiträge 167. Göttingen.

BEUTLER, J. (2015) 'Von der johanneischen Gemeinde zum Relecture-Modell', *Theologie und Philosophie* 90/1, 1–18.

BIERINGER, R. (2007) '"Greater than Our Hearts" (1 John 3:20): The Spirit in the Gospel of John', *Bible Today* (Collegeville, MN) 45/5, 305–9.

BIERINGER, R. (2008) '"I am ascending to my Father and your Father, to my God and your God" (John 20:17): Resurrection and Ascension in the Gospel of John', in Koester and Bieringer (eds) (2008): 209–35.

BIERINGER, R. (2014) '"Ihr habt weder seine Stimme gehört noch seine Gestalt je gesehen" (Joh 5,37): Antijudaismus und johanneische Christologie', in Verheyden et al. (eds) (2014): 165–88.

BIERINGER, R., D. POLLEFEYT, and F. VANDECASTEELE-VANNEUVILLE (eds) (2001a) *Anti-Judaism and the Fourth Gospel*. Louisville, KY.

BIERINGER, R., D. POLLEFEYT, and F. VANDECASTEELE-VANNEUVILLE (2001b) 'Wrestling with Johannine Anti-Judaism: A Hermeneutical Framework for the Analysis of the Current Debate', in Bieringer, Pollefeyt, and Vandecasteele-Vanneuville (eds) (2001a): 3–37.

BIRD, A. (2013) *Thomas Kuhn*. Durham.

BLANK, J. (1959) 'Die Verhandlung vor Pilatus Joh 18,28–19,16 im Lichte johanneischer Theologie', *Biblische Zeitschrift* 3, 60–81.

BLANK, J. (1964) *Krisis. Untersuchungen zur johanneischen Christologie und Eschatologie*. Freiburg.

BLANK, J. (1977–81) *Das Evangelium nach Johannes* I–III. Geistliche Schriftlesung 4/1–3. Düsseldorf.

BOER, M. C. DE (2015) 'The Original Prologue to the Gospel of John', *NTS* 61, 448–67.

BOISMARD, M-E. (1953) *Le prologue de saint Jean*. Lectio divina 11. Paris.

BORGEN, P. (1965) *Bread from Heaven. An Exegetical Study of the Concept of Manna in the Gospel of John and the Writings of Philo*. Supplements to Novum Testamentum 10. Leiden.

BORGEN, P. (1970) 'Observations on the Targumic Character of the Prologue of John', *NTS* 16, 288–95.

BORGEN, P. (1972) 'Logos was the True Light: Contributions to the Interpretation of the Prologue of John', *NT* 14/2, 115–30.

BORGEN, P. (1987) 'The Prologue of John–as Exposition of the Old Testament', in Borgen, *Philo, John and Paul. New Perspectives on Judaism and Early Christianity*. Atlanta, GA: 75–101.

BORGEN, P. (1997) 'John 6: Tradition, Interpretation and Composition', in Culpepper (ed.) (1997): 95–114.

BORGEN, P. (2014) *The Gospel of John. More Light from Philo, Paul and Archaeology.* Supplements to Novum Testamentum 154. Leiden.

BOYARIN, D. (2001) 'The Gospel of the *Memra*: Jewish Binitarianism and the Prologue to John', *Harvard Theological Review* 94/3, 243–84.

BROWN, R. E., S.S. (1966–70) *The Gospel According to John.* Anchor Bible 29–29A. Garden City, NY.

BROWN, R. E., S.S. (1967) 'The Paraclete in the Fourth Gospel', *NTS* 13, 113–32.

BROWN, R. E., S.S. (1970) 'Rev. Herbert Leroy', *Rätsel und Missverständnis*, *Biblica* 51/1, 152–4.

BROWN, R. E., S.S. (1979) *The Community of the Beloved Disciple.* New York.

BROWN, R. E., S.S. (2003) *An Introduction to the Gospel of John*, ed., updated, introduced, and concluded by F. J. Moloney, S.D.B., New Haven, CT.

BROWN, S. (2015) 'What Is Truth? Jesus, Pilate, and the Staging of the Dialogue of the Cross in John 18:28-19:16a', *CBQ* 77/1, 69–86.

BROWN, T. G. (2003). *Spirit in the Writings of John. Johannine Pneumatology in Social-Scientific Perspective.* Journal for the Study of the New Testament Supplement Series 253. London.

BUCH-HANSEN, G. (2010) *»It is the Spirit that Gives Life«. A Stoic Understanding of Pneuma in John's Gospel.* Beihefte zur Zeitschrift für die neutestamentliche Wissenschaft 173. Berlin.

BULTMANN, RUDOLF (1923) 'Der religionsgeschichtliche Hintergrund des Prologs zum Johannesevangelium', in Bultmann (1967) *Exegetica Aufsätze zur Erforschung des Neuen Testaments*, ed. E. Dinkler. Tübingen: 10–35.

BULTMANN, RUDOLF (1925) 'Die Bedeutung der neuerschlossenen mandäischen und manichäischen Quellen für das Verständnis des Johannesevangeliums', in Bultmann (1967) *Exegetica Aufsätze zur Erforschung des Neuen Testaments*, ed. E. Dinkler. Tübingen: 55–104.

BULTMANN, RUDOLF (1941) *Das Evangelium des Johannes.* Kritisch-exegetischer Kommentar über das Neue Testament II, 10. Auflage. Göttingen.

BULTMANN, RUDOLF (1965), 'Zur Geschichte der Lichtsymbolik im Altertum', in Bultmann, *Beiträge zum Verständnis der Jenseitigkeit Gottes im Neuen Testament.* Darmstadt: 7–42.

BURGE, G. M. (1987) *The Anointed Community. The Holy Spirit in the Johannine Tradition.* Grand Rapids, MI.

BURGE, G. M. (2006) 'Revelation and Discipleship in St. John's Gospel', in Lierman (ed.) (2006): 235–54.

BURKETT, D. (1991) *The Son of the Man in the Gospel of John.* Journal for the Study of the New Testament Supplement Series 56. Sheffield.

BURKHALTER, S. (2014) *Die johanneischen Abschiedsreden Jesu. Eine Auslegung von Joh 13–17 unter besonderer Berücksichtigung der Textstruktur.* Judentum und Christentum 20. Stuttgart.

BUSSE, U. (2013) '*Logos*, Jesus en God in Johannes 1:1-5: 'n Tekstuele analise', *Acta Theologica* 33/2, 20–36.

BUSSE, U. (2014) 'Theologie oder Christologie im Johannesprolog?', in Verheyden et al. (eds) (2014): 1–36.

BYRNE, B. (2014) *Life Abounding. A Reading of John's Gospel.* Collegeville, MN.

CARMICHAEL, C. M. (1996) *The Story of Creation. Its Origin and Interpretation in Philo and the Fourth Gospel.* Ithaca, NY.

CARTER, W. (2008) *John and Empire. Initial Explorations.* New York.

CHATMAN, S. (1978) *Story and Discourse. Narrative Structure in Fiction and Film.* Ithaca, NY.

CHIBICI-REVNEANU, N. (2007) *Die Herrlichkeit des Verherrlichten. Das Verständnis der δόξα im Johannesevangelium.* Wissenschaftliche Untersuchungen zum Neuen Testament 2.231. Tübingen.

CIRAFESI, W. V. (2014) 'The Johannine Community Hypothesis (1968–Present): Past and Present Approaches and a New Way Forward', *Currents in Biblical Research* 12/2, 173–93.

COLOE, M. L. (2001) *God Dwells with Us. Temple Symbolism in the Fourth Gospel.* Collegeville, MN.

COLOE, M. L. (2009) 'Temple Imagery in John', *Interpretation* 63/4, 368–81.

COLOE, M. L. (2011a) 'John's Portrait of Jesus', in *The Blackwell Companion to Jesus*, ed. D. R. Burkett. Chichester: 64–80.

COLOE, M. L. (2011b) 'Theological Reflections on Creation in the Gospel of John', *Pacifica* 24, 1–12.

COLOE, M. L. and T. THATCHER (eds) (2011) *John, Qumran, and the Dead Sea Scrolls.* Early Judaism and Its Literature 32. Atlanta, GA.

CONWAY, C. M. (1999) *Men and Women in the Fourth Gospel. Gender and Johannine Characterization.* SBLDS 167. Atlanta, GA.

CONWAY, C. M. (2002) 'The Production of the Johannine Community: A New Historicist Perspective', *JBL* 121/3: 479–95.

CORDERO, M. G. (1993) 'El "Logos" de Filón y el "Logos" del prólogo al Cuarto Evangelio', *Ciencia Tomista* 120: 209–42, 433–61.

COSGROVE, C. H. (1989) 'The Place Where Jesus Is: Allusions to Baptism and the Eucharist in the Fourth Gospel', *NTS* 35, 522–39.

COX, R. (2007) *By the Same Word. Creation and Salvation in Hellenistic Judaism and Early Christianity.* Beihefte zur Zeitschrift für die neutestamentliche Wissenschaft 145. Berlin.

CULPEPPER, R. A. (1975) *The Johannine School. An Examination of the Johannine School Hypothesis Based on the Investigation of the Nature of Ancient Schools.* SBLDS 26. Missoula, MT.

CULPEPPER, R. A. (1981) 'The Pivot of John's Prologue', *NTS* 27, 1–31.

CULPEPPER, R. A. (1983) *Anatomy of the Fourth Gospel. A Study in Literary Design.* Philadelphia, PA.

CULPEPPER, R. A. (1995) 'The Plot of John's Story of Jesus', *Interpretation* 49/4, 347–57.

CULPEPPER, R. A. (ed.) (1997a) *Critical Readings of John 6.* Biblical Interpretation Series 22. Leiden.

CULPEPPER, R. A. (1997b) 'John 6: Current Research in Retrospect', in Culpepper (ed.) (1997a): 247–57.

CULPEPPER, R. A. (1998) *The Gospel and Letters of John.* Interpreting Biblical Texts. Nashville, TN.

CULPEPPER, R. A. (2001) 'Anti-Judaism in the Fourth Gospel as a Theological Problem for Christian Interpreters', in Bieringer, Pollefeyt, and Vandecasteele-Vanneuville (eds) (2001): 61–82.

CULPEPPER, R. A. (2008) 'Realized Eschatology in the Experience of the Johannine Community', in Koester and Bieringer (eds) (2008): 253–76.

CULPEPPER, R. A. (2009) 'The Quest for the Church in the Gospel of John', *Interpretation* 63/4, 341–54.

CULPEPPER, R. A. (2013) 'C. H. Dodd as a precursor to narrative criticism', in Thatcher and Williams (eds) (2013): 31–48.

CULPEPPER, R. A. and F. F. SEGOVIA (eds) (1991) *The Fourth Gospel from a Literary Perspective*. Semeia 53. Atlanta, GA.

CULY, M. M. (2010) *Echoes of Friendship in the Gospel of John*. New Testament Monographs 30. Sheffield.

DAHL, N. A. (1962) 'The Johannine Church and History', in *Current Issues in New Testament Interpretation*, FS Otto A. Piper, eds W. Klassen and G. F. Snyder. New York: 124–42. (Quoted from J. Ashton, ed. (1997), 147–67.)

DAHL, N. A. (1990) '"Do not wonder!" John 5:28–29 and Johannine Eschatology Once More', in *The Conversation Continues. Studies in Paul and John in Honor of J. Louis Martyn*, eds R. T. Fortna and B. R. Gaventa. Nashville, TN: 322–36.

DANKER, F. W. (2000) *A Greek-English Lexicon of the New Testament and other Early Christian Literature*. Chicago, IL.

DENAUX, A. (ed.) (1992) *John and the Synoptics*. BETL 101. Leuven.

DETTWILER, A. (1995) *Die Gegenwart des Erhöhten. Eine exegetische Studie zu den johanneischen Abschiedsreden (Joh 13,31–16,33) unter besonderer Berücksichtigung ihres Relecture-Charakters*. FRLANT 169. Göttingen.

DETTWILER, A. and J. ZUMSTEIN (eds) (2002). *Kreuzestheologie im Neuen Testament*. WUNT 151. Tübingen.

DEVILLERS, L. (2012) 'Le prologue du quatrième évangile, clé de voûte de la littérature johannique', *NTS* 58/3, 317–30.

DIETZFELBINGER, C. (2004²) *Das Evangelium nach Johannes*. Zürcher Bibelkommentare 4.1–2. Zürich.

DILLON, J. (1996/1977) *The Middle Platonists 80 B.C. to A.D. 220*. London.

DILLON, J. (2008) 'Philo and Hellenistic Platonism', in *Philo of Alexandria and Post-Aristotelian Philosophy*, ed. F. Alesse. Leiden: 223–32.

DODD, C. H. (1953a) *The Interpretation of the Fourth Gospel*. Cambridge.

DODD, C. H. (1953b) 'Eternal Life', in Dodd, *New Testament Studies*. Manchester: 160–73.

DODD, C. H. (1963) *Historical Tradition in the Fourth Gospel*. Cambridge.

DONAHUE, J. R. (ed.) (2005) *Life in Abundance. Studies of John's Gospel in Tribute to Raymond E. Brown, S.S.*, Collegeville, MN.

DUKE, P. D. (1985) *Irony in the Fourth Gospel*. Atlanta, GA.

DUNDERBERG, I. (1994) *Johannes und die Synoptiker*. Annales Academiae Scientiarum Fennicae/Dissertationes humanarum litterarum 69. Helsinki.

DUNN, J. D. G. (1971) 'John VI–An Eucharistic Discourse?', *NTS* 17, 328–38.

EDWARDS, R. B. (1988) '*XAPIN ANTI XAPITOΣ* (John 1.16): Grace and the Law in the Johannine Prologue', *JSNT* 32, 3–15.

ENGBERG-PEDERSEN, T. (ed.) (2001) *Paul Beyond The Judaism/Hellenism Divide*. Louisville, KY.

ENGBERG-PEDERSEN, T. (2004) 'The Concept of Paraenesis', in *Early Christian Paraenesis in Context*, eds J. M. Starr and T. Engberg-Pedersen. Beihefte zur Zeitschrift für die neutestamentliche Wissenschaft 125. Berlin: 47–72.

ENGBERG-PEDERSEN, T. (2010) *Cosmology and Self in the Apostle Paul. The Material Spirit*. Oxford.

ENGBERG-PEDERSEN, T. (2012) '*Logos* and *Pneuma* in the Fourth Gospel', in *Greco-Roman Culture and the New Testament. Studies Commemorating the Centennial of the Pontifical Biblical Institute*, eds D. E. Aune and F. E. Brenk. Supplements to Novum Testamentum 143. Leiden: 27–48.

ENGBERG-PEDERSEN, T. (2013a) 'Philosophy and Ideology in John 9–10', in *'The One Who Sows Bountifully'. Essays in Honor of Stanley K. Stowers*, eds C. Johnson Hodge, S. M. Olyan, D. Ullucci, and E. J. Wasserman. Providence, RI: 295–306.

ENGBERG-PEDERSEN, T. (2013b) 'Philosophy and Ideology in John 9–10 Read As a Single Literary Unit', *Histos* 7, 181–204.

ENGBERG-PEDERSEN, T. (2015) 'A Question of Genre: John 13–17 as *Paraklēsis*', in *The Gospel of John as Genre Mosaic*, ed. K. B. Larsen. Studia Aarhusiana Neotestamentica 3. Göttingen: 283–301.

ENGBERG-PEDERSEN, T. (2016) 'Stoicism in Early Christianity: The Apostle Paul and the Evangelist John as Stoics', in *The Routledge Handbook of the Stoic Tradition*, ed. J. Sellars. London: 29–43.

ENGBERG-PEDERSEN, T. (2017) 'The Cosmology of the Raising of Lazarus (John 11–12)', in *Coming Back to Life. The Permeability of Past and Present, Mortality and Immortality, Death and Life in the Ancient Mediterranean*, eds F. S. Tappenden and C. Daniel-Hughes. Montreal. Online: <http://comingbacktolife.mcgill.ca>.

FINNERN, S. (2010) *Narratologie und biblische Exegese*. WUNT 2.285. Tübingen.

FÖRSTER, H. (2013) 'Die Perikope von der Hochzeit zu Kana (Joh 2:1–11) im Kontext der Spätantike', *NT* 55/2, 103–26.

FÖRSTER, H. (2014) 'Die johanneischen Zeichen und Joh 2:11 als möglicher hermeneutischer Schlüssel', *NT* 56/1, 1–23.

FORTNA, R. T. and T. THATCHER (eds) (2001). *Jesus in the Johannine Tradition*. Louisville, KY.

FREY, J. (1997) *Die johanneische Eschatologie I. Ihre Probleme im Spiegel der Forschung seit Reimarus*. WUNT 96. Tübingen.

FREY, J. (1998) *Die johanneische Eschatologie II. Das johanneische Zeitverständnis*. WUNT 110. Tübingen.

FREY, J. (2000a) *Die johanneische Eschatologie III. Die eschatologische Verkündigung in den johanneischen Texten*. WUNT 117. Tübingen.

FREY, J. (2000b) 'Das Bild als Wirkungspotential. Ein rezeptionsästetischer Versuch zur Funktion der Brotmetapher in Joh 6', in *Bildersprache verstehen. Zur Hermeneutik der Metapher und anderer bildlicher Sprachformen*, ed. R. Zimmermann. Übergänge 38. Munich: 331–61.

FREY, J. (2002) 'Die *theologia crucifixi* im Johannesevangelium', in Dettwiler and Zumstein (eds) (2002): 169–238.

FREY, J. (2003) 'Das Vierte Evangelium auf dem Hintergrund der älteren Evangelientradition', in Söding (ed.) (2003): 60–118.

FREY, J. (2004a) 'Auf der Suche nach dem Kontext des vierten Evangeliums: Eine forschungsgeschichtliche Einführung', in Frey and Schnelle (eds) (2004): 3–45.

FREY, J. (2004b) 'Licht aus den Höhlen? Der "johanneische Dualismus" und die Texte von Qumran', in Frey and Schnelle (eds) (2004): 117–203.

FREY, J. (2005) 'Eschatology in the Johannine Circle', in Van Belle et al. (eds) (2005): 47–82.

FREY, J. (2006) 'Zu Hintergrund und Funktion des johanneischen Dualismus', in Sänger and Mell (eds) (2006): 3–73.

FREY, J. (2008a) '"… dass sie meine Herrlichkeit schauen" (Joh 17.24): Zu Hintergrund, Sinn und Funktion der johanneischen Rede von der δόξα Jesu', *NTS* 54/3, 375–97.

FREY, J. (2008b) 'Grundfragen der Johannesinterpretation im Spektrum neuerer Gesamtdarstellungen', *Theologische Literaturzeitung* 133, 743–60.

FREY, J. (2012) 'Was trägt die johanneische Tradition zum christlichen Bild von Gott bei?', in Frey and Poplutz (eds) (2012a): 217–57.

FREY, J. (2013a) *Die Herrlichkeit des Gekreuzigten. Studien zu den Johanneischen Texten I*, WUNT 307. Tübingen.

FREY, J. (2013b) '"Die Juden" im Johannesevangelium und die Frage nach der "Trennung der Wege" zwischen der johanneischen Gemeinde und der Synagoge', in Frey (2013a): 339–77.

FREY, J. (2013c) 'Wege und Perspektiven der Interpretation des Johannesevangeliums: Überlegungen auf dem Weg zu einem Kommentar', in Frey (2013a): 3–41.

FREY, J. (2014) 'How did the Spirit become a Person?', in Frey and Levison (eds) (2014): 343–71.

FREY, J. and J. R. LEVISON (eds) (2014) *The Holy Spirit, Inspiration, and the Cultures of Antiquity. Multidisciplinary Perspectives.* Ekstasis: Religious Experience from Antiquity to the Middle Ages 5. Berlin.

FREY, J. and U. POPLUTZ (eds) (2012a) *Narrativität und Theologie im Johannesevangelium.* Biblisch-Theologische Studien 130. Neukirchen-Vluyn.

FREY, J. and U. POPLUTZ (2012b) 'Narrativität und Theologie im Johannesevangelium', in Frey and Poplutz (eds) (2012a): 1–18.

FREY, J., J. ROHLS, and R. ZIMMERMANN (eds) (2003). *Metaphorik und Christologie.* Theologische Bibliotek Töpelmann 120. Berlin.

FREY, J. and U. SCHNELLE (eds) (2004) *Kontexte des Johannesevangeliums. Das vierte Evangelium in religions- und traditionsgeschichtlicher Perspektive.* WUNT 175. Tübingen.

FREY, J., J. G. VAN DER WATT, and R. ZIMMERMANN (eds) (2006) *Imagery in the Gospel of John. Terms, Forms, Themes, and Theology of Johannine Figurative Language.* WUNT 200. Tübingen.

GARDNER-SMITH, P. (1938) *Saint John and the Synoptic Gospels.* Cambridge.

GARSKÝ, Z. (2012) *Das Wirken Jesu in Galiläa bei Johannes. Eine strukturale Analyse der Intertextualität des vierten Evangeliums mit den Synoptikern.* WUNT 2.325. Tübingen.

GERHARDSSON, B. (1961) *Memory and Manuscript. Oral Tradition and Written Transmission in Rabbinic Judaism and Early Christianity.* Acta Seminarii Neotestamentici Upsaliensis 22. Lund.

GLANCY, J. A. (2005) 'Torture: Flesh, Truth, and the Fourth Gospel', *Biblical Interpretation* 13, 107–36.

GLASSWELL, M. E. (1985) 'The Relationship between John and Mark', *JSNT* 23, 99–115.

GODET, F. (1869) *Commentar zu dem Evangelium Johannis*. Hannover.

GOULDER, M. D. (1992) 'John 1,1–2,12 and the Synoptics', in Denaux (ed.) (1992): 201–22.

GREENE, J. R. (2013) 'Integrating Interpretations of John 7:37–39 into the Temple Theme: The Spirit as Efflux from the New Temple', *Neotestamentica* 47/2, 333–53.

GROSSOUW, W. K. (1966) 'A Note on John XIII 1–3', *NT* 8/2–4, 124–31.

HAENCHEN, E. (1963) 'Probleme des johanneischen "Prologs"', *ZTK* 60, 305–34.

HAHM, D. E. (1977) *The Origins of Stoic Cosmology*. Columbus, OH.

HAHN, F. (1985) 'Das Glaubensverständnis im Johannesevangelium', in *Glaube und Eschatologie*, FS W. G. Kümmel, eds E. Grässer and O. Merk. Tübingen: 51–69.

HAKOLA, R. (2009) 'The Burden of Ambiguity: Nicodemus and the Social Identity of the Johannine Christians', *NTS* 55/4, 438–55.

HARNACK, A. (1892) 'Über das Verhältnis des Prologs des vierten Evangeliums zum ganzen Werk', *ZTK* 2, 189–321.

HARRILL, J. A. (2008) 'Cannibalistic Language in the Fourth Gospel and Greco-Roman Polemics of Factionalism (John 6:52–66)', *JBL* 127/1, 133–58.

HARRIS, J. RENDEL (1916) 'The Origin of the Prologue to St. John's Gospel', *Expositor* 12, 147–70, 314–20, 388–400, 415–26.

HEIL, J. P. (1995a) *Blood and Water. The Death and Resurrection of Jesus in John 18–21*. Catholic Biblical Quarterly Monograph Series 27. Washington, DC.

HEIL, J. P. (1995b) 'Jesus as the Unique High Priest in the Gospel of John', *CBQ* 57/4, 729–45.

HEILMANN, J. (2014) *Wein und Blut. Das Ende der Eucharistie im Johannesevangelium und dessen Konsequenzen*. Beiträge zur Wissenschaft vom Alten und Neuen Testament 204. Stuttgart.

HENGEL, M. (1987) 'The Interpretation of the Wine Miracle at Cana: John 2:1–11', in *The Glory of Christ in the New Testament. Studies in Christology in Memory of George Bradford Caird*, eds L. D. Hurst and N. T. Wright. Oxford: 83–112.

HILL, C. E. (2006) 'The Fourth Gospel in the Second Century: The Myth of Orthodox Johannophobia', in Lierman (ed.) (2006): 135–69.

HIRSCH-LUIPOLD, R. (2002) *Plutarchs Denken in Bildern. Studien zur literarischen, philosophischen und religiösen Funktion des Bildhaften*. Studien und Texte zu Antike und Christentum 14. Tübingen.

HIRSCH-LUIPOLD, R. (2006) 'Klartext in Bildern. ἀληθινός κτλ., παροιμία – παρρησία, σημεῖον als Signalwörter für eine bildhafte Darstellungsform im Johannesevangelium', in Frey, van der Watt, and Zimmermann (eds) (2006): 61–102.

HOEGEN-ROHLS, C. (1996) *Der nachösterliche Johannes. Die Abschiedsreden als hermeneutischer Schlüssel zum vierten Evangelium*. WUNT 2.84. Tübingen.

HOEGEN-ROHLS, C. (2004) 'Johanneische Theologie im Kontext paulinischen Denkens? Eine forschungsgeschichtliche Skizze', in Frey and Schnelle (eds) (2004): 593–612.

HOFIUS, O. (1987) 'Struktur und Gedankengang des Logos-Hymnus in Joh 1 1–18', *ZNW* 78/1, 1–25.

HORSLEY, R. and T. THATCHER (2013) *John, Jesus, and the Renewal of Israel*. Grand Rapids, MI.

HOSKYNS, E. C. (1947) *The Fourth Gospel*, ed. Francis N. Davey. London.

HÜBNER, H. (ed.) (1999) *Die Weisheit Salomons*. Das Alte Testament Deutsch/ Apokryphen 4. Göttingen.

HUNT, S. A., D. F. TOLMIE, and R. ZIMMERMANN (eds) (2013) *Character Studies in the Fourth Gospel. Narrative Approaches to Seventy Figures in John*. WUNT 314. Tübingen.

HYLEN, S. (2005) *Allusion and Meaning in John 6*. Beihefte zur Zeitschrift für die neutestamentliche Wissenschaft 137. Berlin.

HYLEN, S. (2009) *Imperfect Believers. Ambiguous Characters in the Gospel of John*. Louisville, KY.

JENNINGS, M. (2013) 'The Fourth Gospel's Reversal of Mark in John 13,31–14,3', *Biblica* 94/2, 210–36.

JONGE, M. DE (1977) *Jesus: Stranger from Heaven and Son of God. Jesus Christ and the Christians in Johannine Perspective*. Society of Biblical Literature Sources for Biblical Study 11. Missoula, MT.

JONGE, M. DE (1992) 'The Radical Eschatology of the Fourth Gospel and the Eschatology of the Synoptics: Some Suggestions', in Denaux (ed.) 1992, 481–7.

JOUBERT, J. (2007) 'Johannine Metaphors/Symbols Linked to the Paraclete-Spirit and Their Theological Implications', *Acta Theologica* (South Africa) 27/1, 83–103.

KAESTLY, J-D., J-M. POFFET, and J. ZUMSTEIN (eds) (1990) *La communauté johannique et son histoire. La trajectoire de l'évangile de Jean aux deux premiers siècles*. Genève.

KAMMLER, H-C. (1996) 'Jesus Christus und der Geistparaklet: Eine Studie zur johanneischen Verhältnisbestimmung von Pneumatologie und Christologie', in *Johannesstudien. Untersuchungen zur Theologie des vierten Evangeliums*, eds O. Hofius and H-C. Kammler. WUNT 88. Tübingen: 87–190.

KÄSEMANN, E. (1957) 'Aufbau und Anliegen des johanneischen Prologs', in *Libertas Christiana*, FS Delekat, eds W. Matthias and E. Wolf. Munich: 75–99.

KÄSEMANN, E. (1966) *Jesu letzter Wille nach Johannes 17*. Tübingen.

KEEFER, K. (2006) *The Branches of the Gospel of John. On the Reception of the Fourth Gospel in the Early Church*. Library of New Testament Studies 332. London.

KELLUM, L. S. (2004) *The Unity of the Farewell Discourse. The Literary Integrity of John 13.31–16.33*. Journal for the Study of the New Testament Supplement Series 256. London.

KIEFFER, R. (1992) 'Jean et Marc: Convergences dans la structure et dans les détails', in Denaux (ed.) (1992): 109–25.

KIRK, D. R. (2012) 'Heaven Opened: Intertextuality and Meaning in John 1:51', *Tyndale Bulletin* 63/2, 237–56.

KOESTER, C. R. (1989) 'Hearing, Seeing, and Believing in the Gospel of John', *Biblica* 70/3, 327–48.

KOESTER, C. R. (1990) '"The Savior of the World" (John 4:42)', *JBL* 109, 665–80.

KOESTER, C. R. (2003/1995) *Symbolism in the Fourth Gospel. Meaning, Mystery, Community*. Minneapolis, MN.

KOESTER, C. R. (2008a) *The Word of Life. A Theology of John's Gospel*. Grand Rapids, MI.

KOESTER, C. R. (2008b) 'Jesus' Resurrection, the Signs, and the Dynamics of Faith in the Gospel of John', in Koester and Bieringer (eds) (2008): 47–74.

KOESTER, C. R. and R. BIERINGER (eds) (2008) *The Resurrection of Jesus in the Gospel of John*. WUNT 222. Tübingen.

KUHN, H-W. (1966) *Enderwartung und gegenwärtiges Heil*. Studien zur Umwelt des Neuen Testaments 4. Göttingen.

KUHN, T. S. (1957) *The Copernican Revolution*. Cambridge, MA.

KUHN, T. S. (1962) *The Structure of Scientific Revolutions*. Chicago, IL.

KÜMMEL, W. G. (1980) *Einleitung in das Neue Testament*. Heidelberg.

KYSAR, R. (1997) 'The Dismantling of Decisional Faith: A Reading of John 6:25–71', in Culpepper (ed.) (1997a): 161–81.

KYSAR, R. (2005) *Voyages with John. Charting the Fourth Gospel*. Waco, TX.

LABAHN, M. and M. LANG (2004) 'Johannes und die Synoptiker: Positionen und Impulse seit 1990', in Frey and Schnelle (eds) (2004): 443–515.

LANG, M. (2004) 'Johanneische Abschiedsreden und Senecas Konsolationsliteratur: Wie konnte ein Römer Joh 13,31–17,26 lesen?', in Frey and Schnelle (eds) (2004): 365–412.

LARSEN, K. B. (2008) *Recognizing the Stranger. Recognition Scenes in the Gospel of John*. Leiden.

LARSEN, K. B. (2009) 'At sige ret farvel: Jesus' afskedstale i genrehistorisk belysning (Joh 13–17)', in *Hvad er sandhed. Nye læsninger af Johannesevangeliet*, eds G. Buch-Hansen and C. Petterson. Frederiksberg: 85–102.

LEE, D. A. (1994) *The Symbolic Narratives of the Fourth Gospel. The Interplay of Form and Meaning*. Journal for the Study of the New Testament Supplement Series 95. Sheffield.

LEE, D. A. (2002) *Flesh and Glory. Symbol, Gender, and Theology in the Gospel of John*. New York.

LEE, D. A. (2012) *Hallowed in Truth and Love. Spirituality in the Johannine Literature*. Eugene, OR.

LEISEGANG, H. (1919) *Der Heilige Geist. Das Wesen und Werden der mystisch-intuitiven Erkenntnis in der Philosophie und Religion der Griechen*. Leipzig.

LEISEGANG, H. (1922) *Pneuma Hagion. Der Ursprung des Geistbegriffs der synoptischen Evangelien aus der griechischen Mystik*. Leipzig.

LÉON-DUFOUR, X. (1980–1) 'Towards a Symbolic Reading of the Fourth Gospel', *NTS* 27, 439–56.

LÉON-DUFOUR, X. (1988–96) *Lecture de l'évangile selon Jean*. 4 vols. Paris.

LÉON-DUFOUR, X. (1990) 'Spécificité symbolique du langage de Jean', in *La communauté johannique et son histoire*, eds J. D. Kaestili, J. M. Poffet, and J. Zumstein. Genève: 121–34.

LEONHARDT-BALZER, J. (2004) 'Der Logos und die Schöpfung: Streiflichter bei Philo (Op 20–25) und im Johannesprolog (Joh 1,1–18)', in Frey and Schnelle (eds) (2004): 295–319.

LEROY, H. (1968) *Rätsel und Missverständnis. Ein Beitrag zur Formgeschichte des Johannesevangeliums*. Bonner biblische Beiträge 30. Bonn.

Lestang, F. (2013) 'Qui sont les "Juifs" dans l'évangile de Jean?', *Spiritus* 211, 208–22.

Levine, A-J. (ed.) (2003) *A Feminist Companion to John*. 2 vols. London.

Levison, J. R. (2009) *Filled with the Spirit*. Grand Rapids, MI.

Liddell, H. G., R. Scott, and H. S. Jones (eds) (1940) *A Greek-English Lexicon*. Oxford.

Lierman, J. (ed.) (2006) *Challenging Perspectives on the Gospel of John*. WUNT 2.219. Tübingen.

Lieu, J. M. (1988) 'Blindness in the Johannine Tradition', *NTS* 34, 83–95.

Lieu, J. M. (1999) 'Temple and synagogue in John', *NTS* 45/1, 51–69.

Lieu, J. M. (2001) 'Anti-Judaism in the Fourth Gospel: Explanation and Hermeneutics', in Bieringer et al. (eds) (2001): 101–17.

Lieu, J. M. (2008) 'Anti-Judaism, the Jews, and the Worlds of the Fourth Gospel', in Bauckham and Mosser (eds) (2008): 168–82.

Lincoln, A. T. (1998) '"I am the Resurrection and the Life": The Resurrection Message of the Fourth Gospel', in *Life in the Face of Death. The Resurrection Message of the New Testament*, ed. R. N. Longenecker. Grand Rapids, MI: 122–44.

Lincoln, A. T. (2000) *Truth on Trial. The Lawsuit Motif in the Fourth Gospel*. Peabody, MA.

Lincoln, A. T. (2005) *The Gospel According to Saint John*. Black's New Testament Commentary. London.

Lincoln, A. T. (2008) 'The Lazarus Story: A Literary Perspective', in Bauckham and Mosser (eds) (2008) 211–32.

Lindars, B. (1981) 'John and the Synoptic Gospels: A Test Case', *NTS* 27, 287–94.

Loader, W. (1992) *The Christology of the Fourth Gospel. Structure and Issues*. Beiträge zur biblischen Exegese und Theologie 23. Frankfurt am Main.

Long, A. A. (1982) 'Soul and Body in Stoicism', *Phronesis* 27, 34–57.

Long, A. A. (1996) *Stoic Studies*. Cambridge.

Long, A. A. and D. N. Sedley (eds) (1987) *The Hellenistic Philosophers*. 2 vols. Cambridge.

Lowe, M. (1976) 'Who Were the Ἰουδαῖοι', *NT* 18, 101–30.

Lozada, F. and T. Thatcher (eds) (2006) *New Currents through John. A Global Perspective*. Society of Biblical Literature Resources for Biblical Study 54. Atlanta, GA.

Mackay, I. D. (2004) *John's Relationship with Mark. An Analysis of John 6 in the Light of Mark 6–8*. WUNT 2.102. Tübingen.

Malherbe, A. J. (2000) *The Letters to the Thessalonians*. Anchor Bible. New York.

Malherbe, A. J. (2014) *Light from the Gentiles. Hellenistic Philosophy and Early Christianity. Collected Essays, 1959–2012*, eds C. R. Holladay, J. T. Fitzgerald, G. E. Sterling, and J. W. Thompson. Leiden.

Malina, B. J. and R. L. Rohrbaugh (1998) *Social-Science Commentary on the Gospel of John*. Minneapolis, MN.

Manns, F. (2012) 'A Jewish Approach to the Gospel of John. Part One: A Methodological Problem', *Antonianum* 87/2, 259–79.

Manns, F. (2012) 'II. Some Jewish Traditions in the FG', *Antonianum* 87/3, 549–608.

Manns, F. (2012) 'Some Jewish Traditions in the FG. Terza parte', *Antonianum* 87/4, 743–83.

Marcus, J. (2009) '*Birkat-Ha-Minim* Revisited', *NTS* 55, 523–51.

Maritz, P. and G. Van Belle (2006) 'The Imagery of Eating and Drinking in John 6:35', in Frey, van der Watt, and Zimmermann (eds) (2006): 333–52.

Martyn, J. L. (1986) 'Source Criticism and Religionsgeschichte in the Fourth Gospel', in Ashton (ed.) (1986): 99–121.

Martyn, J. L. (1996) 'A Gentile Mission that Replaced an Earlier Jewish Mission?', in *Exploring the Gospel of John. In Honor of D. Moody Smith*, eds R. A. Culpepper and C. C. Black. Louisville, KY: 124–44.

Martyn, J. L. (2003/1968) *History and Theology in the Fourth Gospel*. Louisville, KY.

Meeks, W. A. (1966) 'Galilee and Judea in the Fourth Gospel', *JBL* 85, 159–69.

Meeks, W. A. (1967) *The Prophet-King. Moses Traditions and the Johannine Christology*. Supplements to Novum Testamentum 14. Leiden.

Meeks, W. A. (1972) 'The Man from Heaven in Johannine Sectarianism', *JBL* 91, 44–72.

Meeks, W. A. (1976) 'The divine agent and its counterfeit in Philo and the Fourth Gospel', in *Aspects of Religious Propaganda in Judaism and Early Christianity*, ed. E. Schüssler Fiorenza. Notre Dame, IN: 43–67.

Meeks, W. A. (1990) 'Equal to God', in *The Conversation Continues. Studies in Paul and John in Honor of J. Louis Martyn*, eds R. T. Fortna and B. R. Gaventa. Nashville, TN: 309–21.

Menken, M. J. J. (1997) 'John 6:51c–58: Eucharist or Christology?', in Culpepper (ed.) (1997a): 183–204.

Mlakuzhyil, G., S. J. (1987) *The Christocentric Literary Structure of the Fourth Gospel*. Analecta Biblica 117. Rome.

Moloney, F. J. (1993) *Belief in the Word. Reading John 1–4*. Minneapolis, MN.

Moloney, F. J. (1996) *Signs and Shadows. Reading John 5–12*. Minneapolis, MN.

Moloney, F. J. (1997) 'The Function of Prolepsis in the Interpretation of John 6', in Culpepper (ed.) (1997a): 129–48.

Moloney, F. J. (1998a) *Glory not Dishonor. Reading John 13–21*. Minneapolis, MN.

Moloney, F. J. (1998b) *The Gospel of John*. Sacra Pagina 4. Collegeville, MN.

Moloney, F. J. (2003) 'Can Everyone be Wrong? A Reading of John 11.1–12.8', *NTS* 45, 505–27.

Moloney, F. J. (2005) 'The Gospel of John: The Legacy of Raymond E. Brown and Beyond', in Donahue (ed.) (2005): 19–39.

Moloney, F. J. (2012a) 'Recent Johannine Studies: Part One: Commentaries', *The Expository Times* 123, 313–22.

Moloney, F. J. (2012b) 'Recent Johannine Studies: Part Two: Monographs', *The Expository Times* 123/9, 417–28.

Moloney, F. J. (2013) *Love in the Gospel of John. An Exegetical, Theological, and Literary Study*. Grand Rapids, MI.

Moser, M. (2014) *Schriftdiskurse im Johannesevangelium. Eine narrativ-intertextuelle Analyse am Paradigma von Joh 4 und Joh 7*. WUNT 2.380. Tübingen.

Müller, U. B. (1974) 'Die Parakletvorstellung im Johannesevangelium', *ZTK* 71, 31–77.

Munck, J. (1950) 'Discours d'adieu dans le Nouveau Testament et dans la littérature biblique', in *Aux sources de la tradition chrétienne. Mélanges offerts à M. Maurice Goguel à l'occasion de son soixante-dizième anniversaire*, eds O. Cullmann and P. Menoud. Neuchâtel: 155–70.

NAGEL, T. (2000) *Die Rezeption des Johannesevangeliums im 2. Jahrhundert. Studien zur vorirenäischen Aneignung und Auslegung des vierten Evangeliums in christlicher und christlich-gnostischer Literatur*. Arbeiten zur Bibel und ihrer Geschichte 2. Leipzig.

NEYREY, J. H. (2009) *The Gospel of John in Cultural and Rhetorical Perspective*. Grand Rapids, MI.

NG, WAI-YEE (2001) *Water Symbolism in John. An Eschatological Approach*. New York.

NICHOLSON, G. C. (1983) *Death as Departure. The Johannine Descent-Ascent Schema*. SBLDS 63. Chico, CA.

NICKLAS, T. (2001) *Ablösung und Verstrickung. 'Juden' und Jüngergestalten als Charaktere der erzählten Welt des Johannesevangeliums und ihre Wirkung auf den impliziten Leser*. Regensburger Studien zur Theologie 60. Frankfurt am Main.

NIELSEN, J. T. (2006) 'The Lamb of God: The Cognitive Structure of a Johannine Metaphor', in Frey, van der Watt, and Zimmermann (eds) (2006): 217–56.

NIELSEN, J. T. (2009) *Die kognitive Dimension des Kreuzes. Zur Deutung des Todes Jesu im Johannesevangelium*. WUNT 2.263. Tübingen.

NOBILIO, F. (2007) 'The Implied Definition of the Prophet and Its Middle Platonic Trajectory in the Gospel of John', *Neotestamentica* 41/1, 131–56.

O'DAY, G. R. (1986a) *Revelation in the Fourth Gospel. Narrative Mode and Theological Claim*. Philadelphia, PA.

O'DAY, G. R. (1986b) 'Narrative Mode and Theological Claim: A Study in the Fourth Gospel', *JBL* 105/4, 657–68.

O'DAY, G. R. (1991) '"I Have Overcome the World" (John 16:33): Narrative Time in John 13–17', *Semeia* 53, 153–66.

O'DAY, G. R. (1995a) *The Gospel of John*. The New Interpreter's Bible 9. Nashville, TN.

O'DAY, G. R. (1995b) 'Toward a Narrative-Critical Study of John', *Interpretation* 49/4, 341–6.

O'DAY, G. R. (1997) 'John 6:15–21: Jesus Walking on Water as Narrative Embodiment of Johannine Christology', in Culpepper (ed.) (1997a): 149–59.

O'DAY, G. R. (2004) 'Jesus as Friend in the Gospel of John', *Interpretation* 58/2, 144–57.

O'DAY, G. R. (2013) 'Martha: Seeing the Glory of God', in Hunt, Tolmie, and Zimmermann (eds) (2013): 487–503.

O'DAY, G. R. and S. E. HYLEN (2006) *John*. Louisville, KY.

OKURE, T. (1988) *The Johannine Approach to Mission. A Contextual Study of John 4:1–42*. WUNT 31. Tübingen.

OLSSON, B. (1974) *Structure and Meaning in the Fourth Gospel. A Text-Linguistic Analysis of John 2:1–11 and 4:1–42*. Coniectanea Biblica New Testament Series 6. Lund.

PAINTER, J. (1979) 'Johannine Symbols: A Case Study in Epistemology', *Journal of Theology for South Africa* 27, 26–41.

PAINTER, J. (1980–1) 'The Farewell Discourses and the History of Johannine Christianity', *NTS* 27, 525–43.

PAINTER, J. (1991) *The Quest for the Messiah. The History, Literature and Theology of the Johannine Community*. Edinburgh.

PAINTER, J. (2008) '"The Light Shines in the Darkness...": Creation, Incarnation, and Resurrection in John', in Koester and Bieringer (eds) (2008): 21–46.

PAINTER, J. (2013) 'The Fourth Gospel and the founder of Christianity: The place of historical tradition in the work of C. H. Dodd', in Thatcher and Williams (eds) (2013): 257–84.

PAINTER, J. (2014) 'The Prologue as an Hermeneutical Key to Reading the Fourth Gospel', in Verheyden et al. (eds) (2014): 37–60.

PARSENIOS, G. L. (2006) '"No Longer in the World" (John 17:11): The Transformation of the Tragic in the Fourth Gospel', *Harvard Theological Review* 98/1, 1–21.

PARSENIOS, G. L. (2005) *Departure and Consolation. The Johannine Farewell Discourses in Light of Greco-Roman Literature.* Supplements to Novum Testamentum 117. Leiden.

PARSENIOS, G. L. (2010) *Rhetoric and Drama in the Johannine Lawsuit Motif.* WUNT 258. Tübingen.

PARSENIOS, G. L. (2015) Rev. Frey, *Die Herrlichkeit des Gekreuzigten* (Frey 2013a). *Religious Studies Review* 41/1, 26–7.

PASTORELLI, D. (2006) *Le Paraclet dans le corpus johannique.* Beihefte zur Zeitschrift für die neutestamentliche Wissenschaft 142. Berlin.

PETERSEN, N. R. (1993) *The Gospel of John and the Sociology of Light. Language and Characterization in the Fourth Gospel.* Valley Forge, PA.

PETERSON, R. A. (2013) 'Union with Christ in the Gospel of John', *Presbyterion* (St. Louis, MO) 39/1, 9–29.

PHILLIPS, P. M. (2006) *The Prologue of the Fourth Gospel. A Sequential Reading.* Library of New Testament Studies 294. London.

PHILLIPS, P. M. (2013) 'The Samaritans of Sychar: A Responsive Chorus', in Hunt, Tolmie, and Zimmermann (eds) (2013): 292–8.

PIERCE, M. N. and B. E. REYNOLDS (2014) 'The Perfect Tense-Form and the Son of Man in John 3:13: Developments in Greek Grammar as a Viable Solution to the Timing of the Ascent and Descent', *NTS* 60/1, 149–55.

POPLUTZ, U. (2007) 'Das Drama der Passion: Eine Analyse der Prozesserzählung Joh 18,28–19,16a unter Berücksichtigung dramentheoretischer Gesichtspunkte', in Van Belle (ed.) (2007): 769–82.

POPLUTZ, U. (2012) 'Die Pharisäer als literarische Figurengruppe im Johannesevangelium', in Frey and Poplutz (eds) (2012a): 19–39.

POPP, T. (2001) *Grammatik des Geistes. Literarische Kunst und theologische Konzeption in Johannes 3 und 6.* Arbeiten zur Bibel und ihrer Geschichte 3. Leipzig.

POPP, T. (2004) 'Die Kunst der Wiederholung: Repetition, Variation und Amplifikation im vierten Evangelium am Beispiel von Joh 6,6–71', in Frey and Schnelle (eds) (2004): 559–92.

PORSCH, F. (1974) *Pneuma und Wort. Ein exegetischer Beitrag zur Pneumatologie des Johannesevangeliums.* Frankfurter Theologische Studien 16. Frankfurt.

POTTERIE, I. DE LA (1955) 'De interpunctione et interpretatione versuum Joh. i, 3.4', *Verbum Domini* 33, 193–208.

POTTERIE, I. DE LA (1960) 'Jésus roi et juge d'après Jn 19,13: *ekathisen epi bēmatos*', *Biblica* 41, 217–47.

POTTERIE, I. DE LA (1968) 'L'exaltation du Fils de l'homme (Jn. 12, 31–36)', *Gregorianum* 49/3, 460–78.

POTTERIE, I. DE LA (1977) *La vérité dans saint Jean.* Analecta biblica 73–4. Rome.

POTTERIE, I. DE LA (1984) 'Structure du prologue de saint Jean', *NTS* 30, 354–81.

POTTERIE, I. DE LA (1988) '«C'est lui qui a ouvert la voie»: La finale du prologue johannique', *Biblica* 69/3, 340–70.

RABENS, V. (2012) 'Johannine Perspectives on Ethical Enabling in the Context of Stoic and Philonic Ethics', in van der Watt and Zimmermann (eds) (2012): 114–39.

RAHNER, J. (1999) 'Missverstehen, um zu verstehen: Zur Funktion der Missverständnisse im JohEv'. *Biblische Zeitschrift* 43, 212–19.

REBELL, W. (1987) *Gemeinde als Gegenwelt. Zur soziologischen und didaktischen Funktion des Johannesevangelium.* Beiträge zur biblischen Exegese und Theologie 20. Frankfurt.

REINHARTZ, A. (1992) *The Word in the World. The Cosmological Tale in the Fourth Gospel.* SBLMS 45. Atlanta, GA.

REINHARTZ, A. (1998) 'The Johannine Community and Its Jewish Neighbors: A Reappraisal', in Segovia (ed.) (1998a): 111–38.

REINHARTZ, A. (ed.) (1999a) *God the Father in the Gospel of John.* Semeia 85. Atlanta, GA.

REINHARTZ, A. (1999b) 'Introduction: "Father" As Metaphor in the Fourth Gospel', in Reinhartz (ed.) (1999a): 1–10.

REINHARTZ, A. (1999c) '"And the Word Was Begotten": Divine Epigenesis in the Gospel of John', Semeia 85, 83–103.

REINHARTZ, A. (2001a) *Befriending the Beloved Disciple. A Jewish Reading of the Gospel of John.* New York.

REINHARTZ, A. (2001b) '"Jews" and Jews in the Fourth Gospel', in Bieringer et al. (eds) (2001): 213–27.

REINHARTZ, A. (2009) 'Judaism in the Gospel of John', *Interpretation* 63/4, 383–93.

RESE, M. (2014) 'Johannes 3,22–36: Der taufende Jesus und das letzte Zeugnis Johannes des Täufers', in Verheyden et al. (eds) (2014): 89–98.

RESSEGUIE, J. L. (2001) *The Strange Gospel. Narrative Design and Point of View in John.* Biblical Interpretation Series 56. Leiden.

RESSEGUIE, J. L. (2005) *Narrative Criticism of the New Testament. An Introduction.* Grand Rapids, MI.

REYNOLDS, B. E. (2007) 'The Testimony of Jesus and the Spirit: The "We" of John 3:11 in Its Literary Context', *Neotestamentica* 41/1, 157–72.

REYNOLDS, B. E. (2013) 'Apocalypticism in the Gospel of John's Written Revelation of Heavenly Things', *Early Christianity* 1, 64–95.

RICHTER, G. (1970) 'Die Fleischwerdung des Logos im Johannesevangelium', *NT* 13, 81–126.

RICHTER, G. (1977) *Studien zum Johannesevangelium*, ed. J. Hainz. Biblische Untersuchungen 13. Regensburg.

RICOEUR, P. (1975) *La métaphore vive.* Paris.

RICOEUR, P. (1976) 'Metaphor and Symbol', in *Interpretation Theory. Discourse and the Surplus of Meaning.* Fort Worth, TX: 45–69.

RIDDERBOS, H. (1966) 'The Structure and Scope of the Prologue to the Gospel of John', *NT* 8/2–4, 180–201.

ROCHAIS, G. (1985a) 'La formation du Prologue (Jn 1.1–18) (I)', *Science et Esprit* 37/1, 5–44.

Rochais, G. (1985b) 'La formation du Prologue (Jn 1,1–18) (II)', *Science et Esprit* 37/2, 161–87.

Ruckstuhl, E. (1987/1951) *Die literarische Einheit des Johannesevangeliums*. Novum Testamentum et Orbis Antiquus 5. Freiburg.

Ruckstuhl, E. and P. Dschulnigg (1991) *Stilkritik und Verfasserfrage im Johannesevangelium. Die johanneischen Sprachmerkmale auf dem Hintergrund des Neuen Testaments und des zeitgenössischen hellenistischen Schrifttums*. Novum Testamentum et Orbis Antiquus 17. Freiburg.

Runia, D. T. (1993) 'Was Philo a Middle Platonist? A difficult question revisited', *Studia Philonica Annual* 5: 112–40.

Sabbe, M. (1992) 'The Trial of Jesus before Pilate in John and its Relation to the Synoptic Gospels', in Denaux (ed.) (1992): 341–85.

Sandmel, S. (1962) 'Parallelomania', *JBL* 81, 1–13.

Sandnes, K. O. (2005) 'Whence and Whither: A Narrative Perspective on Birth ἄνωθεν (John 3,3–8)', *Biblica* 86/2, 153–73.

Sänger, D. and U. Mell (eds) (2006) *Paulus und Johannes. Exegetische Studien zur paulinischen und johanneischen Theologie und Literatur*. WUNT 198. Tübingen.

Schenke, L. (1997) 'The Johannine Schism and the "Twelve" (John 6:60–71)', in Culpepper (ed.) (1997a): 205–19.

Schnackenburg, R. (1957) 'Logos-Hymnus und johanneischer Prolog', *Biblische Zeitschrift* 1, 69–109.

Schnackenburg, R. (1965–84) *Das Johannesevangelium*, 4 vols. Herders theologischer Kommentar zum Neuen Testament (TKNT) IV/1–4. Freiburg.

Schneiders, S. M. (1985) 'The Foot Washing (John 13.1–20): An Experiment in Hermeneutics', *Ex Auditu* 1. 135–46.

Schnelle, U. (1989) 'Die Abschiedsreden im Johannesevangelium', *ZNW* 80/1, 64–79.

Schnelle, U. (1992) 'Johannes und die Synoptiker', in *The Four Gospels 1992*, FS Franz Neirynck, eds F. Van Segbroeck, C. M. Tuckett, G. Van Belle, and J. Verheyden. BETL 100. Leuven: 3.1799–1814.

Schnelle, U. (1996) 'Die Tempelreinigung und die Christologie des Johannesevangeliums', *NTS* 42. 359–73.

Schnelle, U. (1998) 'Johannes als Geisttheologe', *NT* 40. 17–31.

Schnelle, U. (2003) 'Theologie als kreative Sinnbildung: Johannes als Weiterbildung von Paulus und Markus', in Söding (ed.) (2003): 119–45.

Schnelle, U. (2008) 'Cross and Resurrection in the Gospel of John', in Koester and Bieringer (eds) (2008): 127–51.

Schnelle, U. (2008/1998) *Das Evangelium nach Johannes*. Theologischer Handkommentar zum Neuen Testament 4. Leipzig.

Schnelle, U. (2009) 'Die johanneischen Abschiedsreden und das Liebesgebot', in Van Belle, Labahn, and Maritz (eds) (2009): 589–608.

Schnelle, U. (2010) 'Aus der Literatur zum Johannesevangelium 1994–2010. Erster Teil: Die Kommentare als Seismographen der Forschung', *Theologische Rundschau* 75, 265–303.

Schnelle, U. (2011) 'Die Reihenfolge der johanneischen Schriften', *NTS* 57/1, 91–113.

SCHNELLE, U. (2013) 'Aus der Literatur zum Johannesevangelium 1994–2010. Zweiter Teil: Eschatologie und Abschiedsreden', *Theologische Rundschau* 78, 462–504.

SCHNELLE, U. (2014) 'Johannes 16 im Rahmen der Abschiedsreden', in Verheyden et al. (eds) (2014): 425–46.

SCHNELLE, U. (2015) 'Das frühe Christentum und die Bildung', *NTS* 61/2, 113–43.

SCHNELLE, U., M. LABAHN, and M. LANG (eds) (2001) *Neuer Wettstein I/2. Texte zum Johannesevangelium*. Berlin.

SCHOLTISSEK, K. (1999a, 2000, 2002, 2004) 'Johannes auslegen I, II, III, IV', *Studien zum Neuen Testament und seiner Umwelt* 24, 35–84; 25, 98–104; 27, 117–53; 29, 67–118.

SCHOLTISSEK, K. (1999b) 'Neue Wege in der Johannesauslegung: Ein Forschungsbericht I', *Theologie und Glaube* 89, 263–95.

SCHOLTISSEK, K. (1999c) 'Abschied und neue Gegenwart: Exegetische und theologische Reflexionen zur johanneischen Abschiedsrede', *Ephemerides theologicae Lovanienses* 75, 332–58.

SCHOLTISSEK, K. (2000) *In Ihm sein und bleiben. Die Sprache der Immanenz in den Johanneischen Schriften*. Herders biblische Studien 21. Freiburg.

SCHOLTISSEK, K. (2001a) 'Neue Wege in der Johannesauslegung: Ein Forschungsbericht II', *Theologie und Glaube* 91, 109–33.

SCHOLTISSEK, K. (2001b) 'Eine Renaissance des Evangeliums nach Johannes. Aktuelle Perspektiven der exegetischen Forschung', *Theologische Revue* 97, 267–88.

SCHOLTISSEK, K. (2004) '"Eine grössere Liebe als diese hat niemand, als wenn einer sein Leben hingibt für seine Freunde" (Joh 15,13): Die hellenistische Freundschaftsethik und das Johannesevangelium', in Frey and Schnelle (eds) (2004): 413–39.

SCHOLTISSEK, K. (2014) Rev. Frey, *Die Herrlichkeit* (2013c), *Theologische Literaturzeitung* 139, 576–9.

SCHRAGE, W. (1997) 'Der gekreuzigte und auferstandene Herr: Zur *theologia crucis* und *theologia resurrectionis* bei Paulus', *ZTK* 94, 25–38.

SCHWANKL, O. (1995) *Licht und Finsternis. Ein metaphorisches Paradigma in den johanneischen Schriften*. Herders biblische Studien 5. Freiburg.

SCHWARTZ, E. (1907, 1908) 'Aporien im vierten Evangelium'. Nachrichten von der Königlichen Gesellschaft der Wissenschaften zu Göttingen: Philologisch-historische Klasse (1907) 342–72; (1908) 115–48; 149–88; 497–650.

SEDLEY, D. (1982) 'On Signs', in *Science and Speculation. Studies in Hellenistic Theory and Practice*, eds J. Barnes, J. Brunschwig, M. Burnyeat, and M. Schofield. Cambridge/Paris: 239–72.

SEEBERG, R. (ed.) (1915a) *Das Johannesevangelium*. Kassel.

SEEBERG, R. (1915b) 'Der Apostel Johannes und sein Evangelium'. Einleitung in Seeberg (1915a): 3–21.

SEELIG, G. (2001) *Religionsgeschichtliche Methode in Vergangenheit und Gegenwart. Studien zur Geschichte und Methode des religionsgeschichtlichen Vergleichs in der neutestamentlichen Wissenschaft*. Arbeiten zur Bibel und ihrer Geschichte 7. Leipzig.

SEGOVIA, F. F. (1982) 'John 13:1–20: The Footwashing in the Johannine Tradition', *ZNW* 73, 31–51.

SEGOVIA, F. F. (1991a) *The Farewell of the Word. The Johannine Call to Abide.* Minneapolis, MN.

SEGOVIA, F. F. (1991b) 'The Journey(s) of the Word of God: A Reading of the Plot of the Fourth Gospel', *Semeia* 53, 23–54.

SEGOVIA, F. F. (1995) 'The Significance of Social Location in Reading John's Story', *Interpretation* 49/4, 370–8.

SEGOVIA, F. F. (ed.) (1998a) *'What is John?' Volume II: Literary and Social Readings of the Fourth Gospel.* Society of Biblical Literature Symposium Series 7. Atlanta, GA.

SEGOVIA, F. F. (1998b) 'Inclusion and Exclusion in John 17: An Intercultural Reading', in Segovia (ed.) (1998a): 183–210.

SEGOVIA, F. F. (1998c) 'Reading Readers Reading John: An Exercise in Intercultural Criticism', in Segovia (ed.) (1998a): 281–322.

SEGOVIA, F. F. (2006) 'The Counterempire of God: Postcolonialism and John', *Princeton Seminary Bulletin* 27/2, 82–99.

SEIM, T. K. (1994) *The Double Message. Patterns of Gender in Luke-Acts.* Studies of the New Testament and its World. Edinburgh.

SEIM, T. K. (2005) 'Descent and Divine Paternity in the Gospel of John: Does the Mother Matter?', *NTS* 51, 351–75.

SEIM, T. K. (2010) 'Motherhood and the Making of Fathers in Antiquity: Contextualizing Genetics in the Gospel of John', in *Women and Gender in Ancient Religions. Interdisciplinary Approaches*, eds S. P. Ahearne-Kroll, P. A. Holloway, and J. A. Kelhoffer. WUNT 263. Tübingen: 99–123.

SEIM, T. K. (2011) 'Baptismal Reflections in the Fourth Gospel', in *Ablution, Initiation and Baptism. Late Antiquity, Early Judaism, and Early Christianity*, eds D. Hellholm et al. Beihefte zur Zeitschrift für die neutestamentliche Wissenschaft 176/1. Berlin.

SHERIDAN, R. (2010) 'John's Gospel and Modern Genre Theory: The Farewell Discourse (John 13–17) as a Test Case', *Irish Theological Quarterly* 75, 287–99.

SHERIDAN, R. (2013) 'Issues in the Translation of οἱ Ἰουδαῖοι in the Fourth Gospel', *JBL* 132, 671–95.

SIEGERT, F. (2004) 'Der Logos, "älterer Sohn" des Schöpfers und "zweiter Gott": Philons Logos und der Johannesprolog', in Frey and Schnelle (eds) (2004): 277–93.

SKINNER, C. W. (2013) *Characters and Characterization in the Gospel of John.* Library of New Testament Studies 461. London.

SMITH, D. M. (2003) 'The Contribution of J. Louis Martin to the Understanding of the Gospel of John', in Martyn (2003): 1–18.

SMITH, D. M. (2005) 'Future Directions of Johannine Studies', in Donahue (ed.) (2005): 52–62.

SMITH, J. Z. (1970) 'The Influence of Symbols upon Social Change: A Place on Which to Stand', *Worship* 44/8, 457–74.

SMITH, J. Z. (1990) *Drudgery Divine. On the Comparison of Early Christianities and the Religions of Late Antiquity.* Chicago, IL.

SÖDING, T. (ed.) (2003) *Johannesevangelium—Mitte oder Rand des Kanons?* Quaestiones disputatae 203. Freiburg.

STALEY, J. (1986) 'The Structure of John's Prologue: Its Implications for the Gospel's Narrative Structure', *CBQ* 48, 249–64.

STERLING, G. E. (1993) 'Platonizing Moses: Philo and Middle Platonism', *Studia Philonica Annual* 5: 96–111.

STIBBE, M. W. G. (1991) 'The Elusive Christ: A New Reading of the Fourth Gospel', *JSNT* 44, 20–39.

STIBBE, M. W. G. (1992) *John as Storyteller. Narrative Criticism and the Fourth Gospel.* Society for New Testament Studies Monograph Series 73. Cambridge.

STIBBE, M. W. G. (ed.) (1993) *The Gospel of John as Literature. An Anthology of Twentieth-Century Perspectives.* New Testament Tools and Studies 17. Leiden.

STIBBE, M. W. G. (2006) 'Telling the Father's Story: The Gospel of John as Narrative Theology', in Lierman (ed.) (2006): 170–93.

STOVELL, B. M. (2012) *Mapping Metaphorical Discourse in the Fourth Gospel. John's Eternal King.* Linguistic Biblical Studies 5. Leiden.

STRECKER, G. (1960) 'William Wrede: Zur hundertsten Wiederkehr seines Geburtstages', *ZTK* 57/1, 67–91.

STUBE, J. C. (2006) *A Graeco-Roman Rhetorical Reading of the Farewell Discourse.* Library of New Testament Studies 309. London.

STURDEVANT, J. S. (2014) 'Incarnation as Psychagogy: The Purpose of the Word's Descent in John's Gospel', *NT* 56/1, 24–44.

TALBERT, C. H. (1992) *Reading John. A Literary and Theological Commentary on the Fourth Gospel and the Johannine Epistles.* New York.

THATCHER, T. (2000) *The Riddles of Jesus in John. A Study in Tradition and Folklore.* SBLMS 53. Atlanta, GA.

THATCHER, T. (2006) *Why John Wrote a Gospel. Jesus—Memory—History.* Louisville, KY.

THATCHER, T. (ed.) (2007) *What We Have Heard from the Beginning. The Past, Presence, and Future of Johannine Studies.* Waco, TX.

THATCHER, T. (2009) 'Riddles, Repetitions, and the Literary Unity of the Johannine Discourses', in Van Belle (ed.) (2009): 357–77.

THATCHER, T. (2014) 'The Rejected Prophet and the Royal Official: A Case Study in the Relationship between John and the Synoptics', in Verheyden et al. (eds) (2014): 119–48.

THATCHER, T. and S. D. MOORE (eds) (2008) *Anatomies of Narrative Criticism. The Past, Present, and Futures of the Fourth Gospel as Literature.* Society of Biblical Literature Resources for Biblical Study 55. Atlanta, GA.

THATCHER, T. and C. WILLIAMS (eds) (2013) *Engaging with C. H. Dodd on the Gospel of John. Sixty Years of Tradition and Interpretation.* Cambridge.

THEOBALD, M. (1988) *Die Fleischwerdung des Logos. Studien zum Verhältnis des Johannesprologs zum Corpus des Evangeliums und zu 1Joh.* Neutestamentliche Abhandlungen Neue Folge 20. Münster.

THEOBALD, M. (1990) 'Geist- und Inkarnationschristologie: Zur Pragmatik des Johannesprologs (Joh 1,1–18)', *ZTK* 112, 129–49.

THEOBALD, M. (1992) 'Gott, Logos und Pneuma: Trinitarische Rede von Gott im Johannesevangelium', in *Monotheismus und Christologie. Zur Gottesfrage im hellenistischen Judentum und im Urchristentum,* ed. H-J. Klauck. Quaestiones disputatae 138. Freiburg: 41–7.

THEOBALD, M. (2002) *Herrenworte im Johannesevangelium.* Herders biblische Studien 34. Freiburg.

THEOBALD, M. (2003) 'Eucharistie in Joh 6: Vom pneumatologischen zum inkarnationstheologischen Verstehensmodell', in Söding (ed.) (2003): 178–257.

THEOBALD, M. (2006a) 'Paschamahl und Eucharistiefeier: Zur heilsgeschichtlichen Relevanz der Abendmahlsszenerie bei Lukas (Lk 22,14–38)', in Theobald and Hoppe (eds) (2006): 133–80.

THEOBALD, M. (2006b) 'Das Johannesevangelium—Zeugnis eines synagogalen "Judenchristentums"?' in Sänger and Mell (eds) (2006): 107–58.

THEOBALD, M. (2007) 'Leib und Blut Christi: Erwägungen zu Herkunft, Funktion und Bedeutung des sogenannten "Einsetzungsberichts" ', in *Herrenmahl und Gruppenidentität* ed. M. Ebner. Quaestiones disputatae 221. Freiburg: 121–65.

THEOBALD, M. (2009) *Das Evangelium nach Johannes. Kapitel 1–12.* Regensburger Neues Testament. Regensburg.

THEOBALD, M. (2010a) *Studien zum Corpus Iohanneum.* Tübingen.

THEOBALD, M. (2010b) ' "Der älteste Kommentar zum Johannesevangelium" (R. F. Collins)?', in Theobald (2010a): 41–75.

THEOBALD, M. (2012) 'Was und wen hat Jesus angekündigt? Das Rätsel um den Parakleten im johanneischen Schrifttum', in *Hat Jesus Muhammad angekündigt? Der Paraklet des Johannesevangeliums und seine koranische Bedeutung,* ed. T. Güzelmansur. Regensburg: 73–207.

THEOBALD, M. and R. HOPPE (eds) (2006) *'Für alle Zeiten zur Erinnerung' (Joh 4,7). Beiträge zu einer biblischen Gedächtniskultur.* Stuttgarter Bibelstudien 209. Stuttgart.

THÜSING, W. (1960) *Die Erhöhung und Verherrlichung Jesu im Johannesevangelium.* Neutestamentliche Abhandlungen 21. Münster.

THYEN, H. (2007a) *Studien zum Corpus Ioanneum.* WUNT 214. Tübingen.

THYEN, H. (2007b) 'Ὁ γέγονεν: Satzende von 1,3 oder Satzeröffnung von 1,4?', in Thyen (2007a): 411–17.

THYEN, H. (2015/2005) *Das Johannesevangelium.* Handbuch zum Neuen Testament 6. Tübingen.

TIELEMAN, T. (2014) 'The Spirit of Stoicism', in Frey and Levison (eds) (2014): 39–62.

TILBORG, S. VAN (2005) 'Cosmological Implications of Johannine Christology', in Van Belle et al. (eds) (2005): 483–502.

TOBIN, T. H., S. J. (1990) 'The Prologue of John and Hellenistic Jewish Speculation', *CBQ* 52, 252–69.

TOLMIE, D. F. (1998) 'The Characterization of God in the Fourth Gospel', *JSNT* 69, 57–75.

TOLMIE, D. F. (2013) 'Pontius Pilate: Failing in More Ways Than One', in Hunt, Tolmie, and Zimmermann (eds) (2013): 578–98.

URBAN, L. and P. HENRY (1979–80) ' "Before Abraham Was I Am": Does Philo Explain John 8:56–58?', *Studia Philonica* 6, 157–93.

VARGAS, N. M. (2014) 'Ἀγαπάω, ὑπάγω, and δοξάζω: Juxtaposed, Yet Tightly-Knit Themes in John 13,31–35', in Verheyden et al. (eds) (2014): 371–95.

VERBEKE, G. (1978) 'La philosophie du signe chez les stoïciens', in *Les Stoïciens et leur logique,* ed. J. Brunschwig. Paris: 401–24.

VERHEYDEN, J. (1992) 'P. Gardner-Smith and "the Turn of the Tide" ', in Denaux (ed.) (1992): 423–52.

VERHEYDEN, J., G. VAN OYEN, M. LABAHN, and R. BIERINGER (eds) (2014) *Studies in the Gospel of John and its Christology*, FS G. Van Belle. BETL 265. Leuven.

WAHLDE, U. C. VON (1981) 'The Witnesses to Jesus in John 5:31–40', *CBQ* 43, 385–404.

WAHLDE, U. C. VON (1981–82) 'The Johannine "Jews": A Critical Survey', *NTS* 28, 33–60.

WAHLDE, U. C. VON (1995) 'Community in Conflict: The History and Social Context of the Johannine Community', *Interpretation* 49/4, 379–89.

WAHLDE, U. C. VON (2013) 'C. H. Dodd, the historical Jesus, and realized eschatology', in Thatcher and Williams (eds) (2013): 149–62.

WALTER, N. (1985) '»Hellenistische Eschatologie« im Neuen Testament' in *Glaube und Eschatologie*, FS W. G. Kümmel, eds E. Grässer and O. Merk. Tübingen: 335–56.

WATSON, F. (1987) 'Is John's Christology Adoptionist?', in *The Glory of Christ in the New Testament. Studies in Christology in Memory of George Bradford Caird*, eds L. D. Hurst and N. T. Wright. Oxford. 113–24.

WATT, J. G. VAN DER (2000) *Family of the King. Dynamics of Metaphor in the Gospel according to John*. Biblical Interpretation Series 47. Leiden.

WATT, J. G. VAN DER (2005) '*Double entendre* in the Gospel According to John', in Van Belle et al. (eds) (2005): 463–81.

WATT, J. G. VAN DER (2006) 'Ethics alive in imagery', in Frey, van der Watt, and Zimmermann (eds) (2006): 421–48.

WATT, J. G. VAN DER (2007a) *An Introduction to the Johannine Gospel and Letters*. London.

WATT, J. G. VAN DER (2007b) 'I Am the Bread of Life: Imagery in John 6:32–51', *Acta Theologica* (South Africa) 27/2, 186–204.

WATT, J. G. VAN DER (2009) 'Repetition and Functionality in the Gospel According to John: Some Initial Explorations', in Van Belle et al. (eds) (2009): 87–108.

WATT, J. G. VAN DER (2011a) *Eschatology in the New Testament and Some Related Documents*. WUNT 2.315. Tübingen.

WATT, J. G. VAN DER (2011b) 'Eschatology in John—A Continuous Process of Realizing Events', in van der Watt (ed.) (2011a): 109–40.

WATT, J. G. VAN DER (2013) 'Symbolism in John's Gospel: An evaluation of Dodd's contribution', in Thatcher and Williams (eds) (2013): 66–85.

WATT, J. G. VAN DER (2014) 'Laying Down Your Life for Your Friends: Some Reflections on the Historicity of John 15:13', *Journal of Early Christian History* (Pretoria) 4/2, 167–80.

WATT, J. G. VAN DER and R. ZIMMERMANN (eds) (2012) *Rethinking the Ethics of John. »Implicit Ethics« in the Johannine Writings*. Kontexte und Normen neutestamentlicher Ethik III. WUNT 291. Tübingen.

WEISSENRIEDER, A. (2014a) 'Spirit and Rebirth in the Gospel of John', *Religion and Theology* (Leiden) 21/1–2, 58–85.

WEISSENRIEDER, A. (2014b) 'The Infusion of the Spirit: The Meaning of ἐμφυσάω in John 20:22–23', in Frey and Levison (eds) (2014): 119–51.

WELLHAUSEN, J. (1907) *Erweiterungen und Änderungen im vierten Evangelium*. Berlin.

WENGST, K. (1981) *Bedrängte Gemeinde und verherrlichter Christus. Der historische Ort des Johannesevangeliums als Schlüssel zu seiner Interpretation*, Biblisch-theologische

Studien 5. Neukirchen-Vluyn. Also:... *Ein Versuch über das Johannesevangelium* (Munich 1990 and 1992).

WENGST, K. (2000/2001) *Das Johannesevangelium I–II.* Theologischer Kommentar zum Neuen Testament 4/1–2. Stuttgart.

WENHAM, D. (2006) 'Paradigms and Possibilities in the Study of John's Gospel', in Lierman (ed.) (2006): 1–13.

WICK, P. (2004) 'Jesus gegen Dionysos? Ein Beitrag zur Kontextualisierung des Johannesevangeliums', *Biblica* 85, 179–98.

WILCKENS, U. (1996) 'Christus traditus se ipsum tradens: Zum johanneischen Verständnis des Kreuzestodes Jesu', in *Gemeinschaft am Evangelium*, FS W. Popkes, eds E. Brandt, P. S. Fiddles, and J. Molthagen. Leipzig: 363–84.

WILCKENS, U. (2003) *Der Sohn Gottes und seine Gemeinde. Studien zur Theologie der Johanneischen Schriften.* FRLANT 200. Göttingen.

WILLIAMS, C. H. and C. ROWLAND (eds) (2013) *John's Gospel and Intimations of Apocalyptic.* London.

WILLIAMS, P. J. (2011) 'Not the Prologue of John', *JSNT* 33/4, 375–86.

WINDISCH, H. (1926) *Johannes und die Synoptiker. Wollte der vierte Evangelist die älteren Evangelien ergänzen oder ersetzen?* Untersuchungen zum Neuen Testament 12. Leipzig.

WINTER, M. (1994) *Das Vermächtnis Jesu und die Abschiedsworte der Väter. Gattungsgeschichtliche Untersuchung der Vermächtnisrede im Blick auf Joh. 13–17.* FRLANT 161. Göttingen.

WITETSCHEK, S. (2012) 'Der Teufel steckt im Detail: Eine Anmerkung zu Joh 13,2', *Biblische Zeitschrift* 56/5, 264–73.

WREDE, W. (1900) Rev. W. Baldensperger, *Der Prolog des vierten Evangeliums.* Göttingische gelehrte Anzeigen 162/1, 1–16.

WREDE, W. (1901) *Das Messiasgeheimnis in den Evangelien. Zugleich ein Beitrag zum Verständnis des Markusevangeliums.* Göttingen.

WREDE, W. (1907) 'Charakter und Tendenz des Johannesevangeliums', in Wrede, *Vorträge und Studien.* Tübingen: 178–231.

WREDE, W. (1971) *The Messianic Secret*, trans. J. C. G. Greig. Cambridge.

ZELYCK, L. R. (2013) *John among the Other Gospels. The Reception of the Fourth Gospel in the Extra-Canonial Gospels.* WUNT 2.347. Tübingen.

ZIMMERMANN, R. (2003a) 'Paradigmen einer metaphorischen Christologie: Eine Leseanleitung', in Frey, Rohls, and Zimmermann (eds) (2003): 1–34.

ZIMMERMANN, R. (2003b) '"Du wirst noch Grösseres sehen..." (Joh 1,50). Zur Ästhetik der Christusbilder im Johannesevangelium – Eine Skizze', in Frey, Rohls, and Zimmermann (eds) (2003): 93–110.

ZIMMERMANN, R. (2004) *Christologie der Bilder im Johannesevangelium. Die Christopoetik des vierten Evangeliums unter besonderer Berücksichtigung von Joh 10.* WUNT 171. Tübingen.

ZIMMERMANN, R. (2006) 'Imagery in John: Opening up paths into the tangled thicket of John's figurative world', in Frey, van der Watt, and Zimmermann (eds) (2006): 1–43.

ZIMMERMANN, R. (2008a) 'The Narrative Hermeneutics of John 11: Learning with Lazarus How to Understand Death, Life, and Resurrection', in Koester and Bieringer (eds) (2008): 75–101.

ZIMMERMANN, R. (2008b) 'Symbolic Communication between John and His Reader: The Garden Symbolism in John 19–20', in Thatcher and Moore (eds) (2008): 221–35.

ZIMMERMANN, R. (2012) 'Narrative Ethik im Johannesevangelium am Beispiel der Lazarus-Perikope Joh 11', in Frey and Poplutz (eds) (2012a): 133–70.

ZIMMERMANN, R. (2014a) 'Figurenanalyse im Johannesevangelium: Ein Beitrag zu Sinn und Wahrheit narratologischer Exegese', *ZNW* 105/1, 20–53.

ZIMMERMANN, R. (2014b) 'From a Jewish Man to the Savior of the World: Narrative and Symbols Forming a Step by Step Christology in John 4,1–42', in Verheyden et al. (eds) (2014): 99–118.

ZORRILLA, H. (1995) 'A Service of Sacrificial Love: Footwashing (John 13: 1–11)', *Direction* 24/1, 74–85.

ZUMSTEIN, J. (1996) 'Narrative Analyse und neutestamentliche Exegese in der frankophonen Welt', *Verkündigung und Forschung* 41, 5–27.

ZUMSTEIN, J. (2004/1999) *Kreative Erinnerung. Relecture und Auslegung im Johannesevangelium*. Abhandlungen zur Theologie des Alten und Neuen Testaments 84. Zürich.

ZUMSTEIN, J. (2006) 'Das hermeneutische Problem der johanneischen Metaphern am Beispiel der Hirtenrede (Joh 10)', in Sänger and Mell (eds) (2006): 159–75.

ZUMSTEIN, J. (2007) *L'Évangile selon Saint Jean (13–21)*. Commentaire du Nouveau Testament IVb. Genève.

ZUMSTEIN, J. (2008) 'Jesus' Resurrection in the Farewell Discourses', in Koester and Bieringer (eds) (2008): 103–26.

ZUMSTEIN, J. (2009) '"Ich bin das Brot des Lebens": Wiederholung und Variation eines johanneischen Ego-Eimi-Wortes in Joh 6', in Van Belle et al. (eds) (2009): 435–52.

ZUMSTEIN, J. (2012) 'Interpréter le quatrième évangile aujourd'hui: Questions de méthode', *Revue d'Histoire et de Philosophie Religieuses* 92/2, 241–58.

ZUMSTEIN, J. (2014) *L'Évangile selon Saint Jean (1–12)*. Commentaire du Nouveau Testament IVa. Genève.

ZUMSTEIN, J. (2016) *Das Johannesevangelium*. Kritisch-exegetischer Kommentar über das Neue Testament 2. Göttingen.

INDEX LOCORUM

GENERAL INDEX

Made in the USA
Monee, IL
04 February 2023

27110706R00240